"Be prepared to read it at least twice to start; once to grasp the dramatic sweep of this **historic accomplishment,** and then another read with pen and pad as you prepare yourself to do your part in the great struggle ahead. . . . **Dr. Horowitz lifts you to a plateau of knowledge with this imperative resource that succinctly distills the essence of the greatest issues of our time."** —Donald W. Scott, M.A., MSc.
President: The Common Cause Medical Research Foundation

"For conspiracy 'doubters,' here is a book to sink your teeth into. In this **powerful cutting-edge piece of research, Dr.** Horowitz breaks new **ground by documenting the deliberate contamination of whole populations** by various means. . . . No more denial, an end to scoffing at the sinister agenda of depopulation, **here is the proof you've demanded."**
—Rick Martin
Book Review, *The Spectrum*

Death in the Air **presents harrowing proof, using primary documentation,** to show that our own, and other governments, are experimenting on the domestic populations . . . **No one has done as daring an investigation of the "Industrial–Military–Congressional–Complex's" medicalized weapons program, as Horowitz. This is a superlative job!**
—Zohara M. Hieronimus
Award Winning National Radio Broadcaster, Host of "Future Talk"

"*Death in the Air* is intensely researched and referenced. It removes any doubts that we are the victims of a global conspiracy that intends to kill millions of people slowly, painfully, and expensively through the multi-directional delivery of chronic diseases."
— Don Harkins
Book Review, *The Idaho Observer*

"Horowitz provides stunning support for his claim that populations are being seeded with biological time bombs . . . One can draw an enormous amount of vital information from this book. It has our strongest recommendation."
— Michael L. Culbert, Sc.D.
Book Review, *The ICHF Newsletter*

"Dr. Horowitz has made another important research contribution to the struggle against continuing worldwide covert medical genocide."
— Alan Cantwell, Jr., M.D.
Author, *The Cancer Microbe:*

DEATH IN THE AIR:
GLOBALISM, TERRORISM & TOXIC WARFARE

Leonard G. Horowitz, D.M.D., M.A., M.P.H.

AUTHOR OF THE NATIONAL BESTSELLER,
EMERGING VIRUSES: AIDS & EBOLA—NATURE, ACCIDENT OR INTENTIONAL?

BY LEONARD G. HOROWITZ

Deadly Innocence

Healing Celebrations

Taking Care of Yourself

Dentistry in the Age of AIDS

AIDS, Fear and Infection Control

Healing Codes for the Biological Apocalypse

Emerging Viruses: AIDS & Ebola—Nature, Accident or Intentional?

There is no proletarian, not even Communist, movement, that has not operated in the interest of money, in the direction indicated by money—and that without the idealists among its leaders having the slightest suspicion of the fact.

—Oswald Spengler,
Decline of the West

Wherever a lessening of population pressures . . .
can increase prospects for such stability,
population policy becomes relevant to resource supplies
and to the economic interests of the United States. . . .
[and its allies.]

—Nelson Rockefeller's protégé, Henry Kissinger,
National Security Special Memorandum 200, 1974 p. 43.

In our dreams we have limitless resources and the people yield themselves with perfect docility to our molding hands. The present educational conventions fade from our minds and, unhampered by tradition, we work our good will upon a grateful and responsive rural folk.

—John D. Rockefeller,
discussing the objectives of Rockefeller Philanthropies
Occasional letter No. 1 of the Rockefeller's General Education Board

With our great influence in publishing and publicity we are able to selectively popularize theorists whose views are incidentally beneficial, compatible, or at least not in conflict with our own goals. This way we obtain sincere, energetic activists to propagate our desires without having to reveal our [financial] motives or even existence. . . . [Thus], the brilliant researchers and experimenters who make most of the break-throughs earnestly believe that their techniques are destined strictly for the betterment of mankind.

—Anonymous
Transcripts of the Global Elite

Tetrahedron
Health science communications
for people around the world
Publishing Group

Cover art design by Leo Tanguma
Manufactured in the United States of America

10 9 8 7 6 5 4 3 2 1

Library of Congress Cataloging Requested
Horowitz, Leonard G.
Death in the Air: Globalism, Terrorism & Toxic Warfare
p.   cm.
Includes bibliographical references and index.
1. Viral Disease   2. Public Health
—West Nile Virus;   3. HIV/AIDS
4. Toxicology—Malathion—Centers for Disease Control—
—Aerial Spraying;   5. Biological Warfare—CIA
—Immunology;   6. Political Science
7. Genetics   8. Mind Control
—Human Genome Project; 9. Population Control
10. New World Order/Globalism
I. Title.

LC Control Number: 2001 130459

ISBN: 0-923550-30-5

Additional copies of this book are available for bulk purchases.
For more information, please contact:
Tetrahedron • Suite 147, 206 North 4th Avenue • Sandpoint, Idaho 83864,
1-800-336-9266, Fax: 208-265-2775, E-mail: tetra@tetrahedron.org,
URL web site: http://www.tetrahedron.org

Fourth printing

DEDICATED TO THE ARMY
OF HEALTHCARE PROFESSIONALS,
ALLIED ACADEMICIANS,
AND RESEARCH SCIENTISTS
WHOSE HUMANITARIAN MOTIVES
MADE THEM HIGHLY SUSCEPTIBLE
TO "BEHAVIORAL MANAGEMENT,"
AND WHO
—LIKE GOOD "MANCHURIAN CANDIDATES"—
UNWITTINGLY COMMITTED MURDER AND GENOCIDE
IN THE NAME OF "PUBLIC HEALTH."
MAY THIS WORK SERVE TO BREAK
THE SPELL UNDER WHICH THEY OPERATE.

Contents

x

Illustrations

Figures

Abbreviations

AEC—Atomic Energy Commission
AIDS—acquired immune deficiency syndrome
ASCC—American Society for Cancer Control
ATCC—American Type Culture Collection
BW—Biological weapons
BL—Burkitt's lymphoma
CACTUS—Citizens Against Chemtrails U.S.
CBW—chemical and biological warfare
CDC—Centers for Disease Control and Prevention
CDFA—California Department of Food and Agriculture
CFR—Council on Foreign Relations
CIA—Central Intelligence Agency
CIC—Counterintelligence Corps
CME—Continuing Medical Education
CRI—Chemtrail Related Illness
CSHL—Cold Spring Harbor Laboratories
DARPA—Defense Applied Research Programs Agency
DCI—Director of Central Intelligence
DHEW—U.S. Department of Health, Education and Welfare
DHS—California Department of Health Services
DNA—deoxyribonucleic acid
DNREC—Delaware Dept. of Natural Resources and Envir. Control
DoD—U.S. Department of Defense
EBV—Epstein–Barr virus
ECT—Electroconvulsive (shock) therapy
ERTS—Earth Resources Technology Satellite
FBI—Federal Bureau of Investigation
FELV—Feline (cat) leukemia virus
FCRC—Frederick Cancer Research Center
FDA—Food and Drug Administration
FOIA—Freedom of Information Act
GAO—U.S. General Accounting Office
GRIC—Gay related immune deficiency
HESIS—Calif. Health Evaluation Systems and Information Service
HBV—hepatitis B virus
HIV—human immunodeficiency virus
HTLV—human T-lymphocyte leukemia virus
IARC—International Agency for Research on Cancer
ICCS—International Cancer Control Society

IDA—International Development Association
IPCC—International Panel on Climate Change
KAC—Kaiser Aluminum Corporation
KACC—Kaiser Aluminum and Chemical Corporation
LBI—Litton Bionetics, Inc.
MIT—Massachusetts Institute for Technology
MKNAOMI—CIA code for secret biological weapons program
MKULTRA—CIA code for mind/population control program
MSD—Merck, Sharp & Dohme
NAS—National Academy of Sciences
NASA—National Aeronautics and Space Administration
NATO—North Atlantic Treaty Organization
NBRL—Naval Biomedical Research Laboratory
NCI—National Cancer Institute
NGO—Nongovernmental organization
NIAID—National Institute for Allergies and Infectious Diseases
NIH—National Institutes of Health
NOAA—National Oceanographic and Atmospheric Administration
NRC—National Research Council
NFS—National Forest Service
NSA—National Security Agency
NSF—National Science Foundation
NYCBB—New York City Blood Bank
NYCDoH—New York City Department of Health
NYUMC—New York University Medical Center
RAPID—Resources for the Awareness of Population and
     International Development
SKMCC—Sloan–Kettering Memorial Cancer Center
SOD—Special Operations Division of the U.S. Army
SSI—Strategic Studies Institute
SVCP—Special Virus Cancer Program
SV40—simian virus 40
UNFPA—U.N. Fund for Population Activities
USAF—United States Air Force
USAID—United States Agency for International Development
USDA—United States Department of Agriculture
USGS—United States Geological Survey
USGSC—United States Global Security Council
USPHS—U.S. Public Health Service
VEE—Venezuelan equine encephalitis
WASPS—White Anglo–Saxon Protestants
WHO—World Health Organization
WNV—West Nile virus

Preface

As an investigative journalist who travels extensively across the western hemisphere, I often get my "homework" assignments from airport newsstands. Since 1990, I've been tracking U.S. Government cover-ups in the health science domain. My special interests lie in "emerging viruses," "bioterrorism," and "media propaganda." As a graduate of Harvard School of Public Health, and a post-doctoral researcher in media persuasion technologies, I have, for the past decade, conducted highly controversial investigations, published stunning government records, and exposed the purveyors of propaganda surrounding today's deadliest microbes. I have documented the agents and agencies directly responsible for bioengineering and transmitting many of the world's most feared viruses and bacteria. With no support from America's mainstream media, my job has been to raise public awareness regarding these "covert operations," to help the intelligent minority survive what might best be called "global genocide."

Having spent most of my adult life residing near Boston, America's medical mecca, the news of massive Malathion and Anvil sprayings there during the summer of 2000 for "disease prevention via mosquito control" grabbed my attention.[1] In Massachusetts and Rhode Island, as was done the previous year in Connecticut, New York, and New Jersey, public health officials were promoting the spraying without any mention of possible side effects. Questionable reports issued by The Massachusetts Department of Public Health alleged the discovery of a West Nile Virus (WNV) "in an adult dead crow found July 22 in a wooded area near Willow Pond in Jamaica Plain [adjacent Roxbury], Massachusetts"— a predominantly African–American Boston suburb. The discovery, they said, necessitated massive pesticide sprayings.

"Odd," I thought, "of all the places in Massachusetts or New England the crow could have landed, it dropped dead on a Black community in South Boston."

The official press notice cited the alleged need to deliver "ground or aerial larvicide and ground adulticide treatments around positive WNV findings." Thus, potentially lethal and extensive spraying of immune system ravaging chemicals began.

That same week, on Friday, July 28, 2000, with heightened fear of a biological apocalypse at hand, the Reuters news agency in Washington announced that the U.S. military's use of anthrax vaccine had come under

XV

intense scrutiny and additional fire.[2] Dr. David A. Ashford, of the Centers for Disease Control and Prevention (CDC), was quoted as stating "we do not have any specific information on the efficacy of the existing vaccine for the prevention of inhalational anthrax and we probably never will." The article suspiciously recalled the largely ignored findings by Dan Burton's congressional investigating committee issued *six months earlier.* The February 2000 report by the House of Representatives' Committee on Government Reforms called for the suspension of the anthrax vaccine program. Not only was the vaccine's inefficacy determined by the committee, but also the risk of side effects was found to be 175 times greater than defense department officials initially assured the Food and Drug Administration (FDA) and military personnel receiving the vaccine.

The same Reuters report previewed the likelihood that the FDA would approve an obscure antibiotic, ciprofloxacin, over better-known penicillins and doxycyclines to prevent deaths from anthrax inhalations. The standard antimicrobials, the article speculated, might be less effective than ciprofloxacin, due to the development of antibiotic resistant strains of anthrax. According to the *Physician's Desk Reference*, the risks of ciprofloxacin administration are numerous and severe.

The very next day, Saturday, July 29, 2000, the nation's principle news agency, the Associated Press (AP), announced the unprecedented move by the FDA to legislate ciprofloxacin as the drug of choice against anthrax. This synchronous announcement was said to help the Bayer Corporation of West Haven, Connecticut market its product. Conveniently, for the corporation, the FDA's action was said to be "part of an organized effort by federal agencies to prepare the nation to respond to biological attack." FDA committee chairman, Dr. L. Barth Reller, of Duke University, said, "the unanimous vote of the committee 'is clearly linked' to the unusual circumstances of preparing for a possible terrorist attack . . . . The CDC also is poised to stockpile the drug," AP reported.[3]

What very few people realized as these announcements broke was that all of these events were economically and politically related. The alleged "outbreak" of WNV set the stage for "emergency" sprayings of Malathion and Anvil. Official predictions of an imminent anthrax holocaust led to the FDA's similarly unprecedented approval of Bayer Corporation's ciprofloxacin to prevent anthrax infection. These events were best explained by what modern military officials term fear-based PSYOPs and preparedness for "non-lethal warfare" bordering on what past Central Intelligence Agency (CIA) director James Woolsy referred to as "industrial espionage."[4] Readers will become very familiar with these terms in this book, particularly the phrase non-lethal warfare. This phrase relates to an economic substitute for war in which populations are exposed to multiple chemical and biological agents effecting chronic illnesses and often slow death.

Indeed, these news stories demonstrated a new form of "bioterrorism" not perpetrated by "radical factions" in the traditional sense, but by official agent radicals espousing pseudoscience. This form of "white-collar bioterrorism" reflects Machiavellian theory in practice. That is, creating biological and chemical problems and the fears surrounding them, then the costly solutions which naturally earn vast revenues for "Fourth World" multinational corporations. Few knew the companies involved here and elsewhere were principle players in what author Martin A. Lee called the "re-awakening beast."[4]

The above ideation prompted the research and discussions relayed in this book. As a long term resident of the state of Massachusetts, and a former member of the state's Public Health Association, I felt personally accountable for alerting my many friends there regarding the Anvil sprayings. This was *my* profession—public health—that was administering this potentially deadly aerosol. A few of my Harvard acquaintances were directly involved in Massachusetts's "mosquito control" effort that should have more accurately been called "population control."

Arguably, this sounds like foolish conspiracy theory. Acceptance is not easy in this regard. Coming to terms with such facts leads, by necessity, through Elizabeth Kubler Ross's "death and dying" process. In her model, denial is always the first step in integrating a horrifying painful reality. It is not pleasant to consider the possibility that many of our public servants cannot be trusted, but even worse, that friends and family members may have been injured or killed by such biochemical attacks.

The risk of denial here, however, is most serious. Ignorance sustains denial. Ironically, denial sustained is not ignorant bliss. Given the contemporary risks of biological and chemical warfare and population control discussed in the forthcoming chapters, ignorance is likely to be most deadly.

Thus, *DEATH IN THE AIR: GLOBALISM, TERRORISM & TOXIC WARFARE* is really about lifesaving revelations regarding contemporary biochemical warfare, and what you need to know to make reasonably informed, potentially lifesaving, decisions in an era that might be called globally genocidal.

I gratefully acknowledge the work of Ms. Betsy Russell-Manning for prodding me to begin this book. She approached me in August, 2000 at the International Cancer Control Society (ICCS) meeting in Hollywood and suggested that I update her lovingly compiled *Malathion: Toxic Time Bomb.*[5] In the early 1990s, Betsy was likewise urged to write a book on the subject of toxic warfare by her friends and colleagues, particularly Lorraine Rosenthal, President of the ICCS. Thus, my labors are largely thanks to them.

Much like my earlier work, *Emerging Viruses: AIDS & Ebola—Nature, Accident or Intentional?*, this text was written primarily for intelligent lay readers, health professionals, academicians, and scientists—public opinion leaders with the potential to sway political attitudes and legislative actions in an effort to stop toxic pesticide sprayings and other unwarranted risks.

I worked to sound several alarms here that some say are false. For the sake of those who would challenge my theories and concerns here, I reprinted the most damning documents for everyone's consideration. If I might be shown a more rational way to interpret these documents and their implications concerning world health and global economics/politics, I would be grateful.

Other authors have adequately addressed the sequestered risks of consumable poisons including fluoride and chlorine in water supplies, artificial food and beverage sweeteners, and mercury amalgam dental fillings. I will not reinvent these wheels here.

Alternatively, this book prepares new ground and deals almost exclusively with the relatively new concept of "non-lethal" cofactor induced diseases. To effect these, two primary delivery vehicles are clear: 1) atmospheric and 2) bloodborne. Thus, I focus on aerosol sprays and seemingly unrelated vaccinations in this book.

In *Taking Care of Yourself* and *Healing Celebrations*, I relayed the most practical advice—self-care steps—people can follow to prepare their defenses against the current and coming plagues of cancers, autoimmune diseases, and novel infectious diseases. These included information and recommendations for: 1) detoxification from chemical exposures, 2) deacidification for defense against infectious diseases, remission of cancers, and reversals of autoimmune and neurological ailments, 3) boosting natural immunity wholistically, 4) oxygenation therapies for miraculous recoveries, and 5) bioelectric modalities including related forms of spiritual healing. Many people have appreciated these and experienced healing following these recommendations. These educational offerings may be recognized as even more valuable in light of the revelations provided here. This awareness empowers people to make more informed choices for health and longevity in every aspect of life.

In essence, this book details the primary manners in which population control programs are being conducted and "non-lethal" warfare is being waged on the generally unwitting masses. This knowledge is provided to help defend the public's health, promote well-being, and stop what might be called global genocide.

Dr. Len Horowitz

References

1) The Commonwealth of Massachusetts Executive Office of Health and Human Services, Department of Public Health. West Nile Virus Detected in Massachusetts. Press release issued by MDPH on July 26, 2000. Available from http://www.state.ma.us/dph/media/pr0726.htm.

2) Bussey E and Stern P. U.S. military use of anthrax vaccine under fire. Reuters news service. Friday, July 28, 2000. Available from http://news. lycos.com/headlines/Health/article.asp?docid=RTHEALTH-ANTHRAX&date=20000728.

3) Associated Press. FDA advisory panel urges approval of anthrax drug. *Las Vegas Review-Journal*. Saturday, July 29, 2000 p. 6A.

4) Lee M. *The Beast Reawakens*. Boston: Little, Brown & Company, 1997.

5) Russell-Manning B. *Malathion: Toxic Time Bomb*. San Francisco: International Cancer Control Society, 1990.

Chapter 1.
Public Health and U.S. National Security: New Challenges from Globalism to Bioterrorism

> "All propaganda has to be popular and has to adapt
> . . . to the perception of the least intelligent of those
> towards whom it intends to direct itself. My adver-
> saries . . . applied the one means that wins the easi-
> est victory over reason: terror and force. . ."
>
> Adolf Hitler, *Mein Kampf*, 1933

Hints of CIA involvement in the debut of the West Nile virus (WNV) came less than a year earlier with the 1999 publication of Richard Preston's *New Yorker* feature entitled, "West Nile Mystery: How did it get here? The CIA would like to know."[1] (See figure 1.1.) Then, the alleged outbreak of a type of arbovirus—so named for its treelike shape similar to the Eastern Equine Encephalitis (EEE) virus or the St. Louis virus (SLV)—provided an excuse to spray "mosquitoes," as well as millions of predominantly Jewish, Black, and Hispanic residents in the tri-state metropolitan region.

Preston's propagandist practices and his links to the Alfred P. Sloan Foundation, the CIA, and the cancer industry's heart—the Sloan-Kettering Memorial Cancer Center in New York, were thoroughly exposed in *Emerging Viruses: AIDS & Ebola—Nature, Accident or Intentional?* (Tetrahedron Publishing Group, 1997).[2] Preston's best known work, *The Hot Zone*,[3] catapulted him to national acclaim as the chief voice in mainstream media bent on broadcasting "imminent" attacks by "mysterious" viruses and angry "bioterrorists." True to his racist benefactors, he has historically depicted Arabs, Blacks, and/or Muslims as his chief suspects.

The word "bioterrorism" in this book reflects a broader sense of the word. It includes frightening Americans into accepting virtually any official prescription, including experimental and risky vaccinations or chemical applications for anthrax, WNV, and far more. For instance, the interim sprayings of Malathion and Anvil—immune suppressive, carcinogenic, and highly lethal toxins—are deemed appropriate precautionary measures against each proclaimed WNV outbreak. For the propagandist's purpose of fear induction, Preston's prose is consistently suited.

I first linked Richard Preston to CIA counterintelligence activities through my independent investigation into the origin of the Ebola virus. Ebola, the ideal biological weapon that kills nine-out-of-ten humans within three weeks of infection, emerged first in three European *vaccine* production laboratories, virtually simultaneously, in 1967. Then named the "Marburg virus" (after the Marburg, Germany, address of the Paul Ehrlich Institute, wherein one of the first outbreaks took place), consensus held that this virus arrived in Europe in a shipment of nearly 500 African monkeys. The scientific literature, mainstream media, and Richard Preston, never once disclosed the name of the infamous monkey supplier—Litton Bionetics.

Figure 1.2 shows that the mysterious Bionetics is merely listed in the *Congressional Record* as a leading biological weapons contractor for the U.S. military.[2] One of its most important contracts is reprinted in Figure 1.3. Rather than reporting obvious associations between biological weapons producers' weapons testing, and related "outbreaks," Preston advanced a theory on Ebola's origin totally void of factual evidence and scientific merit. Ebola, he claimed, came from the deep dark Kitum Cave near the West Nile region of Central Africa.

Incidentally, Kitum Cave, according to suppressed National Cancer Institute (NCI) documents, was Preston's metaphor for Litton Bionetics's research lab. Here, in the West Nile valley region of Uganda, currently the heart of the African AIDS belt, Bionetics collaborated, from the early 1960s through 1978, with the International Agency for Research in Cancer (IARC). Suspiciously, given the history of the cancer industry as will be discussed later, the IARC was funded by the U.S. National Institutes of Health, but centered in France! This is an early indication of the global nature of biomedical research and the biological weapons industry. Near the actual Kitum Cave, in Northwest Uganda, Litton Bionetics and NCI scientists experimented on non-human primates *and* African villagers according to eyewitness testimony.[4] As this book was being completed, the same

Fig. 1.1. CIA Propagandist Richard Preston Presents WNV Feature in *The New Yorker*

White collar "bioterrorist" and CIA propagandist Richard Preston commands a feature story on the mysterious West Nile virus outbreak of 1999 in *The New Yorker*. Exposed as a purveyor of similar disinformation regarding Ebola outbreaks in *Emerging Viruses: AIDS & Ebola—Nature, Accident or Intentional?*, Dr. Horowitz documented Preston's ties to the Rockefeller–Sloan cancer consortium intimately linked to the production, testing, and transmission of such viruses by biological weapons contractors and population controllers.

Fig. 1.2. U.S. Army Biological Weapons Contractors for Fiscal Year 1969

The following list contains the major contractors and amounts of each contract.

Contractor	Fiscal year 1969
Miami, University. of Coral Gables Fla	$645,000
Herner and Co., Bethesda, Md	518,000
Missouri, University of, Columbia, Mo	250,000
Chicago, University, of Chicago, Ill	216,000
Aerojet-General Corp., Sacramento. Calif	210,000
★Bionetics Research Laboratories, Inc., Falls Church, Va	180,000
West Virginia University, Morgantown, W. Va	177,000
Maryland. University of, College Park, Md	170,000
Dow Chemical Co., Midland, Mich	158,000
Hazelton Laboratories, Inc., Falls Church, Reston, Va	145,000
New York University Medical Center, New York, N.Y	142,000
Midwest Research Institute, Kansas City, Mo	134,000
Stanford University, Palo Alto, Calif	125,000
Stanford Research Institute, Menlo Park, Calif	124,000
★Pfizer and Co., Inc., New York, N.Y	120,000
Aldrich Chemical Co., Inc., Milwaukee, Wis	117,000
Computer Usage Development Corp., Washington, D.C	110,000
New England Nuclear Corp., Boston, Mass	104,000

Source: Department of Defense Appropriations For 1970: Hearings Before A Sub-committee of the Committee on Appropriations House of Representatives, Ninety-first Congress, First Session, H.B. 15090, Part 5, Research, Development, Test and Evaluation of Biological Weapons, Dept. of the Army. U.S. Government Printing Office, Washington, D.C., 1969, p. 689.

Ebola virus suddenly reemerged inexplicably in this same area of northwest Uganda.

At the time Ebola first broke, the president of Bionetics—a medical subsidiary of the mega-military weapons contractor Litton Industries—was Roy Ash. Mr. Ash became director of American industry by appointment of his personal friend, Richard Nixon, beginning in 1969. That year, Nelson Rockefeller's protégé, Dr. Henry Kissinger, received the position Nixon also considered for Mr. Ash—National Security Advisor overseeing CIA, FBI, and foreign policy.[2]

Foreshadowing the Rockefeller family's involvement in global genocide that is evidenced in the pages ahead, author G. Edward Griffin, in *World Without Cancer*, cited Litton's strong direction from Rockefeller's "pyramid of power."[5] A spider's web of connections best describes the suspicious outbreaks of AIDS in New York and Ebola in Uganda, the alleged WNV outbreak in New York, Rockefeller links to the cancer industry directed from New York, and Rockefeller ties to the manufacture of carcinogens, particularly Malathion by American Cyanamid, and Anvil, Malathion's replacement, by Rockefeller's own Chevron Corporation. American Cyanamid is a huge subsidiary of American Home Products Corporation, as well as owner of Lederle Labs. Dr. James B. Fisk, director of American Cyanamid, Dow Corning, and Rockefeller's Chase Manhattan Bank, was also, during the last half of the twentieth century, on the Board of Overseers of the Sloan-Kettering Memorial Cancer Center (SKMCC) in New York City.

The Origin of the Cancer Industry and Modern Medicine

In *Murder by Injection: The Story of the Medical Conspiracy Against America*,[6] author Eustace Mullins detailed numerous financial and administrative links between Rockefeller-directed holdings and cancer industry kingpins Albert Lasker and Elmer Bobst. Mullins, well known for his staunch anti-globalist and early anti-Semitic writings, factually described Albert Lasker and his wife Mary, who numerous other authors credited for marketing into existence, mostly for the benefit of the Rockefeller family, the entire cancer and related American pharmaceutical industries. Elmer Bobst, nicknamed "the Vitamin King," was Lasker's partner in establishing the American Cancer Society's immortality in the early 1940s. Bobst later became president of other Rockefeller directed holdings including Hoffman LaRoche and Warner-Lambert. Bobst is further credited for having brought Richard Nixon to power, and because of his wealth and political influence, persuaded Nixon to wage his failed "War on Cancer." It was during this "war" that cancer viruses, many functionally and descriptively identical to the human immunodeficiency viruses (HIVs) associated with AIDS, were produced, cultured, and tested by Bionetics under the contract seen in figure 1.3. From here, as increasing numbers of authorities now admit, many of these man-made viruses were transmitted to humanity through contaminated vaccines. Some claim these contaminations were intended to destroy undesirable populations.[2, 7]

Indeed, the "War on Cancer," according to the evidence advanced in *Emerging Viruses: AIDS & Ebola—Nature, Accident or Intentional?*, was a direct result of, and benefit to, Rockefeller holdings. Rockefeller Standard Oil business managers and legal directors, John Foster and Allen Dulles, had initiated the partnership between the

Fig. 1.3. Litton Bionetics Contract Report to Investigate Viral Carcinogenesis in Primates by Developing HIV/AIDS-like ("Type-C" RNA Retro-)Viruses 1962–1972

BIONETICS RESEARCH LABORATORIES, INC. (NIH-71-2025)

Title: Investigations of Viral Carcinogenesis in Primates

Contractor's Project Directors: Dr. John Landon
                                 Dr. David Valerio
                                 Dr. Robert Ting

Project Officers (NCI): Dr. Roy Kinard
                         Dr. Jack Gruber
                         Dr. Robert Gallo

Objectives: (1) Evaluation of long-term oncogenic effects of human and animal viral inocula in primates of various species, especially newborn macaques; (2) maintenance of monkey breeding colonies and laboratories necessary for inoculation, care and monitoring of monkeys; and (3) biochemical studies of transfer RNA under conditions of neoplastic transformation and studies on the significance of RNA-dependent DNA polymerase in human leukemic tissues.

Major Findings: This contractor continues to produce over 300 excellent newborn monkeys per year. This is made possible by diligent attention to reproductive physiological states of female and male breeders. Semen evaluation, artifical insemination, vaginal cytology and ovulatory drugs are used or tried as needed.

Inoculated and control infants are hand-fed and kept in modified germ-free isolators. They are removed from isolators at about 8 weeks of age and placed in filtered air cages for months or years of observation. The holding area now contains approximately 1200 animals up to 5 years old. Approximately 300 are culled every year at a rate of about 25 per month. This is necessary to make room for young animals inoculated with new or improved virus preparations.

During the past year macaques were inoculated at birth or in utero with the Mason-Pfizer monkey mammary virus, Epstein-Barr virus, Herpesvirus saimiri, and Marek's disease virus. EB virus was given with immunostimulation and immunosuppression (ALS, prednisone, imuran). Australia antigen was given to newborn African green monkeys.

The breeding and holding colonies were surveyed for antibody to EBV. All breeders were positive and their offspring contain maternal antibody for several months. Colony-born offspring that have lost maternal antibody and are sero-negative will be surveyed periodically for conversion to the EB positive state.

An RNA-dependent DNA polymerase similar to that associated with RNA tumor viruses was detected in human leukemic cells but not in normal cells stimulat by phytohemagglutinin. The enzyme was isolated, purified and concentrated 200-fold, making possible its further characterization and study in relation to the leukemic process in man.

Significance to Biomedical Research and to the Program of the Institute: Inasmuch as tests for the biological activity of candidate human viruses will not be tested in the human species, it is imperative that another system be developed for these determinations and, subsequently for the evaluation of vaccines or other measures of control. The close phylogenetic relationship of the lower primates to man justifies utilization of these animals for these purposes. Further study of altered transfer RNA and polymerase enzymes would determine their significance in neoplastic change and provide a basis for selection of therapeutic agents.

Proposed Course: Continuation with increased emphasis on monitoring and intensive care of inoculated animals to determine if active infection occurs, effects of infection, and degree of immunosuppression when used. Further studies of human neoplasms at a molecular level will continue.

Date Contract Initiated: February 12, 1962.

Source: NCI staff. *The Special Virus Cancer Program: Progress Report #8*. Office of the Associate Scientific Director for Viral Oncology (OASDVO). J. B. Moloney, Ed., Washington, D. C.: U. S. Government Printing Office, 1970, p.104-05

Rockefeller family and Germany's leading industrial organization—the international chemical and pharmaceutical cartel, I.G. Farben. These partnerships began before, and extended beyond, World War II. Allen Dulles was director of American intelligence at that time. He established the CIA largely as a cover organization for Third Reich intelligence groups led by Reinhard Gehlen—The Gehlen Org, and Kurt Merk—The Merk Net[work]. Project Paperclip, the Nazi exfiltration program that helped approximately 2,000 scientists and technicians, Hitler's finest, come to America, was directed by these Rockefeller front men along with General Alexander Bolling and Henry Kissinger. This latter fact comes from Managing Editor of *Newsweek,* Walter Isaacson, from his biography of Kissinger. Among Paperclip's most valuable draftees was Erich Traub—Hitler's top biological weapons developer and world-class cancer virologist. Dr. Traub, and his assistant, went to work for the U.S. Navy beginning in 1948. The Navy has consistently been at the forefront of America's biological weapons research and development.[2,7]

At the end of WWII, I.G. Farben, hatched largely through the combined efforts and assets of Bayer Co. (Farbenfabriken vorm. Friedrich Bayer & Co. of Leverkusen), BASF (Badische Anilin und Soda-Fabrik of Ludwigshafen), Hoechst (Farbewerke worm. Meister Lucius und Bruening of Loechst am Main), and Agfa (Aktiengesellschaft fuer Anilinfabrikaten of Berlin), was broken up into a variety of chemical and pharmaceutical companies that dominate these industries today.[8] These Farben-Rockefeller enterprises, according to G. Edward Griffin, based on his meticulous review of U.S. *Congressional Records* from that period, included Sterling Drug and American Home Products (AHP), the parent company for American Cyanamid.[5] It was against AHP that attorney Dennis C. Sweet, III won a landmark $400 million settlement in 1999 for their dietary drug dealings with "fen-phen."[9]

Reflecting on small related details in *Emerging Viruses: AIDS & Ebola—Nature, Accident or Intentional?*, in a letter addressed to the President of American Cyanamid by a Lederle official, a "Cytomegalovirus [herpes virus] Contingency Plan" was discussed to deal with the ongoing problem of potentially lethal monkey cancer viruses, and contaminated oral polio vaccines. It was known by the 1970s that polio vaccine recipients, coinfected with monkey kidney tissue derived DNA viruses, would be at grave risk for cancer. The Lederle communiqué mentioned that safety guardians at the FDA, aware of the contaminations, continued to license the risky vaccine anyway. This

7

was another morbid example of U.S. public health officials turning a blind eye to politically and economically unsavory issues, particularly when Rockefeller profits were at stake.[2] A similar pattern of negligence, if not treason, involving these same parties, will be seen later regarding Malathion and Anvil sprayings and official stonewalling. Author Elaine Feuer cited other FDA injustices in her fine work *Innocent Casualties: The FDA's War Against Humanity.*[10]

At this early juncture, readers might feel uncomfortable with use of terms like "genocide" and "treason" in text related to generally esteemed public health agencies and officials. This was not done for sensationalism. These words most aptly describe the proceedings evidenced by the discussions and documents in this book. The term "genocide" is simply defined as "the mass murder of populations for political, economic, and/or ideological reasons." "Treason" is defined as, "the betrayal of trust, treachery; [and] the offense of attempting . . . to overthrow the government of the state . . ." As you will increasingly see, my use of these terms is contextually accurate.

Further stretching a conspiracy theorist's imagination, while introducing the topic of genocide, George H.W. Bush, at the time Elmer Bobst was coaching and bankrolling Richard Nixon's successful election bid, stood beside his grandfather's best friend, General William Draper III, to warn congressional legislators about the imminent national security threat posed by burgeoning Third World populations. Black Africans were particularly troublesome they said, as did George's grandfather, Prescott, during the 1920s. Prescott, at that time, had joined financial forces with John D. Rockefeller, the Draper family, and the Royal Family of England, to fund the initial research that led to the first racial hygiene programs. It was first called "eugenics." Later, it was renamed "population control," as actively practiced in "family planning," and "maternal and child health" clinics that administer infanticide and dubious vaccination programs. These topics will be discussed in great detail later. Today, eugenics is better known as "The Human Genome Project" which is still heavily funded by the Rockefeller and Sloan Foundations, as is Cold Spring Harbor Labs wherein much of this research continues in New York.[2, 7, 11]

The Bush and Draper population concerns prompted Henry Kissinger to begin writing the infamous *National Security Special [i.e., Secret] Memorandum 200: Implications of Worldwide Population Growth for U.S. Security and Overseas Interests.*[12] Submitted before he left his NSA advisor post in 1974, and declassified December 31,

1980, the document called for massive Third World depopulation. As *NSSM 200* was being prepared, George H.W. Bush was appointed to serve as CIA director.[2, 12]

Following Nixon's fall from grace and Kissinger's loss of his NSA post, the Rockefeller-directed depopulation agenda gained added force during the Carter administration with Zbigniew Brzezinski as NSA chief. This book's color gallery, and Chapter 18, documents a virtual all out war against Black people waged by American officals and covert operations as discussed in National Security Memorandum–46.

According to two previous CIA directors—Richard Helms and William Colby—as published in U.S. *Congressional Records*, Dr. Kissinger oversaw the development of biological weapons for covert operations including depopulation programs.[2, 12]

To the time of this writing, Dr. Kissinger has remained a leading foreign policy advisor for American presidents, as well as on the Board of Advisors of the Merck pharmaceutical company—another firm largely supported and directed by Rockefeller/Sloan Foundation investments,[13] and in days past, by I.G. Farben officials.[2, 5, 7, 14]

Curiously, the President of Merck, George W. Merck, was America's biological weapons industry director for most of the Cold War. This, according to a U.S. Army publication celebrating Fort Detrick's fiftieth anniversary as America's biological weapons testing center.[15]

According to CBS News correspondent Paul Manning, who credited Allen Dulles for much of his information, on August 10, 1944, the lion's share of the Nazi war chest, that is, the working capital of the I.G. Farben–Rockefeller chemical–pharmaceutical cartel, went largely to George Merck's company.[14]

At that time, along with Nazi pilfered gold, Allen Dulles helped to export leading Nazi officers and scientists through "rat lines" from Germany to other nations. The intelligence apparatus used the American Red Cross (ARC), and false ARC identifications, as one vehicle for transporting many war criminals. Conveniently, the Rockefeller family largely controlled the ARC as well as the CIA.[2]

Given the above history, it is reasonable to speculate that the infamous German intelligence "Merk net" was directed by members of the Merck pharmaceutical family, particularly since the names of extradited war criminals were commonly changed by the CIA by one letter for protection in future intelligence operations. For instance, Klaus

Barbie, "the butcher of Lyon," had his name changed to "Barbier," thus averting future identification during background checks.[2]

Modern Treachery

In 1993, CIA director James Woolsy testified before a congressional investigating committee concerned with the agency's French operations. Woolsy stated, "With the end of the Cold War, the CIA must enter the era of economic espionage." In the language of espionage, a French columnist explained, this meant "the CIA will henceforth do many services for American enterprises which take the trouble to ask it for 'help' in both counterespionage and espionage itself."[2]

Considering the history of the powerful people and their positions relayed above, it is not unreasonable to suspect a conspiracy to direct, at minimum, propaganda, if not global genocide under the auspices of "public health" or "population management."

This consideration might seem unconscionable were it not for the definitive links between companies like Litton, the CIA, and the Rockefeller-I.G. Farben cartel—the global chemical and pharmaceutical monopoly. In fact, I.G. Farben's building, that was used by top SS officials of the Third Reich, became the CIA's European headquarters immediately following the war. For its global investors, the marble decorated I.G. Farben building was intentionally spared from allied bombings. It was originally built by the "Bayer Pharmaceutical" consortium that included the distributors of aspirin *and* heroin to U.S. markets by the "Farbenfabriken of Elberfeld Co., 40 Stone Street, New York" according to a 1906 *Medical Observer* advertisement. Relatedly, the Merck Pharmaceutical Company became the world's chief distributor of pharmaceutical grade cocaine and morphine.[16]

It is no secret that the black market for these drugs became largely controlled by the CIA, with involvement by the Bush family in America.[17]

Links to the WNV

In his 1999 pre-Halloween "DISPATCH" in *The New Yorker*, Richard Preston treated us to another trick. Concerning at least five people who supposedly died in the New York City area from WNV (six at the time of this writing), Preston reported the CIA's concern was that the outbreak might have been a bioterrorist attack. "How else did it get here?" he asked.

Then he explained, "The West Nile virus was first identified by virologists in 1937 in the West Nile district of Uganda."[1] Reading between the lines, Preston neglected to explain where these pioneering virologists came from and who funded them. Given the above introduction to "public health" and "national security," the answer is predictable and very easily corroborated by a review of the scientific and historic literature.

Beginning in the 1920s the fields of cancer, virology, and "public health" were, for all practical purposes, entirely funded by the Rockefeller family in cooperation with Alfred P. Sloan, chief benefactors and directors of the later developed SKMCC.[18, 19]

By 1930, John D. Rockefeller's Standard Oil Company had "married" the I.G. Farben chemical/pharmaceutical cartel. Farben's directors—the cream of the SS and Third Reich—decided that Jewish people would best serve as slave labor in their corporate "concentration camps." Hitler's "racial hygiene program," historic documents showed, evolved from the "public health" and "scientific eugenics" efforts of the Rockefeller family, the British Royal Family, and other powerful political notables including Prescott Bush—George H. W. Bush's grandfather. It was Rockefeller money that primarily built the Kaiser Wilhelm Institute for Eugenics, Anthropology and Human Heredity in pre-Nazi Germany, forerunner to today's Cold Spring Harbor Labs' operation. Then, the Rockefellers instilled Ernst Rudin as the institute's director. He later became Hitler's chief racial hygienist. Margaret Sanger, the grand matriarch of "family planning," and "world population control," worked vigorously, at that time, to herald the necessary elimination of "dysgenic" people—mainly Blacks and the mentally retarded.[2, 7, 20]

As mentioned, Erich Traub, a world class cancer virologist, became Hitler's biological weapons chief, and following World War II was paid $65,000 annually, plus benefits, to work for the U.S. Navy's Biological Research Laboratory (NBRL) collaborating largely with the University of California at Berkeley and Irvine.[2]

Thus, Richard Preston's failure to mention these details was not likely an honest oversight. Erich Traub apparently received Rockefeller support, in one form or another, before, as well as after, WWII. Erich Traub's early work was likely being funded by the Rockefeller–

Sloan cancer directorship that first "discovered" the WNV in 1937, possibly as part of a biological weapons and/or eugenics program ongoing at that time in Uganda.

Subsequent efforts in the West Nile district of Uganda by "virologists" working for the Rockefeller cancer consortium also included the testing of the first cancer chemotherapeutic–a derivative of mustard gas used during World War I. The chemical toxin, Sloan investigators claimed, was highly effective in stopping the growth of cancer. Their promotions failed to mention it did the same for people.[18, 19]

Buried Intelligence Behind Propaganda Lines

A Litton Bionetics report to the NCI in 1971 listed virtually every virus, viral recombinant, and infectious agent under study by the world's leading primate cancer researchers, vaccine developers, and biological weapons contractors. It lacked mention of EEE, SLV, or WNV. Instead, only one encephalitis virus was cited——"Dawson's encephalitis" virus—likely deriving its name not from the West Nile district of Uganda, but from a Rockefeller-linked cancer investigator by the name of Dawson who was clearly affiliated, by NCI contract, with Litton, the IARC laboratory, and, by association, the CIA.[2]

Unfortunately, Preston did not relay this politically incorrect background in *The New Yorker*—the Rockefellers' home weekly.[1] Throughout his article, Preston merely weaved a web of paranoia-inciting intrigue regarding the mysterious New York outbreak. "People are bystanders," he claimed, "caught in the cross-fire—bitten by chance by an infected mosquito."

More intriguing, but less politically correct, in 1975, according to the *Congressional Record*, during Frank Church's investigation of the CIA for illegally storing and testing biological weapons, CIA officials testified that they had developed a new weapon that fired a micro-dart to administer toxins, viruses, or other infectious biologicals. It felt like a "mosquito bite" when it hit.[2]

Later, in the article, Preston advanced an alternative hypothesis to explain the WNV outbreak by articulating the suspicions of Ken Alibek, a Russian biological weapons ace, employed by the CDC and American intelligence. Alibek had conveniently defected to America, just in time, to join Preston and a cadre of CIA bioterror propagandists at the forefront of a full-fledged attack on the public's mind, as well as U.S. National Security. The outbreak might be a bioterrorist attack,

Alibek lamented. After all, Preston quoted the Secretary of the Navy, Richard Danzig, as saying bioterrorists could easily get away with such a naturally appearing outbreak. Danzig then relayed what a "top scientist who advises the FBI," had told him. This "person who has been deeply involved with bioterror planning" explained, "If I was planning a bioterror event, I'd do things with subtle finesse, to make it look like a natural outbreak. That would delay the response and lock up the decision-making process." Preston's prose is interesting, if not treasonous—delivering attack strategies to potential enemies.

Furthermore, as you will see later in a contribution made by the editor of the *Idaho Observer*, Don Harkins, Richard Danzig's statement regarding the planning of a bioterrorist event is completely false, misleading, and self-serving for those who have activated their own domestic bioterrorist agenda. Traditional headline-seeking bioterrorists would gain nothing from making an outbreak seem natural. Alternatively, this would be the method of choice for population control activists working covertly.

For critical readers, this raises the question of motive. What incentive might there be for U.S. military officials to instruct potential terrorists how they might best operate to penetrate our defenses, but additionally, to inundate the public with bioterrorist propaganda that best masks their own malicious capabilities and ongoing genocidal activities? The answer lies in the unconscionable destruction of America as the pre-eminent super-power.

A Question of Motive

I first grasped the rationality and gravity of this thesis during my investigation of Gulf War Syndrome (GWS). As detailed in *Healing Codes for the Biological Apocalypse*, the evolution of "secret societies," including the Skull & Bones and CFR, foreshadowed the military and medical experiments that gave rise to GWS. Members of the cryptocracy, including George H. W. Bush and James Baker III, were heavily implicated.[21]

For instance, based on reputable sources, George H. W, Bush's Secretary of State, James Baker III, was reported to have owned part of the vaccine manufacturing company against whom ailing Gulf War veterans had filed a lawsuit. Moreover, Mr. Bush is said to have been a major shareholder in that company—Tanox Biosystems of Houston.[22]

In fact, Bush became a board director at Tanox-affiliated Baylor College of Medicine after leaving his CIA directorship. Tanox was closely linked to Dr. Shyh-Ching Lo, who, under employment by— The Armed Forces Institute of Pathology, isolated and patented a "Pathogenic Mycoplasma" originally taken from an AIDS patient, that somehow contaminated many of the vaccines given to allied military personnel traveling to the Gulf. Only the French soldiers who did not receive the American made vaccines did not develop GWS.[21]

Further, what would seem inconceivable without seeing the documents reprinted in *Healing Codes for the Biological Apocalypse*, Tanox and Baylor College of Medicine first tested their Mycoplasma-infected vaccines on Huntsville, TX prisoners. As a result, the prisoners, and others in the community with whom the prisoners made contact, developed GWS long before the Gulf War. Thus, GWS could have been, and probably was, predicted and effected. [21, 22]

Given the evolution of, in George H.W. Bush's words, "a New World Order," largely advanced by secret agents, and a history of genocidal practices involving "dispensable" populations, GWS was reconcilable, as was the question of motive. The U.S. military, generally comprised of nationalistic, sovereign-thinking, patriotic individuals who pledged to kill and die to defend the U.S. Constitution against all foreign and domestic enemies, represented a "clear and present danger" to the evolving New World Order. Thus, the military might have been targeted for culling, defunding and demoralizing—roughly where it stood by the end of the Clinton administration.

In the eyes of a secret global war-making cabal, why would America be an exception? Like millions of people and numerous nations worldwide who had been sacrificed over the centuries to promote "peace on earth," the United States would have to pay its share of the price. Quoting from the oligarchy's *Report From Iron Mountain* (the summary section was reprinted in *Healing Codes*), "War as a system of gross population control to preserve the species cannot fairly be faulted."[23]

More WNV Propaganda

Preston, in another *New Yorker* article (Mar. 9, 1999), bragged about getting inside information regarding biological warfare and bioterrorism even before CIA chiefs. He said CIA officials have relied on him for intelligence![24]

Regarding the WNV story, however, Preston risked losing even lay reader credibility by providing an inane argument amid more of the steady stream of anti-Iraqi propaganda familiar to intelligence observers. An alleged Iraqi dissident author in hiding, Mikhael Ramadan, a Saddam Hussein look-alike, Preston wrote, had predicted "that Saddam would unleash a virus just months before the same one broke out unexpectedly in New York . . . It was enough to make any bioweapons analyst at the CIA feel uneasy." Citing Saddam's alleged interest in a WNV strain, Preston and Ramadan conveniently omitted American contractors' voluminous contributions to Iraq's biological weapons arsenals. These included strains of WNV, as detailed later. Following a lengthy and frightening discussion, this pair of propagandists admitted that the prospect of using the West Nile encephalitis virus in New York for traditional bioterrorism was absolutely stupid. The fact is "it only killed a few people and a lot of crows."

Preston did not discuss, nor rule out, the greatest likelihood that the WNV outbreak was a CIA brokered event, orchestrated for propaganda purposes to prepare the public's mind to willingly accept neurotoxic carcinogenic sprayings. This seemingly insane notion will be heavily supported in the pages ahead.[1]

Subliminal Racism

Veteran observers will recall similar racist propaganda successfully used in recent years against Muslims or Iraqi nationals labeled as bioterrorists. Two years ago, Larry Wayne Harris, claiming to be a CIA microbiologist, set the Internet abuzz with claims that Muslim women were bringing vials of anthrax into the United States in their crotches. Weeks later, Harris was observed at a national "Preparedness Exposition" demonstrating microbial incubators and spraying devices that, he said, could be used for bioterrorism.

Further investigation, including interviews with some of Harris's intimates, revealed that he had most likely been mind-manipulated by CIA controllers for counterintelligence purposes. Even without this knowledge, I was able to predict, six months in advance, Harris would be used in a bioterror campaign at a critical time. On the eve of the Clinton administration's announcement threatening renewed war with Iraq, as United Nations Secretary Kofi Anan was making a final bid with Hussein to avert further conflict, Harris was being set up for arrest in Las Vegas on possession of what was thought to be anthrax. His arrest made front-page national news, as did the CIA's message that bioterrorists are everywhere, particularly in the Arab world.[25]

Dr. Alibek later stated that he had informed people on Capitol Hill that the West Nile outbreak was suspicious. "I told them, 'It will not be possible to say whether or not it is terrorism unless we have a thorough study.' We need to take these situations with a high degree of seriousness," he cautioned.

Congressional Dysfunction

In fact, such in-depth study by congressional investigators has been chronically lacking; apparently by design. For example, when Congressman Dan Burton's (R-Indiana) Government Reforms Committee met later that month to examine suspicious ties between biological weapons contractors, defense department contracts, and vaccine industry practices, they decided not to examine the documents I was officially requested to send Beth Clay, the hearings coordinator. The reprinted contracts in *Emerging Viruses: AIDS & Ebola—Nature, Accident or Intentional?* linked Litton Bionetics to the first Ebola virus, and the Merck company to the hepatitis B vaccines administered by 1975 to gay men in New York City and Blacks in Central Africa, apparently tainted with HIV or its precursor(s). These documents were deemed too controversial for the committee's focus. Burton's group was simply unwilling to air the facts in light of the fiction considered gospel by the "scientific concensus" regarding AIDS and sacred cow vaccinations.

As Secretary of the Navy, Richard Danzig, admitted in Preston's malignant spoof, "Even if you suspect biological terrorism, it's hard to prove. It's equally hard to disprove. This is more illuminating of my prediction that we won't necessarily know when bioterror has occurred than it is of illuminating . . ." government sanctioned bioterrorists.[1]

Thus, congressional investigators, like public health officials, won't risk their careers unearthing fundamentally objectionable truths about covert U.S. military biological warriors like Secretary Danzig. Forget that his department has been at the forefront of biological weapons research and development since Erich Traub's enlistment into the U.S. Navy, or that Navy personnel have been periodically abused in biological weapons tests. As will be documented later, the U.S. Navy has been at the helm of ways to disseminate lethal biologicals in collaboration with the CIA and British MI6 "black ops" since the 1940s. Legislators simply have "no ears" to hear this truth.

Foreshadowing "Chemtrail" Technology

Revolting as all of this may seem, the CIA and U.S. Navy, working in tandem with the Army, haven't spared military, or civilian populations, from contemporary germ warfare "experiments" or outright biological attacks. Frank Church's investigating committee learned, for instance, that the "USS Coral Sea anchored in Kampton Roads, and the USS F.D. Bailey at sea off [the] entrance to Kampton . . ." had been sprayed at least seventeen times with biological agents ranging from strains of Bacillus (physically similar to anthrax) to *E. coli*.[1]

Mutant strains of *E. coli* had been prepared by CIA contractors and included lethal varieties for potential use as bioweapons that likely included strain 157. This strain was responsible for dozens of deaths and the suspicious takeover of the Hudson Beef Company by Clinton family friend, Don Tyson, and his Springdale, Arkansas-based Tyson Foods Company.[21] More on this later.

Likewise, civilians in the New York subway system, under the skies of San Francisco, and in the tunnels of the Pennsylvania Turnpike, had been sprayed with biological inhalants. Similarly, in 1999, U.S. legislators learned that as many as 200,000 Gulf War troops were unwittingly used in AIDS vaccine experiments wherein portions of the AIDS virus, HIV, were recombined with the "Pathogenic Mycoplasma" cited earlier. [21]

Therefore, it is no wonder, regarding the 1999 WNV outbreak, and subsequent pesticide sprayings for similarly alleged purposes, Richard Preston concluded, "This valley in New Jersey reminded me in a strange way of Kitum Cave, . . . a haunting place I'd seen some years ago."[1]

The toxic exposures about which he wrote, and additional ones in the pages ahead, were more hauntingly reminiscent of a litany of crimes against humanity, violations of the Nuremberg Code, by agents who have consistently conducted global depopulation for Malthusian eco-genocide.

As with the recounting of these facts, the following chapters present an alternative, highly unsettling, and heavily documented view of contemporary "public health" as it relates to "non-lethal" toxic warfare that includes white-collar bioterrorism. Most people believe that the "public health" community heroically defends against such attacks. Unfortunately, as the following chapters document, "public health," as a branch of medical science, most actively promotes and veils the waging of class warfare and global genocide.

The following chapters detail our entrance into an era of accelerated depopulation, and the methods and materials, particularly airborne, by which the vast majority of us are being affected and ultimately killed.

References

1) Preston R. West Nile [Virus] Mystery: How did it get here? The C.I.A. would like to know. *The New Yorker*, Oct. 18 & 25, 1999. pp. 90-108.

2) Horowitz L and Martin J. *Emerging Viruses: AIDS & Ebola—Nature, Accident or Intentional?* Rockport, Masssachusetts: Tetrahedron Publishing Group, 1997.

3) Preston R. *The Hot Zone*. New York: Random House, 1994.

4) Eye witness testimony that African villagers were used in lethal vaccine experiments during the 1950s to early 1960s in this precise area, home to an "American medical research laboratory," was provided by C. Sally, M.D., an African physician and post-doctoral laboratory assistant who worked there at that time. According to Dr. Sally, mosquitoes were blamed, then as well, for spreading Burkitt's lymphoma to Black children, though, he said, his colleagues knew better. The truth was that experimental vaccines had delivered the cancer virus through the mothers to their infants. Dr. Sally's audiotaped testimony is included in: "Horowitz 'On Vaccines'" from Tetrahedron Publishing Group (1-888-508-4787), 1998, by this author.

5) Griffin GE. *World Without Cancer*. Westlake Village, CA: American Media, 1997.

6) Mullins E. *Murder By Injection: The Story of the Medical Conspiracy Against America*. Staunton, VA: The National Council for Medical Research, 1988.

7) Horowitz L and Emory D. "The Nazi-American Biomedical Biowarfare Connection." Sandpoint, Idaho: Tetrahedron Publishing Group (1-888-508-4787), 1998.

8) Borkin J. *The Crime and Punishment of I.G. Farben: The Unholy Alliance Between Hitler and the Great Chemical Combine*. The Free Press (Barnes & Noble Books), 1997.

9) Gary WE, Hitt J, Pires Jr., Scruggs RF and Sweet DC. Making the case for racial reparations. *Harper's Magazine* 2000;301;1806:38.

10) Feuer E. *Innocent Casualties: The FDA's War Against Humanity*. Pittsburgh, PA: Dorrance Publishing Co., Inc., 1996.

11) Blowen M. 'Nazi Medicine' demands to be seen. *The Boston Globe*. Tuesday, April 26, 1997, p. D8; See also: Lee MA. The Nazi past underlying politics today. *Los Angeles Times*, Sunday June 25, 2000, p. M2&M6.

12) Kissinger H. *National Security Special Memorandum 200: Implications of Worldwide Population Growth for U.S. Security and Overseas Interests*. December 10, 1974. Classified by Harry C. Blaney, III. Declassified by the White House on December 31, 1980. NSIAD-ROS-89-4. Available through The National Archives.

13) Isaacson W. *Kissinger: A Biography*. New York: Simon & Schuster, 1992, p. 734.

14) Manning P. *Martin Bormann: Nazi in Exile*. Secaucus, NJ: Lyle Stuart Inc., p. 134.

15) Covert N. *Cutting Edge: A History of Fort Detrick, Maryland, 1943-1993*. Fort Detrick, MD: Public Affairs Office (HSHD-PA), Headquarters U.S. Army Garrison, 1993.p. 17.

16) Advertisements published in the journals *Medical Observer*, Philadelphia, 1906 and *Chemist and Druggist of Australasia*, February, 1908.

17) Blum W. The CIA & Drugs. *Prevailing Winds: The Journal of Current Events, Politics, History and Health*, Number Six, January-April, 200.

18) Starr P. *The Social Transformation of American Medicine: The rise of a sovereign profession and the making of a vast industry*: New York: Basic Books, Inc., 198.

19) Lynes B. *The Cancer Cure That Worked! Fifty Years of Suppression*. Queensville, Ontario: Marcus Books, 1987, pp. 30-32.

20) Kuhl S. *The Nazi Connection: Eugenics, American Racism, and German National Socialism*. New York: Oxford University Press, 1994.

21) Horowitz L and Puleo J. *Healing Codes for the Biological Apocalypse*. Sandpoint, Idaho: Tetrahedron Publishing Group, 1999. pp. 251-253.

22) McAlvany DS. Special Report: Germ Warfare Against America: The Desert Storm Plague and Cover-up. *The McAlvany Intelligence Advisor*, August, 1996, pp. 1-40 (Bush connections to Tanox see p. 27). This information was verbally confirmed by Garth Nicolson, Ph.D., previously with the Univ. of Texas and currently in Irvine, CA at the Institute for Molecular Medicine, during a personal communication with this author.

23) Lewin LC et al., *Report From Iron Mountain on the Possibility and Desirability of Peace*. New York: The Dial Press, 1967, pp. 79-101.

24) Preston R. Biological Armageddon: Is it too late to stop the new weapons of mass destruction? *The New Yorker*, March 9, 1998, pp. 52-65.

25) Martin R. Setup from the start!: Emerging information about arrests of "bio-terrorists." *The Phoenix Contact* 1998(March 3);20;2:1-25. For the evidence see "Larry Wayne Harris" downloadable articles through the archives at www.tetrahedron.org. 19) Lynes B. *The Cancer Cure That Worked! Fifty Years of Suppression*. Queensville, Ontario: Marcus Books, 1987, pp. 30-32.

20) Kuhl S. *The Nazi Connection: Eugenics, American Racism, and German National Socialism*. New York: Oxford University Press, 1994.

21) Horowitz L and Puleo J. *Healing Codes for the Biological Apocalypse*. Sandpoint, Idaho: Tetrahedron Publishing Group, 1999. pp. 251-253.

22) McAlvany DS. Special Report: Germ Warfare Against America: The Desert Storm Plague and Cover-up. *The McAlvany Intelligence Advisor*, August, 1996, pp. 1-40 (Bush connections to Tanox see p. 27). This information was verbally confirmed by Garth Nicolson, Ph.D., previously with the Univ. of Texas and currently in Irvine, CA at the Institute for Molecular Medicine, during a personal communication with this author.

23) Lewin LC et al., *Report From Iron Mountain on the Possibility and Desirability of Peace*. New York: The Dial Press, 1967, pp. 79-101.

24) Preston R. Biological Armageddon: Is it too late to stop the new weapons of mass destruction? *The New Yorker*, March 9, 1998, pp. 52-65.

25) Martin R. Setup from the start!: Emerging information about arrests of "bio-terrorists." *The Phoenix Contact* 1998 (March 3);20;2:1-25. For the evidence see "Larry Wayne Harris" downloadable articles through the archives at www.tetrahedron.org.

Death in the Air

Chapter 2.
Death in the Air

"Malathion is a dangerous neurotoxin. The whole
purpose of its development was to destroy living
organisms. . . ."

California Senator Tom Hayden, 1994

On July 1, 2000, Badische Anilin und Soda-Fabrik of
Ludwigshafen (BASF), one of the founding mega-firms in the
global I.G. Farben chemical/pharmaceutical cartel, completed its acquisition of American Cyanamid's "crop protection business" in the
United States, Canada, Europe, and Mexico. The acquisition demonstrated the incestuous relationship between Cyanamid, an American
Home Products company inexorably linked to Rockefeller/Farben
pharmaceutical holdings, and BASF, equally linked to the German–
American biomedical chemical cartel. The takeover advanced BASF
"to the top tier of global crop protection companies," according to a
press release distributed by the companies.[1] Along with the acquisition
came a number of insecticides that contained Cyanamid's Malathion.

Until recently, Malathion was one of the most commonly used organophosphate insecticides. It was used throughout the world to control pests infesting greenhouses, ornamentals, agricultural crops, stored
grain, livestock, forests, households, and gardens. Commercial, industrial, and government uses made up most of the U.S. market. This included its use in schools, restaurants, warehouses, manufacturing
plants, and widespread pest control such as "emergency" mosquito
spraying programs like the one administered in response to alleged
WNV outbreaks.[2]

Contributing to Malathion's wide appeal was its "relatively low"
acute toxicity for mammals. Like other pesticides, however, including
DDT, Malathion had been proven to cause numerous irreversible health
problems in humans and other living things. That is why Malathion
began its decline from its "most favored" pesticide status during the
1990s.

In short, Malathion posed a far greater risk than most suspected by reading its label. During the latter part of the twentieth century, studies confirmed Malathion's link to genetic damage, cancer in laboratory animals and possibly humans, vision impairment, and many other health problems in humans and animals.

Registered by Cyanamid for American use in 1956, the company reported that between 1961 and 1973, 1.4 million pounds of Malathion were applied "for living quarters" in pest control, and to "protect" American soldiers in Vietnam.

By 1990, approximately 15 million pounds of Malathion had been used in America.[3] Agriculturally, Texas, Oklahoma, California and Pennsylvania led the rest of the United States in applying annually more than 200,000 pounds each.

Although American Cyanamid was the first producer of Malathion, the U.S. Environmental Protection Agency (EPA) listed 342 registrants, either manufacturers or formulators of Malathion; and 1218 product registrations as of 1987.[2]

The Varied Uses of Malathion

In a scientific review article published in the Winter of 1992 *Journal of Pesticide Reform*,[4] author Loretta Brenner provided a detailed analysis of Malathion. She summarized its uses "in a wide variety of situations." It was said to "provide broad spectrum control of many insects and mites, especially household pests, aphids, spider mites, and scales." Malathion was also used extensively in mosquito, grasshopper, and gypsy moth eradication programs. Mediterranean fruit flies and other pests also seemed susceptible. Among its uses, besides "regulatory pest control," listed by the California Department of Pesticide Regulation, "transplants and root stock" usage led the way with more than 300,000 pounds used in the state in 1990. "Alfalfa," "landscape maintenance," and "structural pest control" completed the top five uses, each applying more than 200,000 pounds to varied environments annually.[4]

Other uses of Malathion, sold under several trade names alone or in formulas, included ground and aerial spraying, foggers, paints, baits, pet collars, animal dust bags and dips, and cattle feed blocks.[2,5]

The following facts concerning human exposures were excerpted from Ms. Brenner's article:

Malathion's widespread use makes potential for human exposure high. The National Institute for Occupational Safety and Health estimates that between 20,000 and 100,000 workers are occupationally exposed to Malathion in the U.S. For example, grain elevator workers in Louisiana were exposed to grain dust contaminated with 0.17 to 32 parts per million (ppm) of Malathion. In another incident, office workers complained of headaches and nausea after working in a room adjacent to a pesticide storage shed for a mosquito control program. Investigation showed that Malathion was still evaporating from a wall where a pesticide spill had occurred five years earlier. In California, where physicians make mandatory reports of pesticide-related illnesses, Malathion was the third most frequently reported pesticide. Malathion caused five times more occupational illnesses, per pound sold, than did the average pesticide [based on 1981 and 1985 reports].

Human Exposures From Spraying Programs

According to Dr. Jorge R. Mancillas, a University of California neurobiologist, formerly affiliated with the Salk Institute, the question as to how much Malathion exposure people received was critical yet confusing. In an effort to stop a 1990 spraying campaign in California aimed at the Mediterranean fruit fly (Medfly), he warned the public regarding the false and misleading testimonies offered by state officials. Here is his scientific assessment regarding the "critical question" of Malathion exposures during spraying programs as in the case of New York's WNV campaign:

State officials repeatedly bring out the importance of the concept of dosage and claim that the doses applied are very low, too low to cause any harm. The first flaw with their argument is that they are not monitoring what doses people are being exposed to, but at best what amounts are being applied to the ground.

But let us examine this question using their figures. The EPA has established that the "No Observable Effect Level," that is, the amount below which no effects are observed is 0.2 mg per kilogram (kg) of body weight. Based on that they have established a Provisional Acceptable Daily Intake level of 0.02mg per kg of body weight . . . .

Now, if you look at the State Department of Food and Agriculture's own figures of how much they are spraying, their official notices say that they are spraying 0.000049 ounces per acre. That sounds like very little, right? However, if you convert that to milligrams, it comes to 1.4 mg per square foot. That is, there are 1.4 mg of Malathion spread over each square foot. This means that a 50 lb child (22.7 kgs) would have to be exposed to the Malathion found in 1/3 of a square foot to exceed the EPA's acceptable intake level, and to the amount of Malathion in 3.5 square feet to have observable effects. If you have a child playing in the grass, a sand box, or on a slide, drinking from a public fountain, or elsewhere in a park, or in his home, he can easily be exposed to that amount.

We have also recently learned from scientists working for the California Department of Health Services that the amounts of Malathion are closer to 1.9 mg per square foot and that the distribution is not homogeneous, having found areas where the concentration was around 5 mg per square foot. Is it, therefore, surprising that so many people in the sprayed areas are reporting adverse health effects?[3]

Dr. Mancillas went on to explain that a number of physicians in Los Angeles had documented people who displayed the classical symptoms of Malathion toxicity during and following the county's spraying. "I am told by Dr. Thrasher," he wrote, "that he has documented thousands of calls made to one of the non-governmental Malathion hotlines and found that close to 15,000 people reported classical symptoms of Malathion poisoning. That is not unreasonable if you consider that over a million people are being exposed, and that figure would represent something between 1-2% of that population."[3]

Common Reports of Illness from Pesticide Spraying

It is sobering to reflect on this information, particularly in light of the fact that approximately 16 million Americans are hypersensitive to pesticides in the first place. That means that more than five percent of the public exposed to even smaller doses of Malathion, or other neurotoxic pesticides such as Anvil, are likely to become very ill.[6]

"Exposure due to drift and over spray," Ms. Brenner continued, "can also be problematic." She reviewed several studies in this regard, including the cases that developed when a "homeowner adjacent to a school in Arizona sprayed his garden with Malathion. The spray drifted into the school ventilation system and caused nearly 300 elementary school children to be hospitalized with headaches, nausea, and breathing difficulties."[4,7]

Furthermore, during the 1990 Medfly aerial spray program in Los Angeles, much like the 2000 mosquito control program in New York, sporting fields were targeted while youth leagues played ball. In Los Angeles, most of the children and their fans reported symptoms, including nausea, headaches, skin rashes and hives, sore throats, and irritated eyes. In New York, most of the bystanders ran for their lives.[3]

A number of more disturbing reports were compiled and published for the International Cancer Control Society by Betsy Russell-Manning.

One such case involved Twila Niblack, and her three-year-old daughter Jenisee. Believing in the official safety assurances issued by public health officials in their "Notice of Aerial Treatment," she and Jenisee "watched the helicopters spray" Malathion without any concern. The following day Jenisee lost her appetite and couldn't get to sleep. Hours later she remained bedridden and agitated. The child's eyelids blinked rapidly as she shook, swayed "as if drunk" on her way to the bathroom, and then lost all control of her bladder and bowel functions. A trip to a hospital emergency room proved useless. By then Jenisee was drooling, and as if retarded, "her tongue was hanging out of her mouth." Several hospital visits later, Jenisee was admitted for intensive care, diagnosed with organophosphate poisoning, given Atropine, and subsequently improved. Ms. Niblack wrote and circulated her story in an effort to persuade public health officials to change their notices to better prepare people to prevent spraying program injuries.[3]

California State University professor, Luane Oberholtzer, relayed her similar toxicity reaction. She described her experience as follows:

> I became very ill early on with "flu-like" symptoms (sore throats, headaches, malaise, aching and muscle spasms in arms and legs) following the first [aerial] spraying [for the Medfly]. By the 2nd and 3rd spraying I was experiencing serious central nervous system symptoms.

> I began having extreme memory loss along with the inability to concentrate. I had a slurring of speech and my jaw became very unresponsive. I had a vocabulary loss where I simply couldn't find words, and even very simple ones. For instance, if I started to say, "I am going to close the door," by the time I got to the end of the sentence, "door" wouldn't be there. I came to the point where I literally could not lecture. I had to start substituting other activities in my classes. I was also extremely depressed.

When asked by her interviewer, Betsy Russell-Manning, if her depression resulted from her memory deficits and lack of concentration, or some other source, Luane replied:

> I was clinically depressed. I was chemically depressed; a great deal of crying, and vague thinking patterns. I couldn't focus my thoughts. I couldn't plan my classes. I have never gone into a class unplanned.

You just don't go into a 4-hour class unplanned. I would just wander into the class and feel guilty I hadn't done any preparation. It was really awful.

First I went to a physician and he said I just had the "flu." I was about six weeks into this when I talked to some people in our area who understood the harm Malathion can do and then I took a homeopathic remedy for Malathion. A mild form of the only known antidote, which is Atropine. It is something you don't fool around with either; but I thought about it for a long time and then I did take the homeopathic form. . . . Within two-and-a-half days the symptoms were greatly improved. It was astounding. This simply reinforced my own feelings that my symptoms were due to organophosphate poisoning, because you don't respond to an antidote unless you have been poisoned.

I work in one spray area, and I live in another spray area. So I would be sprayed one day at home and go to school the next day and be sprayed again. It would be a double exposure for me. There was really no way to escape it. Until finally I decided to leave home and stay in a motel or with relatives during the spraying times, plus take my homeopathic remedy.[3]

Professor Oberholtzer concluded that she has yet to fully recover, but, using homeopathies, she was on the mend.

Mode of Neurotoxic Action

As detailed above, Malathion's acute toxicity is registered early on the central and peripheral nervous systems. This is explained by its primary mode of action as a neurotoxin.

Very simply, Malathion is an inhibitor of acetylcholinesterase— the enzyme responsible for controlling acetylcholine, the chemical that is primarily responsible for propelling skeletal nerve impulses and functioning muscles throughout the body. By blocking this enzyme's function, Malathion literally knocks out all control of the central nervous system.

More technically, Malathion, and related thiophosphonates, stimulate and subsequently block, the nicotinic receptor sites of skeletal muscles. This results initially in a tetanus-like condition, muscle spasms and pain, followed quickly by muscle weakness and then complete paralysis.

These compounds, Malathion, its relatives, and other pesticides including Malathion's modern substitute, Anvil, require breakdown or "biotransformation" by the liver and its enzymes, particularly those in the "cytochrome P450 system." Such neurotoxins are thus metabolized into other more, or less, harmful compounds—active "oxon" metabolites.

A primary problem, grossly overlooked by government officials instigating pesticide-spraying programs, rests in the sub-optimal cytochrome P450 liver enzymes produced by increasingly larger populations, both infants and adults.

Neonates, for instance, have far less active liver enzymes than do adults. Thus, they are far more sensitive to these chemicals than adults, "mainly because of a slower rate of detoxification of the active metabolite," according to genetic neurobiologists reporting in the journal *Teratology*.[8] These doctors further found that drug metabolizing systems are less well developed in the fetus than the neonate, and the human fetus is apparently much more sensitive to pesticide exposures than adults.

As a result, these authors warned pregnant mothers concerning their exposure to Malathion in anti-lice shampoo. In anti-lice solutions, the level of toxic exposure may not be enough to harm the mother, but due to "placental transport and fetal exposure," neurological dysfunction and genetic mutations in the fetus may develop causing birth defects in the newborns.[8]

According to Fred Nelson, Director of the National Foundation for the Chemically Sensitive, many people have inadequate levels of cytochrome P450 liver enzymes—phosphosulphotransferase and/or glucose 6 phosphatases—for coping with pesticide exposures. Many, he submitted, have liver damage for various reasons from alcoholism and aspartame intake to hepatitis B or C infections. Through these assaults, people lose their ability to produce "adequate amounts of liver enzymes; so that when you inhale, or gain [exposure] to pesticides through skin absorption, which is even more dangerous than inhalation, you do not detoxify or break [neurotoxins] down from fat storable to water excretable [metabolites]. . . ."

You then, consequently, develop increased blood saturation levels of neurotoxic pesticide. When such elevated blood levels occur, then the blood–brain barrier becomes saturated. Then "ion exchange transference across the blood–brain barrier occurs; so your brain gets poisoned by the organophosphates. . . ." Director Nelson continued to explain that "this also happens with carbamates, and the organochlorine pesticides. . . . We have probably 5 to 10 million people chronically effected in a very bad way, and a total of 30% of the population are affected to some degree."

Malation's More Toxic Metabolites

Dr. Melvin Reuber became a "whistle blower" in this field. The highly distinguished scientist, previously with the Frederick Cancer Research Laboratory—the National Cancer Institute's and U.S. military's top biological and chemical weapons testing facility—reported on the "mountains of evidence concerning the harmful effects of Malathion to humans" documented as far back as 1940–50. Concerning the conversion of the organophosphates that takes place in the liver, he explained that Malathion is "metabolized to malaoxon, and malaoxon is many thousands of times more toxic than Malathion."[9]

Another professor, Sumner M. Kalman, M.D., of the Department of Pharmacology at Stanford University, presented more neurotoxicity information regarding Malathion in the form of an affidavit submitted to Santa Clara County officials. In his effort to halt their spraying program, Dr. Kalman wrote:

> The organophosphorus insecticides are highly reactive chemicals. They combine irreversibly with critically important molecules in the body. This is the basis for their combination with acetylcholinesterase causing paralysis of nerve, nerve-muscle, and some nerve-nerve functions. In severe cases this interaction causes respiratory depression, even respiratory arrest. Motor weakness, twitching of muscles, and an unsteady gait may appear. There are disturbances of the heart, blood pressure, intestine, and central nervous system. Some of these effects may be counteracted by appropriate treatment if carried out in time. But such treatment may have to be carried out for many days, even weeks. And in some cases of poisoning, signs and symptoms persist after recovery. This feature of poisoning due to organophosphorus pesticides concerns me very much. The combination between pesticides and body proteins is an irreversible one. This means that the localized damage persists at least until these proteins are replaced by formation of newly-made molecules . . . . From all that I know about drugs and other toxic materials, I believe that we put certain individuals at risk if we permit aerial spraying of Malathion.[10]

Obviously, given this background, and the caliber of scientists and physicians who take exception to the gross spraying of neurotoxic pesticides such as Malathion and Anvil, official reports that objectors represent an unscientific fringe are gross lies.

In 1997, Colonel Jack Kingston, recently retired from the Pentagon's Joint Chiefs of Staff, explained to me that, "the best covert operation is one that takes place in broad daylight in front of everyone's eyes, yet no one sees it." In the next chapter, as I discuss Malathion's toxicity, and thereafter, other "public health" practices that expose unwitting millions to other lethal chemicals and biologicals, Col. Kingston's instruction may be recalled, along with the ultimate source of these chemicals—the Rockefeller/I.G. Farben cartel.

References

1) BASF publicity department. Acquisition of crop protection business from American Cyanamid. http://www.basf.com/businesses/consumer/agproducts/our_group/about.html.

2) U.S. EPA. Office of Pesticides and Toxic Substances. *Guidance for the reregistration of pesticide products containing Malathion as the active ingredient*. Washington, D.C.: U.S. Gov. Printing Office, 1988.

3) Russell-Manning B. An interview with Jorge R. Mancillas, Ph.D. In: *Malathion: Toxic Time Bomb, The Poisoning of Our People*. San Francisco: Cancer Control Society, 1990, p. , 48, 82.

4) Brenner L. Malathion. *Journal of Pesticide Reform*. 1992;12;4:29-36

5) *Farm Chemicals Handbook*, Willoughby, OH: Meister Publishing Company, 1991.

6) Jaffe R. 16 million Americans are sensitive to pesticides. Press release, April 2, 1990. Serammune Physicians Lab, 11100 Sunrise Valley Drive, Reston, VA 22091.

7) Revere, DT and Rigg M. Insecticide sends 296 kids to hospitals. *Arizona Daily Star*, April 25, 1987, p. 1.

8) Lindhout D and Hageman G. Amyoplasia congenita-like condition and maternal Malathion exposure. *Teratology* 1987;36:7-9.

9) Reuber M. Lecture on Malathion. Franklin High School, Series of Lectures on the Dangers of Malathion. March 1990. In: *Malathion: Toxic Time Bomb, The Poisoning of Our People*. Russell-Manning B., ed. San Francisco: Cancer Control Society, 1990, pp. 101-104.

10) Kalman S. Affidavit of Sumner M. Kalman, M.D. Presented to the Santa Clara County commissioners in response to suspend Malathion sprayings. March 24, 1981. In: *Malathion: Toxic Time Bomb, The Poisoning of Our People*. Russell-Manning B., ed. San Francisco: Cancer Control Society, 1990, p. 203.

Chapter 3.
Pesticide Toxicity

"In spite of the large-scale use of Malathion in
aerial applications . . . there's been no attempt to
actually measure the exposure and uptake . . .
under representative spray conditions."

Samuel Epstein, M.D., 1994
Member, EPA Pesticide Subcommittee of the Health
Advisory Committee

Aerial sprayings of neurotoxic pesticides have become commonly accepted practices despite their risks being inadequately considered. Just how safe Anvil, Malathion, and the array of organophosphate insecticides, including Parathion is, is not even a rational question. "There really is no need to discuss it," cancer chemical expert Dr. Melvin Reuber, reported. Data from the 1950s and 1960s prove pesticides to be extremely dangerous. In Japan, for example, over a 17-year period, there were 19,500 cases of phosphate insecticide poisoning, including more than 9,000 deaths. In another small country, Finland, 286 deaths were reported over six years. In Denmark, in the same period, another 273 deaths occurred. "In California between 1957 and 1960," Dr. Reuber recalled, "there were 950 cases of poisoning, . . . including 790 agricultural, 90 industrial and 70 other causes."[1] Though these numbers may seem small, they represent a fraction of the inadequately reported cases. Mass intoxication of thousands of citizens poisoned by gross organophosphate contamination of foods was heralded in India, Singapore, Mexico, Egypt, and elsewhere.[1] Yet, despite the established toxicity to humans, widespread pesticide sprayings continue.

For decades, numerous investigators have called for more research leading to a better understanding of the extent to which insecticides intoxicate people, though more is known about such agents than most chemicals. Organophosphate pesticides, in particular, have been exhaustively studied. "This is not only because of their use as a pesticide," Dr. Reuber admitted, "but because the U.S. Government, [and] the military, had keen interest in their uses of nerve gases to be used in war."[1]

Having served at the top military biochemical weapons testing laboratory in the U.S.—Fort Detrick—Dr. Reuber noted organophosphate insecticides evolved out of Germany's intense interest in war gases. Though he did not mention the I.G. Farben/Rockefeller chemical cartel's part in these developments, or their central role in gassing millions of holocaust victims to death, he did make curious note of America's inheritance of organophosphate "insecticides" from Cyanamid in 1946. This, of course, was perfectly timed with the infiltration of America's chemical, pharmaceutical, and scientific communities by "Project Paperclip" scientists who had previously worked for I.G. Farben and the Third Reich. (See figure 3.1.)

Thereafter, "in a very few years," Dr. Reuber explained, pesticides became widely used in American agriculture, though from the very beginning," he cautioned, "they were recognized as dangerous to humans."[1]

Double-Talk Regarding Human Toxicity

In 1952, a highly esteemed chemical investigator, DeBoise, wrote, "The high inherent toxicity of the organophosphates and the lack of substantial differences in the toxicity of these compounds from mammals and insects, emphasizes the necessity of obtaining thorough understanding of the effects, which these agents may have on man and domestic animals."[1]

Despite DeBoise's urgent recommendation, to date, according to Steven Ross, President of the World Research Foundation, the "data gaps" concerning these neurotoxic pesticides have not been filled. One simply gets double talk from government and industry officials, he said. "We are having a little bit of difficulty here understanding what these people are talking about," Mr. Ross testified during the Los Angeles City Council hearings of 1989 concerning the aerial spraying of Malathion. "The data gaps are filled and they are content [officials say]. But we have from the EPA that there are data gaps. We hear from the state, saying, they believe the data gaps are filled. I then have another EPA letter saying the data gaps are not filled and then [another] letter directly from the governor's office saying, 'There are still data gaps in exactly the areas of our concern,'" which included acute and chronic human toxicity, along with genetic and reproductive disturbances.[2]

Fig. 3.1. I.G. Farben Building in Frankfurt—Producers of Early War Gases and Pesticides

The I.G. Farben–Rockefeller chemical and pharmaceutical cartel complex in Germany (above) remained protected from allied bombings during WWII to become the CIA's headquarters following the war. Germany's leading industrial organization, whose subsidiaries produced the earliest pesticides, drugs, and war gases, including Zyklon B (below), largely dictated economic and industrial policies to Hitler and his financial minister Martin Bormann. The cartel arrangement between Rockefeller's Standard Oil Company and Farben included a noncompetitive sharing of global revenues from the petrochemical and pharmaceutical industries. Photos courtesy of the National Archives, Griffin *op. cit.*, and Borkin *op. cit.*

Apparently, according to scientific studies, humans are more susceptible to many pesticides, including Malathion and Parathion, than experimental animals. In 1953, for instance, scientists published a report in the *American Journal of Medicine* describing the first signs and symptoms of organophosphate poisoning. They included: "headache, nausea, vomiting, squinting, blurred vision, myosis, weakness, diarrhea, abdominal pain, and pallor and skin rashes."[1]

In moderate to severe cases of pesticide poisoning, the signs and symptoms include: breathing problems, "salivation, lacrimation, muscle fatigue, shock, cardiac arrhythmias, coma and death."[1]

It should be noted that mány of these early symptoms mimic flu-like symptoms, and may be confusing to physicians presented with the challenge of diagnosing insecticide toxicity. Flu-like illnesses have been mysteriously on the rise and are discussed in greater detail in Chapter 11, particularly as this medical dilemma relates to chemical and biological cofactors.

In most cases of acute pesticide neurotoxicity, Dr. Reuber reported, "giddiness, tension, anxiety, restlessness, emotional mobility, excessive dreaming, insomnia, nightmares, headaches, tremors, apathy, withdrawal, depression, drowsiness," and concentration difficulties occurred.

Anecdotally, after living in New Jersey, New York, and metropolitan Boston for most of my life, then moving to the great Northwest, I noticed a great difference in the "tension" levels exhibited by people in these different parts of the country. Was it a simple coincidence that the above signs and symptoms of acute neurotoxic effects of pesticide poisoning were routinely exhibited by people from the northeastern part of the United States? Could the jet stream have carried huge amounts of sprayed organophosphates into the northeast states? According to a U.S. Geological Survey report provided later, this is likely. Is it also possible that the increased unfriendliness and anxiety exhibited generally in that part of the world might be linked to increased exposure to these neurotoxins aside from traffic congestion, fossil fuel emissions, and population density problems? These "data gaps" are not likely to be filled by government or industry any time soon.

In her compilation of articles and government documents in *Malathion: Toxic Time Bomb,* author/editor Betsy Russell-Manning discussed case reports of poisoning with Parathion, Mevinphos, and Malathion, which "indicated that 4 to 9 percent of acutely poisoned individuals experienced delayed or persistent neurological and psychiatric effects such as agitation, insomnia, weakness, nervousness, irritability, forgetfulness and confusion, and depression; persistent mental disturbances reported as delirium, combativeness, hallucinations, or psychosis."[4]

Again, concentrations of pesticides that might be considered safe for healthy persons, might not be so for others. Those with respiratory diseases, such as asthma or emphysema, the very young or the very old, those with cardiovascular diseases, those with skin sensitivity and skin diseases, or with previous exposure to insecticides, were warned by the California Department of Health in 1980 to steer clear of exposures. Those with depressed immune systems, and children prescribed Malathion by public health and school officials, for instance, for the treatment of head lice, were far more likely to become hypersensitive than healthy adults. Also, individuals with mental health problems, particularly those taking additional neuroactive medications may become hypersensitive to pesticides. Dr. Reuber also added liver disease patients, and alcoholics, to this official list of hyper-susceptibles.[1]

The acute oral lethal dose, that is, the LD_{50}—the dose required to kill half of a test population, human or animal—varies between 1522 to 1945 milligrams per kilogram of body weight (mg/kg). According to Ms. Brenner's report in the *Journal of Pesticide Reform*, "less than 5 ounces would be fatal to a 70 kilogram human."[3]

Expanding on the effects of Malathion on the skin and eyes, Brenner wrote:

> Repeated exposure to Malathion has caused allergic responses in humans, guinea pigs, and mice. A single exposure to the skin of a 10 percent Malathion solution induced contact sensitization in almost half of human volunteer subjects, and once sensitized, very weak dilutions of Malathion (1ppm [about the amount of fluoride the U.S. Public Health Service recommends for community water supplies]) would trigger skin reactions. Technical Malathion is mildly irritating to the eyes, can cause temporary visual disturbances, and questions remain regarding its ability to produce external eye irritation.[3,5]

Chronic Toxicity From Pesticide Exposure

Clearly, Malathion, among the most studied pesticides, has never been proven safe for human exposure in any adequate manner. This is likely why government "authorities" turned to the less studied Anvil as a replacement for Malathion during the 1999–2000 WNV spraying program. In addition to acute toxicity, Malathion exposure has been associated with a variety of long term consequences, chronic diseases, which are central to the debate as to whether or not governments should be allowed to spray citizens, unwittingly and largely unwillingly, including children.

Malathion's chronic toxicity problems, for example, can be divided into the following primary areas: carcinogenicity, mutagenicity or teratogenicity, birth and other reproductive effects, and immune system effects. These areas will be explored in the next sections. With all of these, you should keep in mind that "data gaps" persist, particularly in the areas of delayed effects regarding neurotoxicity, inhalation risks, contaminated food consumption, and the breakdown products from organophosphate metabolism.

Carcinogenicity

Based on the literature review conducted by Brenner[3] and others,[4-13] organophosphate usage has been linked to human cancer. The first scientific study in which this was concluded involved the increased risk of non-Hodgkin's lymphoma in farmers from Iowa and Minnesota.[6] Disease risks were increased for those men who had previously handled Malathion, and significantly increased for farmers exposed to Malathion before 1965. Risks were higher for people managing livestock than for others using Malathion for crops.

In a second study, a similarly increased risk of non-Hodgkin's lymphoma was found among Nebraska farmers deploying Malathion.[7]

Likewise, a national study of flourmill workers showed significantly increased risk of developing this form of white blood cell cancer in direct relation to hours worked. It is well known that Malathion is commonly used for insect control in flourmills.[8]

Even reassessed studies at the National Cancer Institute (NCI) showed an association between Malathion and malaoxon exposures and malignancies of the endocrine glands, brain, liver, lung and blood in rats and mice. The NCI, whose history shows a gross dereliction of duties insofar as safeguarding the public's health is concerned (as will be discussed in greater detail later), in the wake of a rapidly growing cancer industry, collected data they first insisted showed nothing. Later, following Dr. Reuber's review of their data, other toxicologists from the EPA, including the esteemed Dr. Brian Dementi, concluded that these organophosphates showed "a positive oncogenic response."[9,10,11]

Embarrassed by the implied fraud, the NCI reconsidered its original study and determined that, indeed, they had overlooked the significant associations determined by independent analysts. They finally admitted the existence of a Malathion dose-dependent increase in rat thyroid tumors, and left it at that.[12]

Brenner also learned that "tumors of the adrenal glands and leukemia have also been associated with Malathion exposure." Moreover, rats exposed to malaoxon developed benign breast tumors.[3]

In light of newer evidence linking Malathion exposure to cancer, in 1991, the EPA requested that American Cyanamid investigators conduct three new cancer studies on their product.[5]

Teratogenicity (Mutagenicity)

Organophosphates, including Malathion, undoubtedly cause genetic damage in exposed bacteria, animals, fish, and humans. Still, Malathion is alleged to be among the "safest" pesticides in use today.

In an update found on the Internet entitled "Malathion and Genetics" Wayne Sinclair, M.D., and coauthor Richard W. Pressinger, reported on their review of the medical literature on this topic. They collected studies at the University of South Florida that showed Malathion exposures caused "birth defects in turtles and frogs, gill damage in fish, bizarre swimming behaviors in fish, and damage to shrimps' ability to locate food."[13]

After considering the broad consequences of their findings, they begrudgingly wrote, "There goes the food chain!"

In other reports they learned that "birth defects and increased infections" affected second-generation animals, "even when no defects were seen in the first generation of offspring." This, they reported, implied "subtle genetic damage that would otherwise be missed in most birth defect studies."

A Rutgers University study showed that Malathion caused heart defects in one species of fish.

"All in all, I was overwhelmed with the amount of research showing how Malathion can cause serious damage to wildlife in so many ways," wrote Dr. Sinclair. "God help our marine life in the lakes, rivers, and in Tampa Bay when it rains since that is where much of the

Malathion goes—right down the storm drain and into the rivers and bay."

Dr. Sinclair's reference to Tampa Bay reflected the great concern numerous citizens voiced, along with legislative backers, in August 1997, when the Clearwater, Sarasota, and Tampa areas were sprayed with Malathion by black helicopters for an alleged "Medfly Eradication Program."

"Remember this point," Dr. Sinclair urged, "the 1989 Bulletin of Environmental Contamination Toxicology states that 25% of the sprayed Malathion is still present in the water after two weeks and 10% is still present after 30 days."

The doctor relayed a story of meeting face-to-face with a University of Florida Professor who stated that "Malathion was degraded after several hours."

"Nonsense!" Dr. Sinclair returned. Fortunately, he said, he was able to counter the disinformation during their Lakeland, Florida community hearing where he "set the record straight" for the audience. He happened to hold "the journal article in [his] hand at the time."

Mutation research showed Malathion was "more powerful than five other pesticides in causing a problem known as 'cell cycle delay,' which means that cells do not grow as quickly, as is 'characteristic for many mutagens' according to the scientists," the Sinclair–Pressinger team reported. "The bottom line is that although it takes more Malathion than other pesticides to cause death, it takes less Malathion than many other pesticides to cause birth defects, immune weakening, and genetic damage." This makes Malathion an excellent non-lethal warfare agent/carcinogen as discussed later.

The authors concluded, "The available evidence, indicates that technical grade, or other than pure Malathion [such as that used in spraying programs] has the potential to produce genotoxic effects in mammalian systems. The results of the available studies on the genotoxicity of Malathion can be summarized as follows:

> In test animals, technical grade Malathion appears to have the potential to produce chromosomal changes.
>
> In humans, the genotoxic effects of Malathion have not been adequately studied. In human and animal cells in culture, both technical grade and purified Malathion appear to produce cytogenetic damage, including chromosomal aberrations . . ."[13]

Other animals genetically damaged by Malathion exposures include mice and hamsters.[3]

Have you ever wondered how the strain of bacteria known as *E. coli* evolved from being the benign germ that everyone carries to the dreaded killer that is recognized today as *E. coli*$_{157}$? Authorities and the media warn incessantly about the risk of bacteria mutating to become far more virulent, and perhaps even treatment resistant, following antibiotic use. What they fail to mention, because it is politically incorrect, is that even bacteria such as *Escherichia coli* have been routinely altered genetically *in labs* and in nature *by contact with organophosphate pesticides.*[3]

Regarding the few human studies on record at the time of her writing, Brenner offered a review of the relevant literature. She reported that the frequencies of chromosomal damage from Malathion exposures was "significantly higher in cotton field workers" than for other pesticides.[3] A study published in the German journal *Humangenetik,* showed that increased chromosomal breaks occurred after acute Malathion poisonings in humans. Moreover, human blood cells were observed to undergo similar alterations.[14,15,16]

Malathion, scientific reports also concluded, caused exchanges of genetic material within amino acid base pairs of chromosomes, called "sister chromatid exchanges." This occurred in human fetal as well as blood cells.[15,16,17,18]

For future generations, Malathion's effects may be worse. Besides having been proven to cause genetic mutations at doses far below levels that induce acute toxicity, the aberrational effects of organophosphates in general appear to be cumulative.[19]

Birth Defects

In a 1987 issue of *Teratology*, Netherlands researchers D. Lindhout, from the Genetics Department at Erasmus University, and G. Hageman, at the Institute of Human Genetics in Amsterdam, combined their data to report on a mother who had rinsed her hair with lotion containing Malathion during her pregnancy. Technically, they described her baby's postmortem examination as follows:

> The muscles of the extremities, and thoracic and abdominal wall were almost completely replaced by fatty tissue. The thymus was enlarged. The heart showed right atrial dilatation and right ventricular hypertrophy. Macroscopically, there was no obvious lung hypoplasia, but there

were minor microscopic signs of pulmonary tissue hypoplasia. The thymus was enlarged. The heart showed right atrial dilatation and right ventricular hypertrophy. Macroscopically, there was no obvious lung hypoplasia, but there were minor microscopic signs of pulmonary tissue hypoplasia. The spinal cord was remarkably thin on gross examination . . . [20]

Loretta Brenner also summarized the scientific literature concerning related birth defects thusly:

In the San Francisco Bay area, a two-year study examined the relationship between aerial sprays of Malathion for Medfly and the occurrence of congenital anomalies and low body weights. The researchers found no definitive associations, but they also admit to limitations in their data and analysis. However, they did find positive associations between Malathion exposure in individual years and increases in ear anomalies, bowing of leg bones, clubfoot, and other deformities.

Malathion has also been associated with birth defects in domestic and laboratory animals. In rabbits, Malathion crosses the placenta and acts on the central nervous system. Injection of Malathion into the yolk sac of chicken eggs caused reduced growth and weakening of a leg bone, increased production of insulin, reduced chick weights, reduced hatch, short legs, nerve damage two to six weeks after hatching, sparse plumage, growth reduction and beak defects.[3]

Reproductive Effects

Since human study reports on the full reproductive effects of Malathion probably disappeared along with German scientists at the end of WWII, with the Nuremberg Code and "informed consent" safeguards, the human reproductive effects of pesticide exposure are currently limited or uncertain. This, of course, is not the case for lower species.

Juvenile male rats given daily doses of Malathion showed reduced sperm-forming cells.[21,22] Additionally, in two cancer studies, pregnant rats exposed to Malathion gave birth to lower weight pups, and they gained less weight during recovery. Their rat babies showed more hemorrhage spots as well.[5] More rat studies showed second-generation offspring weighed less than controls when their grandparents were exposed to Malathion. These rats also had greater susceptibility to "ring-tail disease."[23]

In pregnant rabbit studies, 50 and 100 mg doses per kilogram per day of Malathion induced lower maternal weight gain and increased incidence of dead fetuses being absorbed, not aborted, by the mother. A significant number of mothers died as well at every dose level.

Sheep studies revealed Malathion caused increased abortions, still-births, and lowered birth weights. More severe outcomes were prompted by earlier, or longer duration, exposures.[24]

Immunotoxicity

As described earlier, contemporary spraying programs for mosquito and fruit fly eradication expose massive numbers of people to toxic pesticides causing a significant percentage, especially the hypersensitive, to exhibit flu-like or allergic symptoms.[5]

In keeping with the hypothesis that "public health" practices today may be effecting "non-lethal" military operations, laboratory animal studies showed that immune system dysfunction was evidenced in mice at doses far below those causing cholinesterase inhibition and neurotoxic symptoms.[3] That means that the subtle subclinical effects on the immune system took place to cause the exposed rodents to become more susceptible to infections such as flu viruses and more. Likewise, the effects of pesticide exposure in humans may place people at higher risk of developing opportunistic infections.

Furthermore, chemical impurities in most pesticide brews, such as the often used technical grade Malathion, as will be discussed in greater detail in the next chapter, can disrupt immunological functions far more than pure Malathion.[3]

In summary, the immune system effects of pesticide spraying(s) often translate into serious health consequences. Immunosuppression causes people to become more susceptible to opportunistic infections, including bacteria, viruses, parasites, and fungi, including yeasts. This has also been demonstrated in the scientific literature, particularly in people with a history of liver problems.[3]

Miscellaneous Toxic Effects of Malathion

"Between 1957 and 1971," Brenner reported, "Japanese school children experienced a tremendous increase in cases of myopia, (near-sightedness)," that corresponded to increased exposure to organophosphate insecticides, especially Malathion. In one study of children from the agricultural region of Saku, investigators recorded vision impairment among 98% of them. This illness is now called "Saku disease."

More recently, in California, a lawsuit was filed on behalf of a 15-year-old boy "who was declared legally blind after being outside while helicopters were spraying Malathion." An expert opthalmologist and a pesticide expert agreed in court that the boy likely developed Saku disease.[3]

Studies showed that repeated Malathion exposures produced liver toxicity regardless of the organism's nutritional status. However, malnourished animals, especially those on low protein diets, showed increased risk of Malathion toxicity and liver damage. "This is due, at least in part, to the malnourished liver's decreased ability to detoxify Malathion," Brenner explained. According to investigators, inadequately fed individuals may be more prone to pesticide toxicity.

Likewise, government officials have been advised to assess a community's nutritional health status before subjecting its people to toxic Malathion exposure(s). Despite this warning, however, this preventive practice has generally escaped attention.[3]

This concludes a chapter that relays scientific evidence and facts concerning pesticide toxicity, acute and long-term, particularly regarding the most commonly sprayed product, Malathion. In the next chapter, I will reflect on, in contrast, what people have been told by governing officials, and alleged "public health servants," regarding the practice of spraying neurotoxic pesticides and related chemicals on unwitting populations.

References

1) Reuber M. Lecture on Malathion. Franklin High School, Series of Lectures on the Dangers of Malathion. March 1990. In: *Malathion: Toxic Time Bomb, The Poisoning of Our People*. Russell-Manning B., ed. San Francisco: Cancer Control Society, 1990, pp. 101-104.

2) Ross S. Testimony before the Los Angeles City Council Arts, Health & Humanities Committee, 1989. In: *Malathion: Toxic Time Bomb, The Poisoning of Our People*. Russell-Manning B., ed. San Francisco: Cancer Control Society, 1990, pp. 145-46.

3) Brenner L. Malathion. *Journal of Pesticide Reform*. 1992;12;4:29-36

4) Russell-Manning B. *Malathion: Toxic Time Bomb, The Poisoning of Our People*. San Francisco: Cancer Control Society, 1990, p. vi.

5) Kizer KW. *Health risk assessment of aerial application of malathion-bait*. Summary report. Sacramento, CA: California Department of Health Services, 1991.

6) Cantor KP et al. Pesticides and other risk factors for non-Hodgkin's lymphoma among men in Iowa and Minnesota. *Cancer Res.* 1992;52:2447-2455.

7) Weisenburger DD *et al*. A case-control study of non-Hodgkins lymphoma and agricultural factors in eastern Nebraska (abstract). *Am. J. Epidemiol.* 1988;128:901.

8) Alavanja MCR. Blair A and Masters MN. Cancer mortality in the U.S. flour industry. *J. Nat. Can. Inst.* 1990;82;10:840-848.

9) Reuber, M.D. Carcinogenicity and toxicity of Malathion and malaoxon. *Environ. Res.* 1985;37:119-153.

10) Gross A. (U.S. EPA office of Pesticides Programs senior science advisor). Carcinogenicity of Malathion. Memo to Kevin Keaney, U.S. EPA office of Pesticide Programs. April 24, 1984; See also: Food Chemical News. Malathion "D" oncogene classification likely from peer review group. *Pesticides and Toxic Chemical News* 1990(Feb. 14):32.

11) In recent years, not only has the NCI blocked effective action on the development of highly promising, low risk, anticancer treatments, but also stalled the released of substantial documentation linking the U.S. Atomic Energy Commission, and their radiation experiments, to scores of cancer cases throughout America. *Emerging Viruses: AIDS & Ebola—Nature, Accident or Intentional?*, (Tetrahedron Publishing Group, 1996) by this author, contains vastly more about the NCI's dishonorable services to humanity during the Special Virus Cancer Program.

12) Huff JE, et al. Malathion and malaoxon: histopathology reexamination of the National Cancer Institute's carcinogenesis studies. *Environm. Res.* 1985;37:154-173.

13) Sinclair W and Pressinger RW. Malathion and genetics: Malathion can cause mutations to our human genetic structure. Distributed over the Internet from http://nchem.com/malathio.htm; see also: http://www.safe2use.com/poisons-persitices/pesticides/malathion/genetics.htm.

14) van Bao T, et al. Chromosome aberrations in patients suffering from acute organic phosphate insecticide intoxication. *Humangenetik* 1974;24:33-57.

15) Herath JF et al. Genotoxicity of the organophosphorus insecticide Malathion based on human lymphocytes in culture. *Cytologia* 1989;54:191-195.

16) Garry FT, et al. Preparation for human study of pesticide applicators: sister chromatic exchanges and chromosome aberrations in cultured human lymphocytes exposed to selected fumigants. *Terato. Carcino. Mutato* 1990;10:21-29.

17) Sobti RC, Krishan A and Pfaffenberger CD. Cytokinetic and cytogenetic effects of some agricultural chemicals on human lymphoid cells *in vitro*: organophosphates. *Mut. Res.* 1982;102:89-102.

18) Sarma GP and Sobti RC. Cytotoxic, cytokinetic and cytogenetic effects of agricultural chemicals *in vitro* and *in vivo*. *Gen. Toxicol.* 1987;30;3:167.

19) Nicholas AH, Vienne M and Van Den Berghe H. Induction of sister-chromatid exchanges in cultured human cells by an organophosphorus insecticide: Malathion. *Mut. Res.* 1979;67:167-172.

20) Lindhout D and Hageman G. Amyoplasia congenital-like condition and maternal malathion exposure. *Tetraology* 1987;36:7-9.

21) Krause W. Influence of DDT, DDVP, and Malathion on FSH, LH and testosterone serum levels and testosterone concentration in testes. *Bull. Environ. Contam. Toxicol.* 1977;18;2:231-242.

22) Krause W, Hamm K and Weissmuller J. Damage to spermatogenesis in juvenile rat treated with DDVP and Malathion. *Bull. Environ. Contam. Toxicol.* 1976;15;4:458-462.

23) Kalow W and Marton A. Second generation toxicity of Malathion in rats. *Nature* 1961;192;4801:464-465.

24) Thathoo AK and Prasad MC. Gestational disorders associated with Malathion toxicity in sheep. *Indian Vet. J.* 1988;65:379-382.

Chapter 4.
Public Health Propaganda
and Missing Data

"Why shouldn't the state first have the
responsibility to prove that spraying is safe?
It is a simple matter of burden of proof."

Councilman Joel Wachs, 1990
Hearing before Los Angeles commissioners

In three previous books I addressed propaganda wars waged against people in America and abroad by public health officials and U.S. Government spin-doctors.

Deadly Innocence (1993) unraveled the mystery of a Florida dentist, David Acer, who infected his patients with HIV/AIDS. Here American government and public health officials reported the dentist was a "nice guy." They alleged he was "unwilling to harm a fly." In contrast, the documented evidence showed that Dr. Acer maintained a *classic* organized serial killer personality profile, crime scene profile, and developmental history. All variables were virtually identical to thirty-six serial killers studied by the FBI.

In *Emerging Viruses: AIDS & Ebola—Nature, Accident or Intentional?* (1996), I traced the development of viruses, functionally and descriptively identical to HIV and Ebola, to the West Nile region of Northwest Uganda. There, military–medical operations and vaccine experiments were ongoing involving the biological weapons contractor, Litton Bionetics. Under National Institutes of Health (NIH) contracts, Bionetics shipped contaminated monkeys and chimpanzees to New York City, where Dr. Maurice Hilleman received them to develop Merck pharmaceutical company vaccines. Figure 4.1 shows this contract, circulated at the NCI at the time the first GRID/AIDS cases were being diagnosed in New York City. As described therein, these vaccine experiments focused on the "type-C" cancer retroviruses with simultaneous "coinfections" with herpes viruses such as the Epstein–Barr virus that caused the never before seen leukemia-sarcoma-lymphoma cancer complex later called GRID and AIDS. The most implicated vaccine trigger for HIV/AIDS was the 1974-1975 experimental hepatitis B vaccine given simultaneously to gay men in New York City and Blacks in Central Africa. Rather than admitting the serious implications of their contaminated vaccine program, government officials, including Litton's "project officer for the National Cancer Institute," Dr. Robert Gallo, explained that HIV/AIDS simply came from African monkeys. What they did not tell, and I showed, is what Gallo and his Bionetics colleagues *did* to those monkeys to produce these unique "type-C" class of retroviruses. (See also figure 18.10, page 460.)

Finally, in *Healing Codes for the Biological Apocalypse* (1999), Dr. Joseph Puleo and I exposed the passage of ancient sacred knowledge involving physics, mathematics, genetics, language, music, spirituality, and healing, and the arcana's current use by global leaders of the international chemical/pharmaceutical cartel, in their efforts to survey, manipulate, control, enslave and even kill world populations. The Human Genome Project, they proclaimed, would significantly help promote health in the twenty-first century. What they did not tell is that the Rockefeller-linked Cold Spring Harbor Labs, home to the Human Genome Project, and original eugenics research that Hitler later termed "racial hygiene," was also deeply invested in HAARP—the electromagnetic transmission bases in Alaska, New York, and elsewhere, that has aimed its frequency generators to control weather and apparently populations as well. This new manner of conducting what I called "biospiritual warfare" in that book, and "non-lethal technotronic warfare" in this work, is further detailed in forthcoming chapters.

Each time I investigated, I discovered and reported the deceptive propaganda used to confound the issues and confuse the public. Each time, fear was used to manipulate and control the mass mind—a form of officially sanctioned "terrorism." Each time, truth was held hostage and citizens were mortally victimized.

In this book, again, with the spraying of pesticides for alleged biological "emergencies," truth is the first casualty of governing agents and agencies. In this brief chapter, I compare fiction with facts while addressing the machinations used by public health officials to defend what is indefensible. Their effective ploys involve three general areas: 1) the misrepresentation of adequacy in scientific data, 2) making false and misleading claims, and 3) bureaucratic "buck-passing."

Figure 4.1. One of Several NIH African Primate Supply Contracts to Litton Bionetics From 1962-78

LITTON BIONETICS, INC. (NO1-CP-6-1006)

Title: Operation of a Facility to Provide and Maintain Subhuman Primates for Cancer Research

Contractor's Project Director: Dr. John Cicmanec

Project Officers (NCI): Dr. Garrett V. Keefer
Dr. Jack Gruber

Objectives: The objective of this contract is the maintenance of monkey breeding colonies and laboratories necessary for inoculation, care, and monitoring of primates.

Major Findings: During this report period efforts continued to provide both New World and Old World primates and biological materials from these animals for use by cancer research investigators. The New World breeding colony now has 458 animals representing twelve species; 131 live births occurred in the breeding colony during this report period including 22 infants born in the cotton-topped marmoset (Saguinus oedipus) colony. The cotton-topped marmoset has been identified as an endangered species, which means they can no longer be imported into this country.

Approximately 208 macaques comprising three species were in the Old World breeding colony. A small breeding colony of gibbon apes (Hylobates lar) was also maintained. One hundred and eight live births occurred in the Old World breeding colony, which included five births in the gibbon ape breeding colony. One hundred and seventy-seven animals were assigned to 22 active special studies during this report period.

In support of these efforts, personnel in the Department of Pathology performed 200 complete necropsy procedures involving the preparation of 2,535 microslides (42 with special stains). The surgery team performed 24 major procedures to support the program, and the Department of Microbiology continued its support by performing specimen cultures, antibiotic sensitivity testing, and environmental monitoring. The Hematology Section performed 1,495 complete blood counts. Thirty-nine coagulograms, 1,432 clinical chemistry procedures, and 13 bone marrow biopsies were processed. Routine monitoring and cataloging of specimens continued in the Parasitology Section. A total of 296 tissue or serum samples were transferred or sent to outside investigators.

Significance to Biomedical Research and the Program of the Institute: Inasmuch as experimentation for the biological activity of candidate human cancer viruses will not be carried out on humans, it is imperative that another system be developed for these determinations and subsequently for the evaluation of vaccines or other measures of control. The close phylogenetic relationship of the lower primates to man justifies utilization of these animals for these purposes.

Proposed Course: This contract will continue the following activities: the maintenance of breeding colonies of nine different species of New World primates; production of 100 to 150 infants of various species of both Old World and New World primates for use in experimental studies; continuing efforts in the establishment of a breeding colony of gibbon apes; and the long-term holding and study of experimental animals inoculated by collaborating investigators. All of the systems needed for the production, hand rearing, isolation, and proper care of the primate species represented are included within this program.

Date Contract Initiated: February 12, 1962

From: NCI Staff. *The [Special] Virus Cancer Program [SVCP]*. U.S. Department of Health, Education and Welfare. Washington, D.C.: Public Health Service, National Institutes of Health, Division of Cancer Cause and Prevention, June 1978, pp. 249-50. Library call number: E20.3152:V81/977 and 78-21195.

Advancing Deception

The first two methods of deception cited above are adequately demonstrated in a letter sent to California citizens by Department of Health Services Director Kenneth W. Kizer, M.D., M.P.H.[1] The letter portrayed a scientific grasp of Malathion spraying issues, and typified deception while minimizing the risks posed by organophosphate exposures. The official wrote in 1990:

Dear Fellow Californian:

There has been considerable recent public concern expressed about the health effects of the Malathion-bait being used to eradicate the Mediterranean fruit fly (Medfly) in southern California. I am writing this letter to tell you that these outdoor, nighttime applications present no significant health hazard to persons living in the sprayed areas.

Malathion has been widely used throughout the world for decades. More is known about the health effects of Malathion than any other similar pesticide. Malathion is among the safest insecticides in use, being commonly used around the home, in gardens and in orchards. It is used at much higher concentrations than used in the spray program for the treatment of head lice in both children and adults. It is used in numerous veterinary products, and it has been used (at significantly higher concentrations) in mosquito abatement programs throughout the world (including southern California) for many years.

The Malathion-bait is being applied to the sprayed areas in very small doses. Each acre sprayed will receive 2.8 ounces (about 1/3 of a cup) of Malathion. In such small doses, Malathion is not dangerous to people or animals. Also, it is important to emphasize that in this program the Malathion is not being sprayed such as done in mosquito abatement programs. Instead, the Malathion is contained in corn syrup bait, and this bait is what is being sprayed. There is essentially no evaporation of Malathion from the bait.

To help address the public health concerns that have been expressed about the current Malathion program, the Department has established a Public Health Effects Advisory Committee, similar to what has been done to address previous Malathion spray programs in California and many other issues. This committee will provide an open scientific and medical forum to address public health concerns about the Medfly Project. About twenty-five physicians and scientists with relevant expertise (e.g., toxicology) make up the committee.

Although the current eradication effort may be inconvenient or even unpleasant for some persons, allowing the Medfly to become established in southern California would be much worse from a public health perspective. For example, if the Medfly becomes established in California, we fear that home gardeners and farmers would make much greater use of pesticides that are far more dangerous than Malathion in attempts to control the pest. Also, the fumigation process that would be required to prepare agricultural products for export from the Medfly area, would expose workers to highly toxic fumigant pesticides. Similarly, we are concerned that having Medfly maggots in fruits and vegetables would discourage people from eating these products. This is worrisome since we know Californians currently do not eat fruits and vegetables, and many types of cancer, heart disease and other conditions could be prevented if people ate more fruits and vegetables.

Sincerely,

Kenneth W. Kizer, M.D., M.P.H.
Director

Refuting Deceptions

Considering each paragraph above for its intent and/or deceptive content, Dr. Kizer began his letter addressing the "concern expressed about the health effects " of the program. In other words, if opponent activists had not brought the issues to light, and to the floor of debate, Dr. Kizer would not have written this letter and proceeded without remiss to conduct "business as usual" insofar as spraying large under-educated populations.

The "nighttime applications," he implied, made the program safer. Not so for the children who play on contaminated fields and lawns the next mornings.

The applications presented "no significant health hazard to persons living in sprayed areas," he claimed. Obviously, based on the scientific evidence relayed previously and later in this chapter, this statement is completely false and misleading.

Paragraph two stated that Malathion had been used "throughout the world for decades," implying it must, therefore, be safe. This is reminiscent of cigarette advertisements in medical journals that touted certain brands that sold most.

"More is known about the health effects . . . than any other similar pesticide," the letter stated. Odd then that EPA and other government officials cited the *lack* of important data in response to citizens and scientists opposed to the sprayings. Further misleading was the statement that other pesticides had not been studied as much as Malathion, making it, therefore, the choice insecticide for public safety. In fact, regardless of the relative amount of scientific evidence compiled on Malathion, it is virtually all negative and frightfully incriminating.

"Malathion is among the safest insecticides in use." However, according to Fort Detrick cancer researcher, Melvin Reuber, M.D., this statement does not mean it is safe. On a lethal dose relativity scale, Malathion toxicity has been compared by scientists to "two of the deadliest substances known to man"—dioxin and botulism.[2]

Dr. Kizer emphasized its widespread use "around the home, in gardens, and in orchards" in order to relay a sense of general acceptance rather than the true awareness that American Cyanamid's advertising and marketing efforts during the 1950s and 1960s were highly effective in propelling the toxic chemical into virtually every home in America.

Moreover, the use of the toxin, at higher concentrations than called for in the Medfly program, for head lice lotions, for instance, did not make either applications safe as Dr. Kizer implied. Dr. Kizer did not mention the deadly effects of both of these practices for certain unfortunate individuals, as discussed previously.

His reference to "significantly higher concentrations" of Malathion being used for "mosquito abatement programs" portended higher mortality and morbidity might be expected from these programs, yet, these were ongoing at the time of this writing for the alleged WNV outbreaks in New York, New Jersey, and New England.

Nowhere in Dr. Kizer's announcement, did he mention the far more toxic metabolites (breakdown products) of Malathion, or similarly, the extraordinarily lethal contaminants resident in technical grade Malathion-bait combinations used for spraying.

In paragraph three, Dr. Kizer falsely claimed that the "very small doses" applied to each acre of sprayed land, "2.8 ounces (about 1/3 of a cup)," is not dangerous to people or animals. As discussed previously, according to University of California neurobiologist Dr. Jorge Mancillas, formerly with the Salk Institute, Dr. Kizer's claim that the doses applied are too low to cause any harm is flawed for at least two reasons. First, "public health" officials do not monitor what doses people are exposed to, but "at best what amounts are being applied to the ground."[3] Second, using the EPA's established, "No Observable Effect Level," that is, the amount below which no effects are observed is expressed as 0.2 mg per kg of body weight. This means, following Dr. Mancillas's analysis, there are 1.4 mg of Malathion spread over each square foot of sprayed acreage. Again, in his words, "This means that a 50-pound child (22.7 kgs) would have to be exposed to the Malathion found in 1/3 of a square foot to exceed the EPA's acceptable intake level, and to the amount of Malathion in 3.5 square feet to have observable [toxic] effects. If you have a child playing in the grass, a sand box, or on a slide, drinking from a public fountain, or elsewhere in a park, or in his home, he can easily be exposed to that amount."

Further in paragraph three, Dr. Kizer asserted that the sprayed Malathion is bound, thus stabilized, in "a corn syrup bait." It is therefore likely that it may remain toxic for longer periods. Again, as determined by Dr. Sinclair, "the 1989 Bulletin of Environmental Contamination Toxicology stated 25% of the Malathion is still present in contaminated water after two weeks and 10% is still present after 30 days."

Dr. Kizer did not tell that individuals with economic and/or political incentives to defend pesticides staffed the committee his department had established to field inquiries, and abate the public's concern. Public health and petrochemical industry funds are never spent hiring detractors, or promoting views that conflict with theirs. Thus, Dr. Kizer's claim that, "This committee will provide an open scientific and medical forum," was obviously false, as was his promotion of committee persons as having "relevant expertise." Such committee persons, with their frequently intense bias, might more accurately be called "indoctrinated cult leaders." Thus, one cannot expect rational unbiased discourse to result from such hearings.

The final paragraph of Dr. Kizer's letter implied a positive risk/benefit ratio had been rationally and responsibly established for the spraying program. The minor risks, inconvenience, or unpleasantness "for some persons," Dr. Kizer claimed, was well offset by the benefits "from a public health perspective." As mentioned in the introduction to this book, this form of coercion violates the primary premise of bonafide public health policy. Legitimate public health policy legislation is supposed to be based on having conducted definitive scientific investigations into both the risks and benefits of the proposed action. Regarding these spraying initiatives, much like vaccination programs that will be discussed later, these studies are nonexistent. As Dr. Mancillas pointed out, officials "are not monitoring what doses people are being exposed to," and therefore never learn what consequences these toxic exposures relay.[3,4]

Considering Dr. Kizer's concerns, if gardeners and farmers made greater use of pesticides more dangerous than Malathion, then public health authorities should have targeted these people with more effective preventive messages, including the use of less toxic natural pest control alternatives which abound, yet are infrequently part of official discussions. Moreover, public health officials should have pressured dangerous pesticide manufacturers to cease and desist instead of purchasing and defending toxic products, which by the way, according to numerous reports, has failed miserably in ridding sprayed regions of Medflies or other targeted pests.[5]

Finally, if Dr. Kizer and his colleagues in public health were so concerned about people's malnutrition, then they should have their states' attorneys file lawsuits against pesticide manufacturers, as was done against the tobacco industry, to have *them* clear their products of toxic ingredients, and fund educational campaigns for prevention through healthy nutrition. Dr. Kizer's claim of concern regarding Californians not eating "enough fruits and vegetables" to prevent heart disease and cancer, can be seen in this light as lethal lip service, if not gross negligence.

More Expert Testimony

In contrast to Dr. Kizer's superficial deceptions, the testimony of Dr. Samuel Epstein before governmental hearings committees is persuasive and revealing.[6] Dr. Epstein is among the foremost experts in the field of chemical toxicity, and a regular scientific heavyweight for citizen advocacy groups at governmental hearings. He is a medical pathologist by training, and a toxicologist at the University of Illinois. Dr. Epstein served as a consultant to several congressional committees, and was instrumental in forwarding efforts by Vietnam War veterans to gain compensation for a broad array of illnesses, including cancers from military exposures to Agent Orange. During the 1990s drives to stop aerial spraying of Malathion in California, Dr. Epstein provided the following testimony that directly contradicted the distortions issued by Dr. Kizer. Attorneys posed the following questions for the people's defense. Dr. Epstein's comments reflected the true state of pesticide science as of 1990. His testimony also documented the research that should be conducted in the public's interest before the spraying of any pesticide or toxic chemical occurs in populated areas. Dr. Kizer's and other public health officials' superficial allegations of safety must be reconsidered in light of the following more expert assessment.

Finally, and most importantly, Dr. Epstein's professional analysis should be used very assertively in future debates concerning pesticide sprayings including those for the WNV. Permission is granted to reprint any, or all, of chapters one through six, for distribution to concerned citizens or groups defending against such abusive "public health" practices.

Dr. Epstein: . . . The Environmental Protection Agency has specified a very, very wide range of what they call "data gaps." That's areas of deficiency of information, and I will itemize these for you. But with particular reference to one aspect . . . carcinogenicity studies.

Attorney: Is at least one element of that process, the issue of what information is needed before a pesticide can be safely used?

Dr. Epstein: Correct.

Attorney: Can you share with us what information is necessary before a degree of comfort could be developed that a pesticide can be safely used?

Dr. Epstein: Yes . . . . I should mention that as a member of the EPA Pesticide Subcommittee of the Health Advisory Committee, I play a role in drawing up and delineating some of these requirements.

"First of all is the data efficacy on the pesticide. Obviously it has to be useful.

"Next is the question of the composition of the pesticide. Even though the EPA still does not request disclosure of information on ingredients other than active ingredients, there are general requirements for disclosure of information on the total ingredients in a pesticide. And, I should explain, at this stage, we divide ingredients in pesticides in[to] so-called 'active ingredients,' [and 'inert' ingredients]. By 'active' we don't mean active as far as nontarget organisms like humans are concerned, but 'active' as far as the pesticides are concerned, as far as the pests.

"Then there are other ingredients called 'inerts.' Now, 'inerts' aren't [inert. They] are ingredients which are inert in relation to pesticidal activity but which, in fact, can be much more important than the active ingredient from the point of view of effects on humans. [Such] inerts can include asbestos, benzene, carbon tetrachloride, propane oxide, and dioxin. A very wide range of ingredients . . . whose presence in general is not disclosed and whose presence in fact is critical because the toxic effects in humans may be far more dependent on those undisclosed ingredients.

"And in the case of Malathion, I would say secret ingredient. And I'll provide the basis for the term 'secret ingredient' at the appropriate stage in this collogues.

"The question of the inerts, namely, the additives, the contaminants, is a matter of paramount public health significance. There has been serious discussion in Congress on the necessity of complete ingredient disclosure.

"Just to give you an example . . . [other than] Malathion, . . . pesticides called Chlordane and Heptachlor, which until recently have been widely used for eradication of termites. Now, . . . when you look at the label, you just see Chlordane and Heptachlor. You don't see on the label any reference to 45 other ingredients in this formulation.

"The next is the physicochemical characteristics of the pesticide. What are the vapor pressures? What is the volatility? What is the solubility? What is the stability? What is the stability of the active ingredients? Will, in fact, they persist in the environment? Will they accumulate in the environment, and how is this information derived?

"In addition, what is the stability of the inerts? Again, I'll give you an example. For Herbicide 2,4,5-T, which is 50 percent the component of Agent Orange, 2,4,5-T degrades rapidly in the course of a month in the environment. And after a few months you see pretty little of it; however, there is a contaminant. There's a series of contaminants in 2,4,5-T—dioxanes, which will persist not for years, but for decades. So the question of stability of the pesticide has to take into account, besides the active ingredient, the so-called inert ingredients.

"I emphasize, again, the word 'inert' relates only to the effect on target species. It has no relevance whatsoever to toxic effects in humans.

[Meaning, they may be extremely toxic to humans, yet their risks are not generally considered.]

"Now, the next physiochemical contribution is the binding properties. Does it bind to soil? Does it bind to particulates, and what are the degradation products in the body? Will these pesticides, . . . change or degrade into something which is very much more toxic both in the body and in the environment? And that's a highly pertinent question as far as Malathion is concerned, which we'll come to.

"Then the next is the question of the method of application. The method of application is critically important because it has direct bearing on questions of human dosage and uptake. How is it going to be applied? Is it going to be applied aerially? Is it going to be applied by local spray, by certified pest control applicator? Is it going to be just for agricultural products or domestic products? And are there going to be baits and traps?

"Then, in general, one wants to go into the questions, for this pesticide, of the information on the routes of human exposure. Are the routes going to be by skin, by inhalation, by ingestion in our foodstuff? And based on this information, it's possible to develop theoretical information on the uptake or absorption from air and water and food and the . . dosage, which you or I will get from the use of this. And also what we call the metabolism. How this . . . pesticide will behave in the body, . . its breakdown products, and its contaminants, and its additives. . . . The question of ingredient identity is critical and inerts are critical to the assessment of safety.

"Now, let's move on to more substantial issues, namely, the question of what are the adverse effects, the toxic effects? First of all, as far as toxic issues in general, what information do you need before you can make any comments on the safe use of pesticides?

"You need to know what are the acute effects, effects at high dosage, and you study these in two or three species of rodents and dogs. You find out the dose required to produce fatal effects by different routes, by injection route, by inhalation. You find out dose, the lowest dose, from which you can detect 'LOEL'—the Lowest Observable Effect Level, and 'NOEL'—No Observable Effect Level. And you try to then determine from that the 'ADI.' It's a concept developed by the World Health Organization (WHO)—the Acceptable Daily Intake.

"Now, of course, you also study these things in humans. You base the information on humans on experimental data. You also go into questions of sensitization and allergic effects, and also you take into account any information you have had on accidental poisoning.

"Now, the information on acute toxic effects of pesticides has to be qualified by information on potentiation. Will other pesticides magnify, and potentiate, and increase the effects of that pesticide? Will there be synergistic interactions between this and other pests and other chemicals? . . . .

"Then moving on you look at sub-acute effects. These are effects at lower doses over longer periods of time. You look at chronic effects, long-term exposure both in experiments on the animal and in humans. You look at these, characterize them in relation to the dosage to the organs in the humans and animals, and to how reversible these effects are.

"Now you come to a specific subset of chronic effects, and these include neurotoxic or neurobehavioral effects. These are on the nervous system relating to a wide range of problems which we can discuss, specifically in relation to Malathion [and other pesticide] behavior: abnormal learning, reproductive effects, birth defects, miscarriages, are there any genetic abnormalities which can result in the genetic propagation of adverse genetic diseases?

"And some genetic effects can also be related to cancer. If you produce genetic effects in body cells, . . . this can be associated with carcinogenic effects. If you produce mutations in germ cells of the testes, then you can induce effects which will propagate to the next generation. . . .

"Then after the pesticide has reached commercial use, you do the surveillance and ongoing considerations of safety. Embrace what's happening to the general population.

"And then, all in all, as a final comment on information of which you need before you can safely use a pesticide, there are certain factors which make you extremely stringent and extremely cautious in your requirements for this information. And that is, if the pesticide is going to be used in such a way as large bodies of the human population is going to be exposed.

"If they're going to be exposed in manners which are poorly predictable and for which you don't have adequate dosage—dosimetry data, for particular pesticides, where you have aerial applications, where it's difficult to identify dosage and uptake data and also problems of drift.

"That, in a large nutshell, is the kind of information one needs to have before one can safely talk about the safe use of a pesticide."

Attorney: You spoke of the need to have different or additional information if the pesticide is to be used over more heavily populated, than over essentially agricultural areas. . . . Is it correct that prior to . . . the 1990s, . . . Malathion was not used in urbanized areas to anything like the extent that it is today?

Dr. Epstein: . . . Well, in fact, there's been large-scale aerial application of Malathion or organophosphates in Japan since about 1957. And studies in Japan from '57 have clearly demonstrated a wide range of serious optical damage, damage to the eye, which I will review for you at the appropriate stage.

"And as a [result] of this, in the early 1970s, the Japanese government banned the aerial application."

Attorney: Are you familiar with the literature concerning the exposure to the dosage of aerial Malathion spraying in California in the fruit fly eradication efforts?

Dr. Epstein: I think in general, yes.

Attorney: Is it your understanding that at least recently the application has been approximately 2.8 fluid ounces per acre in a Malathion-bait spray that is admitted from helicopters?

Dr. Epstein: My understanding was that it's somewhere between 2.4 and 2.8 ounces per acre. I'm not quite sure which of the two it is, and I calculate that to be about 1.6 milligrams per square foot.

Attorney: Why is that important, 1.6?

Dr. Epstein: Well, you know, you and I don't go around in an acre. At least I presume you don't. . . . If you want to talk about your exposure from skin contact, I think it's easier to comprehend it in terms of square foot, than it is to an acre. At least to me. I just find that helpful to think of it in terms of [1.6] milligram[s] per square foot.

"Now, it's my understanding that in 1981, when we were dealing with the early eradication programs, and I remain to be corrected in this, that we were talking about 91 percent, [to] 92 percent pure Malathion. Although I really stand to be corrected, now, I believe it's the 95 percent pure [that is currently in use]. So we are talking about 95 percent pure and about 2.4 to 2.8 ounces an acre. And I understand that the current program calls for a minimum of three applications.

Attorney: . . . . Now, does Malathion break down into a different, or related, toxin that also is worth inquiring into?

Dr. Epstein: Yes. In fact, when we go into the questions of acute toxicity, I'll point this out. But essentially, when you talk about exposure, you have to take into account three factors. One is the Malathion itself. Two is a breakdown product called *"malaoxon" which is much more persistent and very much more toxic than Malathion.* And then you have a series of impurities in the Malathion which loosely we can call thioates, T-H-I-O-A-T-E-S, which *about eight thioates are present in Malathion.* [Emphasis added]

"And it's my understanding on the basis of documentation that I've seen, that *the presence of these impurities had been kept secret from the Department of Health Services (DHS) by the California Department of Food and Agriculture.* That is, in spite of the repeated references in 1980 and 1981 documentation by DHS to the need for such information [the information was there, but buried by the CDFA]. But that's another point.

"So when you're talking about dosage and exposure, you want to know, one, what is the Malathion level at any particular time. What's the malaoxon level, and what are the thioate levels. And you need to have this information in air, in water, in food and in the work place. In correction, I should mention in review of DHS documentation in 1980, there was the belief, the unsubstantiated belief, that exposure to malaoxon is insignificant. I have data to prove the contrary; that *exposure to malaoxon is highly significant, and we are dealing with a material which is 25 to 40 times more toxic.*" [Emphasis added.]

Attorney: Well, doctor, let me understand this. The danger, to what-ever extent it exists, of exposure limit to being, in effect, struck by this droplet on its way from the helicopter to the ground?

Dr. Epstein: Well, that's one of them. Any one of them [presents risks]. The others include, of course, skin contact . . . on soil but also on im-pervious surfaces and roads where stuff may land. And also skin con-tact from swimming pools where the Malathion will be rapidly oxidized to malaoxon by the . . . water.

"Essentially, when you drop this stuff from helicopters, you're produc-ing a toxic fog—an atmospheric fog of Malathion and malaoxon which is generated from sprayed droplets and mass fallout deposition.

"And the gas phase [of] pesticides is of extreme importance. In fact, you can identify the gas-phase particide in all areas monitored includ-ing flagged hospitals [where spraying was not permitted], and any at-tempts to eliminate certain areas from the aerial spray, I can only say, are minimally successful. And in addition, you can demonstrate high pesticide value in shallow stagnant pools, in dry streambeds, etcetera.

"Now, I should point out that when you spray the Malathion from the air, in addition to the cutaneous route of exposure, that's the route which I believe is the predominant route, there is also very significant exposure by inhalation. And if you compare—if you do monitor out-door air and indoor air, you see that over a three-day period . . . you get a gradual decrease in the air of the toxic fog . . . of Malathion level. But with a sharp increase of malaoxon, which is the derivative, which is 25 to 40 times more toxic.

"And you find much higher levels, of course, outdoors than you do indoors, ratio of about eight to one. . . . But I emphasize that the impli-cation . . . from reports . . . namely, the stuff just sits on the ground, and the only problem is if you have contact with it, I would say that's highly misleading. There are data, clear data, which show that there's gas phase Malathion and malaoxon in the area, which is generated from spray droplets and mass fallout deposition.

"I should also point out that this information is consistent with some studies going back to the 1967 studies by Wolf in . . . which he studied exposure levels of people outdoors during aerial sprays and people indoors during aerial sprays. He did analyses of dermal exposure (i.e., skin exposure), and really found substantially high levels.

"Now, . . . I think the evidence shows that the predominance of exposure is cutaneous for the Malathion, and we don't have good data on malaoxon, but I presume it's the same for malaoxon. We have no data for thioates. We have no data that I am aware of on the rate of degradation of thioates after spraying. And in general, I would say there are some substantial data gaps on degradation on Malathion, malaoxon, and accolating impurities in water, soil, impervious surfaces, and food, not so much under model conditions, but under representative spray conditions.

"There are data which suggest that Malathion is more persistent than has hitherto been considered. Now, one of the major problems in this area is that . . . in spite of the large-scale use of Malathion in aerial applications for the last ten years, there's been no attempt, or if there has been any attempt at these data I've missed it, or they haven't been published; there's been no attempt to actually measure the exposure and uptake of different members of the population under representative conditions.

"These aren't difficult matters. You can take blood or urine and you can measure the level of metabolites. To the best of my knowledge this hasn't been done on any scale. To the best of my knowledge there's been no studies done on the uptake of the accolating impurities. I want to come back to accolating impurities because these are extremely toxic. We're not talking about something there isn't—these accolating thioates, impurities, are the major determinants of toxic adverse effects."

Dr. Epstein completed this first part of his testimony by saying, "I find it difficult to comprehend why over the course of a year such minimal information on symmetry uptake and exposure seems to be unavailable. . . ."

Cognitive Dissonance Regarding "Public Health"

Relating to Dr. Epstein's cognitive dissonance over public health policy makers' apparent negligence in this matter, not long ago, a woman outraged by my statements concerning the generally overlooked lethal contaminations of standard vaccines asked, "How can you make such claims? How can you say the FDA has 'turned a blind eye to as many as 100 simian monkey cancer viruses per dose of Lederle's oral polio vaccine?'"

"Because," I replied, "that is the testimony of Dr. W. John Martin, M.D., Ph.D., who tested these vaccines for the FDA between 1976 and 1980, along with the testimony of attorney Walter Kyle, who has litigated related cases."

Then I added, "Let me ask you a question. You've lived a fairly long and successful life. The outcomes you have produced in your life have all been a result of your conscious choosing, have they not?"

She replied affirmatively.

"Well then, what makes you think that the outcomes of public health policy, made by rational, highly educated health professionals, have not occurred due to conscious choices made by powerful and successful individuals?"

She stared at me dumbfounded.

"The fact that we are witnessing an unprecedented increase in cancers, new infectious diseases, and global pandemics that are widely reducing certain populations, is not happening by serendipity," I asserted. "They are happening by conscious choice. You may not want to admit this because your loving parents instilled ethics, morals, and higher values in you. That's why you can't conceive that policy makers are actually getting away with murder, but these data speak of the ongoing atrocity. Global genocide, in the name of 'public health,' is occurring by the conscious choice of partially and/or wholly aware leaders. Most people may be living in denial, but that's a poor excuse when lives are at stake and people are being killed."

References

1) Kizer K. Letter to California citizens concerning aerial spraying of Malathion for the eradication of the Mediterranean fruit fly (Med fly). August, 1990. In: *Malathion: Toxic Time Bomb, The Poisoning of Our People.* Russell-Manning B., ed. San Francisco: Cancer Control Society, 1990, p. 21.

2) Reuber M. Lecture on Malathion. Franklin High School, Series of Lectures on the Dangers of Malathion. March 1990. In: *Malathion: Toxic Time Bomb, The Poisoning of Our People.* Russell-Manning B., ed. San Francisco: Cancer Control Society, 1990, p. 102.

3) Russell-Manning B. An interview with Jorge R. Mancillas, Ph.D. In: *Malathion: Toxic Time Bomb, The Poisoning of Our People.* San Francisco: Cancer Control Society, 1990, pp. 48, 82.

4) Similarly, with vaccines, public health agencies do not monitor, with any preventive effectiveness, what contaminations are relayed through injections. Nor do they collect adequate data on persons injured by vaccines. According to the CDC, during the 1990s, less than one percent of actual injuries were reported. That meant, in essence, the authorities might have maimed far more people than they helped with these programs conducted in the name of "public health." See also: Horowitz L. *Horowitz on Vaccines.* Rockport, MA: Tetrahedron Press, 1998; and Centers for Disease Control and Prevention documentation concerning vaccine injury reporting.

5) Carey JR. Med flies have been here in California for a long time, and we may never have gotten rid of them. Speech before the California State Assembly, August 1990. In: *Malathion: Toxic Time Bomb, The Poisoning of Our People.* Op. cit., p. 210.

6. Epstein S. Expert witness testimony in a court of law against the aerial spraying of Malathion in El Cajon, California. In: *Malathion: Toxic Time Bomb, The Poisoning of Our People.* Op. cit., pp. 173-188.

6) Ross S. Testimony before the Los Angeles City Council Arts, Health & Humanities Committee, 1989. In: *Malathion: Toxic Time Bomb, The Poisoning of Our People.* Ibid., pp. 145-46.

7) Brenner L. Malathion. *Journal of Pesticide Reform.* 1992;12;4:29-36

Chapter 5.
Contaminations and Cover-ups

"The presence of these impurities had been
kept secret . . ."
Samual Epstein, M.D., Ph.D.,
U.S. Congressional hearing in 1990

The contaminations and cover-ups in public health methods and materials perceived by citizens to be pure is a sordid chapter in American history. The focus of this chapter, bearing on aerosol pesticide sprayings, and of Chapter 14 concerning toxic vaccine injections, provides two glaring examples of how public health practices, unproven by science, if not heavily condemned by it, have been carried out in the name of "prevention." Both examples reflect mass murder in the name of medical science. Sloppy science and/or bureaucratic–political expediency cannot alone account for the mounting morbidity and mortality resulting from these programs. Rather, a covert Malthusian eco-genocide is strongly suggested as evidenced by the documentation and discussions in the forthcoming chapters, especially chapters fifteen through eighteen. Undoubtedly, multinational corporations are making vast fortunes by delivering such lethal products to world markets that puppet politicians readily condone if not legislate. Something insidious appears in the depth and rational interpretation of these data. Professionally perpetrated genocide best explains contemporary public health policy outcomes as well as many of our current and coming plagues.

In the previous chapters, I reviewed expert testimonies and relevant scientific literature regarding pesticide sprayings. These accounts lead to the conclusion that far more toxicity may accrue from the contaminants found in commercial pesticides than from their active ingredients. This is certainly the message relayed by Dr. Samuel Epstein in the last chapter. This information is relevant here as well as when considering the subject of "Contaminations and Cover-ups."

Dr. Lappe's Story

A telling saga in this regard was that offered by Dr. Mark Lappe, a pathology professor at the University of California, Berkeley, and former Director of California's Hazard Evaluation System and Information Service (HESIS).

Dr. Lappe was given the authority to compile a report regarding the safety of Malathion aerial spraying. He returned an original report noting that the aerial spray should be limited to pure Malathion, not "technical grade," sometimes called "commercial grade," as these contained, he learned from experts like Dr. Epstein, too many more toxic contaminants. He also submitted his report on "safe crawl" recommendations for children residing in areas being sprayed. His figures for these crawl areas were altered by his politically pressured superiors, and his recommendations for pure Malathion went ignored. He was ordered to edit his report or face being fired. When he refused, he was discharged.

After his dismissal, in a newspaper interview, Dr. Lappe inquired, "Is it worth asking what the response of any government agency would have been if experimental data and conclusions were altered in the manner that my report was in 1980? Such manipulation of data and distortion of clearly stated conclusions regarding residual concerns of safety might well be labeled fraud."

Author Betsy Russell–Manning reviewed Dr. Lappe's story, and published his detailed report and testimonies.[1] She documented the activities of Dr. Beverlee Myers, Director of the California Department of Health Services at the time Dr. Myers was in charge of "damage control" from Dr. Lappe's professional termination. Dr. Myers signed a report falsely declaring aerial spraying of Malathion over large northern California urban populations to be "safe." "There will be no significant health risks," she assured in her memorandum to Director Richard Boeringer of the Department of Food and Agriculture. This was what he wanted to read.[2]

According to Russell-Manning's investigation, numerous other discrepancies between scientific knowledge and public health assurances were found. Dr. Myers's report, for instance, "listed chronic effects of Malathion and acute effects." These effects were prefaced by numbers (from 1-15) of referenced medical journals and personal communications. "I looked up the journals listed," Russell-Manning wrote, "the referenced sections and many journals gave negative conclusions regarding the safe use of Malathion for living beings." Reference number three, for instance, "Y. Iwata," U. C. Riverside. In Dr. Iwata's reply to Dr. Myers regarding malaoxon, "he recommended that sprayed areas be monitored, which was apparently never done."[1]

In late 1980, as Dr. Lappe reiterated his concern over possible health risks, he added the results of his study group's findings concerning the likelihood of children developing cancer in the sprayed areas. His group concluded that the risk was approximately five cancers per million, which is five times higher than acceptable by government standards.

What followed was best told by a group of professionals from the Foundation for Advancements in Science and Education.[3] Five authors published their independent analysis, which summarized Dr. Lappe's persecution as follows:

> Lappe . . . sent [his findings] to his immediate superior, and member of the California Medical Association's Subcommittee on Clinical Ecology, Dr. Ephraim Kahn.

> Kahn returned Lappe's assessment with this handwritten memo: "Note that we've cut the infant's crawl area to 6 ft. square [approximately the size of an open newspaper]. This brings the risk to approximately 10^{-6}" [a reduction of precisely one fifth, which brought the risk to within the acceptable limit]. Lappe says that when he objected to this seemingly arbitrary calculation, he was told "that's just the way it's going to be."

> When asked about this memo in a June 7, 1989 telephone interview, Kahn initially stated, "There are no such memos."

> When told of the existence of the memo, however, Kahn argued that the analysis showing Malathion's safety had been based on "one after another worst case assumptions," and that the analysis, therefore, showed that the spraying operation would be safe.

> According to a record in state files, on December 15, 1980, Lappe and Dr. Kim Hooper sent a diplomatic memo to Kahn voicing their disagreement with the position the department had taken on Malathion. "We believe," the two wrote, "that on the issue of Malathion's possible chronic toxicity . . . the data suggest that Malathion may actually have adverse properties only imperfectly studied to date. In our view, the final report could better convey this sense of uncertainty. As written, it may give the erroneous impression that all of the data are in, and thus, inadvertently give a complete 'clean bill of health' to a substance whose chronic toxicity is currently being evaluated."

Despite Lappe's and Hooper's concern, the Health Department issued its final report, with Health Services Director Beverlee Myers asserting that the operation would involve "no significant health risks." The decision to omit Lappe's warning was especially important in light of the HESIS mandate, particularly section 429.11 of the Health Safety Codes [which stated]:

> Whenever the repository [of information on commercially used chemicals] receives a request about toxicity information on any other chemical, in addition to providing available information about the known toxic effects of exposure to the chemical, the repository shall also notify the requester of any determination by any state agency or federal agency that the chronic health effects data on the chemical is inadequate or incomplete.[3]

Dr. Lappe's story documented the manner in which public health and safety officials coerce compliance with predetermined policies and outcomes. When later interviewed, Kahn offered a different assessment of the circumstances surrounding the Malathion spraying operation. He stated that the Health & Safety Code section governing HESIS would not apply to large aerial spraying activity, claiming that this code pertains solely to occupational health exposures "which are of an entirely different magnitude."[4]

In this regard, Betsy Russell–Manning wrote:

> Kahn stated that Lappe and Hooper "were not in the business of evaluating projects of this type." Curiously, Kahn also said that it was he who assigned Lappe and Hooper to evaluate the Malathion spraying operation.
>
> Kahn believes that the public was confused about the Malathion spraying operation and that people felt there was a clear-cut division between the "good guys"—farm-workers, environmentalists, and the "bad guys"—pesticide sprayers, manufacturers, and the agriculture industry. Lappe simply "could not see himself in a position of being on the wrong side," and had typed up the memo disagreeing with the department's position on Malathion, "so that he could make it part of the public record, and so disassociate himself," says Kahn.
>
> Kahn claimed that Lappe told an environmental group, Citizens for a Better Environment (CBE), that such a memo had been prepared "so that they could [under the public records act] come and say they wanted to see that memo."

Upon the release of the health department's report on Malathion, CBE did file a public records request for the agency's files on Malathion. Kahn denied having refused the request, although he stated that there were some working drafts of the Malathion analysis and report, which he felt were "legitimately" not part of available records. CBE files showed that the group then approached Lappe who turned over the files. Approximately two weeks later, Kahn walked into Lappe's office with a memo detailing a letter Lappe was to write and sign.

"I was to write a letter which would recant and say that I did not believe that there were any substantive differences between what I actually wrote, what our risk assessment was, and what the Department interpreted it to be," said Lappe, who now teaches clinical ethics and health policy at the University of Illinois at Chicago. "Kahn gave me the specific points the department wanted me to include in the letter and told me to write it and sign it. I refused. A few weeks later I was fired."

Kahn categorically denied Lappe's charge, stating that he never asked Lappe to sign any such memo and that it was not he who urged Lappe's removal, but "people above me." Lappe, said Kahn, had been "a little bit like a loose cannon."[3]

Heavy Metal Contaminants and More Cover-ups

Just as vaccines, discussed in Chapter 14, challenge the immune system with ingredients such as stabilizers and sterilizers including aluminum, mercury (until 2000), formaldehyde and formalin derivatives, and others called "adjuvants," such as "squalene," so too do the contaminants in pesticide sprays. These leave people more susceptible to secondary diseases and opportunistic infections.

As one physician on the Public Health Effects Advisory Committee explained during the 1990 Malathion controversy in California, potentially harmful spray contaminants included "malaoxon, isomalathion, OO, AS, OOS, Tri-methyl dithioates, and other products that are formed, along with Malathion, and/or during its breakdown. . . . mercaptains; other sulphur containing chemicals, and heavy metals."

A published list of the top sixteen Malathion spray impurities is presented in figure 5.1.

Mention of these biologically risky agents is most commonly avoided by officials in charge of spraying, and their cohorts in public health. They have also been known to routinely conceal laboratory data

Fig. 5.1. Sixteen Major Malathion Impurities

1 Diethyl fumarate 0.90%
2 Diethylhydroxysuccinate...0.05%
3 0,0–Dimethyl–phosphorothioite..0.05%
4 0,0,0–Trimethyl–phosphorothioate 0.45%
5 0,0,0–Trimethyl–phosphorodithioate...............................1.2%
6 Ethyl nitrite 0.03%
7 Diethyl mercaptosuccinate...0.15%
8 S–(1,2–Dicarbethoxy)–ethyl–0
   S–dimethyl phosphorodithioate (isomalathion)...........................0.20%
9 S–(1–Carbemethoxy–2–carbethoxy)
   ethyl–0,0–dimethyl phosphorodithioate...............................0.60%
10 Bis–(0,0–Dimethyl–thiomophosphoryl) sulfide.............................0.30%
11 Diethyl methylthiosuccinate 1.00%
12 S–Ethy–0, 0–dimethyl phosphorodithioate.........................0.10%
13 S–(1,2–Dicarbethoxylt) ethyl–0, 0, dimethly phosphorothioate...0.10%
14 Diethyl ethylthiosuccinate 0.10%
15 Content of water 0.07%
16 Acidity as H_2SO 0.05%

From: Russell-Manning B. *Malathion: Toxic Time Bomb, The Poisoning of Our People.* San Francisco: Cancer Control Society, 1990, p. 195.

unsupportive to their various causes. The following story is another example of official repression of critical data.

Malathion: Toxic Time Bomb author Betsy Russell–Manning asked Jack Thrasher, Ph.D., a heavy metals expert and pesticide analyst, "What are the concentrations of lead, nickel, and chromium found in Malathion spray?"

Dr. Thrasher replied, "They aren't releasing the concentrations found until they have a meeting with the state . . ."

"Why wasn't this done before?"

"The state has always found negative results," Thrasher returned. "They reported negative results. Somehow the City Council got hold of some samples from the last spraying and they found heavy metals, chromium, nickel and lead . . . above the state's allowable standards."

In fact, the lab report, later released, showed *numbing* amounts of these toxic metals were emanating from the spray helicopters. The exposure levels for example, ranged in three tests from 1.67 micrograms (mcgs) to 2.84 mcgs of chromium. The public health exposure limit, according to "Proposition 65 Regulatory Limits" was .001 micrograms per day. That is, *exposure levels occurring during the spraying campaign were more than 1,000 times higher than those allowed by law.*

Ms. Russell–Manning asked if this was normal for "technical grade malathion?"

"Yes," Dr. Thrasher replied. "They would more than likely be there, [but] you would have to look for them. They use various types of heavy metals as catalysts in the organic chemical [manufacturing] process."

"Nickel causes cancer," the concerned journalist interjected.

"So does chromium. Chromium is extremely carcinogenic."

"I am in shock," Russell–Manning admitted.

"I am not surprised," the expert said. "It's a hell of a contamination load."

Toxic Impurities and Immune Suppression

Chief among the toxic effects of pesticide spray impurities are their immunological reactions. Kathlene Rodgers, Ph.D., investigated the effects of Malathion and thioate impurities on the human immune system for more than a decade. Through research conducted in her laboratory at the University of Southern California she became interested in the Malathion spraying controversy, and determined to contribute to the public health and political dialog ongoing in her area in 1990. The following is an excerpt from her report to Assemblywoman Sandra Tanner regarding the "effects of Malathion on the immune system." These include macrophage stimulation and placing individuals at higher risk of immune diseases. While considering the following effects of pesticide exposures, it should be recalled that Malathion was commonly promoted as among the safest, most heavily investigated pesticides.

Dr Tanner wrote:

> These studies on the impurities [of malathion] show that oral administration of the impurities to mice suppressed the immune response transiently. These effects were mediated by alterations in macrophage function similar to those observed following an inflammatory stimulus (i.e., an irritation). I have published three papers on the effects of Malathion (purified, not technical grade which is being sprayed) on the immune system. These studies showed that Malathion, at doses that are non-cholinergic (that is, do not affect nerve function), stimulated the immune system. These alterations in immune function are also through

effects on macrophage function. It should be noted that nonspecific enhancement of immune function is also potentially harmful. There are many diseases mediated by enhanced immune function, such as allergy. Current studies are ongoing to determine the dose of Malathion that does not affect immune function, the mechanism by which Malathion alters macrophage function, and the effects of technical Malathion on immune function.

In the past, the effects of purified Malathion on the immune system have been studied and the effects of technical Malathion are unknown. The impurities in Malathion have separate effects on the immune function and affect the metabolism of Malathion. Published studies indicate that Malathion may affect the immune system through a metabolite. Since the impurities in Malathion block the breakdown of Malathion, through carboxyesterases, into nontoxic derivatives, the technical grade of Malathion may be more toxic to the immune system, as it is to the nervous system, than purified Malathion.

Studies by other investigators have shown that Malathion can cause an allergic response (which would be in keeping with the data regarding immune enhancement above). Milby and Epstein conducted studies in normal human volunteers in which a solution of 10% Malathion (95% pure) in ethanol was applied under occlusive dressings for 2 days. Such an exposure sensitized 45% of the exposed men. Application of a 1% solution of Malathion in the same study did not sensitize any of the exposed persons. In this same study, persons who were occupationally exposed to Malathion were studied and . . . only 3-5% were sensitized. The reason for the discrepancy between these populations may be due to the low concentration of Malathion being used during occupational exposure (i.e., 0.9%). Since the Malathion being sprayed is a relatively high concentration (i.e., approximately 22%), there is a possibility of dermal sensitization to Malathion. Several other studies in other animals, such as guinea pigs, mice, and rats, have shown that allergic reactions occur in animal models.

The long-term health effects of Malathion on the immune system are unknown, nor can it be predicted from the animal studies discussed above. However, I do not believe that sufficient data are available to say that Malathion has absolutely no health effects. In the current situation, it is impossible to tell what are real health effects and what is imagined. Although immunotoxicology (effects of chemicals on the immune system) is not currently used in making policy decisions and most of the current studies are in animals, I think these data should be considered.[8]

Spraying As "Reckless Irresponsibility"

The congressionally recognized expert in pesticide toxicity, Dr. Samuel Epstein, had more to say. At the end of his California legal deposition, the people's attorney asked him, "Doctor, you've reviewed for us at length a number of areas of concern that you have about the existing literature and existing data, as well as what you have described as substantial data gaps. Based on the work you have performed on this subject, have you formed an opinion with regard to the risk to public health of engaging in an aerial program of spraying Malathion-bait proposed for at least two more applications?"

Dr. Epstein replied, "Well, based on some thirty years experience, and as advisor to decision-making bodies at the executive and legislative levels, and I'm choosing my words with caution, I can only characterize this program as demonstrating reckless irresponsibility.

"I say this for some reasons which I've given already, and all the more so in view of the fact that warnings, explicit, unequivocal warnings, on the need for information in many of these areas was clearly articulated by the Department of Health Services in 1980. Substantial literature has grown up since 1980.

"Both CDFA and EPA fully admit the existence of data gaps, and this . . . it's not as if we're talking about small-scale spot applications in one narrow area. To contemplate large-scale aerial applications of this, compounded by the lack of any informational system for surveillance for acute effects, for looking at the chronic effects, compounded by the suppression of information by CDFA [and] from the DHS regarding highly toxic impurities, I think that I can only restate my serious misgivings in this area, and to restate that I believe it [aerial spraying] reflects, and I hesitate to use harsh words of this kind, reckless irresponsibility."[9]

•

References

1) Russell-Manning B. An interview with Jorge R. Mancillas, Ph.D. In: *Malathion: Toxic Time Bomb, The Poisoning of Our People*. San Francisco: Cancer Control Society, 1990, pp. 48, 82.

2) Myers B. Interoffice memorandum from the Director of the California Department of Health Services to the Director of the Department of Food and Agriculture. December 16, 1980. In: *Malathion: Toxic Time Bomb, The Poisoning of Our People*. Russell-Manning B., ed. San Francisco: Cancer Control Society, 1990, p. 160.

3) Beckmann S. Hansen J, Skolnik R, Ullman P and Warner R. The controversy over the 1981 aerial spraying of malathion and the subsequent firing of the HESIS Director Marc Lappe, Ph.D. In: *Malathion: Toxic Time Bomb, The Poisoning of Our People*. Russell-Manning B., ed. San Francisco: Cancer Control Society, 1990, p. 161.

4) These authors, including health attorney Joan Hansen, in their analysis of the case and laws governing it, determined that "Kahn is incorrect on this point." For the complete discussion see Russell-Manning's text cited in reference No. 1.

5) Satcher D. Immunization a must: Protects all. *USA Today*, August 19, 1999, p. 12A.

6) Horowitz LG. *Emerging Viruses: AIDS & Ebola—Nature, Accident or Intentional?* Rockport, MA: Tetrahedron Press, 1998.

7) Shorter E. The Health Century: A companion to the PBS television series. New York: Doubleday, 1987, pp. 67-69; 195-204. The recorded admissions are published on audiotape in: Horowitz L. *Horowitz on Vaccines*. Rockport, MA: Tetrahedron Press, 1998.

8) Rodgers K. Effects of Malathion on the immune system: A letter to Assemblywoman Sandra Tanner and Ms. Virginia Johanssen. In: *Malathion: Toxic Time Bomb, The Poisoning of Our People*. Op. cit., p. 196.

9) Epstein S. Expert witness testimony in a court of law against the aerial spraying of Malathion in El Cajon, California. In: *Malathion: Toxic Time Bomb, The Poisoning of Our People*. Op. cit., pp. 173-188.

Chapter 6.
"Emergency" Powers, Lethal Actions, CIA Propaganda, and Legislative Incompetence

"The reoccuring emergency is not an emergency
at all—rather, it is an indication of poor planning,
decision making, or administration. . . scientific
double-speak masquerading as science. . . ."

David Polcyn, Ph.D., 1994
Professor, California State University
Testimony before the U.S. House of Representatives

While the American news media might wish to claim innocence concerning its role in disseminating deceptive information impacting the public's health, many in the media are also partly responsible for the tragic consequences of what amounts to toxic warfare being waged against unwitting citizens.

Mainstream media has consistently allowed itself to be used, and abused, by public health and political officials. This failure to discern fact from fiction, risk from benefit, that is, the lack of in-depth and unbiased investigative reporting, has done more to further "bioterrorist" agendas, from within our own agencies of government, than the world's leading radical factions have brought to bear.

For instance, in 1998, Dan Rather reported on the CBS Evening News the "emergency" spraying of Malathion by "black helicopters" simultaneously over Miami Beach and Los Angeles for an alleged "fruit fly infestation." My familiarity with public health, "pest" control, population reduction, and propaganda campaigns in support of these, caused me to pause. In considering Rather's message as he showed the military helicopters flying above downtown Miami, I thought it odd that there would be: 1) emergency fruit fly infestations in urban settings as most pest captures I knew were in rural areas (or later you will read, in organic, not traditional, agricultural zones where pesticide-free rotting fruit exists); 2) sudden simultaneous infestation of the same species more than three thousand miles apart. In this case, it seemed too convenient that U.S. disease control and agricultural officials, together with the military, had decided to kill, like "two birds with one stone," two fruit fly infestations with one helicopter dispatch; and 3) the predominant "fruit flies" in Miami Beach and Los Angeles were elderly Jewish, Hispanic, and Black. This occurred at the same time Rockefeller population controllers had just published their desire to eradicate about half of the U.S. population.[1] Who better than these "pests" might they desire to spray?

Moreover, I knew that Dan Rather could not be trusted, as he had personally admitted in June 1992, being used for CIA cover stories and counterintelligence propaganda programs.

The CIA and the Media

During the CBS News special report on "Watergate: The Secret Story," Rather revealed that much of what the news media reported was censured by political bigwigs. Through the CIA, FBI and FCC, he said, politically correct positions were guarded and counterintelligence campaigns were waged and won. For instance, the "anchorman"—a term curiously related to a man directing conditioned behavior in the field of psychology known as neurolinguistic programming, or NLP—noted that during the Nixon administration, the CIA "had ways of influencing a lot of [media] people on the beat, either through their editors or publishers or through granting of favors, all the ways that guys, politicians from county courthouses and city halls and state legislatures do it, but in very sophisticated ways . . ."[2]

In *Deadly Innocence: The Kimberly Bergalis Case*, my ninth book, I first reported that on Tuesday evening September 7, 1993, the *CBS Evening News* aired another "Reality Check." Dan Rather reported that the United States government spent between $2.5 and $3 billion of taxpayer money every year on public relations campaigns. The administration directed 10,858 federal public affairs workers to generate a barrage of press releases that targeted the media and impacted the news the public received. In essence, Rather said, "critics say too much taxpayer money is being spent by the government to say nice things about itself."[3]

In an eye-opening exposé, *Keeping America Uninformed*, Donna Demac traced the demise of America's free press largely back to the FBI and CIA during the Nixon era. Demac wrote:

> ... Richard Nixon, for example, for whom journalists were a persistent headache, eventually had intelligence agents wiretapping reporters' telephone lines, opening their mail, and raiding press offices. Such measures were believed to have ended when Nixon left office....

> The Reagan administration also authorized the FBI and CIA to search newsrooms and institute a stream of ad hoc restrictions. It was primarily interested, however, in designing laws and regulations that would outlast the administration and reposition the media as a subordinated source of information about the actions of government.[4]

According to the Church Committee, by February 1976 fifty American journalists were working for the CIA. Carl Bernstein wrote for *Rolling Stone* that according to CIA documents, "more than 400 American journalists . . . in the past 25 years have secretly carried out assignments for the CIA." Such efforts, wrote Bernstein, contributed to the distortion of news at home as well as abroad. Bernstein's partner during his Watergate investigation, Bob Woodward, was heavily implicated as a CIA propagandist in *Emerging Viruses: AIDS & Ebola— Nature, Accident or Intentional?*

The authors of *Covert Action Information Bulletin* wrote in 1977:

> The CIA has at various times owned or subsidized more than 50 newspapers, news services, radio stations, periodicals and other communications entities, sometimes in the U.S. but mostly overseas. Another dozen foreign-based news organizations, not CIA-financed, were infiltrated by paid CIA agents. Nearly a dozen American publishing houses, including some of the most prominent names in the industry, have printed at least a score of the more than 250 English-language books financed or produced by the CIA since the early 1950s, in many cases without being aware of the Agency involvement. A substantial number of the bogus news stories planted abroad were published as genuine in the United States, a phenomenon the CIA calls "blowback," "replay" or "domestic fallout."[5]

The famous American statesman, the late Adlai Ewing Stevenson said, "Those who corrupt the public's mind are more evil than those who steal from the public's purse."

Unfortunately, the purveyors of public health propaganda are guilty on both counts. Ironically, taxpayers pay their salaries, as well as for their disinformation—financially and with their lives.

Global Patriotism Versus Legislative Dysfunction

In the words of Sean MacBride, the former Foreign Minister of Ireland, and 1974 Nobel Peace Prize recipient, despite his "deep affection for, and tremendous admiration of, the United States and its people," this International Peace Bureau president warned:

> I came to the conclusion that all the values that made me admire the American people were being eroded by the covert operations of the CIA and kindred secret bodies . . .

> Time after time the United States has generously aided other countries threatened by famine or disaster. The survival of this great tradition is of importance, not only to Americans, but also to all freedom loving people in the world.

> But in my view, the survival of this great democracy is now being gravely threatened by the covert criminal actions of the Central Intelligence Agency and its associated services. If the United States is to be protected from this grave danger, it is essential that the activities of this secret agency should be fully exposed to the people of the United States.

> . . . I am a fierce believer in the democratic system of governments. Among the democracies, the Constitution of the United States can be, and has proved to be, a bastion of civil liberty.

> However, democracy and the rule of law could not survive side by side with a state agency that engages in covert operations ranging from assassinations to levying mercenary armies. Even if there is, now, an attempt being made by some to check the activities of the CIA and the other United States intelligence agencies, the whole concept of a secret government and army within a government is a menace to the democratic system.[6]

Since there is no evidence to suggest Sean MacBride's decades old prose is inaccurate, the greatest danger "We the People of the United States" and freedom loving citizens around the world face is the likelihood that America's "democracy" is already extinct.

I have spent many fruitless hours on Capitol Hill in search of heroes. I came to the conclusion that our elected officials were merely puppets for shadow governors who pulled their political strings in a pseudo-democracy that is actually international corporate fascism masquerading.

If you find this hard to believe you are not alone. It seems most people have difficulty reaching this conclusion given the extraordinary anguish accompanying the realization. The false hope that each "democratic" election and political contrivance brings makes it even more difficult to accept the traumatic reality underlying contemporary politics. The most common reaction is to choose denial and avoidance as coping strategies.

There is some consolation in knowing this situation is not peculiar to contemporary history, or even to the United States. On the verge of his revolution against the global colonialists of England, the great American patriot Patrick Henry warned,

> It is natural for man to indulge in the illusions of hope. We are apt to shut our eyes against a painful truth, and listen to the song of that siren till she transforms us into beasts. Is this the part of wise men, engaged in a great and arduous struggle for liberty? Are we disposed to be the number of those who, having eyes, see not, and having ears, hear not, the things which so nearly concern their temporal salvation? For my part, whatever anguish of spirit it may cost, I am willing to know the whole truth; to know the worst, and to provide for it.[7]

The CIA's Black Helicopters

As part of this "reality check," to wake up "those who, having eyes, see not, and having ears, hear not," it is proper to recognize who controls at least some of the helicopters spraying pesticides over public skies. At least in California, the culprit again was determined to be the CIA. This was discussed in a feature story in California's *Phoenix* newspaper.[8]

Evergreen Helicopters, the only company contracted to spray Malathion during the 1980 Medfly eradication program, had links to the CIA dating back to 1976, according to the report by three investigative journalists, Diana Hembrae, A. Jay Fields, and Geoffrey Dawn.

According to their article, Evergreen Helicopter purchased Intermountain Aviation—a CIA "proprietary" in 1976. The CIA funded and operated company served as a front for clandestine activities such as those making headline news during the Reagan and Bush administrations.

In July 1980, *Aviation Weekly* reported that the company became linked to the CIA when it bought Intermountain. Calling the CIA link "a sometimes bothersome connection," the text said that Evergreen "was marked with the CIA brand" when it relocated to Marana, Arizona from Montana to take over the former Intermountain facility. The initial discovery of the CIA's link to Intermountain came during a congressional hearing, the article said.

Ties between Evergreen and the CIA were "strengthened," when the company hired two former agents. One was made the chief executive officer, and the other became a Washington consultant according to *Aviation Weekly*. Though the names of the two men were not published, Hembrae, *et al.*, learned that "one of the agents in question was George Dooie, who had directed a number of CIA-controlled airlines."[8]

The investigators' *Phoenix* article went on to provide a revealing account of the agent's affiliation with the Medfly eradication program as follows:

A CIA agent for 17 years, Dooie became a consultant to Evergreen at the time it purchased Intermountain, and was also appointed to Evergreen's board of directors. An Evergreen spokesperson has recently stated that he "could neither confirm nor deny" Dooie's present role in Evergreen operations.

These allegations surfaced . . . during a weekly talk show led by Rav Taliaferro of KGO radio.

An employee at the State Medfly Project told a local county supervisor that "things were crazy . . . the phone was ringing off the hook" after Taliaferro's broadcast, and Project Director Jerry Schribner called KGO to publicly denounce the talk show. Dismissing Evergreen's alleged ties with the CIA as "irrelevant," Schribner declared, "I don't care whether they are [connected with the CIA] or not."

In the same talk show, Taliaferro discussed Evergreen's controversial herbicide spraying in Scottsdale, Arizona, and its role in secretly transporting the Shah of Iran from Panama to the Azores, the first step of his journey to exile in Egypt. Both allegations were confirmed by *Aviation Weekly*, which said that Evergreen's president Delford Smith had "no qualms" about aiding the Shah's flight.

"I thought the Shah had been a pretty genuine friend to America . . . We knew the trip had been blessed by the U.S. government," the magazine quoted the Evergreen chief as saying. "The White House chose Evergreen as an intermediary because it could react quickly," Smith concluded.

The aerospace weekly also informed us that "working for the CIA might not be all that bad: 'they pay their bills,'" he [Smith] said. And though Smith denies knowledge of a CIA–Evergreen connection, he is quoted as admitting that "unknown to us," the airline might have performed some jobs with CIA connections.

In fact, the CIA created Intermountain during the 1950s to maintain and store their aircraft, the *Phoenix* reporters determined. It was soon used as a training site for foreign and American mercenaries assigned by the agency to "black ops," including war projects related to promoting unrest in Southeast Asia and in Central Africa. Its facilities grew, fueling suspicions, particularly when casual viewers saw military aircraft with bomb bays. The company later used CIA money to expand its hangers in efforts to avert such sightings.

"Intermountain's most controversial operation," the *Phoenix* article said, "was its role as a conduit for the sale of B-26 bombers to Portugal, which used the planes to wage war in its African colonies. Official U.S. policy had banned all weapons sales to Portugal . . . [T]he illegal arms sale resulted in a U.S. Justice Department investigation."

During the next decade, the company's cover became transparent. So it was forced, in one agent's words, "to operate under deeper cover." Thus, in 1976, Intermountain sold out to Evergreen.

Aerial spraying of pesticides became a major activity of Evergreen Helicopters in 1978. During these early decades, Evergreen sprayed more than 2 million gallons of chemicals over foreign soils and greater concealed amounts domestically. Fierce opposition confronted the CIA-linked mission directors conducting genocidal operations here in the United States.

For example, "In Scottsdale, Arizona" the *Phoenix* reported, "Evergreen Helicopters was contracted to spray three chemicals on the cotton fields of a Pima Indian reservation. Many Native Americans fell ill from valley fever and hepatitis shortly after the spraying, and a congressional inquiry revealed that the reservation had been saturated with over 20 chemicals.

"In Oregon and northern California, Evergreen was hired by timber companies to spray weed killers 2,4-D and 2,4,5-T herbicides developed at the U.S. Army Germ Warfare Center in 1945. In 1978, a group of Oregon doctors linked the spraying with a sharp increase in miscarriages and deformed babies in coastal Oregon.

"Dr. Renee Scrimham, an Oregon physician, told the *L.A. Times* that she had seen three cases of anencephalus (infants born without brains) in four years of practice—an incidence thirteen times higher than the national average. The mother of one of the babies . . . told reporters that she had 'seen the helicopters overhead and smelled the chemicals'" while pregnant.

"[More] recently, cases of acute pesticide related health problems are being reported from areas that have been heavily sprayed with Malathion" by Evergreen Helicopters, Hembrae, *et al.* concluded.[8]

"Bioterrorism" for Economic Espionage

In *Healing Codes for the Biological Apocalypse*, Dr. Puleo and I discussed the use of a new form of "bioterrorism" waged by multinational corporations with ties to the ruling families of the world—the oligarchy with financial links to the Rockefeller–Farben chemical/pharmaceutical cartel and the global military–medical–industrial complex.[9]

This form of "bioterrorism" employed the principle of "Problem/Reaction/Solution," explained deftly by author and Illuminati investigator, David Icke.[10] It is based largely on Machiavellian theory whereby creating a problem prompts the economic opportunity for a solution. In today's global health arena, there is great incentive to manufacture health and environmental problems, have mainstream media herald them, thereby inducing anxiety, even hysteria, which leads to mass consumption of expensive chemical or pharmaceutical solutions. Thus, people's desire for, and acceptance of, a quick fix or resolution to the manufactured problem is engineered. I have repeatedly observed this dynamic in the realm of infectious diseases. In the context of this book, examples include annual flu predictions and vaccine shortage warnings, as well as the WNV "outbreak" prompting spraying programs.

Healing Codes for the Biological Apocalypse provided another compelling example of this new form of "bioterrorism." It related to "economic espionage," or in Past CIA Director James Woolsy's words, "industrial espionage." The following excerpt, based on the scientific literature, cited the manufacture of proteins responsible for "mad cow disease," called "prions," by altering *E. coli* bacteria "through recombinant DNA techniques."[9] It may be recalled that, *E. coli* is one of the most commonly used bacteria for germ warfare research and development. As mentioned in Chapter 1, the 157th strain of *E. coli* was likely a man-made hybrid later associated with the deaths of many children at a Jack-in-the-Box restaurant in Texas, as well as the recall of 25 million pounds of Hudson Beef Company meat just before Tyson Foods purchased the company. The Tyson takeover was likely an industrial espionage operation.

How had I drawn this seemingly outrageous conclusion?

My initial suspicion was based on a review of a U.S. *Congressional Record* that showed *E. coli* had been one of the principle germs manipulated by CIA and Army biological weapons contractors.

Later I read James Woolsy's statement, "With the end of the Cold War, the CIA must enter the era of economic [or industrial] espionage." This function would be served, it was intimated, on behalf of American corporations that requested such CIA assistance.

With that knowledge, the week the CDC announced an alleged outbreak of *E. coli* from Hudson, I predicted, before more than 700 people during lectures, of the likely "takeover of Hudson Beef by a large competitor. . . . You can't trust the CDC whatsoever," I warned during lectures.

One week later, newspapers heralded the takeover of Hudson by Tyson Foods. Hudson's stock had plummeted by a third following the fright and beef recall. Tyson took advantage of the media (and likely CIA) manufactured business opportunity.

Reuters reported that the "U.S. chicken processor Tyson Foods Inc., has agreed to buy Hudson Foods Inc. in a deal worth about $650 million, a week after Hudson Foods agreed to sell its only raw hamburger plant to [Tyson competitor] IBP Inc. . . . Merrill Lynch & Co. Inc. analyst Leonard Teitelbaum was cited in one story as saying the acquisition will add to Tyson's earnings immediately and he called the deal favorable to both parties, although the value was at the 'bottom end' of what he would consider a fair price for Hudson Foods."

This occurred despite the fact that meat inspectors and public health officials never confirmed the contaminations came from the Hudson plant.

Tyson, I realized, had most likely gotten away with a ruse.

Then, a similar ruse was orchestrated a few months later, but this time it was a chicken influenza "outbreak" in Asia. Recalling the Tyson scam from *Healing Codes for the Biological Apocalypse:*

> On December 23, 1997, the Associated Press reported that a 60-year-old woman had died of "suspected bird flu." The U.S. Government immediately announced it would halt "all chicken imports from China in a move to curb the spread of the virus."
>
> The virus—A H5N1—according to the report, "has long been known to infect birds but appeared in humans for the first time this year."
>
> "Oh come on!" I protested, knowing that such cross-species transmission was extremely difficult and rare. Far likelier than a spontaneous cross-species leap, the chicken influenza viruses had, like *E. coli*, been most likely mutated in a lab. This I knew had been routinely done with chicken sarcoma viruses at the University of California under the direction of Dr. Peter Duesberg of AIDS-virus fame. Duesberg and other NCI colleagues had routinely cultured chicken viruses in human cells in an effort to get them to adapt their protein coats before jumping species. All I could do was shake my head as I thought, "This looks like another setup for some other ruse."
>
> Days later it was announced the horrible outbreak required the slaughter of 1.2 million Asian chickens, and perhaps cats, dogs, and other animals as well! Asian chicken farmers were overwhelmed with concern and pressured to massacre their flocks.
>
> Few knew that prior to these events, Tyson was vying to bring the Asian poultry industry into its worldwide monopolistic fold. The emergency primarily targeted Tyson's Asian competition—mostly small chicken farmers. What was most likely a CIA-directed "outbreak" conveniently required the annihilation of Tyson's competitors. That would have been a very effective, albeit immoral, industrial espionage operation.[9]

Morality, however, had not been one of Tyson's features. The Springdale, Arkansas-based company showered gifts upon Clinton administration policy makers like former Agriculture Secretary Mike Espy. Don Tyson, in fact, was one of Bill Clinton's "closest friends and biggest supporters," according to Arkansas state trooper Larry Patterson's testimony before the grand jury that investigated Tyson's unethical and illegal conduct.

In fact, many Americans can recall the hoopla over Hillary Clinton making more than $100,000 virtually overnight in the commodities market in 1978. The cattle-trading tip came from James Blair, chief counselor at Tyson Foods.

Don Tyson had also been Bill Clinton's top fundraiser during his Gubernatorial election. In return, the governor, and later president, eased regulations on Tyson's chicken industry. This allowed continued pollution of America's rivers and streams with chicken waste. Espy tidied up the meat packing industry, but killed the proposal to do the same for chicken processors, sixty-six of which, in America in 1998, were owned by Tyson. Thanks to Tyson and Clinton cronies, and their "environmental protection" efforts, in northwest Arkansas alone more than 500 miles of rivers were dangerously polluted and, at the time of this writing, were off-limits to swimmers.[9]

Finally, as this book went to press, Tyson Foods and the CIA were apparently at it again with the fright over an international foot-and-mouth disease outbreak. *USA Today* reported on March 15, 2001 that the mass slaughter of cattle was certain to raise beef costs to Tyson's primary U.S. competitor, IBP, which Tyson had unsuccessfully attempted to purchase four times previously. The newspaper reported that because of the outbreak, Tyson's $30 per share offer for IBP stock valued at only $24.11 was likely to be accepted in the $3.2 billion deal.[13]

What if Medfly "Infestations" Were Not Simply "Eradication" Ruses

The "problem/reaction/solution" dynamic involving economic or "industrial espionage," as cited in the examples above, applied to the alleged threats of insect "infestations" as well. Illuminated here is the utility of eradicating a problem that was the cryptocracy's creation in the first place. Insofar as periodic pesticide spraying programs, and more recently Anvil sprayings in the northeastern U.S., one can assume, tallying all of the preceding discussions, that economic motives may be at least part of the impetus for these programs, programs that have consistently failed to accomplish their alleged objective, that is, "to safely eradicate insect pests."

However, what if economic espionage was *not* the primary objective behind these "public health" programs? What if an even more sinister motive was being applied here? The state-of-the-art and the method of choice in conducting warfare on targeted populations, including genocidal campaigns, was by the early 1990s determined to be "non-lethal military warfare" or principally "toxic warfare."

Advancing a horrifying possibility that modern pesticide spraying programs and, as will be discussed, vaccination campaigns, have been principally covert genocidal campaigns, the first step would be to show that the "infestations" as well as the "eradications" were fantasy; more accurately "science fiction."

For this, consider the submission by Professor David M. Polcyn, Ph.D., of the Department of Biology at California State University in San Bernardino, to the Committee on Agriculture, U.S. House of Representatives, on May 5, 1994.[11] What follows is his transcribed appeal to legislators to recognize that the problem with California's pests cannot, has not, and will never, be addressed by spraying pesticides. In fact, he submitted, the "eradication" program likely facilitated the Medfly establishment, which he also reported, is not expressed in legitimate "infestations." Finally, he rationally and scientifically argued that true "emergencies" have never been recurring as agriculture and public health authorities had alleged. Here are the relevant excerpts from his lengthy testimony before the U.S. Congress:

> Contrary to how some would prefer to portray me, I am definitely *not* anti-agriculture. Rather, I think agriculture has as much to lose from the failed programs as do the millions of citizens who are and have been sprayed with thousands of gallons of Malathion against their wishes and the wishes of their elected officials. I am only concerned with the continued spread of the Medfly, and believe, after extensive review of the literature and program, that the continued spread of the Medfly in southern California is the *result of*, not *despite*, the failed unscientific efforts of the CDFA and USDA.
>
> Let me begin by emphatically stating that the Medfly program is a scientific problem. More specifically it is a biological phenomenon. Although there are obvious economic and political ramifications, first and foremost it is a scientific phenomenon. The Medflies are biological organisms displaying biological characteristics and responding to biological and physical parameters of their environments. Therefore, the solutions to the Medfly problems must be based on sound science; whether or not the solutions make political or economic sense, or meet the needs of political or economical expediency, the solutions must be based on sound science. Solutions based on, or driven by, bureaucratic and political needs or desires may suffice as very short-term band-aids, but they will not solve the problems, and the problems we are experiencing are becoming worse by the year.[11]

Dr. Polcyn continued before the U.S. House of Representatives:

Although not officially termed "infestations" each year by the CDFA/ USDA, Medflies have been captured in the Los Angeles area numerous times since 1975. Repeat "infestations" occurred in 1980, '81, '82, '84, '86, '87, '88, '90, '91, '92, '93, and now a record number and dispersion of "infestations" in 1994. The initial "infestations" (1975 and 1980) have spread from a single county (Los Angeles) to currently including four counties (Los Angeles, Orange, San Bernardino and Riverside). After every "infestation," the CDFA/USDA has declared the Medfly "eradicated," only to call each successive "infestation," a "new introduction." The recurring emergencies have been dealt with using either Malathion and/or sterile insect releases. Over the years thousands of Medflies have been captured, with all but one captured in nonagricultural areas (i.e., backyards, parks, etc.). The single exception was in an organic (pesticide-free) citrus grove, which has since been sprayed with Malathion and had its natural balance of insects severely disrupted. **The Medflies have never been found within a traditional agricultural setting**, yet the claim is repeatedly made that agriculture as we know it in California will collapse unless the State takes quick and decisive action to eradicate the pest. [Emphasis not added.]

Although aerial applications of Malathion have been used extensively in the past to eradicate the Medfly, other alternatives exist (nematodes, natural parasites, bacteria, etc.) Due to a lack of urgency in bringing most alternatives to fruition, the only alternative to pesticide use to date is the use of sterile flies. However, the CDFA and USDA have used the excuse "we have exhausted our supply of flies," for many years, and despite building a new facility in Hawaii, we are once again caught in a very predictable situation of having too few flies to treat the current infestation. Thus, they are resorting to the treatments of yesteryear— pesticides.

While I have serious problems believing that the pesticide treatment protocols are sufficient to eradicate the Medflies (and do believe a concerted biological control effort has a much higher probability of success, as well as acceptance by the affected citizens), my discussion today will center on the underlying basis for the program in the first place—the presence of the Medfly. Although these might seem like things we *must* already be fully knowledgeable about (and in fact we *should* be fully knowledgeable about), I would like to address basic issues relating to questions such as "Do we know where the Medfly is and where it isn't?" and "Do we know when our eradication programs have been effective in eradicating the Medfly?" Unfortunately, the answer to all of these is "No." We are seriously ignorant of the most basic information necessary to plan, implement and successfully carry out an eradication program.

. . . Thus, to believe the CDFA/USDA theory of recurring multiple introductions followed by multiple eradications, one has to not only ignore
the scientific models widely used to understand pest introductions and
spread, but must also rely on numerous farfetched assumptions about
the distribution and dynamics of illegal fruit introductions. Yet the myth
continues . . .[11]

Dr. Polcyn concluded his testimony with a plea for an "independent
scientific review" of the matter, since he made it quite clear that decisions were not being made based on knowledge that "should" and
"must" be known, and that the correct intelligence *is* known, but simply
not used. In this final statement, as with the problem/reaction/solution
machination, he shared that the "recurring emergency is not an emergency at all." The embolden and other emphasis was his:

> **A reoccurring emergency is not an emergency at all—rather, it is an
> indication of poor planning, decision-making, or administration**. How
> much of this is based on flawed science is hard to determine, but it is
> abundantly clear that there is a fundamental problem with the way
> science is being handled within the Medfly eradication program. Many
> scientists, myself included, are asking for a truly independent review of
> the program from a purely scientific perspective. We want the program
> brought out into the open, out from behind the facade of a recurring
> emergency and from behind the thin veil of science. With no offense to
> legislators, I would suggest that most politicians couldn't tell good
> science from bad science, especially since the CDFA and USDA have
> proven to be very effective at scientific double-speak masquerading as
> science. I would plead for the legislators to support an independent
> panel of scientists, experts in their fields but *independent of agricul-
> tural biases and conflicts of interest.* Such a panel could be compiled
> by either the National Academy of Sciences [NAS], or the California
> Academy of Sciences, or another similar scientific non-agricultural-body
> of scientists. Let the scientists review the scientific merits of the pro-
> grams and report back to the appropriate legislative bodies. Unfortu-
> nately, it appears that only through legislative hearings and indepen-
> dent scientific evaluation will we be able to alter the ineffective pro-
> grams currently embraced by CDFA and USDA. *The perpetuation of
> the current program is a lose-lose situation*, bad for the citizens experi-
> encing repeated sprayings of Malathion, and bad for the agricultural
> community faced with continued spread of the Medfly. Fifteen years of
> repeat Medfly infestations is evidence that something is *very* wrong
> and needs fixing, and neither CDFA nor USDA appears to be up to the
> task.[11]

In his 1906 account of developing food and drug laws, novelist Upton Sinclair wrote in *The Jungle,* "it is difficult to get a man to understand something when his salary depends on his not understanding it."

To date, Dr. Polcyn's recommendations for an independent scientific review of pesticide spraying programs has yet to be done, again, not because it isn't justified, but because politicians are incapable of extricating themselves from certain economic allegiances. Asking Capitol Hill legislators to effectively intervene was naive, on Dr. Polcyn's part. Even if the NAS had been invited to peer review the matter, as you will soon learn, no fair scientific assessment could be expected.

As Dr. Polcyn intimated, and as detailed more completely in upcoming chapters, behind the thin veil of science in matters such as pesticide spraying and vaccination programs, lies a thinner veil of legislative competence in actions perceived to be rational for public health. Too often, by way of legislation, shadow governors representing petrochemical/pharmaceutical interests have advanced hidden agendas to extend a new form of global corporate control. As detailed in the forthcoming chapters, in this "New World Order," evolved from chaos, people are often viewed as dispensable commodities at best, and at worst, burgeoning and threatening excess populations.

Nay-sayers find this difficult to believe. Most people can not conceive that contemporary spraying and vaccination programs are pseudo-scientifically driven practices. Most people never seriously investigate the issues or ask, "How have we come to know what we know?"

To date, public health programs have tended to mainly target minority, native, and economically disadvantaged populations. By definition and scientific outcome, these actions have tended to be genocidal. Consequently, we might ask if there has been a deliberate and systematic effort to destroy certain racial and/or political groups for economic, and as later chapters argue, ideological reasons.[12] The answer is clearly, "Yes."

In this context of genocide, it is alarming that this country's most powerful policy-makers have considered it urgent, in 1998, to reduce the U.S. population by 50%.[1] Thus, we see that people are being killed slowly through cofactor methods of intoxication as delivered by petrochemicals, pharmaceuticals, and/or biologicals, in the name of public health. In the next chapters, I will lay more of the scientific and historic groundwork for this horrific thesis to be seriously considered, if not proven.

References

1) Negative Population Control, Inc. Why we need a small U. S. population: And how we can achieve it. *Foreign Affairs*. New York: Council on Foreign Relations, 1996, Volume 75; No. 2. See also documents and discussion in: Horowitz and Puleo, *Healing Codes for the Biological Apocalypse*. Sandpoint, Idaho: Tetrahedron Publishing Group, 1999, pp. 250-252.

2) CBS Evening News. Watergate: The secret story CBS News special program. June 17, 1992. Available through Burrelle's Information Services.

3) CBS Evening News with Dan Rather and Connie Chung. "Reality Check: The Government's PR Machine." September 7, 1993.

4) Demac DD. *Keeping America Uninformed*. New York: The Pilgram Press, 1984, pp. 91-92.

5) Covert Action Information Bulletin. Turner's "Born Again" CIA. In: *Dirty Work: The CIA in Western Europe*. P. Agee and L. Wolf, eds. Secaucus, NJ: Lyle Stuart Inc., 1977. p.313.

6) MacBride S. Preface. In: *Dirty Work-2: The CIA in Africa*. Ray E. Schaap W., Van Meter K and Wolf L eds. Secaucus, NJ: Lyle Stewart, Inc., 1979, pp. xiii-xiv.

7) Henry P. Speech in Virginia convention. Richmond, VA. March 23, 1775. In: *Bartlett's Familiar Quotations*. E.M. Beck, ed. Boston: Little, Brown and Company, 1980, p. 383.

8) Hembrae D, Fields AJ and Dawn G. Medfly helicopters linked to CIA. *Phoenix: A Worker Controlled Newspaper*. November 19 - December 2, 1981. p. 1.

9) Horowitz L and Puleo J. *Op. cit*. pp. 236-239.

10) Icke D. *And the Truth Shall Set You Free*. Cambridge, England: Bridge of Love Publications, 1995.

11) Polcyn DM. Testimony before the Department of Operations and Nutrition Subcommittee, Committee on Agriculture, U.S. House of Representative, Washington, DC, May 5, 1994.

12) Webster M. *Merriam Webster's Collegiate Dictionary, Tenth Edition*. Springfield, MA: Merriam-Webster, Incorporated, 1994, p.486.

13) Valdmanis T. Foot-and-mouth disease worries can cost money: From McDonald's to airlines, profits are on the line. *USA Today*, Thursday, March 15, 2001, p. B 1.

Chapter 7.
Anvil Instead of Malathion

"What is food to one,
is to others bitter poison. . . .
From the heart of this fountain of delights
wells up some bitter taste to choke them
even amid the flowers."

Titus Lucretius Carus, 99–55 B.C.
On the Nature of Things

When the WNV was alleged to have "first appeared" in NYC, most people had never heard the word "Anvil," and had not clued in to what it was or did.

The Chevron Corporation produced the primary ingredients in Anvil. According to the company and the New York City Department of Health (NYCDoH), it provided "a safer" alternative pesticide substitute for Malathion. The sudden change was likely spurred by the intense controversy surrounding Malathion's published problems as detailed earlier. You might also recall that Malathion was also deceptively promoted as among the "safest" pesticides during the 1980s and early 1990s spraying programs.

Anvil, according to NYCDoH literature, "is a pyrethroid-based pesticide registered for use in mosquito control by the Environmental Protection Agency and New York State Department of Environmental Conservation. It is effective against adult mosquitoes, including the Culex species, which transmitted West Nile virus last year. Anvil is registered for use against mosquitoes in swamps, marshes, and outdoor residential and recreational areas. It has low toxicity to humans, mammals, and the environment. In three decades of its use, there have been no reports of toxic effects of Anvil to people, pregnant women, pets, or other mammals. Mild eye and skin irritation may occur with exposure to Anvil, which can be treated by washing the eyes and skin thoroughly with water after contact."[1]

The main active ingredient in Anvil is *Sumithrin*, "a synthetic pesticide similar to a natural pesticide produced by chrysanthemum flowers." Sumithrin, the NYCDoH reported, "quickly breaks down in
sunlight and water, and will not cause damage to the environment."

They warned, however, that "children or adults who have asthma
or a respiratory condition should stay inside if spraying occurs. In addition, windows and doors should be closed and air conditioners should
be shut off."[1]

As this sounded much like Malathion advertisements a decade earlier, I decided to investigate Anvil further. The public relations director
for Zanus Corporation in Belgrade, Montana, said to be the source of
this pesticide, was kind enough to fax me the Material Safety Data
Sheet (MSDS) on the product.[2] As I read this, I realized the NYCDoH
pronouncements followed the tradition of Malathion endorsements—
pure propaganda, if not downright lies.

Anvil, the MSDS forms stated, was manufactured by Clark Mosquito Control Products, Inc. of Roselle, Illinois. The label displayed
three categories of special relevance: "Hazards to Humans and Domestic Animals," "Environmental Hazards," and "Physical or Chemical
Hazards." These read as follows:

HAZARDS TO HUMANS AND DOMESTIC ANIMALS—Harmful if
absorbed through the skin. Do not induce vomiting because of aspiration pneumonia hazard. Avoid contact with skin, eyes, or clothing. In
case of contact, flush with plenty of water. Wash with soap and water
after use. Obtain medical attention if irritation persists. Avoid contamination of food and feedstocks.

ENVIRONMENTAL HAZARDS—Do not contaminate untreated
water by cleaning of equipment. Cleaning of equipment or disposal of
wastes must be done in a manner that avoids contamination of bodies
of water or wetlands. For terrestrial uses, do not apply directly to water;
or to areas where surface water is present or to intertidal areas before
the mean high water mark.

PHYSICAL OR CHEMICAL HAZARDS—Do not use or store near
heat or open flame.[2]

Furthermore, under "Statement of Practical Treatment" the label
read:

IF SWALLOWED: Call a physician or Poison Control Center immediately. Do not induce vomiting because of aspiration pneumonia hazard.

IF IN EYES: Flush eyes with plenty of water. Call a physician if irritation persists.

IF ON SKIN OR CLOTHING: Remove contaminated clothing and wash before reuse. Wash skin with soap and warm water. Get medical attention if irritation persists.

IF INHALED: Remove victim to fresh air. If not breathing, give artificial respiration, preferably mouth to mouth.

For information regarding medical emergencies or pesticide incidents, call the Informational Poison Center at 1-888-740-8712.[2]

My first thoughts, after reading the above, was of the likelihood that New York health commissioners had not heeded the warning on Anvil's label concerning the flow of this chemical into "areas where surface water" was present, sewers and waterways, and onto surfaces contacted by humans.

I also realized that the inhalation warning would be contrary to the aerial spraying that had occurred over several heavily populated areas of New York. For instance, spraying the air over Staten Island is detailed in the next chapter. Here, *Newsday* reported that helicopters sprayed Anvil in broad daylight upon mostly minority children playing in parks and athletic fields.[3]

Further analyzing the information on Anvil's MSDS form under the heading "Principal Hazardous Components," listed was:

Sumithrin [3-Phenoxybenzyl-(1RS, 3RS; 1RS, 3RS) 2,2-cimethyl-3-2(2-methlyprop-2-enyl] cyclopropane-carboxylate)

Piperonyl Butoxide [Alpha-(2-(1 butoxyethoxy)-4,5-methylenedioxy-2-propyltoluene]

White Mineral Oil and Aromatic Hydrocarbon

Following this, the form included "Health Hazard Data," that stated:

EXPOSURE LIMITS: Not established by OSHA or ACGIH.

I thought it risky, indeed, that the human exposure limits had not been established, yet these chemicals were being sprayed all around humans.

Under the heading "EMERGENCY FIRST AID," the label gave the following warnings:

SKIN CONTACT: CAUTION. Can cause a burning sensation on more sensitive areas (face, eyes, mouth). Prolonged or repeated exposure can cause irritation and reddening of the skin, possibly progressing into dermatitis. Immediately flush affected area . . .

EYE: CAUTION. Can cause temporary irritation, tearing, and blurred vision. Immediately flush with large amounts of water for at least 15 minutes. If irritation persists, get medical attention.

INHALATION: CAUTION. Excessive inhalation can cause nasal and respiratory irritation. Remove affected person to fresh air. Give oxygen, if necessary. If breathing has stopped, administer artificial respiration and get medical attention immediately.

INGESTION: CAUTION. Can cause stomach irritation, resulting in nausea, cramps and vomiting. Excessive ingestion can cause nervous system disorders such as fatigue, dizziness, headaches, lack of coordination, tremors and unconsciousness. Do not induce vomiting because of aspiration pneumonia hazard. Call a physician or poison control center.

Next, under "Environmental Protection Procedures," the MSDS listed "Spill Responses," "Storage," and "Waste Disposal." These sections read:

SPILL RESPONSE: Shut off ignition sources. Stop release, if possible without risk. Dike or contain release, if possible, and if immediate response can prevent further damage or danger, isolate and control access to the release area. Take actions to reduce vapors. Absorb with appropriate absorbent. For large spills, collect product into drums, etc., via drains, pumps, etc. Clean spill area of residues and absorbent. Contaminated absorbent and wash water should be disposed of according to local, state and federal regulations.

STORAGE: Store containers upright and closed. Store in areas that are cool, dry and well-ventilated. Keep away from heat, ignition sources and strong oxidizers. Emptied containers may retain product residues.

WASTE DISPOSAL: Do not contaminate water when disposing of equipment wash waters. Do not discharge effluent containing this product into lakes, streams, ponds, estuaries, oceans, or other waters unless in accordance with the requirement of a National Pollutant Discharge Elimination System (NPDES) permit, and the permitting authority has been notified in writing prior to discharge. Do not discharge effluent containing this product into sewer systems without previously notifying the sewage treatment plant authority. For guidance, contact your State Water Board or Regional Office of the EPA. Do not mix with other waste materials.[2]

After reading this last paragraph I wondered what might happen if the sewer runoff containing the pesticide reached the Hudson River, Long Island Sound, or the Atlantic Ocean? One possibility came a few days later with a telephone call from a marine biologist, and former water commissioner from the State of Florida, Mr. William Winkler. His report is provided in Chapter 9 in a "case study" in water pollution/contamination, government cover-ups, and non-lethal warfare.

Cancer Link to Anvil's Sumithrin

I searched the Internet to see if I could locate any data on Anvil's main ingredient—Sumithrin. Immediately, a cancer study popped up in a NIH restricted website.[4] The abstract was all that was available to unauthorized parties. Entitled, "Estrogenic Potential of Certain Pyrethroid Compounds in the MCF-7 Human Breast Carcinoma Cell Line," the abstract revealed that "Estrogens . . . clearly influence reproductive development, senescence, and carcinogenesis. Three pyrethroid insecticides studied, including Sumithrin, caused a significant increase in the production of messenger RNA as a trigger for cancer cells grown in culture. The findings suggested that "pyrethroids should be considered to be hormone disrupters, and their potential to affect endocrine function in humans and wildlife should be investigated."

Once again, I considered it odd that this toxic pesticide was likely to produce cancer and sterility in humans, yet the NYCDoH and the CDC was touting its safety and instigating programs whereby populations might be massively exposed for no proven benefit.

Chevron Today

Finally, over the Internet, I learned that Chevron, a Rockefeller company, produced the main toxic/carcinogenic ingredients for Anvil. Here was the text posted under "Chevron Today:"

> Chevron Corporation, one of the world's largest integrated petroleum companies, is involved in every aspect of the industry, from exploration and production to transportation, refining and retail marketing, as well as chemicals manufacturing and sales. It is active in more than 100 countries and employs about 31,000 people worldwide.

The Chevron Way

Chevron takes pride not only in its products and services, but also in the way it conducts its worldwide operations. The company's principles and values are embodied in *The Chevron Way*, which provides an integrated framework for its strategies and goals. The company's Mission and Vision statements are part of The Chevron Way.

MISSION: We are an international company providing energy and chemical products vital to the growth of the world's economies. Our mission is to create superior value for our stockholders, our customers and our employees.

VISION: Our vision is to be "Better than the Best," which means: Employees are proud of their success as a team; customers, suppliers and governments prefer us; competitors respect us; communities welcome us; and investors are eager to invest in us.

Our primary objective is to exceed the financial performance of our strongest competitors. Our goal is to be No. 1 among our competitors in Total Stockholder Return for the period 2000-2004. We will balance long-term growth and short-term results in pursuit of this objective.

1999 Highlights

Chevron's 1999 net income was up 55 percent from 1998, to $2.070 billion [$2,070 million], and operating earnings were $2.3 billion, up from $1.9 billion in 1998. Worldwide liquids production was up 2 percent to a record 1.13 million barrels a day, and oil and gas reserves additions exceeded production for the seventh straight year. The company eliminated $500 million from the 1999 cost structure, and also benefited from a recovery in oil prices.

In 1999 Chevron declared a dividend increase for the 12th straight year.

Financial Highlights

(Millions of dollars, except per-share data)

Net income: $2,070

Sales and other operating revenues: $35,448

Capital and exploratory expenditures: $6,133

Total assets at year-end: $40,668

Total debt at year-end: $8,919

Stockholders' equity at year-end: $17,749

Cash flow from operating activities: $4,481

Per-share data:

Earnings (basic): $3.16

Earnings (diluted): $3.14

Cash dividends: $2.48

Stockholders' equity: $27.04

Return on average stockholders' equity: 11.9%

Return on average capital employed: 9.4%

OPERATING HIGHLIGHTS

• At more than 1.5 million barrels a day, 1999 crude oil and gas production was the highest in the company's history.

• International net liquids production climbed for the ninth straight year, up 7 percent over 1997.

• Additions to reserves exceeded production for the sixth consecutive year. The company replaced 109 percent of production (excluding sales and acquisitions).

• Worldwide proved reserves were more than 6.2 billion barrels of oil and equivalent gas at year-end.

Chevron Around the World

EXPLORATION AND PRODUCTION (UPSTREAM)

Chevron explores for and produces crude oil and natural gas in 25 countries. In the United States, major producing areas include the Gulf of Mexico, California, the Rocky Mountains and Texas. Outside the United States, Chevron production areas include Angola, Nigeria, Canada, the North Sea, Australia, Indonesia, Kazakhstan, Venezuela, Republic of Congo, Thailand, China and Papua New Guinea. Major exploration areas include the above, as well as Azerbaijan, Bahrain and Qatar. . . .

REFINING/MARKETING/TRANSPORTATION (DOWN-STREAM)

Chevron is one of the largest U.S. refiners, with principal facilities at El Segundo and Richmond, Calif.; Pascagoula, Miss.; Salt Lake City; El Paso, Texas; and Honolulu. The company turns crude oil into a variety of products, including motor gasoline, diesel and aviation fuels, lubricants, asphalt and chemicals.

Chevron also is one of the largest U.S. marketers, selling refined products through 7,900 retail outlets. It is one of the top three gasoline marketers in 14 states, with primary markets in the fast-growing West, Southwest and South.

The company is the leading marketer of aviation fuels in the West [Meaning it is likely the chief, if not sole supplier, of the JP-8 jet fuel that contains ethylene dibromide (EDB)—the chemical carcinogen that was removed from unleaded gasolines due to its immune toxicity and cancer causing risks, but currently is implicated in the "chemtrail" controversy discussed later.[5]], the top seller of asphalt nationwide and the leading single-brand marketer of heavy-duty and industrial oils in North America.

In Canada, Chevron operates a refinery and is the leading marketer of transportation fuels with 200 outlets in British Columbia.

CALTEX

In more than 60 countries throughout Africa, Asia and the Middle East, Chevron operates through Caltex, its 50 percent-owned affiliate. Through its subsidiaries and affiliates, Caltex is involved in refining, distribution, shipping, storage, marketing, supply and trading. Caltex owns interests in 13 fuel refineries, with equity throughput of nearly 850,000 barrels a day in 1998. In addition, it has interests in two lubricant refineries, six asphalt plants, 17 lubricating oil blending plants and more than 500 ocean terminals and depots. It has a retail network of more than 8,000 service stations and is a leading fuels marketer in the Asia-Pacific region, with 1998 refined products sales of nearly 1.2 million barrels per day.

CHEMICALS

Chevron is a leading petrochemicals and plastics manufacturer. Major products include styrene, polystyrene and olefins, as well as additives for fuels and lubricants. The company has plants in nine states and is expanding several U.S. facilities to boost overall production. The company also has plants in Brazil, France, Japan and Singapore, and through affiliates and subsidiaries, operates or markets in more than 80 countries. The company is growing internationally, adding major facilities in Saudi Arabia and China.

SHIPPING

Chevron Shipping Company has one of the world's largest tanker fleets and is ranked at or near the top of the industry based on its environmental and safety record. It owns and operates 34 tankers — and charters about the same number — for shipping crude oil and refined products around the globe. The company is building four new double-hulled tankers, with the last to be delivered by 2000. At that time, Chevron will have 14 double-hulled vessels in its fleet.

"Protecting People and the Environment"

Chevron's goal is to be the industry leader in safety and health performance, and to be recognized worldwide for environmental excellence. All Chevron operations use the company's "Protecting People and the Environment" program, which sets forth 102 specific practices in 10 broad categories.

Chevron also sponsors numerous conservation, education and community awareness projects; funds environmental research; donates land for conservation and habitat restoration; and sponsors employee volunteer efforts. For example, in Papua New Guinea, Chevron established a precedent-setting partnership with the World Wildlife Fund to protect one of the world's most sensitive rain forests.

In 1997, Chevron joined three other companies in ceding exploration rights to some 320,000 acres of coastal waters, paving the way for the first national maritime conservation area on Canada's west coast. Efforts such as this have won Chevron numerous awards from environmental organizations throughout the world.

For instance, in recognition of its commitment to protecting the environment, Chevron has received both the Nigeria Environmental Society's Environmental Excellence Award and the Nigerian Federal Environmental Protection Agency's excellence award.

Supporting Local Communities

Chevron shares its resources and expertise to become a partner with the communities in which it operates.

For example, Tengizchevroil, Chevron's joint venture in the Republic of Kazakhstan, has funded health programs, built a medical clinic, donated emergency vehicles and medical equipment, constructed housing, and provided machinery and personnel for a host of local projects. In Angola, Chevron has given medical supplies and organized vaccination and health education programs; trained teachers and equipped local schools; and paved roads and drilled water wells. In Nigeria, Chevron is training young men and women in such marketable skills as welding, and computer and secretarial proficiency. The company also has worked with fishermen and farmers to develop a community fish farm project. In addition, Chevron builds hospitals and schools.

More than 100 Years of Growth

Chevron Corporation started business in Los Angeles in 1879 as the Pacific Coast Oil Company. In 1900, *the thriving company was acquired by John D. Rockefeller's Standard Oil Trust.* The breakup of the trust in 1911 led to the formation of the Standard Oil Company of California. In the 1920s and 1930s, the company began investing in international exploration and made the first major discoveries in Bahrain and Saudi Arabia.

In 1936, in partnership with Texaco, it formed Caltex, bringing in new markets in Asia, Africa and Europe.

After World War II, continued expansion led to major discoveries in Indonesia, Australia, the U.K. North Sea and the Gulf of Mexico.

In 1984, the company nearly doubled its size by acquiring Gulf Oil Corporation in what then was the largest corporate merger in U.S. history. That same year, Standard also changed its name to Chevron, the well-known brand name of many of its products.

In 1993, Chevron achieved another milestone when it joined the Republic of Kazakhstan in the largest joint venture between a Western company and a member of the former Soviet Union. A new company, Tengizchevroil, was formed to develop the Tengiz oil field, the largest discovery in the past 30 years.[6]

I included the above lengthy sample of Chevron propaganda to relay the gargantuan dimension of only this small portion of the Rockefeller's petrochemical/pharmaceutical holdings. The Rockefeller family is like a central cog in the globalists' wheel of fortune. As the coming chapters reveal, they not only played a crucial role in the early laboratory developments surrounding the WNV, and many other contemporary pathogens and plagues, but through their global entities and corporate networks, the Rockefellers have routinely practiced Machiavellian eco-genocide. Creating such problems and solutions to justify and effect non-lethal military/public health operations, that coincidentally serve lucrative depopulation functions, their scientific "service" to humanity is destined to effect a "New World Order" with far fewer more easily controlled people.

References

1) New York State Department of Health. Literature displayed on http://www.health.state.ny.us/nysdoh/consumer/environ/anvil.htm. For information about the West Nile virus, people were instructed to call the New York City Department of Health West Nile Information Line, 24 hours a day, seven days a week, at (877) WNV-4NYC or (877) 968-4692.

2) MSDS form for Anvil, prepared by Chevron Corporation, Trade Name: ORTHO HOME & GARDEN INSECT KILLER FORMULA II, MSDS Serial Number: BSCRW, Hazard Characteristic Code: F1 . Available from Zanus Corporation, P.O. Box 169, 1897 Airport Road, Belgrade, MT 59714; (800) 347-7783, (406) 388-5740; email: ZANUSCO1@MSN.COM. Chevron listed its non-proprietary main ingredients in its pesticide as CYCLOPROPANE CARBOXYLIC ACID,2,2-DIMETHYL-3-(2-METHYL-1-PROPENYL)-, (1,3,4,5,6,7-HEXAHYDRO-1,3-DIOXO-2H- (ING 2); Ingredient: CYCLOPROPANE CARBOXYLIC ACID, 2,2-DIMETHYL-3-(2-METHYLPROPENYL)-, M-PHENOXYBENZYL ESTER; **(SUMITHRIN),** and ISOINDOL-2-Y1) METHYL ESTER; (TETRAMETHRIN).

3) Williams F. Bug bombers stray and spray. Staten Island Advance, August 31, 2000; Available at: http://baltech.org/lederman/spray/905staten.html

4) Go V,1 Garey J, Wolff MS,2 and Beatriz G.T. Pogo, BG. Estrogenic Potential of Certain Pyrethroid Compounds in the MCF-7 Human Breast Carcinoma Cell Line. *Environ Health Perspect* 1999;107;3:173-177. [Online 21 January 1999] http://ehpnet1.niehs.nih.gov/docs/1999/107p173-177go/abstract.html. Complete article was said to be available through the Environmental Health Information Service, for members only. EHIS Technical Support was available at: ehis@niehs.nih.gov; 919-541-3841.

5) Thomas W. Mystery contrails: Poison from the sky. Document available on www.Islandnet.com/~wilco/. Also personal communication from Will Thomas, February 26, 1999, following his second national broadcast on "The Art Bell Show" wherein this information was also provided. See also: Staff reporters. Art Bell says everybody is sick: Watch those contrails in sky! *Contact: The Phoenix Educator*, February 16, 1999, Vol. 23, No. 13, pp. 1, 8-9. Independent investigator Jay Reynolds countered the Thomas and Bell reports. See: "Contrail Controversy" in FTP file at www.tetrahedron.org.

According to Will Thomas (personal communication April 25, 2000), he was able to locate a patent, held by the Hughes Corporation, for the development and deployment of an aluminum oxide atmospheric spraying device as discussed in Chapter 10. He and other authors theorize, and strongly suspect, this "weather modification" method might somehow serve to increase transmission of certain electromagnetic frequencies, like those produced by projects HAARP and EISCAT, for behavior modification and global population control. For more details contact Will Thomas at: wilco@islandnet.com.

In addition, see website http://www.contrailconnection.com/ for excellent color photographs of chemtrails spraying from the tail sections of aircraft whose jet engines are devoid of contrails.

Another website, http://www.earthfiles.com/earth039.html, shows chemtrails, one formed at a 90 degree angle in Three Rivers, Michigan, that according to Centers for Disease Control and Prevention, Toxicology Information Branch administrator George Prince, represents a "scary hoax." According to Prince, "extremely small quantities" of ethylene dibromide (EDB) have mysteriously been included in jet fuels. He also wrote, "Unless there is indeed the broad conspiracy . . . ambient air monitoring efforts conducted by the U. S. Government, state governments, and private and public research institutions would detect any widespread levels that might pose a threat to health." He responded to questions at 1-888-42-ATSDR, or by e-mail at ATSDRIC@cdc.gov.

6) Chevron profile available at http://www.chevron.com/about/frame.html

Chapter 8.
West Nile Virus
In New York City

"The virus has for decades made its home
in several U.S. research laboratories . . .
including Rockefeller University in Manhattan
and Yale University in New Haven, Connecticut.
In fact, investigators there were the first to grow
and study the WNV in the United States.
The work began in the 1950s when unidentified
viral samples from around the world arrived at
Rockefeller University on a steady basis."

New York Newsday, Sept. 29, 1999

Among the few investigative journalists who have pierced the false reality bubble and risen above the fear that supports the media's conspiracy of silence, is New York's Robert Lederman. This author and artist discerned the Rockefeller connection to New York's WNV "outbreak," along with the media's deadly deceptions, long before anyone else, and splattered the Internet and New York alternative presses with his revealing exposés. His reporting of the nightmarish spraying of Anvil over this region's population during the Summer of 2000 provided a prime example of non-lethal Rockefeller-sanctioned genocide.

Having pieced together several bits of seemingly disparate data, Lederman's findings reinforced my concerns regarding the apparent use of non-lethal warfare against U.S. citizens. In fact, no rational explanation can be made for the "emergency" WNV "outbreaks" in America's northeast, and subsequent pesticide spraying programs, than a direct attack on people's neuroendocrine and immune systems to facilitate infectious diseases, increased cancer rates, and sterility along with an array of other multifactorial illnesses.

That is, the Rockefellers and their cryptocracy were applying a "Russian biological cocktail" for inconspicuous genocide as the evidence indicated occurred with AIDS and GWS. Again, these nightmarish accusations are reconcilable given the currently available evidence.

The first Lederman article I read was sent to me by a leading naturopathic physician, Dr. Carolyn Bormann, in Los Angeles. "Every Child and Senior to Take West Nile Vaccine," read the headline.[1] Lederman drew largely on reports in New York's *Daily News*,[2] *Newsday*,[3] and the *New York Times*,[4] to reveal a conspiracy between high level politicians representing globalists' interests including Mayor Guilliani, the Rockefeller family and their pharmaceutical companies, and CIA-linked biowarfare officials.

Other investigative journalists including Canada's "chemtrail" expert William Thomas, San Francisco's freedom fighter D. Jennifer Hewitt, and emerging diseases researcher Patty Doyle, later bolstered Lederman's findings.

Ms. Doyle unearthed a Plum Island biological weapons laboratory contract that held direct relevance to the WNV outbreak. Suggesting industrial espionage and foul play, she discovered evidence linking key bioweapons experts, vaccine industrialists, and government officials to the likely release of the mysterious virus from the Plum Island biowarfare lab off Long Island, New York in the summer of 1999. One of the few "Level-5" biowarfare labs in the United States, "Plum Island has long worked on secret biowarfare projects including West Nile and Japanese Encephalitis," Will Thomas wrote.[5]

Linking AIDS and GWS to WNV issues, Ms. Doyle learned that an Iraqi bioweapons investigator, Dr. Jawad Al Aubaidi, worked with *Mycoplasma incognitas*, the agent largely responsible for the symptoms of AIDS and GWS, at Plum Island before returning to Baghdad preceding the Gulf War. As detailed below, Dr. Joshua Lederberg, the President of Rockefeller University, and Director of the American Type Culture Collection (ATCC), was likewise exposed during the 1994 U.S. Senate Hearings investigating GWS for having aided Iraq's biowarfare efforts by shipping a variety of lethal biologicals including the WNV to Sadam Hussein's laboratories for years preceding the war.[6]

As a bird-borne virus often carried by crows, Ms. Doyle initially considered the Plum Island bioweapons operation to be the chief reservoir of the WNV because of the lab's long history of using birds in its human virus transmission studies. Plum Island had also been cited for numerous EPA safety violations. Additionally, on Aug. 2, 1993, the

New York Daily News reported that "[t]he discovery of the remains of at least 10 dead birds in a courtyard of Plum Island's research laboratory for exotic animal diseases is being investigated by Agriculture Department scientists."[5]

Ms. Doyle began to suspect foul play, white-collar bioterrorism, and industrial espionage when she learned that the Director of Plum Island's biowarfare program, Dr. David Huxsoll, was an alumnus of Fort Detrick bioweapons testing facility in Frederick, Maryland. So was Col. Jerry Hauer, the Head of the Office of Emergency Management (OEM) for New York City during the 1999 WNV "emergency."[5]

An additional alumnus of Fort Detrick was Dr. Col. Thomas Monath of OraVax Corporation. Dr. Monath's part, described in greater detail below, was made clear during a meeting between Dr. Monath, Dr. Hauer, and Dr. Lederberg with President Clinton in the Truman Room at the White House a year *before* the WNV outbreak in New York.

Based on her findings, Ms. Doyle concluded that the sudden emergence of WNV, never before a public concern, was likely a deliberate release to "test that city's biowarfare response, and make at least one corporation a sizable profit."[5]

The OraVax WNV Vaccine Scam

Ms. Doyle's research showed that in March, 1998 OraVax corporation, the sole maker of WNV vaccine, was facing bankruptcy and was about to be delisted from the NASDAQ. A few weeks later, in April, the infamous White House meeting took place.

"That same month," Will Thomas recalled, "OraVax was rescued from insolvency by a $343 million contract from the CDC for smallpox vaccine . . . The company later received $1.8 million from the National Institute of Allergy and Infectious Diseases for a vaccine against dengue fever—a tropical 'break bone fever' that has now migrated into the southern United States."[5]

Ms. Doyle also copied *Federal Register* records that showed on March 22, 1996, the Peptide Therapeutics Corporation began developing a vaccine for the prevention of WNV-related Japanese encephalitis using its ChimeriVax technology. These findings were also relayed in the *London Financial Times* on August 1, 2000. Here, Peptide Therapeutics was reported to be a "UK biotech company" awarded "a $3,000,000 grant to develop a new vaccine to combat the mosquito-borne West Nile virus. . . . The vaccine will be developed at OraVax, Peptide's U.S. subsidiary, using the company's proprietary ChimeriVax technology." The article also credited the V.P of Oravax, Dr. Thomas Monath, for having worked "behind the scenes with Mayor Guilliani, former OEM chief Jerry Hauer, . . . [and] the CDC since the very beginning of this issue."[1]

The year Peptide Therapeutics began developing a WNV vaccine, Dr. Monath's Oravax Corporation was granted a license by the U.S. Army biowarfare lab at Ft. Detrick to manufacture a similar "Japanese encephalitis vaccine derived from a genetically-altered virus" the Army had created. The WNV was simply a variation of Japanese encephalitis, Ms. Doyle learned.

Quite suspiciously, "field tests began in the fall of 1999—the same time encephalitis broke out in Queens and spread throughout New York City," Will Thomas reported.

Then, on August 1, 2000 OraVax was awarded a $3 million contract from the NIH to "fast track" its research and development of the encephalitis vaccine that they had already developed in 1996![5]

Robert Lederman reported that Dr. Monath retired from Fort Detrick to become the Vice President of Research & Medical Affairs of the Peptide Company synchronously advising New York City's Mayor Guiliani to begin pesticide spraying operations to combat the WNV "crisis" that was said to have killed seven people in 1999.

Ms. Doyle suspected that the WNV was deliberately deployed in New York City for at least two reasons: 1) to instigate "a bioterrorism preparedness drill," and 2) to create "a multimillion dollar market" for OraVax's Japanese Encephalitis (JE)/WNV vaccine.

To support her thesis, she documented that "Dr. R.E. Shope also worked with Dr. Thomas Monath of OraVax on that [WNV] vaccine. Dr. R. E. Shope also served," to the time of this writing, "on the same bioterrorism preparedness committee as Dr. Jerry Hauer, formerly of the New York City Dept. of Emergency Management. Both Dr. Shope and Dr. Hauer have been advocates of 'real life' bioterrorism preparedness drills."[5]

Likewise, Mr. Lederman's article expertly fingered Dr. Monath. "Wow!" *Newsday* quoted the OraVax and Peptide official. "This is the biggest arbovirus story of the last 50 years." While most people "reacted to the news about West Nile virus appearing in New York City with either horror or yawning indifference," Lederman wrote, Dr. Monath became "exhilarated."[3]

Why did the Army choose Monath and his company to produce the only WNV vaccine? By unearthing suspicious, if not incriminating, connections between Dr. Monath and the highest-level politicians involved in this apparent charade, Lederman answered:

> Mayor Guilliani keeps referring to the CDC as the source of the order to massively spray NYC with toxic pesticides. Monath . . . according to *Newsday*, has been closely advising the CDC and the Guilliani administration since the first day of the so-called NYC epidemic. . . .
>
> In August of 1998—approximately a year before the NYC outbreak—Dr. Monath met with President Clinton and attempted to sell him on the idea of stockpiling millions of dollars worth of OraVax vaccines. With Monath were some heavy hitters—Attorney General Janet Reno, the head of the CIA, Jerry Hauer—Giuliani's Office of Emergency Management Commissioner, and Dr. Joshua Lederberg—former president of Rockefeller University in NYC [wherein investigators had been experimenting with WNV for decades].[4,8]

Newsday sourced this later claim in September 1999. The article said that although epidemiologists suspected WNV had suddenly and inexplicably emerged in humans or animals in the Western Hemisphere, "the virus has for decades made its home in several U.S. research laboratories . . . including Rockefeller University in Manhattan and Yale University in New Haven, Connecticut. In fact, investigators there were the first to grow and study the WNV in the United States. The work began in the 1950s when unidentified viral samples from around the world arrived at Rockefeller University on a steady basis."[9]

"Dr. Lederberg of Rockefeller University," Lederman referred to, as "another key name on the West Nile and biowarfare front." He headed a 1994 Pentagon study on Gulf War illness, which "falsely concluded that no American service personnel in the Gulf had been exposed to biological warfare material. Dr. Lederberg headed the study while he was the Director of the American Type Culture Collection (ATCC)."[1]

As previously mentioned, ATCC was forced to admit to Congress having shipped 70 containers of biological weapons samples to Sadam Hussein's laboratories including the WNV.[1] The order to blow up their major storage arsenal at Khamisiyah—that is, destroy the evidence— Lederman attributed to former President George H.W. Bush. It is certain, however, General Norman Schwartzkopf gave the go-ahead.[10]

Lederman explained that the CIA, and also the CDC, were caught in the same lie. "When the Mayor, the CDC and the media insist on referring to it as the, 'mysterious, never before seen in North America, deadly WNV,'" Lederman quoted reports, "they are knowingly disinforming the public."[1]

Additionally suspicious was Dr. Tracy McNamarra, the Bronx Zoo pathologist who initially identified the WNV, allegedly in dead crows. She reported to the NY City Council that she also trained at the Plum Island lab.

"Plum Island has been cited by the NY State Attorney General for dumping dead animal carcasses and releasing various live experimental lab subjects," Lederman wrote. "NYC area labs like Plum Island not only inject crows—the birds that the Mayor keeps announcing have been 'discovered' before each spraying, but many of these labs have been breeding WNV and malaria-infected mosquitoes as well; genetically altering them, and preparing to release them into the environment."[12]

During the aptly named Rockefeller Hearings before the U.S. Congress in 1994, government officials admitted "to more than 50 years of biowarfare experiments carried out on hundreds of thousands of unsuspecting American citizens," Lederman continued. "While it might seem comforting to dismiss these ideas as paranoid, in the context of the Rockefeller Hearings there can be no doubt that such programs exist and are increasingly being implemented at the highest levels of government."[1]

Finally, Lederman pointed appropriately to the fact that, Mayor Guilliani may be "nothing more than a puppet following orders." The orders, he concluded, had to have come from the CIA.

"The CDC's efforts on infectious diseases are overseen by the CIA.[48] Guilliani admits he gets all of his 'ideas' from the Manhattan Institute, a right wing think tank started by William Casey, Reagan's CIA director. [President] GW Bush proudly admitted that next to the Bible, the Manhattan Institute was his greatest inspiration. Bush's father was himself a former CIA director whose family was among Hitler's biggest supporters. The Manhattan Institute is funded by Rockefeller's Chase Manhattan Bank, which publicly admitted it helped Hitler loot the vaults of occupied Europe."[1]

Some Communities Said "No!" to Pesticide Sprayings

Not every public official, of course, was like Mayor Guilliani. Some refused to force their electorate to submit to pesticide sprayings. Several communities, led by concerned citizen activists and responsible politicians, many of whom had received Lederman e-mails, just said, "No!"

Among the first to resist the CDC's recommendations was the city of Schenectady, New York.[16] Health authorities there became concerned about the cost and efficacy of the spraying program. Following their lead, other upstate cities and counties followed.

According to a report in the *Albany Times Union*,[16] wet weather and cooler temperatures contributed to the decision, "At this point," said Jack Parisi, the county's director of environmental health, "we're not rescheduling, and at this stage of the season, I don't think we will reschedule. It's just not effective." Parisi, only weeks earlier, had testified "before a packed crowd at the Rotterdam Senior Services Center that spraying Anvil was the best means for combating the West Nile virus," the Albany paper reported.

The virus had allegedly been detected in 15 dead crows, blue jays and hawks in the Capital Region of upstate NY. "Schenectady had a seventh bird test positive . . . ," the article said, and went on to explain the rationale behind the spraying program and the officials' decision to stop it:

> Health officials spray a two-mile radius from where infected birds are found, but the increasing number of positive birds is making spraying expensive.

> "We were caught in the middle of the season and we had a positive bird and everybody panicked," Parisi said. "But as it spreads . . . we just can't spray here and spray there."

> Rensselaer and Albany counties have only postponed spraying Anvil. Albany County is expected to make a final decision on whether to spray a second time today.

> Part of the reason for Schenectady's reluctance to spray a second time is the estimated cost of $65 per mile.

Schenectady paid $16,000 for the first round of spraying earlier this month, which covered areas where the first two positive birds were found. The second round for Schenectady County, which was scheduled for last night and would have covered five dead bird locations, would have cost the county $60,000.[16]

As detailed earlier, given the likelihood that spraying companies and helicopter dispatchers, such as Evergreen's Intermountain in California, were CIA fronts, at these prices, not only was Anvil's manufacturer, principally Rockefeller's Chevron Corporation, making a killing, financial and otherwise, but these fees likely helped finance additional CIA covert operations.

The Albany Times article continued:

The weather has also been a factor. Anvil only kills mosquitoes when droplets of the chemical make contact with them in the air. When temperatures dip down to the low 60s the mosquitoes carrying the disease aren't out. "The effectiveness of the chemical goes way down at the 60 plateau," said Wayne Crans, director of mosquito research at Rutgers University in New Brunswick, N.J.

The first round of spraying in the Capital Region was delayed by rain showers that blew through the region. . . . "When we made the decision we were hearing temperatures in the high 40s, rainy and thunderstorms," said Steve Nelson, spokesman for Rensselaer County, which is putting off making a final decision on spraying until weather conditions change, more birds test positive for the virus, or if a local person tests positive for West Nile encephalitis, a rare brain infection that occurs in only 1 percent of all people with the virus.

Consequently, rather than spraying a pesticide likely to kill humans as well as mosquitos, Schenectady County officials planned to "aggressively larvicide." A "bacteria that eats mosquito larvae" had apparently been genetically engineered by the same industry that delivered the WNV to humanity in the first place. Authorities chose to drop this germ warfare agent into "catch basins and storm drains" to hopefully rid the public of infected mosquitos. "Since the mosquito carrying the virus has an average life span of two to three weeks," the article concluded, "over time the adults will naturally die off."[16]

References

1)) Lederman. R. Every child and senior to take West Nile vaccine. Published on the Internet at http://www.operair.org/alerts/artist/nyc.html. See also: http://baltech.org/lederman/spray.

2) Gittrich G. Biotech company takes shot at vaccine. *Daily News,* August 21, 2000. Available at http://www.nospray.org/

3) Staff. Deadly discovery. *Newsday*, September 25, 1999. Available at: http://baltech.org/lederman/spray/802vaccine.html

4) *Times* staff. Germ defense plan in peril as its flaws are revealed. *New York Times*, August 7, 1998. Available from http://info.med.yale.edu/EIINet/MonathSeminar.html

5) Thomas W. *Probing The Chemtrails Conundrum.* Available from www.islandnet.com/wilco; E-mail: wilco@islandnet.com

6) Riegle, Jr. DW and D'Amato A. U.S. Chemical and Biological Warfare-related Dual Use Exports to Iraq and Their Possible Impact on the Health Consequences of the Persian Gulf War. United States Senate, 103rd Congress, 2d Session, May 25, 1994, p. 47.

7) DEPARTMENT OF DEFENSE. Notice of Intent To Grant an Exclusive License of a U.S. Government-Owned Patent agency: U.S. Army Medical Research and Materiel Command, DOD. *Federal Register*: March 22, 1996 (Volume 61, Number 57, Page 11812]

8) White House Press Corps. President Clinton to roundtable on genetic engineering and biological weapons. High-level scientists in attendance. Newswire. Washington: D.C., April 10, 1998. OCT 10.04.98.16:53. Downloadable from German newspaper *Das Zeitung* at: http://www.netlink.de/gen/Zeitung/1998/980410a.htm.

9) Staff. Area Labs Have Long Studied Virus /Yale, Rockefeller began tests in '50s. *Newsday*, Sept. 29, 1999, p. A28.

10) Gulf War syndrome, as a classical outcome and example of non-lethal warfare, is discussed in detail in Chapter 12; See also: Horowitz LG, Riley J, Nicolson G and Richard L. *Gulf War Syndrome: The Spreading Epidemic Cover-up.* Sandpoint, Idaho: Tetrahedron Publishing Group, 1998.

11) *Post* staff. *CIA knew of chemical weapons at Iraqi depot, agency reveals.* *The Washington Post*, April 10, 1997, pg. 1.

12) Lederman references: http://abcnews.go.com/onair/CloserLook/wnt000719_CL_mosquitoes_feature.html, which indeed reports the genetic engineering of mosquitoes for malaria and WNV transmission trials.

13) Although Lederman is likely correct in this statement, technically only AIDS science, not all infectious diseases, has been publicly revealed as being under CIA oversight. See: Gellman B. AIDS is declared threat to security. *Washington Post* Online, Sunday, April 30, 2000; p. AO1. (See: http://www.washingtonpost.com/wp-dyn/articles/A40503-2000Apr29.html); see also: National Intelligence Council staff. The Global Infectious Disease Threat and Its Implications for the United States. "[P]roduced under the auspices of David F. Gordon, National Intelligence Officer for Economics and Global Issues," Lt. Col. (Dr.) Don Noah of the Armed Forces Medical Intelligence Center and George Fidas of the National Intelligence Council, chaired and submitted by John C. Gannon. NIE 99-17D, January 2000, pp. 4, 27, 29-30. (See: http://www.cia.gov/cia/publications/nie/report/nie99-17d.html)

Regarding author and artist Robert Lederman, he is a regular columnist for the *Greenwich Village Gazette* (See: http://www.baltech.org/lederman/ for an extensive archive of Lederman columns), *The Shadow, The African Sun Times, The Vigo-Examiner* (see: http://www.vigo-examiner.com/archive.htm) and *Street News.* He has written hundreds of published essays concerning Mayor Rudolph Guilliani, and because of this, has been "falsely arrested *41 times* to date for his anti-Guilliani activities. He has never been convicted on any of the charges set against him. He is best known for creating hundreds of paintings of Mayor Guilliani as a Hitler-like dictator. Mr. Lederman, the President of A.R.T.I.S.T. (Artists' Response To Illegal State Tactics) may be reached at: robertlederman@worldnet.att.net; (718) 743-3722.

For a detailed exposition on the West Nile virus issue Lederman refers to: http://www.nospray.org/ and for archived Lederman articles see: http://www.levymultimedia.com; http://www.levymultimedia. com/lederman/index.htm] for an article on the Manhattan Institute go to http://www.konformist.com/2000/rudyg.htm. Finally, if you would like to help oppose the spraying, please write to the No Spray Coalition, PO Box 334, Peck Slip Station, NYC, NY 10272-0334, or call the No Spray hotline at (718) 670-7110.

14) Cappiello. D. Officials cool to spraying for virus. *Albany Times Union,* Thursday, August 24, 2000. Available on the Internet at: http://www.timesunion.com/AspStories/story.asp?storyKey=40133 &category=F.

15) New York State Department of Health. Literature displayed on http://www.health.state.ny.us/nysdoh/consumer/environ/anvil.htm. For information about the West Nile virus, people were instructed to call the New York City Department of Health West Nile Information Line, 24 hours a day, seven days a week, at (877) WNV-4NYC or (877) 968-4692.

16) Cappiello. D. Officials cool to spraying for virus. *Albany Times Union,* Thursday, August 24, 2000. Available on the Internet at: http://www.timesunion.com/AspStories/story.asp?storyKey=40133 &category=F.

Chapter 9.
Reports From the Front on Non-lethal Warfare
by
Leonard Horowitz
and William Winkler

"If it is true that this is being done for genocide,
you can't ethically and morally do that to people.
I simply can't condone people doing this in the
name of public health. It's *unconscionable.* Especially when so many disenfranchised people don't
know what's going on. These people have rights
to life too."

Adam Evans, M.P.H., 2000
Senior Public Health Advisor,
New York City Department of Health,
regarding Anvil sprayings for the West Nile virus

During the Gulf War it was called "Iraq's Yellow Rain." Generi-
cally, it is better known as the "Russian biological cocktail." It is
the method of choice for conducting contemporary biochemical warfare. Simply stated, toxic warfare can be most insidiously and destruc-
tively administered when populations are exposed to combinations of
biological and chemical agents in a mixed "cocktail." This best explains several widespread contemporary pathologies such as Gulf War
syndrome and the general malaise of humanity.[1]

Agricultural researchers, for example, according to a special report
in the *American Spectator,* have found that a biochemical weapon
called aflatoxin "potentiates both T-2 and another 'yellow rain' component called DAS (diacetoxyscirpenol)." The end result is increased
harm to exposed populations caused by the actions and interactions of
the combined agents.

The following reports and chapters detail what, in effect, amounts
to the targeting of American citizens with Russian biological cocktails.

Above all, the information relays the recognition that despite a huge public outcry against such toxic exposures, public health officials have been mostly unwitting facilitators and accomplices to this form of "non-lethal" warfare.

The Spraying of Staten Island

On August 31, 2000, the *Staten Island Advance* published an article that described the horrific "stray" spraying of people on Staten Island, New York, mostly children, with the toxic pesticide—Anvil 10:10. Allegedly a "public health" emergency management program to irradicate mosquitoes infected with the WNV, staff writer Frank Williams documented "hundreds of moms, dads and kids" running for cover as black military helicopters "doused ball fields, a golf course and a residential area" with their neurotoxic payloads.

"Helicopters that city officials said would only spray over '*unpopulated areas,*'" Williams wrote, "instead spewed their pesticide cloud over surprised and frightened Islanders . . . . Hundreds of children playing on football and baseball fields in Travis had to dodge the mist."

"Our policy, in general, has been to use helicopters in mainly non-residential areas not accessible to all-terrain vehicles," defended city spokeswoman Sandra Mullin of the Health Department. "If this incident reflects a veering away from the designed route, that's something we want to look into."

In other words, public health officials were not even cognizant of the manner in which the spraying program was being carried out. They needed to "look into" it.

"We certainly apologize to any individuals over whom the helicopters may have flown and put in the way of the Anvil we were spraying," Mullin said.

City officials had promised that helicopter sprayings would avoid populated or environmentally sensitive areas. To accomplish this they scheduled sprayings for daylight hours to provide pilots with good visibility. "How they failed to recognize a golf course, youth ball fields and the residential area near High Rock Park—all areas where people claimed choppers doused them last night—remains unclear," reporter Williams wrote.

He further documented how "parents became aware of the mist falling from a low-flying chopper over the three fields of the Staten

Island Boys' Football League . . . , kids were quickly hustled into cars—shoulder pads and all—and suddenly found themselves going home. A practice was canceled soon after the helicopter arrived at 6:45 p.m. . . . A scrimmage game went on, but was delayed until the spraying was over. During a time-out, dozens of children huddled for cover under the concessions stand's awning. . . .

"'The helicopter flew by four times. I think the borough president needs to get a call,' said Kathleen Collins of West Brighton, who was watching her 8-year-old son, Michael, play. She said she sat in her car, cradling her 1-month-old daughter, Kayla, during the dousing. 'This is a field full of children—and many of them aren't even playing.'"

Many parents criticized the government's vague spraying program that was said to target "unpopulated" areas.

"Unpopulated? You can't get more populated than a field full of kids having fun," said Great Kills resident Joe Yacca, who was also baby-sitting his nephew, Michael.

"'I got spray on me and I'm annoyed,' said Carol Aponte of Travis, who was with her sons, Jonathan, 8, and Steven, 10. 'We had no idea. It was supposed to be only unpopulated areas.'"[2]

The article went on to describe the surprise of football league officials who said they were not informed their field would be under helicopter attack.

"We would never have had practice if we knew about the spraying. We thought they were only spraying unpopulated areas, but we're populated," said Sandy Scott, league treasurer. "We received no notice at all."

"It was unclear," wrote Williams, "who in city government, if anyone," was responsible for "notifying specific youth leagues or public recreation areas—like city-owned LaTourette Golf Course, where complaints from pesticide-covered golfers were heard . . .

"We have in many instances been working with the borough presidents' offices to identify leagues to notify them," said health department official Mullin. "We may not have reached every league but we certainly have attempted to do it. This could be a situation that we may not have been aware of."

The Borough President, Guy V. Molinari, exemplifying the bureaucratic shuffle while effectively circumventing official accountability in the matter, reported that the Health Department "never asked us to notify anyone." Furthermore, he objected, the notion of contacting the entire league was "outrageous. . . . 'We just don't have the resources and staff to do this,' he said. 'All we can do is take information from the Health Department and relay it to the public.'"

When Ms. Mullin was contacted to respond to Molinari's comments, she said, "We've been working with all elected officials through announcements in the media in an attempt to get the word out."

Community School Board chairwoman Eleanor Conforti was at the Mid-Island Babe Ruth League's Travis baseball field during the spraying. She was hit with pesticide along with "two teams and two full bleachers."

"I'm appalled at this. I'm just so upset because all these kids are here," said Ms. Conforti. "This is a crowded field and you're telling me this is uninhabited?"

Golfers were also running for their lives. Lou Pinheiro, 43, and his tee partner Robert Trimarchi, 35, recalled their ordeal on the fourth hole of LaTourette Golf Course. "There were at least 100 people out there and they were spraying right over us." said Pinheiro. "When everybody was leaving, they sprayed right over the parking lot."

"Those condominiums on Forest Hill Road were being sprayed too," said Trimarchi. "It's very irresponsible to be spraying people in the early evening."

Kevin Calabrese, who lived in a house adjacent High Rock Park said his block was sprayed also.

"I came back from the store at around 7 p.m. and they were spraying when I tried to get in my house," Calabrese recalled. "The same thing happened the last time they sprayed from helicopters."

The Edgeville resident said when the spraying began people started running from the park for shelter.

"I don't understand why the park wasn't closed—especially since they were spraying," Calabrese lamented.

These "killing fields" were allegedly near a "remote . . . industrial corridor," on Staten Island's West Shore. City official alerts only disclosed that aerial spraying would target this area from 6:30 to 9:00 P.M. Additional aerial sprayings, they warned, were scheduled the next morning from 5:00 to 6:30. Trucks were also reported by Williams to have sprayed "all over the Island . . . between 10:00 last night and 5:00 this morning."[2]

A NY Public Health Professional's Lament

Mr. Adam Evans, Senior Public Health Advisor for the New York City Department of Health, working within the state's correctional facilities, provided a personal account of the year 2000 Anvil sprayings.

"I first became aware of a perceived threat from the WNV sometime in 1999," Mr. Evans told me. "There was some talk of spraying in the inner city, in particular Central Park, which runs for miles from 59th Street to 110th. There were rumors of a mosquito borne illness. It was said to require the spraying of a pesticide—it may have been Malathion that was first considered or used."

"What were you thinking at the time?" I asked Mr. Evans as we sat poolside in Montego Bay, Jamaica in late September 2000.

"I wasn't very suspicious, at first. I simply figured authorities with reasonable judgment decided to spray a few insects. . . .

"My suspicions were only raised after the media heralded the discovery of [allegedly] infected crows. There were a few cases of elderly people, allegedly stricken with the virus in the suburbs that made me consider the potential benefits of the spraying program.

"Not long after that, after hearing another news report about the spraying, my mind strangely jumped to the deadly gas spraying episode that took place in the Japanese subway system a few years ago. I had a horrible thought that, 'What if this spraying program was infiltrated by terrorists?'

"I didn't think too much about it again until I saw televised news reports that sprayings were being carried out in the suburbs. Water samples from area pools and ponds were being analyzed for potential pesticide contamination. Dead insects were being collected and analyzed. Many citizen advocates were voicing concern, if not outrage, that such sprayings might be affecting humans as well as insects."

"How much of this dissent reached the news in New York?" I asked.

"There was a great deal of media coverage concerning the alleged need to spray, but far less regarding the potential threat to the public's health. I recall repeatedly watching coverage on Eyewitness News, UPN Channel 9, and the CBS Evening News on Channel 2," Mr. Evans said.

Indeed, I too watched New York's Channel 2 News coverage on the Anvil spraying program on Sunday night September 24, 2000 while I was in Jamaica. The segment showed spraying trucks operating at night in a rural setting near grocery stores. Reporters discussed the outrage of citizens, and one legislator, over the contamination of fresh fruit and vegetables being displayed outdoors by urban grocers, then bought and eaten by the public.

"At this point, my thoughts turned to the children, and people with respiratory problems being exposed during the sprayings," Mr. Evans continued. "I considered the likelihood that some of the sprayed pesticide might also filter out into water systems through direct contamination and sewer run-off. I had not learned much about Anvil, but professing ignorance is a poor excuse for a public health professional in this matter affecting the public's health.

"There were many people in the suburbs that were against the sprayings. Thoughts of cancer and other illnesses made people apprehensive. There were no side effects predicted or discussed by the news media. This alarmed me.

"What was also strange was that there were no Black people who had been infected by the WNV, yet there was clearly a targeting of minority neighborhoods by the spray trucks and helicopters.

"Then the issue, and my concerns, struck closer to home. My mother lives in the Washington Heights section of New York City. One afternoon, the spraying trucks heavily sprayed her neighborhood just around 5:00 P.M. People were complaining about the broad daylight spraying at the height of rush hour."

"What are the demographics of the Washington Heights section of New York City?" I asked.

"The demographics there include largely poor Black and Hispanic populations. There are also a lot of white elderly people on fixed incomes. Many of the immigrants living there are illegal. This made me additionally suspicious.

"At the beginning of the spraying program, Mayor Guilliani had not announced the spraying times, until there was a public outcry. Then he began to announce the sprayings. But during *this* episode, it seemed very odd to me that he had made no announcement.

"Every afternoon my mother comes home from work using the subway system. This day she, and thousands of other commuters, received a frightening dose of pesticide as she disembarked the subway tunnel at 137th Street in upper Washington Heights.

"The potentially catastrophic event was reported that night on the 10 o'clock news on UPN Channel 9.

"Most of those people who commute that way, and were in the area at that time, were immigrants. Many, if not most, do not speak English very well, if at all. As a public health professional I felt very ashamed that the Public Health Department of NYC for whom I work, entirely disregarded this risk by issuing no forewarning.

"I thought, *why would they be spraying at that time of the day, potentially exposing so many people to a toxic pesticide?* It made me wonder whether this was done for a reason other than for public health. These were human "mosquitoes" now being sprayed.

"It was as if there was little to no regard for the health of Black and Hispanic people, children of color, the elderly, even white people who have been living there for years.

"Meanwhile, the media was reporting the need to keep young children indoors during spraying periods, turn air conditioners off, close people's doors and windows, and above all keep the elderly with weakened immune systems and respiratory problems including asthma and emphysema indoors, or better yet, away from spraying areas altogether.

"But here in my mother's neighborhood, without warning, they were disregarding every public health precaution.

"What I also realized about the Washington Heights section of New York is that it was composed of mainly politically disenfranchised people. Largely a population of immigrants, many undocumented illegal aliens live there, who for that reason avoid political or legal involvement. They would not have complained, and ultimately did nothing about the rush hour spraying.

"I was also very disappointed, and rightfully concerned, that the Mayor's office, Public Health Department, and news media never mentioned what the symptoms of pesticide toxicity might be for those seeking this knowledge and possible care for pesticide poisoning. Such warnings, I realized, should have been posted in several languages throughout the city, even if it was an "emergency" response to the virus. To my knowledge, however, this was never done. I'm certain these warnings were not posted in the upper parts of the city.

"All of this made me consider the possibility that this spraying program was something other than a legitimate public health measure. Later, I began to consider the alternatives. That the consequences of such a program might more reasonably reflect human population control than insect control.

"Meanwhile, people generally remained unconcerned about the health consequences of the spraying program. Everyone seemed more concerned about being bitten by mosquitoes carrying WNV than pesticide toxicity. This was due to the very effective media coverage concerning the perceived threat. Newsreels repeatedly showed pictures of dead crows and mosquitoes. Yet, friends and several colleagues expressed concern about the long term effects of the pesticide program including cancer."

"Were you aware of any immediate casualties of the spraying program in New York?" I asked.

"Indeed," Mr. Evans continued, "after the sprayings, a lot of people were ending up in the emergency rooms of local hospitals with sore throats, skin and eye irritations, and respiratory problems. I personally observed this at the Westchester Medical Center and Valhalla Hospital in Westchester. These increased emergency room visits were also reported to some extent in local news reports. Channel 7, ABC News, for instance, broadcast such a report."

"Had the concept of downright genocide ever entered your mind?" I asked.

"I've tried not to think about that, but the possibility could be very real.

"My wife, Madelyn, who is the Assistant Coordinating Manager of HIV Services at Metropolitan Hospital Center, in Manhattan, had talked about that possibility regarding HIV/AIDS. It has remained highly suspicious why this pandemic has struck principally minority populations in the United States. Minorities considered 'over populated,' and social misfits, including IV drug users. Getting rid of populations considered excessive and socially undesirable is conveniently the outcome of HIV/AIDS. People, particularly Blacks, are dropping like flies."

"What would you recommend as far as constructive political action in this regard?" I queried.

"I believe that people should be informed about the potential dangers of spraying. People need to be better educated in general. We need to let people of all races know that such spraying programs could pose long-term health risks.

"If it is true that this is being done for genocide, you can't ethically and morally do that to people. I simply can't condone people doing this he name of public health. It's *unconscionable*. Especially when so many disenfranchised people don't know what's going on? These people have rights to life too."

"Are you aware of the terms "non-lethal military warfare," and the "Russian biological cocktail" method of killing and maiming people?" I asked.

"No."

I explained both phrases to the public health director following which he responded:

"If depopulation is the objective of the spraying campaign, I can't even respond to this. No one effectively can. It's a no win situation. You need social activism on a scale that is virtually unachievable today. Too many people are afraid to learn the truth, and respond to it. Many people, because of their political or economic positions, simply don't want to get involved. Too many are living in denial. Most people don't have the time for political activism. That, perhaps, too is by design. By keeping people preoccupied with achieving their basic needs, they have little time for anything else.

"But I believe, given knowledge, people can choose to do what's right. My upbringing, the way I was raised," Mr. Evans continued, "was to do what's right. This situation makes me pause to think what to do if what you suspect is true. If the spraying programs are for the economic and political gain of a select few public health policy manipulators, then I certainly want to know the truth, proclaim it, and provide for it.

"When I'm gone, whose to say things will be different. But it's up to me now to try to leave something more beneficial for my children. It's important for me to know I did the right thing, and my children to know this as well.

"Ultimately it begs the question of free will," Mr. Evans concluded. "Are we experiencing God's will for depopulation, or man's will for depopulation? If it's God's will for depopulation, I can accept that. But this may very well be a case wherein powerful people are deciding the future health or disease, longevity or premature demise, of populations without giving anyone an educated choice in the matter. That's a violation of God's will that included empowering people, His children, with free will to help decide their fates. This is simply wrong and abhorrent."[3]

The Toxic Slick That Went Unreported

Synchronously, as I was compiling the previous chapter's information on Anvil, I received a call from Mr. William J. Winkler, a marine biologist from Ocean View, Delaware.[4] "Have you any idea what might be floating down the east coast, threatening the beaches and swimmers, intoxicating scores of children in its path?" he asked.

Having no idea what he was talking about, I asked, "Could you elaborate?"

He then described an approximately "20-mile long toxic slick," confirmed by aerial surveillance, that had floated southward along the mid-Atlantic coast during July and August along with the receding Labrador current. The "slick," that turned yellow and red as it rolled through coastal surf, had left dozens of people, mostly children, intoxicated and neurologically impaired. Mr. Winkler had been collecting the data on many of these cases for weeks.

"I'm certain it's a neurotoxin," he said. "I've conducted a series of studies on mice using the sample I collected off Bethany Beach in Delaware. The experimental rodents showed similar symptoms of toxicity as the swimmers have. . . . I've spoken with many parents of hospitalized children. They all report similar symptoms of neurotoxicity and hypersensitization."

The biologist then recited a series of the most common complaints that immediately reminded me of pesticide poisoning. The case histories and list of ailments included: burning eyes, skin rashes, headaches, general malaise and flu-like symptoms, nausea and vomiting, numbness and tingling of arms and legs, dizziness and balance and movement difficulties, muscle spasms, and even convulsive seizures.

"No one in any government position is doing a damn thing about this," Mr. Winkler said. "I've contacted the EPA, and several state and federal agencies as well. I've only gotten the run-around. I have a sample that needs analysis, but the commercial labs that can tell me what this stuff is are either under direct government control, or so heavily influenced by state and federal agencies that they are unwilling to perform the analyses. Can you make any recommendations, and do you have any idea of what we might be dealing with here?" he asked.

"I would certainly put potential pesticide poisoning on the top of my differential diagnosis list," I replied. "But, I would be extremely careful about where you send your sample. Definitely don't send the entire sample anywhere. Such evidence has a knack for disappearing."

I relayed to him the mysterious disappearance of a "chemtrail" specimen that fell from the sky in northern Idaho that my research colleague, Dr. Joseph Puleo, had collected. He suspected it contained immune toxic chemicals including ethylene di-bromide, and possibly pathogenic microbes. He had mailed his entire sample to a highly regarded university affiliated lab. The sample inexplicably disappeared before the analysis could be done.

As a result of this urging, Mr. Winkler only sent half of his sample to a bonifide laboratory where, as feared, it was promptly "lost."

"I would also be careful with whom you entrust this information, or attempt to involve in your investigation," I offered.

"I've thought about that," Mr. Winkler said. "I don't really know who I can trust. Prior to hearing you on "Coast to Coast" the other night, I had sent letters with documented cases off to a number of public health officials and government agencies. To date, they haven't even been decent enough to return my telephone calls. Now I don't feel they are trustworthy."

"Get copies of your data and documents off to a dozen or more friends or colleagues that you are certain you can trust. That will help safeguard your findings. Instruct them, if something unfortunate should happen to you, that incapacitates you, that they should carry on the investigation and public awareness campaign," I recommended. "Take extremely good notes during your study. Document the names of everyone you speak to in the course of your work. Include me, if you will, in your list of entrusted colleagues. Send me a copy of your findings to date, right away, and I'll help you put together a press release as soon as possible.

Mr. Winkler agreed to e-mail me a copy of his investigation records including two letters he had written to public officials. His letters and summaries of neurotoxicity cases, mostly affecting children following their beach or ocean exposures, follow.

A Written Appeal to Public Health Officials

On August 25, 2000, Mr. Winkler sent a letter to Mr. Chuck Davidson, Unit Manager in the Department of Public Health of Sussex County, Delaware. It relayed the following information:

As I said in our phone conversation today I saw what I [first] believe[d] to have been a Red Tide (Reddish-brown water) on the Delaware Atlantic coastline on August 11, 2000. The backwash of the wave from the beach turned yellow. I videotaped the phenomenon and took a gallon water sample. . . .

At approx 4:00 P.M. on that day, I called DNREC [Department of Natural Resources and Environmental Control] emergency response office and spoke to Ms. Tucker, the dispatcher. I asked her what was the Emergency Response truck doing at the north side of Indian River Inlet at approximately 1:00 P.M. the same day. Her response was, "We think we've had a spill." I asked her, "What kind of a spill?" She responded, "We don't know," but it has been reported as far north as the C&D Canal!

I said this is great; here I am surfing with my son and two of his friends in this stuff. I told her I was going to call Shirley Price, my State Representative, which I did, to find out what is going on and why they are not closing the beaches.

On August 12th, I told Rep. Price what had occurred and she said it sounded like she'd better find out what is going on. Rep. Price contacted DNREC Emergency Response and she told me that they told her the yellow stuff in the water was pollen, that we had a lot of pollen lately. When Rep. Price told me that, I said, "Shirley, come on, what is pollinating this time of the year, besides that, the wind was blowing onshore from the east for the past two days." She agreed with me. It couldn't be pollen; there was no pollen on our cars or sidewalks. We both agreed to keep checking.

On Saturday, August 12, 2000, at 4:05 P.M, I left a message at [DNREC director] Jack Pingree's home and said that he should close the beaches until DNREC determined what the "Red Tide" and yellow water was.

[About a half-hour later,] at approximately 4:30 P.M., Mr. John Morman of DNREC Emergency Response came to my store with another gentleman to pick up the water sample that I had taken the day before of the Red Tide. I told him that I had researched Red Tides on a National Oceanographic and Atmospheric (NOAA) web site and that the Red Tide could be a toxic dinoflagellate called *Gymnodinium breve*. (The website is http://www.marinelab.sarasota.fl.us/~mhenry/ wredtide.) *G. breve* could have been brought up in the Gulf Stream and blown in from the east winds that we had for two days.

I suggested [to Mr. Morman] closing the shell fishing beds since clams can concentrate up to 10,000 times the toxin from the dinoflagellate. He said there was no evidence of the yellow stuff in the water today.

They saw nothing he said. Before they (the DNREC) decided what to do, they had to have a consultation and department discussion, I was told.

L.L. [another Ocean View resident, whose name, along with all other citizens described in this report is withheld for privacy, but may be made available at the subjects' discretion by contacting Mr. Winkler.4] came into my nautical store [a couple of days later, on] August 16th. I asked her if she had noticed the discoloration in the ocean water on the 11th or 12th of the month. She said on Saturday, August 12th, from her 3rd floor apartment at Sea Colony, she could see that the water was dark colored, brownish she said. But by . . . the 15th, her kids said the water wasn't brown anymore, it was bluer (referring to the ocean view in front of the Sea Colony).

Below is a list of [additional community persons and vacationers] . . . , who have experienced side effects from the phenomenon . . . that occurred on August 11th and 12th . . . and was dispersed by a storm on August 13th. This may still be occurring, [at the time of this writing] especially in our back bays (e.g., Indian River Bay, Rehoboth, and possibly Assawoman Bay).

Initial Reports of Cases

Under "Possible Neurotoxin Effects," Mr. Winkler relayed the following cases of apparent neurotoxicity from the off-color ocean exposures.

I [first became concerned about possible "Red Tide" neurotoxicity when I] experienced three severe muscle contractions, almost epileptic, on the evening of Aug. 11th while sleeping. The first occurred in my neck/shoulder muscle that violently snapped my head into my pillow. I actually heard my neck crack and very cautiously massaged my neck muscles, thinking, *What the hell was that!* A few minutes later, my back went into violent spasms. Thank God, only once. Then I felt a spasm in one of my legs, and that was it. My neck and shoulder muscles still ache as of today, 2 weeks later.

On August 18, 2000, S.H. gave me her testimony. She and her three children were staying at Ashwood St. in Bethany Beach. Two of her children that were in the water most of the day on August 11th, kept complaining to her that they had difficulty in breathing and one had a skin rash. I put her right on the phone with Dr. Bruce Richards, Executive Director of Inland Bay's [medical clinic]. The concern on her face was very apparent as she talked to him. She then gave the phone to me, and Dr. Richards said (per my notes of that day at 12:30 P.M.) that these were definite symptoms of neurotoxicity. Even the rash was [apparently] a symptom of neurotoxicity.

Dr. Richards then informed me that he would relay the matter during an upcoming luncheon to Dr. Sergio Huerta, and would tell Dr. Huerta of what S.H. told him of her children having these symptoms.

On August 19th, a lifeguard at Sea Colony Beach, D.G., told me that he noticed the water to be reddish-brown, and that all the lifeguards were commenting about the color—"the worst" they had ever seen it, he said. The morning of August 12th, [the day after the first beach exposures] he woke up with what he described as "lock jaw." He was hardly able to open his mouth for a day and a half.

A customer in my store, J.F., informed me on August 19th, that she too saw "yellow foam" on a local beach. Shortly thereafter, the week of August 12th through the 19th, she suffered eye irritation.

That same day, on August 19th, an adult swimmer died in waste deep water in Ocean City, Maryland while boogie boarding. Witnesses said he just stood up and fell flat on his face into the water, where he drowned. Resuscitation kept him alive for a while but he died on the way to the hospital.

On August 20th I called the Maryland Medical Examiner's Office at 410-333-3271 and they gave me the physician on call: Dr. Locke (410-333-4980). I told him about the "Red Tide" we had here in Delaware that extended approximately twenty miles from Cape Henlopen to Fenwick Island. Also, that we had muscle spasms reported, possibly from a neurotoxin. I suggested since the news reported the man who drowned was prone to spasms, that the "Red Tide" neurotoxin could have triggered his epileptic seizure. I suggested they check the man's nasal cavities, lungs and blood for a marine neurotoxin. He said they would.

On Aug 25th I spoke to Dr. Locke again, and told him of more cases [in our State] being found with neurotoxin-like symptoms. I asked if they had discovered any neurotoxins in the corpse of the swimmer. He said he was looking into the marine "neurotoxins" and "other things."

Again, on August 19th, a Mrs. D.G. and her two children went boating from Vines Creek, on the Indian River, to Lewes. They traveled through the Indian River Bay, Rehoboth Bay and through the Rehoboth-Lewes Canal and back. They never went in the water. Both of her children suddenly developed severe breathing problems and itching eyes.

Her daughter's eyes became very red and swollen and she also said that her stomach was "killing her." A cold washcloth applied to her eyes that evening made her eye pain and itching worse. My experience with marine neurotoxins is that cold enhances the effect of the toxin and heat diminishes the effect . . . According to N.C., a Mrs. L.W. reported that her daughter became extremely ill after swimming in the ocean on Aug 11th or 12th. The little girl was taken to the hospital. N.C. said they couldn't figure out what was wrong with her.

On August 22, 2000, my son and I, along with a friend and his four-year-old son, went to the beach. That night the little boy became severely ill with vomiting.

Mr. Winkler wrote, "I hope you can figure out what is going on here, Mr. Davidson." He then closed by providing his contact information.[4]

The following week, on August 27, 2000, Mr. Winkler sent another letter to the Health Department, several more public officials, and local media contacts. What follows is his report of what he continued to suspect was a "red-tide phenomenon:"

"Continuation of Investigation"

August 26th, 2000 at approximately 2:10 P.M., I called a local marina and spoke to its owner, T.C. I asked her if she had noticed any customers with eye irritation, difficulty in breathing or nausea, especially in children. She said, "No."

I told her what some people had experienced on the ocean and bays. Then she asked, "Were there any other symptoms?"

"Muscle spasms," I replied.

She then said that she had dizziness lately as did her mother and a friend. She explained that one week before, while she was sleeping, she had the worst leg cramp ever in her life. That day she had gone in the water, wading. She said she wondered how that came about since she hadn't done any strenuous work. I told her that I had experienced a similar reaction to my ocean exposure on August 11, as had Sea Colony beach lifeguard, D.G., on August 12.

On August 26th at approximately 2:20 P.M, I called the Beebe Emergency Center in Millville, Delaware (302-539-8450). I spoke with a nurse, named Debbie, and asked her if anyone was coming in with similar symptoms of neurotoxicity. The nurse said they have had a lot of people come in with eye irritation in the past two weeks, but now a lot are coming in with dizziness. I faxed her my three-page letter from August 25th—my report to the Department of Health (302-537-1713). She said she would give a copy to [the hospital toxicologist,] Dr. Levelly.

The next day I telephoned to confirm with Debbie that she had passed the report on to Dr. Levelly. She said she saw him read the report, although he didn't say anything, or seem to have any reaction.

Later that day, on August 27th, M.S., a nurse who teaches at Sussex Tech School came into my nautical store. After talking to her she said that about two weeks previously she was in Rite Aid drug store, on Route 26 near Ocean View, getting a prescription for her son. The pharmacy cashier mentioned to her that they were having a run on eye irritation medication.

So following our conversation, later that afternoon, I called, out of curiosity, the Rite Aid in Selbyville, about 10 miles [inland] from Ocean View. The pharmacist said that they had no run there on eye medication; in fact, it has been relatively slow even on ear infection medication, and that inland people were not suffering the effects seen on the coast.

Synchronously, shortly after my call to the Rite Aid drugstore in Selbyville, again on August 27th, the chief pharmacist from Happy Harry's drugstore on Route 26 in Bethany Beach walked into my store. Happy Harry's is the closest pharmacy to the ocean. Herb announced that, indeed, there had been a lot of eye irritation medication sold in the past two weeks, and that ear infection medication has slowed down. . . .

I speculated that the apparent "Red Tide" might have consisted of dinoflagellates that had consumed the bacteria in the water, since they are filter feeders; thereby, reducing the incidence of swimmers ear, but increasing the neurotoxicity problem in local waters as the dinoflagellates grew.

Again on August 27th, another customer, B.U., came into my store, and following my question concerning the "Red Tide" she replied that about two weeks earlier, she and her husband were listening to a local radio talk show discussing the "high winds that blew the water onto the beach leaving a yellow foam behind." She said that several people had called in to report the phenomenon. . . .

Still later that afternoon, others provided additional confirmations and information: Mrs. S.P. said that on August 10th through the 12th she saw "a yellow-green color" as the waves broke on to State Park beach as she drove south from South Bethany.

Also driving by this beach the week of August 14th through the 18th was Mrs. T.M. and her daughter. T.M. reported that her daughter complained of something in her eye, but they couldn't see anything. Additionally odd was that she and her daughter both suffered insomnia, as my son and I had, for four nights in a row after surfing on August 11th.

Around 4:00 P.M. that afternoon, I called my son Bill. I asked him, "How are you feeling, and has your insomnia resolved?" He told me he "hurt all over. It even hurts to sit down," he said. "This is really weird." Furthermore, he reported that he and his wife were still experiencing insomnia.

I told him I thought whatever was in the water was a neurotoxin that could be absorbed through the skin. So I warned him to stay out of the water until we knew what was going on. Usually, he surfs about every other day as he had since the August 11th red/yellow tide phenomenon. "Something is in the ocean and bay waters," I said. "Steer clear of them."

After speaking with Bill, beginning at approximately 4:30 P.M. [on August 27, 2000], I thought it best to call some of the other people who had reported symptoms to me earlier, to see if they had also developed insomnia, and how they were feeling. . . .

A more recent and severe case involved a 6-year-old boy who, after a full day of swimming, collapsed with seizures later that night. His parents initially thought their child was kidding and told him to go to bed.

He seemed well enough the next day, so the family swam for three more days. By the forth day the young boy's skin began to peel, he broke out with oral blisters, spiked a fever, and suffered a series of epileptic-like seizures. They rushed him to Beebe Hospital Emergency Room. Later they moved him to Children's Hospital in Wash. D.C. where he was diagnosed with Coxsackie virus. Shortly thereafter, the boy's two siblings developed similar symptoms.

Another child, from a different family, also developed similar symptoms, but no seizures. The Beebe Hospital staff could not diagnose the problem. Following two weeks they performed a spinal tap on the child, which led to a diagnosis of "bacterial meningitis."

I spoke to one of the doctors who attended this child in the emergency room at Beebe. He came into my store. He knew nothing of the letter I had sent to our Public Health Department. He said, "This could explain a lot—the eye burning, skin peeling, and more." He took Mr. Davidson's name from me and said that he was going to call him at the Public Health Department on September 14, 2000.

Finally, a friend of mine who kayaks regularly in the ocean and neighboring waterways complained of burning sensations in both arms from his elbows down. His pains felt worse, he said, when he put them in water. [This suggested that possibly residual neurotoxin was being activated by water or rehydration.]

I have spoken with many people who have none of the symptoms reported above. They all have one thing in common: THEY HAVE NOT BEEN NEAR THE OCEAN OR BAY!

I provided all the names and telephone numbers of the above affected families and people to public health officials in a letter I sent them of August 25, 2000. As I patiently awaited their official response, which I never got to any satisfaction, I learned of several other cases of apparent neurotoxicity associated with contaminated beach water exposures in my area. One was a 40-year-old Rehoboth area surfer about whom an acquaintance alerted me; another was a 3-year-old boy who went into the water according to a local news report. Both subsequently convulsed with seizures. The 3-year-old boy died on the beach.

Another case involved a second surfer that spit up blood and showed marked signs of neurotoxicity. He went to a local Dr. Shoemaker, who found him to be the "worse case" he had ever seen to fail a neurotoxin contrast eye test! The blood flow into his retina, the doctor recorded, was only about 125 units compared to normal, which is above 600. I likewise suffered this effect, but less seriously. My retinal blood flow was a little over 300. Physiologically, neurotoxins, apparently like the one(s) we were exposed to, constrict blood vessels that feed the retina. Thus, I learned, such CDC approved tests are an excellent place to begin to identify cases of environmental neurotoxicity.

These symptoms and cases reflect something very different from a standard red tide. Typically, red tide neurotoxicity can occur from shellfish poisoning mostly associated with the New England, Florida, or Pacific coasts from June through October. Symptoms include paresthesias of the mouth, lips, face and extremities, visual disturbances, nausea, vomiting, diarrhea, and in more severe cases, muscle weakness, and respiratory and general paralysis. These symptoms usually dissipate within a few hours or certainly a few days. Not so for what we were dealing with here in Delaware.

Assigning Theoretic Causes

Naturally, I considered the possibility that these neurotoxic effects might have been caused by a red tide; particularly since the ocean water had turned red and yellow. However, brevetoxins from the red tides do not cause seizures, intoxication of beachgoers and coastal by-passers, or hemoptysis—coughing or spitting up blood! I questioned, *What else besides brevetoxins and red tides could have caused these crippling and terminal effects?*

Other alternatives I considered included a toxic release from a chemical plant, or a spill from a garbage barge. Such instances had been reported previously. One barge dumped toxic waste at the mouth of the Delaware Bay instead of 40 miles out to sea as per their legal requirement.

I also considered the possibility that the mosquito spraying of Anvil 10:10 in New York and New Jersey triggered neurotoxic pollution of the waterways enroute to the ocean. Dr. Horowitz advanced this consideration. He suggested this was likely since the pesticide label particularly warned against water pollution with this deadly neurotoxin. No doubt much of the spraying that was done during the summer along coastal northeastern states had washed into the waterways leading to the ocean. Had these WNV sprayings culminated in a 20-mile "red tide-like" neurotoxic slick that floated south along the Atlantic coast to the Delaware Bay following the receding Labrador current? This was certainly a grave possibility.

I was really thrown for a loop when bizarre "jellyfish" began washing up on our shores. Photographs of these objects are seen in figures 9.1 and 9.2. To the layperson these "jellyfish" appeared real. But as I later learned they were not "normal." The "Type-I" jellyfish was synthetic. It was composed of a type of plastic that became jelly-like when wet.

People who stepped on the "Type-II" jellyfish, thinking they were benign, reported to me that they squirted a clear substance that caused the skin on their exposed feet to chap and peel. I decided to investigate these objects for myself, and confirmed their reports.

The Type-II had more natural features including white radial symmetry lines emanating from their centers. When I dried the Type-II creatures they turned clear-like and literally disintegrated without a trace left behind. On the beaches, they were simply and rapidly absorbed like liquid into the sand.

The top convex side of the fake (Type-I) organism felt smooth to the touch, but the bottom seemed sticky, like it was designed to attach to something. Thus, I wondered whether these unique non-creatures were some kind of government experiment, perhaps used to help clean up, or absorb the neurotoxic chemicals making people sick. They were certainly related to the red/yellow toxic tide insofar as oddity is concerned. I still have no idea what they are, but I stored plenty of samples for serious investigators.[4]

What hampered my investigation most was the cost involved in testing water samples and exposed symptomatic people for neurotoxins. Most neurotoxins are fat-soluble. This means that in the case of, let's say, the red tide brevetoxin, the nerve poisons are absorbed into the fat cells of your body within 24 seconds of entering your blood stream through normal breathing. This was determined by the United States Army's Dr. Mark Poli in Fort Detrick, Maryland, in a 1990 study of intravenous brevetoxin injections.[5]

The scientific community remains at odds regarding the wide array of effects synthetic neurotoxins have on the body, or how long they stay in the fatty tissues. Some doctors say that they accumulate over time with additional exposures.

Fig. 9.1. Synthetic "Jellyfish" Discovered On Delaware Shores in August, 2000 by Marine Biologist Bill Winkler

Type I Found Sept. 16, 2000 at Fenwick Island State Park, Delaware
By John and Sharon Stewart

The "Type-I" plastic "jellyfish." One side appeared "adhesive." Beneath this adhesive layer was a lanolin-like layer that apparently held a toxic chemical. While wet, or in the water, these appeared as "pieces of jellyfish." During the Summer of 2000 many beachgoers were "stung" by these. These people did not develop welts as they would have if they had been stung by true jellyfish. They developed chemical burn-like red marks and skin rashes. In contrast to these, the "Type-II" specimens were perfectly round, crystal clear, and held a toxic liquid. No known jellyfish store and/ or release such liquid. Found by John and Sharon Stewart on Fenwick Island State Park, Delaware. Photograph contributed by Mr. William Winkler.

Doctors also have no standard protocols for treating chemical neuro-toxicity. Using shellfish toxicity as a model, some doctors believe that the anti-cholesterol drug cholestyramine can bind chemically with brevetoxins and remove them from the body through the small intestine. In any case, there is general agreement that detoxification is difficult for neurotoxic pesticide poisoning.

Following my fruitless attempts to get local politicians, environmental protection agents, public health officials, and media reporters to respond in kind, that is, investigate my findings, I ended up calling the Federal Bureau of Investigation (FBI). They sent an agent to my store. He said he had checked with counter-terrorism and it was not that; so it was not his "jurisdiction." He also said that I had done a good job exposing an earlier outbreak of Chattonella, but if I brought out these "jelly things," that I could be arrested for "environmental terrorism."

After he left, I called the Weidner Environmental and Natural Resources Law Clinic in Wilmington, DE, and explained the entire affair. People in charge there were concerned, but not surprised. They agreed to help me pro bono.

Officials at Weidner filed Freedom of Information Act (FOIA) requests to the following agencies: the Delaware Dept. of Natural Resources and Environmental Control (DNREC), the U.S. Coast Guard, the National Oceanographic and Atmospheric Administration Satellite Division, and the Delaware Department of Public Health (DDPH). To the time of this writing, we have only received FOIA requests back from DNREC, DDPH and the Coast Guard.

The DNREC mostly replied by e-mail. Officials there stated that they were aware of a bloom of some sort coming out of the Roosevelt Inlet on the Delaware Bay on August 15, 2000. Photos taken from an aircraft showed the bloom and the DNREC's e-mail reconfirmed it. They provided nothing to indicate the nature of the bloom, and failed to include a discussion of results from testing water samples taken from the bloom, inlet and bay. The bloom may have come out of the inlet and followed the bay's coastline for two to three miles before it washed into the Atlantic. Here is where the pilot said the bloom dispersed.

Keep in mind that I reported the colored water on August 11, 2000— four days before the "flyover." Then, two days later, we had a mild nor'easter and all the red water was blown up onto the beach where yellow-green foam carpeted the beach. At that time, and following my initial contacts with them, DNREC officials reported to the press and others that they saw no evidence of a bloom. Incompetence or cover-up could explain this glaring discrepancy. I strongly suspect the later. Here's why:

Fig. 9.2. Unusual "Jellyfish" Discovered On Delaware Shores in August, 2000 by Marine Biologist Bill Winkler

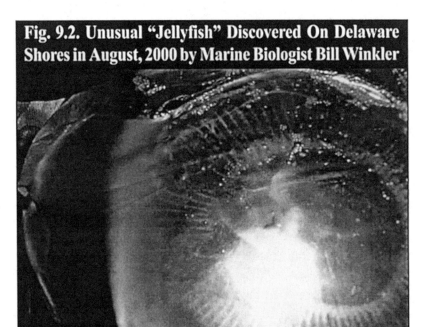

The "Type-II" jellyfish. Lay persons might be seriously "stung" by this benign looking jellyfish that is perfectly round, crystal clear, with white and gray striations eminating from the center. Unlike the "Type-I" plastic "jellyfish," these creatures were blown up, similar to baloons, with toxic irritating liquid in their centers, possibly due to osmotic differentials from aluminum contaminted seawater. No known jellyfish store and/or release such liquid. Photograph courtesy of Mr. William Winkler, Ocean View, Delaware.

Chemical analysis of the water samples taken by DNREC on August 13, 2000 showed what they called "normal" levels of chemicals found in the ocean. They omitted some damning details. Their complete chemical analysis was censured before it was sent to Weidner under the FOIA request. Investigators at Weidner documented that DNREC officials omitted one important chemical—aluminum. Through an anonymous collaborator inside the DNREC, I obtained a copy of the original chemical analysis that showed levels of aluminum from 2,015–2,066 micrograms per liter of water. That is *extremely* high. The normal level of aluminum in seawater is 0.01 milligrams/liter. This equals 1.0 micrograms/liter. Thus, their censored analysis showed more than 2,000 times higher levels of aluminum than normal.

Why aluminum? No one seems to know for sure at this time, but at least I was able to rule out suspected pesticides such as Anvil and Malathion that do not contain aluminum. However, it is odd that out of 106 standard elements in the periodic table, knowledge of this one— aluminum— was censored by the DNREC. As you will read in the next chapter, aluminum is intimately linked to the atmospheric "seeding" and spraying technology patented by the Hughes Corporation to [allegedly] abate global warming. It is possible that at least some of the dramatic rise in sea water aluminum concentrations the DNREC's report censored may be directly attributable to the fallout from chemtrail-related aluminum-oxide about which you will shortly read. Heavy jet fuel sprayings containing aluminum would be expected to settle inland, wash into the waterways, and collect in bays like the one here in Delaware.

The DNREC was not the only agency to delete or lose vital data. Equally transparent, the U.S. Coast Guard did virtually the same thing concerning a different set of findings. Their reply to our FOIA request included a "Marine Casualty Investigation Report" last updated on August 29, 2000 as shown in figure 9.3. The document stated that one of their vessels was called to investigate "a report of a red substance floating on the water along SFC along Dewey Beach." Apparently, "Indian River personnel observed by boat a reddish slush-type material/*product* with numerous jellyfish *swimming* in each." The Coast Guard reported taking samples along with "DNREC Personnel." They then white-washed their findings and concluded, contrary to the DNREC's report of no evidence indicating a bloom, "It was determined to be a 'Red-Tide;' non-harmful and non-hazardous. Case closed."

I italicized the words "product" and "swimming" in the above quotes to emphasize that 1) they did obtain a product descriptively similar to the specimens that I collected and detailed above, and 2) Coast Guard officials alleged these jellyfish were swimming. In fact, only the "Type-II" jellyfish might have been observed swimming at the time of the "Red-Tide" bloom/no bloom. The fact that this report stated both Coast Guard crew members and DNREC personnel obtained the same samples at the same time, yet came to conflicting conclusions, neither one reflecting the full evidence in my possession, suggests a coverup and/or conspiracy which, I believe, transcends these obviously incompetent agencies.

Suspiciously, as Dr. Horowitz disclosed in *Healing Codes for the Biological Apocalypse*, besides their link to aluminum oxide spraying devices discussed in the next chapter, the Hughes Corporation is heavily involved in electromagnetic energy and disease research closely linked to project HAARP and its related technologies.[6] [A detailed review and update on these developments is provided in forthcoming chapters.] Thus, the association of Hughes with HAARP, prion disease research, electromagnetic implants for surveillance and population control, ARCO, the British Royal Family, the Rockefellers' Standard Oil Company, and the "human genome project," might explain why these local officials seem so incompetent and reluctant to tell the truth. Our toxic aluminum and political experience here in Delaware may be, unfortunately, linked to global petrochemical industrialists advancing some form of population control operation that supercedes state and federal laws for the sake of "U.S. National Security."

Another aluminum hypothesis, likewise placing petrochemical and pharmaceutical companies under suspicion, stems from the fact that just west of Cape Henlopen Point, where the bay meets the ocean, the Barcroft Company, of Lewes, DE, owned by Aventis Pharmaceuticals (a subsidiary of Rhône-Poulenc Rorer Inc., that was sold to American Home Products [AHP] in May 2000) processes aluminum and magnesium for pharmaceuticals. Such products include over-the-counter antacids like Maalox (Novartis Consumer Subsidiary of Sandoz and Ciba) and Mylanta (J&J–Merck Consumer).[7] They have a discharge pipe that runs into the bay. The excessive aluminum might have come from there. In this case, the disturbing associations between AHP and the Rockefeller–I.G. Farben cartel, as well as the Sandoz and Merck pharmaceutical companies, with the CIA and related neurotoxic research and development, suggests the need for further investigation into this curious coincidence of elevated aluminum levels, in a milieu with synthetic jellyfish, at a time when Alzheimer's disease and dementia rates are skyrocketing,[8,9] and while non-lethal warfare is apparently being waged against unwitting populations.

In this regard, the unprecedented appearances of the "Type-I" and "Type-II" jellyfish might be reconciled. An initial laboratory analysis on the "Type-II" revealed high concentrations of "a binding agent" (according to the chemist) capable of binding aluminum and/or toxic chemicals. This was likely related to the numerous feet injuries associated with the high concentrations of caustic skin-peeling chemicals polluting the sand on which these "jellyfish" dried and dissolved. The "Type-I" jellyfish also appeared to have a unique adhesive side. The presence of these binding and/or adhesive features in/on these unique creatures possibly suggests people at the helm of advanced research and industry were aware of the need to clean up toxic agent(s) through some novel binding/adhesive technology. This might also explain the osmotic accumulation of toxic fluid inside the "Type-II" jellyfish.

On the Broadkill River is a plastics plant. The Broadkill empties into the Delaware Bay through the Roosevelt Inlet. People in Lewes, Delaware, just east of the inlet, testified that for the past two years they have seen pieces of plastic-like stuff resembling the "Type-I" jellies on their beaches. Unfortunately, they did not think to collect samples of these for analysis.

The DDPH and the Centers for Disease Control and Prevention (CDC) exchanged one letter Weidner officials obtained through the FOIA. Ironically, the CDC actually commended the public health department for their diligence in getting word out to people about the water problems. The DDPH officials stated that with all the media coverage, they did not have one complaint due to the water. They obviously discounted or censored the five typed pages I sent them documenting, as above, the numerous injuries sustained by beachgoers due to the mysterious "red tide."

Regarding the "good job" the DDPH did in getting media coverage concerning the ocean toxicity, none of the three coastal newspapers printed the health advisory at all. Only two did a story on my Chattonella dinoflagellate research. I took my complaint to the State and learned that there is no law that mandates a newspaper print a health advisory. State officials were supposedly looking into correcting the matter. I will not rest until they do.

I called local talk radio shows many mornings to get the truth out to people in this area at risk. I've advised others to do the same.

The NOAA satellite data is expected to arrive as this book goes to press. The NOAA asked the Weidner organization for a 60-day extension to comply with their FOIA request. Hopefully, once we review these photos and related data, more truth will surface as to what happened here in ocean-side Delaware the summer of 2000.

It is obvious to me that whoever is pulling the political strings on the seemingly puppet government administrators, they do not want American citizens to know the truth about what is happening to us and our environment. People are dying due to man-made chemicals and biological pollutants intoxicating our biosphere. Must we write this off as "survival of the fittest or wealthiest?"

I cannot take this mildly. Many people have told me to drop this investigation and my truth-telling efforts by saying such disclosures might "affect tourism." "Do you know what that will do to business around here?" one acquaintance asked. Yet the bottom line is not money, it's us—the people who live here. Would you, if you knew the truth, not tell your friends and loved ones, your community, risks you knew existed in your air, food, or water? I must because it seriously impacts public health.

By writing this account, and getting truth out every way I can, more citizens are likelier to join in the effort to right serious wrongs in this country. Though you may consider me a fool or naive, the America I love, and serve to protect, stands for truth and justice. If we have

Fig. 9.3. U.S. Coast Guard "Marine Casualty Investigation Report" on "Red-Tide" Jelly Fish and "Product."

```
MCIR  .               MARINE CASUALTY INVESTIGATION REPORT              28SEP00

CASE NUMBER,,/ MC00010866  INV INIT/ TMP  PORT/ PHIMS LAST UPDATE/ 29AUG00
CASUALTY TYPE: VESSEL/    PERSONNEL/    FACILITY/   POLLUTION/ X MARPOL/
INCIDENT DATE/ 25AUG00 TIME/ 1200  KNOWN/      ESTIMATED/ X  REF CASE/
NOTIFY DATE../ 25AUG00 TIME/ 1730  REPORTER TYPE/ PARTY,NEC
SUBJECT....../ RED TIDE/DEWEY BCH/UNFOUNDED    LOCAL FILE REFERENCE/
LOCATION...../ ATLANTIC OCEAN, DEWEY BEACH,DE        LOCAL CODE/
INCIDENT STATUS: VERIFIED/     NOT VERIFIED/ X  VERIFIED, NOT REPORTABLE/
NOTIFY/                              ACTION: CTP/ X  RETURN/    (TO IAPR)

                --- VALIDATION AND ENDORSEMENT ---
            END/FWD END/CLS RETURN  USER-ID           NAME              DATE
INVESTIGATOR:   X                   TPARTISS   MST1 THOMAS M PARTISS   29AUG00
UNIT COMMAND:        X              TPARTISS   MST1 THOMAS M PARTISS   29AUG00
DIST REQ?  :
HQ   REQ?  :

                --- GENERAL INFORMATION ---
CITY/ REHOBOTH              ST/ DE WATERBODY/ SOUTH ATLANTIC OCEAN COASTAL
RIVER MILE/              LATITUDE/ N 38-42.0       LONGITUDE/ W 75- 4.0
CAS SUMMARY:TYPE/ POLLUTION    CLASS/ NONE
            POSSIBLE DRUG INVOLVEMENT?/ N  PUBLIC VESSEL/      BOATING/
            DEATHS/    0  MISSING/   0   INJURED/   0   TOTAL DAMAGE/
ENV IMPACT: MODE/ WATER    SEVERITY CATEGORY/ NS     MATERIAL CATEGORY/
            OSC/ USCG  EPA REGION/ 2   CLEANUP REQ?/ N
            RESPONSE BY NSF?/ N    NSF TIME TO RESPOND/   0 HOURS
            NOTIFICATION FROM NRC?../ N   NRC CASE../
            NOTIFICATION FROM APHIS?/ N   APHIS PORT/

                --- INCIDENT BRIEF ---
MSD PERSONNEL INVESTIGATED A REPORT OF A RED SUBSTANCE FLOATING ON THE WATER
SFC ALONG DEWEY BEACH, DE.  STA. INDIAN RIVER PERSONNEL OBSERVED BY BOAT A
REDISH SLOSH-TYPE MATERIAL/PRODUCT W/ NUMEROUS JELLY FISH SWIMMING IN EACH.
EACH AREA WAS APPROX. 200 YDS LONG.  NO ODOR OF OIL OR SHEENING.  NOTHING
OBSERVED ON SHORE AREAS.  SAMPLES TAKEN BY BOAT CREW AND DNREC PERSONNEL.  IT
WAS DETERMINED TO BE A "RED-TIDE"; NON-HARMFUL & NON-HAZARDOUS.  CASE CLOSED.

                --- ACTIONS REPORTED ---
SEL     CASE SUPPLEMENTS          SEL     EVENT SUPPLEMENTS
 1  WITNESS LIST........(IAWL)/ X  14  COLLISION OR GROUNDING.(MCCG)/  0
 2  COMDT RECOMMENDATION.(MCCR)/   15  EQUIP FAILURE..........(MCDR)/  0
 3  CASUALTY DETAILS.....(MCDD)/   16  FLOOD,CAPSIZE,SINKING..(MCFC)/  0
 4  NARRATIVE SUPPLEMENT.(MCNS)/   17  FIRE,EXPLOSION.........(MCFB)/  0
 5  PERS ACTION RECOMMEND(MCPA)/ 0 18  HUMAN FACTORS SUPP....:(MCHF)/  0
 6  POLLUTANT DETAILS....(MCPD)/ 0 19  HAZ MAT INVOLVEMENT....(MCHM)/  0
 7  MARPOL DETAIL SUP....(MCMD)/ 0 20  LIFESAVING SUPPLEMENT..(MCLS)/  0
 8  OPERATIONAL CONTROLS (PSOC)/ 0 21  PERSONNEL CASUALTY.....(MCPC)/  0
 9  PERSONNEL INVOLVEMENT(MCPI)/ 0 22  STRUCTURAL FAILURE.....(MCSF)/  0
10  SMI SUPPLEMENT.......(MCSI)/ 0
11  TOWING SUPPLEMENT....(MCTS)/ 0
12  SUBJECT SUPPLEMENT...(MCSS)/
13  WEATHER FACTORS......(MCWX)/

VESSELS INVOLVED/  0
                                              SUPPLEMENTS
FACILITIES INVOLVED/  1                      P     P P S
   FIN         NAME              CATEGORY    D     A I I
UNKLAND   UNKNOWN LAND SOURCE    SHORELINE

                --- INVESTIGATION RESOURCES UTILIZED ---
            ACTIVITY     TOTAL   ------- RESOURCE CATEGORY -------
            CATEGORY     HOURS   REGULAR RESERVE CIVILIAN OTHER
```

Report shows the sampling of a "product" mixed with "swimming" jellyfish along with a "Red-Tide" bloom that was denied by the Delaware Department of Natural Resources and Environmental Control. The fact that this report stated both Coast Guard crew members and DNREC personnel obtained the same samples at the same time, yet came to two completely opposite conclusions, reflects incompetance and coverup.

moved away from what America stands for then we must move back. The power of pens remains mightier than swords. Write your truths for public consumption. Call radio talk shows to defend "justice for all." Consistently pressure your legislators to make needed changes, and demand honest and complete answers to pressing questions. Ask *hard* questions like, "Who did the testing?" Ask for copies of test results. Keep the pressure up until you achieve your goals. If a significant minority of people did this, we might all live a lot healthier and happier.

References

1) Adams JR. Iraq's yellow rain: The hellhole spectator. *American Spectator*, Special Report: The weapons behind the latest crisis, March 1998. Available on: http://www.amspec.org/archives/98-03_adams.html

2) Williams F. Bug bombers stray and spray. Staten Island Advance. August 31, 2000, p. 1. Available from: http://baltech.org/lederman/spray/905staten.html

3) Personal communication from Mr. Adam Evans, Senior Public Health Advisor for the New York City Department of Health, poolside in Montego Bay, Jamaica, September 26, 2000.

4) Personal communication from William J. Winkler, II. Mr. Winker can be contacted at: P.O. Box 1400 Ocean View, DE 19970. Telephone 302-537-5334.

5) Dr. Mark Poli's address was given as: Biological Weapon's Center, U.S. Army Toxicology Division, Ft. Detrick, Fredrick, MD. 21702-5011. The information on Dr. Poli's experiment came from Dr. Ritchie Shoemaker's book, *Pfiesteria: Crossing Dark Water*, 1998.

6) Horowitz L and Puleo J. *Healing Codes for the Biological Apocalypse.* Sandpoint, Idaho: Tetrahedron Publishing Group, pp. 435-437.

7) According to information available on Aventis's website at: http://www.aventispharma-us.com/pressreleases/05_02_00B.html, and Novartis's website at: http://www.info.novartis.com/weare/index.html:

On May 2, 2000, Aventis Pharmaceuticals announced an agreement to sell their 312-acre Collegeville campus to American Home Products—chief among the Rockefeller–I.G. Farben pharmaceutical cartel's progeny. The facility then became the "global headquarters for Wyeth-Ayerst, the pharmaceutical division of American Home Products. The facility was formerly the global headquarters, combining Corporate, Research and Development and U.S. Commercial activities of Rhône-Poulenc S.A.'s pharmaceutical business . . . prior to Rhône-Poulenc's merger last year [1999] with Hoechst AG to form Aventis."

The corporate headquarters of Aventis Pharma was cited as Frankfurt, Germany. "Aventis Pharma comprises Aventis Pasteur, a world leader in vaccines, with corporate headquarters in Lyon, France, and Aventis Behring, a world leader in therapeutic proteins, with corporate headquarters in King of Prussia, Pa." the new release stated. "Aventis S.A." was identified as "a world leader in life sciences. Focused on two core business areas - pharmaceuticals and agriculture - Aventis is dedicated to improving life through the discovery and development of innovative products in the fields of prescription drugs, vaccines, therapeutic proteins, crop production and protection, animal health and nutrition. With global corporate headquarters in Strasbourg, France,

Aventis employs around 95,000 people in 150 countries and recorded unaudited pro forma sales in 1999 or euros 20.5 billion (US$20.7 billion).

In April 1996, the shareholders of Sandoz and Ciba agreed to merge two Basel-based Swiss enterprises. It was, at the time, the largest corporate merger in world history. When the announcement was made, Marc Moret, Chairman of the Board of Sandoz, stated: "The globalization of markets, and therefore of competition, is taking on gigantic proportions. And the long-term success of the company depends to an ever greater degree on being among the best in our fields of activity."

> The advantages of this merger of equals are clear. "Strategically, the new company moves into a worldwide leadership position in life sciences," explained Alex Krauer, Chairman of Novartis and former Chairman and CEO of Ciba, "Novartis holds the number two position in pharmaceuticals, *number one in crop protection* [including pesticides; emphasis added.], and has tremendous development potential in nutrition. A consistent commitment to innovation and an impressive lead in emerging technologies constitute the basis for solid and sustainable growth. The strategic focus on life sciences requires the demerger of the Specialty Chemicals Division of Ciba and the Construction Chemicals of Sandoz."

> With the European Union approved merger in July 1996, the U.S. Federal Trade Commission agreed to the formation of the new company in the fall of the same year.

As disclosed by retired British Secret Service agent, Dr. John Coleman, in his monumental *Conspirators' Hierarchy: The Story of the Committee of 300*, Sandoz was responsible for developing LSD, and selling it to the U.S. Central Intelligence Agency (CIA) for distribution throughout America, particularly on college campuses, for the "drug cult." In Dr. Coleman's words:

> Tavistock and Stanford Research . . . turned up the heat for social change in America. . . . It became popular to "drop out" and wear dirty jeans, go about with long unwashed hair. The "beat generation" cut itself off from mainstream America. . . . The newly created group and its "lifestyle" swept millions of young Americans into the cult. American youth underwent a radical revolution without ever being aware of it, . . . and thus reacting in a maladaptive manner against its manifestation, which were drugs of all types, marijuana, and later Lysergic acid, "LSD," so conveniently provided for them by the Swiss pharmaceutical company, SANDOZ, following the discovery by one of its chemists, Albert Hoffman, how to make the synthetic ergot amine, a powerful

mind-altering drug. The Committee of 300 financed the project through one of their banks, S.C. Warburg, and the philosopher, Aldous Huxley, carried the drug to America. . . .

The descendants of the British East India Company were delighted with the success of their drug-pushing program. Their disciples became adept in the use of lysergic acid (LSD) so conveniently made available by patrons of the drug trade . . . The new "wonder drug" was promptly distributed at all rock concerts and on college campuses in free sample packages. The question that begs to be asked is, "What was the FBI doing while all this was going on?" [Neglecting the historic links between the British East India Company and the] . . . British controllers and bankers who grew fat and intolerant on the enormous amounts of money that poured into the coffers of the British East India Company from the wretched Chinese coolies opium trade. BEIC profits, even in those years, far exceeded the combined profits made in a single year by General Motors, Ford and Chrysler in their heydays. The trend in making huge profits out of drugs was carried over into the 1960s by such "legal" drug death merchants such as Sandoz . . . .

The Merck pharmaceutical company will be additionally discussed in forthcoming chapters.

8) Zalta P, et al., Alzheimer dementia and the aluminum hypothesis. *Medical Hypotheses* 26:139-142.

9) Editorial staff. Growing evidence for aluminum/Alzheimer's link. *Clinical Psychiatry News* (Dec. 1988), p.2.

Chapter 10.
Chemtrails: Compromising Public Health and Civil Confidence

by William Thomas

"My office has received a number of letters from people who want to know if our Armed Forces, charged with protecting us, could have injured them or their loved ones through indiscriminate open-air testing with disease-producing agents. They do not like the idea that they may have been guinea pigs in germ warfare experiments. . . . The American people have a right to know what is going on around them, and I hope this hearing will help resolve their lingering doubts."

Senator Lowell Schweiker, 1977
Hearings on Biological Testing Involving
Human Subjects by the Department of Defense

Blue skies showed them best. Sometimes silver, often painted all white, huge air-refueling planes wove broad white plumes that instead of quickly dissipating like normal contrails lingered for hours. In a process U.S. Air Force Weather Force specialists call "aerial obscuration," skies became completely overcast, despite forecasts calling for sunny weather.

Since 1998, military and civil aviation officials have insisted that sky trails, striking enough to stop traffic and bring families outside to photograph precisely spaced grid patterns and perfectly intersected X's were "normal flight operations."

But many sightings were taking place far from navigation beacons and established air routes. Since when, for instance, did "scheduled air traffic" suddenly appear, saturating rural skies for weeks, only to abruptly cease, then start up again weeks later?

Pilots, police officers, former military personnel and thousands of other observers insisted that they had never seen so many jet trails at once; often at altitudes below which commercial jetliners were seen leaving no contrails at all.

In the words of eyewitnesses across the United States:

• "I've lived here for 26 years never seeing this number of contrails at once."

• "One morning I saw so many I almost had a car accident. They were X'ing, probably 50, 100 of them, as far as I could see. A lot of X's and parallel lines. Definitely not normal air traffic."

• "They looked like they were playing tic-tac-toe up there. You know darn well it's not passenger planes."

• "I am under the understanding that we have regular flight patterns. This however, broke all the rules, as these patterns criss-crossed one another over a dozen times."

• "The day starts out clear, and then they come, from the east, in a fan-shaped spread, laying down the trails. By noon, or early afternoon, the sky was solidly overcast. I'm a retired airline pilot. I know a chemtrail from a contrail!"

Contrail or Chemtrail

Along busy jet routes, cirrus clouds can form around particles of jet pollution. With more than *62 million* commercial and military flights taking place every year over the United States alone, scientists say that the pollution and moisture from so many jet engines has increased cloud cover by as much as *5%* since the jet age took off.

But federal aviation authorities state that aircraft condensation trails usually dissipate within 50 seconds, like the wake behind a boat.

Contrails are formed when hot, moist engine exhaust momentarily condense stratospheric ice crystals into wispy trails, like breath exhaled on a cold day. As NASA explained, "Contrails only form at very high altitudes (usually above 8 km) where the air is extremely cold (less than -40°C). If the air is very dry, contrails do not form behind airplanes. . . . Cirrus cloud formation is not expected to occur with relative humidities of less than 70%."[1] Correlating official meteorological readings with days of heavy "chemtrail" sightings over Santa Fe, New Mexico, researcher Clifford Carnicom determined suspicious conditions of *30% humidity or less* at altitudes where persistent white plumes criss-cross the sky.[2]

The New Pandemic

Contrails do not make people sick. Yet many observers became ill within hours of chemtrail exposures. Depending on what age, general health, and immunity they had, the congestion and dry hacking cough, fierce headache and gushing nosebleeds, suffocating asthma attacks, stiff necks and aching joints, twitching eyelids, dizziness, and inability to concentrate or remember simple errands very often began within 24 hours of these sightings. There was no fever accompanying this unusual "flu-like" illness. Yet the ensuing symptoms onslaught was more drastic than any similar illness. Pneumonia, heart problems, and even death followed in many cases.

Since such sightings and illnesses began in 1998, through the year 2000, the CDC reported 52 weeks of "epidemic" levels of fatalities from flu-like illness, pneumonia, and related cardiac arrest.[3]

Because no samples from these high-altitude "chemtrail" plumes were ever collected and analyzed, to the time of this writing, no scientific link between chemtrail sprayings and these illness could be determined. But in a correlation that is dubiously coincidental, hospital admissions following heavy "spray days" across the U.S. jumped to *nearly double* normal peak flu-season rates, even in states that reported only "mild" flu outbreaks.[4]

In The Beginning

The first widespread reports of intense chemtrail activity came in November 1998. A registered nurse was driving north in Michigan while watching unusual "stripes" being formed in the sky," she wrote. "It appeared as if someone took white paint on their fingers and from north to south ran their fingers through the sky. These contrails were evenly spaced and they covered the *whole* sky!"

When she finished the next home visit about 45 minutes later, the nurse came outside to find the whole sky was white. Within 24 hours she became very weak and feverish.

Her asthma began to act up. Her patients, friends and family members came down with the same symptoms at the same time, while at the local hospital, nurses and physicians began complaining of "being extremely busy with respiratory diagnoses."[5]

By mid-December, Florida hospitals were filled to capacity. In Raleigh, North Carolina, admissions at Durham regional hospital jumped from 184 patients a day to 247. It was forced to refer incoming patients elsewhere.[6]

Two days later, the *Philadelphia Daily News* reported that emergency room patients were overflowing into the hallways at West Jersey Hospital "as a wave of respiratory illnesses swept the area."[7]

By January 25, 1999 there was a 24-hour waiting period to get into hospitals in New York, and many other states. The following day, local San Francisco TV stations reported that emergency rooms were so inundated with "flu-like" cases ambulances were being turned away.[8]

Three days later, a Portland person heard on the radio that the hospitals in Portland were jammed up with people coming in. Plus, in Eugene, he wrote, "it seems like everyone is coming down with something. My wife and I saw some rainbow-colored clouds yesterday. We are calling them chem-clouds."[9]

Bakersfield, California was another epicenter of chemtrail sightings. During heavy chemtrail activity in early February 1999, one resident wrote: "Holy molly! It's been all over the news about hospital admissions . . . emergency rooms full, etc. I teach at South Bakersfield High School and I've never seen so many kids with asthma and bronchitis."[10]

In Austin, Texas, a man married to a nurse took their six-year-old daughter to the store. In the parking lot she pointed to the sky and said, "Look daddy, it's tic-tac-toe." He looked up and saw a "giant pattern of huge contrails. Four of them crossed in a perfect tic-tac-toe." Soon after this sighting, local hospitals begged his wife and other nurses to work extra shifts. There were no empty hospital beds in the city.[11]

After heavy chemtrail activity in Chandler, Arizona, a resident reported that "the doctor's offices and hospitals were totally packed the next week, and one of the nurses I spoke to said they didn't know what was wrong with everyone."[12]

On January 31, a Lake Havasu physician told *Today's News Herald* "that a nameless virus is bringing at least 10 patients a day into her office and driving some into the hospital, but laboratory tests show only a few are suffering from Type A or other identifiable strains of influenza."[13]

In Castle Rock, Colorado: "The emergency room was filled with people and the prescription line was out the front door. The woman doctor told my wife, 'You don't have to say anything, everyone here has the same thing.' And she told my wife it was a new bacterium that they can't fight. She said 'your sickness will last for up to three months.'"[14]

International Reports of Chemtrail Sightings

The mystery pandemic was not confined to the United States. On January 27, 1999, a man living near Birmingham, England was walking to work around 4:45 PM. "The sky was clear and the sun was out," he reported. "Looking up, I saw one branch of an 'X'-shaped contrail was already present and a large aero plane was forming the second branch. This aircraft was flying much lower than normal commercial airliners that I normally see, and as I watched, it clearly flew so as to form a distinct 'X' in the sky."[15]

Other X's were videotaped over London, and at least one driver stared as a strange "gel just globed onto my car windshield, seemingly out of nowhere. I couldn't wipe it off even with a towel and some screen wash." He fell sick the next day.[16]

Many others were already ill. On January 7, 1999 the BBC reported that 97,100 people in England and Wales had fallen ill with flu-like symptoms in *a single week*. The outbreak swamped ambulance services and emergency rooms. GPs who would normally receive 1,200 calls a month, received 1,000 calls in just *one* day.[17]

Many cases were fatal. The BBC reported that 8,100 people— mostly elderly—died from sudden severe upper respiratory ailments during the last week of December and the first two weeks of January, 1999, *double* the normal number of flu fatalities. Refrigerator trucks were used to haul corpses away.[18]

Less than two weeks later an Akron, Ohio resident reported: "The trails above our home are lower and wider. *How long has this been going on?* Our kids are coming up with throat, lung, and upper respiratory ailments that no one can figure out."[19]

Not a Normal Flu

By the week ending February 13, 1999, the CDC reported "Deaths from influenza and pneumonia in a sampling of 122 cities were at epidemic levels for the third consecutive week." The CDC's definition of influenza included "influenza-like illness and/or culture-confirmed influenza."[20]

But lab tests for influenza kept coming up negative. Robert Page, director of the Chemung County Health Department in Elmira, New

York, told reporters "We know there's a lot of sickness, but our diagnosis shows that it's not the flu."[21]

MDs across America told the *New York Times* and other newspapers:

- "This is the worst crisis I have seen."
- "We have people double- and triple-parked in the ER on stretchers."
- "Respiratory and gastrointestinal illnesses are filling up the beds."
- "It was surprising to me how sick they got and how quickly it happened."
- "The increase in respiratory infections may not be due to the flu."
- "We know there's a lot of sickness, but our diagnosis shows that it's not the flu."
- "We've seen a lot of cases that you can't typically classify as flu."
- "We don't know what it is or where it came from."

Suspected Fatalities From Chemtrails

Similar reports and many sudden fatalities also appeared to follow chemtrail sprayings. Typical of many reports, one woman from Russell Springs, Kentucky, wrote "[m]y uncle who has always been healthy, had to go to the hospital because he couldn't breathe. Well, he died in the hospital. He wasn't even sick!"[22]

In another suspected chemtrail calamity, "Mrs. Betty Marlin and Mrs. Pricilla Cisneros both died suddenly of pneumonia which overtook them so fast that family members did not even have time to get their families together."[23]

From Utah, another woman wrote, "We've had an unusually mild winter here . . . Warm sunny days, dry climate. Not the sort of weather you would associate with such a widespread pneumonia epidemic. Within weeks of each other, the mothers of two of my closest friends passed away. Both died of a pneumonia that overtook them so quickly that there was no time to even prepare family members. On one of the local news channels, there was a special report about the hospitals in Provo, Utah being filled to capacity with cases of pneumonia."[24]

That spring, in another state, a nurse reported emphatically that "a number of people have died, and are dying this very day . . . it is not one or two a week or month who are dying, but several people die *each day* from 'flu-like' symptoms just in her hospital alone, when, in fact, no known flu strains are present."[25]

The Atypical Flu Returns and Spreads

The influenza-like pandemic of 1999–2000 was a virtual repeat of the previous year's plague.

One distraught father of a stricken child in Salt Lake City questioned, "*If* this was a virus as they say, then why did it suddenly appear within 24 hours of each time the aircraft flew, and affected so many people at the same time? And *if* this was a virus as they say, then why is it that no one has been able to define what kind of virus it is? When I first took my son to the hospital, it was as if they expected that they would be inundated with sick kids. It almost makes me wonder if they knew what was up before things went down."[26]

A December 3, 1999 letter from a Georgian observer succinctly summarized the worsening situation:

Greetings! I'm reporting to you from Cobb County in the Atlanta, Georgia metro area. We've had *heavy* contrail spraying here this week. This past Thursday, I drove from Atlanta to Nashville. There were heavy chemtrails in X grid patterns, as well as some more circular type patterns all along the way. It was by far the heaviest spraying I've seen this year, and over such an extensive area!

In Dalton, you could actually see it hanging in the air down at the ground level. I have had a sore throat, fatigue and lots of muscle aches and pains since I returned. Also, many of the people I know in Atlanta are also ill with cold type symptoms that just keep lingering.

On the local evening news here in Atlanta (Channel 2—the ABC affiliate) Glen Burns, the meteorologist, showed time-lapse photography of the contrails over Atlanta. All he said was, that we have a lot of jet activity in Atlanta. He actually showed an X pattern over the Atlanta skyline and said, "Would you look at that? It looks like a tic-tac-toe board out there!"[27].

In the week leading up to Christmas 1999, Canadian outbreaks occurred in Vancouver, Edmonton, Calgary, Regina and London, Ontario. Montreal General Hospital had to put 34 of its emergency-room patients on stretchers in the hallway, while the Royal Victoria treated 21 patients in its corridors.

In Toronto, where heavy chemtrail spraying was also observed, 21 of 25 hospitals closed their overcrowded emergency rooms and turned ambulances away. At one point, only two of 25 hospitals were accepting patients. The Hospital for Sick Children saw more than 250 children in its emergency room on a single day, while Peterborough Regional Hospital received a record-breaking 307 patients.[28]

In Saskatchewan, the nurses union told the CBC the medical situation was so serious that the hospital wouldn't have been able to handle a car accident.[29]

Also in the first days of 2000, a woman from Down Under wrote:

I have just returned from a two-day bout in the hospital with pneumonia. Small town, a whopping seven in hospital, five of which had pneumonia, the rest had lung problems of various sorts. Spraying has occurred so we can see it for the past eight weeks nonstop, including at night, even on full moons. The moon turns green in a sea of fluorescent green mist. . . . I'm mad as hell. Sick as a dog, as are my three kids. My local doc is also mad as hell, as he can't do anything about it for fear of losing his license.[30]

Whatever was happening, it was highly unusual. The CDC "Influenza Summary Update" for the week December 12 through December 18, 1999 found that while deaths attributed to pneumonia and influenza were above the epidemic threshold, only "24% of specimens tested by WHO [World Health Organization] and NREVSS [National Respiratory and Enteric Virus Surveillance System] laboratories for influenza were positive."[31]

Elsewhere across the USA, the CDC found "the percentage of specimens testing positive for influenza ranged from 2% to 15%."

In other words, according to this official infectious disease-tracking agency, between 76 and 98 percent of acutely ill patients jamming doctors' offices and emergency rooms *did not have the flu.*[31]

The Millennium Bug was biting people, not computers. On New Year's Day, British hospitals were once again stuffing corpses into trailers. After nearly *40% of elderly victims* died, a spokesman at Conquest Hospital told reporters, "We can't stack bodies up in the corridor."[32]

Back in the USA, the *Wichita Eagle* reported that this year's "virus invades the lungs, killing even healthy people in four or five days."[33]

As Los Angeles staggered under an onslaught of hospital admissions as dire as any biowar scenario, Northridge Hospital nursing supervisor, Silvia Mieure, told reporters, "I don't think anybody really knows what's causing it. Maybe it's a new strain."[34] Maybe it was a chemtrail strain. AP neglected to report skies webbed by criss-crossing spray planes. According to one eyewitness, "Unbelievable chemtrail sprayings" took place December 4th and 5th over Los Angeles and Orange County involving "dozens of trails" laid down from 9:00 A.M. to noon, "until the entire sky was covered."

Bringing Biochemical Warfare Home

These reports, and dozens more like them, were reminiscent of jammed field hospitals in Saudi Arabia following attacks on U.S. Marine positions by SCUD warheads filled with chemical and biological agents. The many first-hand accounts in *Bringing The War Home* told of similar symptoms of exposure.[35] Besides respiratory problems, mental and emotional problems, as well as twitching eyelids characteristic of neurological damage, often followed chemical exposures. Some exposed citizens reported other symptoms including burning semen, lethargy, confusion, dizziness, chills, vision problems, and many other symptoms several investigators have linked to Mycoplasma infections and GWS.

Was a "weaponized" vector of Gulf War Illness spreading among the civilian population?

Professor Colman Salloway, an epidemiologist at the University of New Hampshire, was surprised to learn that his university, like most doctors' offices and clinics across the country, had been treating the "flu" symptomatically. No cultures had been taken to test for the "Type A" Sydney influenza said to be afflicting students.

Prof. Salloway saw that an illness referred to by students nationwide as "the plague" was most likely a Mycoplasma infection. "The symptoms of the Mycoplasma are similar to that of the Type A Sydney; they both cause upper respiratory infection," Dr. Salloway wrote. "The difference between them is that the Mycoplasma leaves a cough that can last up to four weeks. The influenza is a five to seven day disease."[36]

A pet pathogen of bioweaponeers, the tiny Mycoplasma, responsible for transmissible Gulf War illness, also triggers autoimmune dysfunction and sudden severe pneumonia. Few medical laboratories have the specialized equipment needed to test for a pathogen one-tenth the size of normal bacteria.

Though Mycoplasma rarely infects the blood, *Mycoplasma fermentans* was modified for experimental vaccine research by Dr. Shyh-Ching Lo for the Armed Forces Institute of Pathology. The patent, assigned to the American Registry of Pathology, and reprinted in Dr. Horowitz's book *Healing Codes for the Biological Apocalypse*, described the isolation and cloning of a "Pathogenic Mycoplasma" capable of inducing pneumonia, chronic fatigue, respiratory distress, lupus-like illness, as well as the symptoms of AIDS.[37]

Six years later, Mycoplasmas began showing up among victims of Chemtrail-Related Illness (CRI).

By 2000, rates of Mycoplasma infection, particularly pneumonia variants, were rising steeply across the USA. This was no surprise to Dr. Garth Nicolson at the Institute for Molecular Medicine in Irvine, California. The Nobel-nominated microbiologist, and his equally prestigious wife, Nancy, codiscovered modified *Mycoplasma fermentans* as the primary infectious agent linked to GWS.[37]

Since the 1970s, researchers injected U.S. military volunteers with Mycoplasma. Iraqi BW expert Dr. Jawad Al Aubaidi later worked on Mycoplasmas alongside his American counterparts at Plum Island, before returning to Baghdad for the "Mother of All Deceptions" that left at least 200,000 American soldiers stricken with deadly degenerative diseases. Al Aubaidi was murdered in 1995—long after pathogenic Mycoplasma wound up in supposedly "attenuated" anthrax vaccines given to Desert Storm soldiers along with experimental AIDS vaccines.[38]

Dr. Nicolson also discovered how experimental Mycoplasma vaccines given to Huntsville prisoners in the early 1970s resulted in the deaths of at least 42 inmates. Prison workers like Candace Brown became infected and took the Mycoplasma home. Her son got sick, and according to San Antonio's Eyewitness News, in a town of 35,000, nearly 300 people simultaneously "came down with rare neuromuscular diseases"—including CFIDS, MS, lupus, fibromyalgia, cancer, meningitis and Epstein-Barr.[39]

Gulf War veterans and chemtrail victims reported similar symptoms, but CRI did not appear to be contagious. Instead, CRI most often appeared as an acute allergic reaction to something toxic in the chemtrail fallout. People whose immune systems were especially susceptible, or who had been repeatedly "sensitized" by concentrations of chemtrail fallout, seemed to be at greatest risk.

Fungus Among Us

The "myco" in Mycoplasma suggests "fungus." *While there is no evidence that Mycoplasma is present in chemtrails*, the prevalence of chills without fever, a persistent cough, and lingering malaise, strongly suggests a fungal infection.

Botanist Bruce Tanio's list of reported fungal-related symptoms is familiar to many sufferers of CRI: "Depression, anxiety, sudden mood swings, lack of concentration, drowsiness, fatigue, insomnia, poor memory, headaches, light headedness, abdominal pain, gas, bloating, indigestion, heartburn, constipation, diarrhea, and pain of muscles and/or joints."[40]

In late 1999, the *Idaho Observer* published, "Last year, north Idaho naturopaths determined that the upper respiratory infections that would drag on for months were not viral or bacterial but were fungal." In a survey among 179 patients complaining of CRI, Idaho naturopath Dr. Joseph Puleo found that:

- 22% had been to a hospital emergency room
- 34% exhibited rashes and sores
- half or more had experienced disorientation and suffered from stiff neck and gastro-intestinal problems
- 72% had a sore throat
- 78% reported severe headaches
- 81% complained of congestion
- Almost everyone surveyed experienced short-term memory loss and had difficulty in concentrating

A compelling finding was that *fully 99% were found to have fungus in their blood.*[41]

Just as chemtrails have been mistaken for normal contrails, extremely toxic *Stachybotrys* molds responsible for spreading Sick Building Syndrome in warmer wetter climates may have been masking even more dangerous "weaponized" fungi responsible for massive overnight outbreaks of inexplicable illness across the United States, Canada, and other nations.

Dr. Barbara Herskovitz is a researcher specialized in Sick Building Syndrome. Herskovitz pointed out "black" research at Lawrence Livermore and other national laboratories investigating black molds as biowarfare agents. Herskovitz commented:

Even the EPA is being very evasive on this issue. On the conspiracy theory side, there are those who believe that "stachy" and other toxic molds were being tested at labs for defense purposes and "got away" from the researchers; became airborne and ended up contaminating cities. Or *else* [they] were part of an experiment and were sprayed over the city and . . . the rest is history. There is some credence to this theory when you look at how fast these toxins have established a toe-hold in the last decade.[42]

Additionally confusing is the fact that fungal invaders have also predisposed people to secondary bacterial infections. Dr. Puleo reported that "among those with that horrible cough, low fluctuating body temperatures between 95.6–97.6, their conditions encouraged bacterial infections."[41]

All of this lends credence to the theory advanced by Dr. Horowitz in this book concerning the contemporary use of toxic warfare in the "Russian biological cocktail" form.

50 Years of Biowarfare Testing On Americans

Credence tends toward certainty for many following a review of *Congressional Record*s from 1977 and 1994, along with recently declassified British defense documents, that detailed 50 years of "open air" tests that used ships and spray-equipped aircraft to spread biological warfare "simulants" on hundreds of cities across the U.S., Canada and the U.K.

Even as atomic weapons tests were being conducted upwind of U.S. cities to study the effects of fallout on unsuspecting residents, airborne biowarfare tests began in earnest in 1957 and 1958 when a cargo plane criss-crossed the country spraying carcinogenic zinc cadmium sulfide. A U.S. Army report stated, "Virtually, the whole country of the United States was covered with this material." Small particles were chosen, the army said, because it approximated "that which is considered most effective in penetrating into the lungs."[43]

In the United States, such experiments are still allowed under legal loopholes and provisions. Initially, the U.S. Code Title 50, Section 1520, effective through the late 1990s, stated that the Secretary of Defense may conduct tests or experiments "involving the use of a chemical agent or biological agent on a civilian population . . . if related to research activity." But, the revised law stipulated: "Only if informed consent to the testing was obtained from each human subject in advance of the testing on that subject," and corporate contractors paid for the tests, not taxpayers![43, 44]

Low Level Spraying

Evidence is mounting that such biowar tests on North Americans are continuing.

In November, 1998, veteran health researcher Erminia Cassani began investigating a series of rooftop level drops of powder and gel-like material on residences in Ontario and in many areas of the U.S.

Normally taking three or four days to grow in a Petri dish, Cassani's first gel sample from a Michigan suburb spread "all over the plate" within 48 hours. The head of the testing lab had never seen anything grow so quickly. "Where did you get this bio-hazardous material?" she asked Cassani.[44]

The lab found *Pseudomonas fluorescens* bacteria, along with a common "restrictor enzyme" used in biolabs to restrict, or cut, DNA when transferring genetic traits between different microorganisms.[45] In another report,[46] a "day-glo" bacterial marker was also found in gel dropped by a prop-plane flying at roof-top level on what may have been a landing approach to a nearby airfield.

Pseudomonas, Staphylococcus, and Streptomyces fungus predominated in the Michigan samples, and predated widespread outbreaks of "staph" and "strep" infections in that state and nearby Illinois. Other found fungi included the "black mold" Nigrospora, and *Aureobasidium pullans*. Both organisms can lead to a severe upper respiratory infection, even pneumonia.

Similar samples were taken from an aluminum-sided structure in Pennsylvania after a neighbor watched a "huge, dull gunmetal gray, unmarked" plane flying so low it almost hit his barn. Windows shook as the plane—possibly a C-130 Hercules—sprayed several sides of his neighbor's three-story farmhouse with a gel-like substance that, as in Michigan, proved extremely difficult to remove.[47]

When Cassani took the year-old Pennsylvania sample to the same lab, technicians again found Streptomyces and "an overpowering amount" of *Bacillus amyloliquefaciens*. *Turicella otitidis* also turned up, along with Rhizomucor mold.[48]

Then, in March, 1999 residents of the small Ontario town of Espanola began experiencing severe respiratory problems. Strange aches and pains also became endemic over a 50-mile area following what appeared to be deliberate spraying by high-flying U.S. Air Force tankers. Former Ontario Provincial Police Officer Ted Simola reported lingering X's and numerous contrails—some of which "just ended" as if they had been shut off, but remained in the sky.

On November 18, 1999 a petition signed by about 550 Espanola residents was submitted to the Canadian Parliament in Ottawa demanding an end to the aerial spraying. Still the Ministry of Environment insisted that the air was safe to breathe.

But chemtrails were not residents only concern. At nearby Birch Lake on July 18, 1999, a retired couple was sitting on their patio when a huge gray Hercules glided silently over the roof of their home trailing a reddish-brown powder that covered their patio, dock, and neighbor's dock, before coating McGregor Bay.

Erminia Cassani arrived soon afterwards. She learned that the retirees, their neighbors, a nephew who swam in the lake and even their neighbor's dog had all become ill the next day. When tested, Cassani's sticky red blood samples included pathogenic Pseudomonas, Staphylococcus and bacilli similar to the Pennsylvania and Michigan material. The fungi found at Birch Lake also included a primitive mold, as well as Penicillium and Acremonium—"a rather nasty organism," Cassani commented, "found most frequently in AIDS patients."[48]

Erminia Cassani also interviewed officials and eyewitnesses in Utah after 29 rooftop-level flyovers dropped "goo" there, too. A public health statement later identified the material as "sewage" dropped by a pilot "prankster." He was said to have done this "twenty-nine times!"

Cassani said "we have similarly described planes at opposite ends of the country, and at least one instance in Canada, dropping similar substances on residential homes."[48, 49]

In a possibly unrelated story published in the March/April 1997 edition of the *Portland Free Press*, investigative reporter John Titus documented the diversion of an estimated 42 former Navy P-3 Orions and *spray-equipped Air Force C-130's* from fire-fighting duties with the U.S. Forest Service to the CIA. "The C-130 scandal is but the tip of an iceberg," Titus wrote, "with dozens of companies and individuals operating beyond the Forest Service and congressional oversight."

The Air Force Responds

Responding to citizen complaints of high-altitude chemical emissions from aerial tankers, air force pilots explained that they routinely dump fuel to lower landing weights.

This is not good news. Lab test MEL 97-1140 done in September, 1997 on a sample of JP-8 jet fuel by Aqua Tech Environmental Labs in Ohio found 51 toxic petroleum substances, including benzene, carbon tetrachloride, chloromethane, toluene, styrene, and trace amounts of ethylene dibromide (EDB).[49]

Banned in a rare emergency order by the Environmental Protection Agency in 1983, EDB is a potent pesticide. The *Hazardous Chemicals Desk Reference* and the EPA's seven page "hazard summary" both label EDB a "confirmed carcinogen."[50]

Mark Witten, a respiratory physiologist involved in an official U.S. Air Force JP8 study at the University of Arizona, told *Scientist* magazine in March, 1998 that crew chiefs "seem to have more colds, more bronchitis, more chronic coughs than the people not exposed to jet fuel."[51]

While there are no studies nor evidence that show EDB in jet fuel has caused harm to people, chemically sensitive persons exposed to jet fuel fallout from greatly increased aerial activity are experiencing the symptoms Witten described.

Equally suspicious is the wholesale "push" of experimental flu, pneumonia, migraine, and meningitis vaccines in the wake of chemtrail spraying. Callers of special 1-800 "flu-tracking" numbers are told that they must first qualify for these studies by contracting specific symptoms within a specific radius of exposure during a specific time-frame.[52]

A Chemtrail Cull?

Wealthy American family foundations, whose 1930s statewide eugenics program inspired Hitler's pogroms against the gypsies and the Jews, have long targeted the elderly, minorities, the weak and "unfit." Since then, "population control" has become much more sinister than abortions.

Research by Dr. Len Horowitz linked Litton Bionetics, the Merck pharmaceutical company, the U.S., Canadian and British military, and powerful families in the U.S. and Britain with 70 years of research and clandestine testing of nearly undetectable bioweapons capable of culling so-called "human weeds" and "unfit, useless eaters" whose support drains government and corporate coffers.[37]

On January 25-26, 2000, a little-publicized meeting took place at the Center for Strategic and International Studies in Washington, D.C. The high-level gathering confronted the urgent task of "Assessing the Economic, Political, and Strategic Implications of the Simultaneous Aging of the Major Industrial Nations."

President Clinton was invited to give a key address. Other attendees included such aging luminaries as former Vice President Walter Mondale, former Japanese Prime Minister Ryutaro Hashimoto, former National Security Advisor Zbigniew Brzezinski, former Secretary of Defense James Schlesinger, and former Chairman of the U.S. Federal Reserve Paul Volcker.

Big money also showed up in the personages of the chief economist for the Deutsche Bank, the International Monetary Fund, as well as representatives from Barclays, Goldman Sachs, the World Bank, the head of CSIS (Canada's equivalent to the CIA), the Minister of Labor and Social Affairs, Federal Republic of Germany, and the U.S. Secretary of the Treasury.[53]

What did they decide to do about penurious pensioners? Give them pneumonia? While the conclusions of the millennial meeting were not publicized, many chemtrails commentators are convinced that this secret spray program is aimed at eliminating the weak, the sick and the elderly, while jacking up pharmaceutical profits.

Lending support to this theory of Machiavellian practice, by October 30, 2000 CNN reported that flu vaccine prices "have shot up nearly 200% in some areas of the country to as much as $100 a vial."[54]

While there is as yet no conclusive evidence that intensive aerial spraying observed over 14 allied nations is part of a planned depopulation campaign, renewed calls for a cull have come from Earth Summit's Maurice Strong, Ted Turner, Prince Philip, and the late Jacques Cousteau. It is clear that at the very least, mounting fatalities among the elderly does not concern the faceless elite responsible for chemtrails.

An Aerosol Vaccine?

Could widespread aerial spraying be an attempt to inoculate people against a stridently advertised biowarfare threat as some have speculated?

After looking at the evidence, an anonymous medical doctor decided: "Aerial spraying of a vaccine would be exceedingly inefficient. Cost would be prohibitive. This is why I do not think the mass secret immunization theory is plausible."

While not directly related to chemtrails, the leading expert on low-level spraying, Erminia Cassani commented that the organisms contained in the samples she collected "are not viruses and they are not capable of becoming antigens to any viral-based disease."

Nor are bacteria found in her powder and gel samples "of the type and caliber to create any type of bacteriological immunity against such killer attacks as anthrax." Even more telling, these air-dropped materials are also "not of respirable size, i.e. too big to be breathed in by any human pulmonary system."[55]

Dr. Horowitz responded to the benevolent government theory of chemtrail-induced immunity by writing, "It is a stretch for me to speculate that the same military-medical-industrialists that have clearly articulated their desire to reduce half of the earth's present population, would spray periodically for humanity's salvation. Given the preponderance of incriminating evidence, and documented history of non-lethal warfare activities that remain to be reconciled, the heroic vaccination explanation of chemtrails is not tenable."

Casual Observers Decide Weather or Not

Sudden weather changes—including falling temperatures, high winds, and heavy precipitation—often follow where chemtrail grid patterns have been laid out *ahead of approaching fronts.* "Can it be that the contrails reported in the Bakersfield area are related to the 6-inches of snowfall in Bakersfield?" one resident wrote from that desert town. "If not, it's an interesting coincidence."[56]

In the winter of 1998, former Raytheon missile technician Tommy Farmer videotaped heavy chemtrail formations the day before 90 tornadoes struck Tennessee and three adjoining states. Tornadoes are summertime phenomena. This Arkansas correspondent described "heavy spraying" on January 19th and 20th, 1999. "On the 21st, Arkansas had the worst outbreak of tornadoes on record, killing many people. The spraying has continued," he said. "I spent eight years in the military and was around many different kinds of aircraft and I have never seen anything that left contrails such as these."[57]

In Utah that month, nationally syndicated radio talk show host David John Oates and Clyde Lewis—a well-known talkshow host in Salt Lake City, fell ill. Mr. Lewis recalled, "I did not know of the impact of such things until a four-line [chemtrail] grid was made over the Cottonwood, Utah area. Three-line grids were seen three days before. The temperature in Utah was 62° and dropped to 10°; 90 mile-an-hour winds took place and clouds rolled in dropping six-inches of snow." The men then became ill.[58]

A West Virginia resident reported that, "Hospitals are full. Doctors say 'near epidemic,' 'schools [are] closed.' People have 'sinus infections to pneumonia,' blamed on the weather. By the way, the temp here in Charleston today was 75°. Tonight it will go down to 30° with snow this weekend. The planes are still making waves over the skies!"[59]

In Pittsburgh, Kansas, another citizen wrote:

It's incredibly rare that we have a plane come in here. I've lived here for more than 10 years, jets going overhead is a *very* uncommon thing. These jets flew over about three different nights. I've watched the "contrails" myself. I remember thinking how 'different' they seemed, wondering why they just hung there, thinking how much it looked like somebody took a thick paintbrush and drew a couple of lines across the sky. The weather here has been crazy. Literally, during the day walking around with no shoes and a T-shirt. That *very* night, snow, light hail, and ice on the ground. Few days later, comfortable again.[60]

Clouds, Chemtrails and HAARP

Weather modification involving the seeding of existing clouds with silver iodide has been routinely conducted for decades.[61] More recently, the air force admitted to spraying chemicals that *created* clouds. An official air force study, *Weather as A Force Multiplier: Owning The Weather In 2025* described how jet tankers flown by "Weather Force Specialists" were being deployed to spray chemicals that form "cirrus shields."

Visibly similar to the dispersion of chemtrails, experts agreed that such large-scale tinkering with cloud cover could trigger trouble. Acting as a complex planetary thermostat, clouds cool the Earth by reflecting sunlight. Clouds also heat the atmosphere by trapping outgoing heat. As a NASA scientist told the *Rocky Mountain News*, "A small tip in one direction or another can eliminate global warming, or *greatly enhance it*."[62]

Contravening a U.N. agreement not to use the environment as a weapon, the U.S. Air Force admitted it is also upsetting the weather "by adding small amounts of energy at just the right time and space." Previously known as the High Altitude Auroral Research Project, HAARP is operating a transmitter powerful enough to make the "air glow" near Gakon, Alaska. From computer-couples to similar smaller "ionospheric heaters" located in Puerto Rico and other far-flung locales, this joint Navy-Air Force project is "significantly altering" the ionosphere 1,200 miles away.[63]

One aim is to control the weather by bending the jet stream. However, heat transfer at lower altitudes more directly influences local rain and wind. HAARP's intense radio-frequency beam passes right through this region, unless HAARP has a target to heat. This may best explain [El Nino and] the chemtrail phenomena.

Adding iron oxide to the atmosphere, similar to the particles found in chemtrail fallout, allows the sun, or HAARP, to heat the weather-forming troposphere.

Alternately, strands of extremely fine polymers could be sprayed into the upper atmosphere to be heated by HAARP. Wafting slowly earthward in thousands of gossamer strands similar to the "cobweb-like" material drifting down to drape porches, power lines, and police cruisers across the United States, these polymers would tend to disintegrate rapidly from moisture, handling, and abrasion on the ground.

After the Environment News Service advanced this weather modification theory, HAARP's inventor Bernard Eastlund wrote to say that "The experiments described by Thomas seem technically feasible. Recent work on polymeric additives for microwave absorption has been done for commercial curing applications so the polymer fibers are available."[64]

Dr. Nick Begich, author of *Angels Don't Play This HAARP*, and other experts also worry that HAARP's 20 to 30 hertz emissions can trigger changes in brain chemistry. Experiments show that neurochemicals released at these frequencies can alter thoughts and emotions leading to anxiety, inability to concentrate, and depression.[63]

Other studies reviewed by Dr. Horowitz and Dr. Puleo previously,[39] and Dr. Horowitz and Dr. Begich in a later chapter in this book, strongly suggest a negative impact on human immunity from such low-level non-ionizing frequency radiations.[39]

Planetary Emergency

Could a grave global crisis be motive behind such a citizen sickening response as chemtrail sprayings? Might the primary threat be coming from the sun?

When Dr. Edward Teller, a leading climatologist, stood to address an "International Seminar On Planetary Emergencies" in 1998, the Earth's lowest temperatures had just been found to be heating up more than 2° Fahrenheit per century. Parts of Antarctica were warming at *ten times* this global rate. Heatstruck, Adele and Chinstrap penguin colonies were going extinct on the Antarctica Peninsula. There, stunned scientists clad in windbreakers strolled in unprecedented rain showers and marveled at a first-time profusion of wildflowers.[65]

The year before, while the father of the H-bomb was busy co-authoring a paper on reducing global warming through a massive geoengineering effort, warming oceans and the "Super storms" they spawned were already wreaking havoc. The strongest *El Nino* ever recorded saw tropical marlin and mahi-mahi caught off the coast of Washington state, as torrential rains flooded Germany. The first "Category 6" hurricane ever recorded packed sustained winds of 200 mph off the coast of Southeast Asia.[66]

Solar radiation levels were also rising rapidly. U.S. farmers alone were losing more than $3 billion a year to crops damaged by UV light. As an epidemic of sun-induced cataracts swept North America, the EPA sharply revised its estimates of skin cancer deaths from 9,300 to 200,000 over the next 50 years. According to *Earth Island Journal*, insurance losses from extreme weather events hit a record $92 billion—three-times the annual dollar cost of the Vietnam War.

Bigger than big oil and the international trade in arms, insurance corporations are one of the world's largest sources of investment capital. Reeling from catastrophic storm losses up *1,500%* over the previous decade, this powerful lobby pressed Ottawa, Washington, and Whitehall to turn down the heat on global warming. If global warming bankrupts global insurers, they warned, the resulting "domino effect" might wipe out Wall Street and the banks.

Teller's "Sunscreen"

Teller offered an affordable quick fix that would allow petroleum-fueled profits and pollution to continue. Dusting off suggestions from the 1960s, the scientist who had once proposed detonating atomic bombs to carve harbors out of U.S. coastlines now urged countries to spray a protective chemical "sunscreen" into the upper atmosphere.[65]

Computer simulations run by climate modelers Ken Caldeira and Bala Govindasamy at Lawrence Livermore National Laboratory showed that if 1.7% of incoming sunlight was reflected back into space, doubling CO_2 emissions within the next 40 years would result in *no net warming* on 85% of Earth's surface. The chemical cloud cover would also significantly reduce levels of solar radiation reaching the ground.[68]

It could be done. With the Cold War officially over and nearly 700 air-to-air refueling tankers in its active inventory, the U.S. Air Force had the planes and the personnel to conduct a sustained aerial spray campaign.

And it was cheap. The sunscreen models showed that the greenhouse effect could be averted at a spray program price of $1 billion a year—just 1% of the projected cost of cutting carbon emissions back to 1990 levels.

But Caldeira worried that further cooling the stratosphere would form more CFC-collecting ice-clouds, like those already eating continent-size ozone holes over both rapidly melting poles. Teller's stratospheric spray program, Caldeira concluded, "could destroy the ozone layer."[68]

Other influential scientists saw merit in Teller's proposal. Representing consensus among leading climatologists, the International Panel on Climate Change was predicting a heating trend hotter than any seen in the last 10,000 years. As if confirming the location and timing of most chemtrail sightings, the IPCC also reported that much of the current warming is over "the mid-latitude continents in winter and spring."

In late summer, 2000, I obtained a restricted-circulation IPCC draft document intended to advise global policy makers on ways to counter the accelerating effects of atmospheric warming. Completed on May 15, 2000, IPCC-WGIII TAR SOD points in part to Teller's sunscreen to raise this planet's reflective albedo.[69]

According to this IPCC study, spraying *10 million tons* of sun-light-reflecting aerosols "would be sufficient to increase the albedo of the Earth by ~1%. Recent analyses using the CCM3 climate model suggested, however, that a 1.7% decrease in solar luminosity would closely counterbalance a doubling of CO_2 at the regional and seasonal scale."[70]

But the confidential high-level study went on to mention two "key problems:" the unknown consequences of altering atmospheric chemistry, and "the associated whitening of the visual appearance of the sky."

Patenting the Sky

This sunscreen technology already existed. A 1975 U.S. Navy "Contrail Generation Patent" described a "Contrail generation apparatus for producing a powder contrail having maximum radiation scattering ability."[1] (See figure 10.1.)

Intended to produce an easily observed chemical trail behind target drones, the patent noted that the military invention is also suitable "to generate contrails or reflective screens for any desired purpose."

Decades later, environmental consultant Mike Castle discovered another practical spray patent. Assigned to the Hughes Aircraft Company in 1991, "Stratospheric Welsbach Seeding for Reduction of Global Warming" described a patented process for scattering aluminum oxide particles to reflect incoming sunlight.[72] (See figure 10.2.)

Welsbach materials are oxides of metals that also convert heat trapped by greenhouse gases near the Earth's surface into far-infrared wavelengths that radiate back into space. They are especially beneficial if sprayed at night, when the IPCC says "land temperatures have generally increased more than daytime temperatures."

Recognizing that the resulting milky white skies may prove unpopular, the Hughes patent nevertheless suggested that these very tiny aluminum flakes could be added to the fuel of jet airliners, so that the particles would be emitted from the jet engine exhaust while the airliner was at its cruising altitude. This alone could explain the chemtrail phenomenon.[72] (See figure 10.3.)

The patent stated:

A desired material for the stratospheric seeding has a reflection coefficient close to unity for near IR radiation, and a reflection coefficient close to zero (or emissity close to unity) for far IR radiation. . . .

Fig. 10.1. U. S. Patent Assigned to the U.S. Navy for "Light Scattering Pigment Powder Particles for Maximum Radiation Scattering."

Inventor(s): Werle; Donald K. , Hillside, IL
Kasparas; Romas , Riverside, IL
Katz; Sidney , Chicago, IL
Applicant(s): The United States of America as represented by the Secretary of the Navy, Washington, DC
Issued/Filed Dates: Aug. 12, 1975 / July 22, 1974
Application Number: US1974000490610

—

July 22, 1974 AE Application data

Abstract–
Light scattering pigment powder particles, surface treated to minimize inparticle cohesive forces, are dispensed from a jet mill deagglomerator as separate single particles to produce a powder contrail having maximum visibility or radiation scattering ability for a given weight material.

Attorney, Agent, or Firm: Sciascia; Richard S.; St. Amand et al.

Title US1619183* 3 /1927 Bradner et al. US2045865* 6 /1936 Morey US2591988* 4 /1952 Willcox US3531310 9 /1970 Goodspeed et al. **PRODUCTION OF IMPROVED METAL OXIDE PIGMENT** USR0015771* 2 /1924 Savage

CLAIMS:

1. Contrail generation apparatus for producing a powder contrail having maximum radiation scattering ability for a given weight material, comprising:

   a. an aerodynamic housing;

   b. a jet tube means passing through said housing, said tube means having an inlet at a forward end of said housing and an exhaust at a rearward end thereof;

   c. a powder storage means in said housing;

   d. a deagglomeration means also in said housing;

   e. means connecting said powder storage means with said deagglomeration means for feeding radiation scattering powder from said powder storage means to said deagglomeration means;

   f. the output of said deagglomeration means dispensing directly into said jet tube means for exhausting deagglomerated powder particles into the atmosphere to form a contrail; and

   h. means for controlling the flow of said powder from said storage means to said deagglomeration means. . . .

Fig. 10.2. U. S. Patent Assigned to Hughes Aircraft Co. for Atmospheric Spraying with Aluminum Oxide (Al₂O₃) For Allegedly Reducing Global Warming Through "Seeding"

United States Patent [19]

Chang et al.

[11] **Patent Number:** **5,003,186**

[45] **Date of Patent:** Mar. 26, 1991

[54] STRATOSPHERIC WELSBACH SEEDING FOR REDUCTION OF GLOBAL WARMING

[75] Inventors: David B. Chang, Tustin; I-Fu Shih, Los Alamitos, both of Calif.

[73] Assignee: Hughes Aircraft Company, Los Angeles, Calif.

[21] Appl. No.: 513,145

[22] Filed: Apr. 23, 1990

[51] Int. Cl.⁵ G21K 1/00

[52] U.S. Cl. .... 250/505.1; 250/504 R; 250/503.1; 244/158 R

[58] Field of Search .... 250/505.1, 504 R, 503.1, 250/493.1; 244/136, 158 R

[56] References Cited

U.S. PATENT DOCUMENTS

3,222,675 12/1965 Schwartz 244/158
4,755,673 7/1988 Pollack et al. 250/330

Primary Examiner—Jack I. Berman
Attorney, Agent, or Firm—Michael W. Sales; Wanda Denson-Low

[57] ABSTRACT

A method is described for reducing atmospheric or global warming resulting from the presence of heat-trapping gases in the atmosphere, i.e., from the greenhouse effect. Such gases are relatively transparent to sunshine, but absorb strongly the long-wavelength infrared radiation released by the earth. The method incudes the step of seeding the layer of heat-trapping gases in the atmosphere with particles of materials characterized by wavelength-dependent emissivity. Such materials include Welsbach materials and the oxides of metals which have high emissivity (and thus low reflectivities) in the visible and 8–12 micron infrared wavelength regions.

18 Claims, 2 Drawing Sheets

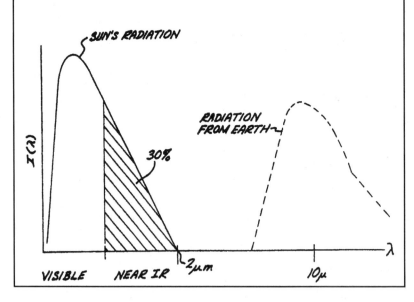

Another class of materials having the desired property includes the oxides of metals. For example, *aluminum oxide (Al$_2$O$_3$) is one metal oxide suitable for the purpose* and which is relatively inexpensive. . . . This suggests that the particle seeding should be done at an altitutude on the order of 10 kilometers. *The particles may be seeded by dispersal from seeding aircraft; one exemplary technique may be via the jet fuel as suggested by prior work regarding the metallic particles.* Once the tiny particles have been dispersed into the atmosphere, the particles may remain in suspension for up to one year. . . . The method of claim 1 wherein said material comprises aluminum oxide. . . .[73] [Emphasis added.]

Aluminum oxide can withstand temperatures far higher than jet engine exhausts. While highly abrasive in larger sizes, a former engineer for Alcoa aluminum explained that aluminum in the 10 to 100 micron size range called for in the sunscreen patent would simply polish jet turbine blades without harming them. The engineer added that this "very fine, talcum-like" aluminum powder would appear as a *"pure white plume"* in the sky.[73]

Proof that sunscreen studies by Edward Teller, the Lawrence Livermore Lab, and the IPCC might already be ongoing came in the summer of 1999 when the rainwater samples collected after heavy chemtrail spraying over Espanola were analyzed by an Ontario laboratory. In addition to small amounts of mica and quartz used by the U.S. Air Force in weather modification, the lab tests turned up *aluminum* at 7- times government-permissible safe levels.[74] Not 2,000 times above normal seawater aluminum levels reported in the previous chapter by William Winkler, but suspicious enough to warrant special consideration.

The Neurotoxicity and Infectivity of Aluminum

Aluminum is a neurotoxin capable of dulling concentration and reasoning ability. By blocking nerve impulses from being properly conducted to and from the brain, dizziness, memory loss, impaired coordination, involuntary tremors, speech disorders, and a loss of balance and energy can result.[75]

Linked to Alzheimer's and osteoporosis, ingesting aluminum can also cause gastro-intestinal problems, weak and aching muscles, headaches, lethargy, fatigue and flu-like symptoms that leave the body vulnerable to opportunistic infections—including Mycoplasma.

Fig. 10.3. Chemtrail Photographs Showing Persistent Milky White Cloud Formations Over Atlanta, GA and Indianapolis, IN

Atlanta (2000) above and Indianapolis (1999) below. Two previous blue skies are partly to completely obscured by persistent chem-clouds formed from jet emissions. Chevron, a Rockefeller company, is the chief producer of jet fuel supplied to the aviation industry.   Photos courtesy of William Thomas, 2001

What about the fungal and possible viral components of chemtrail contamination? If not deliberately introduced into a climate modification program, could malevolent microorganisms be piggybacking on the plumes?

A series of balloon flights made high above the U.S. during the 1960s collected stratospheric samples that surprisingly swarmed with live bacteria and fungi, as well as viruses bigger than any known at the time.[76]

Far from being deterred by lack of oxygen, frigid cold, and intense radiation, fungal spores can survive in space. In October 2000, the *Boston Globe* reported that "especially aggressive" forms of Aspergillus, Penicillium and Cadesporium infested the aging Russian space station. Possibly mutated by solar radiation, the ferocious fungi were overgrowing a musty, moldy Mir.[77]

Since chemtrails are spread over populated areas where sun shading is most needed, it is reasonable to conclude that these aluminum-laden plumes are bringing down sky-dwelling viruses, fungi and bacteria into human respiratory systems unable to recognize or resist these mutant alien invaders.

Dr. Robert Folk, a Geology Professor Emeritus at the University of Texas, strengthened this possibility. He discovered even smaller nannobacteria, "possibly an order of magnitude more abundant than normal bacteria."[78]

Folk chose a lightweight metal as a matrix to grow bugs too small to be seen by optical microscopes. Viewed under electronic magnification, Folk found many diverse kinds of swarming nannobacteria. The bacteria were feasting (he called it "metabolizing") on . . . *aluminum*!

Follow the Conductor

What happens when megatons of conductive chemicals and metals are added to the atmosphere? With cell phone and microwave towers, radio and television transmitters, power lines, orbiting radars, and a silent cacophony of other electrical emitters producing invisible "smog" shown to disrupt brain and body cells, chemtrails could be inadvertently conducting these electromagnetic energies into antennas called human beings.

In early October 2000, on what one resident described as "a rare cloudless north central Florida day," his father-in-law complained that his ball game on the Dish Satellite TV had just winked out. He walked outside "expecting to see a big thunderhead in the signal path." Much to his surprise, "the sky was perfectly clear - except for one greatly expanded airplane trail right in the signal path. It was blocking about 50% the blue sky behind it. In a few minutes the prevailing winds moved it out of the signal path and the satellite TV system resumed working."

This signal-savvy sleuth suggested that if it is "correct about aluminum being sprayed into the atmosphere, this would be one way to detect it. There are a lot of small satellite dishes in use. I was really quite surprised that a white trail in the sky could reduce the satellite signal that much," he said.[79]

Who or What is the Target?

Could copiously applied climate modification chemistry be an unintended form of chemical-biological attack, or are chemtrails being aimed directly at people?

U.S. Gulf War veterans know the signs of chemical–biological exposure. In July, 2000, one marine who survived the sickening Scuds wrote to friends concerning chemtrails. "Keep me posted on this, my mother is very ill in the hospital with bacterial pneumonia and atrial fibrillation. This occurred 48 hours after chemtrail spraying. She was fine before and perfectly healthy, and now she is coughing up blood. What the hell is this? What the hell have these bastards done now?"[80]

After a Toronto music promoter noted the prevalence of spray planes over outdoor concerts, CACTUS (Citizens Against Chemtrails U.S.) organizer Kim Weber reported from Ohio on Oct. 14, 2000, that large gatherings appear to be attracting spray planes. She wrote:

> It started bright and early. By 9:30 a.m., as folks started coming into town for the home football game at OSU and the morning parade down High Street, it was quite obvious that *people*, yes, *people* were the target. TV sports news even showed heavy chemtrails right over the freaking stadium. We also had military jets fly over. By mid-afternoon, the sky was milky opaque and smelled to high heaven. We stayed indoors.[81]

Thus, in response to the questions posed four paragraphs above, the answer is likely a little of both.

Chemtrail Non-lethality for Global Depopulation

As mentioned, chemtrail exposures are associated with flu-like, toxic metal and fungal-type symptoms. As chemtrail sprayings continue, year-round "flu," headaches, allergies, and lethargy are increasingly seen as "normal" in the U.S. and other countries. At the same time public health officials are warning of an imminent global influenza pandemic with catastrophic mortality and morbidity.[23, 33]

Masked by public acceptance of the flu as a perennial nuisance, particularly for the immune compromised, influenza's extremely contagious nature, debilitating symptoms, and propensity to kill the weak, provides the ideal cover for chemtrail-linked toxic warfare. Unfortunately, besides the information provided above, there is even more evidence supporting this theoretic nightmare.[82]

For instance, in 1970, immediately after National Security Adviser Henry Kissinger called for drastic Third World depopulation, which sparked secret congressional subsidies into a new generation of bioweapons that Litton Bionetics engineered, one contract called for the testing of special *strains of "influenza" and "Para influenza" viruses.* As reported by Dr. Horowitz in *Emerging Viruses: AIDS & Ebola— Nature, Accident or Intentional?*, these flu viruses were recombined with leukemia viruses for its only rational use—population reduction. Much like the AIDS virus, these new strains could be more rapidly spread to cause slow, non-traceable genocide.[85]

On December 29, 1999, the *London Sunday Times* warned readers that the WHO had called on every country to prepare for a pandemic similar to the Spanish Flu that swept the world in 1919, killing 40 million people. Whitehall worried that one in four people could be infected by this "lethal strain of flu" which had yet to be identified.[83]

The CDC, however, told a different story in its "1999-2000 Influenza Season Summary." The "disease cowboys" wondered if the year's "higher-than-expected percentage" of pneumonia and influenza deaths was really due to influenza activity, new reporting techniques, or *"respiratory illness"* due to some other factor.[84]

Will Thomas is a veteran investigative journalist and author of *Scorched Earth, Bringing The War Home,* and *Probing The Chemtrail Conundrum.* Published in eight countries, with translations into French, Dutch and Japanese, Mr. Thomas's feature articles have won four Canadian writing awards. His Gulf War documentary, "Eco War," won the 1991 U.S. Environmental Film Festival's "Best Documentary Short."

William Thomas's documentary, "Chemtrails: Mystery Lines In The Sky" was being released at the time of this writing.

Additional information regarding Mr. Thomas's background and writings can be accessed through his website: http://www.islandnet.com/wilco.

[Editor's note: This chapter regarding the chemtrail phenomenon was based largely on personal communications with the author as detailed in the following reference section. Readers will note the extensive reliance on personal communications relaying much empirical data—observations and testimonies which, though numerous enough to sound an alarm, do not scientifically substantiate the theories of cause and effect advanced herein.

Mr. Thomas's chapter, potentially relevant to the subject of non-lethal warfare, was commissioned by Dr. Horowitz with the hope that this contribution might provoke more serious scientific study from which more reliable and definitive conclusions regarding these data might evolve.]

References

1) Runyan C. Jets linked to global warming.*The Worldwatch Report,* September 30, 1998.

2) Personal communication from Clifford Carnicom. See also "Chemtrail Message Board" 6/27/00 at www.carnicom.com; see also: http://techreports.larc.nasa.gov/ltrs/refer/1997/NASA-97-rp1404.refer.html

3) See: http://asd-www.larc.nasa.gov/SCOOL/contrails.html; see also: www.mmm.ucar.edu/asr97/science_high.html; and see also: www.carnicom.com

4) CDC staff. CDC 1999-2000 *Influenza Season Summary - Pneumonia and Influenza Mortality.* Atlanta: Centers for Disease Control and Prevention. Available from http://www.cdc.gov/ncidod/diseases/flu/weekly.htm; see also: CDC. Influenza Vaccination Update. *Clinician Reviews* 9(8):101-102, 1999; and see also: www.medscape.com/13583.rhtml.

5) Burcum J. Minnesota *Star Tribune,* Feb. 23, 1999.

6) Personal communication from Kim Korte, RN, December 20, 1998.

7) Personal communication from anonymous e-mail sender that read: "January typically is a busy month for all hospitals because respiratory ailments increase and people come in for elective surgery that they have postponed until after the holidays. But in Raleigh, North Carolina *The News and Observer* reported that in early January, 1999, the number of patients at Durham regional hospital jumped from 184 patients a day to 247. On January 5, the hospital's Emergency Services broadcast a message to ambulance drivers that the hospital was not receiving any more patients."

8) Personal communication from anonymous e-mail sender that read: "On January 7, 1998, the *Philadelphia Daily News* reported that: Emergency room patients overflowed into the hallways at West Jersey Hospital in Berlin, New Jersey yesterday "as a wave of respiratory illnesses swept the area." The Emergency Room at the University of Pennsylvania - up 25% since Christmas - largely due to respiratory illness. The Children's hospital reports patient occupancy is 89% - compared with an average 76% - mostly pneumonia, bronchial problems, and asthma. Seven to 10 hospitals a day over the past few days have asked fire rescue to divert patients to other institutions. Dr. Herbert Patrick of Thomas Jefferson University. "We know what its not. But we don't know what it is or where it came from," said Patrick, an expert on respiratory illnesses."

9) Rushlo M. Flu Cases Flood Emergency Rooms. Associated Press, December 29, 1999.

10) Personal communication from Kathy Armstrong, Jan 26, 1999.

11) Personal communication from Mike Burns, Jan. 29, 1888.

12) Personal communication from Steve Faulk, Feb. 1, 1999

13) Personal communication from "John," entry not dated.

14) Personal communication from "BJ," entry not dated.

15) Channel 4000 News, St. Paul, Minnesota, December 16,1999; See: http://www.Channel4000.com/health/storieshealth-stories-19991216-174956.html

16) Personal communication from Art Bentley, Feb. 2, 1999

17) Personal communication from Tony Banderaz, entry not dated.

18) Personal communication from Richard Ayliffe, February 2, 1999.

19) Personal communication from Nancy Court, entry not dated.

20) BBC staff/ Flu kills thousands. Print News, January 14, 1999; See: http://news.bbc.co.uk/hi/english/health/newsid%5F255000/255244.stm

21) *Ibid.*

22) Personal communication from Victoria Bay, Jan. 16, 1999.

23) CDC staff. Influenza Summary Update for the week ending February 12, 2000, Atlanta: Centers for Disease Control and Prevention; available at http://www.cdc.gov/ncidod/diseases/flu/weekly.htm

24) Quinn K. article in the *Star-Gazette* Elmira, NY, March 12, 1999.

25) Personal communication from "Nicholis," entry not dated.

26) Personal communication from Janine T Gardner, entry not dated.

27) *Ibid.*

28) Thomas, W. *Probing The Chemtrail Conundrum.* Gabriola Island, BC: Essence Publications, 1999.

29) Personal communication from Lauren Reed, December 5, 1999.

30) Foss K. Hospitals reeling from flu onslaught and influenza outbreaks occurring up to six weeks earlier than expected in cities across Canada. *Ottawa Citizen,* December 29, 1999; see also: Cherney E. Flu victims crowd nation's hospitals. *The National Post,* December 28, 1999, available at: http://www.nationalpost.com/news.asp?f=991228/161819&s2=national

31) CBC Radio News, Dec. 29, 1999; available at: http://cbc.ca/cgi-bin/templates/NWview.cgi?/news/1999/12/29/canflu991229

32) Open Letter To Janelle Bankroft Senior Environmental Health Officer, Byron Shire Council, from Gary Opit, Environmental Consultant, Aug. 2, 2000.

33) CDC staff. Influenza Summary Update for the week December 12 through December 18. Atlanta: Centers for Disease Control and Prevention. Available at: www.cdc.gov/ncidod/diseases/flu/weekly.htm

34) Hall E. More flu-hit hospitals are forced to use lorries as morgues. *The London Telegraph,* Volume 1688, January 8, 2000. Available at: http://www.telegraph.co.uk/et?ac=001851641145319&rtmo=r3hE93tX&atmo=gggggggK

35) Shideler K. Kansas flu is deadliest in years. *The Wichita Eagle.* February 10, 2000. Available at: http://www.wichitaeagle.com/news/health/docs/fludeaths0209_txt.htm

36) Staff reporter. Virulent flu strain taxing Southern California hospitals. Associated Press, December 18, 1999.

37) Thomas, W. *Bringing The War Home.* Gabriola Island, BC: Earth Pulse Press 1998; see also: Horowitz and Puleo, *Op cit.,* 1999.

38) U. New Hampshire. University Wire. February, 16 1999.

39) Horowitz L and Puleo J. *Healing Codes For The Biological Apocalypse.* Sandpoint, ID: Tetrahedron Publishing Group, 1999, p.267.

40) Thomas, *Op cit.* 1999, p.283; see also: Horowitz and Puleo, *Op cit.,* 1999.

41) Personal communication from Patty Doyle, Oct. 25, 2000; see also: Scott D. The Linking Pathogen in Neuro-Systemic Diseases, Chronic Fatigue, Alzheimer, Parkinson's, & Multiple Sclerosis. *Journal of Degenrative Diseases,* Aug. 6th, 2000; see also: Hylak G. Sophisticated Bio-Technology, Military Operations, Diminished Accountability, And The Adulterated Stream Of Medical Information; A Criminal And Unholy Design Where Mycoplasma Meets The Public Health? Health Law Hilary Term, Thomas M. Cooley Law School, 1998.

42) News staff. KENS 5 Eyewitness News. SanAntonio, Nov. 2, 2000; see also: www.immed.org/illness/autoimmune_illness_research.html

43) Thomas *Op cit.,* 1999; see also: AIDS Treatment Data Network website at: http://www.aidsinfonyc.org/network/simple/fungal.html

44) *Ibid.;* For Erminia Cassani's material go to: http://www.moonbowmedia.com/ei/goo.htm

45) Personal communication from Barbara Herskovitz. November 27, 1999.

46) *St. Louis Post-Disptach* July 14, 1994.

47) Horowitz and Puleo, *Op cit.,* 1999.

48) Aqua Tech Environmental Labs, Melmore, OH 44843-9990, Lab number MEL 97-1140; Date submitted 9/17/97; Report Approved by Wado E. Bayer; Sample ID: Jet Fuel; Found 51 toxic substances related to fuel - including: Benzene, Carbon Tetrachloride, Chloromethane, Dichloromethane, Dichlorodiflouromethane, 1,1 and 1,2 Dichloroehtane, Ethylbenze, Styrene, Toluene, and 1,2 Dibromethane (EDB).

49) Lewis, R. J. Sr. *Hazardous Chemicals Desk Reference* Second edition, 1991; see also: Foster H. Mishandling Of Pesticide Contamination Called "Government At Its Worst." *Seattle Post-Intelligencer,* March 22, 1999.

50) *Scientist* March, 1998

51) Redden J. The Satanic Nazi Flu Conspiracy. An interview with Dr. Len Horowitz. *The Konformist*, April 8, 2000.

52) Center for Strategic and International Studies. Conference on "Assessing the Economic, Political, and Strategic Implications of the Simultaneous Aging of the Major Industrial Nations," Washington, D.C., January 25-26, 2000.

53) Cohen E. Flu Vaccine Costs Climb To Nearly $100 A Vial, CNN Headline News, October 30, 2000.

54) Personal communication from "JK." Entry dated only 1999.

55) Personal communication from Tommy Farmer dated January, 1999.

56) Personal communication from Clyde Lewis, EarthBroadcasting reporter/ Ground Zero host. Entry not dated.

57) Personal communication from "Roxie," dated February 11, 1999.

58) Personal communication from "Steph," entry not dated.

59) Freyman R. Kansas Counties Oppose Fooling Mother Nature, *Governing Magazine,* October, 1999.

60) Col Tamzy J. House, Lt Col James B. Near, Jr., LTC William B. Shields, Maj Ronald J. Celentano, Maj David M. Husband, Maj Ann E. Mercer, Maj James E. Pugh U.S. Air Force. *USAF 2025 - Weather As A Force Multiplier: Owning The Weather,* August 1996. Available at: www.au.af.mil/au/2025/ contact.htmAir Force 2025.

61) Scanlon B. CSU Will Lead Nasa Cloud Study $145 Million Project Is Designed To Improve Weather Forecasts, Study Global Warming. *Rocky Mountain News,* December 30, 1998, p. 5A.

62) U.S. Air Force Geophysics Laboratory and the Office of Naval Research. Plans and Activities Report: RFP N00014-91-R-0001, February, 1990.

63) Thomas, *Op cit.,* 1999; based on personal communication from Bernard Eastlund, January, 1999; see also: Manning J and Begich N. *Angels Don't Play This HAARP: Advancers in Tesla Technology.* Anchorage, AK: Earthpulse Press (P.O. Box 201393, Anchorage, AK 99520), 1995.

64) Burke N. New Non-Lethal Weapons Systems May Be Used Against U.S. Citizens. An interview of Dr. Nick Begich, M.D; see also: http:// www.leadingedgenews.com/Nonlethalwarfare.htm,and see also: http://www.earthpulse.com/haarp/index.html

65) Staff reporter. Penguin data in the Antarctic reveal serious reductions in numbers. *Los Angeles Times*, September 4, 1997.

66) Staff reporter. *The New York Times*, September 9, 1997.

67) Staff reporter. *Fortune,* September, 1997.

68) Staff reporter. Project Chariot: Alaskan Roots of Environmentalism. *Alaska History Magazine* Vol. 4, No. 2, Fall, 1989; see also: www.bullatomsci.org/issues/2000/mj00/mj00perkovich.html; and see also Vandergraft DL. Project Chariot: Nuclear Legacy of Cape Thompson. Anchorage, Alaska: Cartographic Unit, Division of Realty U.S. Fish & Wildlife Service.

69) Jones N. Office Fights Over The Air Conditioning May Pale In Comparison To Global Bickering Over A Dimmer Switch On The Sun. *New Scientist,* September 23, 2000; see also: Staff reporter. The Planet Needs a Sunscreen. *The Wall Street Journal,* October 17, 1997.

70) Roberts G. Jr. Tinkering with global climate very risky, says researcher. *The Hayward Daily Review,* December 19, 1999; ee also http://www.agu.org/cgi-bin/waisgate?WAISdocID=407311789+20+0+0.

71) Kauppi P, Sedio R, Apps M and Cerri C *et al.* Reservoirs and Geo-Engineering: Chapter 4. In: *GOVERNMENT / EXPERT REVIEW IPCC-WGIII TAR SOD,* May 15, 2000.

72) Contrail Generation Apparatus For Producing A Powder Contrail Having Maximum Radiation Scattering Ability. Inventor(s): Werle; Donald K., Kasparas; Romas , Katz; Sidney, Issued/Filed Dates: Aug. 12, 1975 / July 22, 1974 Application Number: US1974000490610

73) U.S. Patent #5003186US1990000513145 Filed: March 26, 1991 / April 23, 1990. Stratospheric Welsbach Seeding For Reduction Of Global Warming. Inventors: Chang; David B. , Tustin, CA Shih; I-Fu , Los Alamitos, CA. Hughes Aircraft Company. See: http://www.patents.ibm.com/details?pn= US05003186__

74) Personal communication from Ben McNenly, June 26, 2000.

75) Balch J. and Balch P. *Prescription For Nutritional Healing,* pg.122.

76) Hoyle F. *The Intelligent Universe: A New View of Creation and Evolution* London: Michael Joseph Limited, 1983, p 100.

77) Karash Y. Space Fungus: A Menace to Orbital Habitats. Moscow: Space.com, July 27, 2000. See: www.space.com/news/spacestation/space_fungus_000727.html

78) Folk R. Nanobacteria: Surely Not Figments, But What Under Heaven Are They? Department of Geological Sciences, University of Texas, Austin, Texas 78712, March 4, 1997.

79) Personal communication from Charles Shumate, October 17, 2000.

80) Personal communication from Kim Weber, CACTUS organizer, Oct. 14, 2000.

82) Personal communication from "Laurie," Oct. 22, 2000.

83) Personal communication from Annette M. Patterson, RMT, November, 29, 2000. See also: www.wellbeinginst.com/curiousthings.htm

84) Open Letter To Janelle Bankroft Senior Environmental Health Officer Byron Shire Council from Gary Opit Environmental Consultant, August 2, 2000.

85) Horowitz L and Martin WJ. *Emerging Viruses: AIDS and Ebola—Nature, Accident or Intentional.* Rockport: MA: Tetrahedron Publishing Group 1999, pp. 62 and 166.

86) The *London Sunday Times,* December 29, 1999.

87) Borenstein S. Scientists Fear Flu Pandemic Could Strike At Any Time. Knight Ridder News Service, September 14, 2000; see also: Staff reporter. Survive Y2K, and Another Bug May Get You. *The National Journal,* November 13, 1999.

88) CDC staff. Influenza Summary Update for the week ending May 20, 2000. Atlanta: Centers for Disease Control and Prevention; see also, Thomas, Op cit., 1999.

Chapter 11.
Higher Forms of Killing:
"Non-lethal" Warfare

"To date, the United States has been trapped between classic diplomatic table-thumping and indiscriminate economic sanctions on the one hand, and major military intervention on the other hand. But a new and effective middle option may emerge in the future, . . . This potential new option could come in the form of nonlethal warfare.

"This report recommends that the Clinton administration . . . pushes ahead on these fronts, and the Defense Department engages in a much more serious and systematic evaluation process . . . to determine just how useful nonlethal weapons might be and set policy accordingly."

Richard L Garwin, 2000
Independent Task Force Report
Council on Foreign Relations

At the U.S. Government's top-secret Los Alamos Laboratory in New Mexico, in 1991, a U.S. Global Strategy Council (USGSC) think tank met to pioneer a new future for "global conflict" short of war. The Research Director of the USGSC, Janet Morris, and the council's chairman, Ray Cline, former Deputy Director of the CIA, forged the creation of a Non-lethality Policy Review Group, led by Major General Chris S. Adams. Adams, retired from the United States Air Force (USAF), and former Chief of Staff of the Strategic Air Command, led the group in establishing guidelines to help military commanders to think in terms of "non-lethality," rather than employing traditional lethal forces.[1]

Following these preliminary meetings, as I explained in *Healing Codes for the Biological Apocalypse*,[2] Janet Morris issued several papers promoting the concept of "non-lethal warfare." She and her associates advanced certain key areas of military preparedness research. "These included technologies directed at the destruction of weapons of war, but also an increased focus on antipersonnel electromagnetics."[1]

Electromagnetic military technologies, based on the pioneering work of Nicola Tesla, had proven profoundly effective in altering human behavior and metabolism, including neuroendocrine systems and related immunological functions. In other words, Morris, *et al.,* recommended a "Star Wars"-type population control project for America.[2]

The U.S. Army War College's Strategic Studies Institute (SSI) in Pennsylvania soon advanced parallel recommendations. A 1994 paper originating there entitled, "The Revolution in Military Affairs [RMA] and Conflict Short of War," argued that many "American strategic thinkers believe that we are in the beginning stages of a historical revolution in military affairs." The changes were destined to affect not only "the nature of warfare," but also the "global geopolitical balance." Accordingly, the RMA included, according to investigative journalist Jim Keith, "a number of new avenues of warfare research that should be pursued, specifically 'behavior modification' and 'technology designed specifically for conflict short of war, especially psychological, biological, and defensive technology.'" It was also determined that psychological warfare employing various methods of propaganda, "public research" included, would be necessary to successfully conduct non-lethal warfare and achieve its objectives.[1]

This chapter addresses these political and military realities, namely, the combined use of biological, chemical and electromagnetic weapons of mass destruction for "non-lethal warfare."

Promoting Non-lethality for Law Enforcement

Medical doctor Nick Begich, whose publication *Angels Don't Play This HAARP,* which exposed Alaska's project HAARP, and gained him international recognition, examined non-lethal policy recommendations by the U.S. Air Force. The recommendations, he read, gave highest priority to the development of "technologies most likely to get dual use, i.e., law enforcement and military applications." According to the military, non-lethal weapons were to be used on both foreign *and* domestic "adversaries."[4]

The definition of "adversary" had been "significantly enlarged in the policy," Dr. Begich reported. The term "adversary" was used "in its broadest sense, including those who are not declared enemies but who are engaged in activities" authorities wish to stop. According to the Defense Department draft, this policy did "not preclude legally authorized domestic use of the non-lethal weapons by United States military forces in support of law enforcement."

Consequently, Dr. Begich questioned, "Who are the enemies that are engaged in activities that government authorities wish to stop? What are those activities, and who will make the decisions to stop these activities? An important aspect of non-lethal weapon systems is that the name non-lethal is intentionally misleading. The policy added, 'It is important that the public understand that just as lethal weapons do not achieve perfect lethality, neither will non-lethal weapons always be capable of precluding fatalities and undesired collateral damage.' In other words," Dr. Begich clarified, "you might still destroy property and kill people with these new weapons. . . . In Orwellian double speak; what is non-lethal can be lethal."[4]

In fact, the extent to which non-lethal weapons have advanced in recent years in domestic law enforcement is enlightening. In 1997, for instance, following a six month national trial, the British Metropolitan Police began using a toxic chemical spray known as "the CS aerosol incapacitant. This became a tactical option for police officers." In a report circulated over the Internet by Nicholas Mackay, a Police Constable for the Metropolitan Police Firearms Unit in England, the "CS irritant" was described as "a less than lethal device or weapon, which in essence can be defined as having the potential ability of incapacitating a subject with a reduced likelihood of long term injury or fatality."

Constable Mackay acknowledged the development of "a vast array of chemical and other non-lethal devices offered on the world-wide market and used by various police and law enforcement agencies around the world." Unfortunately, an air of secrecy surrounded this subject, which the British police officer likened to "a turning point in the whole concept of officer safety and the dawn of a new debate."

Mr. Mackay, whose wife had fallen victim to a violent crime, argued for continued research, development, and implementation of such non-lethal technologies in law enforcement and crowd control because, as he put it, "current non-lethal alternatives are not only ineffective but also detrimental to the safety of the officers concerned."

He cited, for example, "cross contamination" as one drawback of non-lethal chemical weapons. "Any use of CS irritant in a confined area without the use of protective respirators," Mr. MacKay wrote, "will lead to a high degree of officer contamination and jeopardize further officer safety."

Despite such risks, he argued, the new non-lethal technologies may serve as adjuncts to traditional defense and law enforcement applications including firearms, batons, and shields. "Ideally," he wrote, they would be "suitable for dealing with violent berserk suspects, perhaps intoxicated, possibly armed with offensive weapons, both in premises and outdoors."

In conclusion, Constable Mackay wrote, "Non-lethal devices should not be seen to be replacing in any way the use of justifiable lethal force. They should be seen to be bridging the current gap in our tactical response when dealing with violent scenarios."[3]

CIA Projects MKNAOMI and MKULTRA

As detailed in the next chapter,[2,4,5] the CIA's top secret project MKULTRA provided the methods and materials to insidiously conduct non-lethal warfare, particularly against unwitting civilian populations, fully integrating biological, chemical, as well as electromagnetic capabilities, and cloaked by counterintelligence propaganda.

In fact, the entire American biological warfare effort, code-named project MKNAOMI, was, in fact, a subordinate part of the CIA's "Program of Research in Behavioral Modification," that is, PROJECT: MKULTRA. In other words, as evidenced in figure 11.1, by the early 1950s the CIA administered a project to develop and test biological agents that would, "under operational conditions," precisely affect aspects of human behavior—thinking, feeling, and acting. The purpose was to render targeted populations helpless and susceptible to attack, manipulation, and even complete control.[6]

Thus, primary emphasis of MKULTRA was on *controlling human behavior* and populations, and the principle methods used to accomplish this were biological and radiological. The radiological methods included the use of electromagnetic frequencies deployed to affect individuals and large populations. The biological materials included bacteria, viruses, and fungi. As documented in *Healing Codes for the Biological Apocalypse,* Mycoplasma, yeast, and other fungi were researched, developed, and even transmitted to infect, affect and even kill plants, animals, and humans. This was clearly inferred when the Senate Select Committee on Intelligence reported that in addition to the CIA's interest in biological weapons for use against humans, it also asked the Special Operations Division (SOD) at Fort Detrick, Maryland "to assist CIA in developing, testing, and maintaining biological

Fig. 11.1. *Congressional Record* **of CIA Biological Weapons Project MKNAOMI As Part of Top Secret Mind Control Project MKULTRA**

PROJECT MKULTRA, THE CIA'S PROGRAM OF RESEARCH IN BEHAVIORAL MODIFICATION

JOINT HEARING

BEFORE THE

SELECT COMMITTEE ON INTELLIGENCE

AND THE

SUBCOMMITTEE ON HEALTH AND SCIENTIFIC RESEARCH

OF THE

COMMITTEE ON HUMAN RESOURCES

UNITED STATES SENATE

NINETY-FIFTH CONGRESS

FIRST SESSION

AUGUST 3, 1977

Printed for the use of the Select Committee on Intelligence
and Committee on Human Resources

U.S. GOVERNMENT PRINTING OFFICE

96-408 O   WASHINGTON : 1977

For sale by the Superintendent of Documents, U.S. Government Printing Office
Washington, D.C., 20402
Stock No. 052-070-04357-1

Fig. 11.1. MKNAOMI and MKULTRA Cont.

that no damage was done to individuals who volunteer for the experiments."⁵ Overseas interrogations utilizing a combination of sodium pentothal and hypnosis after physical and psychiatric examinations of the subjects were also part of ARTICHOKE.

The Office of Scientific Intelligence (OSI), which studied scientific advances by hostile powers, initially led BLUEBIRD/ARTICHOKE efforts. In 1952, overall responsibility for ARTICHOKE was transferred from OSI to the Inspection and Security Office (I&SO), predecessor to the present Office of Security. The CIA's Technical Services and Medical Staffs were to be called upon as needed; OSI would retain liaison function with other government agencies.⁶ The change in leadership from an intelligence unit to an operating unit apparently reflected a change in emphasis; from the study of actions by hostile powers to the use, both for offensive and defensive purposes, of special interrogation techniques—primarily hypnosis and truth serums.

Representatives from each Agency unit involved in ARTICHOKE met almost monthly to discuss their progress. These discussions included the planning of overseas interrogations⁷ as well as further experimentation in the U.S.

Information about project ARTICHOKE after the fall of 1953 is scarce. The CIA maintains that the project ended in 1956, but evidence suggests that Office of Security and Office of Medical Services use of "special interrogation" techniques continued for several years thereafter.

3. MKNAOMI

MKNAOMI was another major CIA program in this area. In 1967, the CIA summarized the purposes of MKNAOMI:

(a) To provide for a covert support base to meet clandestine operational requirements.

(b) To stockpile severely incapacitating and lethal materials for the specific use of TSD [Technical Services Division].

(c) To maintain in operational readiness special and unique items for the dissemination of biological and chemical materials.

(d) To provide for the required surveillance, testing, upgrading, and evaluation of materials and items in order to assure absence of defects and complete predictability of results to be expected under operational conditions.⁸

Under an agreement reached with the Army in 1952, the Special Operations Division (SOD) at Fort Detrick was to assist CIA in developing, testing, and maintaining biological agents and delivery

⁵ Memorandum from Robert Taylor, O/DD/P to the Assistant Deputy (Inspection and Security) and Chief of the Medical Staff, 3/22/52.
⁶ Memorandum from H. Marshall Chadwell, Assistant Director, Scientific Intelligence, to the Deputy Director/Plans (DDP) "Project ARTICHOKE," 8/29/52.
⁷ "Progress Report, Project ARTICHOKE," 1/12/53.
⁸ Memorandum from Chief, TSD/Biological Branch to Chief, TSD "MKNAOMI: Funding, Objectives, and Accomplishments," 10/18/67, p. 1. For a fuller description of MKNAOMI and the relationship between CIA and SOD, see p. 360 ff.

agents and delivery systems," and to study the use of biological agents against crops, animals, and enemies.[6] (See figures 11.1 through 11.4.)

Early Toxic Clouds and Encephalitis Sprayings

As seen in figures 11.3 and 11.4, biological weapons tests included "anticrop" and "antipersonnel" studies employing "high efficiency . . . Airborne Spray Tank[s]." "An important advance in field evaluation was the development of a miniature spraying system for disseminating liquid agents" from airplanes, the U.S. Army Chemical Corps reported in a declassified document dating back to the mid-1950s. Figure 11.4 shows that progress was being made toward the "standardization of a strain of Venezuelan equine encephalomyelitis"—a virus immunologically distinct from the Japanese and St. Louis varieties of encephalitis virions, but pathologically related to the West Nile virus nonetheless.

The same page reported the performance features of unspecified biological agents tested through "dissemination in a visible cloud of smoke." The toxic cloud's visibility along with the delayed "time of onset of symptoms" were cited as shortfalls for this series of BW experiments. However, considering contemporary practices of non-lethal warfare that have emerged from this early work, including visible "chemtrail" sprayings, and their delayed results, that was discussed in Chapter 10, such features may be seen as manageable if not desired.

Vaccines As Killing Co-Factors

Furthermore, in figure 11.3, the Army's "Biological Warfare Research and Development" 1950s update heralded the "first time . . . use of human volunteers in the evaluation of such agents." The "quantitative assessment of BW agents and vaccines," the document stated, had been "approved by the Surgeon General and the Secretary of the Army."

The testing of vaccines during these human BW trials may be falsely assumed to be for disease prevention and defensive purposes. When considering non-lethal biological and chemical warfare, however, the opposite may be true. That is, vaccines, researchers realized, may be used to deliver pathogenic cofactors required for disease expression.

Pathology textbooks from that era, in fact, noted this to be the case for viral encephalomyelitis in particular. The *Synopsis of Pathology*

Fig. 11.2. Declassified U.S. Army Chemical Corps Document Showing Genetic Engineering of Fungi with Viral Nucleic Acids by 1962

SECRET   SECRET

SUMMARY OF MAJOR EVENTS
and
PROBLEMS

United States Army Chemical Corps (U)

FISCAL YEARS 1961 - 1962

CLASSIFIED BY:
DOD DIR 5200.1R

JUNE 1962   REVIEW ON: JUNE 1992

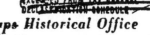

U.S. Army Chemical Corps Historical Office
Army Chemical Center, Maryland

SPECIAL HANDLING REQUIRED
NOT RELEASABLE TO FOREIGN NATIONALS
EXCEPT NONE BY AUTHORITY OF OCCMLO
12 Mar 62

THIS DOCUMENT
REGRADED UNCLASSIFIED
THEN SEPARATED FROM
CLASSIFIED DOCUMENTS
PAGES 109 + 110

SECRET

SECRET

COPY 6 OF 35 COPIES

CBR-8-1794-62

OCMH, SC No: 116226

Fig. 11.2. Chemical Corps Document Continued

SECRET

(S) Research on new agents has tended to concentrate on viral and rickettsial diseases. A whole range of exotic virus diseases prevalent in tropical areas came within the screening program in FY 1961 - 62, with major effort directed at increased first-hand knowledge of these so-called arbor (i.e., arthropod-borne) viruses. The importance of epidemiological studies in connection with this area of endeavor was being emphasized. A major step forward was achieved in the development of a better known agent, the virus of psittacosis, when stabilization of the dry agent through addition of a small amount of monosodium glutamate was successfully demonstrated. This accomplishment eliminated one of the principal difficulties in the path of future development of this agent.[25]

(S) In the realm of bacterial and fungal agents, the causative organisms of histoplasmosis, leptospirosis, and cryptococcosis reached the laboratory screening stage. Work on Bacillus anthracis, an agent which has been the subject of more or less concern to the Corps for many years, went forward in the area of process research, particularly in the evaluation of drying methods. But the crucial problem of providing adequate assessment of human susceptibility to this agent remains to be solved.[26]

(U) One of the most striking lines of inquiry in the Corps program was the basic research being done by the Biological Laboratories on the genetic factors underlying the infectivity of micro-organisms. Nucleic acids carrying infectivity factors were isolated from viruses. First attempts at inducing new

---

[25] Goodlow interv, 16 Feb 62.

[26] (1) Ibid. (2) Technical Program Review & Analysis, Bio Labs, Jan - Mar 62, p 24.

SECRET PAGE 127 OF 195 PAGES

COPY 6 OF 35 COPIES

Fig. 11.2. Chemical Corps Document Continued

CONFIDENTIAL

combinations of genetic factors through the mixture of infectious nucleic

acids from different sources were undertaken in FY 1962. Studies of bacterial

genetics were also in progress with the aim of transferring genetic determi-

nants from one type of organism to another.[27]

Alarms

(C) A landmark in the long development of a practical automatic field

alarm for G and V agents was reached early in the third quarter of FY 1962,

when the E41R3 point detection alarm was accepted by the Army for limited

production, thereby fulfilling at least a portion of the existing Qualitative

Military Requirement for automatic alarms. The E41R3, which operates through

a color reaction on a treated wet tape and a color-actuated audio signal, is

a modified version of the E41R1 discussed in the FY 1960 Annual Summary.[28]

The modifications were those suggested by deficiencies revealed during Arctic

Test Board tests of the earlier model in FY 1961. Approval of the alarm for

limited procurement (to satisfy an immediate operational requirement for 400

alarms) came in January of 1962.[29]

(C) An active program toward the development of a long path infra-red

(LOPAIR) system for area scanning alarms reached the contracting stage before

the end of FY 1962. The E49 LOPAIR system, selected for development, was the

---

27

(1) Goodlow Interv, 16 Feb 62. (2) Technical Program Review & Analysis,
Bio Labs, Oct - Dec 61, pp 17 - 18.

28

Summary of Major Events and Problems, FY 60, pp 117 - 18.

29

CCTC Items 3934, 26 Dec 61, and 3950, 23 Jan 62..

CONFIDENTIAL PAGE 103 OF 133 PAGES
COPY 6 CF 35 COPIES

noted that "Acute disseminated encephalomyelitis occurs after certain infectious diseases (notably measles, mumps, smallpox, and chickenpox) and vaccination for smallpox and rabies. . . . Some workers believe that the viruses of the antecedent diseases or *those introduced by vaccination* are etiologically involved, either directly or by inducing cerebral anoxia. . . . The most widely held theory [in 1972], however, is that an autoimmune mechanism is responsible for the disease."[7] [Emphasis added.]

Such brain infections were microscopically associated with extensive demyelinization of nerve fibers; particularly those neighboring blood vessels that supply brain cells with oxygen.

Relatedly, "slow viruses" including the "kuru" agent—the name initially given to "prion" proteins associated with mad-cow-related illnesses such as "Creutzfeldt-Jakob disease" (CJD)—were studied to elucidate their delayed initiation of brain lesions. Slow viruses were also suspected, at that time, of causing other diseases including multiple sclerosis, Parkinson's disease, amyotrophic lateral sclerosis (ALS) or Lou Gehrig's disease, and Altzheimer's presenile dementia. Since that time, these diseases have become pandemic and are still widely suspected as being attributable to vaccines due to their autoimmune features.[7]

The Gulf War Example of Non-lethality

As relayed earlier, the concept of manufacturing biological problems, such as the WNV, with lucrative chemical and pharmaceutical solutions such as Anvil and the WNV vaccine was not new. Precedence for the Machiavellian practice of creating an enemy against which to wage non-lethal warfare had been set at least once a decade earlier in 1989. As advanced in *Healing Codes for the Biological Apocalypse*, Gulf War Syndrome (GWS) can be best understood in this context of "non-lethal warfare"—a practical application of biological and chemical cofactor facilitated disease and depopulation that required intensive propaganda to cover.

Maintained to the time of this writing as a medical mystery, research had determined that GWS was the result of chemical *as well as* biological exposures.[8] Debilitating vaccines had been used to deliver both infectious Mycoplasma strains as well as harmful chemicals. Squaline, only associated with "experimental" vaccines had been found in many of the sick veterans. This "adjuvant," or additive, de-

Fig. 11.3. U.S. Army Documents Demonstrating "High Efficiency Airborne Spray Tank" Use During Human Biological Warfare Experiments

UNCLASSIFIED

CONFIDENTIAL

    Considerable progress, on the other hand, was made in the development of anticrop agents. Research resulted in improved field evaluation of potential agents, addition of 4-fluorophenoxy-, acetic acid as a standard-type agent, and demonstration of the high efficiency of the Aero 14A Airborne Spray Tank. (SECRET)

    Whereas the previous chemical anticrop agents, butyl 2,4-dichlorophenoxyacetic acid and butyl 2,4,5-trichlorophenoxyacetate were useful for curtailing the growth of broadleaf plants, the new standard-type agent, 4-fluorophenoxyacetic acid, reduces the yields of wheat and rice materially when applied in militarily feasible quantities. The agent is produced industrially by chemical companies and is available on the open market. [56] (SECRET)

    An important advance in field evaluation was the development of a miniature spraying system for disseminating liquid agents from an L-19 airplane. This system makes practicable the testing of undiluted agents on field grown crops. An effort is being made to mount the system on a truck, which can then be used at Camp Detrick. (CONFIDENTIAL)

    In conjunction with the Navy, tests were made of the Aero 14A

56
Chemical anticrop agents are discussed in:
(1) Technical Progress FY 1954, pp.56-58.
(2) Annual BW Project Report.

REGRADED UNCLASSIFIED ORDER SEC ARMY BY TAG PER 791934

PAGE 10 OF 11 PAGES

COPY 2 OF 25 COPIES

UNCLASSIFIED

CONFIDENTIAL

Fig. 11.3. Biological Warfare Experiments Cont.

UNCLASSIFIED

46

<u>Biological Warfare Research and Development</u>

<u>For the first time since the Chemical Corps embarked on a BW</u>
<u>program, permission has been granted for the use of human volunteers</u>
<u>in the evaluation of agents. A plan, drawn up at Camp Detrick, for</u>
<u>the quantitative assessment of BW agents and vaccines has been</u>
<u>approved by the Surgeon General and the Secretary of the Army. It</u>
<u>is being planned to have the work carried on under contract in a</u>
<u>medical school.</u>   (SECRET) [47]

The funds available for BW during the fiscal year amounted to
$25,440,000. By 30 June, $21,966,000 (86%) were obligated. The
failure to fully obligate the funds were due to delays caused by
earlier <u>attempts to place the entire BW program under contract.</u>
Approval was obtained from higher authority to continue obligation
of 1954 funds through 30 September 1954. [48]   (CONFIDENTIAL)

---

[46]
Unless otherwise noted, the section on BW is based on an interview with Dr. Charles Phillips, Camp Detrick, 28 Jul 54.
The Eighth Annual Report, Cml C Biol Labs, was not scheduled for
publication until 16 Sep 54, and was therefore not available
for this Summary History.
[47]
DF, DC CmlO to Hist O, OCCmlO, 3 Jun 54, sub: Summary List for
Historical Report.
[48]
Review and Analysis of Chemical Corps Program, 4th Qtr FY 1954.

PAGE, 6 OF 11 PAGES

COPY 2 OF 25 COPIES

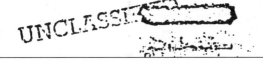

UNCLASSIFIED

pressed their immune systems.[9] Then the troops were exposed to other drugs and chemicals such as the pesticide pyridostygmine bromide.[8, 9] Finally, despite a concerted effort by Pentagon officials, including former President of Rockefeller University, Joshua Lederberg, who led the Pentagon's study into GWS, to confuse and deceive the public, final evidence proved Dr. Lederberg and the Pentagon had outright lied. Not only had allied troops been exposed to biological and chemical weapons during the war and its aftermath, but Dr. Lederberg's organization, American Type Culture Collection (ATCC) had been found during a congressional investigation to have shipped 70 loads of biological warfare samples including anthrax, botulinum toxin, and the West Nile virus (WNV), to Iraq shortly before the war.[10]

According to Senator Don Riegle's report on GWS, the pyridostygmine bromide that was given to troops in an effort to avert the toxic symptoms of nerve gas attacks, actually gave many of the troops the illnesses the drug was taken to prevent. The array of side effects were virtually the same as those experienced as a result of pesticide exposures. Here is the excerpt from the Senate's final report regarding pyridostygmine bromide:

> During House of Representatives hearings in 1993, Carol Picou, assigned to a combat support hospital during the Gulf War, recalled that when the ground war began, "we were ordered to take the drug pyridostygmine to protect us against chemical attack. Within one hour of taking the drug, I began to experience serious side-effects, such as uncontrollable twitching eyes, runny nose, excessive frothing from the mouth, neck and shoulder pain." Dr. Sidney Wolfe, director of the Public Citizen's health research group, who filed a suit against use of the drug, said it was administered so sloppily that nobody knew who took it. Major General Blanck said that there was a risk of minor side effects, but that these were worthwhile to be "prepared for exposure to deadly biological and chemical warfare agents."

> . . . Brian Martin also claimed to have had side effects from the drug pyridostygmine. According to Martin, the drug made him jittery and made his vision "jiggle."

> Steve Hudspeth, assigned to the 1454th Transportation Company, also reported getting very sick from the nerve agent pretreatment pills. He reported severe nausea and diarrhea that did not abate until he stopped taking the pills after two days. He recalled thinking that "if I'm going to feel like this I might as well be dead." Mr. Hudspeth currently suffers from memory loss, fatigue, sore muscles and joints, insomnia,

Fig. 11.4. U.S. Army "Antipersonnel" Experiments Including Encephalitis Virus Testing, and Spray "Dissemination in a Visible Cloud of Smoke"

SECRET

the M44 generator cluster respectively.[22] The Standard B classification represents the interim character of the new agent which in some respects - its prolonged time of onset of symptoms (at least two to three hours), and its dissemination in a visible cloud of smoke - falls short of optimum performance.

(C) Research was resumed during the FY 1961 - 62 period on botulinum toxin, the substance responsible for botulism. The research project on the crystalline toxin was the responsbility of CRDL, but some of the work was done by the Biological Laboratories acting as a sub-contractor. Problems in bio- assays and dissemination methods were a major concern during the period.[23]

(S) Progress toward standardizing new BW agents was slowed in 1961 - 62 by the lack of adequate extra-continental test facilities in which agent- munition combinations could be fully assayed without the limitations necessary in less remote test areas. Lack of the data such a test program could provide was responsible for the inability of the Chemical Corps to gain approval at the outset of the period for the standardization of a strain of Venezuelan equine encephalomyelitis. The requirement, new in FY 1961, that agents be type classi- fied only in conjunction with munitions, was itself a limiting factor in consequence of the small range of formulated Army requirements for BW anti- personnel munitions.[24]

---

[22]   CCTC Item 3960, 26 Feb 62.

[23]   Quart Hist Rpt, CRDL, Jan - Mar 62 .

[24]   (1) Interv, Hist Off with Dr C.G. Ash, Hq EDCCM, 27 Dec 61. (2) Interv, Hist Off with Dr R.D. Housewright, Bio Labs, 16 Feb 52. (3) Interv, Hist Off with Dr R.J. Goodlow, Bio Labs 15 Feb 62. For creation of Deseret Test Facility to expedite extra-continental test programs, see Chap I, above.

SECRET PAGE 126 OF 163 PAGES

COPY 6 OF 35 COPIES

cough, some night sweats, diverticulitis, diarrhea, kidney stones, bloody stools, urinary urgency, growth on his eye, rashes, tingling and itching sensations, and depression and irritability.

Chemically related to pesticides, nerve agents such as Sarin, Soman, Tabun, and VX kill [like Malathion and Anvil], by interfering with the metabolic processes, and cause a buildup of a chemical messenger in the human metabolic process called acetylcholine, which operates in the gap between the nerve and the muscle cells. A buildup of acetylcholine may cause drooling, excessive sweating, cramping, vomiting, confusion, irregular heartbeat, convulsions, loss of consciousness and coma. Little, however, is known about the consequences of *non-lethal* exposure to these toxins. [Emphasis added.]

Nerve gas pretreatment drugs such as pyridostygmine bromide, paradoxically, also meddle with these metabolic processes by creating carbamate-inhibited acetylcholinesterase, which interferes with the actions of nerve gas—theoretically permitting the process to be partially reversed.[11]

The case histories and testimony recorded above, as well as the explanation of the victim's complaints relating to acetylcholine metabolic inhibition, were virtually identical, in terms of symptoms, with cases discussed earlier in this book resulting from Malathion-bait spray exposures with subsequent toxicity.

Unconscionable as it may seem, these effects could have easily been predicted, if not planned, to occur in the Gulf War troops. Given all the research that war departments do to "protect" military personnel, plus the stacks of scientific literature generated by the chemical and pharmaceutical companies, such illnesses, drug interactions, and side effects are readily predicted by pharmacists and toxicologists who certainly advise military officials. Economic reward and/or intent to do harm then, not negligence, much like the conclusion I reached earlier concerning "public health" pesticide spraying and vaccination programs, was likewise the most rational explanation for GWS. All fit neatly into the non-lethality and population control picture.

Supporting the intentional theory of intoxicating allied troops in a non-lethal manner were the legal documents reprinted in *Healing Codes for the Biological Apocalypse*.[12] Some of these showed that risky "experimental" AIDS vaccines were given to unwitting troops *enroute* to the Middle East. Some of the vaccines contained "pathogenic Mycoplasma." This germ maintained the "stealth-like" ability to evade the human immune system. It dove deep within cell nuclei.

194

There, this likely laboratory engineered microbe became very difficult to diagnose, and even harder to treat.

The lead Mycoplasma expert, Dr. Shyh-Ching Lo published in both his patent report, as well as in the esteemed journal of *Clinical Infectious Diseases*, that this microbe was responsible for virtually all of the symptoms attributed to HIV, as well as cases of chronic upper respiratory infections—flu-like illness resistant to almost all antibiotics.[13] Suspiciously, beginning in 1998, epidemics of such bizarre flu-like illnesses began circulating around the world.[12]

Furthermore, evidence compiled by lawyers for the class of people sickened by *Mycoplasma incognitas* and related illnesses, from Huntsville, Texas, revealed more astonishing documents. These, also published in *Healing Codes for the Biological Apocalypse*, showed that Baylor College of Medicine investigators conducted studies on Huntsville prison inmates beginning in 1968. Mycoplasma inoculations, as well as Mycoplasma vaccination studies, were listed as having begun in 1970 under U.S. Army contracts. Baylor's contract raised the spectre of "ethnic cleansing" or racial genocide. It discussed herpes virus type 2 that was studied in different parts of the world where Christian, Muslim, Black, and Jewish women were investigated for cervical cancer tendencies.

Other studies ongoing at that time, as stated in Chapter 1, included the herpes-type viruses, including Epstein–Barr and cytomegalovirus currently associated with additional cancers and the CFIDS epidemic. Infectious CFIDS was virtually nonexistent before 1968, that is, before these studies began. In addition, Epstein–Barr, linked to lymphomas (originally called Burkitt's lymphoma in Black children) I determined, originated, like WNV, in the West Nile Valley of Northwest Uganda at the Rockefeller and Bionetics linked IARC.[5]

The Hegelian Dialectic and Gulf War Syndrome

Consistent with earlier discussions regarding the vital role played by psychological operations and propaganda in support of non-lethal warfare, we would expect to find such PSYOPs operating across the spectrum of contemporary illnesses, and indeed we do. The following discussion of the Hegelian dialectic provides some examples of this deceptive social control activity.

Georg Wilhelm Friedrich Hegel (1770-1831), the famous eighteenth century German philosopher, elaborated a revolution in thought

195

based on "dialectical logic." Political scientists, including Communists Karl Marx and Vladimir Lenin, were largely credited with having perfected the logic's practice in dialectical propaganda.

That is, Hegel advanced the logic that two opposite realities negate each other; yet, the two are expressed in a third condition of human experience he termed "synthesis." It was this "synthesis," Hegel reasoned, that gave rise to human "intellect," or more accurately in terms of political propagandists, synthesized or artificial intelligence.

In other words, social scientists working for political propagandists learned that if people were presented with one "fact" or "thesis," then later learned a second most opposite "fact" or "antithesis," then a state of dissonance termed "synthesis" could be engineered which left people confused and largely disinterested in the entire subject. HIV/AIDS and GWS are two classic examples of this Hegelian dialectic in public health and U.S. military practice.

With HIV/AIDS, the first "fact" heralded in 1984 by Dr. Robert Gallo at the NCI was that a single virus—HTLV-III/HIV-1—caused the syndrome known as AIDS. A multi-billion dollar industry sprang from this announcement. Two years later, Dr. Gallo's colleague and NCI retrovirus collaborator, Dr. Peter Duesberg, suddenly advanced the "antithesis." He stated that HIV had little to do with the spectrum of illnesses Dr. Gallo had blamed on that virus. Largely as a result of this, and other dialectics being played out in the media, the public became confused and increasingly disinterested in the entire subject of HIV/AIDS. Meanwhile, its death toll continued mounting in minority, apparently targeted, populations.

A similar campaign and outcome was successfully managed following the identification of GWS. Initially, the Pentagon blamed the condition on military service stress, as in "post traumatic stress disorder." Ailing veterans were sent to psychiatrists and generally prescribed Prozac as the "treatment" of choice. Later, when verifiable evidence emerged that military personnel had indeed been exposed to biological and chemical weapons, the Pentagon advanced a new, more scientific, thesis—side effects from combined chemical and drug exposures had left the veterans sick. Soon, this thesis too was widely recognized as flawed. Some saw it as part of the Pentagon's continuing effort to cover-up known biological and chemical exposures of Gulf War troops who had received risky experimental vaccines along with toxic war exposures. The Pentagon's thesis was then followed by claims of cover-up by the CIA, and their "antithesis" that many veterans were suffering from chemical warfare exposures. The CIA never mentioned, however, the implicated vaccines. As with the confusion over the etiology of AIDS, GWS investigators were largely left stymied by the intellectual "synthesis" of conflicting reports.

It should also be understood that every thesis or antithesis advanced, as in the above examples, has an element of truth. In the case of HIV/AIDS, host immunosuppression is a defining characteristic of this type of retroviral (initially known as "type-C" cancer virus) infection, even though the disease onset and course depends on various other cofactors such as the presence of Epstein–Barr virus or the Mycoplasma agent.

Likewise with GWS, the fact is that ailing veterans *had* been exposed to several risky biologicals and chemicals while under increased military stress. I refer to this selective truth telling as the "80:20 rule" in counterintelligence propaganda. In essence, approximately 80 percent of every thesis or antithesis used to produce "synthesis" is accurate. The other 20 percent is either slightly twisted, or misses the most important fact(s) altogether; which, given these correct details, would paint totally different pictures reflecting the truest most disturbing realities.

According to *The Washington Post*, a leading voice for counterintelligence along with the *NY Times* and *LA Times*, the CIA knew that chemical weapons were being stored for use against allied forces.[14] The agency spent three years after the war, however, denying that fact. *The Post* made no mention of the CIA's additional knowledge that biological weapons were also in Hussein's cache. Here they only wrote:

> The CIA disclosed Wednesday that it had received numerous warnings starting in 1984 that chemical weapons were stored in an Iraqi depot those U.S. soldiers blew up shortly after the Persian Gulf War.

> The agency added that it had failed to adequately alert the armed forces of the danger.

> The disclosure contradicted three years of CIA accounts of what it knew about poison-gas weapons in Iraq, including a statement made six weeks ago by acting CIA Director George J. Tenet. He said then that the CIA had not specifically identified the Khamisiyah weapons site as a chemical weapons area prior to its destruction by U.S. forces in March 1991. . . .

Intelligence support before, during and after the war should have been better," said Robert D. Walpole, chairman of the task force. "If you're looking for an apology that we should have given this information out sooner, I'll give that apology. We should have gotten it out sooner."[14]

As a matter of fact, CIA officials Tenet and Walpole only disclosed the chemical weapons portion of the truth because of severe pressure placed upon them mostly by American Gulf War Veterans Association Director, Retired Reserve Captain Joyce Riley. Ms. Riley, herself made sick by Mycoplasma infection that she believes came from contaminated military vaccines, compiled much of the most damning evidence including video footage concerning the Khamisiyah arsenal demolition and subsequent widespread chemical fallout. Apparently, soldiers assigned to blow up the site escaped with a video showing the names and places of origin of many of the weapons. One seen in a three-hour video entitled, *Gulf War Syndrome: The Spreading Epidemic Cover-up* (Tetrahedron Publishing Group, 1998; 1-888-508-4787) clearly read, "Shipped from Oklahoma City, Oklahoma." Thus, the CIA was forced to make this limited apology to save what could have become a major disgrace.[15]

The Protocols for "Non-lethality," Propaganda, and Global Control

Indeed, globalists have traditionally used Hegelian dialectics, and the press, to facilitate social control and population management. Historically, through the press, genocide has been covered up far more than it has been properly exposed. Globalists have relied heavily on the mass media to maintain certain deceptions, just as they do today surrounding the practice of non-lethal warfare.

The oldest document that describes such practices and objectives, one that additionally supports the theory that numerous plagues have been instigated by globalists, is *The Protocols of the Elders of Sion.*

As evidenced in *Healing Codes for the Biological Apocalypse*, Masonic leaders have consistently encrypted intelligence, as well as disseminated counterintelligence, to achieve their colonialistic goals and their continued acquisition of power. Virtually all impartial investigators have concluded that the early Masonic society—the Prieuré de Sion—is still effectively operating "behind the scenes" to orchestrate the economic alignment of the superpowers for global governance. Many believe that the New World Order is a direct result of the Prieuré de Sion.[12]

Freemasons, and not Jewish globalists, per se, as many have contended, had originally written *The Protocols of the Elders of Sion*, traditionally considered among the most anti-Semitic documents in the world. In their meticulously referenced book *Holy Blood/Holy Grail*, three investigators—Michael Baigent, Richard Leigh, and Henry Lincoln—definitively determined *The Protocols* to have Masonic origin. The work had been grossly demonized following its early rewriting into its current anti-Semitic form. Used to inspire Jewish hate during the Russian pogrom, and the subsequent rise of the Third Reich, the document hinted at the use of non-lethal warfare to achieve globalistic objectives. It also clearly articulated its authors' desire to direct global fascism. Furthermore, it provided the precise methods for achieving such extensive social and global control. Dating back to a Masonic meeting directed by the early European banking mogul Mayer Amschel Rothschild in 1773, the relevance of *The Protocols* to contemporary globalization seems too uncanny to be ignored.[12]

Considering the conducting of non-lethal warfare in the twenty-first century, *The Protocols* stated, "Our States, marching along the path of peaceful conquest, has the right to *replace the horrors of war by less noticeable and more satisfactory sentences of death,* necessary to maintain the terror which tends to produce blind submission."

Mention has already been made regarding the use of terrorism, bioterrorism included, to induce fear for successful population manipulation.

The second protocol stated that "in the hands of the States of today there is a great force that creates the movement of thought in the people, and this is the press. The part played by the press is to keep pointing out requirements supposed to be indispensable; to give voice to the complaints of the people, and to express and to create discontent. It is in the press that the triumph of freedom of speech finds its incarnation. . . . Through the press we have gained the power to influence while remaining ourselves in the shade; thanks to the press we have got the gold in our hands, notwithstanding that we have had to gather it out of oceans of blood and tears. . . .

"Moreover, [Protocol No. 5 stated] the art of directing masses and individuals by means of cleverly manipulated theory and verbiage, by regulations of life in common, and all sorts of other quirks, in which the [manipulated] understand nothing, belongs likewise to the specialists of our administrative brain.

199

"For a time perhaps we might be successfully dealt with by a coalition of the [manipulated] of all the world: but from this danger we are secured by the discord existing among them whose roots are so deeply seated that they can never now be plucked up. . . .

"The principle object of our directorate consists in this: to debilitate the public mind by criticism; to lead it away from serious reflections calculated to arouse resistance; to distract the forces of the mind towards a sham fight of empty eloquence. . . . [Our] orators will speak so much that they will exhaust the patience of their hearers and produce an abhorrence of oratory.

"In order to put public opinion into our hands we must bring it into a state of bewilderment by giving expression from all sides to so many contradictory opinions and for such a length of time as will suffice to make the [manipulated] lose their heads in the labyrinth and come to see that the best thing is to have no opinion of any kind in matters political . . . .

"In counties known to be progressive and enlightened we have created a senseless, filthy, abominable literature . . . in order that the masses themselves may not guess what they are about we further distract them with amusements, games, pastimes, passions, people's palaces [etc.] . . ."

As continued in Protocol No. 7, "We must compel the governments of the [manipulated] to take action in the direction favored by our widely conceived plan, already approaching the desired consummation, by what *we shall represent as public opinion, secretly prompted by us through the means of the so-called "Great Power"—the press,* which, with a few exceptions that may be disregarded, is already entirely in our hands. . . . [Emphasis added.]

"In a word, to sum up our system of keeping the governments of the [manipulated] . . . in check, we shall show our strength to one of them by terrorist attempts and to all, if we allow the possibility of a general rising against us, we shall respond with the guns of America, or China, or Japan. . . ."

And to facilitate the New World Order, "Protocol No. 10" documented, "By such measures we shall obtain the power of destroying, little by little, step by step . . . the constitutions of States to prepare for the transition to an imperceptible abolition of every kind of constitution, and then the time is come to turn every form of government into our despotism.

"The recognition of our despot may also come before the destruction of the constitution; the moment for this recognition will come
when the peoples, utterly wearied by the irregularities and incompetence—a matter which we shall arrange for—of their rulers, will
clamor: 'Away with them and give us one king over all the earth who
will unite us and annihilate the causes of discords—frontiers, nation-
alities, religions, state debts—who will give us peace and quiet, which
we cannot find under our rulers and representatives.

"But you yourselves perfectly well know that to produce the possibility of the expression of such wishes by all the nations it is indispensable to trouble, in all countries, the people's relations with their
governments so as to utterly exhaust humanity with dissension, hatred,
struggle, envy, and even by the use of torture, by starvation, *by the
inoculation of diseases*, by want, so that the [manipulated] see no issue
than to take refuge in our complete sovereignty in money and in all
else."

The emphasis on inoculated diseases in the above paragraph was
added due to its striking relevance to GWS and other vaccine induced
injuries discussed herein and in this author's earlier works.

Finally, "Protocol No. 12" also dealt extensively with the press
and the globalists' capacity to direct it, as discussed earlier, along with
the public's mind. It answered its own rhetorical question, "What is the
part played by the press today? It serves to excite and inflame those
passions, which are needed for our purpose, or else it serves selfish
ends of (other) parties. It is often vapid, unjust, mendacious, and the
majority of the public have not the slightest idea what ends the press
really serves. We shall saddle and bridle it with a tight curb: we shall do
the same also with all productions of the printing press [book publish-
ers], for where would be the sense of getting rid of the attacks of the
press if we remain targets for pamphlets and books?

"The produce of publicity, which nowadays [late 1700s] is a source
of heavy expense owing to the necessity of censoring it, will be turned
by us into a very lucrative source of income to our State: We shall lay
on it a special stamp tax and require deposits of caution-money before
permitting the establishment of any organ of the press or of printing
offices [e.g., similar to the functions of the U.S. Federal Communications Commission]; these will then have to guarantee our government
against any kind of attack on the part of the press. For any attempt to
attack us, if such still were possible, we shall inflict fines without

mercy. . . . The pretext for stopping any publication will be the alleged plea that it is agitating the public mind without occasion or justification. I beg you to note that among those making attacks upon us will also be organs established by us [like the Astroturf and fraudulent "grassroots" organizations discussed in Chapter 14], but they will attack exclusively points that we have predetermined to alter.

"Not a single announcement will reach the public without our control. Even now we are already attaining this inasmuch as news items are received by a few agencies, in whose offices they are focused from all parts of the world. These agencies will then be already entirely ours and will give publicity only to what we dictate to them. . . .

"Literature and journalism are two of the most important educative forces and therefore our government will become proprietor of the majority of the journals. This will neutralize the injurious influence of the privately owned press and will put us in possession of a tremendous influence upon the public mind. . . . If we give permits for ten journals, we shall ourselves found thirty, and so on in the same proportion. This, however, must in no way be suspected by the public.

"For which reason all journals published by us will be of the most opposite, in appearance, tendencies, and opinions, thereby creating confidence in us and bringing over to us our quite unsuspicious opponents, who will thus fall into our trap and be rendered harmless.

"In the front rank will stand organ[ization]s of an official character [such as the American medical and public health associations, the World Health Organization, the National Press Club, etc.]. They will always stand guard over our interests, and therefore their influence will be comparatively insignificant.

"By discussing and controverting, but always superficially, without touching the essence of the matter, our organ[ization]s will carry on a sham fight . . . with the official newspapers (operating) solely for the purpose of giving occasion for us to express ourselves more fully . . . (Superficially, self-generated) attacks upon us will also serve another purpose, namely, that our subjects will be convinced of the existence of full freedom of speech, and so give our agents an occasion to affirm that all organ[ization]s which oppose us are empty babblers, since they are incapable of finding any substantial objections to our orders.

"Methods of organization like these, imperceptible to the public eye, but absolutely sure, are best calculated to succeed in bringing the attention and the confidence of the public to the side of our government. Thanks to such methods, we shall be in a position as from time to time may be required, to excite or to tranquilize the public mind on political questions, to persuade or to confuse, printing now truth, now lies, facts or their contradictions, accordingly as they may be well or ill received, always very cautiously feeling our ground before stepping upon it. We shall have a sure triumph over our opponents since they will not have at their disposition organ[ization]s of the press in which they can give full and final expression to their views owing to the aforesaid methods of dealing with the press. We shall not even need to refute them except very superficially."[2]

Reflecting on the above *Protocols of the Elders of Sion*, they obviously foreshadowed contemporary globalization, the use of non-lethal warfare, and the mass mind-controlling propaganda required to propagate it.[16, 17]

Prospects for America: The Rockefeller Panel Reports and Carnegie Endowment

In keeping with the above revelations concerning the fields of public opinion and persuasion, contemporary culture clearly reflects these activities largely, if not entirely, attributable to the global elite. In fact, the entire Gestalt of American values, attitudes, and behavior has precipitated from PSYOPs largely directed by America's wealthiest families.

Though this may seem to be an unsubstantiated claim, the following pertinent history substantiates this fact.

During the mid-1950s—the heart of the Cold War period—liberal historian Arthur Schlesinger wrote, "Our shops overflow with gadgets and gimmicks; consumer goods of ever-increasing ingenuity and luxuriance pour out of our ears. But our schools become more crowded and dilapidated, our teachers more weary and underpaid, our cities dirtier, our roads more teeming and filthy, our national parks more unkempt, our law enforcement more overworked and inadequate. . . ."[18]

Schlesinger was referring to a cultural crisis, partly real but mostly fabricated, opulent Americans were seeking greater meaning in their lives. Following the Soviet Union's successful launch of Sputnik in October 1957, and a review of "secret documents" by "the more romantically inclined and liberal political, intellectual, and economic elites," according to Whitney Museum of Art author and historian Marcus Raskin, a search began for a "National Purpose" for all Americans. This, the sequestered commission texts predicted, "would stiffen the will . . . so that the public would stay the course of the United States as Leader of the Free World, improve the quality of American life, and escape the aimlessness which various social commentators of the period had identified."[19]

The contents of these classified commission reports were persuasive enough to prompt American hagiographers and their venerated subjects to join the campaign to define the "National Purpose." Henry Luce, the publisher of *Time* and *Life*, committed America's most prominent magazines to the effort. Not long after, President Eisenhower appointed another Commission on National Goals, which, according to Raskin, gave the search for "National Purpose . . . the imprimatur of political establishment solidity."[20] ("Imprimatur," according to *Webster's Dictionary*, means "approval or distinction." It also means "approval of a publication under circumstances of official censorship." Both meanings fit Raskin's discussion.)

Coordinated with this effort, and largely controlling it behind the scenes, was the Rockefeller family and the Rockefeller Brothers Fund. History recalls that Dwight David Eisenhower, though an esteemed army general and American president, was no blind devotee of the "military–industrial complex." He was personally acquainted with its ruthlessness. As a member of the Council on Foreign Relations (CFR) he knew his colleagues, the Rockefellers, were acting as America's helmsmen directing the country through the international sea of military and economic possibilities.

Quoting Eisenhower's farewell address to the American people on January 17, 1961, "This conjunction of an immense military establishment and a large arms industry is new in the American experience. . . . In the councils of government [he was undoubtedly including the Council on Foreign Relations], we must guard against the acquisition of unwarranted influence, whether sought or unsought, by the military–industrial complex. The potential for the disastrous rise of misplaced power exists and will persist."

Not to be outdone by any of this, and as part of the effort to establish a "National Purpose" in the hearts and minds of all Americans, the Rockefeller Brothers Fund, according to Raskin, "sponsored a series of Panel reports which were governed by the conception that *a prudent corporate and military leadership of the National Security State could link guns, butter, and the new technology of missile and nuclear weap-*

ons production to the cause of Freedom and the Free World. (At the time, important words were written with initial capital letters.)" These various commissions established by the Rockefellers and the president, Raskin reported, "had an eerie character, reminiscent of the Empire of Kakania, the fictional Austro-Hungarian empire in Robert Musil's novel *Man Without Qualities,* where a commission was appointed by the powers that be (soon to be powers that were) to give new life to the Kakania empire and purpose to its people."[21] [Emphasis added.]

While discussing AIDS during my lectures, I routinely tell audiences that "everything you know about AIDS is a complete deception. Let me rephrase that," I add. "Everything you know about everything is a complete deception." Laughter always follows.

Indeed, a bit of comic relief might be welcome given the seriousness of this subject. These historic facts indicate that as a nation, "We've been had!" Our world view has been shaped by the same forces against whom Eisenhower, Senators Barry Goldwater and Jesse Helms, and others have warned. Mistake this not as a liberal versus conservative issue. The evidence indicates American people across the political spectrum have had their "National Purpose" defined by international bankers and global industrialists for their sole purpose to exercise their power, wealth, and mostly concealed, often genocidal, agendas. For all practical purposes then, this defining of our "National Purpose" by "corporate and military leadership of the National Security State," so that when we buy "butter" it feeds weapons production and the latest technologies for killing people; all for "the cause of Freedom and the Free World," is a *scam* so large that most people—the media-opiate slaves they've become—can not even fathom it.

This is not the first time, nor will it be the last, that critics have wailed against the usurpers of American values, attitudes and behaviors. Those who have educated the public into ignorant states of dimwittedness have heard this complaint several times before. More than a century ago, on April 20, 1884, Pope Leo XIII warned brethren throughout the Catholic world that Masonic leaders had attempted "to control the education of youth, and mold it to its own godless pattern."[22] In 1954, an unprecedented Congressional investigation into tax-exempt foundations identified a similar villain and agenda afoot. The Committee stumbled upon the rewriting of American history by the Rockefeller and Carnegie oligarchy.

Norman Dodd, Research Director for the Congressional Committee, found the following stunning statement of insidious purpose in the archives of the Carnegie Endowment:

> The only way to maintain control of the population was to obtain control of education in the U.S. They realized this was a prodigious task so they approached the Rockefeller Foundation with the suggestion that they go in tandem and that the portion of education which could be considered as domestically oriented be taken over by the Rockefeller Foundation and that portion which was oriented to International matters be taken over by the Carnegie Endowment.[23]

Naturally, the Rockefeller Foundation consented, and the rest is history?

References

1) Keith J. *Mind Control World Control: The Encyclopedia of Mind Control.* Kempton, IL: Adventures Unlimited, 1997, pp. 264;267-269.

2) Horowitz L and Puleo J. *Healing Codes for the Biological Apocalypse.* Sandpoint, Idaho: Tetrahedron Publishing Group, pp. 118-120; 125-130; 435-437.

3) Mackay N. Non Lethal Devices: The Violent Man Scenario. Part One: Current Tactics & Debate. *A time for change?*, 1998; http://www.keme.co.uk/~mack/Contents.htm

4) Burke K. An interview with Dr. Nick Begich on "New Non-lethal Weapons Systems Used Against U.S. Citizens." Anchorage, AK: Earthpulse Press, 1998; www.earthpulse.com.

5) Horowitz LG and Martin JW. *Emerging Viruses: AIDS & Ebola—Nature, Accident or Intentional?* Rockport, MA: Tetrahedron Press, 1998, pp. 275-329; 401-440; for Sloan connections see pp. 476-479.

6) Senate Select Committee on Intelligence. *PROJECT MKULTRA, The CIA's Program of Research in Behavior Modification.* Joint Hearing Before the Select Committee on Intelligence and the Subcommittee on Health and Scientific Research of the Committee on Human Resources, United States Senate, Ninety-fifth Congress, First Session, August 3, 1977. Washington, D.C.: U.S. Government Printing Office, 1977, pp. 388-390.

7) Secret Summary of Major Events and Problems, United States Army Chemical Corps, Fiscal Years 1961-1962. U.S. Army Chemical Corps Historical Office, Army Chemical Center, Maryland. Declassified document CBR-S-1794-62, OCMH, SCNo. 116226, released June, 1992; see also: Anderson WAD and Scotti TM. *Synopsis of Pathology, Eighth edition.* St. Louis: The C.V. Mosby Company, 1972, p. 202-203 for information relating to encephalomeylitis virus and slow virus infections.

8) Nicolson GL and Nicolson NL. Chronic fatigue illnesses associated with service in Operation Desert Storm. *Townsend Letter for Doctors*, 1995; see also: Gill K. Doctor ties gulf war illness to anti-chemical pills. *USA Today*, Thursday, March 28, 1996; and News staff. Gen. Powell: Chemical alarms sounded frequently in gulf war. *Chicago Tribune*, Dec. 3, 1996 Sec. 1, p. 6.; and Hanchette J. Iraq showdown is centered on biochemicals. *USA Today*, Monday, Nov. 17, 1997, p. 13A.

9) Rodriguez PM. Sickness and Secrecy: Why do antibodies for an experimental immune-system-affecting adjuvant show up in the bloodstreams of Gulf-war vets who are sick with a variety of illnesses? Insight Magazine, August 25, 1997, pp. 7-12.

207

10) U.S. Senate. *U.S. Chemical and Biological Warfare-related Dual Use Exports to Iraq and Their Possible Impact on the Health Consequences of the Persian Gulf War.* A Report of Chairman Donald W. Riegle, Jr, and Ranking Member Alfonse M. D'Amato of the Committee on Banking, Housing and Urban Affairs With Respect to Export Administration, 103d Congress, Session 2d, May 25, 1994, pp. 38-47.

11) *Ibid.*, pp. 136-137.

12) Horowitz and Puleo. *Op cit.*, pp. 307-308; 262-270; 281-283; 371-405; see also: Baigent M, Leigh R and Lincoln H. *Holy Blood, Holy Grail.* New York: Dell Publishing, 1983.

13) Lo SC, Wear DJ, Green SL, Jones PG and Legrei JF. Adult respiratory distress syndrome with or without systemic disease associated with infection due to Mycoplasma fermentans. *Clinical Infectious Diseases* 1993;17 (Suppl. 1): S259-63.

14) Post staff. *CIA knew of chemical weapons at Iraqi depot, agency reveals. The Washington Post,* April 10, 1997, pg. 1.

15) White House Press Corps. President Clinton to roundtable on genetic engineering and biological weapons. High-level scientists in attendance. Newswire. Washington: D.C., April 10, 1998. OCT 10.04.98.16:53. Downloadable from German newspaper *Das Zeitung* at: http://www.netlink.de/gen/Zeitung/1998/980410a.htm.

16) Lewin LC, et al. *Report From Iron Mountain on the Possibility and Desirability of Peace.* New York: The Dial Press, 1967.

17) Keith J. *Op cit.*, pp. 264; 267-269.

18) Schlesinger, quoted in Herbert von Borch, *The Unfurnished Society.* New York: Hawthorne Publishers, 1962, p. 85.

19) Raskin M. Ed Kienholz and the Burden of Being an American. In: *Kienholz: A Retrospective.* New York: Whitney Museum of American Art. 1996, pp. 38-43.

20) *Goals for Americans: Programs for Action in the Sixties. Comprising the Report of the President's Commission on National Goals and Chapters Submitted for the Consideration of the Commission.* Englewood Cliffs, New Jersey: Prentice-Hall, 1960.

21) Rockefeller Brothers Fund. *Prospect for America: The Rockefeller Panel Reports.* Garden City, New York: Doubleday & Co., 1961.

22) *Humanum Genus Encyclical Letter of His Holiness Pope Leo XIII on Freemasonry,* (originally published on April 20, 1884; republished, Hawthorne, CA: Christian Book Club of America, 1982, p. 27.

23) "Norman Dodd radio interview." May 30, 1977, distributed by *American Opinion*, 395, Concord/Belmont, MA, 02178.

Chapter 12.
The CIA's Population Control
Projects: MKULTRA and MKNAOMI

"In the Army's tests, as with those of the CIA,
individual rights were also subordinated
to national security considerations;
informed consent and followup examinations of subjects
were neglected in efforts to maintain the secrecy of the tests."

U.S. Senator, Frank Church, Chairman
Foreign and Military Intelligence
Book I, Final Report 94th Congress, 2d Session, 1976.

America's most renowned program in which non-lethal warfare methods and materials were advanced was the CIA's top secret mind control and population control programs MKULTRA and MKNAOMI. Begun in the 1950s, both were allegedly terminated in 1970. We know, however, from the documentation in *Emerging Viruses: AIDS & Ebola*, that this was clearly not the case.[1,2] Lawmakers and the public had been deceived by false assurances from Henry Kissinger and President Nixon that America's offensive biological and chemical weapons programs had been halted.

In 1975, Frank Church's Congressional investigating committee learned that the most important of all CIA MKULTRA records had been "destroyed by Technical Services Division personnel acting on the verbal orders of Dr. Sidney Gottlieb, Chief of TSD [Technical Services Division]." Dr. Gottlieb testified, and former CIA Director Richard Helms confirmed, "that in ordering the records destroyed, Dr. Gottlieb was carrying out the verbal orders of then DCI [Director of Central Intelligence] Helms."[1]

So, if one wanted to find any remaining MKNAOMI—biological weapons research and development documents—alternative investi·

tive channels would need to be followed. Even then, only limited evidence might be gathered.

One example of this was apparent in figure 11.2. By reading the Army Chemical Corps documents certain references to top secret MKULTRA and MKNAOMI activities are implied and reasonably enlightening. The text discussed the use of "bacterial and fungal agents" that were recombined with genetic material "carrying infectivity factors . . . isolated from viruses." As seen in the "CONFIDENTIAL" document beginning in 1962, that is, when the "Special Virus Cancer Program" began, "new combinations of genetic factors through the mixture of infectious nucleic acids from different sources were undertaken. . . ."[2]

As introduced in Chapter 1, Dr. Shyh-Ching Lo's "Pathogenic Mycoplasma" work has relevance here, as does research concerning the "mad cow disease" protein (prion) agent. Dr. Lo's Armed Forces Institute of Pathology labor and patent application[3] referred to prion pioneer Carlton Gajdusek's work on AIDS virus-related hybridization projects akin to Robert Gallo's efforts with U.S. Army biological weapons contractor Litton Bionetics.[2] *Scientific American* author Mark Rogers from the Biotechnology Center at the University College in Dublin, Ireland, reported that prion crystals had been manufactured in labs "through recombinant DNA techniques" from *E. coli* bacteria.[4] Likewise, Gajdusek had written concerning the *"artificial manmade nature of the [kuru] epidemic"* associated with prion proteins.[5] Furthermore, University of Chicago Howard Hughes Medical Institute researcher Susan Lindquist *et al.* published that "prion-like proteins exist in yeast [fungi]," and pass in mammalian brains between cells as they function as infectious agents. Additionally, these researchers showed that such prions, devoid of genetic material, may still pass between generations of fungi.[6] Finally, concerning the prion's potential for bioelectrical activation, Professor Jacques Benveniste, a leading expert in bioelectric medicine at the University of Paris, theorized that prion crystals vated, and became pathogenic, by shape shifting as a gnetic frequencies impacting their protein structure.[7] wledge in mind, the U.S. Army document shown in evidences a link between biological weapons refungal diseases, and protein crystal research for d control and population control mission, suggestive rion research and associated brain disorders. Based

Fig. 12.1. Senate Committee's Report on the Testing and Use of Chemical & Biological Agents By the U.S. Intelligence Community

XVII. TESTING AND USE OF CHEMICAL AND BIOLOGICAL AGENTS BY THE INTELLIGENCE COMMUNITY[2]

Under its mandate[1] the Select Committee has studied the testing and use of chemical and biological agents by intelligence agencies. Detailed descriptions of the programs conducted by intelligence agencies involving chemical and biological agents will be included in a separately published appendix to the Senate Select Committee's report. This section of the report will discuss the rationale for the programs, their monitoring and control, and what the Committee's investigation has revealed about the relationship among the intelligence agencies and about their relations with other government agencies and private institutions and individuals.[2]

Fears that countries hostile to the United States would use chemical and biological agents against Americans or America's allies led to the development of a defensive program designed to discover techniques for American intelligence agencies to detect and counteract chemical and biological agents. The defensive orientation soon became secondary as the possible use of these agents to obtain information from, or gain control over, enemy agents became apparent.

Research and development programs to find materials which could be used to alter human behavior were initiated in the late 1940s and early 1950s. These experimental programs originally included testing of drugs involving willing human subjects, and culminated in tests using unwitting, nonvolunteer human subjects. These tests were designed to determine the potential effects of chemical or biological agents when used operationally against individuals unaware that they had received a drug.

The testing programs were considered highly sensitive by the intelligence agencies administering them. Few people, even within the agencies, knew of the programs and there is no evidence that either the executive branch or Congress were ever informed of them. The highly compartmented nature of these programs may be explained in part by an observation made by the CIA Inspector General that, "the knowledge that the Agency is engaging in unethical and illicit activies would have serious repercussions in political and diplomatic circles and would be detrimental to the accomplishment of its missions."[3]

Fig. 12.1 Senate Committee's Report Cont.

The research and development program, and particularly the covert testing programs, resulted in massive abridgments of the rights of American citizens, sometimes with tragic consequences. The deaths of two Americans[3a] can be attributed to these programs; other participants in the testing programs may still suffer from the residual effects. While some controlled testing of these substances might be defended, the nature of the tests, their scale, and the fact that they were continued for years after the danger of surreptitious administration of LSD to unwitting individuals was known, demonstrate a fundamental disregard for the value of human life.

The Select Committee's investigation of the testing and use of chemical and biological agents also raise serious questions about the adequacy of command and control procedures within the Central Intelligence Agency and military intelligence, and about the relationships among the intelligence agencies, other governmental agencies, and private institutions and individuals. The CIA's normal administrative controls were waived for programs involving chemical and biological agents to protect their security. According to the head of the Audit Branch of the CIA these waivers produced "gross administrative failures." They prevented the CIA's internal review mechanisms (the Office of General Counsel, the Inspector General, and the Audit Staff) from adequately supervising the programs. In general, the waivers had the paradoxical effect of providing less restrictive administrative controls and less effective internal review for controversial and highly sensitive projects than those governing normal Agency activities. . . .

---

[1] Senate Resolution 21 directs the Senate Select Committee on Intelligence Activities to investigate a number of issues:

" (a) Whether agencies within the intelligence community conducted illegal domestic activities (Section 2(1) and (2));

" (b) The extent to which agencies within the intelligence community cooperate (Section 2(4) and (8));

" (c) The adequacy of executive branch and congressional oversight of intelligence activities (Section 2 (7) and (11));

" (d) The adequacy of existing laws to safeguard the rights of American citizens (Section 2 (13))."

[2] The details of these programs may never be known. The programs were highly compartmented. Few records were kept. What little documentation existed for the CIA's principal program was destroyed early in 1973.

[3] CIA Inspector General's Survey of TSD, 1957, p. 217.

[3a] On January 8, 1953, Mr. Harold Blauer died of circulatory collapse and heart failure following an intravenous injection of a synthetic mescaline derivative while a subject of tests conducted by New York State Psychiatric Institute under a contract let by the U.S. Army Chemical Corps. . . .

on this knowledge, prion diseases such as Creutzfeldt–Jakob disease in humans are not only likely manmade, but may be aerially transmitted and electromagnetically induced or enhanced.

As seen in the previous chapter, a link between electromagnetic technologies and biological and chemical warfare is certain. Applications ranged from purely defensive to clearly offensive. The former is found in the declassified document shown in figure 11.2. Here "infrared" scanning systems were developed to quickly identify infectious agents or toxic substances in the field of military operations as early as 1962. Offensively, figure 11.4 documented that U.S. Army contractors were involved in research and testing of "antipersonnel" biologicals including a new "crystalline toxin" derived from *Clostridium botulinum* (botulism), like toxic prion crystal production from *E. coli*,[2,4] that might be disseminated "in a visible cloud of smoke."

It should be recalled that this entire biological weapons program, Project MKNAOMI, was a subordinate part of the larger Project MKULTRA for mind control and population control. Infectious crystalline agents disseminated through aerosol sprays that were potentially responsive to electromagnetic impulses were apparently considered important, even during this early period of "antipersonnel" research and development.[5] The fact that today's pandemics of prion diseases may be a direct result of these programs is, quite literally, mind-blowing.

MKULTRA for Mind and Population Control

According to the *Congressional Record*, MKULTRA began with a proposal from the Assistant Deputy Director for Plans, Richard Helms, to the DCI, outlining a special funding mechanism for highly sensitive CIA research and development projects that studied the use of biological and chemical materials in altering human behavior.

The hearings revealed that MKULTRA had been "approved by the DCI on April 13, 1953, along the lines proposed by ADDP [Assistant Deputy Director for Planning] Helms."[1]

The entire operation was kept top secret primarily because Americans themselves were to be placed at risk as targets for the research and developments. In this regard, the Senate report stated, "Part of the rationale for the establishment of this special funding mechanism was its extreme sensitivity. The Inspector General's survey of MKULTRA in 1963 noted the following reasons for this secrecy:

a. Research in the manipulation of human behavior is considered by many authorities in medicine and related fields to be professionally unethical, therefore the reputation of professional participants in the MKULTRA program are on occasion in jeopardy.

b. Some MKULTRA activities raise questions of legality implicit in the original charter.

c. A final phase of the testing of MKULTRA products places the rights and interests of U.S. citizens in jeopardy.

d. Public disclosure of some aspects of MKULTRA activity could induce serious adverse reaction in U.S. public opinion, as well as stimulate offensive and defensive action in this field on the part of foreign intelligence services.[1]

Additional evidence that such secret experimentation on U.S. citizens continued despite Nixon's signing of the Geneva accord in 1971 is shown in figures 12.1 and 12.2. The first of these documents came from the 1976 "Foreign and Military Intelligence, Book I, Final Report of the Senate Select Committee to Study Governmental Operations with Respect to Intelligence Activities." The document discussed "Testing and Use of Chemical and Biological Agents by the Intelligence Community." It stated:

Research and development programs to find materials which could be used to alter human behavior were initiated in the late 1940s and early 1950s. These experimental programs originally included testing of drugs involving witting human subjects, and culminated in tests using unwitting, non-volunteer human subjects . . . Few people, even within the agencies, knew of the programs and there is no evidence that either the executive branch or Congress were ever informed of them. The highly compartmented nature of these programs may be explained in part by an observation made by the CIA Inspector General that, "the knowledge that the Agency is engaging in unethical and illicit activities would have serious repercussions in political and diplomatic circles and would be detrimental to the accomplishment of its missions."

The research and development program, and particularly the covert testing programs, resulted in massive abridgements of the rights of American citizens, sometimes with tragic consequences. . . .[8]

The second document, figure 12.2, showed biological testing had been authorized to continue well into the 1990s. This "Title 1520" of the "United States Code Annotated Title 50, on War and National Defense" was widely circulated among U.S. patriots, Christians, and mili-

Fig. 12.2. United States Annotated Title 50. War and National Defense. Chapter 32—Chemical and Biological Warfare Program. Approved 1-16-96

§ 1520. Use of human subjects for testing of chemical or biological agents by Department of Defense; accounting to Congressional committees with respect to experiments and studies; notification of local civilian officials

(a) Not later than thirty days after final approval within the Department of Defense of plans for any experiment or study to be conducted by the Department of Defense, whether directly or under contract, involving the use of human subjects for the testing of chemical or biological agents, the Secretary of Defense shall supply Representatives with a full accounting of such plans for such experiment or study, and such experiment or study may then be conducted only after the expiration of the thirty-day period beginning on the date such accounting is received by such committees.

(b)(1) The Secretary of Defense may not conduct any test or experiment involving the use of any chemical or biological agent on civilian populations unless local civilian officials in the area in which the test or experiment is to be conducted are notified in advance of such test or experiment, and such test or experiment may then be conducted only after the expiration of the thirty-day period beginning on the date of such notification.

(2) Paragraph (1) shall apply to tests and experiments conducted by Department of Defense personnel and tests and experiments conducted on behalf of the Department of Defense by contractors.

(Pub.L. 95-79, Title VIII, § 808, July 30, 1977, 91 Stat. 334; Pub.L. 97-375, Title II, § 203(a)(1), Dec. 21, 1982, 96 Stat. 1822.)

The above text has been reset verbatum from: United States Code Annotated: Title 50, War and National Defense, Chapter 32—Chemical and Biological Warfare Program, Title 50:1520 on the Use of human subjects for testing of chemical or biological agents by Department of Defense. January, 1996, pp. 510, This represents a revision from "1977 Act. House Report No. 95-194 and House Conference Report No. 95-446, see 1977 U. S. Code Cong. and Adm. News, p. 537.

tia groups as evidence of the government's malfeasance. This 1996 document reiterated and clarified authorizations detailed in 1977 and again in 1982. This update covered the "Use of human subjects for testing of chemical or biological agents by the Department of Defense; accounting to Congressional committees with respect to experiments and studies;" [and] notification, not permission, of one unspecified local civilian official.

Thus, this document stated that the only requirement for defense and intelligence agencies that wish to authorize the exposure of unwitting citizens to lethal biological or chemical agents was the notification of one local civilian official. This was required "in the area in which the test or experiment is to be conducted . . . in advance of such test or experiment" by thirty days.[9]

The circulation of this document created such popular outrage that Senator John Glenn was obliged to sponsor a revised proposal titled: "Bill S-193 HUMAN RESEARCH SUBJECT PROTECTIONS ACT OF 1997." The bill was sent to the Senate's Labor and Human Resources Committee for final consideration and approval. It was subsequently modified to require military, medical, and intelligence contractors to fund the human experiments. No longer would taxpayers be forced to fund their own manipulation, intoxication, and/or demise.[10] Yet, according to the final "Repeal Restrictions," biological and chemical testing on U.S. citizens could continue under the guise of "medical, therapeutic, pharmaceutical, agricultural, industrial, or research activity." This allowed for alleged "protection against toxic chemicals or biological weapons," or "any law enforcement purpose, including any purpose related to riot control" providing "informed consent to the testing was obtained from each human subject in advance . . ."[11]

Even considering these concessions, there was no assurance that biological, chemical, and/or electromagnetic tests, if not full scale applications, would not be conducted by highly compartmentalized factions, operating independently, within the national security apparatus.

Although these government investigations and documents raised a few eyebrows, they did little more than that. It appeared that government oversight committees were doing their jobs so taxpayers could rest assured. However, very little technical knowledge and too few specifics were ever discussed during related Senate committee hearings. In some cases, legislators were even given false and misleading information from the intelligence community. As a result, the public has remained at risk for manipulation and experimentation.

Non-lethal Electromagnetic Warfare

Another example of such gross deception is shown in figure 12.3—a declassified U.S. government memorandum discussing some intricacies of project BLUEBIRD. Notice the deletion of critical facts. The document and project is of particular relevance to this book as it concerns the use of "sound" and the application of "ultrasonics, UHF, vibrations, monotonous sounds, concussion, etc., etc.," for hypnosis, mind control, and behavior change. The project also employed the study and use of dietary factors and foods as toxin delivery systems.

Such research foreshadowed the "mad cow disease" pandemic and the addition of highly toxic substances, such as the artificial sweetener aspartame, to foods and beverages. Other manipulations such as community water fluoridation and chlorination—sacred cows to public health—may serve alternative population control functions.[12]

In contrast to the documented facts, the 1976 Senate Select Committee's report described the CIA's project BLUEBIRD/ARTICHOKE as simply "the earliest of the CIA's major programs involving the use of chemical and biological agents. The Director approved project BLUEBIRD in 1950." Its less offensive objectives aside from general population control were:

> (a) Discovering means of conditioning personnel to prevent unauthorized extractions of information from them by known means, (b) investigating the possibility of control of an individual by application of special interrogation techniques, (c) memory enhancement, and (d) establishing defensive means for preventing hostile control of Agency personnel."[8]

Without mentioning precise details, the *Congressional Record*s provided knowledge that the earliest BLUEBIRD experiments involved extensive use of biologicals, chemicals, drugs, sound and electromagnetic frequencies for inducing various states of mental incapacitation, persuasion, and even death.

Most revealing, and reflective of early non-lethal warfare innovations, the declassified document in figure 12.3 showed the initial use of "Bacteria, Plant Cultures, Fungi, [and] Poisons of Various Types" were already being considered as *cofactors*, or *delivery systems*, for mind and personnel control by the early 1950s. Though BLUEBIRD's targets were allegedly limited to individuals, BLUEBIRD evolved into ARTICHOKE and ultimately to the PHOENIX II project—also called the MONTAUK program. This activity endeavored to develop technologies and the wherewithal for "electronic multidirectional targeting of select populations." This implied the capability of directing multiple electromagnetic frequencies to various targeted populations. This program description and purpose was akin to those provided by project HAARP as detailed in Chapter 15.[13]

Figure 12.4 provides a listing of the major electromagnetic mind-control projects administered by the CIA and branches of the U.S. military. The next section covers their most relevant achievements.

Early Electromagnetics for Mind-Control

According to *Operation Mind Control*,[13] a definitive effort by investigative journalist Walter Bowart, the earliest "wireless" mind-control experiments evolved by the late 1960s. Figure 12.4 lists these special electromagnetic mind control and population control programs. By then, the "remote control" of human cognition without the use of implanted electrodes was being pioneered by a research team at the University of California's Space and Biology Laboratory at the Los Angeles Brain Research Institute. There, Dr. W. Ross Adey developed ways of stimulating the brain using low-level electromagnetic pulses. Bowart detailed the novel methods Adey used. In one experiment, Dr. Adey analyzed the brain waves of chimpanzees that were performing tasks that involved learning. He attempted to control the rate at which the chimps learned by applying force fields to the outside of the head to alter behavior, moods, and attention. Dr. Adey's research indicated that his subjects were able to remember new information faster and better with stimulation."[14]

Following the alleged assassination of John. F. Kennedy by Lee Harvey Oswald with, according to most authorities, support from the CIA, Richard Helms sent a memo to Warren Commissioners. Helms, once again, was the initiator of project MKULTRA. In his letter, Helms referred to "biological radio communication" as having something to do with the assassination. Although he failed to fully explain, he did relate his comments to electronic brain stimulation research that was underway in the United States and Russia. "Current research," Helms wrote, "indicates that the Soviets are attempting to develop a technology for control in the development of behavioral patterns among the citizenry of the USSR in accordance with politically determined requirements of the system. Furthermore, the same technology can be applied to more

Fig. 12.3. United States Government Office Memorandum Concerning the CIA's 1950 Top Secret Mind Control Project Bluebird

Office Memorandum • UNITED STATES GOVERNMENT

A/B, 4, 23/32

TO :

Via :

FROM :

A

DATE: 3 March 1952

SUBJECT: Attached.

1. The attached memorandum is an Eyes Only report for your study and consideration.

2. The writer has set down personal comments relative the Bluebird operation and particularly contributions or rather lack of contributions to this effort by OSI. The writer has also commented relative matters involving the medical staff in relation to the Bluebird program.

3. The paper is not an official document, but rather a confidential report for I & SO information only.

4. If you have no further use for it after reading, I will retain it in our controlled files.

A

219

Fig. 12.3. Mind Control Project Bluebird Cont.

1) **Sound**

What use can be made of sound for Bluebird
application? Consider ultra-sonics, UHF,
vibrations, monotonous sounds, concussion,
etc., etc. (The Agency has contributed
██████ recently to the "Side Tone Delay" --
a related matter but the answers along these
lines are a year away probably.)

H-B/3

2) **High and Low Pressures, Various Gases**

Use of gas as in the air-tight chambers and
the effects of various gases or lack of oxygen
on individuals should be studied. The effects
of high and low pressures and certain gases
are reported to be being considered b██████
██████████), but pressure chamber
there has not been built.

H-B/6
B

-3) **Use of Hypnotic Techniques and Chemicals in
Connection with the Polygraph**

Some work has been done by the writer and his
associates in the hypnotic field with interesting results; however, insufficient work has
been done to specifically state that individuals
controlled by hypnotism or operating under post-
hypnotics could

    A) beat the polygraph

    B) or take the polygraph examination
    without being detected.

Information relative chemicals and drugs which
could be used in beating the polygraph is very
sketchy and inaccurate. This type of testing
cannot easily be carried on within the Agency
and the few tests that have been observed by
the writer were very poorly controlled and the
results at best were confusing.

4) **Use of Bacteria, Plant Cultures, Fungi, Poisons
of Various Types, Etc.**

Whether any of these elements would be useful
in Bluebird techniques are unknown to the writer
and to date, research has developed no information

-13-

Fig. 12.3. Mind Control Project Bluebird Cont.

that is useful along these lines. What effect
these elements would have on individuals who
are under control is unknown. However, certain
of these elements could produce bodily conditions
such as high fever, delirium, etc., but it is
doubted if these conditions could be exploited
advantageously.

5) Diet

If individuals under strict control are continuously fed food or liquid containing high quantities of salt, spices, etc. or if certain basic
food elements (such as fats, starches, proteins,
etc.) are continuously removed from the diet of
controlled individuals, will they or can they
thus be conditioned for Bluebird techniques?

There is considerable literature to indicate
that a standard Soviet and satellite technique
is the use of food containing high salt content,
which produces thirst in the subject to be in-
terrogated. The exact reasons for this are unknown, but a number of intelligent guesses can
be made.

O.   FURTHER COMMENTS RELATIVE ELECTRO-SHOCK

As has been noted above and in conversation, there has been
a considerable amount of discussion relative possible uses of
electroshock as a weapon by Bluebird.

It has been reported to the writer that ███████████, referred **C**
to above, believes that the electroshock or post electroshock coma
can be used obtaining information from individuals. According **A**
to ████████████████████ and his associates have been able
to obtain information from subjects after the electroshock convulsion and during the coma period following the convulsion after
the initial electroshock. There is very little information on this
technique and while we are not certain that individuals who are
attempting to conceal information could be forced to give up information through this method, the idea may have some merit, but
it is apparently in experimental form only and has not been widely
tested. At least as far as the writer knows there is little, if
any, literature available relative this technique.

-14-

sophisticated approaches to the 'coding' of information for transmittal to population targets in the 'battle for the minds of men.'"[14]

Helms's comments regarding the broad application of electromagnetic population controlling technologies were based partly on knowledge that, since 1961, Drs. W. Fry and R. Meyers at the University of Illinois had used *ultrasonic waves to develop brain lesions in test subjects*. Their research, according to Bowart, "demonstrated the great advantage of ultrasonics over the psychosurgical techniques which implanted electrodes in the brain. By using low-energy sound beams, Fry and Meyers stimulated or destroyed neural tissue at the point of focus of the beams without cutting or drilling into the brain."[14]

Not long after, Dr. Peter Lindstrom at the University of Pittsburgh developed "prefrontal sonic treatment" to effectively produce a lobotomy in patients with severe psychiatric disorders or untreatable pain. He used a single unfocused sound beam to kill specific nerve fiber tracts leaving adjacent cells healthy.[14]

At the same time, scientists found that monotonous rhythms could produce drowsiness and hypnotic inductions, and that specific frequency flashing strobe lights could initiate seizures in epileptics.[14]

Along with these discoveries the CIA secretly funded studies designed to test the effects of various vibrations on the brain. In one such experiment, researchers suspended a tin sheet from the ceiling connected to an electrical wave generator operating at ten cycles per second. When very large field strengths were coupled with very small volt strengths, and oscillated at the alpha frequency of brain function, human volunteers reported extremely unpleasant sensations.[14]

Similarly, at the Brain Research Institute in California, researchers examined additional effects of oscillating electromagnetic fields (EMFs) on human behavior. They exposed subjects to extremely small EMFs for only fifteen minutes and observed measurable degeneration of simple task performance.[14]

"These and other experiments," Bowart concluded, "led the cryptocracy to study the effects of very-low-frequency sound (VLF)—the opposite of ultrasonics—as an instrument of war. *Research revealed that there is a natural wave-guide between the ionosphere and the earth, which could be used to propagate very-low-frequency radiation, and guide it to selected locations on the earth.* Studies showed that this low-frequency sound subtly affected the electrical behavior of the brain in much the same way that Dr. Adey's studies had shown."[14]

Emphasis was added in the above paragraph due to special relevance to later discussions concerning projects such as HAARP and the Phoenix II project. These were virtually the same experiments that led authorities to realize the potential use of such applications, operating today to affect behavior and induce certain diseases in large populations, among these, possibly Alzheimer's presenile dementia and Creutzfeldt–Jakob disease.

Race to Control Minds and Induce Illnesses

The alpha-wave frequency of the human brain is known to be between eight and twelve hertz or cycles per second. "The ionospheric wave-guide oscillates at eight hertz, making it a good harmonic carrier of low-frequency sound (LFS) waves," according to Bowart and his scientific sources. These long waves are virtually impossible to detect. According to Pentagon studies, LFS waves might be successfully used to reduce the productive capacity of civilian populations during times of war.[13]

Dr. Frank Barnaby, Director of the Stockholm International Peace Research Institute, voiced a related concern. He warned of military and intelligence agency use of this technology as follows:

"If methods could be devised to *produce greater field strengths of such low-frequency oscillations, either by natural (for example, lightning) or artificial means, then it might become possible to impair the performance of a large group of people* in selected regions over extended periods."[15] [Emphasis added.]

Thus, early researchers found that ultrasonics, or very-low-frequency sound, harmonized with alpha rhythms, might lull large populations into suggestive states wherein radio waves, as well as television, could then be used to implant suggestions. These suggestions could then affect, if not control, the attitudes and behavior of the targeted masses.

By 1933, Soviet scientists had also studied microwave irradiation to cause central nervous system changes and affect behavior. During mind control studies they observed that even low intensity microwave radiation could dangerously alter normal brain wave rhythms. Such manipulations caused drastic alterations in perception—sense of time loss included—*and even hallucinations. In addition, Russian investigators learned that microwave exposures caused changes in protein metabolism and protein composition, altered white blood cell and im-*

Fig. 12.4. Major U.S. Military and Intelligence Agency Electromagnetic Mind-Control Projects

Project Moonstruck, 1952, CIA:

Description—Electronic implants in brain and teeth

Targeting—Long range; Implants introduced during surgey or sur-
reptitiously during abduction.

Frequency range: HF–ELF transceiver implants.

Purpose: Tracking, mind and behavior control, conditioning, programming, covert operations.

Functional Basis: Electronic stimulaton of the brain, E.S.B.

Project MK-ULTRA (BLUEBIRD/ARTICHOKE), 1953, CIA:

Description—Electronics and electroshock

Targeting—Short range.

Frequency range: VHF, HF, UHF, modulated at ELF. Local
transmission and reception.

Purpose: Programming behavior, creation of "cyborg" mentalities.

Effects: Narcoleptic trance states, programming by suggestion.

Functional Basis: Electronic dissolution of memory, E.D.O.M.

Project ORION (DREAMLAND), 1958, U.S.A.F.:

Description—Drugs, hypnosis, and ESB

Targeting—Short range, in person.

Frequency range: ELF modulation. Transmission and reception by
radar and microwaves.

Purpose: Top security personnel debriefing, programming, insure
security and loyalty.

Effects: Narcoleptic trance states, programming by suggestion.

Functional Basis: Electronic dissolution of memory, E.D.O.M.

Project MK-DELTA (DEEP SLEEP), 1960, CIA:
Description—Fine-tuned electromagnetic subliminal programming.

Targeting—Long range.

Frequency range: VHF, HF, UHF, modulated at ELF. Transmission and reception through television and radio antennae, power lines, mattress spring coils, modulation on 60Hz wiring.

Purpose: Programming behavior and attitudes in general population.

Effects: Fatigue, mood swings, behavior dysfunction and criminality.

Project PHOENIX II (MONTAUK), 1983, U.S.A.F., NSA:
Description—Electronic multi-directional targeting of select population groups.

Targeting—Medium range.

Frequency range: Radar, microwaves, EHF, UHF modulated with gigawatt through terawatt power.

Purpose: Loading of Earth grids, planetary sonombulescence to stave off geological activity, specific-point earthquake creation, population programming for sensitized individuals.

Pseudonym: "Rainbow," ZAP.

Project TRIDENT, 1989, ONR, NSA:
Description—Electronic directed targeting of individuals or populations

Targeting—Large population groups assembled.

Frequency range: VHF, HF, UHF, modulated at ELF. Local transmission and reception.

Purpose: Crowd dispersion and others.

Display: Black helicopters flying in triad formation.

Adopted from "Major Electromagnetic Mind-Control Projects" report in Contact: The Phoenix Educator, July 14, 1998, p. 5.

mune system functions, and created hormonal imbalances—especially those linked to altered thyroid activity, chronic fatigue, and male sterility.[14]

These low intensity microwave capabilities, as will be reconsidered later, are noteworthy with respect to contemporary epidemics including the prion protein induced Creutzfeldt–Jakob disease, immune system diseases such as AIDS and Mycoplasma related flu-like illnesses, the Gulf War Syndrome, as well as chronic fatigue and male sterility.

Bowart also recalled the 1962 fracas between the United States and Russia over the microwave bombardment of the U.S. Embassy in Moscow. He noted very few details regarding the issue in the news. "Perhaps," he speculated, the CIA "feared that any claim that *microwave radiation could affect human behavior* would bring great restrictions on the use of radar, *microwave relays*, and on booming microwave oven sales. But a less obvious reason suggests itself: the cryptocracy did not want to draw attention to its own use of such radiation in mind manipulation and population control."[14]

Expert Detractors and Advocates

Despite these historic facts, during the 1970s and early 1980s, most U.S. scientists remained skeptical that there was an advancing field of bioelectric population control.[14]

Dr. Elliot S. Valenstein, the author of *Brain Control*, was one whose comments reflected such bias, or scientific naiveté, concerning this burgeoning field. He wrote, "The reports of new technical developments for brain stimulation have led to concern that it will be used as the basis of an 'electroligarchy' where people could be virtually enslaved by controlling them from within their own brains . . . there is actually little foundation for the belief that brain stimulation could be used as a political weapon. It doesn't make sense. Anyone influential enough to get an entire population to consent to having electrodes placed in its head would already have his goal without firing a single volt." Obviously, Dr. Valenstein's research and conclusion missed the entire field of wireless communications and their military applications.[16]

Dr. Willard Gaylin somewhat concurred with Dr. Valenstein, but added that drugs and the media are far better tools for population control. Consistent with the knowledge advanced herein, Dr. Gaylin wrote,

"Drugs, brainwashing by control of the media, exploitation of fears through forms of propaganda, and indoctrination through the sources of education, particularly if preschool education or neonatal conditioning . . . becomes an approved practice, all seem more likely methods of totalitarian control."[17]

Finally, as an example of how amiss expert scientific opinions can be, Dr. Steven Rose, a British biochemist objected: "Unlike ancient maps marked 'here be monsters,' there will not be . . . brains transplanted into bodies or bottles, thought, memory or mind control, telepathic communication or genetic engineering, artificial intelligence or robots . . . I believe them impossible—or at least improbable; more importantly because scientific advance and its attendant technology only comes about in response to social constraints and social demands in the direction of these lurid potential developments, they do not represent, in a world beset with crises and challenges to human survival, serious contenders for our concerns."[18]

History has proven such naysayers wrong. As Bowart explained, such off base remarks by esteemed scientists could have been expected "when science is developed in a piecemeal, compartmentalized fashion, as it is under the direction of the cryptocracy. . . . Where the public is kept ignorant, and where scientists themselves are manipulated by the grant system, the balance upon which" such denials rest, heavily favors deception.[14]

For every scientist who has denied the practice of mind control, however, there were those who took a shining to the advancing technology for improved prospects for social control. One example was social psychologist Kenneth B. Clark, who said, "Given the urgency of the immediate survival problem, the psychological and social sciences must enable us to control the animalistic, barbaric and primitive propensities in man and subordinate these negatives to the uniquely human moral and ethical characteristics of love, kindness, and empathy . . . We can no longer afford to rely solely on the traditional prescientific attempts to contain human cruelty and destructiveness."[19]

Further advancing this thesis were Drs. Stephen Rosen, a scientist at IBM and Olaf Helmer, a founding member of the Institute for the Future. Rosen predicted a time when physical medicine would combine with the behavioral sciences to produce a new level of social control. Helmer envisioned a state in which "slave robots" were likely to be developed from advances in mind control technologies.[14]

References

1) Senate Select Committee on Intelligence. *PROJECT MKULTRA, The CIA's Program of Research in Behavior Modification.* Joint Hearing Before the Select Committee on Intelligence and the Subcommittee on Health and Scientific Research of the Committee on Human Resources, United States Senate, Ninety-fifth Congress, First Session, August 3, 1977. Washington, D.C.: U.S. Government Printing Office, 1977, pp. 388-390.

2) Secret Summary of Major Events and Problems, United States Army Chemical Corps, Fiscal Years 1961-1962. U.S. Army Chemical Corps Historical Office, Army Chemical Center, Maryland. Declassified document CBR-S-1794-62, OCMH, SCNo. 116226, released June, 1992; see also: Anderson WAD and Scotti TM. *Synopsis of Pathology, Eighth edition.* St. Louis: The C.V. Mosby Company, 1972, p. 202-203 for information relating to encephalomeylitis virus and slow virus infections.

3) Lo SC. Pathogenic Mycoplasma. United States Patent number 5,242,820, September 7, 1993. Assigned to the American Registry of Pathology, Washington, D.C. For cell cytoplasmic degenerative changes including vacuolization, see p. 63; and Lo SC, Wear DJ, Green SL, Jones PG and Legier JF. Adult respiratory distress syndrome with or without systemic disease associated with infections due to *Mycoplasma fermentans. Clinical Infectious Diseases* 1993;17(Suppl 1):S259-63.

4) Contributing scientists. Ask the experts: Medicine—"What is a prion? Specifically, what is known about the molecular structure of prions and how they cause infections such as Creutzfeldt-Jakob disease? *Scientific American* Internet publication. Available from file:///A/medicine14what is a prion.html.

5) The U.S. Army Chemical Corps' reference to "crystalline toxin" reinforces the findings reported in: Scott D and Scott W. *The Brucellosis Triangle.* Sudbury, Canada: The Chelmsford Publishers (Box 133, Station B, Sudbury, Canada. P3E 4N5. [705-670-0180]), 1998 pp. 44-57.

The Scotts' investigation also determined that on January 3, 1946, George W. Merck, as U.S. biological weapons industry director, reported to the Secretary of War, Henry Stimson, on the "Production and isolation, for the first time, of a crystalline bacterial toxin, which has opened the way for the preparation of a more highly purified immunizing toxoid." In the same report, Merck noted significant advances in the biological warfare arena had been made concerning human immune mechanisms.

The remainder of this fascinating and relevant research section dealt with Carlton Gajdusek's earliest studies. As an expert in "protein chemistry" and "blood electrolyte balance," Gajdusek used Australian aboriginal and New Guinean populations to advance his career. These remote tribes, the Scotts concluded, had originally been infected with prion crystals by Japanese bioweapons researchers. Gajdusek's Australian assignment had been granted by his "biowar friend from Walter Reed Army Institute of Research, Joseph E. Smadel."

Most revealing in *The Brucellosis Triangle* is the Scotts' simple explanation of blood protein crystallization with relevance to Gajdusek's knowledge and research including his published report that the kuru epidemic was "manmade." The Scotts quoted Gajdusek as writing: "Continued surveillance has revealed no alteration in the unusual pattern of kuru disappearance, which indicates the *artificial man-made nature of the epidemic*. Kuru virus clearly has no reservoir in nature and no intermediate biological cycle for its preservation except in humans." [Emphasis added.]

The above "conclusion by Gajdusek," the Scotts reported, "fits the template of a Japanese-created infection as part of their biological warfare research."

6) Burton B. New type of DNA-free inheritance in yeast is spread by a "mad cow" mechanism. *Cell*, May 30, 1997. Press release from the University of Chicago. Available from: http://www.ucmc.uchicago. edu/news/1997/ prionfibers.html.

7) Personal communication from Dr. Benveniste during a "clustered water" conference sponsored by CellCore International Corporation in Irvine, California, June 8, 1999.

8) The entire text in figure 10.1, reset for clarity, came verbatim from: Senate Select Committee. *Foreign and Military Intelligence, Book I, Final Report of the Senate Select Committee to Study Governmental Operations with Respect to Intelligence Activities.* 94th Congress, 2nd Session. Report 94-755. Washington, D.C.: U.S. Government Printing Office, April 26 (Legislative Day, April 14),1976, pp.385-386.

9) United States Code Annotated: Title 50, War and National Defense, Chapter 32—Chemical and Biological Warfare Program, Title 50:1520 on the Use of human subjects for testing of chemical or biological agents by Department of Defense. January 1996, p. 510.

10) Osborn K. Senator John Glenn introduces human research subject protection act of 1997. *Russian River Times*, 2;24, November 17, 1997, p. 1.; Letter to U.S. Senator John Warner's Office from political activist June S. Heyman, Tues, Nov. 18, 1997;

11) Excerpt from 50USC Annotated, p. 138. 50 Sec. 1520 Repealed: Sec. 1520. Repealed. Pub. L. 105-85, Div. A, Title X sec. 1078 (g), Nov. 18, 1997, 111 Stat. 1916. See also Sec. 1520a. Restrictions.

12) An interesting literature review article on fluoride, entitled, "Fluoride and Stupidity. Part 1. Sickness Control 101. was written by Tom Swanson of Bright Ideas Consulting. Copies are available by e-mailing him at: tswans@Alaska.NET.

13) Anonymous Internet source. "Major Electromagnetic Mind-Control Projects." *Contact: The Phoenix Educator*, July 14, 1998, p. 5.

14) Bowart W. *Operation Mind Control*. New York: Dell Publishing Co., Inc., 1978, pp. 257-271.

15) Barnaby F. *New Scientist*, June 17, 1976.

16) Valenstein E. *Brain Control*. New York: Wiley, 1973;

17) Gaylin WM, Meister JS and Neville RC. *Operating on the Mind*. New York: Basic Books, 1975;

18) Rose S. *The Conscious Brain*. New York: Knopf, 1976.

19) Clark K. *American Psychological Assoc. Monitor*, October, 1971.

Chapter 13.
Globalism: An Essay and Reality Check

"A popular Government without popular information or the means of acquiring it, is but a Prologue to a Farce or a Tragedy or perhaps both. Knowledge will forever govern ignorance, and a people who mean to be their own Governors, must arm themselves with the power knowledge gives."

James Madison, Aug. 4, 1822
Letter to W.T. Barry in G.P. Hunt, ed.,
IX The Writings of James Madison 103 (1910)

There was a time when the phrase "New World Order" inspired right wing patriots and Christian fundamentalists to rale in distress against an insidious foe directing societies and economies towards globalism and the Armageddon. This is obviously no longer the case. The intriguing phrase linked to the back of every dollar bill—"Novus Ordo Seclorum"[1]—and what many authors claim are "secret societies" directed by Anglo-Saxon oligarchs,[2] was also cited in the October, 2000 issue of the *American Journal of Public Health*. The article by medical sociologist Stephen J. Kunitz was entitled "Public Health Then and Now—Globalization, States, and the Health of Indigenous People."[3]

From the Department of Community and Preventive Medicine at the University of Rochester, Professor Kunitz reviewed literature that linked declines in health, longevity, and numbers of indigenous populations to the same "well-to-do WASPS (White Anglo-Saxon Protestants)" condemned by political right-wingers and societally conscious liberals. Despite the ongoing genocides that he documented, however, this obviously liberal-leaning social scientist concluded that, "The consequences of globalization are mixed, and for the indigenous peoples of poor countries globalization has *potentially* important benefits."

The emphasis on the word "potentially" is mine. It emphasizes my opinion that Dr. Kunitz's highly professional prose was tainted by what might be called "wishful thinking," at best, or "lethal fantasy" at worst. It reflected a common bias among academicians, engineered by the same *potential* saviors about whom Dr. Kunitz wrote. Could it be that the entire context within which Dr. Kunitz and other academicians operates, including such avenues of academic expression as the *AJPH*, has been heavily influenced, if not completely shaped, by the non-governmental and private organizations that Dr. Kunitz posited may help save minority populations from extinction? If that is so, and I believe it is, then his analysis, scholarly as it may seem, represented little more than propaganda for those directing New World Order globalization—popular persuasion in the realm of social science.

Let's review the facts.

Globalism and Native Life Expectancy

Dr. Kunitz defined globalization as "[t]he increasing integration of world capital and trade flows." It was also "[a] social process in which the constraints of geography on social and cultural arrangements recede and in which people become increasingly aware that they are receding."[3]

What was most vexing about Dr. Kunitz's article was that it heralded, in the first line of the abstract, the *potential* benefits of globalization while his text relayed data that reflected the grave risks and high tolls of such "progress."

"[N]ow, as in the past, states have dominated indigenous peoples primarily for purposes of their own economic growth," he wrote. "[T]here is no assurance that all countries will benefit equally, or that some will benefit at all, from the global economy that has emerged since World War II. Indeed, many skeptics, of whom I am one, believe that globalization may have profoundly deleterious effects on some states and may well increase inequality among them. The erosion of sovereignty may mean that states cannot protect their industries and local employment; that laws protecting the environment and the health and safety of workers are weakened; that social spending is reduced; and that national economies are controlled by the flow of international capital. . . ."

"The widening of income differences among regions," he argued, "and the actual downturn in income" in many, was "congruent with the decline of life expectancy" in many African and Eastern European nations. "And both absolute and relative decline in income do not bode well for indigenous peoples in poor countries."

Why not? Dr. Kunitz answered that "indigenous people stand in the way of exploitation of the natural resources that poor countries must undertake in order to participate in the global economy." He stated that this would raise their "standard of living," although others have argued otherwise.[4]

An Alternative View of "Western Progress"

Professor T. Adeoye Lambo, the Vice-Chancellor of the University of Ibadan, Nigeria, where he was formerly Head of the Department of Psychiatry and Dean of the Faculty of Medicine, had argued before the WHO, in 1971, that such globalization—evangelizing the Western way of life and economically driven social services, in contrast to traditional native ways of living—was highly, possibly irreversibly, destructive. "Men in many advanced countries . . . are so engrossed in their various occupations, in manufacturing superfluous goods, in buying and selling, in searching for affluence, in accumulating wealth, in altering their environment, in building for the future, and in rushing hither and thither, that they have no time left to wonder what it is all about," Dr. Lambo said.[4]

Believing that capitalistic expansion and globalism led only to mass "disillusionment," Lambo expressed the African position of "doubt whether material prosperity is necessarily synonymous with successful living."[4]

"There is no doubt that this preoccupation with affluence tends to destroy traditional cultures, or at least to transform them," he lectured. "[T]he modified cultures weaken dependencies of individuals on family, clan, shrine, and community, and it is this break in the affective bond which is at the root of the contemporary conflict agitating the mind of the African" and other native people.[4]

Lambo cautioned against the negative "impact of the western style of life, including technology, on the family 'tradition' or 'atmosphere,' its interests and amusements, its resources for occupying and developing rather than repressing the growing mind, its social ideals and customs."[4]

"It is important to remember," he said, "that the fundamental basis of African cultures attributes all values, categories of thought, and significant content of thought to the group. Because of the nature of this cultural environment . . . he does not interpret reality in relation to the temporal environment but in terms of the relations of men to other men, and of men to the supernatural. . . ."[4]

Despite acknowledging western medicine's "remarkable development" in providing drugs to combat "infectious diseases and disorders of metabolism," Lambo cited its weaknesses:

> The patient himself was provisionally ignored; he was merely the incidental battlefield of a bacteriological conflict, or the irrelevant container of fascinating biochemical processes. The prestige of discoveries made along these lines encouraged the injudicious to formulate practically all ailments, even the psychoneuroses, in terms of internal medicine, with no reference to the integrative levels of the instincts, the emotions, the personality, and the ecology.[4]

Largely rejecting western medical modes and WHO pharmaceutical campaigns, Lambo urged the adoption of "a well-designed programme of preventive medicine in many fields, involving the social sciences and mental health . . . in order to obviate the necessity of building expensive institutions for curative purposes."[4]

Lambo continued his tirade against western globalization by citing the symptoms of discontent and disease that it spreads. Included here were "[v]arious feelings [such as] complete lack of interest in, or lack of capacity to control, events on which well-being depends; overt human responses to change, including anxiety and fear; an extreme sense of insecurity, lack of purpose and direction; severe manifestations of depersonalization and derealization, including confusion of identity; conflicts generated by incompatible values characterized by the sense of social isolation, [and] self-estrangement."[4]

It occurred to me that Dr. Lambo had diagnosed the chief complaints and psycho-social pathology underlying disillusionment, crime, and violence in America as well.

Genocidal Effects of Globalization

To lend support to Dr. Lambo's concerns, in each country affected by globalization, Dr. Kunitz reported, "life expectancy of indigenous people is substantially less than that of nonindigenous people. . . . [H]igh national wealth is associated with changes in values and policies in important segments of the dominant society . . ." This ultimately left most minority populations disenfranchised and susceptible to continued virulent manipulation.

Examples of this, provided by the University of Rochester medical sociologist, included "Amazonia" and native America.

In Brazil, he reported, agricultural expansions left six aboriginal tribes extinct. Between the early 1900s and 1957, when Brazilian anthropologist Rebeiro conducted his analysis, the Indian population declined from about 1 million to less than 200,000. "In areas of pastoral expansion (cattle raising)," Dr. Kunitz wrote, "thirteen tribes disappeared. In areas of extractive activities (rubber and nut collecting, diamond prospecting, etc.), a phenomenal fifty-nine tribes were destroyed." The military "worked a 'global transformation' in the Brazilian mining sector that . . . had emerged between the military government and a number of large multinational corporations."[3]

"But it was not only multinational corporations that were involved" in the Amazonian genocide, he stated. U.S. government agencies such as the Agency for International Development (USAID) and others, including: the U.S. Geological Survey, the Inter-American Development Bank, and the World Bank provided additional capital for projects that involved "not only mining but highway and dam construction, cattle ranching, and farming on large tracts cleared from the forest."

Clearly, Dr. Kunitz reiterated, this globalistic effort caused catastrophic effects in Amazonia. "The rain forest turned out to be ecologically far more fragile than had been supposed," he wrote, "and the result of all these development activities has been ecologic destruction that has attracted world attention. The Indians who stood in the way of development were also largely destroyed."

Within twenty years of the insurgence by global agencies to sponsor regional development in Brazil, "epidemics of measles, tuberculosis, and other infectious diseases had begun to spread" among native populations. "Prospectors, ranchers, the military, and hired killers murdered large numbers," Dr. Kunitz reported. "Destruction of hunting,

fishing, and farming areas contributed to malnutrition and outright starvation among the Indians."[3]

Continuing to describe these genocides, Dr. Kunitz quoted British
anthropologist L. Rabben:

> Describing the result of a 3-year gold rush in the late 1980s in part of
> Amazonia, Rabben observed that 65% of the indigenous population
> was infected with malaria, whereas before the rush malaria had been
> rare. "Among the Yanomani, 35 percent were malnourished, and 76
> percent were anemic; 13 percent of children lost one or both of their
> parents." Dispersion of survivors, coupled with high death rates, "dev-
> astated Yanomani culture and disaggregated Yanomani society in many
> areas."

> These ecologic and human catastrophes have been facilitated by inter-
> national capital, expertise, and markets—that is to say, by globaliza-
> tion. The rapidity with which the calamity has occurred is remarkable,
> but the process is not so different from, and no more rapid than, what
> occurred in settler societies of the past. What is very different is that
> there have been witnesses who have reported it internationally in great
> detail.[3]

Foundations and Non-governmental Organzations (NGOs) to the Rescue?

Given all of the above indications of globalism inexorably linked
to acts of genocide, how did Dr. Kunitz defend his statement that "there
may also be benefits from globalization, including *benefits* for indigenous peoples in poor countries?"

As "people become increasingly aware" of globalization, Dr.
Kunitz observed, along with economic advantages accumulating in the
wealthiest sectors, the values and attitudes of the privileged majority
shifted toward human advocacy, minority rights, and environmental
concerns. He credited globalism for better communications and increasing media savvy among victimized people, helping to bring world
attention to regional injustices. This had resulted in, he alleged,
"greater safeguards of the land and natural resource rights of indigenous peoples in projects supported by . . ." multinational political and
economic organizations including the International Labor Organization, the Organization of the American States, the Inter-American Development Bank, the World Bank, and the United Nations. He credited

the United Nations for having developed treaties and policies recognizing the rights of indigenous peoples. "When they violate those agreements," he wrote, "individuals and groups often bring the violations to the attention of the UN. This is one of the ways in which the Working Group on Indigenous Populations has attempted to publicize violations of the right of indigenous peoples."

Thus, Dr. Kunitz claimed, globalism had facilitated "the growth of NGOs that *attempt* to influence international policies to advance agendas involving protection of the environment and of indigenous peoples. Just as it was well-to-do people from the East and West Coast of the United States who first attempted to protect the environment and American Indians," he wrote, "it was now pressure groups in the rich countries of the North who were trying to protect the environment and indigenous peoples of the poor countries of the South . . ." [Emphasis added.]

As the director of one such NGO who has, since 1978, attempted to "influence international policies" to protect minority, and other unwitting populations, from ongoing atrocities perpetrated by military–medical–pharmaceutical–industrialists upon whose broad shoulders globalism rests, I have credited the Internet and grassroots activism far more than an allegedly free press, foundations, or agencies largely funded, if not established, by the same international industrialists and world banking institutions whose aim it has been since at least the late 1800s to colonialize the globe.

Having myself matriculated in Dr. Kunitz's department under the tutelage of the brilliant and kind medical sociologist Dr. Andrew Sorenson, I am surprised that the professor missed mentioning the sociopolitical and economic ties between chief globalists influencing health care and world pharmaceutics today, having "emerged" as Dr. Kunitz correctly stated, since World War II—the Rockefeller–IG Farben consortium.

This was, after all, no mystery at the time Dr. Kunitz wrote his article. Even mainstream newspapers and television had reviewed books like Martin Lee's *The Beast Reawakens*[5] and Boston College's chairman of the Fine Arts Department, John J. Michalczk's, "Nazi Medicine."

Regarding the latter, *The Boston Globe* was brave enough to print, "America was in the Reich's shadow. Years before the Nazis, American experiments in racial engineering and genetic superiority were financed by the Rockefeller Foundation and Andrew Carnegie under the category of eugenics."[6] More revealing were works cited in the reference section of this chapter.[7-11]

When I submitted a rebuttal to Kunitz's report to the *AJPH*, I dared not mention specific names of corporate culprits in order to satisfy "peer review." Such poignant references might have troubled the editors with legal concerns, and possibly lost advertising revenues. The journal's full-page color ads were all paid for by the subsidiaries of these genocide-linked mega corporations.[6-11] As shown in figure 13.1, Mary Northridge, the journal's editor, rejected the submission nonetheless.

Linking the NGOs to Genocide

It was also no secret that USAID, cited by Dr. Kunitz as playing a collaborative role in the Amazonian genocides, provided cover for the CIA to infiltrate African nations during the mid-1970s to foment political unrest and even wars.[12] As the Vietnam War was winding down, and Nixon's "War on Cancer" was heating up, Sub-Sahara Africa, in particular, became the target of numerous clandestine activities designed to influence Black-ruled governments, events, organizations, or persons in support of U.S. foreign policy. Such intrusions were conducted in such a way that the involvements of U.S. Government affiliated agencies were not apparent. Other organizations used to conceal intelligence operations and position agents in various parts of Africa were PUSH (People to Save Humanity), AFRICARE, CARE, the Peace Corps, The Rockefeller and Ford Foundations, the World Bank, and more.[12]

American intelligence's primary focus then was Third World depopulation as articulated in Henry Kissinger's 1974, initially classified, publication *National Security Secret Memorandum 200*.[13] Later, as shown in figures 18.14 and 18.15, Kissinger's successor, Zbigniew Brzezinski, articulated U.S. security policy that extended Black African genocides to American Blacks. He set to motion, or more accurately continued, covert intelligence operations that kept American Blacks leaderless and lacking social-political cohesion. As Dr. Lambo reasoned, this downright malicious policy had predictably devasting and genocidal effects on Africans and Black Americans. Rationale for such atrocities was expressed most clearly in both national security memoranda.

Fig. 13.1. *AJPH* Rejection Letter to Dr. Horowitz

 American Public Health Association
800 I Street NW • Washington, DC 20001-3710
(202) 777-APHA • Fax: (202) 777-2534 • comments@apha.org • www.apha.org

December 13, 2000

Leonard G. Horowitz, DMD, MA, MPH
Tetrahedron
206 North 4th Avenue
Suite 147
Sandpoint, ID 83864

RE: 00/048E:"Globalism: An Alternative View

Dear Dr. Horowitz:

Thank you for sending us your paper. After careful editorial review, we regret to inform you that we cannot publish your manuscript in the Journal. The potential to advance public health research, policy, practice and education is our foremost consideration. Other criteria guide us in our decision-making process, including balance among topics covered, fit with planned theme issues, and interest to our readers and the general public.

We receive many valuable papers that we must turn down. We wish you success in publishing elsewhere.

Sincerely,

Mary E. Northridge, PhD
Editor

GLOBAL HEALTH   129TH ANNUAL MEETING • OCTOBER 21-25, 2001 • ATLANTA, GEORGIA

A standard letter for rejecting authors' submissions sent by *APHA* journal editor Mary E. Northridge to Dr. Horowitz . The submission covered the information presented in this chapter concerning globalism and its genocidal aspects, but without citing specific globalists.

.۱elson Rockefeller's protégé, Dr. Kissinger, overseeing CIA operations as the National Security Advisor under Richard Nixon wrote, " . . . the U.S. economy will require large and increasing amounts of minerals from abroad; especially from less developed countries. That fact gives the U.S. enhanced interest in the political, economic, and social stability of the supplying countries. Wherever a lessening of population pressures through reduced birth rates can increase the prospects for such stability, population policy becomes relevant to resource supplies and to the economic interests of the United States."[14]

David Rockefeller's protégé, Brzezinski, stated likewise that "preventive operations" were required "in order to impede durable ties between U.S. black organizations and radical groups in African states." These actions were further designed "to sharpen social stratification in the black community, which would increase the widening and perpetuation of the gap between successful educated blacks and the poor, giving rise to growing antagonism between different black groups, weakening . . . the movement as a whole."

As per the projected "Political Effects of Population Factors," Dr. Kissinger wrote, "there is a major risk of severe damage to world economic, political, and ecological systems and, as these systems begin to fail . . . urban slum dwellers may serve as a volatile, violent force which threatens political stability."[13] He thus recommended these and other people in lesser developed nations be culled through a variety of methods involving USAID, the World Bank, and other organizations serving to protect "our humanitarian values."

The cover of Kissinger's NSSM 200 document dated December 10, 1974, is shown in figure 13.2. It is certainly worth the time referencing and reading this document through interlibrary loans.

More Background on a Rockefeller Centered Conspiracy

The best reading, particularly for those inclined to dismiss the conspiratorial nature of contemporary global genocides, is Christopher Simpson's book *The Science of Coercion*. This British journalist documented the manner in which globalists' control of social systems, especially those of *science*, have been maintained since 1945. "[T]he Rockefeller organization," Oxford University Press published, "appears to have been used as a public front to conceal the source of at least $1 million in CIA funds for Hadley Cantril's Institute for International Social Research" at Princeton—among the world's leading in-

Fig. 13.2. *National Security Secret Memorandum 200*

CONFIDENTIAL

NSSM 200

IMPLICATIONS OF WORLDWIDE POPULATION GROWTH
FOR U.S. SECURITY AND OVERSEAS INTERESTS

December 10, 1974

CLASSIFIED BY Harry C. Blaney, III
SUBJECT TO GENERAL DECLASSIFICATION SCHEDULE
OF EXECUTIVE ORDER 11652 AUTOMATICALLY DOWN-
GRADED AT TWO YEAR INTERVALS AND DECLASSIFIED
ON DECEMBER 31, 1980.

This document can only be declassified by the White House.

Declassified/Released on 7/3/15
under provisions of E.O. 12356
by F. Graboske, National Security Council

CONFIDENTIAL

DECLASSIFIED
Authority E.O. 12356

NSIAD-205-89-4

Largely written and promoted by Nelson Rockefeller's protégé Dr. Henry Kissinger, this document strategises U.S. National Security "diplomatic" responses to Third World population that stood in the way of accessing natural resources for globalists' corporate interests.

vestigative centers for economic elitists interested in mass media, social science, and persuasive communications. "Nelson Rockefeller was himself among the most prominent promoters of psychological [warfare] operations."

The $1 million cited above was ridiculously conservative. From 1945 to the present the concealed costs of maintaining "control of [psychological and] social systems" is obviously thousands of times this amount.

Simpson continued:

> Taken as a whole, the evidence thus far shows that a very substantial fraction of the funding for academic US research into social psychology and into many aspects of mass communication behavior during the first fifteen years of the Cold War was directly controlled or strongly influenced by a small group of men who had enthusiastically supported elite psychological operations as an instrument of foreign and domestic policy since World War II. They exercised power through a series of interlocking committees and commissions that linked the world of mainstream academic with that of the US military and intelligence communities. Their networks were for the most part closed to outsiders; their records and decision-making processes were often classified; and in some instances the very existence of the coordinating bodies was a state secret.

Simpson's next paragraphs spoke directly to the publication of Dr. Kunitz's article in the *AJPH* and also to the rejection of my related submission:

> This was not a "conspiracy," in the hackneyed sense of that word. It was rather precisely the type of "reference group" or informal network that is so well known to sociologists. The informal authority exercised by these networks reveals a distinctly centrist ideological bent: Projects that advanced their conception of scientific progress and national security enjoyed a chance to gain the financial support that is often a prerequisite to academic success. . . . [P]rojects that did not meet these criteria were often relegated to obscurity, and in some cases actively suppressed. One result of this selective financing has been a detailed elaboration of those aspects of scientific truth that tend to support the preconceptions of the agencies that were paying the bill. . . .
>
> [T]he "dominant paradigm" of the period proved to be in substantial part a paradigm of dominance, in which the appropriateness and inevitability of elite control of communication was taken as a given. As a practical matter, the key academic journals of the day demonstrated only a secondary interest in what communication "is." Instead, they

concentrated on how modern technology could be used by elites to manage social change, extract political concessions, or win purchasing decisions from targeted audiences. Their studies emphasized those aspects of communication that were of greatest practical interest to the public and private agencies that were underwriting most of the research. This orientation reduced the extraordinarily complex, inherently communal social process of communication to simple models based on the dynamics of transmission of persuasive—and, in the final analysis, coercive—messages.[9]

Giving him the benefit of doubt, one cannot say that Dr. Kunitz, other medical sociologists, and world leading social scientists, have been *witting* agents for coercive elitists' global messages. Nor was his article perceived by most readers as the sophisticated expression of propaganda that it was. Given this more thorough background and analysis, however, and the fact that you can only fool most of the people all the time, readers might now be awakened to the insidious threat that even such "scientific" communications conceal.

Unfortunately, such revelation comes a little too late. Given the urgency of this subject—globalism and widespread acts of genocides accompanying it—the "reawakening beast" does not bode well for the world's fooled, mostly native, minority, and/or ethnic populations.

The U.S. Geological Survey and Global Genocide

Among the U.S. government agencies at the forefront of social engineering, while communicating the "paradigm of dominance," is the U.S. Geological Survey (USGS). Dr. Kunitz credited this organization, along with the World Bank and Rockefeller Foundation, for having funded several South American genocides. This agency, he wrote, provided resources for projects that involved "not only mining but highway and dam construction, cattle ranching, and farming on large tracts cleared from the forest."[3] Their maps detailed everything from water sources and mineral deposits to deforestation and wildlife preserves in regions targeted for corporate expansion. Thus, as a source of hard data for logistical intelligence, USGS mapping, resource projections, and associated pronouncements for the benefit of governments and private concerns, were routinely used to direct Third World developments in various fields in keeping with global, covertly genocidal, agendas.

The U.S. Geological Survey and the WNV

It was, therefore, no surprise that from the beginning of the WNV "outbreak" in the northeastern U.S., the USGS played a leading role in developing and disseminating propaganda in support of official pesticide spraying campaigns. In effect, along with the CDC, the agency became a chief voice articulating the WNV problem, reaction, and solution—Anvil—effectively promulgating non-lethal warfare against humans as well as lower species.

According to the USGS's website, as shown in figure 13.3, the agency began, in the fall of 1999, to test "dead birds for the West Nile virus in support of federal, state, and local wildlife agencies, as well as public health departments and other federal agencies" that utilized dead wild birds as "sentinels for detecting WNV activity in their area." By the fall of 2000, the USGS had helped diagnose and map WNVs in "2370 birds from 8 states and from over 63 species, including 53 free-ranging species . . ." including "16 horses from 5 states." They reported sixteen people had fallen ill to the virus that year "with one human death in New Jersey."[15]

Manipulating the public's collective consciousness with fear, as effective bioterrorists might, the agency heralded concerns of a few "wildlife health biologists" that "the fall 2000 migration of millions of birds from and through the 400 mile wide infected region of the northeastern U.S. may move the WNV southward along the Atlantic and Gulf coast states." Indeed, by year's end, other states, including Maryland and Pennsylvania "reported their first two WNV positive crows . . . ." An additional "19 free-living mammals" in New York were allegedly found infected with WNV "including three species of bats, a raccoon, an eastern chipmunk, and tree squirrels in New York." Seven domestic pets, three rabbits, a chicken, a macaw, a parakeet, and a cockatoo, were also identified as WNV positive and cause for mosquito abatement programs according to the USGS.[15]

Henry Luce's *Time* magazine, discussed later as operating at the forefront of Rockefeller-directed psychosocial shaping of American attitudes, also had much to say about the WNV outbreak, including subtle criticism. In "Your A to Z Guide to the Year in Medicine" (figure 13.5), David Bjerklie *et al.,* wrote: "In the second year of a much feared and overpublicized medical crisis, public-health officials in the Northeast intensified their campaign against mosquitoes infected with the West Nile virus." Despite their complaint concerning the "much

Fig. 13.3. USGS "Fact Sheet" Used to Promote Public Acceptance of Official WNV Policies

science for a changing world

Wild Birds Critical to Understanding the WEST NILE VIRUS

1999: West Nile Virus Emerges In North America

Since the fall of 1999, the USGS has been testing wild birds and mammals for West Nile virus (WNV) infection and incorporating epidemiological data on the West Nile outbreak into a geographic-information system (GIS) for display and analysis. The West Nile virus is an insect-borne virus that had never been reported in the Western Hemisphere. Birds are the natural hosts for this virus, which can be transmitted from infected birds to humans and other animals through the bites of infected mosquitoes. Wild birds, primarily crows, were affected in last year's outbreak in the greater New York City area along with a few other native North American bird species, horses, and people. In 1999, the virus caused encephalitis in 62 people in the New York City area, seven of whom died. Thus far in 2000, eighteen people have been diagnosed with the disease and there has been one fatality.

2000: West Nile Over-Winters and Re-Emerges in Wild Birds and Mammals

This year (2000), wild bird mortality due to WNV was first detected in May in

A USGS pathologist examines a suspect West Nile virus crow.

southeastern New York and northeastern New Jersey. Since then, the disease has continued to expand both geographically and in the number and variety of species infected. The virus has been found in 70 bird species, including 54 free-ranging species from 11 States, ranging from Vermont to North Carolina. Free-living wild mammals in New York were found positive for WNV for the first time this year. Once again the virus was found in horses, causing illness in 38 horses from 6 States. Surveillance efforts have also detected a number of positive mosquito species including species that are active at dawn and dusk and species that are active during the day. The mosquitoes found positive include species that feed on both birds and mammals.

Surveillance of Wild Bird Diffusion of West Nile Virus

Wild bird mortality has been an accurate indicator of the extent of WNV, and it will continue to provide an early warning system for the emergence of the virus in new locations. The probable dissemination of the virus to the South offers new challenges for both public health and wildlife disease specialists. Wildlife involvement in expanding WNV activity in the United States has become more intense and complex with the increasing number and variety of bird species that are testing positive. In September 2000, the USGS alerted Federal and State wildlife and conservation agencies that the fall migration of millions of birds through the 500-mile-wide region where infection has been found will likely move the West Nile virus farther south into the Atlantic and Gulf coast states. USGS scientists are concerned about the wide variety of birds in which WNV has been found and has asked these agencies for assistance in reporting unusual bird mortality.

Wildlife disease scientists from the USGS National Wildlife Health Center (NWHC) are providing diagnostic support to Federal, State, and local wildlife agencies, as well as to public health departments and other Federal agencies that are utilizing dead wild birds as sentinels for detecting WNV in their area. Active surveillance to detect the geographic expansion of the virus is ongoing in collaboration with the U.S. Department of Agriculture, the U.S. Fish and Wildlife Service, the National Park Service, and State wildlife agencies that are sampling free-ranging wild bird populations in the eastern United States from New Hampshire to Louisiana. This year, the USGS-NWHC is working with the Centers for Disease Control in field investigations in New York and New Jersey to determine the level of WNV in wild birds and mosquitoes where WNV-positive dead birds were found.

USGS' Mapping Supports West Nile Control Efforts

Scientists in the USGS Geographic Sciences Branch are providing the Centers for Disease Control and Prevention, as well as public health agencies, with a GIS incorporating Landsat 7 Thematic Mapper imagery, land-use and land-cover data, roads, and hydrography. This data is being used by scientists in the field to identify bird and mosquito habitat and for determining the best locations for placement of mosquito traps. Information from the National West Nile Virus Surveillance System is being used to compile and produce graphical displays and animation showing the pattern and spread of the outbreak. An additional analysis is being performed to detect clusters of infections and, possibly, the geographic origin of the outbreak. The staff of the U.S. National Atlas is creating online, interactive maps to track the geographical spread of the virus.

U.S. Department of the Interior
U.S. Geological Survey

Fact Sheet FS-153-00
November 2000

A typical example of persuasive communications, the above "fact sheet" shows a USGS pathologist examining "a suspect West Nile virus crow" during autopsy. Aside from this morbid image, pictures of a crow and mosquito are seen in the top right. Source: Fact Sheet F5-153-00, November 2000.

feared and *overpublicized*" WNV, the *Time* authors and editors didn't hesitate to dominate the same page with a mosquito picture that told "more than a thousand words" to "spread fear," "loathing," and "the West Nile virus up and down the East Coast." As propaganda, the article helped justify "intensified" pesticide spraying and campaigning expected during the Spring and Summer of 2001.

As seen in figures 13.3 and 13.4, the USGS communications effectively killed several "birds" with each message. Coupling subliminally racist and overtly anti-African messages with threatened American and ecological survival, figure 13.4, displayed the application of classic propaganda. Here the headline of the "USGS Information Sheet" read "African Dust Causes Widespread Environmental Distress." The dubious announcement came at the height of the WNV drama in New York. While the agency endorsed pesticide sprayings across the U.S. without reservations concerning the associated health risks to humans, especially for the manufactured WNV threat in the northeast region, it leveled charges against "the countries of North Africa in the Sahel region" that allegedly applied "large amounts of pesticides, including those banned in the U.S. to fight" locusts. The feature story told of USGS collaboration with NASA officials to study "microbes and pesticides transported across the Atlantic in African soil dust." This, officials said, was a probable risk for increasing epidemics of asthma in children.

In reality, far more scientists held evidence linking childhood asthma to American pesticide sprayings and to vaccine-related immune system dysfunction, hypersensitivity, and allergy, aside from the asthma in increasing numbers of multiple chemical sensitivity cases. Thus, the USGS issued these two distractions along with its anti-African message.

"Conventional wisdom," the USGS published, "says ultraviolet radiation from the sun would kill microbes during the 5 to 7-day trip across the Atlantic. Our studies thus far indicate that hundreds of viable microorganisms are making the aerial journey in each gram of dust apparently protected within the particles or shielded by overlying dust clouds."

Reading between these lines, the USGS thus presented another reasonable explanation, besides jet travel, for African viruses to suddenly appear in the U.S.

Furthermore, forgetting concerns about silver–mercury amalgam dental fillings, or the controversy regarding established toxicity from mercury preserved vaccines, the USGS warned that the small African

Fig. 13.4. USGS Distractive Propaganda Sheet Distributed During WNV Spraying Campaign

USGS
science for a changing world

African Dust Causes Widespread Environmental Distress

Atmospheric transport of dust from North Africa to the western Atlantic Ocean region may be responsible for a number of environmental hazards, including the demise of Caribbean corals, red tides, amphibian diseases, increased occurrence of asthma in humans, and decrease of oxygen (eutrophication) in estuaries. Outbreaks of other unexplained environmental changes also may be attributable to the influx of African dust. Studies of satellite images suggest that hundreds of millions of tons of dust are transported annually at relatively low altitudes across the Atlantic Ocean from the expanding Sahara Desert in Africa to the Caribbean Sea and southeastern United States.

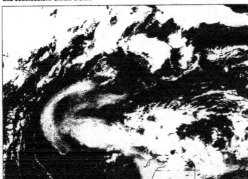

mercury, which is many times greater than amounts normally found in the air. The mercury may have originated from open-pit mercury mines in Algeria and from the rock formations from which the mercury is mined.

At the first sign of locusts, the countries of North Africa in the Sahel region apply large amounts of pesticides, including those banned in the U.S. to fight the pests. These pesticides are also present in the dust reaching the Caribbean and southern U.S.

The satellite image at left, acquired by NASA/Goddard Spaceflight Center's SeaWiFS Project and ORBIMAGE on February 26, 2000, shows one of the largest Saharan dust storms ever observed by SeaWiFS as it moves out over the eastern Atlantic Ocean. Spain and Portugal are at upper right, Morocco is at lower right.

The USGS in collaboration with NASA/Goddard Spaceflight Center began a study to identify microbes and pesticides transported across the Atlantic in African soil dust. Of special interest is asthma, which is becoming prevalent in children of the Caribbean region, especially in Puerto Rico and Trinidad. Conventional wisdom says ultraviolet radiation from the sun would kill microbes during the 5- to 7-day trip across the Atlantic. Our studies thus far indicate that hundreds of viable microorganisms are making the aerial journey in each gram of dust apparently protected within the particles or shielded by overlying dust clouds. Dust from the extraordinary dust event of February 26, 2000, shown above, was collected by researchers at the University of the Azores. The smallest particles (one micrometer) were found to contain 2 parts per million of the element

Brain coral infected with black-band disease. The band of tissue-killing bacterial slime radiates outward like a ringworm at a rate of up to 1 cm per day during summer warm-water conditions. The white area in the center is dead tissue-free coral skeleton. The dead skeleton will be attacked by boring algae, boring sponges, boring clams and parrot fish that will gnaw away the skeleton. Together these organisms remove about 1 cm (1/2 inch) per year. This means that in 100 years, a 1-meter high coral head will be completely consumed and converted to sediment. Black-band disease on brain corals was first reported in Bermuda in the early 1970s, but became rampant in other species in the Florida Keys, and elsewhere, beginning in 1985.

U.S. Department of the Interior
U.S. Geological Survey

USGS Information Sheet
April 2000

Cover photo allegedly showed a microbial and pesticide contaminated dust storm emanating from Africa, crossing the Atlantic, acquired by satellite reconnaissance on February 26, 2000. Credited by the USGS is the NASA/Goddard Spaceflight Center's SeaWiFS Project and ORBIMAGE.[16]

Fig. 13.4. USGS Propaganda Sheet Continued

USGS Plans To Research West Nile Movements In Wildlife

The USGS is initiating studies, in collaboration with the Centers for Disease Control and Prevention, to learn the current geographic extent of WNV, to understand how it moves between birds, mosquitoes, and humans, and to predict future movements of the virus. The 3-year study will utilize active wild bird surveillance along the Atlantic Flyway, with simultaneous collection of mosquitoes, to detect the presence of WNV. The USGS will work with the U.S. Fish and Wildlife Service, the National Park Service, and other Federal agencies to identify appropriate sampling sites spaced along the Atlantic Flyway. Over-wintering birds at sites in Florida will be surveyed. This system, based on the ubiquitous presence of birds and their potential exposure to disease, indicates the diffusion of pathogens across eastern America and provides a mechanism to detect novel pathogens in the environment, their geographic extent, and their relations to the landscape and the environment.

The surveillance system will provide the basic information on the geography of WNV. The combination of this data with

This map shows the cumulative number of wild bird cases of West Nile virus between January 1- October 20, 2000; the counties in green are those in which wild birds tested positive for the virus. National Atlas maps that show the surveillance plans, the geographic locations of animals that tested positive for the West Nile virus, and the species affected are updated weekly on the world wide web at http://www.nationalatlas.gov/virusmap.html.

information about landscape characteristics and weather conditions, over space and time, will provide the data foundation for developing spatial analytical and forecasting models. Hypotheses about the necessary precursor conditions of landscape and weather that enable outbreaks can be formulated and tested.

Determination of the Virulence of West Nile Virus

The USGS is also using its Biological Safety Level 3 containment facility in Madison, Wis. to conduct research studies to determine the virulence of WNV in

crows and waterfowl. The USGS recently reported that a study conducted at this facility demonstrated that in a confined experimental setting, the West Nile virus could be transmitted from crow-to-crow. It had been thought that the virus was transmitted only through the bite of a mosquito.

Additional Information

For more information on the West Nile virus you can access the USGS National Atlas web site at http://www.nationalatlas.gov/virusmap.html and the USGS-Wildlife Health site at http://www.umesc.usgs.gov/http_data/nwhc/news/westnil2.html or contact: Dr. Linda Glaser, USGS, National Wildlife Health Center, (608)270-2446, or Dr. Stephen Guptill, USGS, Geographic Sciences Branch, (703)648-4520.

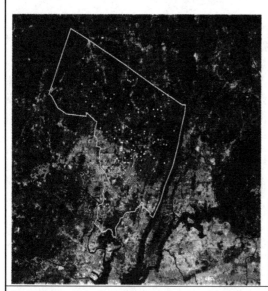

The precise locations of West Nile virus-positive crows enable geographic analysis of the West Nile virus outbreak.

Bergen County, New Jersey	Avian Cases by WEEK
West Nile Virus Outbreak	
157 Confirmed Avian Cases	
May 30 - September 7, 2000	
Landsat 7 Satellite Imagery	
Acquired September 23 and October 2, 1999	
Data Sources	
Bergen County Department of Health Services	
Centers for Disease Control and Prevention	
U.S. Geological Survey	

The USGS, typically known for its mapping services, is shown here delivering maps of WNV associated geography. Of greater service to "spin-doctors" than the health science community, few realize this technology and agency serves population controlling interests more than public health.[12]

Fig. 13.5. Example of West Nile Virus Propaganda— A Form of "Bioterrorism" From *Time Magazine*

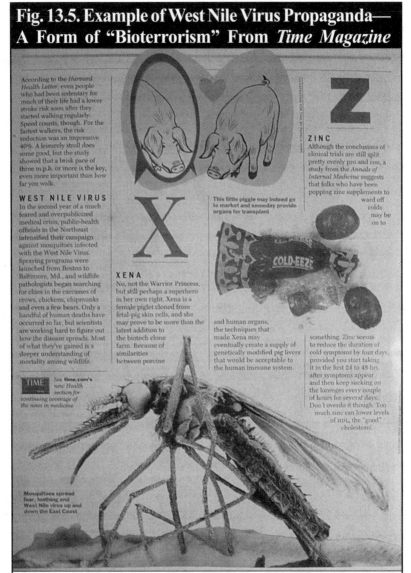

Magazine mogul Henry Luce, publisher of *Time*, *Life* and more of America's most prominent magazines pioneered the effort, during the 1950s, to establish a "National Purpose." Best articulated by the Rockefeller Brothers Fund sponsored Panel reports published in 1961, Eisenhower's Commission on National Goals was directed to the prudence of linking militarism and general consumerism for the "National Security State" and corporate welfare. This page from *Time* adequately exemplifies this subliminal social programming with images of biowarfare—the war against deadly germs—and American consumerism. Source: Rockefeller Brothers Fund, *Prospect for America: The Rockefeller Panel Reports*. Garden City, New York: Doubleday & Co., 1961.

dust particles "were found to contain 2 parts per million of the element mercury, which is many times greater than amounts normally found in the air." These authors speculated that, "The mercury may have originated from open-pit mercury mines in Algeria and from the rock formations from which the mercury is mined." The mercury, fungal spores, and dust from the African continent were all believed to be linked to the mysterious demise of Caribbean coral reefs, the USGS reported.[16]

Figures 13.3 and 13.5 also projected the feared images of mosquitoes, an autopsied crow, and related text to generate public acceptance of official WNV spraying campaigns. As the virus inevitably spread, the USGS reported, they were "providing the Centers for Disease Control and Prevention, as well as public health agencies," with an epidemiological data base and geographic-information system (GIS) "incorporating Landsat 7 Thematic Mapper imagery, land-use and land-cover data, roads, and hydrography." This data was being used "by scientists in the field to identify bird and mosquito habitat and for determining the best locations for placement of mosquito traps," their propaganda stated.

Unfortunately, during earlier investigations, I discovered that virtually all of the satellite reconnaissance systems administered by USAID, NASA, and by association the USGS, for allegedly humanitarian and agricultural purposes had actually been designed, purchased, and directed by NATO officials. In fact, the *Wall Street Journal* had documented many of these transactions along with their corporate beneficiaries. A leader among them was Litton Data Systems—a group intimately connected to NATO satellite reconnaissance efforts, computerized communications systems, and the division of Litton Industries that included their West German Hellige Company and Litton Bionetics–the manufacturers of most of the worlds's most feared and deadly viruses.[12]

Again, it seemed, history was repeating. I learned toward the end of my investigation for *Emerging Viruses: AIDS & Ebola* that during the 1970s German–American military–medical industrialists, intimately linked to NATO, NASA, USAID, the CIA, and the cancer industry's NCI—agencies largely representing globalists' interests—had used "satellite reconnaissance" and "communications systems" as "humanitarian" covers to accomplish genocide in Africa and America.

Advances in satellite and electromagnetic "reconnaissance" technology additionally effecting "non-lethal" warfare on unwitting populations will be discussed in forthcoming chapters.

References:

1) Cook TL. *The Mark of the New World Order*. Springdale, PA: Whitaker House, 1996.

2) van Helsing J. *Secret Societies and Their Power in the 20th Century*. Gran Canaria, Spain: Ewertverlab S.L., 1995.

3) Kunitz SJ. Public health then and now: Globalization, states, and the health of indigenous peoples. *American Journal of Public Health* 2000; 90;10:1531-1539.

4) Lambo TA. The African mind in contemporary conflict: The Jacques Parisot Foundation Lecture, 1971. *World Health Organization Chronicle* 1971;25:8:343-353.

5) Lee MA. The Nazi past underlying politics today. *Los Angeles Times*. Sunday, June 25, 2000, p. M2; See also: Lee MA. *The Beast Reawakens*. Boston: Little, Brown and Company, 1997.

6) Blowen M. 'Nazi Medicine' demands to be seen. *The Boston Globe*, Tuesday, April 26, 1997, p. D8.

7) Kuhl S. *The Nazi Connection: Eugenics, American Racism and German National Socialism*. New York: Oxford University Press, 1994.

8) Borkin J. *The Crime and Punishment of I.G. Farben: The Unholy Alliance Between Hitler and the Great Chemical Combine*. New York: Barnes & Noble, Inc., 1997.

9) Simpson C. *The Science of Coercion: Eugenics, American Racism, and German National Socialism*. New York: Oxford University Press, 1994, pp. 60-62.

10) Manning P. *Martin Bormann: Nazi in Exile*. Secaucus, NJ: Lyle Stuart, Inc., 1981.

11) Griffin GE. *World Without Cancer*. Westlake Village, CA: American Media, 1997.

12) Horowitz LG and Martin JW. *Emerging Viruses: AIDS & Ebola—Nature, Accident or Intentional?* Rockport, MA; Tetrahedron Press, 1998, pp. 251-362;380-381.

13) Kissinger H. *National Security Special Memorandum 200 (NSSM): Implications of Worldwide Population Growth for US Security and Overseas Interests*. December 10, 1974, Classified by Harry C. Blaney, III, and Declassified on December 31, 1980 by order of the White House, p.43.

14) *Ibid.*, p. 10.

15) United States Geological Survey. West Nile Virus. Madison, WI: National Wildlife Health Center; http://www.umesc.usgs.gov/http_data/nwhc/news/westnil2.html.

16) USGS. African dust causes widespread environmental distress. *USGS Information Sheet*. St. Petersburg, FL: U.S. Department of the Interior and U.S. Geological Survey, April 2000, pp. 1-4.

Death in the Air

Chapter 14.
Vaccinations for
Global Genocide

"To produce the possibility of the expression of . . . [global governance] by all nations, it is indespensible to trouble, in all countries, the people's relations with their governments so as to utterly exhaust humanity with dissention, hatred, struggle, envy, and even by the use of torture, starvation, by the *inoculation of diseases*, by want, so that the [manipulated] see no issue than to take refuge in our complete sovereignity in money and in all else."[Emphasis added.]

Protocols of the Elders of Sion, 1773
Global strategists in the Prieuré de Sion

In Chapter 5, expert toxicologist, Dr. Samuel Epstein, referred to contemporary pesticide spraying programs as "reckless irresponsibility."[1] This suitably described the contaminations and cover-ups perpetrated in the name of "public health" conducted and promoted by agencies and individuals historically linked to Rockefeller enterprises and their administrative cryptocracy. This chapter focuses on the same dilemma concerning vaccines. In this regard as well, trusting citizens tolerate, and even defend, legislative mandates and pseudoscientific dogmas which propel vaccination agendas with globally genocidal consequences.

My initial scrutiny of vaccines began following my publication of *Emerging Viruses: AIDS and Ebola* in 1996. The following year, David Satcher, M.D., then Director of the CDC, Surgeon General of the United States at the time of this writing, invited me to Atlanta to "discuss issues of mutual interest." He withdrew his invitation following my candid response. I explained in a letter, that the CDC had helped the Merck pharmaceutical company develop the 1974–1975 hepatitis B vaccine given to gay men in New York City and Blacks in Sub-Saharan Africa that most likely triggered the AIDS pandemic.

Dr. Satcher's response reprinted in 14.1 was much like the firing of Dr. Lappe by his public health superiors. No legitimate scientific or public safety purpose was served by Dr. Satcher's bureaucratic avoidance of the critical vaccine contamination issues I had raised. Once again, a public health official claimed lacking "credible scientific evidence" to defend against the disturbing truth. The reply that I issued following receipt of Dr. Satcher's letter is reprinted in figure 14.2.

Similar to Dr. Beverlee Myers's unconscionable whitewashing of Malathion spraying risks,[2-4] Dr. Satcher did virtually the same concerning carcinogenic vaccine contaminations. Neglecting the critical documents I had produced, he published a letter to the editor in *USA Today* that stated that "serious [vaccine] side effects are extremely rare."[5]

Many reputable scientists had, by the time I contacted Dr. Satcher, advanced serious misgivings concerning vaccine contaminants and their harmful effects. Vaccine risks had, in fact, shone brightly in the national spotlight enough to prompt Dr. Satcher to respond to the growing concern over vaccine-linked epidemics of autoimmune diseases, childhood injuries, and unique cancers that were virtually nonexistent decades before vaccines were introduced. The short list of autoimmune illnesses science had proven were aggravated, if not initiated, by vaccinations included chronic fatigue immune dysfunction, fibromyalgia, Lupus, MS, ALS, type-one (autoimmune) diabetes, Guillain–Barré, Crohn's disease, Steven–Johnson's syndrome, Bell's palsy, and others. Childhood injuries included autism, hyperactivity, and attention deficit disorders, chronic draining ear infections, and increased epidemics of asthma, hay fever, allergies and sudden infant death. Regarding cancer, my research into *Emerging Viruses: AIDS & Ebola* showed that the unique HIV-linked immune suppression, combined with leukemia, lymphoma, and sarcoma cancers—what we call AIDS today—was a bioengineered outcome of cancer virus and vaccine research and development.[6]

In fact, I sent Dr. Robert Gallo's NCI contract reprinted in figure 1.3 to Dr. Satcher for his perusal. Here Gallo and Bionetics directors John Landon and Robert Ting prepared and tested numerous immune system destroying viruses descriptively and functionally identical to HIV. They called them "Type-C" cancer retroviruses at that time. These were bioengineered en masse during the "Special Virus Cancer Program"—the largely funded, mostly secret, NCI effort that ran from the early 1960s to the mid 1970s. This contract preceded the one shown in Chapter 18, figure 18.10.

Fig. 14.1. Dr. Satcher's Letter to Dr. Horowitz Concerning the Triggering of AIDS via Vaccines

DEPARTMENT OF HEALTH & HUMAN SERVICES

Public Health Service

Centers for Disease Control
and Prevention (CDC)
Atlanta GA 30333

MAY 22 1997

Leonard G. Horowitz, D.M.D., M.A., M.P.H.
Tetrahedron Publishing Group
20 Drumlin Road
P.O. Box 402
Rockport, Massachusetts 01966

Dear Dr. Horowitz:

Thank you for your letter concerning the invitation extended to you on February 21 to meet with the Centers of Disease Control and Prevention (CDC) officials to discuss the issue of vaccine contamination and other public health issues.

CDC believes that scientific evidence is the foundation for sound public health policies; however, the allegations contained within your letter do not appear to be based on credible, evidence-based information. I, therefore, believe that a meeting to discuss this issue would not likely serve a useful purpose.

Sincerely,

David Satcher, M.D., Ph.D.
Director

The above letter by CDC Director, David Satcher, was composed in response to the letter sent by Dr. Horowitz, reprinted in *Emerging Viruses: AIDS & Ebola—Nature, Accident or Intentional?* explaining, and documenting, the CDC's role in co-producing the 1974–1975 hepatitis B vaccine that apparently triggered the AIDS pandemic.

Fig. 14.2. Dr. Horowitz's Response to Dr. Satcher

NEWS RELEASE

Release: No. 97-EV/9
Date Mailed: June 18, 1997
For Immediate Release

CDC Director Pulls Invitation to Discuss Controversial Book on AIDS-linked Vaccines

Rockport, MA — Centers for Disease Control and Prevention (CDC) Director David Satcher, challenged by scientists, Black leaders, and citizen groups concerned about vaccination risks, declined to discuss AIDS as a possible outcome of contaminated vaccines with the author of a new and highly controversial book that documents the CDC and Food and Drug Administration (FDA) helped manufacture a vaccine that might have transmitted AIDS worldwide. The exchange between the author of *Emerging Viruses: AIDS and Ebola—Nature, Accident or Intentional?* (Tetrahedron Publishing Group, 1997), Dr. Leonard Horowitz, a Harvard graduate, independent investigator, and internationally known public health authority, and Dr. Satcher, followed a recommendation for a moratorium on vaccines by the Nation of Islam's Health Minister, Dr. Alim Muhammad, and a special legislative committee meeting of the National Medical Association, representing Black physicians of America, in which the book's main thesis, and supportive documentation, was considered. All parties agreed that growing fears over vaccine contaminations, and associated health risks, should be addressed at another meeting proposed, then cancelled, by Dr. Satcher.

Dr. Horowitz, supported by thousands of concerned citizens in a rapidly growing grass roots coalition, accepted Dr. Satcher's invitation in writing contingent upon an official investigation into the role the CDC played in "developing the vaccine that most plausibly delivered AIDS to the world." In his book, two man-made theories of AIDS's origin are advanced and bolstered by astonishing government documents including National Cancer Institute reports showing how much U. S. taxpayers spent for contracts to develop and test immune system destroying viruses on monkeys and humans. According to Dr. Horowitz's theory, the CDC, FDA, and Merck & Company, a leading vaccine manufacturer, developed 200,000 human doses of a potentially contaminated experimental hepatitis B vaccine that was given to thousands of Central Africans, gay men in New York City, and mentally retarded children on Staten Island, simultaneously in 1974— perfect timing for the initial outbreak of AIDS cases in these areas by 1978.

Fig. 14.2. Dr. Horowitz's Response Continued

In an official letter to Dr. Horowitz in which he withdrew his invitation to meet, Dr. Satcher stated the "CDC believes that scientific evidence is the foundation for sound public health policies," and that Dr. Horowitz's allegations "do not appear to be based on credible, evidence-based information."

In response, Dr. Horowitz reported to thousands of Internet-workers, and the press, that Dr. Satcher's comments were false and misleading. "If the CDC truly demanded rigorous scientific proof to support its public health policies," Dr. Horowitz said, then the CDC would also be calling for a moratorium on virtually all vaccinations "which, to date, lack definitive scientific analyses showing positive risk/benefit ratios." In fact, Dr. Horowitz wrote Dr. Satcher, CDC and pharmaceutical company experts "don't really know whether vaccines are harming or killing more people than they are helping or saving."

Likewise, Dr. Horowitz questioned how much scientific evidence the CDC and FDA officials demanded when their "mutual consent was given to blood and pharmaceutical interests to sustain the use of HIV contaminated clotting factor VIII and blood supplies to the public between 1983 and 1986," despite the fact that these officials predicted thousands would die as a result. Furthermore, in 1984, when the hepatitis B vaccine link to the AIDS epidemic was first advanced then investigated by CDC and Merck, Sharp & Dohme collaborators, homosexual men in New York City were known to be the primary and earliest test subjects for the suspected vaccine. Yet the CDC omitted the New York City gay men from their investigation and focused only on Denver and San Francisco populations that had not been immunized using the earliest, most implicated, vaccine lots. "No wonder your 'expert' CDC authors remained 'Anonymous' on this *Morbidity & Mortality Weekly Report*," Dr. Horowitz chided. "I too would feel ashamed to affix my name to such bogus 'science.'"

Regarding Dr. Satcher's inability to see any "credible evidence-based information" in Dr. Horowitz's writings, the author replied, "If he did, he would also see himself and his agency are now fully exposed. And since rumor has it that President Clinton is considering Dr. Satcher for the Surgeon General post, putting on the 'Emperors new clothes' suits him fine—a Black man who can watch his own people, and millions of others, die without seeing anything."

Press release issued by Dr. Horowitz in response to CDC Director, David Satcher's, flippant dismissal of Dr. Horowitz's findings that explained for the first time a vaccine-linked connection between chimpanzee and human AIDS, and the viruses associated with them. This release, neglected by mainstream news sources, was ultimately published in several alternative political and health publications including the *Townsend Letter for Doctors & Patients*, November 1997, Issue #172, p.135.

I also included in my package to Dr. Satcher the contract under which Litton shipped contaminated chimpanzees to the Merck pharmaceutical company for vaccine research beginning in 1971. (See figure 14.3.) This best explained the chimpanzee immunodeficiency virus (SIVcpz) link to HIV. Merck's vaccine chief, Dr. Maurice Hilleman, likewise admitted that he "didn't know we were importing AIDS virus at the time." He later defended such vaccine contaminations saying, "It was good science at the time. . . . You didn't think about these 'wild viruses.'"[7] Dr. Hilleman's hepatitis B vaccine contract is shown in figure 14.4.

Following Dr. Satcher's implied denial of CDC wrongdoing in the manufacture of the AIDS-linked contaminated hepatitis B vaccines, I issued a formal complaint published in several alternative periodicals. (See figure 14.2.) Dr. Satcher's inability to see the incriminating evidence at the time he was being considered for Surgeon General of the United States, I said, was reminiscent of the story told in *The Emperor's New Clothes*.[8] Here was a Black man who could watch millions of his own people in the U.S. and around the world, particularly in Africa, die without seeing anything. The "Surgeon Genocide's" uniform—"The Emperor's New Clothes"—suited him perfectly, I wrote.

Earlier, I defined genocide as the mass murder of people for political, ideological, and/or economic reasons.[9] During the late 1980s experimental tetanus vaccines containing sterilizing "contaminants" were given to millions of unsuspecting women in the Americas and in several Third World nations.[10,11] This will be discussed in greater detail later. By the mid-1990s, substantial percentages of Black and Native American women had become *sterile*, not all due to the corrupted vaccines, but likely a good percentage. This was, of course, a convenient "act of nature" for forces effecting global depopulation including the world's largest vaccine maker—Merck.[11] Merck's place, as well as the Rockefeller Foundation's position, in the hierarchy of depopulation funding organizations is shown in figure 14.5.

You might recall that in the first chapter, I mentioned that Lederle Labs—a medical subsidiary of Cyanamid, Malathion's main manufacturer, a company entirely owned by American Home Products corporation which was largely responsible for the rise of the Third Reich through the development of the Rockefeller–Farben chemical/pharmaceutical cartel, suppressed knowledge that their oral polio vaccines were spreading monkey/human cancer viruses throughout the world.

From the early 1960s, through the 1990s, the viral contaminants per dose unregulated by the FDA remained at 100.[12]

Was it an "accident" or "act of nature," that after HIV had curiously devastated two minority populations by 1995—African (mainly female heterosexual) Blacks and gay American males—by 2000, the epidemic had shifted to strike mainly heterosexual Blacks and Hispanics in America.

Meanwhile, public health units and "family planning" centers continued to attract mainly poor minority groups for "immunizations," offering free vaccines. Had these settings become contemporary concentration camps? Had vaccines become the substitute for Zyclone B gas used for mass extermination of people by the petrochemical cartel during the holocaust? The *Boston Globe* accurately reported, after all, that Nazi medicine fell in the shadow of American medicine—a shadow never extinguished by the light of truth.

Given all of the above, as in *The Emperor's New Clothes*, very few were witting and willing enough to proclaim Dr. Satcher et al., facilitators of a rising Fourth Reich.

Hepatitis B Vaccines for "Mandatory" Genocide

The eventual phase out of the risky live–attenuated and contaminated oral polio vaccine (OPV) by the turn of the century, along with the elimination of mercury-derived toxic sterilizers in vaccines, by no means stopped the ongoing global pharmaceutical-induced genocide. In 1998, the Clinton administration enacted legislation—a "mandate" aside from religious and medical exemptions—that infants be vaccinated against hepatitis B. Twelve-hour-old infants were suddenly forced to begin a virtually useless and highly risky series of three injections.

When I first heard of this I balked at the announcement's incredulity. It seemed to me, as a public health professional who had personally trained more than 20,000 health care workers in Occupational Safety and Health Administration (OSHA) requirements between 1990 and 1995, including hefty hepatitis B—blood borne pathogen—training, that this was completely absurd.

My assessment was soon echoed by Dr. Martin Schecter, Canada's leading AIDS epidemiologist at the University of British Columbia, and Co-chair of the XI International Conference on AIDS. Held in

BIONETICS RESEARCH LABORATORIES (NIH-69-2160)

Title: Support Services for the Special Virus Cancer Program.

Contractor's Project Director: Dr. Robert C. Y. Ting

Project Officer (NCI): Dr. George Todaro

Objectives: To provide a laboratory that will collect, process and test specimens from human and animal sources suspected of containing virus associated antigens or antibodies, and to provide other virology, immunology or cell culture services as required.

Major Findings: Services and resources provided in close collaboration with NCI investigators during the past year include: (1) biochemical studies of cell growth regulation with Dr. Todaro; (2) attempts to isolate a human cancer virus with Dr. Bassin; (3) tests for EBV antigens for Dr. Levine; (4) immunological tests of leukemia patients, including studies of twins, for Dr. Levine; (5) CF tests for gs antigens for Dr. Hellman; (6) membrane antigen preparation from human tissue for Dr. Herberman; (7) collection of familial cancer sera and histories for Dr. Fraumeni; (8) tissue and serum bank for Dr. Levine et al; (9) American Burkitt registry and follow-up; and (10) data processing with Dr. Waggoner.

When abortively transformed cells containing SV40 genome were re-infected with SV40, they had a lower rate of transformation than cells without the genome; thus, the presence of SV40 did not confer immunity.

Fetal thymus cells of dogs were cocultivated with irradiated human sarcoma cells. The dog cells showed degeneration and transformation (chromosome analysis now being done).

Rhesus cell cultures infected with Mason-Pfizer virus showed evidence of transformation and caused regressing tumors when subsequently inoculated into newborn rhesus monkeys.

Cellular immunity studies of leukemia patients, using lymphocyte cytotoxicity and cytotoxicity inhibition tests, suggest that cells of such patients possess leukemia-associated antigens and that a widespread antigen system may be operative in human and animal tumors.

Significance to Biomedical Research and the Program of the Institute: This contract laboratory provides an opportunity for a systematic, large-scale effort to detect viruses and/or viral antigens in human tumor materials (particularly leukemias and sarcomas), using tissue culture, immunological, biochemical and EM techniques. This is a major objective of the SVCP.

Fig. 14.3. Additional Grant Descriptions Cont.

Proposed Course: It is proposed that this contract will continue to supply the necessary supportive services required to meet the needs of the SVCP.

Date Contract Initiated: June 27, 1969

Current Contract Level: $800,000

BIONETICS RESEARCH LABS., INC. (NIH 69-2160)

Title: Support Services for SVCP

Contractor's Project Director: Dr. Robert Ting

Project Officers (NCI): Dr. George Todaro
Dr. Paul Levine
Dr. Robert Bassin

Objectives: To provide a laboratory that will collect, process and test cancer specimens from human and animal sources suspected of containing virus associated antigens.

Major Findings: EBV studies were carried out under the supervision of Dr. Paul Levine. One study initiated and completed during this year was a seroepidemiological study comparing EBV titers in American patients with Burkitt's lymphoma and age-and sex-matched patients with acute lymphocytic leukemia, African Burkitt lymphoma, and non-malignant diseases. The African Burkitt sera were significantly higher than the American Burkitt sera (P<0.005). The role of EBV in human lymphoma was evaluated by immunological techniques detecting humoral and cellular immunity to the virus. The importance of careful clinical evaluation was emphasized by a study of twenty American patients with Burkitt's lymphoma and age and sex matched controls. Treatment and prognosis correlated with EBV titers in both lymphoma and leukemia patients, indicating that seroepidemiological studies which include single samples on a patient may be misleading. The studies clearly demonstrated that American patients with Burkitt's lymphoma, although their histopathology is indistinguishable from African patients, have different immune patterns to EBV.

Five individuals with low titers to EBV who were identified on an earlier study of Hodgkins disease were followed over a three year period. Half the patients developed high titers while the other half maintained low titers.

A study of leukemia in identical twins was initiated to determine whether an antigen could be detected in the cells of a leukemia twin which would not be identified in his normal HLA identical twin. Leukemia-associated antigens were detected in four of the seven families studied to date using the lymphocyte cytotoxicity test. In the animal system, this test is positive only when the lymphocytes are presensitized by an antigen, so that the reactivity of the family members against the leukemic patient's cells but not against the normal twin's cells suggest that an environmental agent, perhaps a virus, is present.

Sera from 43/102 (42%) of breast cancer patients had antibodies to BeLev antigens. Sera from 29% of patient's with sarcomas had detectable antibodies, whereas, 13% of patients with benign breast diseases and 3.6% of normal blood bank donors reacted.

Fig. 14.3. Additional Grant Descriptions Cont.

Significance to Biomedical Research and the Program of the Institute: Provides opportunity for systematic, large-scale effort to detect viruses or viral antigens in human or animal materials using tissue culture, immunological, biochemical and EM techniques. This is a major objective of the SVCP.

Proposed Course: Although this contract will continue to supply necessary supportive services to SVCP, the workscope has recently been divided into three major areas, each being co-directed by a senior investigator at Bionetics and an NCI project officer. Drs. Rein and Todaro will attempt to isolate, characterize, and purify the factor(s) in serum which overcome contract inhibition and regulate the growth of normal and transformed 3T3 cells in culture. Drs. Pienta and Bassin will attempt to rescue and isolate a viral genome in undifferentiated sarcomas from untreated patients by co-cultivation, hybridization, and other techniques. Drs. Levine and Ting will continue studies to detect tumor specific antigens in patients with leukemia, lymphoma and breast cancer. In the leukemia studies, special emphasis will be placed on testing patients who have an identical twin; in the lymphoma studies, the serums of patients in selected disease groups will be tested for antibodies to EBV.

Date Contract Initiated: June 27, 1969

Under NIH contract number 69-2160 documented above, Bionetics researchers attempted to "isolate human cancer" viruses. Specifically, Epstein–Barr (EBV), leukemia, lymphoma, and sarcoma virus particles were studied frequently in age and sex matched American and African patients "in selected disease groups." These contracts were initiated in 1969—approximately ten years before the first AIDS cases began to exhibit the unprecedented leukemia–lymphoma–sarcoma cancer complex coupled with dramatic immune suppression, particularly upon EBV co-factor infection, and on these two specific far-removed continents. As stated in the contract under "Proposed Course," Bionetics collaborators were apparently successful, given the AIDS pandemic, in their "attempt to rescue and isolate a viral genome . . . from untreated patients by co-cultivation, hybridization, and other techniques." This disproves official reports that HIV could not have been "constructed" in labs due to the absence of sophisticated biotechnology allegedly unavailable before the mid-1970s. "Co-cultivation" and "hybridization" refer to the gross mixing, in-vivo and in-vitro of, for instance, leukemia, lymphoma, sarcoma, and EBV particles/genes to create, then "rescue" (i.e., isolate), new mutant strains of deadly viruses that produced AIDS-like symptoms much like HIV. Source: NCI staff. *The Special Virus Cancer Program: Progress Reports #8 (and #9).* Office of the Associate Scientific Director for Viral Oncology (OASDVO). J. B. Moloney, Ed., Washington, D. C.: U. S. Government Printing Office, 1971 (and 1972) and Reference # HE 20.3152:V81. See also: Horowitz LG and Martin WJ. *Emerging Viruses: AIDS & Ebola—Nature, Accident or Intentional?* Rockport, MA: Tetrahedron Press, 1998, for additional discussions.

Fig. 14.3. Additional Grant Descriptions Cont.

BIONETICS RESEARCH LABORATORIES, INC. (NIH 71-2025)

Title: Investigations of Viral Carcinogenesis in Primates

Contractor's Project Director: Dr. Harvey Rabin

Project Officers (NCI): Dr. Roy Kinard
Dr. Jack Gruber
Dr. Gary Pearson

Objectives: (1) Evaluation of long-term oncogenic effects of human and animal viral inocula in primates of various species, especially newborn macaques; (2) maintenance of monkey breeding colonies and laboratories necessary for inoculation, care and monitoring of monkeys; and (3) biochemical studies of transfer RNA under conditions of neoplastic transformation and studies on the significance of RNA-dependent DNA polymerase in human leukemic tissues.

Major Findings: This contractor continues to produce over 300 excellent newborn monkeys per year. This is made possible by diligent attention to reproductive physiological states of female and male breeders. Semen evaluation, artifical insemination, vaginal cytology and ovulatory drugs are used or tried as needed.

Inoculated and control infants are hand-fed and kept in modified germ-free isolators. They are removed from isolators at about 8 weeks of age and placed in filtered air cages for months or years of observation. The holding area now contains approximately 1200 animals up to 5 years old. Approximately 300 are culled every year at a rate of about 25 per month. This is necessary to make room for young animals inoculated with new or improved virus preparations.

New importance is being given to the New World species of monkeys, including squirrel, marmoset, and spider monkeys. Animals currently on study are being actively culled to reflect this change.

Special emphasis has been placed on virological studies characterizing the Mason-Pfizer monkey virus (M-PMV). Seven sublines established from chronically M-PMV-infected rhesus foreskin cultures were shown to be releasing moderately high titers of infectious M-PMV, and in addition seemed to have undergone in vitro transformation. Inoculation of cells of these sublines into newborn rhesus monkeys produced palpable masses at the sites of inoculation. Biopsies performed on these masses and on the regional lymph nodes of the same animals revealed the presence of proliferating virus character- istic of M-PMV by both electron microscopic and cell culture analysis. Proliferating M-PMV was found in the lymph nodes of monkeys inoculated with cell-free M-PMV preparations.

Chromatographic examination of transfer RNA's (tRNA's) from control and virus-transformed rat and mouse embryo cells

Fig. 14.3. Additional Grant Descriptions Cont.

demonstrated differences in phenyl-alanyl-tRNA's and aspartyl-tRNA's. No differences were noted in the elution profiles of seryl-, tyrosyl-, leucyl-, asparaginyl-, or glutaminyl-tRNA.

The effects of 11 rifamycin derivatives on viral reverse transcriptase and on DNA polymerases from human normal and leukemic blood lymphocytes were evaluated. Compound 143-483, 3-formyl rifamycin SV: octyl oxime showed the greatest potency and inhibited all DNA polymerases from both viral and cellular origins.

The contractor also engaged in collaborative studies involving the oncornavirus, RD-114, from a human sarcoma, isolated by Drs. McAllister, Gardiner, and Huebner. The virus is being produced and supplied by Dr. Gilden of Flow Laboratories. Another virus, a human papovavirus associated with progressive multifocal leukoencephalopathy, is being supplied by Dr. Duard Walker for inoculation into newborn monkeys.

Significance to Biomedical Research and to the Program of the Institute: Inasmuch as tests for the biological activity of candidate human viruses will not be tested in the human species it is imperative that another system be developed for these determinations and. subsequently for the evaluation of vaccines or other measures of control. The close phylogenetic relationship of the lower primates to man justifies utilization of these animals for these purposes. Further study of altered transfer RNA and polymerase enzymes would determine their significance in neoplastic change and provide a basis for selection of therapeutic agents.

Proposed Course: The previously mentioned studies will be continued and expanded. Particular attention will be given to research on animals inoculated with candidate human cancer viruses, and investigations will be carried forward into the nature of neoplastic changes and their possible control at the cellular level. Collaborative efforts with other researchers within the SVCP will continue.

Date Contract Initiated: February 12, 1962

Current Annual Level: $2,153,850

Numerous AIDS-like RNA tumor retrovirus hybrids were bioengineered under the above contract. Related efforts began as early as 1962. In Africa, Bionetics-bred monkeys were inoculated with recombinant strains of immune-suppressive carcinogenic viruses acting as cofactors with other biological and chemical agents, as detailed above. For instance, the RD114 virus referred to was a cat/human hybrid that, according to Dr. Gilden, "may be accidentally introduced in a new species, perhaps by vaccine . . ." Note the "Australian antigen" (i.e., hepatitis B virus) given to African green monkeys under contracts numbered 71-2025 and 71-2059. Much evidence strongly suggests vaccine research triggered the AIDS pandemic. Source: Horowitz and Martin, *Op cit.*, p. 511.

Fig. 14.4. Merck Pharmaceutical Company Contract Suggesting an Iatrogenic Origin of AIDS: Early Feline Leukemia/Sarcoma, Herpes virus, and Monkey Cancer Virus Studies That Led to the Pilot Hepatitis B Vaccines Partially Prepared in Chimpanzees, Given to Gay Men in NYC and African Blacks by 1975.

MERCK AND COMPANY, INC. (NIH-71-2059)

Title: Oncogenic Virus Research and Vaccine Development

Contractor's Project Director: Dr. Maurice Hilleman

Project Officers (NCI): Dr. Robert A. Manaker
                        Mr. J. Thomas Lewin

Objectives: To conduct investigations designed to develop vaccines or other agents effective for the prophylaxis and therapy for human neoplasia of suspected viral etiology.

Major Findings: Multiple construction and renovation projects have been involved in the expansion and reorientation for this program. Remodeling of a laboratory, physically separated from the animal tumor virus area, was recently completed and is in use for Herpes simplex type 2 vaccine work. Two rooms (440 sq. ft.) in Bldg. #43 were remodeled and equipped and are in use for the germ-free derivation of kittens for the SPF cat colony breeding nucleus. Plans were completed for the renovation of half of Bldg. #65 (5,940 sq. ft.) for housing an SPF cat colony and for housing experimental cats. The construction and equipping of the new biohazard containment building #26B (12,096 sq. ft.) for laboratory work is progressing on schedule. The projected completion date is September, 1972.

Tumor-specific cellular vaccine development: The preparation and assay of tumor cell vaccines for protective efficacy in the hamster model system was continued at a lower priority level. Testing of adenovirus 31 tumor cell fractions prepared by mechanical disruption of the cells and fractionation by differential centrifugation was completed. None of the vaccines (crude cell homogenate, nuclear fraction-$\omega^2 t = 10^7$ pellet, membrane fraction-$\omega^2 t = 5 \times 10^9$ pellet, particulate fraction-$\omega^2 t = 10^{11}$ pellet, cell sap-$\omega^2 t = 10^{11}$ supernate) protected hamsters against development of tumors when they were challenged by inoculation of viable homologous tumor cells. Work on the preparation of two other types of tumor cell antigens was continued. Cell membranes were prepared from a adenovirus 12 tumor cells by hypotonic extraction and were solubilized by sonication. The solubilized material was fractionated on Sephadex G200

Fig. 14.4. Merck Pharmaceutical Co. Contract. Cont.

columns and the desired fraction concentrated by the Diaflo membrane
technique. The first batch of test and control antigens is on test
for protective efficacy in hamsters. Preparation of additional batches
of antigen for assay is in progress. Technology is still being developed
for the preparation of adenovirus 7 tumor cell membranes by flow sonication and flow zonal centrifugation.

Investigation of the host immunologic response to nonprotective tumor
cell vaccines is being conducted in hamster-tumor model systems. The
first series of experiments was designed to test the effect of inoculation
of known nonprotective vaccines before, simultaneously with, or after
immunization with a known effective vaccine (5×10^6 γ-irradiated tumor
cells). Most of the experiments in this series are on test. Final
results with one of the nonprotective vaccines, SV_{40} tumor cell ghosts
prepared by hypertonic extraction, showed that this vaccine did not
interfere with the ability of the host to reject viable homologous
tumor cells after vaccination with 5×10^6 γ-irradiated SV_{40} tumor
cells.

Attempts to render nonprotective SV_{40} tumor cell vaccines effective by
the administration of poly I:C before, simultaneously with, or after
vaccine, single or multiple doses, or by different routes were not
successful in the hamster model system.

Studies on the role of fetal antigens in tumor immunology are being
conducted in the SV_{40}-hamster model system. In the first series of
experiment, γ-irradiated, 9-12 day gestation fetal cells of multiparous
origin did not protect adult male or female hamsters against tumor
development when challenged with 5000 homologous tumor cells. Experiments
are in progress wherein the vaccines were prepared from primaparous 10-
day gestation embryos and are being tested in the SV_{40} virus-newborn hamster
model system and in the adult hamster-tumor cell challenge system with
a 2500 cell challenge dose.

Virus vaccine development: This project is still in the initial stages.
The work in progress is concerned primarily with basic needs such as
virus propagation, virus concentration and purification, preparation of
specific antisera, and establishment of routine assay procedures.

The KT (Kawakami-Theilen) strain of feline leukemia virus (FLV) was
routinely propagated in roller bottle (1 liter/bottle) suspension cultures
of the virus-shedding FL74c cell line. Ten liter lots of culture fluid
were concentrated (1000x) and purified by flow zonal centrifugation
and isopynic centrifugation on sucrose gradients. Modifications in
technology are still being made to increase the purity of the concentrated
virus. Virus yields of 10^{13} virus particles/ml were readily achieved.

In order to provide an adequate supply of healthy cats for future experimental work, establishment of a specific pathogen-free cat colony was
proposed. The first step, the germ-free derivation of the breeding

Fig. 14.4. Merck Pharmaceutical Co. Contract Cont.

has been in progress for two months. All eight isolators are occupied by kittens (16 females, 7 males) ranging from 1 to 8 weeks in age.

Significance to Biomedical Research and the Program of the Institute:

If viruses are an essential element in the genesis of some human cancers, prophylaxis by vaccines to prevent or minimize infection should provide a rational approach to cancer prevention. This could be accomplished by living or killed virus vaccines or possibly by vaccines of purified virion sub-units. Although greatest benefit could be derived by prevention of infections transmitted horizontally after birth, a potential benefit from vaccines may be derived where viruses are transmitted vertically but do not express their full antigenic complement. Non-oncogenic viruses may function as essential co-factors in expression of neoplasia, and immunity against such secondary agents might prevent expression of the neoplastic state. In addition, vaccination with homologous virus in a virus-dependent cancer may enhance specific humoral antibody or cellular immunity. This research project is of fundamental importance to total program.

Proposed Course: Efforts to prepare tumor-specific cellular antigens for immunoprophylaxis of cancer and to study the immunologic response to such antigens will continue. Tests with poly I:C for adjuvant effect on ineffective cellular vaccines will be completed. Work towards development of a feline leukemia-sarcoma virus vaccine and a herpesvirus type 2 vaccine will be continued as rapidly as possible. If no problems arise, the germfree derivation of kittens for the SPF cat colony should be completed in several months.

Date Contract Initiated: March 1, 1971

Current Annual Level: $1,016,000

Merck and Company, Inc. (NIH-71-2059)

Title: Study of Viruses in Human and Animal Neoplasia.

Contractor's Project Director: Dr. Maurice R. Hilleman

Project Officers (NCI): Dr. Robert A. Manaker
Dr. Jack Gruber

Objectives: To perform investigations designed to develop vaccines or other agents effective for the prophylaxis and therapy of human neoplasia of suspected viral etiology.

Major Findings: This is a new contract.

Significance to Biomedical Research and the Program of the Institute:
Current data support the concept that a virus or viruses are the essential element in most animal tumors studied and that viruses are probably the necessary etiological component in human neoplasia, though expression may be greatly influenced and modified by host and environmental factors. If viruses are the essential element in human cancer, then prophylaxis by vaccines to prevent or minimize infection should provide a rational approach to cancer prevention. This could be accomplished by utilization of live or killed virus vaccines or possibly by vaccines of purified virion subunits.

Fig. 14.4. Merck Pharmaceutical Co. Contract Cont.

Vaccines would obviously provide their greatest benefit in preventing infection with oncogenic viruses transmitted horizontally after birth. However, even the possible vertical transmission of hypothetical neoplastic agents does not rule out a potential benefit from vaccines. Nononcogenic viruses may function as essential cofactors in expression of neoplasia, and immunity against such secondary agents might prevent expression of the neoplastic state. Additionally, antibody or cellular immunity may be enhanced by vaccination with homologous virus in virus-dependent cancer. Obviously this research investigation is of fundamental importance to the goals of SVCP and can make unique contributions to the total program.

Proposed Course: The investigators will devote initial efforts to developing methods for propagation, purification, concentration and specific quantitation of candidate viruses suspected or shown to cause cancer in man. At the present time, investigations will be focused upon herpes-type (DNA) viruses and "B" and "C" type (RNA) particles. Parallel studies to evolve live attenuated and killed virus vaccines in appropriate animal model systems will be conducted. Particular attention will be given to developing and applying optimal methods for viral attenuation, viral inactivation, viral quantitation, vaccine safety assessment, and vaccine potency assay.

Date Contract Initiated: March 1, 1971

"Combine these two diseases—feline leukemia and hepatitis—and you have the immune deficiency" syndrome today called AIDS, said CDC hepatitis B chief Dr. Don Francis at the onset of the pandemic. As stated in the above contract, Merck investigators developed "methods of propagation, purification, concentration, and specific quantitation of candidate viruses suspected or shown to cause cancer in man." Among these was the "KT strain of feline leukemia virus (FLV)" concentrated to "10^3 virus particles/ml." This "C" type (RNA) tumor retrovirus, according to leading expert Dr. George Todaro, was another man-made virus that apparently evolved during similar cancer virus hybridization studies, as in the case of the RD114 cat/human mutant, and/or vaccine experiments involving cross species transfers of infectious particles. As stated above, in response to these laboratory studies, authorities knew as early as 1970 that "non-oncogenic viruses may function as essential co-factors in expression of neoplasia (cancer), and immunity against such secondary agents might prevent expression of the neoplastic state." For this reason, these cancer virus and vaccine studies focused on the herpes type (DNA) viruses, especially EBV, as infectious co-factors to regulate retroviral carcinogenesis along with other chemical immune modulators. Evidence is firmly established, therefore, that the hepatitis B virus and vaccine research, conducted simultaneously in NYC and Central Africa between 1970 and 1975 under the preceding Bionetics and Merck contracts, involving infected monkeys and chimpanzees used for vaccine production, was extremely risky and circumstantially linked to the AIDS pandemic. For primary sources and additional background regarding this important thesis see: Horowitz LG and Martin WJ. *Emerging Viruses: AIDS & Ebola—Nature, Accident or Intentional*? Rockport, MA: Tetrahedron Press, 1998.

Fig. 14.5. Population Control Funding FYs 1993-95

Carnegie Corporation
Planned Parenthood Federation of America $25,000
Sex Infor. and Educ. Council of the US..............$325,000

Clark Foundation
National Abortion Federation $120,000
National Family Planning and Reproductive Health..$110,000
Planned Parenthood Federation of America $200,000
Sex Infor. and Educ. Council of the US................$180,000

Ford Foundation
Population Council $1,749,194
Sex Infor. and Educ. Council of the US..............$255,000

MacArthur Foundation
Population Council $900,000

Mellon Foundation
Population Council $7,170,000

Merck Fund
National Abortion Federation $90,000
Planned Parenthood Federation of America $160,000
Population Council $180,000

Mertz-Gilmore Foundation
Lambda Legal Defense and Education Fund $90,000

Mott Foundation
Planned Parenthood Federation of America $35,006

Pew Charitable Trust
Planned Parenthood Federation of America $130,000
Population Council $300,000
Zero Population Growth $150,000

Rockefeller Foundation
Nat. Family Planning and Reproductive Health.....$20,000
Planned Parenthood Federation of America $130,000
Population Council $1,877,170
Population Institute..$20,000

Vancouver in 1996, it was there that I first presented my thesis linking the hepatitis B vaccines to the AIDS pandemic.[13]

Days following the announcement of the infant "mandate," I told Marty, "Have you heard the news? The Clinton administration has just mandated that twelve-hour-old infants begin their series of three hepatitis B vaccinations."

"No," Marty replied. "That's impossible."

"Really, Marty, I'm not kidding," I defended.

"Len, you don't know what you're talking about," he returned. "In Canada we wait till at least six years of age before we give the hepatitis B vaccine."

This I also thought was ridiculous, but our mutual concern stemmed from the fact that the hepatitis B virus is a *blood borne pathogen*. Above all, it is sexually transmitted. Besides the sexually promiscuous, the only major risk group was intravenous drug users. Combined, sex and drugs accounted for approximately 96 percent of all hepatitis B transmissions. The other 4 percent were predominantly medical and public safety personnel who got splashed with blood or stuck with contaminated needles.[14] Infants were nowhere on that risk list.

My analysis below showed me that the hepatitis B vaccine "mandate" only made sense insofar as *genocide* was concerned. It made no medical or scientific sense. In fact, as time passed, I realized that this was a *classic* example of how pubic health was being used as a cover for conducting toxic warfare.

The following facts, led me to this conclusion:

• 98 percent of the people who became infected with hepatitis B (in the ways noted above) developed lifelong immunity, never become seriously ill, and never passed their infections to others.

• The remaining 2 percent—approximately 4,500 people annually, according to CDC statistics, were largely fatalities. Officials failed to explain to the general public that these people were serious risk takers. In other words, the vast majority of these hepatitis B virus victims were "burnouts"—"doped-up" and "sexed-out" individuals who virtually held death wishes stemming from low self-esteem. The problem was that no matter what one did for these people, without establishing a sense of worthiness and non-narcissistic "self-love," these people remained self and socially destructive.

• The vaccine makers admitted that a full one third of those vaccinated received no benefit whatsoever. Subsequent injections commonly failed to prompt immunity against hepatitis B as well. These people were labeled "long-term non-serum-converters."

• The "mandated" hepatitis B vaccine, that targeted approximately 80 million American infants, children, and teens, unlike naturally induced immunity, wore off every 7–10 years in healthy and immunocompetent adults; far faster in children, the elderly, and immune compromised persons.

• Healthy individuals who developed a "protective immune response" needed to be rechecked every 7–10 years. This required an expensive blood test often not paid for by employers, HMOs, or the poor. Infants, whose immune systems were not even mature at the time of their first hepatitis B injections, like the elderly and immune compromised, required more frequent blood analysis to assure antibody protection. That meant that parents of immunized infants would need to bring their children back during kindergarten or the first grade to have the expensive blood test performed, while they were still at extremely low, or no, risk of infection!

• Another 7–10 years later, the teen would have to be retested a second time, or just assumed to have lost their immunity, and therefore vaccinated again, not once but *three more times*; each time delivering additional risks.

• It is difficult enough to get teenagers to do anything, let alone persuade them to return to their physician's office or health clinic to receive another series of three shots. Compliance rates were expected to fall dramatically. No doubt high school and college entrance "mandates" attempt to compensate for this.

• Still, the above failed to address the high-risk teenagers who, at a young age, begin to experiment with, or routinely practice, sex and drug use. No matter how much money was invested in promoting hepatitis B vaccine compliance as a public health practice among these high-risk takers, it would consistently fail. Of this I was certain, given my review of the research literature and expertise in public health education gained during my post-doctoral degree program in behavioral science/media persuasion from Harvard School of Public Health.

In other words, this official "public health policy" was scientifically unsupportable. In fact, it was downright bogus.

All one needed to do in order to establish that this was not a science-based public health policy, but a political and economic (i.e., genocidal) policy, was to carefully examine the risks of hepatitis B vaccine side effects listed on its package insert, or in the *Physician's Desk Reference.* Here it is written:

> RECOMBIVAX HB and RECOMBIVAX HB Dialysis Formulation are generally well tolerated. No serious adverse reactions attributable to the vaccine have been reported during the course of clinical trials [which, as noted below, only lasted *five days*]. No adverse experiences were reported during clinical trials, which could be related to changes in the titers of antibodies to yeast [but not other agents]. As with any vaccine, there is the possibility that broad use of the vaccine could reveal adverse reactions not observed in clinical trials. In three clinical studies, 434 doses of RECOMBIVAX HB, 5 mcg, were administered to 147 healthy infants and children (up to 10 years of age) who were monitored for 5 days after each dose. Injection site reactions and systemic complaints were reported following 0.2% and 10.4% of the injections, respectively. The most frequently reported system adverse reactions (>1% injections), in decreasing order of frequency, were irritability, fever (≥101°F oral equivalent), diarrhea, fatigue/weakness, diminished appetite, and rhinitis. In a group of studies, 3258 doses of RECOMBIVAX HB, 10 mcg, were administered to 1252 healthy adults who were monitored for 5 days after each dose. Injection site reactions and systemic complaints were reported following 17% and 15% of the injections, respectively. . . .[15]

Merck's list of "adverse reactions" is seen in figure 14.6. The misleading manner in which these reactions rates were expressed here, and in the above paragraph, should be noted. Their text stated "≥1% injections," and, in figure 14.6, as "Incidence Equal to or Greater Than 1% of Injections." This language literally disguised, for casual or lay readers, far greater than 1% of people adversely reacted following each injection. Furthermore, since all of the experimental adults and children who had received the injections were only "monitored for 5 days after each dose," chronic illnesses that resulted from the vaccine could not have been, and were not, tracked. This fact, coupled with the CDC's own admission that *more than 90% of serious vaccine injuries went unreported,* seriously undermined the credibility of the company's information—deceptive propaganda to be more accurate.

Summarizing their data, approximately 17% of vaccine recipients develop a little redness and swelling at the site of injection. About 14% develop a little cold or flu-like symptoms that lasts a few days. Approximately 12–13% develop fevers between 103–105°F for a longer duration, perhaps a week. (Parents then question, "Did I do the right thing by giving my child this vaccine?") Between 9 and 11% react even more seriously with pharyngitis and upper respiratory infections. Somewhere in the neighborhood of 5–8% are affected more adversely. They entered into the realm of possibly long term (i.e., chronic) health consequences including autoimmune diseases and others listed in Merck's report. (See figures 14.6 and 14.7.) Again, though it reads "≥1% of injections," what that really means is "greater than 1% of injections given to people followed for only five days." Between 2 and 5% of vaccine recipients experience delayed, long term, often severe and/or life-threatening illnesses. "Less than 1%," the Merck propaganda submitted, sustain "serious injuries." These serious injuries include chronic crippling rheumatoid arthritis, encephalopathies causing permanent brain damage (e.g., autism, attention deficit and hyperactivity disorders), and death, including sudden infant death (SID).

I projected, therefore, the approximate number of adverse reactions to the hepatitis B vaccine simply by taking the company's propaganda, and multiplying the percentages of adverse reactions by approximately 80 million infants, children, and teenagers targeted for the hepatitis B vaccination in the United States. This analysis yielded, conservatively, approximately 250,000 of our nation's youth over the course of about 10 years, would be crippled, brain damaged, or killed. That meant approximately 25,000 hepatitis B vaccine injured young victims were produced annually. For what? To help save approximately 4,500 burned-out, drugged-out, and sexed-out individuals with subliminal death wishes. So urged the CDC.

I conducted this analysis and predicted this ensuing mortality and morbidity in 1997 as documented on my audiotape, "Horowitz 'On Vaccines.'" In 1998, I was unfortunately proven correct. That year, France suspended its hepatitis B vaccine program for children, "faced with a potential health disaster," the Associated Press reported, "because of fears that the vaccine could cause neurological disorders, in particular multiple sclerosis."[16] When the 1996 hepatitis B vaccine adverse reactions were compiled by the Association of American Physicians and Surgeons (AAPS) for their 1999 report, they tallied *almost 25,000 people were seriously harmed.*[17] An AAPS press release noted that there were 440 deaths, 7,726 emergency room visits, and 2,549 hospital stays in 24,772 reports. Again, this number did not include all of the injured, only those injuries reported which only represented approximately 10% of the total population injured. "About 10% of the patients had not recovered from the adverse effects," the medical

Fig. 14.6. Adverse Reactions From Hepatitis B Vaccine

Incidence Equal to or Greater Than 1% of Injections*

LOCAL REACTION (INJECTION SITE)
Injection site reactions consisting principally of soreness, and including pain, tenderness, pruritus, erythema, ecchymosis, swelling, warmth, and nodule formation

BODY AS A WHOLE
The most frequent systemic complaints include fatigue/weakness; headache; fever (≥100°F); and malaise

DIGESTIVE SYSTEM
Nausea; and diarrhea

RESPIRATORY SYSTEM
Pharyngitis; and upper respiratory infection

Incidence Less than 1% of Injections*

BODY AS A WHOLE
Sweating; achiness; sensation of warmth; lightheadedness; chills; and flushing

DIGESTIVE SYSTEM
Vomiting; abdominal pains/cramps; dyspepsia; and diminished appetite

RESPIRATORY SYSTEM
Rhinitis; influenza; and cough

NERVOUS SYSTEM
Vertigo/dizziness; and pareshesia

INTEGUMENTARY SYSTEM
Pruritus; rash (non-specific); angioedema; and uticaria

MUSCULOSKELETAL SYSTEM
Arthralgia including monoarticular; myalgia; back pain, neck pain; shoulder pain; and neck stiffness

HEMIC/LYMPHATIC SYSTEM
Lymphadenopathy

PSYCHIATRIC/BEHAVIORAL
Insomnia/Disturbed sleep

SPECIAL SENSES
Earache

UROGENITAL SYSTEM
Dysuria

CARDIOVASCULAR SYSTEM
Hypotension
The following additional adverse reactions have been reported with use of the marketed vaccine. In many instances, the relationship to the vaccine was unclear.
Hypersensitivity
Anaphylaxis and symptoms of immediate hypersensitivity reactions including rash, pruritus, uticaria, edema, angioedema, dyspnea, chest discomfort, bronchial spasm, palpitation, or symptoms consistent with a hypotensive episode have been reported within the first few hours after vaccination. An apparent hypsesensitivity syndrome (serum-sickness-like) of delayed onset has been reported days to weeks after

vaccination, including: arthralgia/arthritis (usually transient), fever, and dermatologic reactions such as urticaria, erythema multiforme, ecchymoses and erythema nodosum (See WARNINGS and PRECAUTIONS).
Digestive System
Elevation of liver enzymes; constipation.
Nervous System
Guillain-Barre Syndrome; multiple sclerosis; myelitis including transverse myelitis; peripheral neuropahty including Bell's Palsy; radiculopathy; herpes zoster; migraine; muscle weakness; hypesthesia.
Integumentary System
Stevens-Johnson Syndrome; petechiae. Musculoskeletal System Arthritis.
Hematologic
Increased erythrocyte sedimentation rate; thrombocytopenia Immune System Systemic lupus erythematosus (SLE); lupus-like syndrome.
Psychiatric/Behavioral
Irritability; agitation; somnolence.
Special Senses
Optic neuritis; tinnitus; conjunctivitis; visual disturbances.
Cardiovascular System
Syncope; tachycardia. The following adverse reaction has been reported with another Hepatitis B Vaccine (recombinant) but not with RECOMBIVAX: keratitis.

WARNINGS

Patients who develop symptoms of hypersensitivity [but not "adverse events"] after an injection should not receive further injections of the vaccine (see CONTRAINDICATIONS).
Because of the long incubation period for hepatitis B, it is possible for unrecognized infection to be present at the time the vaccine is given. The vaccine may not prevent hepatitis B in such patients.[This disclaimer also obscures the fact that approximately 30% of vaccine recipients derive no benefit, or immunity, whatsoever from the injections. Thus, these individuals remain susceptible to hepatitis B infection that the manufacturer can then claim was incubating prior to the vaccination.]*

PRECAUTIONS

General
As with any percutaneous vaccine, epinephrine should be available for immediate use should an anaphylactoid reaction occur. Any serious active infection is reason for delaying use of the vaccine except when in the opinion of the physician, withholding the vaccine entails a greater risk. Caution and appropriate care should be exercised in administering the vaccine to individuals with severely compromised cardiopulmonary status or to others in whom a febrile or systemic reaction could pose a significant risk, [or to pregnant or nursing mothers].

Source: Merck & Company, Inc. *Physicians' Desk Reference, 54th Edition 2000.* Montvale, NJ. Medical Economics Company, Inc., 2000, p. 1881. *Misleading statement: see text for detailed discussion.

organizations revealed, "and recovery status was listed as unknown in 33%" of reported cases.[18]

Further, epidemiological analyses revealed additional risks. The incidence of hepatitis B infection in the U.S. in 1996 was reported as four people out of every one hundred thousand. That translated to approximately 10,000 cases annually given about 250 million people in America. However, 98% of these people developed lifelong immunity, and never became seriously ill. In contrast, the risk of serious hepatitis B vaccine reactions, recommended by the CDC, was about four in every one thousand.[18] Thus, the vaccine injury rate amounted to one hundred times the incidence rate for the disease it portended to prevent! Also, in 1996, only 54 cases of hepatitis B were actually reported nationally in children below 1 year of age. But that same year there were 1,080 reported adverse reactions, including 47 infant deaths. Again, with *less than 10 percent being reported.* Any way you ciphered it, the mortality and morbidity from the hepatitis B vaccine was far greater than that caused by the disease.[19]

This evidence prompted the AAPS to petition the Clinton administration to lift its "mandate" on 12-hour-old infant hepatitis B vaccines. Their evidence was not only buffeted by reports from France linking the vaccines to class action lawsuits against SmithKline Beecham, the makers of the French vaccine, but also by a scientific article published in the *Journal of Rheumatology.* Researchers at the University of Western Ontario determined that ten of eleven firemen tested following administration of the hepatitis B vaccination had "fulfilled" all of the "revised American College of Rheumatology criteria for rheumatoid arthritis."[19]

This focus on, and harangue against, the hepatitis B vaccine does not suggest that other vaccines are safer or pose fewer risks. The fact is, no one knows the extent to which vaccines induced various illnesses since long-term vaccine trials in regard to injuries are virtually non-existent.

The Lyme Disease Example

Figure 14.7 reprints SmithKline Beecham's highly touted Lymerix vaccine prescribed to prevent Lyme disease. It showed that more than 25% of people who received the vaccine developed the disease's chronic arthritic symptoms.[15]

It was, therefore, no surprise that within months of its licensing, the FDA was asked to review the vaccine's safety. The New Jersey *Star-Ledger* reported that Lymerix had "come under increasing fire from some doctors and consumers" who believed the vaccine may have caused severe side effects akin to arthritis. The Food and Drug Administration, the paper stated, had decided to step in with a special review of the drug. SmithKline officials, however, remained secure in their belief that the drug was "effective and, more importantly in this case, safe: 'We're not seeing any *unexpected* adverse events coming through,' said spokeswoman Carmel Hogan, 'but we see this very much as an opportunity to put our data out in the public domain.'"

I added the emphasis on the word "unexpected." Indeed, such high rates of arthralgia had been published and expected.

Ms. Hogan's second statement was also an honest admission that the company's Lymerix data had never been seriously reviewed by the public or FDA prior to licensing.

Detractors said that the vaccine contained a protein that caused an untreatable severe form of arthritis in certain, genetically predisposed, patients—about 30 percent of the population!

The company reported that more than 440,000 people had been vaccinated with Lymerix before the review was instigated.

In other words, within a few short months this one vaccine had crippled more than 130,000 Americans.

David Versus Goliath

Among the most dedicated and articulate investigators of vaccine contaminations, risks, cover-ups, and coercive policies intended to have mass populations unwittingly forfeit their right to refuse what amounts to pharmaceutical-induced genocide is Dr. Kristine Severyn. The Director of the Vaccine Policy Institute in Dayton, Ohio, Dr. Severyn has testified before numerous government hearings committees in an effort to bring some level of sound science to policy decisions.

In 1999, Dr. Severyn presented her view of political corruption affecting vaccine science and public health policies to the AAPS.[20] The entire vaccine industry, and the government regulatory agencies entrusted to oversee it, she explained, was rife with fraud. Her lengthy review of relevant data supporting her thesis was presented by invitation of the AAPS at their 56th annual meeting, held that year in Coeur D'Alene, Idaho.

Figure 14.7. The Incidence of Adverse Reactions to Lymerix Vaccine for Lyme Disease Including "Severe Events" After Each Dose and Overall

Table 4. The Incidence of Local and General Solicited Adverse Events (including Severe Events) Reported After Each Dose and Overall

Events	Dose 1		Dose 2		Dose 3		Overall	
	Vaccine (N=402) %	Placebo (N=398) %	Vaccine (N=402) %	Placebo (N=398) %	Vaccine (N=402) %	Placebo (N=398) %	Vaccine (N=402) %	Placebo (N=398) %
Local Symptoms								
Redness, any	21.64[c]	8.29	16.67[c]	7.04	25.12[c]	11.81	41.79[c]	20.85
Redness, severe*	2.2[b]	0.0	1.0	0.0	2.5[b]	0.0	4.2[c]	0.0
Soreness, any	81.59[c]	36.68	76.37[c]	30.90	82.59[c]	52.26	93.53[c]	68.09
Soreness, severe†	1.2	0.0	1.0	0.3	3.0[b]	0.3	5.0[c]	0.0
Swelling, any	14.43[c]	4.27	11.44[c]	3.27	19.15[c]	6.78	29.85[c]	11.31
Swelling, severe*	0.0	0.0	0.0	0.0	0.5	0.0	0.5	0.0
General Symptoms								
Arthralgia, any	11.94[c]	4.52	10.70	8.29	13.43[b]	7.54	25.62[b]	16.33
Arthralgia, severe†	0.7	0.0	0.2	0.3	0.0	0.3	1.0	0.5
Fatigue, any	20.90	16.83	20.15[c]	11.81	21.89[a]	16.33	40.80[a]	32.91
Fatigue, severe†	0.5	0.05	1.5	1.3	1.0	1.0	3.0	2.3
Headache, any	20.65	19.10	14.43	12.31	19.90	18.34	38.56	37.19
Headache, severe†	0.5	0.05	1.2	0.5	1.2	1.8	3.0	2.8
Rash, any	4.23[a]	1.51	4.98[a]	2.01	5.47[b]	1.76	11.69[b]	5.28
Rash, severe*	0.0	0.0	0.0	0.0	0.2	0.0	0.2	0.0
Fever ≥99.5°F	1.49	0.75	1.00	0.50	1.00	1.01	3.48	2.26
Fever >102.2°F	0.0	0.0	0.0	0.0	0.0	0.0	0.0	0.0

*Severe = measuring >3.0 cm and persisting longer than 24 hours.
†Severe = preventing everyday normal activity.
a. p-value <0.05.   b. p-value <0.01.   c. p-value <0.001.

Highlights from Dr. Severyn's revealing presentation are presented below. She began by addressing the "hepatitis B vaccine mandate" that had been successfully opposed by her and the AAPS to the chagrin of its manufacturers and public health proponents. What follows is a David versus Goliath story worth reviewing. Dr. Severyn began:

> The mandate was tagged onto a hazardous waste bill in 1998,[21] through direct lobbying of the Ohio House and Senate health committees by the two manufacturers of hepatitis B vaccine, Merck and SmithKline Beecham. In an effort to reverse the mandate, I wrote an op-ed column about the shady manner in which the mandate was passed,[22] mailed it to all 300-plus newspapers across the state [See figure 14.8.], and met with the head of the House Health Committee. Surprisingly, he introduced legislation to rescind the mandate, and eventually reversed his original support of vaccine mandates.[23]

> Since Ohio was the first state to have such a bill introduced and have legislative hearings scheduled to rescind a hepatitis B vaccine mandate,[24] well-funded organized opposition to our efforts descended from across the country on the statehouse in Columbus, Ohio. A representative of a public relations firm from New York City, hired by the American Academy of Pediatrics and the vaccine manufacturers to deal with hepatitis B vaccine dissent, flew back and forth from New York to Columbus for the hearings. A representative from the CDC flew up from Atlanta to testify. . . . We were definitely out-gunned, financially and otherwise.

Polling, Opinion and Public Health

Despite generating a *Chicago Sun-Times*[25] telephone poll that showed 83 percent of voting parents did not want their children vaccinated with the hepatitis B vaccine, plus marshalling substantial medical and grassroots support through her exhaustive effort, Dr. Severyn lost the battle.

"How did organized medicine get to such a point where informed consent, a basic tenet of ethical medical practice, gets thrown out the window under the guise of 'disease prevention?'" Dr. Severyn asked. After listing all of the violations against civil rights freely perpetrated by vaccine makers and allied government agencies, she answered her own question by reviewing the historical antecedents to "mandatory vaccine" policies:

Fig. 14.8. News Article in Response to Dr. Severyn's Efforts

SOME OPPOSE HEPATITIS VACCINE FOR KIDS

By Kevin Lamb

Children younger than 14 are three times more likely to be killed or "seriously injured" by hepatitis B vaccines than to catch the disease, the Association of American Physicians and Surgeons said in opposing "Ohio's mandate that children entering kindergarten this fall must begin receiving three doses of the vaccine."

An Ohio House committee will continue hearings and possibly vote today on legislation that would suspend the requirement for one year.

"I'm gratified that a physicians' group is courageous enough to finally speak up," said Kristine M. Severyn of Centerville, a pharmacist with a Ph.D. that involved the composition and physical effects of drugs. As director of Ohio Parents for Vaccine Safety, Severyn already had given the Health, Retirement and Aging Committee "letters opposing the mandate from 24 individual physicians.

The American Medical Association and the American Academy of Pediatrics have endorsed the vaccine, but Severyn and the AAPS expressed concern about the organizations' financial ties to vaccine manufacturers. Severyn has a thank-you letter from the AAP for a $100,000 donation in 1988 from Merck & Co., which manufacturers vaccines for hepatitis B and other diseases.

The AAPS statistics came from the federal National Vaccine Information Center's last tabulated year, 1996, when there were 872 "serious adverse events" and 48 deaths associated with hepatitis B vaccinations of children younger than 14, compared with 279 cases of hepatitis B in that age group. "Serious" was defined as requiring an emergency room visit or hospital stay, or causing death or "life-threatening or disabling injuries."

Nevertheless, government health officials cavalierly dismiss reports of serious adverse vaccine effects as coincidental, said Dr. Jane M. Orient, AAPS executive director..

Dr. Virginia Haller, chief of the Ohio Department of Health's family and community health division, calls the vaccine's risks slim and vaccines in general "the No.1 accomplishment in the effort to improve the health and well-being of U.S. citizens." Haller told the House committee that only about one in 600,000 recipients suffers severe allergic reaction to the hepatitis B vaccine and that it successfully immunizes 90 percent to 95 percent of them.

Hepatitis B is not spread by casual contact. The U.S. Centers for Disease Control and Prevention recommends targeting the vaccine to people with the disease's distinct risk factors: multiple sex partners, injection-drug use, frequent occupational exposure to blood and transmission at birth from an infected mother.

Ohio's mandatory hepatitis B vaccine was tacked onto a hazardous waste bill last year without debate because committee chairman Dale Van Vyven, R-Cincinnati, was unaware of opposition. Now Van Vyven plans to introduce two amendments to the bill under consideration.

One would require state health officials to study the vaccine in the next year. The other would enable informed parents to decline any vaccine for personal or religious reasons, in which case schools could not bar their children unless county health officials declare there is a risk the disease will be transmitted at school.

The AAPS said no Ohio school has reported hepatitis B transmission.

Article from the *Dayton Daily News,* Wednesday, April 28, 1999, in response to Dr. Kristine Severyn's grassroots efforts concerning "mandatory" hepatitis B vaccines. Text discusses financial ties between medical organizations and the vaccine makers.

Mandatory vaccination laws are made in state legislatures. The precedent for such laws goes back to a 1905 U.S. Supreme Court decision, *Jacobson v. Massachusetts*.[26, 27] Mr. Jacobson, an adult resident of Cambridge, Massachusetts, refused to be vaccinated, opposing a 1902 Cambridge Board of Health mandate "that all inhabitants of the city . . . be vaccinated. . . ." Jacobsen claimed that he had "suffered seriously from previous vaccination," as did his son. All adults over 21 years of age who refused vaccination were fined $5.00.

The U.S. Supreme Court affirmed the right of the state legislature to enforce mandatory vaccination, claiming it a proper exercise of the state's police power to enact "health laws" reflecting dominant medical beliefs and those of the majority of society. Thus, the opinion of the minority should not subvert the opinion of the majority, or "the interests of the many [should not be] subordinated to the wishes or convenience of the few."

I should emphasize, at this point, the power of *public opinion* in affecting court rulings and legislative decisions. As this history clearly demonstrated, in Dr. Severyn's words, "the opinion of the minority should not subvert the opinion of the majority." For this reason, public opinion research (e.g., surveys and polls), and efforts to manipulate majority opinion through various social science organizations and propaganda programs, have been the foundation upon which multinational corporations have been built. Today's globalists, led by the Rockefeller/I.G. Farben cartel, have historically directed vast media resources to engineer public opinion to facilitate their agendas, including genocide, as will be discussed in greater detail in later chapters.

In this vein, Dr. Severyn noted the controversial nature of vaccine programs, and the Supreme Court's decision that " . . . in a free country, where the government is by the people . . . what the people believe is for the common welfare must be accepted as tending to promote the common welfare, *whether it does in fact or not.*" Dr. Severyn added the emphasis and noted that "until public opinion changes, with subsequent changes in state vaccination laws, the courts will not consider challenges to state vaccination laws."

In summary, vaccination laws and policies are based largely on mass mediated mind control. Courts will not uphold justice, or even sound science, but only the most commonly held beliefs.

As compared with mathematics and physics, described as being "hard sciences," behavioral and social sciences are generally thought to be "soft sciences," somewhat less dependable and persuasive. Yet, the above discussions indicate these "soft sciences" impact most force-

Fig. 14.9. "Miracle Vaccines" in *U.S. News & World Report*: A Classic Example of Media Propaganda

The Pentagon Strategy to Hammer Saddam

How to Use Ritalin the Right Way

Microsoft's Pesky Rival

U.S.News & WORLD REPORT

NOVEMBER 23, 1998   www.usnews.com

Miracle Vaccines

New ways to fight earaches, the flu, strep throat–and maybe even cancer

EXCLUSIVE: Investigating the Embassy Bombings

Dumbing Down the Military

Think Snow: The Best Ski Bargains

Magazine cover shows classic exercise of media propaganda and psychological operations (PSYOPs) consistent with non-lethal warfare. Notice the subtle (subliminal) messages in the margin. Adjacent "Miracle Vaccines," is "New ways to fight earaches, the flu . . . and maybe even cancer" when vaccines have been shown to *cause* these illnesses. "How to use Ritalin the right way" is another example—vaccine induced brain damage is a leading cause of autism, attention deficit and hyperactivity disorders for which children are prescribed Ritalin. Such messages dramatically impact beliefs, attitudes, behavior, and most importantly, public opinions upon which "mandatory" vaccination laws and other public health policies are legislated.

fully Americans' most commonly held beliefs, attitudes and opinions, and these most consequentially effect the laws of the land.

As exemplified in figure 14.9, these media promulgated beliefs, attitudes, and opinions are also why, despite the availability of religious exemptions to legally avoid vaccinations in 47 American states, and personal/philosophical exemptions available in 16, as Dr. Severyn documented, "Across the U.S. less than 2 percent of students in each state take any type of exemption."

In fact, according to a 1997 report of the National Vaccine Advisory Committee,[28] "There appear to be no correlation between states which allow philosophical exemptions and immunization coverage." Moreover, "given the small percentage of children who are currently exempted, philosophical exemptions do not appear to have a major detrimental impact on child health and well-being in the United States." Unfortunately for freedom of choice advocates, however, these two vaccine exemption facts were never publicized, though they obviously should have been.

The Popular Myth of Vaccination Safety

Regarding the reality alluded to above, the safety of any vaccine has yet to be proven. To date, the greatest travesty and injustice in public health is the fact that current vaccination policies violate the fundamental premise upon which the profession of public health is supposed to be practiced. That is, health policies are to "above all, do no harm," or at minimum, if some harm is to be done, that sound scientific studies prove less harm than benefit is being accomplished. These studies are called "cost-benefit," and "risk-benefit" analyses. The trouble is, to date, no definitive "cost-benefit" study has ever been conducted on any of the vaccines. Such studies have been published, but critical reviews revealed they never included all of the costs, such as the costs to society for vaccine injuries and deaths admittedly underreported. Even worse, no risk-benefit study whatsoever has ever been conducted to show that vaccines are not killing and maiming more people than they are helping or saving as detailed above with the hepatitis B and Lyme vaccines.

Dr. Severyn also addressed the issue of vaccine safety this way before the AAPS. "Americans naively assume the CDC's vaccine policies are backed by numerous medical studies proving the vaccines always work and are safe. Nothing could be further from the truth," she said. Using rubella (German measles) as her "prime example," the vaccine expert reported:

> CDC experts admit there really is no evidence supporting the current requirement that seventh-graders and/or college students in most states receive a second dose of rubella vaccine. In February 1996, the director of the CDC's National Immunization Program, Dr. Walter Orenstein, even commented, "We don't have the data to support a second dose of rubella, but we hate to go back."[29] Nevertheless, to facilitate measles outbreak control, students across the U.S. must receive, upon CDC urging, a second dose of the combination vaccine MMR (measles, mumps, rubella) . . . before attending classes. . . .[20]

> The way CDC currently withholds information, circles its wagons, and cites only the studies which support its views, ignoring those studies that don't, one would think that the letters CDC stood for Cover-up, Distortion and Coercion. . . . [or] Coercion, Distortion and Conflict of Interest.

Likewise, given the evidence herein and in my earlier works, I came to the conclusion that America's leading health science and policy making agency might more aptly be called the "Centers for Disease Creation."

Conflicting Interests at the CDC

The CDC's Advisory Committee on Immunization Practices (ACIP) established American vaccination policies. For decades, their recommendations have been heeded by legislatures, and "mandated" by state governments. For more than twenty years, prior to Dr. Severyn's heroic efforts, ACIP operated behind closed doors. Complete independence from vaccine awareness organizations, citizen's rights groups, and other governmental watchdogs ended in 1997, largely due to Dr. Severyn. She explained to members of the AAPS that prior to her activism, unlike all other federal advisory committees, ACIP "chose to make available only heavily-edited minutes," and these, only months after important decisions and subsequent policies were voted into law.

Her battle to make ACIP meeting transcripts public involved a lengthy letter and report writing campaign to "two congressmen and a senator in Washington, D.C." Throughout her campaign, the CDC remained obstinate. Finally, financial pressures from Capitol Hill broke their tradition.

"Congress added a statement in July 1997 to CDC's 1998 appropriations, i.e., the agency's operating budget, . . . instructing CDC to make the transcripts available," Dr. Severyn reported. "Backed into a corner, the CDC relented. At the beginning of the October 22, 1997, ACIP meeting, their Executive Secretary announced that verbatim transcripts would now be available, in his words, '. . . for reasons I won't go into here. . . .'"[20]

But Dr. Severyn's troubles were just beginning. About a year later she learned, during a National Vaccine Advisory Committee meeting, that members were being informed by Human Health Services Agency officials, including their attorney, David Benor, how they might circumvent the Federal Advisory Committee Act, and "not be bothered with public meetings to enact public policy."[20]

Further investigations by Dr. Severyn showed that ACIP members frequently maintained relationships with vaccine makers that grossly demonstrated conflicting interests. While federal law (18 U.S.C. section 208) prohibited "members of federal advisory committees from participating in matters in which he/she, wife, or child, or organization has a financial interest, the conflict of interest can be waived if 'the need for the individual's services outweighs the potential for a conflict of interest created by the financial interest involved."

The law essentially authorized certified pharmaceutical champions to facilitate the government's policymaking process for the benefit of the drug makers.[30]

Amplifying this understanding, Assistant Secretary for Health, Dr. James Mason, wrote in a letter to attorney Jeffrey H. Schwartz of the fledgling activist group Dissatisfied Parents Together (DPT), that given the "[l]imited funding . . . available from the Government for applied research on vaccine immunogenicity and efficacy; therefore, such research is generally funded by pharmaceutical companies. A policy that excludes such scientists would eliminate many university investigators knowledgeable about vaccines."[20]

Dr. Severyn further testified, that she was told by John Livengood, M.D., the Director of Epidemiology and Surveillance Division, at the CDC, involved in managing conflict of interest waivers for ACIP members, "that all ACIP members serve under waivers."[20, 31]

When she alerted Congressman Bob McEwen (D-Ohio) regarding this ACIP conflict of interest problem, the legislator contacted HHS Secretary Louis Sullivan, who turned the problem back over to Dr.

Mason, who then delivered it to the CDC's ACIP staff, their lawyers, and ethics officer, who then returned a verdict to Mr. Sullivan reaffirming "the appropriateness of including individuals as members of advisory groups based on their expertise. . . ."[20]

"In a nutshell," Dr. Severyn summarized, "Dr. Mason told my congressman not to worry because CDC's SOP's (standard operating procedures) were in place which CDC established to define conflicts of interest and keep specific details about conflicts of interest secret from the public. Since a system to monitor conflict of interest was in place, the agency was technically in compliance with the law." In essence, both Dr. Severyn and Congressman McEwen were told to "Buzz off!"

Dr. Severyn learned that the financial disclosure forms of ACIP members were classified intelligence. When citizens requested these forms through the Freedom of Information Officer at the CDC, she explained, everyone was told the forms "are exempt under the provisions of 5 U.S.C. 552(b)(3) of the Freedom of Information Act, which permits nondisclosure of records exempted by other statutes." Here, the Ethics in Government Act prohibited the provision of "financial disclosure documents." Plus, she ascertained, such disclosures, important as they might be in ferreting out unscientific biases and bogus health policies, "constitute(s) a clearly unwarranted invasion of personal privacy," per U.S.C. 552(b)(6) and the HHS "Department's implementing regulation 45 CFR 5.67"[20]

In addition to these political contrivances, Dr. Severyn discovered a policy of allowing nonvoting ex-officios, from various agencies including the FDA, NIH, and Defense Department, to be temporarily "deputized" for special ACIP meetings. During a February 1999 ACIP meeting in Atlanta, she witnessed how "deputized" and virtually all other votes were ultimately generated to favor CDC, vaccination, and pharmaceutical industry policies.[20]

Vaccine Policy Secrecy at the Institute of Medicine (IoM)

Dr. Severyn also discovered how difficult it was for the public to gain access to information concerning vaccines and the establishment of vaccination policies that dramatically affected the public's health. "When the CDC was questioned about the rationale behind its vaccine recommendations, which one assumes would be public information," Dr. Severyn said, "citizens find that agency treats formulation of national vaccination policy as a top military secret." The agency hides ïind a "privacy" clause in the Freedom of Information Act that exempts them from public scrutiny. This loophole is required, the U.S. Department of Justice wrote, to prevent stifling "honest and frank communication within the agency."

Consequently, Dr. Severyn concluded that "[t]he public is left in the dark about the scientific validity behind various CDC vaccination recommendations. . . . U.S. families must live with a government vaccine policymaking bureaucracy which is accountable to no one but itself." The CDC that determined U.S. vaccination policy, Dr. Severyn said, was the same agency that determined whether or not a conflict of interest is significant. "When the public tries to find out just how significant a conflict is, the CDC tells them that the degree of conflict of interest is confidential. When the public questions how a policy is formulated, the CDC tells them that is also confidential. The U.S. Public Health Service says, 'Trust us, we know best.'"

The same is apparently true insofar as pesticide spraying and vaccination programs for alleged WNV outbreaks. Similar conflicts of interest and behind-closed-doors dealings were described in Chapter 8 regarding Dr. Thomas Monath, Vice President of OraVax—sole producers of a vaccine said to be effective against the WNV.

As Dr. Severyn testified, the prestigious National Academy of Sciences, and its division, the IoM, had, over the years, been contracted by the major government health agencies, including the NIH and National Institute for Allergy and Infectious Diseases (NIAID), to "evaluate which vaccines should be put on the fast track." In gauging the IoM's power, Dr. Severyn noted that by the year 2000, six of the fourteen vaccines so authorized by the IoM in 1985 had been licensed, and even "mandated" in some states for daycare or school attendance. These vaccines included: hepatitis B, varicella, rotavirus, hepatitis A, and *Hemophilus influenzae* type B. A report by the IoM in 1999 set "vaccine research priorities in this country for the next 20 years."[20]

Pharmaceutical and Political Bias at the IOM

The IoM, a National Academy of Sciences (NAS) affiliate, is linked by the NAS to the pharmaceutical cartel. It has, like the CDC, an infamous history. As detailed in *Emerging Viruses: AIDS & Ebola— Nature, Accident or Intentional?* the NAS had been funded, from its inception, principally by either Rockefeller family holdings, or their globalist affiliates.

For instance, I documented that the Alfred P. Sloan Foundation—sister organization to the Rockefeller Foundation—both under the direction of Lawrance Rockefeller in the 1960s and early 1970s, had contributed vast sums of money to the NAS's Cold Spring Harbor Laboratory project for "neuroscience," that is, social engineering through public persuasion technologies research and development. In other words, when mass mind control projects needed to be developed and "public opinion" needed to be formed, the Rockefeller/Farben cartel turned to NAS furnished human resources.

I also reported that the NAS–National Research Council (NRC), in 1969, was primarily responsible for advising the Defense Department on everything required to develop and transmit AIDS-like and Ebola-like viruses about *ten years prior* to their first "scientific discovery" or "outbreak." What an amazing feat! How was that accomplished?

Furthermore, related to these viruses and their effects, as detailed in Chapter 18, the NAS–NRC became the leading proponents for global depopulation with its publication of *Beyond Six Billion: Forecasting the World's Population.* The Rockefeller Population Council was heavily represented by the book's leading contributors who hailed from this organization.

The NAS, and its divisions, has traditionally been composed of both the brightest minds as well as the most politically powerful pharmaceutical enthusiasts. An example here, also from *Emerging Viruses,* was Dr. David Baltimore, among the world's leading experts in molecular biology, retrovirology, and biological warfare. In 1969, Dr. Baltimore, a member of the NAS–NRC, was one of the only experts in this field capable of advising DoD officials that, as seen in figure 18.5 and 18.6, AIDS-like and Ebola-like viruses could be mass-produced for biological warfare in "five years" for only $10 million.

Further considering the Rockefeller pharmaceutical influence at the NAS, and all levels of government, the appointment of George W. Merck, President of the Merck Pharmaceutical Company, as overseer of America's biological weapons industry, a position he maintained throughout most of the Cold War, was critical. A major conflicting interest here, never publicly acknowledged, was that George Merck's company—the drug making giant, today the world's leading vaccine producer, received a lion's share of the Nazi war chest. It was no accident that on August 10, 1944, prior to the end of WWII, when the Rockefeller Standard Oil Company and their Farben partners needed to decide where their war profits would go, they elected to invest heavily in the Merck pharmaceutical company.[6]

Infiltrating the Grassroots: "Astroturf" Organizations

Quite befitting discussions on contaminations, cover-ups, and conflicts of interest, Dr. Severyn also indicted a law that gave the NAS–IoM total contract authority over the government's vaccine safety studies. The law was the bogus National Childhood Vaccine Injury Act of 1986, advanced by the highly active "Astroturf" organization called the National Vaccine Information Center, or NVIC.

Like America's biological weapons industry, concealed pharmaceutical interests contaminated the NVIC from its inception. This practice of growing, what has become known as "Astroturf organizations," had become common industry practice by the time Marge Grant—a Wisconsin-based mother whose son had become seriously injured from a vaccine—was invited to appear on the Phil Donohue Show to tell her sad story.

"Astroturf organization" refers to one that is fundamentally financed by, and therefore beholding to, special interests. Like Astroturf in a sports arena, these organizations are rolled out to form the playing field before the "big game." Imitating natural growth, Astroturf organizations are, likewise, misperceived to grow from grassroots support. Due to their well-financed industry backers, such organizations grow rapidly, and soon establish themselves as the principle voices of consumer discontent and activism in their fields. Indeed, much of the information they disseminate supports grassroots activism, otherwise they would be obvious give-aways as special interest cons. Sadly, however, they tend to monopolize media coverage of alternative/grassroots perspectives in their domains. While promoting pro-industry policies in the name of "consumer activism," and by avoiding or suppressing key issues, they tragically misdirect the masses of well-meaning activists into an arena of consumer complacency and pro-corporate policy reforms. The NVIC is a premier example of this false and misleading and controlled form of "consumer activism."

During "The First International Public Conference on Vaccination" in 1997, with Dr. Severyn in attendance, Marge Grant revealed the following information to me. Attorney Jeffrey Schwartz, a co-founder and past president of the NVIC, worked with the organization's primary leader, Barbara Loe Fisher, NVIC president Kathy Williams, and

Stephan E. Lawton, a Washington lobbyist for the American Academy of Pediatrics, to direct the fledgling NVIC and the subsequent passing of The Vaccine Injury Act of 1986—the infamous "no fault" compensation program that freed vaccine makers from liability from law suits brought on by injured parties.

According to a 1984 Gannett News Service report entitled "The Vaccine Machine," supplied to me by Ms. Grant, the bond between Schwartz and Lawton began long before the formation of the NVIC. Gannett authors C. Collins and J. Hanchette wrote: "Until 1979, both [Schwartz and Lawton] worked for then-Rep. Paul Rogers, D-Fla., who, as chairman of the House's health subcommittee, was nicknamed 'Mr. Health' because of his image as guardian of America's physical well-being.

"Rogers led the House fight to pass the 1976 swine flu program." This became the nation's most ambitious, least successful, and most deadly mass immunization program on record. "He also spearheaded the 1976 legislation that made the federal government, rather than vaccine makers, financially liable for injuries resulting from that program.

"During the swine flu episode [in which thousands died as a result of the vaccine and tens of thousands more developed chronic autoimmune disorders], Schwartz worked for Rogers . . . as a member of the professional staff of the House Interstate and Foreign Commerce Committee. At the same time, Lawton, as chief counsel to that committee's Subcommittee on Health and the Environment, which Rogers chaired, was actively involved in the swine flu legislation."

Rogers later became a partner in a powerful Washington legal and lobbying firm that represented, of course, the Merck pharmaceutical company. "Since 1980," the Gannett News authors said, "Rogers also ha[d] been on Merck's board of directors."

Another Rogers aide, Dack Dalrymple, "became a lobbyist for American Cyanamid Co., the parent company of Lederle Laboratories." Mentioned earlier in this book for its cover-up of the cancer viruses spread worldwide through millions of contaminated doses of oral polio vaccine, Lederle is also infamous. Its parent, American Cyanamid Co., you might also recall from earlier chapters, is a subsidiary of American Home Products. Therefore, these firms are direct descendents of the Rockefeller/I.G. Farben pharmaceutical cartel.

"As well as lobbying for pediatricians," Gannett News continued, attorney Lawton worked for "at least two other organizations with a tie to vaccines: the Infectious Diseases Society of America, an organization of specialists in infectious diseases who retain[ed] Lawton to lobby for more government funding of research in their field; and Genetech, a California-based company specializing in genetics research" and vaccine development.

Genetech is also linked to Dr. Don Francis—an ex-CDC hepatitis B vaccine chief and, at the time of this writing, the director of vaccine research at Genetech. Dr. Francis was heavily implicated in *Emerging Viruses: AIDS & Ebola—Nature, Accident or Intentional?* in a conspiracy to cover-up the iatrogenic origin of AIDS that was largely centered in his field of expertise, and at his agency, when he worked at the CDC in the late 1970s and early 1980s.[6]

Prior to Schwartz's and Lawton's involvement, efforts to bring "dissatisfied parents together (DPT)," and subsequently form the NVIC, began when Ms. Grant appeared on the Phil Donohue Show and requested parents contact her if their children, like her son Scott, had been injured by vaccines. "Before I could give the Donohue people my address," Ms. Grant recalled, "Barbara [Loe Fisher] called the station and gave them her number. She said that I was representing her organization. Later when I tried to get the letters of the approximately 4,000 people that replied, I was told by Schwartz that I would have to deal with his attorneys. They never did share [the letters] or turn over my mail to me. It was from this information that Fisher wrote *A Shot in the Dark*."

Alternatively, here is how Barbara Loe Fisher, Kathy Williams, and other NVIC officials promote themselves. From their First International Public Conference on Vaccination, during which five of seven academic investigators/speakers favored vaccines for public health despite their espousing opposing findings, they wrote in their "Official Program:"

> Founded in 1982 as Dissatisfied Parents Together (DPT) by parents of vaccine injured children, the nonprofit, educational organization known today as the National Vaccine Information Center (NVIC) is dedicated to preventing vaccine injuries and deaths through public education. NVIC provides assistance to parents whose children have suffered vaccine reactions; promotes scientific research to investigate vaccine safety and effectiveness as well as to identify factors which place individuals at high risk for suffering vaccine reactions; and advocates the institution of oversight mechanisms within the mass vaccination system to make it safer.

After launching the organized national vaccine safety and informed consent movement in the U.S. in the early 1980s, NVIC's cofounders worked with Congress to create the National Childhood Vaccine Injury Act of 1986. This historic law set up a vaccine injury compensation program and included vaccine safety provisions such as mandatory recording and reporting of hospitalizations, injuries and deaths following vaccination. . . .[32]

Critics contend that the actual result of the NVIC's "historic law" allowed vaccine manufacturers to, literally, get away with murder. By 1997, more than a decade after the law had been established, the billion-dollar consumer funded trust that had been set aside to pay claimants for their injuries and deaths, had reimbursed less than 3,000 people. More than a hundred thousand others failed to qualify after submitting claims, according to Peter H. Meyers, J.D., a Professor of Clinical Law and Director of the Vaccine Injury Project at George Washington University Law School.[33]

Dr. Severyn attributed much of the law's injustice, once again, to the IoM. "The National Childhood Vaccine Injury Act of 1986," she reported, "specified that IoM be contracted to conduct studies on vaccine safety. These studies, which cost taxpayers nearly $2 million, were released in 1991 and 1994," yet failed to adequately deliver definitive safety data. Still, "the 1991 IoM study was used by the Department of Health and Human Services in its 1992 proposal to redefine pertussis vaccine injury. This change in criteria to grant award payments under the Vaccine Injury Compensation Program (VICP) effectively eliminated 90 percent of pertussis vaccine damage claims submitted at that time, pertussis vaccine damage representing almost three-fourths of all VICP claims," Dr. Severyn said.[20]

Legislative Control: Past, Present and Future

In conclusion, the U.S. Congress passed the 1986 National Childhood Vaccine Injury Act with forceful lobbying by the Rockefeller dominated pharmaceutical industry, and a little help from their friends in the "grassroots." The Act effectively protected vaccine makers, largely Merck and American Home Products subsidiaries, from litigations stemming from vaccine injuries. Vaccine manufacturers have openly admitted they make substantial financial contributions to policy setting organizations such as the IoM. Most vaccine officials and "authorities" that have guided vaccine science and policy-making since it began early last century have been paid industry contractors and consultants.[20]

To the time of this writing, the pharmaceutical lobby has remained the most powerful special interest influence on Capitol Hill. Given the omnipotent financial control over health policy and its makers by the chemical and pharmaceutical cartel, an ironic indication of such governmental injustice was recorded by CNN anchorman Bernard Shaw who announced on the eve of the 2000 presidential election that CNN's televised coverage was "brought to you by the American Pharmaceutical Companies, and Ditech financial services."[34]

The public never realized that these two sponsors of election news updates, heralding the Florida "vote scam," were infamously linked to the Rockefellers through I.G. Farben and General Motors Corporation president, Sloan Foundation founder, and Rockefeller cancer industry partner, Alfred P. Sloan. The Ditech Mortgage Company—a General Motors subsidiary—had likewise generated disappointment and controversy shortly before the election when indictments were levied against several of its chief executives for embezzlement.[34]

Within this milieu of fraud, special interest politics, corruption, public persuasion, and resulting genocide, as the election results necessitated George W. Bush's first "presidential decision," he selected his father's Secretary of State—James Baker, III—to legitimize the recount of Florida's critical votes. Concluding this discussion of vaccines for global genocide, again, the public never knew that Mr. Baker had been implicated as co-owner of Tanox Biomedical Systems of Houston, Texas—the chief maker of the Mycoplasma contaminated vaccines given to military personnel enroute to the Middle East, that class action lawyers and expert witnesses claimed initiated Gulf War Syndrome, along with the bizarre "flu-like" upper respiratory infections chronically plaguing millions of Americans at the time of this writing.[35]

References

1) Epstein S. Expert witness testimony in a court of law against the aerial spraying of Malathion in El Cajon, California. In: *Malathion: Toxic Time Bomb, The Poisoning of Our People*. Op. cit., pp. 173-188.

2) Myers B. Interoffice memorandum from the Director of the California Department of Health Services to the Director of the Department of Food and Agriculture. December 16, 1980. In: *Malathion: Toxic Time Bomb, The Poisoning of Our People*. Russell-Manning B., ed. San Francisco: Cancer Control Society, 1990, p. 160.

3) Rodgers K. Effects of Malathion on the immune system: A letter to Assemblywoman Sandra Tanner and Ms. Virginia Johanssen. In: *Malathion: Toxic Time Bomb, The Poisoning of Our People*. Op. cit., p. 196.

4) Beckmann S., Hansen J. Skolnik R, Ullman P, and Warner R. The controversy over the 1981 aerial spraying of Malathion and the subsequent firing of the HESIS Director Marc Lappe, Ph.D. In: *Malathion: Toxic Time Bomb, The Poisoning of Our People*. Russell-Manning B., ed. San Francisco: Cancer Control Society, 1990, p. 161.

5) Satcher D. Immunization a must: Protects all. *USA Today*, August 19, 1999, p. 12A.

6) Horowitz LG. *Emerging Viruses: AIDS & Ebola—Nature, Accident or Intentional?* Rockport, MA: Tetrahedron Press, 1998.

7) Shorter E. The Health Century: A companion to the PBS television series. New York: Doubleday, 1987, pp. 67-69; 195-204. The recorded admissions are published on audiotape in: Horowitz L. *Horowitz on Vaccines*. Rockport, MA: Tetrahedron Press, 1998.

8) Andersen HC. *The Emperor's New Clothes: An All-Star Retelling of the Classic Fairy Tale*. Los Angeles, CA: Starbright Foundation, 1998.

9) *Merriam Webster's Collegiate Dictionary, Tenth Edition*. Springfield, MA: Merriam-Webster, Inc., 1994.

10) Christine M. Anti-immunities in vaccines. *News & Views*, 1997;14;3:1-2. (For copies contact Betty Tannenbaum, Editor, 8520 Bryan Avenue, Richmond Heights, MO 63117; See also: Staff writer. Vaccine against pregnancy now being tested on humans. *St. Louis Globe-Democrat*. Friday, July 11, 1986, p. 32.

11) Roberts D. *Killing the Black Body: Race, Reproduction and the Meaning of Liberty*. New York: Pantheon, 1997, pp. 104-149.

12) Kyle WS. Simian retroviruses, polio vaccine, and the origin of AIDS. *The Lancet* 1992;339:600-601.

13) Horowitz LG, Strecker R, Cantwell A, Vid D, and Grossman G. The mysterious origin of HIV: reviewing the natural, iatrogenic, and genocidal theo-

ries of AIDS. (Abstract) XI International AIDS Symposium. Vancouver, Canada, July 10, 1996.

14) Horowitz LG. *AIDS, Fear and Infection Control: A Professional Development, Risk Management and Practice Building Manual.* Rockport, MA: Tetrahedron, Inc. 1992; See also: Horowitz LG and Kehoe L. Fear and AIDS: Educating the public about dental office infection control procedures. *J. Am. Acad. Gen. Dent.* 1993;41;5:385-392.

15) Silverman E. FDA to Review Safety of Lyme Vaccine. New Jersey *Star-Ledger*, December 19, 2000. Article available through www.nj.com/starledger; for hepatitis B and Lyme vaccine side effects see: *Physicians' Desk Reference: 54th Edition.* Montvale, NJ: Medical Economics Company, Inc. 2000, pp. 1881; 3021.

16) AP staff. France suspends hepatitis B inoculations. *Casper Star-Tribune.* Sunday, October 4, 1998, p. A8.

17) News staff. The case of the hepatitis B vaccine. *The Well Being Journal.* 1999;8;5:6-10.

18) Pope JE, Stevens A, Howson W and Bell DA. The development of rheumatoid arthritis after recombinant hepatitis B vaccination. *J Rheumatol* 1998 Sept;25;9:1687-93.

19) Carnahan A. Hepatitis B vaccine rule stays: House panel declines to exempt school kids. *Rocky Mountain News.* February 9, 1999, p. 12A-13A.

20) Severyn KM. "Mandatory vaccination." A presentation before the 56th Annual Meeting of the Association of American Physicians and Surgeons, Coeur D'Alene, Idaho, October 14, 1999. (Available from Vaccine Policy Institute, 251 West Ridgeway Drive, Dayton, Ohio 45459; 937-435-4750.)

21) Amended Substitute to Senate Bill 153, Ohio 122nd General Assembly, 1997-1998.

22) Severyn KM. Hepatitis B vaccine for Ohio's kindergartners unnecessary, wasteful. *The Cincinnati Enquirer*, January 15, 1999, p. A23; Severyn KM. Has Ohio's vaccine policy gone too far? *Dayton Daily News*, January 27, 1999, p. 9A.

23) Ohio House Health, Retirement and Aging Committee, May 5, 1999. Vote on house Bill 200, Amendment 123-0758.

24) House Bill 200, Ohio 123rd General Assembly, 1999-2000.

25) Hepatitis shots should be OK'd by parents, *Dayton Daily News*, January 27, 1999, p. 8A; Hepatitis B vaccine to get its hearing in Ohio after all, *Dayton Daily News*, March 29, 1999, p. 6A; *Chicago Sun Times*, Morningline Results October 9, 1998, "Do you want your child vaccinated against hepatitis B?" Yes: 17%, No: 83%.

26) *Jacobson v. Massachusetts*, 197 U.S. 11 (1905).

27) Severyn KM. Jacobson v. Massachusetts: Impact on informed consent and vaccine policy. *J of Pharmacy and Law*, 5(2): 249-274, 1996.

28) National Vaccine Program Office. 1997 Annual Report. Centers for Disease Control and Prevention, 1600 Clifton Rd., N.E., Mailstop D-66, Atlanta, GA, 30333.

29) Rubella Elimination Working Group, meeting proceedings, Centers for Disease Control and Prevention National Immunization Conference, Detroit, Michigan, February 13, 1996.

30) 18 U.S.C. section 208 (b)(3).

31) John Livengood, M.D., Medical Officer, Director of Epidemiology and Surveillance Division, CDC, 1600 Clifton Rd., N.E., Mailstop E61, Atlanta, GA 30333. Dr. Severyn instructed interested parties to "[s]ee also, 'Financial Conflicts of Interest and 208 (b)(3) Waivers,' which describes how CDC incorporates 18 U.S.C. section 208 into establishing conflict of interest waivers for ACIP members. The following ten items are defined/described: Prohibition, inherent potential, waivers, integrity of committee, scope of waivers, current direct financial interest, disclosure not required—uncontrolled interests, *de minimus* financial interests—honoraria and travel support for scientific interchange, voting restrictions, and financial disclosure by members. See also, blank waiver form given to the Deputy Ethics Counselor, CDC from the ACIP Executive Secretary, regarding Conflict of Interest Waiver for Participation on the ACIP. (Faxed on December 11, 1996 from Dr. Dixie Snider, Executive Secretary, ACIP.)"

32) Marge Grant, along with her husband Jim, went on to form their own organization, the "Determined Parents to Stop Hurting Our Tots" or DPT-SHOT. They may be reached by calling 920-887-1133, or mail at P. O. Box 543, Beaver Dam, WI 53916. Other reputable contacts regarding vaccines and consumer health advocacy include: Barbara Alexander Mullarkey, Co-Director of the Illinois Vaccine Awareness Coalition (IVAC) available by mail at: P. O. Box 946, Oak Park, IL 60303; and Kristine Severyn, Director, Parents for Vaccine Safety, 251 Ridgeway Drive, Dayton, OH 45459, Telephone: 937-435-4750; and Ingri Cassel–Harkins, Vaccination Liberation, P. O. Box 1444, Coeur d'Alene, Idaho 83816; vaclib@dmi.net.

33) Myers PH. "Vaccination, the law and informed consent." Oral presentation during the First International Public Conference on Vaccination, Alexandria, Virginia, September 14, 1997.

34) CNN Election 2000 News. Coverage of the 2000 presidential election. American Pharmaceutical Industry and Ditech Mortgage Services—election night coverage sponsors cited by anchorman Bernard Shaw on Tuesday, November 7, 2000; See also: "Hoover's Online" (at www.hoovers.com/co/cap-

sule/0/0,2163,57220,00,html) for information concerning Ditech executives "indicted for extortion" and links to General Motors. GM, according to previous MI6 intelligence agent Dr. John Coleman, is controlled by the British Royal Family and Committee of 300 (See: Coleman J. *Conspirators' Hierarchy: The Story of the Committee of 300.* Carson City, NV: America West Publishers, 1992., p.233.

35) McAlvany DS. Special Report: Germ Warfare Against America—The Desert Storm Plague and Coverup. *The McAlvany Intelligence Advisor*, (P.O. Box 84904, Phoenix, AZ 85071) August, 1996, pp. 1-40. For additional connections to George Bush, see p. 27. Mr. McAlvany's statements regarding Mr. Baker were confirmed during a personal communication from Dr. Garth Nicolson who had first hand knowledge regarding the Mycoplasma research conducted at Tanox and the Baylor College of Medicine whereon the Board of Directors sat George H.W. Bush; See also: Horowitz LG and Puleo JS. *Healing Codes for the Biological Apocalypse.* Sandpoint, ID: Tetrahedron Publishing Group, 1999.

Chapter 15.
Non-Lethal
Electromagnetic Weapons

"In carrying on your governments, why should you
use killing at all? Let your evinced desires be for
what is good, and the people will be good. The relation between superiors and inferiors is like that between the wind and the grass. The grass must bend
when the wind blows across it.."
Confucius, 551–479 B.C.
The Confucian Analects

Besides biological and chemical weapons threats, among the "other
factors" associated with increasing worldwide mortality and morbidity, is the subtle but powerful influence of electromagnetic technologies developed for population control in a New Age of non-lethal
weaponry. Much of *Healing Codes for the Biological Apocalypse* was
devoted to investigating the High Frequency Active Auroral Research
Program (HAARP), linked through the ARCO Company and Cold
Spring Harbor Labs to the British Royal and Rockefeller Families respectively. The copyright on HAARP's website text was held by Cold
Spring Harbor Labs—home to the Human Genome Project—the contemporary focus of the century old eugenics movement. It was mainly
these families that initiated eugenics—racial hygiene for the development of a superior human race—during the early 1900s. It is, therefore,
highly suspicious that HAARP, allegedly developed for weather modification, would be linked to the Royal Family through its ARCO company controllers, and to the Hughes Corporation that has been at the
forefront of researching prion crystal diseases like "mad cow" and
Creutzfeldt-Jakob disease (CJD). Hughes company documents showed
they had also developed virtually all of the electromagnetic, satellite,
and biochip technologies required for the most advanced population
control applications consistent with the CIA's mind control and depopulation Project: MKULTRA.[1]

Thus far, this book has largely focused on biological and chemical agents that appear to be part of non-lethal warfare applications. This treatment, however, would be incomplete without including some of the extensive findings and diligent work of medical physician and journalist Nick Begich, M.D., the author of *Angels Don't Play This HAARP: Advances in Tesla Technology*, and the publisher at Earthpulse Press in Anchorage, Alaska.[2]

On October 17, 1998, Dr. Begich presented a report on non-lethal warfare and U.S. Star Wars-type weapon technology before the World Foundation for Natural Sciences in Interlaken Switzerland. Later, reporter Kenneth Burke for *The Leading Edge* interviewed him. The following excerpts are provided with permission from these authors and their publishers. The primary question addressed below is, "What developments have taken place in the field of non-lethal electromagnetic weaponry that could profoundly affect human life as well as planetary ecology in general." Initially, these authors asked, "Is it possible to trigger earthquakes, volcanic eruptions or weather changes by man-made activities? Is it possible to create and direct balls of energy at lightning speeds, to destroy an enemy? Is it possible to manipulate the behavior, and even the memories, of people using specialized technologies?" They answered affirmatively to all of the above.[3]

The New Controversial Technologies

Many of these capabilities and requisite systems are either operational or well on their way to being used in the battlefield. There are many new technologies being developed that will induce profound changes in human behavior and physiological functions from the instillation of artificial memories and delusions to physical ailments. Many of these new weapons are being called "non-lethal" in terms of their effect on people. Conceivably designed to minimize death and be virtually undetectable, death and detection is possible.

On February 5, 1998, the European Parliament's Committee on Foreign Affairs, Security and Defense Policy discussed these new technologies. Dr. Begich was one of those called to testify. One of the points discussed involved the definition of "non-lethal." Part of the definition involved the idea that such weapons would result in a less than 25% kill rate for those exposed. The basic fallacy in this is that under this definition, even land-mines might be considered non-lethal because they fail to kill more than 25% of their victims. Lasers which

The *Death in the Air* bookcover depicts a Nazi–gas-masked–alien stick-ing the dove of peace with his saber. His backdrop projects the horrific images of genocide, particularly affecting Black and Hispanic popula-tions. This and the following related murals were painted by artist Leo Tanguma, October 1995. They adorn the two interconnected halls in Denver Airport's main terminal building. The construction was dedicated by Black and white leaders on behalf of separate Masonic (largely se-cret) segregated societies. This entire building and its contents is dedi-cated to the "New World Airport Commission."

Why might Black and Hispanic genocide victims predominate? The Nazi–alien symbolizes the Nazi-fascist links between contemporary population controllers and the military–petrochemical industrialists accountable for Hitler's rise to power. Elite global industrialists, including the Rockefeller family in America and the Royal Family of England, were primarily re-sponsible for "eugenics," the first "racial hygiene" experiments pio-neered in America against Black and mentally retarded people. The development and use of chemical sprays and gasses for "pest control" and chemical warfare evolved largely from the twentieth century efforts of the I.G. Farben–Rockefeller petrochemical cartel. The "alien phenom-enon," as prescribed in *The Report From Iron Mountain* to facilitate glo-balism through the development of an enemy common to all earth's people, is reflected in the face of the masked Nazi villain who obviously sprays the sick and dying masses as he flies by etherically above the suffering.

Denver International Airport's dedication capstone dated March 19, 1994. The date is significant for its numerical equavalency is nine (9)—representing completion to Freemasons and other global secret society members as detailed in *Healing Codes for the Biological Apocalypse*. Note that the governing elite have apparently established a "New World Airport Commission" for their global reign.

The mural below is a dedication to the extinct species. Against a frightening background of flames and destruction, the foreground depicts several extinct species including the American buffalo, sea turtle, whale, and other animals. Children are seen crying over three open caskets. In these lie the extinct humans—Blacks, Native peoples, and Judeo-Christian Whites.

Deceased Black woman dressed in native African attire representing the Black people of Africa, if not the world—victims of globalism and genocide. The netted sea turtle above the coffin is an ancient spiritual symbol. Black people are generally recognized as being the oldest humans, as well as the most ("soul filled") spritually evolved.

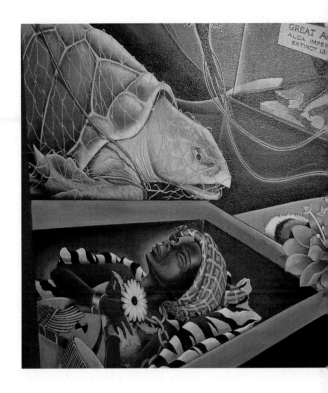

The Indians and native people of the world are represented here. Like Black Africans, natives have been traditionally devoted to spiritual and not physical concerns. American natives never believed in purchasing or owning land that was by nature part of "the Great Spirit." Globalism disregards, if not opposes this spiritual orientation. Thus, these people lie here extinct.

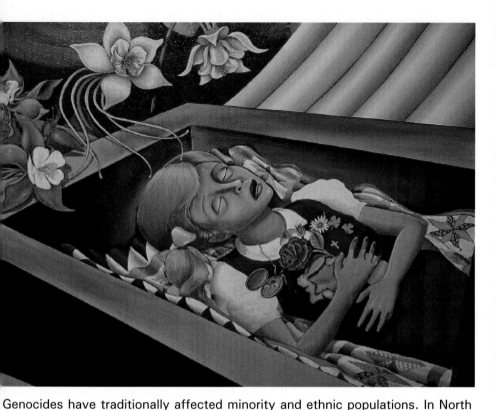

Genocides have traditionally affected minority and ethnic populations. In North America, the white upper and middle classes have largely considered them- selves safe against this type of threat. Non-lethal technologies, and global governors who wield them, know no such limitation. Here, a young blonde- haired woman lies deceased on an American quilt representing the Jewish and Christian people of the world. In her hands, by her heart, she holds the Star of David and the Bible with the cross. Separating the Jewish and Christian symbols is the symbol of the Illuminati, the Rosecrucians, and other secret societies—the red rose. Around her neck is a locket with her family's picture symbolizing the lineage or bloodline liability in this case. For this, and other reasons, globalism has been likened by the Christian community, not incorrectly, as an outcome of "spiritual warfare," and by most Muslim people as part of a "Holy War." To the time of this writing, Jewish people have generally remained, as they did during the rise of the Third Reich, in denial.

The New World Order celebration begins. This colorful mural, also displayed in Denver's "New World Airport" terminal, shows the dead Nazi–alien in the foreground surrounded by children only. Internationally, parents are gone,

symbolic of contemporary globalists efforts to use psychological warfare to subvert the minds of new generations, and decimate the traditional family institution that resists state control. Front and center is, naturally, the "Deutsche Bursche"—the German boy—who pounds the Nazi-alien's sabre with his hammer—the fascist symbol for Communism. Germany's war prone history is solemnly regarded but little understood, as is the British Royal Family's ancestral links as globalists to German war lords and conquerors. Also prominent in the foreground are the Chinese and American children and the British and Italian youth holding their respective flags. The Chinese youth dominates in her match-up symbolic of Revelation's prophesied "End Times" dragon coming from the East to devour the West. The Israeli flag survives too above a cracked tombstone that symbolizes the demise of "War, Violence and Hate."

This mural hangs in Denver Airport adjacent to the one on the preceding page as a tribute to the global extinction of people holding traditional spritual convictions. Represented here, as an outcome of the New World Order, are the world's children celebrating one global religion. This New World religion is predicted to be based on Eastern philosophy as symbolized by the colorful lotus-like flower emitting an aura of white light. In the background, the children, including the "Deutsche Bursche," are dancing joyously. Leading the dance on the left side of the mural is the Scottish Rite Freemason, dressed in his native attire and adorned with Masonic symbols. Trailing behind is a lone African child, seemingly apart from the dance, in his shadow.

The Ozymandias Parade, 1985 by Edward Kienholz of Hope, Idaho and Berlin, Germany. The first of several pieces of "art" reprinted here from *Keinholz: A Retrospective* (1996) courtesy of the Whitney Museum of American Art, The Henry Luce Foundation, the Andew W. Mellon Foundation (linked to the Carnegie Endowment) and others.

Kienholz's Nazi-American war-lord straddles a debilitated Judeo-Christian skeleton. In his hands he controls an electromagnetic signaling device as well as the beckoning symbols of these religions. The book quotes Barnett Newman in 1933: "'It is humanity's tragedy that today its leaders are either sullen materialists or maniacs who express the psychopathology of the mob mind.' . . . Between the macrocosmic dimensions of the Star Wars program and the microcosmic space of AIDS, our new world seems to have produced a sense of crisis and of being out of control." The reality is, the world, along with people's perceptions of it, is being meticulously controlled through agencies and foundations that pioneered the fields of public opinion and persuasion while funding such works of "art." These are the military–industrialists that Kienholz characterized *and* served. The sense that even the wind (nature) whipping the American flag, electronically controlled by a Nazi-American militarist, suggests Kienholz's knowledge of the energy generator reported near his home in Hope.

The Big Double Cross, 1987-89. From his lake view estate in Hope, Idaho, Kienholz brought symbols of militarism and religion together. Reflecting on his benefactors' consensus for one world religion, the Whitney Museum published, "Throughout history, the name of God has been invoked to legitimize bloodshed, carnage, and mass destruction. . . . Jews and Arabs have used military power to force their own ideological imperatives on neighbors with different religious convictions. . . . More than 8 feet high, [this] is one of the most breathtakingly simple elegies to the follies of war. In the artist's own words: 'War in the name of religion is the big double cross.'" A "Double Cross" in that the globalists that instigate wars also finance all the major religions.

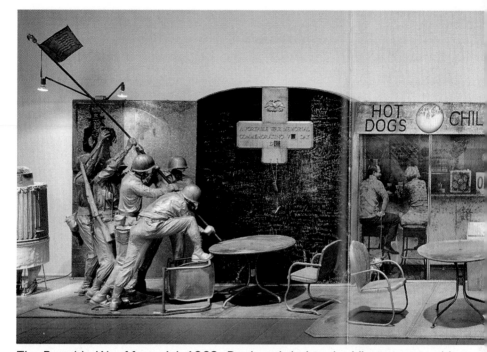

The Portable War Memorial, 1968. Produced during the Vietnam war, this most famous and most famously contrived American war photograph of soldiers erecting the flag on Iwo Jima, stands adjacent a list of 475 nations extinct because of wars. "The power of the work," claimed the Whitney Museum, "emanates from the location of this heroic act: the American diner. . . . metaphorically extending the war machine into the realm of consumption."

That is precisely what was socially engineered as directed by the Rockefeller Brothers Fund in 1961 with reports that drafted a "National Purpose" for America that linked "guns, butter, and the new technology" for "weapons production to the cause of Freedom and the Free World."

My Country Tis Of Thee, 1991 "Pork Barrel" politics as usual. The legislators and business men pledge allegiance to the flag, "while below the waist they enact the never-ending daisy chain of commerce and government."

(Above) The Birthday, 1964. Giving birth to missiles or birth control? The Rockefellers and other prominent globalists that control the media, including this artist's benefactor, media mogel Henry Luce, promote both depopulation options. The woman screams into a bubble so as not to be heard.

76 J.Cs Led The Big Charade, 1992-94. Much of Keinholz's work relays the globalist attitude towards religion. Here, "seventy-six framed icons of Jesus Christ are mounted on the handles of children's wagons . . ." They bear the arms and legs of dismembered baby dolls suggestive of the infanticide theme expressed in the artist's other works. According to the caption in this Whitney Museum publication, the images "seems to associate institutionalized religion with puerile game-playing. . . ." This best displays his and his benefactors denial and disparagement of Christianity as clearly articulated by Richard Jackson, one of Keinholz's best friends. This hunting partner wrote:

> Now when I'm driving in from Spokane to pay my last respects to Ed, I think about religion. Jesus, shit, I think to myself. What about all those terrible things we said up at hunting camp about the pope and all those people? What if there really is a God and He has a Son Jesus Christ? Now we're in real trouble here. Poor old Ed is goin' to go down to hell so fast in that Packard that he's goin' to knock all the fuckin' lights out down there. And then I thought, well Ed isn't going to some terrible place that these other people made up. . . . Ed's going to the happy hunting ground; and believe me folks, the hunting ground is a happy place. Now I see it pretty good. . . . Ed, I'll meet you up at camp.

(Previous page, below) *All have Sinned in Rm. 323*, Tammy Faye Bakker's portrait hangs behind a cross and more prominent television set as Kienholz muses over the public's "obsession with the dirty laundry of public figures, envisioned here as an act of masturbation, a way of 'getting off' on the apparent sins of others. 'Which is the greater sin?'" we are asked.

Many of Kienholz's works contain televisions to symbolize the use of the media to mold society into a perverted and ignorant trance by broadcasting the "people, places, palaces, and passions" prescribed for mass consumption and lethal distraction in the *Protocols of the Elders of Sion*, and other manuals for advancing globalism.

The Double Cross TV, 1987.

Six O'Clock News, 1964
Mickey Mouse makes his debut in Kienholz's collection of television icons. What better way is there to gain control over children's minds?

The Future As An Afterthought, 1962.

A bundle of baby dolls, black, white and brown, are strapped into an atomic mushroom configuration with bicycle peddles symbolizing someone behind the nuclear weapons industry is peddling global infanticide. The Rockefeller family is indicted on both counts.

As the wheel of population control goes round and round the same military–medical–petrochemical industrialists and propaganists are pleased and profiting.

It Takes Two To Integrate, 1961. Kienholz's art deftly depicts American blue collar racism, but conveniently conceals the white collar eugenics programs of his benefactors.

Holdin' The Dog, 1986. America's "Great Northwest," particularly northern Idaho and Montana, are reputed to be neo-Nazi and Ku Klux Klan strongholds. Do you believe everything on TV? This may be Kienholz's biggest "Doublecross." Like his neighbors' reputations, Kienholz's "art" seems to glorify more than condemn racism. The sacrificial dog in this work, a "human victim by proxy, . . . attempts to demystify and demythologize the act of racial violence." "The real shock," we are told in The Whitney Museum's publication (as it falsely blames us—the victims of this mass mediated "art") is the recognition "that this bigotry might be ours. We own it because it possesses us." This possession appears courtesy of *Time* and *Life* magazine founder Henry Luce, the Carnegie endowment, and friends.

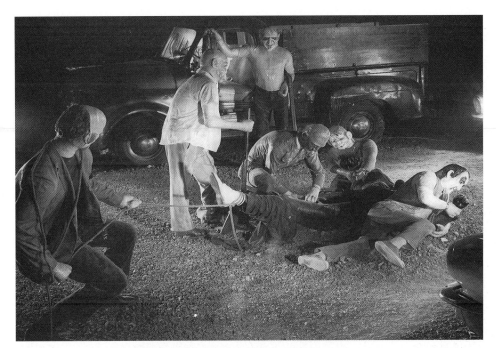

Five Car Stud, 1969-72. In this life size depiction of a racially motivated castration and slaying, five cars drive to the scene of the crime to enjoy the "game" of sterilizing a "Nigger." Reflecting the manner in which Africans and Black Americans have been targeted for genocide by the same global industrials that have hailed Kienholz's "art," this work may be seen much like Norman Mailer viewed grotesque war scenes on television in *Why We Are In Vietnam*—familiarity to the vivid violence breeds acceptance. Kienholz, like other "artists" made famous by the cryptocracy, served his PSYOPs function.

The White Cup, 1984-85. This piece is consistent with David Rockefeller's protégé, Zbigniew Brzezinski's, National Security Memorandum–46 declaring war against African and American Blacks. Policy options for Black genocide included: demonizing and assassinating Black leaders, thus generating "mistrust and hostility . . . giving rise to growing antagonism between different black groups," concomitantly instigating low self esteem and high aggression within the race, and engineering social class warfare as well.

Shown here is the targeted Black male killing himself as he holds a "white cup" suggestive of the WASP power that feeds class warfare to the manipulated faceless fools who consume the white powdered elixirs—cocaines, heroines, amphetamines, and more—certain to destroy their bodies and minds.

permanently blind people also fit this definition, as does "sticky foam" that might kill an adversary if it was sprayed on the victim's face causing a slow and agonizing death by suffocation. Indeed, non-lethals can be extremely lethal.

Thus, many of the panelists concluded that the term non-lethal was inaccurate in describing these new systems. Conference delegates decided the name non-lethal was more like a ploy used by military planners to gain acceptance for the new technology.

Another relevant point made in the hearing was the frequency of use of these weapons in non-combat situations or policing actions. Comparisons between Bosnia and Northern Ireland were made. Investigators determined that in conflicts where rubber bullets and other non-lethal systems were available they tended to be used with greater frequency because the troops using them believed that they would not kill. Others in conflict situations using weapons clearly designed for killing used much greater restraint. As of the date of the hearing, "peace keepers" armed with lethal weapons had not fired a shot in Bosnia whereas in Northern Ireland there were often injuries and deaths from the use of "non-lethals."

Dr. Begich learned that the Scientific Advisory Board of the Air Force produced a most revealing document regarding these new technologies.[4] The Air Force initiated study looked forward to the next century and saw what was possible for new weapons. In one of the volumes published as a result of the study, researchers, scientists and others forecast the following information:

> One can envision the development of electromagnetic energy sources, the output of which can be pulsed, shaped, and focused, that can couple with the human body in a fashion that will allow one to prevent voluntary muscular movements, control emotions (and thus actions), produce sleep, transmit suggestions, interfere with both short-term and long-term memory, produce an experience set, and delete an experience set.[4]

Think about this for a moment—a system that can manipulate emotions, control behavior, put you to sleep, create false memories and wipe old memories clean. Realizing this was a forecast and not necessarily the current state of technology should not cause one to believe that it is not a current issue. These systems are far from speculative. In fact, a great deal of work has already been done in this area with many systems being developed.

Regarding the creation of Manchurian candidates, this forecast went on to discuss the technology:

It would also appear possible to create high fidelity speech in the human body, raising the possibility of covert suggestion and psychological direction. When a high power microwave pulse in the gigahertz range strikes the human body, a very small temperature perturbation occurs. This is associated with a sudden expansion of the slightly heated tissue. This expansion is fast enough to produce an acoustic wave. If a pulse stream is used, it should be possible to create an internal acoustic field in the 5-15 kilohertz range, which is audible. Thus, it may be possible to "talk" to selected adversaries in a fashion that would be most disturbing to them.[4]

The forecast suggested that this would be "disturbing" to victims. Dr. Begich considered this a gross understatement. It would be pure terror and an unprecedented invasion on people's privacy. The entire controversial concept should have caused significant discussion and public debate. In fact, developments in this field have proceeded with virtually no public discourse whatsoever.

Developing Non-lethal Police and Military Policies

On July 21, 1994, Dr. Christopher Lamb, Director of Policy Planning, drafted a Department of Defense directive that established a policy for non-lethal weapons in the United States. The policy was intended to take effect January 1, 1995, and formally connected the military's non-lethal research to civilian law enforcement agencies.[1] The government's plan was to use pulsed electromagnetic and radio frequency systems as a non-lethal technology for domestic Justice Department operations. This combined mission raised additional constitutional questions for Americans regarding the power of the federal government to use military systems in domestic police actions.[5]

More recently, interviews with members of the Department of Defense confirmed the institution of this policy.

The policy statement reiterated, "It is important that the public understand that just as lethal weapons do not achieve perfect lethality, neither will non-lethal weapons always be capable of precluding fatalities and undesired collateral damage." In press statements, governments have continued to downplay the risks associated with such systems, even though the lethal potential is described in the context of their own usage policy.

On the Brink of Depersonalized Psychotronic Warfare

In "The Mind Has No Firewall," an article published in the Spring of 1998 in the U.S. Army War College's Quarterly, *Parameters*, Timothy L. Thomas discussed behavior modification systems of the past, present and future.[6]

For decades, he explained, the United States, the former Soviet Union, and other nations have been involved in developing sophisticated systems for influencing human behavior, along with physical and mental health. The focus of this research was to discover ways of manipulating human behavior in meeting political objectives in the context of war making and defense. What is interesting in all of this is the sophistication of external devices that can alter human nature.

Thomas stated that the Russian military "offered a slightly different slant to the problem, declaring that humanity stands on the brink of a 'psychotronic war' with mind and body as the focus. His article discussed Russian and international attempts to control the psychophysical condition of man and his decision-making processes by the use of VHF-generators, noiseless cassettes, and other technologies.

Thomas's article went on to describe that the aim of these new weapons was to control or alter the psyche or interfere with the various parts of the body in such a way as to confuse or destroy the inner-body signals, which keep the living system operational.

The *Parameters* article described the way "Information Warfare Theory" neglects the most important factor in information warfare—the human being. Humans were considered in information warfare scenarios only in that they could be impacted by propaganda, deceit, and deception—all tools recognized as part of the military mindset and arsenal. Thomas's prose publicly explored a more sinister approach, an approach which must be considered in the context of basic human rights and values; fundamentally and foundationally based on our right to think freely.

"Yet," Thomas explained, "the body is capable not only of being deceived, manipulated, or misinformed, but also shut down or destroyed, just as any other data-processing system. The data the body receives from external sources—such as electromagnetic, vortex, or acoustic energy waves—or creates through its own electrical or chemical stimuli can be manipulated or changed just as the data (information) in any hardware system can be altered."[6]

PSYOPs, C2W and "Open Systems"

The United States military in Joint Publication 3–13.1 referred to the importance of propaganda in conducting non-lethal operations.[7] They discussed the human body in the context of information warfare in addressing "psychological operations (PSYOPs)." This publication noted, "the ultimate target of (information warfare) is the information dependent process, whether human or automated. . . . Command and control warfare (C2W) is an application of information warfare in military operations. . . . C2W is the integrated use of PSYOPs, military deception, operations security, electronic warfare and physical destruction."

The aim of any information war ultimately targets human beings. The policy of the United States military is to target all information dependent systems "whether human or automated," and the definition extends the use of these new technologies to people as if they were just data-processing hardware.

The *Parameters* article went on to discuss the work of Dr. Victor Solntsev of the Baumann Technical Institute in Moscow. He insisted that the human body must be viewed as an open system instead of simply as an organism or closed system. Many Russian researchers, and others going back to at least the early 1970s according to documents held by Dr. Begich and Earthpulse, have held this "open system" approach. What is interesting is that it has taken thirty years to be seen in the open literature as a credible view of reality.

Dr. Solntsev proceeded to suggest that a person's physical environment can cause changes within the body and mind whether stimulated by electromagnetic, gravitational, acoustic, or other stimuli. The same Russian researcher examined the issue of *"information noise" which can create a dense shield between a person and external reality. The noise could be created as signals, messages, images or other information with the target being the "group consciousness." The purpose would be to overload people so that they no longer react normally to external stimuli or information. Such overloading could serve to destabilize judgment,* modify behavior, and/or reduce resistance to covert operations.

In applications crossing biology and cyberspace, according to Solntsev, at least one computer virus has been created that can affect people's psyches. It is referred to as "Russian Virus 666." This virus appears in every 25th frame of a computer visual display where a mix of color, pulse, and patterns were reported to put computer operators into trances. Once in a trance, the subconscious perception of the display can be used to induce heart attacks or to subtly manage or change perceptions of computer operators. This same system could be used in any television or visual broadcast.

In a July 7, 1997 *U.S. News and World Report* article, scientists revealed their efforts to identify specific energy patterns that could be likewise applied to people to produce similar results. The article addressed some of the important public revelations about these new systems. These revelations represented a mere piece of the story. What interests serious observers is why the military has begun to present these new systems to the public through the mainstream media.

It is widely held that art reflects culture. Many argue, on the other hand, that art molds culture. For instance, the broadcast media—including music, television, and film—are recognized as "art" forms. These, authorities argue, have modeled the social behaviors affecting the formation of the sex, drugs, rock-n-roll cultures and more.

In light of the above facts, it is logical to recognize that our culture is being conditioned to accept, and respond to, higher-tech methods of persuasion.

PSYOPs to Persuade the Public to Accept Non-lethal Warfare

An earlier article published by Dr. Begich and Earthpulse illuminated the subject of public persuasion insofar as non-lethal warfare acceptance is concerned. Officially, the campaign is referred to as the "Revolution in Military Affairs," or RMA. The hype encapsulates the idea that military technology has changed to such a degree that the very foundation of war must be, or has been, altered. The paper on this subject was advanced, once again, by the United States Army War College in July 1994.[8] This article suggested that new military technologies could be equated to the introduction of gunpowder to Europe a few centuries ago, or the discovery of the atom bomb in more recent history. The paper also suggested that these new systems may run contrary to American values, and that their introduction might be heatedly opposed by unconditioned individuals. Thus, the authors of the report proposed that in order to introduce these new weapons, American values would have to be changed.

Editorially speaking, it is alarming that military "think-tanks" publish papers in which they propose that commonly held national and human values are insufficient to meet the demands of desired military objectives; in this case introducing new lethal technologies labeled "non-lethal." Dr. Begich asked, "What is wrong with this picture?"

Obviously, military institutions and their extensive C2W PSYOPS mold popular values to their liking. They do not speak for, nor do their actions reflect, popular values or even majority opinions.

The idea, simply put, is that the same technologies that have transformed the American workplace may have no less profound effect on America's warrior status.

The U.S. Army War College report on RMA provided a rationale for "conflict short of war" that included a graduated response to "terrorism, insurgency, or violence associated with narcotrafficking." These growing demands, the military authors advanced, required new weapons along with a change in public opinion. They asserted that this change in opinion did not have to evolve naturally, but could be deliberately shaped by the government. The idea was that belief systems of Americans could be slowly altered to allow the military to introduce their new non-lethal weapons systems.

Lethal Revolution in Unpopular Non-Lethal Warfare

In its purest sense, revolution brings change that is permanent, fundamental, and rapid. The basic premise of the RMA is simple: throughout history, warfare usually developed in an evolutionary fashion, but occasionally ideas and inventions combined to propel dramatic and decisive change. This not only affected the application of military force, but also often altered the geopolitical balance in favor of those who mastered the new form of warfare.

The RMA opposes, military authors insinuate, "people's wars," these U.S. military officials label as Communistic. Russian officials naturally submit they are Capitalistic. The phrase "people's wars" could be equally applied to what occurred in the Philippines and to Eastern Europe's popular revolutions in the late 1980s. These military writers contended that there is a shift to "spiritual" and "commercial" insurgencies, which they do not define well, but imply national security risks to be defended against.

This is much akin to the 1978 National Security Memorandum–46, discussed later in this book, that proved the war against Black people in the United States and Africa was justified by alleged risks to "national security." The thesis that AIDS was an apparent outcome of this "security" operation, and the public's perception regarding this illness and its victims the result of a military PSYOP, may well be the case.

Who, after all, decides what is "spiritually," "commercially," or "politically" correct may be accurately surmised by reviewing the information in the final chapters of this book.

Military authors dismiss such things as the presumption of innocence, the right to disagree with the government, and the right to free expression and movement throughout the world as threats to "national security." At one point in the War College's document the need to use new technology to keep track of Americans traveling out of the United States was discussed. Here was justification for biochips or other surveillance technologies. The article stated:

> While advances in robotics and information technologies may make it possible to perform many commercial activities with fewer employees in dangerous regions, those Americans who are overseas will be more isolated and dispersed. This complicates the main problems of NEOs (noncombatant evacuation operations): identification and notification of the individuals to be evacuated, identification of safe routes, and assessment of threats to the evacuation. Technology could diminish these problems. In the near future every American at risk could be equipped with an electronic individual position locator device (IPLD). The device, derived from the electronic bracelet used to control some criminal offenders or parolees, would continuously inform a central data bank of the individuals' locations.

Eventually such a device could be permanently implanted under the skin, with automatic remote activation either upon departure from the U.S. territory (while passing through the security screening system at the airport, for example) or by transmission of a NEO alert code to areas of conflict. Implantation would help preclude removal of the device (although, of course, some terrorists might be willing to remove a portion of the hostage's body if they knew where the device was implanted). The IPLD could also act as a form of IFFN (identification friend, foe, or neutral) if U.S. military personnel were equipped with appropriate challenge/response devices. The most likely people to receive the implants are military personnel who will be told that this will help rescue them if they are captured. They may be the first, setting the stage for the rest of the country. Will our military personnel object, seeing this as an invasion of their private lives?

Another technology mentioned is a method for interfering with activities the cryptocracy judges to be wrong. In the examples given (drug traffickers and terrorists), most of us would agree intervention should take place at some level. However, the methods contemplated are extreme. Will those with the power to invade the privacy of individuals do so and without just cause? Will the rest of the population trust the holders of the power? The military planners anticipate a resounding, "NO"! Therefore, they propose a series of events to shift the popular view to the opposite extreme. They propose a revolution in popular thought, which will allow for a Revolution in Military Affairs.

At this point in the article, the authors suggested a fictional scenario where the illusion of the need for this kind of control could be created. In the scenario, a plan to desensitize the population to increasing control and, introduction of the new technology, through systematic manipulation and disinformation by the government was initiated. What they advanced is apparently underway as evidenced by today's headline news.

Under their nonfictional scenario, the military's writers heralded, "greatly improved intelligence gathering," in the form of public opinion polling, and public assimilation of propaganda as a "primary component of the RMA, and proposed information warfare capabilities . . ." These "might be ideally suited for helping develop desired emotions, attitudes, or behavior" within targeted populations.

The ICRC on the RMA?

Earthpulse researchers, and intelligent investigators around the world, are questioning the rationality of the RMA. Even within the Rockefeller-linked International Committee of the Red Cross (ICRC), some members are highly suspicious of this movement.

In their report from mid-1994,[9] the ICRC raised a number of points worth considering: The idea of "war without death," the committee noted, is not new but began in the 1950s. Military interest in these systems originally dealt with chemical weapons. Later electronic systems were advanced. The RMA report looked at the ramifications of international law regarding the use of these new technologies. It pointed out weaknesses in the international conventions regarding the use of chemical weapons, which can be extended to these other emerging technologies, as follows. The ICRC wrote:

> Therefore, when the [Chemical Weapons] Convention comes into force next year, activities involving them—activities such as development, production, stockpiling and use—will become illegal, unless their

purpose is a purpose that is expressly not prohibited under the Convention. One such purpose is law enforcement including domestic riot control purposes. Unfortunately, the Convention does not define what it means by law enforcement (whose law? what law? enforcement where? by whom?), though it does define what it means by riot control agent, namely any chemical . . . which can produce rapidly, in humans, sensory irritation or disabling physical effects which disappear within a short time following termination of exposure. States parties are enjoined not to use riot control agents as a method of warfare.[9]

In other words, Dr. Begich reflected, we can use chemical or even electromagnetic weapons on our own citizens, but not in warfare with real enemies who are serious threats to national security.

This explains why the development of some types of non-lethals has moved out of the Department of Defense into the Department of Justice. For the Department of Defense to continue to work on some of these weapons, as instruments of war, it must circumvent illegalities under international law. The ICRC report went on to discuss the shift from weapons of war to police tools, which they called "riot control agents." What does this mean for people?

Ironically, RMA and the growing application of non-lethal technologies by law enforcers places Americans, and citizens of other countries, in a lesser protected class than invading armies. Not coincidentally, this is one of the globalists' chief objectives for instituting a "New World Order," as described in *The Report From Iron Mountain on the Possibility and Desirability of Peace*.[10]

HAARP, EISCAT and the Report From Iron Mountain

At this juncture it may be wise to detail HAARP's capabilities, linked as they were in *Healing Codes for the Biological Apocalypse*, to the Rockefeller-directed Human Genome Project (i.e., eugenics) at Cold Spring Harbor Labs and other operations including HAARP's European counterpart—EISCAT (European Incoherent Scatter Association [Technology]).

In review, HAARP's and EISCAT's capabilities are based on solar dynamics and physics. The sun produces a wide spectrum of electromagnetic effects by producing x-rays, ultraviolet radiation, and various other light frequencies, as well as by emitting magnetic fields. All of these produce profound effects on Earth and its people. Magnetic field phenomena result from the properties of "solar plasma." Solar plasma is the ions and electrons from atoms blown apart at the surface of the sun by its extreme heat.

"When the solar wind plasma reaches the Earth," an international government agency reported, "these embedded magnetic fields interact with the Earth's magnetic field, distorting it to form a compression on the dayside, and a very elongated tail on the night-side, away from the sun. The region within which the Earth's magnetic field is constrained is called the magnetosphere . . . .

"The solar UV, x-rays and charged particles, also ionize the upper part of the Earth's atmosphere resulting in a region, called the ionosphere, which can be studied by radar methods."[1] (See figure 15.1.)

This report, issued by EISCAT—comprised and funded by seven nations: Finland, France, Germany, Japan, Norway, Sweden and the United Kingdom—further explained the "eleven year cycle" of changing electromagnetism surrounding the earth due to changes of the solar wind and plasma.

EISCAT's authors explained that high in the Earth's atmosphere "magnetic field lines provide routes" for particles to "interact with the neutral gas to produce spectacular auroral displays . . . and additional ionization at polar and auroral latitudes. Electric fields and currents are also transferred between the magnetosphere and the auroral zone ionosphere."[1]

The purpose of EISCAT, its promotion stated, was to study these regions with radars "which transmit powerful radio waves into the ionosphere, where a small fraction of the energy is scattered back to the radar receiver. . . . EISCAT uses this technique," the article said, "in the study of solar-terrestrial physics. The scattered signal contains information describing the ionosphere and upper atmosphere."[1]

What EISCAT's report failed to mention was that their "scatter back" could have a profound effect on the weather and all living bioelectric systems including the "open systems" better known as human beings. The authors also neglected to reveal EISCAT's connections to the eugenics-linked Cold Spring Harbor labs and the infamous "atmospheric heating project HAARP."

In other words, what EISCAT's propaganda failed to disclose was that EISCAT represented the quintessential bioelectric technology for population surveillance and military control—key objectives of *The Report From Iron Mountain* and the RMA. In fact, projects EISCAT and HAARP provided the bioelectric technology to kill all "the Iron Mountain birds" with one fell swoop from inner space.

Background On *The Report From Iron Mountain*

Iron Mountain is located close to the town of Hudson, New York. The report by government consultants who met at this site beginning in 1963, briefly described this meeting place as "something out of [an] Ian Fleming" James Bond novel. "It is an underground nuclear hideout for hundreds of large American corporations. Most of them use it as an emergency storage vault for important documents. But a number of them maintain substitute corporate headquarters, as well, where essential personnel could presumably survive and continue to work after an attack. This latter group includes such firms as Standard Oil of New Jersey, Manufacturers Hanover Trust, and Shell."[11]

Standard Oil, of course, is owned principally by the Rockefeller family whose connections to the Committee of 300, NATO and The Club of Rome have been detailed by others including the highly reputable Dr. John Coleman, previously with British Intelligence. Manufacturers Hanover Trust is directed by Gabriel Hague, who is also affiliated with these largely secret organizations. Finally, according to Dr. Coleman, Queen Elizabeth II holds Shell's controlling interests.[12]

The Iron Mountain report,[10] "On the Possibility and Desirability of Peace," was written by anonymous authors and published in late 1967 with an introduction by Leonard C. Lewin who edited the manuscript. Its extraordinary content immediately sparked controversy and criticism of Lewin. Shortly thereafter, he reversed his position and announced that the meeting had not really happened. The report was his own satirical hoax he retracted. By that time, the report had been so widely distributed, and believed, that its readers did not know which Lewin story to trust—the standard "synthesis" from the Hegelian dialectic had been achieved.

Given the relevance of *The Report From Iron Mountain* to Cecil Rhodes's century old quest to "charm young America . . . to share in a scheme to take the government of the whole world" for the "cessation of all wars," as revealed in *Healing Codes for the Biological Apocalypse*, the report was considered legitimate for at least five reasons: 1) someone with Lewin's apparent intimate knowledge of government operations and the globalists' objectives would not likely waste time, nor jeopardize his professional career, by developing and then distributing a hoax in the form of a serious work; 2) the in-depth analysis provided by the work would likely be missing in a satire; 3) a satire would likely include obviously satirical content missing in the final

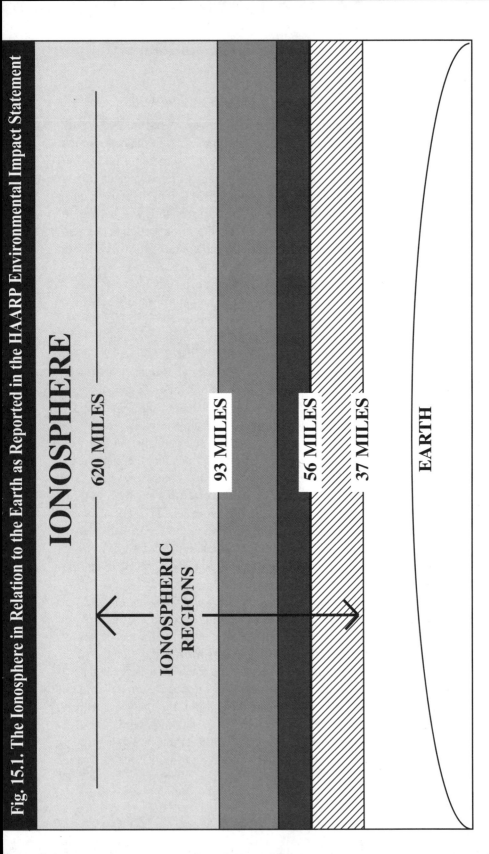

Fig. 15.1. The Ionosphere in Relation to the Earth as Reported in the HAARP Environmental Impact Statement

IONOSPHERE

620 MILES

IONOSPHERIC REGIONS

93 MILES

56 MILES

37 MILES

EARTH

publication; 4) the work was published by an organization with Masonic and secret society connections—The Dial Press, Inc.; and 5) there was precedence for calling a legitimate document a satirical hoax—the old Hegelian "thesis-antithesis-synthesis" model—previously discussed. A similar hoax was successfully performed following the release of *The Protocols of the Elders of Sion*. For all the above reasons, suggestions that *The Report From Iron Mountain* was a satirical hoax were likely designed to confuse—standard PSYOPs.

Following a thorough reading of this report, recalling its authors' chief objective was to devise economic substitutes for global militarization and traditional "peace keeping" programs, I concluded that EISCAT's efforts were, in reality, and quoting directly from the report, intended to develop: 1) as part of the recommended "giant open-end space research program, aimed at unreachable targets . . . [since] space research can be viewed as the nearest modern equivalent yet devised to the pyramid-building, and the similar ritualistic enterprises, of ancient societies;" 2) "a permanent, ritualized, ultra-elaborate disarmament inspection system, and variants of such a system" the best of which is conducted from outer space with the aid of extensive radar and surveillance technology; 3) "massive global environmental pollution" to effect shifting public attitudes and policy-making toward global governance, regulation, and enforcement. This objective included the effects of "global warming" (generated largely by the EISCAT and HAARP atmospheric heaters), as well as "ozone depletion" that presented an international threat by the turn of the century; 4) "an acceptable threat from 'outer space'" or "an established and recognized extraterrestrial menace" that included most of "the alien phenomena" highly publicized in modern times; the cyclic solar flares described by EISCAT that are blamed for "El Nino" and related environmental damage; and the economic gain resulting from related natural disasters including hurricanes, floods, tornados, and earthquakes; 5) "a comprehensive social" control program, or "a modern sophisticated form of slavery," that, as this chapter evidences, is likely linked to the "scatter back" of specific electromagnetic broadcasts capable of modifying, if not completely controlling human health, thought, emotions, and behavior in a program said to be for "public health" and "social welfare;" and 6) a "direct eugenic management" program, or "comprehensive program of applied eugenics" for depopulation which is easily brought about by several of the above EISCAT and HAARP capabilities.[10]

EISCAT, UNFPA and "Applied Eugenics"

The Report From Iron Mountain articulated the need for a "comprehensive program of applied eugenics" to provide the social climate capable of sustaining global governance and peacekeeping. Eugenics—the scientific investigation of genetic differences between the races, including the genetic predisposition for diseases among minority and ethnic groups—will be discussed in greater detail below, particularly as it relates to the field of population studies and population control. As mentioned above, EISCAT's supporting nations included "Finland, France, Germany, Japan, Norway, Sweden and the United Kingdom." Minus the United States, where HAARP is located, these nations have represented the majority of NATO countries. They also just happened to be the chief funding sources for UNFPA—the United Nations Fund for Population Activities.

According to a United Nations report, "The U.N. Fund for Population Activities is the largest multilateral source of external funding for population action programs in developing countries." Between 1969 and 1978, UNFPA "provided over $250 million in support of more than 1,200 population projects in more than 100 countries. In 1977, the Fund's annual budget, obtained from voluntary contributions, exceeded $100 million." The major donors were, once again, the principle NATO nations. "The United States in recent years has provided about 30% of total UNFPA funding."[13]

Bilateral assistance, the report said, came from the NATO countries and Japan. The U.S. program comprised about "two-thirds of the total over the 1965-78 period," and the entire operation was "administered by the Agency for International Development (USAID)."[13]

The "voluntary" contributors funding the lion's share of depopulation operations according to the State Department was the United States through USAID. A number of NGOs (non-governmental organizations) additionally contributed "in recognition of the need for many-sided efforts for effective overall population [control/reduction] assistance to developing countries. The Ford and Rockefeller Foundations have been major supporters of world population programs since 1965."[13]

In other words, U.S. taxpayers along with the Ford and Rockefeller Foundations, provided the money to effectively administer eugenics. This new level of applied eugenics came in 1965 as *The Report From Iron Mountain* was being finalized. Moreover, EISCAT is linked to these same organizations and funding sources.[14]

What is "Ionospheric Heating?"

As initially publicized by Dr. Begich, HAARP's U.S. Patent number 4,686,605 provided for:

A method and apparatus for altering at least one selected region, which normally exists above the earth's surface. The region is excited by electron cyclotron resonance heating to thereby increase its charged particle density. In one embodiment, circularly–polarized electromagnetic radiation is transmitted upward in a direction substantially parallel to and along a field line, which extends through the region of plasma to be altered. The radiation is transmitted at a frequency, which excites electron cyclotron resonance to heat and accelerate the charged particles. This increase in energy can cause ionization of neutral particles which are then absorbed as part of the region, thereby increasing the charged particle density of the region.[2]

The HAARP patent, assigned to ARCO Power Technologies, Inc., a division of the Atlantic Richfield Oil Company, entitled "Method and Apparatus for Altering a Region in the Earth's Atmosphere, Ionosphere, and/or Magnetosphere," was claimed by inventor Bernard J. Eastlund to have several uses. According to Alaskan author Eric Nashlund, who broke the HAARP story in the Australian magazine *Nexus*, these uses included:

. . . total disruption of communications over a very large portion of the Earth . . . disrupting not only land-based communications, but also airborne communications and sea communications (both surface and subsurface) . . . missile or aircraft destruction, deflection or confusion . . . . Weather modification . . . by altering solar absorption . . . ozone, nitrogen etc. concentrations could be artificially increased.[2]

The patent's "prior art" section acknowledged the previous related inventions of inventor Nikola Tesla. His referenced articles had appeared during the late nineteenth and early twentieth century. In the book *Angels Don't Play This HAARP*, Dr. Begich and Jeane Manning reviewed Tesla's earliest applications of this technology. A story featured in the *New York Times* on December 8, 1915, read:

Nikola Tesla, the inventor, has filed patent applications on the essential parts of a machine; possibilities [of which] test a layman's imagination and promise a parallel of Thor's shooting thunderbolts from the sky to punish those who had angered the gods. . . . Suffice it to say that the invention will go through space with a speed of 300 miles a second, a manless ship without propelling engine or wings sent by electricity to any desired point on the globe on its errand of destruction, if destruction [is what] its manipulator wishes to effect.

"It is not a time," said Dr. Tesla yesterday, "to go into the details of this thing. It is founded upon a principle that means great things in peace; it can be used for great things in war. But I repeat, this is no time to talk of such things."[2]

Though he obviously lacked a desire to explore details, Tesla continued:

"It is perfectly practicable to transmit electrical energy without wires and produce destructive effects at a distance. I have already constructed a wireless transmitter, which makes this possible, and have described it in my technical publications, among which I refer to my patent number 1,119,732 recently granted. With transmitters of this kind we are enabled to project electrical energy in any amount to any distance and apply it for innumerable purposes, both in war and peace. Through the universal adoption of this system, ideal conditions for the maintenance of law and order will be realized, for then the energy necessary to the enforcement of right and justice will be normally productive, yet potential, and in any moment available, for attack and defense. The power transmitted need not be necessarily destructive, for, if [people are] made to depend upon it, its withdrawal or supply will bring about the same results as those now accomplished by force of arms."[2]

Though "heating" the atmosphere in the wake of a "global warming crisis" might seem inappropriate to everyone except Satan, the discrepancy might be reconciled with a background check on HAARP's patent assignee. Few realize that the Atlantic Richfield Oil Company is closely linked to the British Royal Family, MI6, the Committee of 300, NATO and the leading globalists' Club of Rome.[12]

Background on ARCO

Dr. John Coleman extensively detailed the hierarchy of these global conspirators. Members of the Committee of 300 include[d] Lord Hartley Shawcross and Sirs Brian Edward Mountain, Kenneth Keith, Kenneth Strong, William Stephenson, and William Wiseman. "All of the foregoing are (or were) heavily involved in key Committee 300 companies which interface with literally thousands of companies engaged in every branch of commercial activity . . . "[12] Regarding Atlantic Richfield and related electric industrialists, Coleman wrote:

MI6 ran a large number of these companies through British intelligence stationed in the RCA building in New York, which was the headquarters of its chief officer, Sir William Stephenson. Radio Corporation of America (RCA) was formed by G. E., Westinghouse, Morgan Guarantee and Trust (acting for the British crown), . . . back in 1919 as a British intelligence center. . .

In addition, another affiliate of RCA was United Fruit, identified as a CIA front that was intimately linked to the assassination of President John F. Kennedy.[12,15]

Coleman continued:

It is obvious that the communications field is tightly controlled. Going back to RCA, we find that its directorate is composed of British-American establishment figures who feature prominently in other organizations such as the CFR, NATO, the Club of Rome, the Trilateral Commission, Freemasonry, Skull and Bones, Bilderbergers, Round Table, Milner Society and the Jesuits-Aristotle Society. Among them was David Sarnoff [RCA's president] who moved to London at the same time Sir William Stephenson moved into the RCA building in New York.

All three major television networks came as spin-offs from RCA, especially the National Broadcasting Company (NBC) that was first, closely followed by the American Broadcasting Company (ABC) in 1951. The third big television network was Columbia Broadcasting System (CBS) which, like its sister companies was, and still is, dominated by British intelligence. William Paley was trained in mass brainwashing techniques at the Tavistock Institute prior to being passed as qualified to head CBS. . . .

On RCA's board sits Thornton Bradshaw, president of Atlantic Richfield and a member of NATO, World Wildlife Fund, the Club of Rome, The Aspen Institute for Humanistic Studies, and the Council on Foreign Relations. Bradshaw is also chairman of NBC. The most important function of RCA remains its service to British intelligence.[12][Emphasis added.]

Dr. Coleman published for posterity the important organizational chart seen in figure 15.2 that summarized the Illuminati's worldwide operations.

"The Real Problem" Regarding HAARP

"The real problem with HAARP," according to "Hugh's HAARP Info Page"—a well publicized and active "primenet.com" website—"is the news blackout."

I disagree. The "real problem" with HAARP is that in virtually one fell swoop from inner space, HAARP provides the capability to fulfill the majority of population policy recommendations advanced in *The Report From Iron Mountain.* Until this was advanced in *Healing Codes for the Biological Apocalypse*, there had been no mention of this critical fact by any previous investigators or author(s).

The "real problem" is that HAARP is a principle part of the "giant open-end space research program" that could easily be used as "a permanent, ritualized, ultra-elaborate disarmament inspection system." As its patent clearly indicated, HAARP's capacity to survey communications and cause "total disruption of communications over a very large portion of the Earth . . . disrupting not only land-based communications, but also airborne communications and sea communications (both surface and subsurface)" was by itself potentially lethal in unprecedented measure.

Worse yet, *The Report From Iron Mountain* called for "massive global environmental pollution," while HAARP and EISCAT demonstrated their hazardous ability to affect solar absorption, nitrogen, and ozone levels. Underwriting the report were petrochemical industrialists who directed nuclear and fossil fuel consumption following their suppression of Tesla's technologies that could have provided clean free energy for everyone by the early 1900s. In an age when widespread global heating and other climatic changes endanger virtually every living thing, technologies being used to "heat up the earth's atmosphere" are not likely benign.

Additionally suspicious, and troubling, is the media's coverage of the "alien phenomenon" during the last part of the twentieth century. In keeping with the Iron Mountain report's recommendation to create "an established and recognized extraterrestrial menace," the HAARP and EISCAT technologies might easily come into play in a "grand finale"— a Hollywoodesque curtain call to end the Old World of managed chaos. Confronting the threat of an extraterrestrial menace, massive communication and energy shut downs, and, as a result, social chaos, including, of course, loss of life—conditions demanding unprecedented forms of social control and non-lethal warfare—all of this seemed peculiarly similar to what the doctors from Iron Mountain prescribed.

Specifically, the atmospheric electromagnetic technologies applied by HAARP, EISCAT, and other "defense" initiatives (including the Montauk and Phoenix II-type projects described later) could acutely, or over the long term, create massive population reduction—death and destruction from natural and man-made disasters. All of this would naturally justify a "flexible" military or FEMA presence as implied in the report.

Further recommended under "the execution of the nonmilitary functions of war," the globalists directing the U.S. Government were advised, by Lewin et al., to extend "war games" methods to social and political systems. Through the creation of "quasi-adversary" proceedings,[10] such as the initiation and funding of bogus (and legitimate) terrorist organizations and events as broadcast by various news agencies,[16] and the social chaos associated with communications and energy systems failures, citizens will desire and demand more government protections, interventions, and control. This context includes the non-lethal warfare technologies extending into routine law enforcement, as well as those allegedly used to defend against "threats from space," or the environment.[10]

Finally, since leading globalists consider "excess population is war material," in the more "peaceful" New World Order, Lewin et al., advised reducing excess populations in the ways cited above, as well as to develop "a comprehensive social" control program—or, as they put it, "slavery" in a technologically modern and acceptable manner. This capability, to provide worldwide technological slavery, is within this technology's extended range. These HAARP and Montauk-like electromagnetic frequency generators, based on Tesla's findings, had been researched and perfected by British, Russian, German, and American intelligence agencies and their contractors as early as the 1940s. The "scatter back" of specific electromagnetic frequency broadcasts are capable of modifying, if not completely controlling, numerous aspects of the human condition. In this context, simple identification and surveillance programs that operate electromagnetically, including "medical biochips," "health passport cards," and other "ID chip" technologies are only part of the applied science of technological slavery and "direct eugenic management" proposed in *The Report From Iron Mountain.*[10]

All of the above are "real problems" with HAARP, EISCAT, and other electromagnetic technologies including the mass media, capable of effecting non-lethal warfare and state-instituted conditioning of targeted populations.

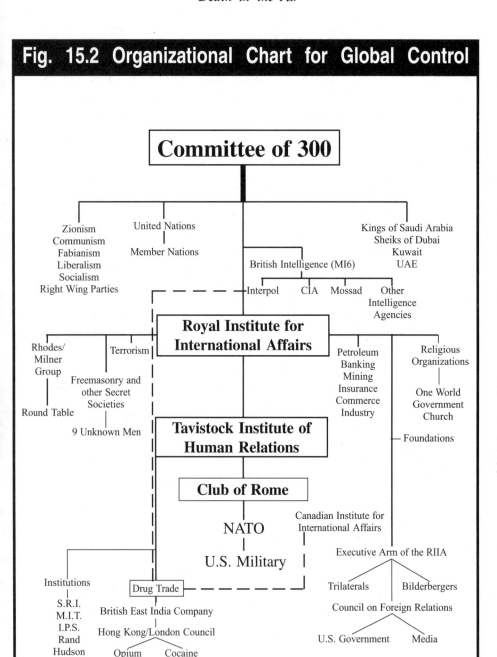

Fig. 15.2 Organizational Chart for Global Control

Committee of 300

Zionism
Communism
Fabianism
Liberalism
Socialism
Right Wing Parties

United Nations

Member Nations

Kings of Saudi Arabia
Sheiks of Dubai
Kuwait
UAE

British Intelligence (MI6)

Interpol   CIA   Mossad   Other
Intelligence
Agencies

Royal Institute for
International Affairs

Rhodes/
Milner
Group

Terrorism

Freemasonry and
other Secret
Societies

Round Table

9 Unknown Men

Petroleum
Banking
Mining
Insurance
Commerce
Industry

Religious
Organizations

One World
Government
Church

Foundations

Tavistock Institute of
Human Relations

Club of Rome

NATO

U.S. Military

Canadian Institute for
International Affairs

Executive Arm of the RIIA

Institutions

S.R.I.
M.I.T.
I.P.S.
Rand
Hudson
Wharton

Drug Trade

British East India Company

Hong Kong/London Council

Opium   Cocaine

Trilaterals   Bilderbergers

Council on Foreign Relations

U.S. Government   Media

Adapted from: Dr. John Coleman's book, *Conspirators' Hierarchy: The Story of the Committee of 300*. Carson City, NV: American West Publishers, 1992, p. 265.

Additional Effects of "High Power Microwaves"

Dr. Begich reviewed a section of the International Red Cross's report that discussed "Future Weapons Using High Power Microwaves." This text described microwave frequencies developed for use in weapons against machines and people. One of the uses described was an Electromagnetic Pulse (EMP) weapon, which gave operators the same ability to wipe out electronic circuits as that provided by nuclear blasts. The main difference, the report acknowledged, was that this new technology was far more controllable. Plus it could be used without violating nuclear weapons treaties. This section of their report described the energy levels needed to cause: tissue to overheat, possible nervous system damage, "byte errors in unshielded computers," and destruction of "unprotected receiver diodes in antennas."

Again, these effects are mediated by radio frequency radiation. The Red Cross's report confirmed that non-thermal effects were being researched, and included damage to human health when the effects occurred "within so-called modulation frequency windows or power density windows." Hertz frequencies are one such window.

The way these weapons work was clearly described when the report noted their effect on machines: "*A HPM (High Power Microwave) weapon employs a high power, rapidly pulsating microwave beam that penetrates electronic components. The pulsing action internally excites the components, rapidly generating intense heat, which causes them to fuse or melt, thus destroying the circuit. . . . HPM (weapons) attack at the speed of light thus making avoidance of the beam impossible*," consequently negating the advantage of weapon systems such as high velocity tactical missiles." In other words, with this kind of weapon no machine, including human, could survive. [Emphasis added.]

Another report on non-lethal technologies, issued by the Council on Foreign Relations,[17] additionally discussed in the next chapter of this book, stated that, "The Nairobi Convention, to which the United States is a signatory, prohibits the broadcast of electronic signals into a sovereign state without its consent in peacetime." This report openly discussed the use of these weapons against terrorists and drug traffickers. The CFR report recommended this be done secretly so that victims never know who issued the attack, or even if there was an attack.[17]

A glitch discussed in the CFR report concerned the use of this technology in violation of United States law, which presumes innocence rather than guilt. In other words, the police, CIA, DEA, or other enforcement organizations would have to be afforded the right to become the judge, jury, and executioner.[17]

Low Level Non-ionizing Radiation Technology

During his presentation in Interlaken, Dr. Begich also considered a document issued by U.S. Air Force Captain Paul Tyler, which reviewed classical theories and recent conflicting research on the effects of low-level non-ionizing electromagnetic radiation. By the 1990s, much debate centered on the classical idea that only ionizing radiation, which generates heat in tissues, can cause reactions in the body. New research indicated that subtle exposures to non-ionizing frequencies and microwaves of energy cause harmful reactions as well.

Tyler wrote in 1984 that, "Even though the body is basically an electrochemical system, modern science has almost exclusively studied the chemical aspects of the body and to date has largely neglected the electrical aspects." Moreover, the use of classical concepts of electrodynamics could not explain "some experimental results and clinical findings" that Tyler and other investigators had observed.

For example, according to classical physics, the frequency of visible light would indicate that it is reflected or totally absorbed within the first few millimeters of tissue, and thus no light should pass through significant amounts of tissue. But it does. Also, classical theory indicates that the body should be completely invisible to extremely low frequencies of light where a single wavelength is thousands of miles long. However, visible light has been used in clinical medicine to transilluminate various body tissues.

In other words, the classical theories are partially wrong in that they do not fully explain all of the reactions observed in the body in response to various non-ionizing electromagnetic frequencies. The Navy has abstracted over a thousand international professional papers by private and government scientists that explore these issues.

Tyler also addressed, "a second area where classical theory fails to provide an adequate explanation for observed effects." This was "in the clinical use of extremely low frequency (ELF) electromagnetic fields." "Researchers," he wrote, "have found that pulsed external magnetic fields at frequencies below 100 Hertz (pulses/cycles per second) will stimulate the healing of non-union fractures, congenital pseudarthroses, and failed arthroses. The effects of these pulsed magnetic fields have been extremely impressive, and their use in orthopaedic conditions has been approved by the Food and Drug Administration."

Tyler noted that, "pulsed electromagnetic fields have been reported to induce cellular transcription," the primary process underlying genetic expression. He discussed the results of this new thinking and the possible effects of these low energy radiations in terms of information transfer and storage, and their effects on the nervous system. Research showed that very specific frequencies caused very specific reactions, and, once a critical threshold was passed, negative reactions frequently occurred.

Dr. Begich cautioned that despite the years of expressed concern over these low frequency energy risks, the non-lethal weapons have advanced. He directed his Interlaken audience to "imagine a world where land mines don't blow up, but give off an eerie sound that makes intruders feel sick. Or a war where attackers don't use missiles to stop tanks but microwaves to shut down engines."[3]

Official Attention to Developing Weapons

At Penn State College, The Institute for Non-Lethal Defense Technologies, in cooperation with the United States Marines, evaluated such weapons developed by military contractors and other organizations.[19] Studies at this institute also addressed the legal, ethical, political, environmental and physical effects of these new technologies. For example, they issued much discussion about the possibilities of creating artificial weather and of controlling the weather. Despite the 1976 signing of an international treaty by the United States banning "geophysical warfare," this has been the subject of ongoing military research for decades.

The use of these new energy weapons is not limited to governments and sophisticated science laboratories. In April 1997, the United States Secretary of Defense, William Cohen commented: "Others are engaging even in an eco-type of terrorism whereby they can alter climate, set off earthquakes and volcanoes remotely through the use of electromagnetic waves."[3]

Natural disaster technology is not really new. It is rooted in 1960–1970s research by American and Russian scientists and continues to appear in numerous articles and reports. As recently reported in the *Wall Street Journal*, the idea of creating artificial weather including cyclones is being explored. The article stated "a Malaysian company,

BioCure Sdn. Bhd., will sign a memorandum of understanding soon with a government-owned Russian party to produce the Cyclone." The deal with the Russians was set up so that if the technology did not work the Malaysians did not have to pay for the attempt. There have been other reports of Russian research in this field.

Concerning other weapons of mass destruction, a 1989 patent held by the United States Department of Energy revealed a most interesting bit of science. The patent detailed a new kind of weapon that allows electromagnetic or acoustic energy to be focused into a tight package and projected over great distances without dissipating. When scientists thought of this energy being projected through the air it was always assumed that the energy would disperse so rapidly that no effect could be realized. This discovery transcended this limitation. The patent stated: "The invention relates generally to transmission of pulses of energy, and more particularly to the propagation of localized pulses of electromagnetic or acoustic energy over long distances without divergence."

As the Klingon battle cruiser attacked the Starship Enterprise, Captain Kirk commanded, "Fire photon torpedoes." Two darts of light sped toward the target and destroyed the enemy's spaceship. Stardate 1989 or 2189, somewhere in intergalactic space, this fantasy has become reality with the ability to launch localized packets of light or other energy which do not diverge as they travel great distances through space. The patent described this energy effect as "electromagnetic missiles or bullets" which could destroy almost any object in its path.

In 1995, Dr. Begich reflected, the funding for Star Wars was widely reported as a dead issue when full funding was defeated by the United States Congress. Star Wars did not end, it was just renamed. In 1996, "the Ballistic Missile Defense Organization [once called the Strategic Defense Initiative] got $3.7 billion. That's up from $2.8 billion in 1995, and is very near the peak level spent during the Cold War."

In another offshoot of the Reagan administration's Strategic Defense Initiative, Dr. Begich explained, satellite-disabling lasers have been developed. A test, at less than full power, was performed at the end of 1997 to demonstrate the ability of the system to hit its target. The demonstration was a success and now many people are concerned that this may have provoked an arms race in space. This is the same concern that was raised when this technology was first discussed in public forums. There was a good deal of antagonism, and yet here we are two decades later delivering on, what was said to be, "impossible" technology.

"Earthpulse takes the position that this approach is highly destabilizing and provocative," Dr Begich told the World Foundation for Natural Sciences, "particularly given the state of domestic policy and ideological shifts taking place in Russia."[3]

"Wildfires" in America's Northwest

Another possible electromagnetic non-lethal operation that involved extensive PSYOPs to cover it were the "wildfires" in the Summer of 2000. Investigative journalist, Rick Martin, in *The Spectrum*[20]—a leading national newspaper dedicated to exposing government insubordination and treasonous public officials—reported "Bizarre Wildfires Expose Sinister Agenda." The veteran author wrote of an alleged scam involving the Federal Emergency Management Agency (FEMA), the mysterious outbreaks of numerous "wildfires" that mostly threatened Idaho and surrounding states, and a suspected HAARP-like energy network involving a U.S. Navy base located south of Hope, Idaho. An aluminum-clad suspected energy generator was officially mapped on National Forest Service land. This site was reported to be graced by an "energy vortex" like the one believed associated with the great Pyramid of Giza. This north Idaho operation lies suspiciously near the American property of the German–international real estate and banking industrialist Klaus Groenke. Mr. Groenke is also on the Board of Trustees, along with Honorary Cofounder Henry Kissinger, of the American Academy of Berlin—a U.S. Diplomatic Service institute. He was also the chief benefactor, friend, and neighbor to the deceased American-German artist Edward Kienholz, whose "art" is partly displayed in this book's gallery.

Remember "Smokey the Bear?" The old National Forest Service (NFS) icon cautioned, "Only you can prevent forest fires!" Indeed, they used to be correctly termed "forest fires," and people were most often responsible for these catastrophic blazes. In recent years the media suddenly changed the vernacular of the phrase to "wildfires"—a word that subliminally suggests a wild, natural, and uncontrollable event. This occurrence too smacks of PSYOPs and non-lethal C2W propaganda.

Government observers can recall the "wildfire" set near Sante Fe, New Mexico, by National Forest Service (NFS) officials earlier in 2000 that threatened, and according to some local reports caused, the release of radioactive material from the Los Alamos National Laboratory. This facility is directed by the Atomic Energy Commission and engaged in the Human Genome Project. The "burn" was started in an alleged effort to prevent such a fire. High winds, that might have been predicted, drove the blaze beyond containment.

Creating Lightning

Most "wildfires" are said to be kindled by lightning. In Dr. Fred Bell's book *Rays of Truth–Crystals of Light*, he discussed the earth's vortices—electromagnetic ley lines—and the technology used to generate thunderstorm-like clouds that hurled lightning bolts to earth.[21] He exquisitely detailed one such event when he experimentally directed "piezoelectric scalar energy" from his living room in Laguna Beach, CA, to create a lightning strike upon the roof of his neighbor's workshop. The roof caught fire! Not being a pyromaniac, he quickly shut down his energy generator and ran down the hill to extinguish the blaze. (See figures 15.3. and 15.4.) Dr. Bell has an impressive government and industry labor record. It included high level consulting work on some of the CIA's most advanced top-secret anti-gravity and time travel projects.

Rick Martin reported that a similar lightning generator is believed to have ignited the majority of "wildfires" suspiciously clustered south and east of the Hope area. (See figure 15.5) Neighboring Canada, with similar geography and weather conditions, showed no such clustering.

"Now we enter into the 'Twilight Zone,'" Martin wrote as he described collaborators' visits to the NFS land in question. "All the roads are blocked off," unlike every other NFS property in that region, "and just in the past year," wildlife behavior became completely bizarre. All wild birds left the area. Neighboring chickens remained "huddled-up in their pen" as though afraid to venture out. Deer and other animals around the area acted "like they're almost in a state of shock," a resident reported. "The deer come walking right up to you, and expect you to feed them. They don't feed on their own. Very, very bizarre!"

A resident of Clark Fork, which neighbors Hope, additionally described the "weirdness" exhibited by domestic pets. "Everybody is calling me to ask, 'Are your animals acting strange?' Usually, my dog follows me *everywhere*. . . . She even lies beneath my bed at night. Suddenly she wouldn't even go to the river with me. She hid under the porch, and I had to call her out. And on certain days she acted really weird when this crazy weather was happening. It was as though she felt vibrations. And my neighbors' dogs and cats [did] too. All the animals

Figures. 15.3. Dr. Fred Bell's Livingroom With Electromagnetic Vortex and Field Generators

The "Basic Quad System Energy Form" arrangement diagrammed above generated the thunderstorm and four lightning strikes depicted below. The first strike occurred in the ocean, the others moved progressively closer to Dr. Bell's house. The fourth strike set fire to a neighbor's workshop roof. Courtesy of Dr. Fred Bell. Reprinted from: Bell F. *Rays of Truth–Crystals of Light.* Laguna Beach, CA: Pyradyne Press, 1999; http://www.pyradyne.com; 1-800-729-2603.

Figures. 15.4. Electromagnetic Lightning Generation Experiment at Laguna Beach, CA

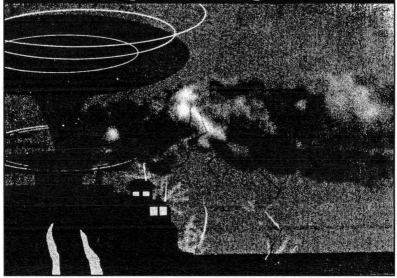

were acting weird around here, and they all acted weird on the same day."

The Idaho resident continued, "We've never seen these types of fires."

Martin, quoted HAARP investigator John Quinn and his Internet news service NewsHawk, Inc. Mr. Quinn said he had received communications from Idaho's neighboring states that metal structures without power or telephone service were somehow "being powerfully charged-up with electrical energy. . . .

"There is, in fact, only one way this can happen," Mr. Quinn advanced. "Through electromagnetic induction via EM/RF transmissions. According to a HAARP consultant who has divulged other information to us, this phenomenon . . . is a direct result of extremely high-powered HAARP transmissions targeting the western U.S.

"Confidential sources have told NewsHawk that HAARP and other related technologies are being used to manifest a 'virtual Venturi device' on a gigantic scale in the upper atmosphere. Science students will remember that a Venturi device can separate warmer air from cooler air and re-direct the different streams with great force. The whole deal is being further intensified by chemtrail spraying of weather modification substances [as discussed by Will Thomas in Chapter 10.]

"This is one of the primary tactics currently being used in the tremendously extensive and severe 'weather war' being waged by federal forces which is causing the Western wildfires to become so extremely destructive." The resulting drought, with reduced hydroelectric energy supplies, suspiciously supports the western state "energy crisis."

Geological scientist Joe Bowling, working in eastern Montana at the time other areas were either burning or at heightened risk of a fire, reported his laboratory's telephone lines were arcing so profoundly that he and his coworkers heard a loud "snap" as the energy discharged from the lines. "The wires were then disconnected from the phone line coming in from the pedestal; there was some concern about damaging the phone which was hooked up. All four conductors and their shielding, each subsequently obtained a sufficient charge to deliver an uncomfortable shock or arc about three centimeters to a ground."

"This happened repeatedly: the conductors were discharged, could be handled without shock, and recharged within a minute or two to their previous charge level. . . ."

Figures. 15.5. Wildfires Clustered Around North Idaho—Site of Suspected Frequency Generator

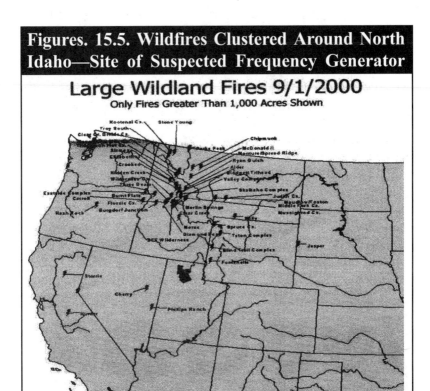

Large Wildland Fires 9/1/2000
Only Fires Greater Than 1,000 Acres Shown

Map generated by the U.S. Geological Survey for Federal Emergency Management and governmental agencies. The U.S.G.S. has also been linked to PSYOP-like propaganda campaigns and documented genocides in lesser developed nations. More acres burned in the nine-month period ending September 2, 2000 (6,482,016) than in any year since such record keeping began in 1987. Statistics and maps courtesy of Rick Martin as published in *The Spectrum*, Sept. 5, 2000.

After checking to make certain their phone systems had no grounding problems or other possibilities, Mr. Bowling concluded that federal agencies and officials were the most reasonable suspects in the generation of such HAARP-like effects including the "lightning" initiated wildfires of 2000.

Eyewitness Accounts and Additional Observations in Hope

Area residents whose properties abut the NFS land reported during lengthy interviews that they observed "bolts of lightning" transmitting during clear weather, from the vicinity of a two-story windowless modern "fire watch station" built with concrete blocks and two doors. Public officials call this building "Lunch Peak." It is situated above the tree line on a mountain clearing approximately five miles into the woods

329

from their home. Subsequent visits to the gated area by them and Don and Ingri Harkins, journalists for *The Idaho Observer,* to obtain photographs, appeared to offend non-uniformed "federal-looking" security agents patrolling the gate and entrance road in unmarked cars. The sneers and body language of these men were interpreted as warnings, enough to put off these visits.

One family, including teenage children, also reported extensive "black helicopter" activity in their area, and the extraordinary delivery by trucks of special cargo—hundreds of limestone blocks each weighing thousands of pounds. They delivered photographic evidence of this, along with proof that the huge pyramid-building-type slabs had been mined in Portugal, and transported to the United States to finally arrive in Hope. (See figures 15.6 and 15.7)

Another area resident, Dr. Joseph Puleo, a naturopathic physician on the Board of Directors of the World Natural Health Organization and coauthor of *Healing Codes for the Biological Apocalypse*, also reported "strange" lightning seemingly coming from this area near his home. Dr. Puleo told Rick Martin, "I went to a concert in Sandpoint, Idaho, and I noticed that the lightning started, and it kept hitting in the same spot. And I said to my wife, 'Now, when did you ever see lightning start, or generate, or hit twice in the same spot?'

"I said to my wife: 'we'd better go. It's in our area. It's in our neighborhood.' That's also what I saw on our way home, following Route 200 in that direction. The lightning kept emanating or striking from that area.

I said: 'You know, that's the oddest thing.' It was the weirdest looking lightning I'd ever seen. . . . It kind of looked like a web effect, like an old cobweb, going out sideways, where pieces were missing. . . ."

"And it occurred over and over again. It radiated out, and I plotted it. The funny part about it is, it ended up somewhere between Trestle Creek Road and Trout Creek Road, in the mountains on the way to Clark Fork. And that was in the general area of the NFS's 'Lunch Peak' building . . ."

Dr. Puleo, who also holds two additional doctorates, one in health science and the other in theology, was additionally aware of the extensive limestone deliveries made to his neighborhood. With his knowledge of the Montauk Project—the top secret MKULTRA project that included electromagnetic earthquake production and population programming (See figure 12.4.)—he told Rick Martin that government agents had to be developing "tetrahedrons" for pyramid energy genera-

Figures. 15.6. The Mining of Limestone Blocks in Portugal: Destination—Hope, ID, U.S.A.

The above photo shows the mining of Portuguese limestone—widely recognized for its energy conducting properties. This document was digitally recorded by the foreign purchasing agent and used to secure the purchase of the stone for shipment to Hope, ID where it is suspected of being used with the building shown in figures 15.7 and 17.5 to generate and transmit electromagnetic energy for various purposes. Among these purposes is the targeted ignition of "wildfires." Hope, ID is also the home of the wealthy German-American real estate industrialist, Klaus Groenke, whose links to artist Edward Kienholz, Rockefeller protégé Henry Kissinger, and international magazine mogul, Henry Luce of the Luce Foundation, raises questions as to his suspected participation in global depopulation and non-lethal warfare efforts waged by the Rockefellers and the global elite. For these purposes, a local "Montauk Project" energy generator would be exceedingly useful.

tion. "The only purpose [for that amount of limestone]," he said, "would be to make a 'Delta-T' [device], which would work like HAARP does to effect the grid-lightning."

"I have a friend from the Forest Service," Dr. Puleo continued. "He was a surveyor. He said they were planting ceramic pyramids in certain places, then installing special magnets in special cases with their black sides up. In some areas they were taking a square mile, and dividing it into quarters and quarters and quarters . . . at 36 per mile. . . . By doing that, they likely created a standing columnar wave array effect. To what degree I don't know, but it would make sense if you read everything on HAARP and you look at the control stations on these maps."

The maps to which Dr. Puleo referred included the "Idaho Panhandle National Forests" map of the Kaniksu National Forest. As shown in figure 15.8, the map includes triangles representing "Hori-

331

Figures. 15.7. "Lunch Peak" Building, Hope, ID, Suspected Site of HAARP-like "Fire Starter"

Long range photograph of "Lunch Peak" near Hope, Idaho that is theorized to be the site of an energy generator that may have sparked lightning-triggered forest fires during the summer of 2000 in the Northwestern U.S. It is marked on maps as a "Permanent Lookout Station." It is surrounded by at least six "Horizontal Control Stations" mostly on the peaks of neighboring mountains. West, approximately 18 miles, and precisely on the "North Parallel," sits one of three nearby "Electronic sites." All of these sites overlook Lake Pend Oreille. The broad rocky and denuded areas surrounding the building protect it from forest fires. Yet, NFS authorities cited a need to wrap the mostly concrete building with "aluminum" allegedly for protection. A straight line connects this building with six other "Horizontal Control Stations" perpendicular to three triangulated "Electronic Sites." The Klaus Groenke estate and the Navy's "Cutthroat" submarine base also lie close to this axis as shown in figure 17.6.

Lake Pend Oreille, the second largest lake west of the Mississippi, was reported to be in use by the U.S. Navy for project "Cutthroat." Project Cutthroat was described by authorities as using an unmanned submarine with ultra-advanced electronics and satellite communications systems for twenty-first century military preparedness.

Mr. Groenke is a leading shareholder in Coca Cola Europe and an international real estate and banking executive. His is also on the Board of Trustees of The U.S. Diplomatic Corps affiliated German–American Academy cofounded by Dr. Henry Kissinger. Mr. Groenke was also a close friend and hearty benefactor to the deceased American–German artist Edward Kienholz, whose works speak volumes concerning the racist and genocidal exploits of leading global industrialists and militarists among whom Mr. Groenke is privileged. (See this book's gallery.) It is not known what function, if any, Mr. Groenke's highly secure home on Hope Peninsula lends to either this possible Montauk-like operation and/or the genocidal conspiracy documented in this book. Suspiciously displayed in metal art on the front of the Groenke lakeside estate is the double X symbol used by Exxon and Maxxam corporations whose operations under the Committee of 300 are central to ongoing depopulation efforts. The "XX" codes for "66," as in the oil industry's Phillips 66. (See Chapter 17 for more details.) Photo courtesy of the NFS.

zontal Control Stations." The "Lunch Peak" building, the researcher noted, had been marked with a very special geometric symbol discussed at length in *Healing Codes for the Biological Apocalypse*—the six-sided hexagonal shaped ring. According to the NFS map this represented a "Permanent Lookout Station."

As will be discussed in greater detail in Chapter 17, this station is surrounded by numerous "Horizontal Control Stations" alleged to be of use only for geographic surveys. Alternatively, Dr. Puleo theorized, the phrase "Horizontal Control" may reference: 1) control of the "standing columnar wave array effect" needed for various HAARP-like applications, and 2) a satellite grid transmission system for various functions including location signaling, surveillance, aerial photography, and/or "psychotronic warfare" for "population control."

Dr. Puleo initially balked at the sight of the hexagonal ringed triangles on the map near "Lunch Peak" where the repeated lightning transmissions had occurred, but the geometry and numerology of these symbols seemed to reflect knowledge of the "ancient arcana"—the awareness of metaphysical principles discussed in *Healing Codes for the Biological Apocalypse*. This related to "spiritual forces" and "spiritual warfare." The most energetically powerful numbers—3s, 6s and 9s—were all represented in the NFS "Horizontal Control and Permanent Lookout Station" symbols. (See figure 15.8 with inset. The nine is deciphered by adding the 3 and 6, [as in "666"]or multiplying them to get 18, then reducing 18 to the Pythagorean single digit integer where 1+8=9.)

Dr. Puleo's other maps, apparently developed by the federal government's chief mapping agency, the U.S. Geological Survey (USGS), discussed earlier in relation to the WNV pesticide propaganda, and global genocide, showed the clustering of fires mentioned above. It was "a strange array in which these fires started," Dr. Puleo noted. "Almost like they're pinpointed [i.e., targeted]. (See figure 15. 5.)

"The Forest Service [and FEMA] came [to Clark Fork, ID]," he continued, "and they wanted to talk to us about evacuation. And so we all went down to find out what was going on. They showed us the fire sites, and [I noted that] these places were in-between markers that I accidentally found about 4 years ago, because of the [Native American] petroglyphs [I was studying] off of the Hope peninsula and Lake Pend Oreille."

Figures. 15.8. Idaho Panhandle Forest Service Legend Showing Symbols for "Horizontal Control Stations"

The NFS's legend shows the use of sacred geometric symbols—the triangle and the hexagon—involving the energetically powerful 3s, 6s and 9s to mark the locations of possible energy generators— "Horizontal Control Stations," and "Permanent Lookout Stations." The triangles mark locations of the control stations. Hexagonal rings reflect the locations of lookout stations. These are located in the vicinity of three triangulated "Electronic Sites" said to be microwave generators near the U.S. Navy's "Cutthroat" Submarine base near Hope, ID where frequent lightning displays and bizarre animal behavior have been repeatedly reported. Courtesy of Dr. Joseph Puleo.

Having explained the above to Rick Martin, Dr. Puleo simplified his theory about "what was going on," and included his understanding of how HAARP technologies are believed to work for population control. "Once they fire up the HAARP generator, the 'Delta-T' energy creates what's called a 'bottle effect,' 'magnetic bottle,' or 'bubble.' Everything within this 'magnetic bottle,' or 'bubble,' is controlled by whatever magnetic fields are within it. But like anything else, it would collapse, unless you had standing columnar waves. . . . [This is the hypothetical function of] the magnets being planted 36 per square mile, so many feet [apart, so that] it keeps the magnetic field from collapsing. So, everything within that 'magnetic bottle' would be controlled by the generated field."

More intelligence linking this suspected weather/population control project to key Committee of 300 organizations, corporations, and political notables is provided in the next chapters. Like the HAARP projects, figure 15.9 additionally links U.S. Dept. of Energy operations in Idaho to the Atlantic Richfield Oil Company (ARCO) controlled by the Royal Family of England.

Other HAARP Capabilities

Other energy weapons seem to depend on similar electromagnetic grid technologies including those capable of creating physical symptoms like seasickness. Others produce signals that can be used to resonate the inner organs to cause pain and spasms, Dr. Begich added. Additional weapons can induce epileptic-like seizures, cause cardiac arrest, prevent sleep, override voluntary muscle movements, or damage the brain.

Russian writer N. Anisimov of the Moscow Anti-Psychotronic Center coined the term "psycho-terrorism." According to Anisimov, psychotronic weapons are those that act to "take away a part of the information which is stored in a man's brain." That has merits for those who seek "horizontal control" over large populations. These weapons can also be used to induce hallucinations, mental sickness, "zombification," genetic mutations, and even death.

Included in this battery of energy devices are VHF generators, X-rays, ultrasound, and radio waves.

Russian army Major I. Chernishev, writing in the military journal *Orienteer* in February 1997, asserted that psychotronic weapons are under development all over the globe. Specific types of weapons noted by Chernishev, not all of which had prototypes at the time, were:

- A psychotronic generator which produced powerful electromagnetic emanation capable of being sent through telephone lines, TV, radio networks, supply pipes and incandescent lamps.

- An autonomous generator, a device that operates in the 10-150 Hertz band, which at the 10-20 Hertz band forms an infrasonic oscillation that is destructive to all living creatures.

335

- A nervous system generator designed to paralyze the central nervous systems of insects, which could have the same applicability in humans.

- Ultrasonic emanations which one institute claimed to have developed. Devices using ultrasound emanations are supposedly capable of carrying out bloodless internal operations without leaving a mark on the skin. They can also, according to Chernishev, be used to kill.

- Noiseless cassettes. Chernishev claimed that the Japanese have developed the ability to place infra-low frequency voice patterns over music, patterns that are detected by the subconscious. Russians claim to be using similar "bombardments" with computer programming to treat alcoholism and smoking.

- The 25th-frame effect alluded to previously—a technique wherein each 25th frame of movie reels or film footage contains a message that is picked up by the subconscious.

- Psychotropics—defined as medical preparations used to induce a trance, euphoria, or depression. Symptoms include headaches, noises, voices or commands in the brain, dizziness, pain in the abdominal cavities, cardiac arrhythmia, or even the destruction of the cardiovascular system.

In 1991, during the course of her research, Dr. Janet Morris, coauthor of *The Warriors Edge*, was given a tour of the Russian Department of Psycho-Correction at the Moscow Medical Academy. Here she was shown a method whereby researchers monitored human minds, and then using infrasound—very low frequency transmissions—messages were transmitted subliminally to individuals' brains.

The Russian research also vigorously explored the military possibilities of ESP, including reading human thoughts, influencing objects at a distance, moving objects with the mind, or directly interfering with the thoughts of other people.

The Russians are not alone. The U.S. has also followed this research path. For example, the issue of acoustic manipulation of the human brain by radio frequency radiation (RFR) was summarized in June 1996, in a document entitled "Human Exposure to Radio-frequency Radiation: A Review Pertinent to Air Force Operations (Al/OE-TR-1996-0035)." The Air Force Materiel Command located at Brooks Air Force Base, in Texas, prepared this document.[22] Their report summarized a number of the studies on the effect of RFR for military applications. This information built on the earlier efforts by the military in RFR research, specifically calling for weapons research in this area. An earlier work prepared to advance this research was put together by the same organization. This was titled the *Radiofrequency Radiation Dosimetry Handbook*, issued by United States Air Force School of Aerospace Medicine, Brooks Air Force Base in Texas. It was published in October 1986.[23] This publication provided an index to research and a summary of findings into the specific radio frequency effects observed on the various parts of the human body.

Information Systems as Non-lethal Weapons

In "Radical Destabilizing Effects of New Technologies" written by Thomas Adams for the U.S. Army War College's publication, *Parameters* (Autumn issue, 1998), three areas continued to grow in importance in both civilian and military environments.[24] These three: information systems, biotechnology, and nanotechnology, were mutually reinforcing in their development and were changing the very nature of knowledge disbursement. Advances in these areas, according to the article, were transferring enormous power and potential to the general public. This presented a clear and present danger to military officials and programs. This new technology, epitomized by the Internet, was viewed as a destabilizing force. Specifically, the article suggested that organized crime, private armies, urban gangs, insurgents, regional separatists, conspiracy theory terrorists, radical cults, and violent environmentalists together with anti-government militias and "hobbyists" who disrupt information systems as a form of recreation, will gain access to this new technology. For this reason, efforts to curtail Internet access and services were recommended.

A prime example of this is the FDA's effort to regulate and censor certain websites that provide health advice unsupportive to the Rockefeller-directed medical–pharmaceutical trades.

The future, to a great extent, is already here. What remains of this predicted future to occur has probably already been designed or will be in the next few years. Already the privacy of individuals is compromised by every purchase made where information is digitized. From the list of goods purchased at the store with a scanner and charged to a debit or credit card to all telephone calls and other forms of communication—all are transparent to those who have access to the systems.

Given the pace of miniaturization, surveillance, and information processing in recent years, it is now possible to monitor all forms of communication, and create miniature surveillance equipment to monitor not only inner cities, but also entire regions.

Non-lethal "Global Management" Issues

As relayed by Dr. Begich, in March 1998, a paper entitled "Non-Lethal Technologies: Implications for Military Strategy," was authored by U.S. Air Force Colonel Joseph Siniscalchi, and published by the Center for Strategy and Technology, Air War College, Maxwell Air Force Base, in Alabama.[25] The paper stated modern military strategists must "focus on Global Management" because of the overriding unifying force demonstrated by the great powers of the United States, Europe, Japan, China and Russia. The chief unifying factor was an interdependent expanding economy. The lack of competing ideologies, with the exception of China, removed, the authors submitted, the primary threats to global security and replaced them with new ones that required new military options and directions. The principle new military threats were identified as groups or "non-state actors" motivated by religious causes, nationalism, ethnic rivalries and narco-interests. Dealing with these groups in the territorial boundaries of other countries, the authors argued, limited military options. The officials insisted that because of the changes in the nature of conflicts short of war, there is increasing need to bring forward the newest weapons with the hope that these new systems will minimize noncombatant casualties, reduce property destruction, and increase control in areas judged to be a threat.

Siniscalchi predicted that the proliferation of first and second-generation non-lethal weapons would occur quickly because these technologies are not unique and the hardware and software is widely available to those with the knowledge to assemble and use them. This is threatening to governments, particularly as developed countries' systems are often more vulnerable to attack.

An additional risk with the use of these new non-lethal systems is the risk of conflict escalation. For example, if a country is unable to counterattack in kind it will likely resort to conventional war fighting methods, terrorism, or weapons of mass destruction, Siniscalchi wrote.

Further complicating matters was the false assumption that non-lethal weapons could be successfully used against "non-state" actors operating with different "logic or rational thought" bases, or dissimilar value-sets. Siniscalchi cautioned against this inaccurate assumption given the history of conflicts involving such players. However, given the possibility of "non-visible combat," enemies may be targeted insidiously with non-lethal force, never knowing who in fact pulled the trigger.

Siniscalchi wrote that non-lethal options might also increase the success of economic sanctions placed against nation states. He advanced the idea that a country's communications, power generation, transfer systems, and all forms of electronic data processing could be shut down. Adding this factor to economic sanctions, he wrote, would increase the immediacy of the effect of such sanctions. He heralded acts of "disrupting television, radio, and commercial communications" to "isolate a state's leadership," or "denying electrical production" to "grind an economy to a halt."

Conclusion

"What has happened in the United States, which has allowed segments of our government to set agendas which run counter to the values most of us hold?" Dr. Begich asked.

"As technology advances, the ability to control populations and manipulate outcomes also advances. Because we know how to control the weather, create earthquakes, force behavioral changes, and manipulate the physiology of people does not mean that we should do so. The age we are in requires even greater safeguards for remaining personal freedoms. If freedom is what the militaries allegedly defend, then maintaining the values underlying freedom is what must be inherent in the actions our governments take in shaping our realities.

"We at Earthpulse believe that the greatest threat to freedom is an over-oppressive and increasingly secretive government. To many, the government has shifted from one 'of the people, by the people, and for the people,' to a government 'of special interests, for their own benefit, at the peoples' expense.' What went wrong, and where it went wrong, to a large extent, is a product of the intelligence bureaucracies that thrive through one administration to the next with unrestrained growth. These secretive intelligence agencies hide more and more of their agendas under a cloak of "national security," while drifting further from the principles which have allowed democratic states to exist. Secret government policy is not sanctioned by the free will of the people, and threatens the foundations of liberty, honest government, and public responsibility.

"The only truly free people are those who live in an open society, a society that cherishes above all the right of men and women to set the values that their public servants, including elected officials, should consistently reflect by their deeds. These are the popularly set values, which must be pressed into the philosophy of all projects, policies, and programs our leaders and governments seek to institute. Our militaries and economic policies are increasingly empty of the values upon which our democratic forms of government rest.

"Our desire then," based on the information this chapter and book presents, "is to put human values ahead of political agendas. It is time to drag our military institutions out from under their veil of secrecy to higher levels of accountability. It is time for all people to recognize and demand that increases in security must not be made at the expense of personal freedom. The rights to 'life, liberty, and the pursuit of happiness,' that include privacy, freedom of speech, and an electromagnetically secure environment in which optimal health can be manifested, must be preserved."[3]

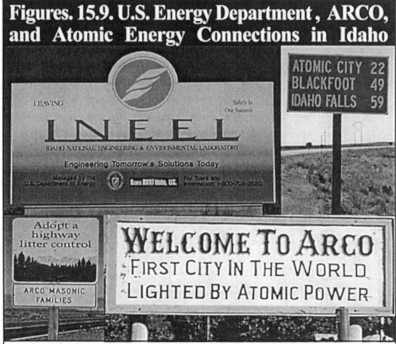

Figures. 15.9. U.S. Energy Department, ARCO, and Atomic Energy Connections in Idaho

Photographs taken on desolate lands within Idaho's National Engineering & Environmental Laboratories (INEEL), among America's leading nuclear waste and research facilities, adjacent to the town of ARCO—obviously named for the petrochemical company principally controlled by the British oligarchy. The three "S" INEEL logo, coding for "666," is fully explained in Chapter 17.

References

1) Horowitz LG and Puleo J. *Healing Codes for the Biological Apocalypse.* Sandpoint, Idaho, 1999.

2) Manning J and Begich N. *Angels Don't Play this HAARP: Advances in Tesla Technology.* Anchorage, AK: Earthpulse Press (P. O. Box 201393, Anchorage, AK 99520), 1995.

3) Begich N and Burke K. New non-lethal weapons systems may be used against U.S. citizens. Report Presented to the World Foundation for Natural Sciences on October 17,1998, Interlaken, Switzerland. Published by The Leading Edge and available on Dr. Begich's website: www.earthpulse.com

4) The Scientific Advisory Board of the Air Force document and reference is available from Dr. Begich at Earthpulse Press, Telephone: 907-694-1277. Fax: 907-696-1277.

5) Lamb C. Department of Defense Policy Planning Draft, July 21, 1994. Document and complete reference is available from Dr. Begich at Earthpulse Press, Telephone: 907-694-1277. Fax: 907-696-1277.

6) Thomas TL. The mind has no firewall. U.S. Army War College Quarterly, *Parameters,* Spring of 1998. . Document and complete reference is available from Dr. Begich at Earthpulse Press, Telephone: 907-694-1277. Fax: 907-696-1277.

7) United States Military Joint Publication 3–13.1. Document and complete reference is available from Dr. Begich at Earthpulse Press, Telephone: 907-694-1277. Fax: 907-696-1277.

8) United States Army War College. Revolution in Military Affairs (RMA), July 1994. Document and complete reference is available from Dr. Begich at Earthpulse Press, Telephone: 907-694-1277. Fax: 907-696-1277.

9) The International Committee of the Red Cross (ICRC). Discussion on the RMA, 1994. Document and complete reference is available from Dr. Begich at Earthpulse Press, Telephone: 907-694-1277. Fax: 907-696-1277.

10) Lewin LC, et al. *Report From Iron Mountain on the Possibility and Desirability of Peace.* New York: The Dial Press, 1967, pp. 79-101.

11) Cook T. *The Mark of the New World Order.* Springdale, PA: Whitaker House, 1996, p. 125.

12) Coleman J. *Conspirators' Hierarchy: The Story of the Committee of 300.* Carson City, NV: American West Publishers, 1992, pp. 52; 159; 182-183; 187.

13) Department of State Staff. World Population: The Silent Explosion. *Department of State Bulletin.* November, 1978. pp. 1-8. The Series were available through the Correspondence Management Division, Bureau of Public Affairs, Department of State, Washington, D.C. 20520.

14) "Programme" from the "4th European Heating Seminar" held on May 16-19, 1995. Following a preliminary presentation entitled, "EISCAT-Heating: results and future prospects," the "US Heater plans (HAARP)" program was presented by M. T. Rietveld. Document available on the Internet at http://eiscate.ag.rl.ac.uk/ and http://www.eiscat.ult.no/heating/semtlks.html.

15) Haslam ET. *Mary, Ferrie & the Monkey Virus: The Story of an Underground Medical Laboratory*. Albuquerque, NM: Wordsworth Communications (7200 Montgomery NE #280, Albuquerque, NM 87109), 1995.

16) McMahon P. FBI battles terrorism in Northwest. *USA Today*, Wednesday, December 23, 1998, p. 3A.

17) Document is available from the The Council on Foreign Relations. See their website: http://www.cfr.org/public/about.html

18) Tyler P. U.S. Air Force research paper on the effects of low-level non-ionizing electromagnetic radiation, 1984. Document and complete reference is available from Dr. Begich at Earthpulse Press, Telephone: 907-694-1277. Fax: 907-696-1277.

19) Reference and/or article from Penn State College, The Institute for Non-Lethal Defense Technologies, in cooperation with the United States Marines is available from Dr. Begich at Earthpulse Press, Telephone: 907-694-1277. Fax: 907-696-1277.

20) Martin R. "Dr. Jekyll" or "Mr. Hyde" Which is FEMA? Bizarre wildfires expose sinister agenda. *The Spectrum* (September 5) 2000;2;4:1-47.

21) Bell F. *Rays of Truth–Crystals of Light*. Laguna Beach, CA: Pyradyne Press, 1999; http://www.pyradyne.com; 1-800-729-2603; 949-499-5940.

22) Air Force Materiel Command. *Human Exposure to Radio-frequency Radiation: A Review Pertinent to Air Force Operations* (Al/OE-TR-1996-0035), Brooks Air Force Base, Texas: June 1996; document and complete reference is available from Dr. Begich at Earthpulse Press, Telephone: 907-694-1277. Fax: 907-696-1277.

23) United States Air Force School of Aerospace Medicine. *Radiofrequency Radiation Dosimetry Handbook*. Texas: Brooks Air Force Base, October 1986; document and complete reference is available from Dr. Begich at Earthpulse Press, Telephone: 907-694-1277. Fax: 907-696-1277.

24) Adams T. Radical Destabilizing Effects of New Technologies.U.S. Army War College: *Parameters*, Autumn, 1998; document and complete reference is available from Dr. Begich at Earthpulse Press, Telephone: 907-694-1277. Fax: 907-696-1277.

25) Siniscalchi J. Non-Lethal Technologies: Implications for Military Strategy. Center for Strategy and Technology, Air War College, Maxwell Air Force Base, Alabama, March 1998; document and complete reference is available from Dr. Begich at Earthpulse Press, Telephone: 907-694-1277. Fax: 907-696-1277.

Chapter 16.
Public Health, American Medicine and the Rockefeller Family

"Any method which appears to offer advantages to
a nation at war will be vigorously employed by that
nation. There is but one logical course to pursue,
namely, to study the possibilities of such warfare
from every angle . . ."

George W. Merck,
President, Merck Pharmaceutical Company,
in his report on biological warfare
to the U.S. Secretary of War, 1942

The shams of "public health," and the shenanigans described in the previous chapters, might be best explained by the substantial interest paid by the Rockefeller family to the entire field. This influence is peddled through pseudo-scientific institutions and agencies, operating both domestically and internationally that ultimately pave the study paths considered legitimate for science to pursue. This power brokering, naturally, depends heavily on "payoffs" and propaganda mechanisms, and extends globally to effect genocide beyond most people's desire to imagine, or will to discover.

As a clinician and health professional educator, it has amazed me for more than a decade that people—including leading academicians, scientists, and health service providers—have remained scatomatous to this widespread Rockefeller influence. Through their foundations and allied institutions, America's wealthiest family has asserted its direction over the fields of public health and medicine for almost a century. Meanwhile, the virtual army of health professionals—people who, mostly for the love of humanity, endured years of dehumanizing indoctrination called medical education, and paid dearly physically and financially—have remained pawns in a global sham.

To facilitate such privately and politically influenced science, propaganda mechanisms, as mentioned, were key. It is no secret, in fact, that worldwide, people have been heavily influenced, if not entirely "brainwashed" by pharmaceutical propaganda. These have routinely included claims made by esteemed scientists in reputable journals that have been, too often, biased by Rockefeller/Farben cartel interests.

USA Today pierced this harsh reality in March 2000, when they questioned, "Who's teaching the doctors?"—a cover story by Dan Vergano. The subheading answered thusly: "Drug firms sponsor required courses—and see their sales rise."[1]

For years, pharmaceutical advertising and marketing firms have been fully accredited as continuing medical education (CME) providers, and have virtually cornered the market in providing such "professional education."

"It is unconscionable," said the editor-in-chief of the *Journal of the American Medical Association*, Catherine De Angelis. Marketing firms "advertise wares under the guise of medical education," and doctors have blindly followed along.

"The drug companies provide 'unrestricted' grants to the marketers who hire the course faculty," Vergano wrote. "But growing numbers of critics say there's nothing unrestricted about the involvement of pharmaceutical companies" in what amounts to professional brainwashing at worst, and professional persuasion at best.

Proponents have argued that pharmaceutical companies survive "through education" to assure that new products are used correctly, said Berton Spilker, an official with the Pharmaceutical Research and Manufacturers of America in Washington, D.C.

Others have rhetorically defended that commercial CME providers employ faculty from leading medical schools. They argue that this practice helps to ensure objectivity, "while delivering updates on drugs to the medical community more quickly than academic educators." Odd that Vergano did not recognize the inherent conflict in his own writing. "[F]aculty from leading medical schools" are "academic educators!"

The *USA Today* article went on to explain how CME firms, "stack their programs with faculty physicians overly friendly to their sponsors' products. Sponsors [then] get a chance to market their products directly to doctors in a venue disguised as education. . . .

"Meanwhile, attempts to change the practice have been rebuffed even as the number of commercial providers has increased." In the spring of 1999, Vergano reported, "a resolution condemning accreditation of commercial CME firms" was signed by "educators from 47 medical schools," and then submitted to the Society for Academic Continuing Medical Education to initiate reforms. A few months later the complaint was tabled because of "the possibility or likelihood of grant money to universities being reduced by pharmaceutical companies," said Ruth Glotzer of Tufts University School of Medicine in Boston, one of the proposal's authors.[1]

Thus, by paving continuing education and academic pathways, and so subsidizing subscriptions to pharmaceutical industry established views, the Rockefeller family's influence in "public health" has been profound.

This chapter addresses, from this politically skewed perspective, the Rockefeller family's staggering influence upon American medicine and world health. Through their foundations, allied agencies, and respected institutions, this family, more than any other, has directed the paths of health science to their economic doorsteps. In light of this coercion, members of the medical mainstream participate in a virtual cult.[2,3]

Early Rockefeller Influence

Before World War II, America's scientific community generally frowned upon U.S. Government investments that implied potential biases in health science and healthcare. Major financing and administration of medical research by federal agencies, in fact, had been generally opposed during peacetime. Only during wars did organizations like the National Academy of Sciences (NAS) or the National Research Council (NRC) receive major federal funding. Both the NAS, established during the Civil War, and its NRC, set up during the First World War, were largely organized to respond to wartime threats including infectious biologicals and toxic chemicals.[2] From at least the early 1900s, Rockefeller appointees and monies shaped these agencies and others.

Naturally, little or no mention of this fact accompanies these organizations' literature. According to their promotions, the NAS is simply "a private, nonprofit, self-perpetuating society of distinguished scholars engaged in scientific and engineering research, dedicated to the furtherance of science and technology and to their use for the general welfare. Upon the authority of the charter granted to it by the Congress in 1863, the Academy has a mandate that requires it to advise the federal government on scientific and technical matters."[4]

Likewise avoiding direct mention of its Rockefeller connection, the NRC was effectively "organized by the National Academy of Sciences in 1916 to associate the broad community of science and technology with the Academy's purposes of furthering knowledge and advising the federal government. Functioning in accordance with general policies determined by the Academy, the Council has become the principal operating agency of both the NAS and the National Academy of Engineering in providing services to the government, the public, and the scientific and engineering communities. The Council is administered jointly by both Academies and the Institute of Medicine."[4]

These details concerning the NAS–NRC are relevant insofar as the development and promotion of vaccines, as discussed earlier, and the development, testing, and deployment of biological weapons and population controlling agents such as HIV through contaminated vaccines as additionally documented below.

Between 1900 and 1940, private foundations and universities financed most medical research. According to Paul Starr, author of *The Social Transformation of American Medicine: The rise of a sovereign profession and the making of a vast industry*, "the most richly endowed research center, the Rockefeller Institute for Medical Research was established in New York in 1902 and by 1928 had received from John D. Rockefeller $65 million in endowment funds." In contrast, as late as 1938, as little as $2.8 million in federal funding was budgeted for the entire Public Health Service. Therefore, it is not difficult to understand how the Rockefeller family came to influence, so heavily, health science and contemporary medicine. Very simply, the Rockefeller family's investment in health research and medical practice predated, and far surpassed, even the U.S. federal government's.[2]

More than the New Deal, the Second World War created the greatest boom in federal government and private industry support for medical research. It was during this time that Rockefeller/IG Farben chemical/pharmaceutical cartel scientists, including German eugenicists then experimenting on Blacks in central Africa, made major advances in biological and chemotoxic warfare. Together with Farben, as discussed earlier, the Rockefeller family had invested heavily, along with the Royal Family of England, Prescott Bush, and other political notables, in forwarding the earliest racial hygiene experiments and promotions.

Early History of Public Health

Prior to the Second World War, German models had heavily influenced American science and medicine. This precedent changed during the 1930s with the Rockefellers' heavy investment in the health sciences at a time when the Nazis were purging Jewish scientists from

German universities and biological laboratories. These changes, according to Starr, significantly altered the course of American health science and medicine. Many of Germany's most brilliant Jewish researchers immigrated to the United States just as the movement burgeoned to privatize war related biological and medical research.[2]

In 1938, as many Jewish scholars emigrated to the United States, the National Institutes of Health (NIH) synchronously established residence in "a privately donated estate" in Bethesda, Maryland, which is still its home today. From here, grants and stipends were awarded to direct the path of health science in America.

In this regard, the NIH—the most powerful and esteemed of all health science agencies in America—might be more honestly seen as a "cover organization," or "front" for its original benefactors, principle among them was the Rockefeller/IG Farben chemical–pharmaceutical and cancer cartel.

In this way, the Rockefeller/I.G Farben medical–industrial complex was fully poised to influence, and take advantage of, the U.S. Congress's "first series of measures to promote cancer research and cancer control."[2]

In 1937, new congressionally supported federal legislation authorized the establishment of the National Cancer Institute (NCI) under the NIH, and, for the first time, "the Public Health Service (PHS) to make grants to outside researchers."[2]

According to Starr's chronology:

> The war gave medical research priority. In July 1941 President Roosevelt created an Office of Scientific Research and Development (OSRD) with two parallel committees on national defense and medical research. The Committee on Medical Research (CMR) undertook a comprehensive research program to deal with the medical problems of the war. The work, costing $15 million, involved 450 contracts with universities and another 150 with research institutes, hospitals, and other organizations. Altogether, some 5,500 scientists and technicians were employed in the enterprise.[11]

Cancer Investigations and Exterminations

Given its early heavy interest in cancer research and eugenics (as detailed more completely in Chapter 18; see figures 18.1 and 18.2), the Rockefeller Institute for Medical Investigations in San Juan, Puerto Rico, initiated a nightmarish series of human investigations. The "Puerto Rican Cancer Experiment," launched in 1931 by program director, Dr. Cornelius Rhoads, caused the deaths of at least

347

thirteen Puerto Rican natives following their purposeful injection with cancerous tissues to determine if cancer might be transmitted that way.[7]

In a letter to his colleague, obtained by the Puerto Rican Nationalist Party, Rhoads expressed his desire to rid the planet of the island's natives. The Puerto Ricans, he reported in his racist tirade, were "beyond doubt the dirtiest, laziest, most degenerate and thievish race of men ever inhabiting this sphere. It makes you sick to inhabit the same island with them."

Expressing his disappointment over the inefficacy of "public health" to deliver genocide to the people of Puerto Rico, the Rockefeller Institute medical director wrote, "What the island needs is not public health work, but a tidal wave or something to totally exterminate the population. It might then be livable."

He concluded his letter by proudly confessing to his serial murders: "I have done my best to further the process of extermination by killing off eight and transplanting cancer into several more. The latter has not resulted in any fatalities so far. . . . The matter of consideration for the patients' welfare plays no role here—in fact, all physicians take delight in the abuse and torture of the unfortunate subjects."[7]

Dr. Rhoads, rather than being held accountable for his crimes against the people of Puerto Rico, was later awarded the Legion of Merit, and then appointed to the staff of the U.S. Atomic Energy Commission (AEC). This was during the 1950s when the commission was carrying out radiation experiments on unwitting hospital patients, mentally retarded children, prisoners, and American soldiers.[7]

The AEC was intimately involved in the NCI's cancer virus research program during the 1960s and early 1970s. Their "Joint AEC–NCI Molecular Anatomy Cancer Program," directed by Dr. Norman Anderson, extensively studied "human embryo tissues during early and mid-gestation." Anderson, and a host of AEC and NCI researchers including Robert Gallo's superior Robert Manaker, injected human fetal specimens with various viral mutants in an effort to develop cancers and vaccines. Among their "major findings," announced in a 1971 Department of Health, Education and Welfare (DHEW) publication, was that by bombarding fetuses with ionizing radiation, the researchers were able to cause tumor-like reactions later in life. Wisely, they did not report where their human trails were being carried out.[7]

More incriminating cancer studies conducted by AEC officials, including the development of airborne viruses that transmitted cancer and other immune system related disorders, were discussed previously.[7] In the final chapter addressing population control, discussions include the most advanced research linking AEC radiation experiments, project HAARP, and twenty-first century eugenics.

The Rhodes–Rothschield–Rockefeller Connection

Digressing a moment for pertinent historic detail, the surname Rhoads or Rhodes are both suspiciously related to Rockefeller money and contemporary acts of genocide. Though the potential blood relationship between Cornelius Rhoads and Cecil Rhodes is not out of the question, again given the cryptocracy's practice of changing names slightly to protect the guilty, there is certainly a political, economic, and ideological kinship between these two men. John Cecil Rhodes, from whom the Rhodes Scholarship was named, had, like Cornelius, no qualms about conducting genocidal operations in Third World nations. The British diamond magnate did so to further colonialist intentions. Curiously, Dr. Rhoads's financial support for genocidal cancer experiments in Puerto Rico derived, at least historically, from John Cecil Rhodes's funding of the Rothschild–J.P. Morgan–Rockefeller banking axis. What follows are some relevant facts:

Frank Aydelotte, American Secretary to the Rhodes Trustees, recalled that, "In 1888 Rhodes made his third will . . . leaving everything to Lord Rothschild"—his mining enterprise financier.

Later, for strategic reasons, Lord Rothschild's son-in-law, Lord Rosebury, replaced his elder as Rhodes's final heir.

Professor Carroll Quigley—President Clinton's teacher and mentor at Georgetown University during the mid–1960s—explained that these financial elite maintained global colonialism among their highest aspirations. In order to accomplish this, secret societies were administered largely on behalf of the Rothschild and Rhodes dynasties. The secret societies in which they invested had inner member structures that were shielded by successively larger outer circles. The central part of the structure was established by March, 1891, using Rhodes's money. Rothschild trustee Lord Alfred Milner directed the organization that was called "The Round Table." This organization "worked behind the scenes at the highest levels of British government, influencing foreign policy and England's involvement and conduct of WWI" and later WWII.[12,14]

According to secret society investigator and author Jan van Helsing, the British Secret Intelligence Service (MI6) evolved largely from efforts of members of the Committee of 300 and The Round Table. Other sources have reported that MI6 has exercised far greater worldwide control than most people realize. More wiretaps in the United States, for instance, have been administered on behalf of MI6 than the CIA. In this regard, Loftus and Aarons reported that, "for the last fifty years, virtually every Jewish citizen, organization, and charity in the world has been the victim of electronic surveillance by Great Britain, with the knowing and willing assistance of the intelligence services of the United States."[13]

To set the stage for the first World War, The Round Table directors developed the "Royal Institute for International Affairs," or RIIA. (See figure 15.2.) It was also known as "Chatham House" and had among its members Lords Albert Grey and Arnold Toynbee. The latter was known as the *éminence grise* (i.e., gray eminence; one exercising un-suspected power) of MI6.[12,14]

Apparently the Masonic influence in the affairs of the world's lead-ing intelligence organization has been striking and esoteric. Even the name "MI6" reflected knowledge of the ancient mystical arcana, as you will soon see.

It was Lord Toynbee of the MI6 who, following "brainstorming" sessions conducted at the Wellington House into ways to condition the public into accepting World War I, delivered the orders from the Com-mittee of 300.[12] Other famous members of the Committee of 300, past and present, are listed in figure 16.1.

Another leading committee member, Lord Rothmere, used his newspapers to test the Wellington House "social conditioning" strate-gies. Following a six-month test period, it was learned that eighty-seven percent of the public had formed their opinions without using critical or rational judgment—the intended result. Thereafter, the English working class, according to van Helsing, "was subjected to sophisticated propa-ganda methods to convince them that they had to send their sons by the thousands to their deaths" in WWI.

In response, Teddy Roosevelt, the 26th President of the United States, complained during his 1912 election campaign, "Behind the vis-ible government there is an invisible government upon the throne that owes the people no loyalty and recognizes no responsibility. To destroy this invisible government, to undo the ungodly union between corrupt business and corrupt politics is the task of a statesman."[12]

Fig. 16.1. Famous Members of the "Committee of 300"

Balfour, Arthur
Brandt, Willy
Bulwer-Lytton, Edward
Bundy, McGeorge
Bush, George H.W.
Carrington, Lord
Chamberlain, Huston Stewart
Constanti, House of Orange
Delano, Family
Drake, Sir Francis
Du Pont, Family
Forbes, John M.
Frederik IX, King of Denmark
George, Lloyd
Grey, Sir Edward
Haig, Sir Douglas
Harriman, Averill
Hohenzollern, House of
House, Col. Edward Mandell
Inchcape, Lord
Kissinger, Henry
Lever, Sir Harold
Lippmann, Walter
Lackhart, Bruce
Loudon, Sir John
Mazzini, Giuseppe

Mellon, Andrew
Milner, Lord Alfred
Mitterand, Francois
Morgan, J. P.
Norman, Montague
Oppenheimer, Sir Harry
Palme, Olof
Princess Beatrix
Queen Elizabeth II
Queen Juliana
Rainier, Prince
Retinger, Joseph
Rhodes, Cecil
Rockefeller, David
Rothmere, Lord
Rothschild, Baron Edmond de
Shultz, George
Spellman, Cardinal
Thyssen-Bornemisza, Baron
Vanderbilt, Family
von Finck, Baron August
von Habsburg, Otto
von Thurn und Taxis, Max
Warburg, S. G.
Warren, Earl
Young, Owen

Adapted from: Jan van Helsing's *Secret Societies and Their Power in the 20th Century*, Gran Canaria, Spain, Ewertverlag S. L., 1995; and Dr. John Coleman's, *Conspirators' Hierarchy: The Story of the Committee of 300*. Carson City, NV: American West Publishers, 1992.

From Shadow Governors to Rockefeller High Finance

The solidification of secret society power in America began in 1776 around the time Adam Weishaupt was establishing the Order of the Bavarian Illuminati on behalf of the Rothschilds. According to van Helsing, the founding of the United States of America was the result of the secret plan carried out by Freemasons beginning in the 17th century. Freemasons had organized the American War of Independence. The U.S. Constitution was penned and signed by Freemasons. Almost a third of American presidents have been Freemasons. The Great Seal of the United States with the pyramid and all seeing eye, the bald eagle that replaced the phoenix, the original thirteen states, stars and stripes, were all adopted symbols of Freemasonry. Though they had been put in place by Weishaupt to convey Rothschild wishes, the symbolism dated back to the Masons of ancient Egypt. The Illuminated pyramid on the American dollar bill was the design of Philip Rothschild as Ayn Rand, his lover, divulged in *Atlas Shrugged*.[12]

Although early American political leaders Benjamin Franklin and Thomas Jefferson heavily favored private centralized banking, in 1790 Alexander Hamilton was appointed secretary of the treasury, and reformed policy heavily favoring his silent benefactors Mayer Amschel Rothschild and his sons. A year later, Hamilton established the "First National Bank of the United States" fashioned after the "Bank of England." The Rothschilds controlled it.[12]

After Mayer Rothschild's death in 1812, Nathan took control over the family fortune and opened the "Nathan Mayer Rothschild & Sons Bank" in London, Vienna, Paris, and Berlin. In America it was represented by J. P. Morgan & Co., August Belmont & Co., and Kuhn Loeb & Company.[12]

During the American Civil War, the Rothschilds financed both sides of the conflict. "The reasons leading to this civil war," van Helsing wrote, "were almost completely due to the actions and provocations of Rothschild agents." One of the troublemakers, founder of the "Knights of the Golden Circle," was George Bickley. Bickley extolled the advantages of succession from the Union by the Confederate States. On the other side, the Rothschild–J. P. Morgan and August Belmont banks financed the Union. In addition, Rothschild's London bank supported the North, while its Paris bank funded the South. It was a glorious business.

President Lincoln finally caught wind of the scam and withheld immense interest payments to the Rothschilds. He then petitioned Congress to print "greenbacks"—dollars over which only the Union held printing power. In response, the furious Rothschilds are said to have arranged his assassination. John Wilkes Booth murdered Lincoln on April 14, 1865. Booth was freed from jail due to the efforts of the Knights of the Golden Circle. He spent the duration of his days living comfortably in England, funded by the Rothschilds.

By the early 1900s, the Masonic-linked "secret societies," including the CFR, held a stranglehold on America's leading social, economic, and political institutions.

In 1913, American banking mogul William Averell Harriman was initiated into the Skull & Bones fraternity. During the "Roaring Twenties" Harriman became the chief Western financier of the Russian government and their Ruskombank—where Max May, a Skull & Bones brother of Harriman, was vice-president. May was simultaneously vice-president of the Guaranty Trust Company controlled by J. P. Morgan and by extension the Nathan Mayer Rothschild Bank. Other Skull & Bones members partnered with J. P. Morgan at that time included Harold Stanley and Thomas Cochran. The capital used to create the Guaranty Trust came from the Harrimans, Rockefellers, Vanderbilts, and Whitneys—all families with blood kin in the Skull & Bones.

Percy Rockefeller represented his family's interest in the Skull & Bones as well as Guaranty Trust, which he directed from 1915 to 1930. Rothschild and Bavarian Illuminati representatives helped establish the Rockefeller's European Standard Oil empire as well as Carnegie's steelworks and Harriman's railroad. The economic result of these investments and associations is diagramed in figure 16.2 depicting the international banking community.

The introduction of the "Federal Reserve System" in 1913 enabled these international bankers to consolidate their American financial powers. Banking chiefs, who were largely supported by the Rothschilds, became the chairmen of the first Federal Reserve Bank of New York.

Following passage of "The Federal Reserve Act," Warburg conspired with others in the U.S. Congress to illegally ratify the 16th Amendment to the Constitution after which Congress deemed it necessary to levy personal income taxes on American citizens. The legislation was required since the United States government could no longer print money to finance its operations due to the controlling forces of the international banking cartel.

Opposition to these fiscal policies came, but was grossly inadequate to quell the changing tide. U.S. Congressman Louis McFadden expressed the sentiments of too few when he decried, "We have in this country one of the most corrupt institutions the world has ever known. I refer to the Federal Reserve Board and the Federal Reserve Bank, hereinafter called the FED. They are not government institutions. They are private monopolies which prey upon the people of these United States for the benefit of themselves and their foreign customers. . . ."[15]

With No Apologies: The Personal and Political Memoirs of U.S. Senator Barry Goldwater expressed the insider's view that The Round Table's cover organization, the CFR, tightly controlled the American political scene with Rockefellers at the helm. "I believe the Council on Foreign Relations and its ancillary elitist groups [referring to the other "secret societies" such as the Skull & Bones] are indifferent to communism. They have no ideological anchors. In their pursuit of a New World Order they are prepared to deal without prejudice with a communist state, a socialist state, a democratic state, monarchy, oligarchy—it's all the same to them."[16]

Rear Admiral Chester Ward of the U.S. Navy, a sixteen-year veteran of the CFR warned, "The most powerful clique in these elitist groups have one objective in common—they want to bring about the surrender of the sovereignty and the national independence of the United States."[16]

". . . Their rationale rests exclusively on materialism," Senator Goldwater added. "When a new president comes on board, there is a great turnover in personnel but no change in policy. For instance (as stated earlier), during the Nixon years Henry Kissinger, CFR member and Nelson Rockefeller's protégé, was in charge of foreign policy. When Jimmy Carter was elected, Kissinger was replaced with Zbigniew Brzezinski, CFR member and David Rockefeller's protégé."[16]

On February 18, 1991, President George H.W. Bush, past CIA director, former CFR chief, and a member of the Skull & Bones, Committee of 300 and its offshoot, The Bilderbergers, addressed the American people during his State of the Union address. "It is big," he said. "A New World Order, where diverse nations are drawn together in common cause . . . Only the United States has both the moral standing and the means to back it up."[17]

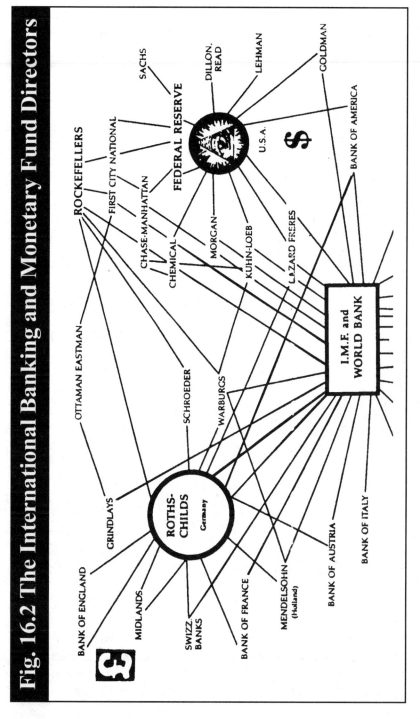

Fig. 16.2 The International Banking and Monetary Fund Directors

Pioneering the Fields of Cancer, Neurotoxicity, and Eugenics

Following the Rothschilds' early financial backing, the Rockefellers exercised significant control over American banking, medicine, and public health. This control was with the help of the foundations established to promote the Committee of 300's New World Order objectives.[18]

In *Emerging Viruses: AIDS & Ebola—Nature, Accident or Intentional?*, the intimate connections between the Rockefeller family and the funding and administration of the Rockefeller Foundation, Alfred P. Sloan Foundation, and the Sloan–Kettering Memorial Cancer Center was heavily documented.

Further implicating the Rockefeller/Farben military–medical influence in the development of the cancer industry, was the recognition that mustard gas—the ethylene derived nerve gas widely used during WWI responsible for killing millions—was what Sloan researchers used to develop the first cancer chemotherapeutic agent. Likewise, the petro-chemical industrialists managed by the Rockefeller/Farben cartel produced the earliest nerve gases.

Author Joseph Borkin made this association very clear in *The Crime and Punishment of I.G. Farben: The Unholy Alliance Between Hitler and the Great Chemical Combine*.[19] Tabun, "a nerve gas so deadly that a drop on the skin killed a victim in minutes, . . . as well as Sarin, a companion nerve gas, had been discovered during I.G. research and development on pesticides . . ." It became "one of Germany's most closely guarded military secrets," intimately shared by Rockefeller Standard Oil officials before WWII. Referred to by the code name "N-Stoff," Tabum was publicized as early as 1902 in the United States.

Although most historians reported that the Germans had sole access to the technology needed to develop these nerve gases, the Rockefeller family and their Standard Oil Company were undoubtedly privy to these developments, and profited greatly, as I.G. Farben's partner, by their trade.

As author G. Edward Griffin reported in *World Without Cancer*, the Rockefeller's Chase Manhattan Bank had been " the principal stock registrar for Farben–Rockefeller enterprises such as Sterling Drug, Olin Corporation, American Home Products, and General Aniline and Film. When Farben's vast holdings were finally sold in 1962, the Rockefeller group was the dominant force in carrying out the transaction."[9]

Rockefeller entry with I.G. Farben into the pharmaceutical field was concealed, Ed Griffin reported, for at least two reasons: "One is the fact that, for many years before World War II, Standard Oil had a continuing cartel agreement not to enter into the broad field of chemicals except as a partner with I.G. Farben which, in turn, agreed not to compete in oil. The other is that, because of the unpopularity of Farben" in America, and "its need to camouflage its American holdings, Standard had concealed even its partnership interest in chemical firms behind a maze of false fronts and dummy accounts."[9]

Griffin further detailed the Rockefeller group's "pyramid of power" through which international corporate control was exercised. The Rockefellers placed influential managers atop a vast number of companies. Included here was Litton Industries—the parent company to Litton Bionetics.[9]

The Rockefellers and Eugenics

Prior to WWII, underlying the close working relationship "between the German and American governments," according to German scholar Stephan Kühl in *The Nazi Connection: Eugenics, American Racism and German National Socialism*, "was the extensive financial support of American foundations for the establishment of eugenic research in Germany. The main supporter was the Rockefeller foundation in New York." According to Kühl, the Rockefellers "financed the research of German racial hygienist Agnes Bluhm on heredity and alcoholism in early 1920." By early 1927, "the Foundation began supporting other German eugenicists, including Hermann Poll, Alfred Grotjahn, and Hans Nactsheim. The Rockefeller Foundation played the central role in establishing and sponsoring major eugenic institutes in Germany, including the Kaiser Wilhelm Institute for Psychiatry and the Kaiser Wilhelm Institute for Anthropology, Eugenics, and Human Heredity."[20]

Kühl, a sociologist and historian at the University of Bielefeld in Germany further chronicled the Rockefeller connection to Hitler's racial hygiene program this way:

> In 1918, German psychiatrist Emil Kraepelin founded the Institute of Psychiatry in Munich, which was taken over by the Kaiser Wilhelm Society in 1924. Ernst Rüdin, later director of the Institute for Psychiatry, headed the Department of Genealogy and Demography. This department—the core of the Institute—concentrated on locating the genetic and neurological basis of traits such as criminal propensity and

mental disease [along with social psychology and herd mentality]. In 1928, the Rockefeller Foundation donated $325,000 for the construction of a new building. The funding of the Institute in Munich was a model that other American sponsors followed. Ironically, the Institute continued to be supported by the money of the Jewish philanthropist James Loeb until 1940.

The actual building of the Kaiser Wilhelm Institute for Anthropology, Eugenics, and Human Heredity in Berlin was also partially funded by money from the Rockefeller Foundation. . . . The Institute concentrated on a comprehensive project on racial variation as indicated by blood groups, and on twin studies, coordinated by Otmar Freiherr von Verschuer. When severe financial problems threatened to close the Institute during the early years of the Depression, the Rockefeller Foundation kept it afloat. At several points, the Institute director, Eugen Fischer, met with representatives of the Foundation. In March 1932, he wrote to the European bureau of the Foundation in Paris, requesting support for six additional research projects. Two months later, the Rockefeller Foundation answered affirmatively. The Foundation continued to support German eugenicists even after the National Socialists had gained control over German science.[20]

"By 1930, the United States and Germany had surpassed Great Britain as the leading forces of the international eugenics movement," Kühl reported. Around that time, Ernst Rüdin took control over the International Federation of Eugenic Organizations (IFEO), whose major administrative offices included "the Eugenics Record Office and the Station for Experimental Evolution in Cold Spring Harbor," New York, currently home to the Human Genome Project, and the "Kaiser Wilhelm Institute in Berlin."[20]

Additional links between Kaiser affiliated organizations and global industrialists' efforts to psychotronically and genetically control humanity are provided below with future implications in the final chapter.

The Secret War Against the Jews

According to authors John Loftus and Mark Aarons, the Rockefellers were principle players in *The Secret War Against the Jews*. "All through the war," they reported, "at least while [Nelson] Rockefeller was in charge" of the Office of Inter-American Affairs—the main foreign intelligence gathering and disseminating body, the Germans received everything they requested, "from refueling stations to espionage bases." Alternatively, the British "had to pay in cash. Behind Rockefeller's rhetoric of taking measures in Latin America for the national defense stood a naked grab for profits. Under the cloak of his official position, Rockefeller and his cronies would take over Britain's most valuable Latin American properties. If the British resisted, he would effectively block raw materials and food supplies desperately needed for Britain's fight against Hitler."[13]

Loftus and Aarons credited the close relationship the Rockefellers maintained with I.G. Farben for their preferential treatment of Hitler over Churchill:

> The Rockefellers just happened to own the largest stock in Standard of New Jersey and were then in partnership with the Nazi-controlled I.G. Farben, which held the second largest share of the Rockefeller-controlled oil company, to develop synthetic gas and rubber. The sources among the former intelligence officers whom we interviewed on the Rockefellers say that the family was in complete agreement with the Dulles brothers and Forrestal on the question of preserving U.S. profits, no matter who won the war.[13]

"In 1936," these authors recalled, "the Rockefellers entered into partnership with [Allen] Dulles's Nazi front, the Schroder Bank of New York, which . . . was a key institution in the Fascist economic 'miracle'" for which Hitler was credited. In 1939, "the Rockefeller-controlled Chase National Bank secured $25 million for Nazi Germany and supplied Berlin with information on ten thousand Nazi sympathizers in the United States. Except for a few months interruption, the Rockefeller-owned Standard Oil Company shipped oil to the Nazis through Spain all throughout the war. . . ."[13]

These investigators judged "the roster of the Rockefeller's known pro-Nazi behavior" as "horrendous." They noted Senator Harry Truman's description of the Rockefellers' company behavior as "treasonous." Indeed, under the U.S. Constitution, it was. "On September 22, 1947," Loftus and Aarons chronicled, Federal Judge Charles Clark issued an opinion against the Rockefellers in a civil case brought against Standard Oil. He stated that the company "can be considered an enemy national in view of its relationship with I. G. Farben after the United States and Germany had become active enemies."[13]

Two months later, merely days before the Rockefeller-controlled United Nations voted on the question of a Jewish "promised land," David Ben-Gurion, and other Jewish intelligence officers, entered Nelson Rockefeller's office. They "arrived with their dossier" of incriminating proof that he had personally "committed treason against the United States of America. . . . They had his Swiss bank records with the Nazis, his signature on correspondence setting up the German cartel in South America, transcripts of his conversations with Nazi agents during the war, and finally, evidence of his complicity in helping Allen Dulles smuggle Nazi war criminals and money from the Vatican to Argentina." Loftus and Aarons documented all of this. "It was the perfect moment for blackmail. . . ," they wrote, and that was the antecedent that prompted Rockefeller to direct the decisive South American vote to form the State of Israel.[13]

Figure 16.3 provides a graphic representation of "The Rockefeller Empire," its relationship to the CFR, other more secretive global organizations, and a few of its corporate/industrial holdings.

Kaiser Permanente and Non-lethal Ethnic Cleansing

One might ask, "Who was Kaiser Wilhelm, and why had the Rockefeller family invested so heavily in a eugenics institute given his name? Further, what, if any, relationships remain in contemporary medicine and public health which reflect these original institutions and their mission to direct global 'racial hygiene'?"

To answer the last of these questions first, in June 1990, the CDC, with the help of Kaiser Permanente, injected more than 1500 six-month-old Black and Hispanic babies in Los Angeles with a "high-potency Edmonston Zagreb (EZ) measles vaccine." Tens of thousands of other infants were similarly treated experimentally in several Third World countries. The shots caused many deaths, but generally resulted in profound chronic immune suppression and greatly enhanced susceptibility to infectious diseases and cancers.

The study was halted in October 1991, after more than a year of repeated reports from vaccine trial sites in Africa that female babies were dying in higher than expected numbers six months or longer after their inoculations.

CDC director David Satcher admitted in a June 17, 1996, *Los Angeles Times* article that an NIH investigation of the 1990–1991 Los Angeles study found that informed consent regulations had been violated because parents were not told their babies would be injected with an experimental vaccine that had never been licensed by the FDA.

"Sorry, sometimes these things just fall through the cracks," another CDC official apologized.

The public learned that Kaiser Permanente's health maintenance organization (HMO) in Northern California had become America's

Fig. 16.3. The Rockefeller Globalist Empire

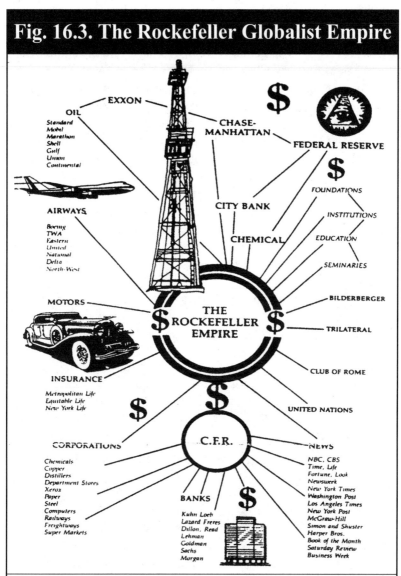

Secretary of the Treasury, Alexander Hamilton, established banking policies favoring his silent benefactors Mayer Amschel Rothschild and his sons. He then established the "First National Bank of the United States" fashioned after the "Bank of England," under Rothschilds' control. The Rothschild & Sons Bank then principally established J. P. Morgan & Co., August Belmont & Co., and Kuhn Loeb & Company. The Guaranty Trust Company was controlled by J. P. Morgan and by extension the Rothschild Bank in partnership with the Harrimans, Rockefellers, Vanderbilts, and Whitneys—all families with blood kin in the Skull & Bones and other secret societies. Rothschild also helped establish the Rockefeller's European Standard Oil empire. The introduction of the "Federal Reserve System" in 1913 enabled these international bankers to consolidate their powers. Banking chiefs, who were largely supported by the Rothschilds and Rockefellers, became the first directors of the Federal Reserve Bank of New York.

premier vaccine testing institution, according to the San Jose *Mercury News*.[21] "But Black, Latino, and American Indian babies bear the brunt of the risk involved in getting vaccines to the market," reported staff writer Ariana Eunjung Cha.

"At least eight out of 14 childhood vaccines approved since 1990 were tested disproportionately in lower-income minority communities" largely through Kaiser's trials in which "the experimental nature of the products and potential dangers weren't properly described to parents."

Consequently, bioethicists criticized the CDC and Kaiser Permanente's "informed consent" policies. "The difficulty we've gotten into is that unfortunately many of those populations are . . . peripheral, poor and ethnic minorities," stated Douglas Diekema, an associated professor of pediatrics and medical history at the University of Washington–Seattle. In the worst case, he added, if these vaccine trials caused major side effects, then "you have just taken advantage of a population."

Officials representing the pharmaceutical industry countered the nationwide critique. "Our trials are mutually beneficial," defended Merck & Company's spokeswoman, Isabelle Claxton. She argued that the obvious ethnic and racial imbalance in vaccine testing was "meaningless." It was "only a problem," she said, "if they were victims . . . if there were some conspiracy to use them as guinea pigs. . . . But there is not."

"The socioeconomic and ethnic imbalance in vaccine studies is the by-product of a testing network that grew out of years of cooperation between the government, pharmaceutical companies and health care providers," Eunjung Cha wrote. "The first tests of new vaccines are usually conducted through academic centers and are funded at least partially by the NIH. The larger vaccine trials that come next can involve tens of thousands of children and take place mostly on Indian reservations or through HMOs like Kaiser Permanente in California, Colorado, Hawaii and Georgia or Group Health Cooperative in Washington."[21]

"Kaiser Permanente Northern California, with 16 hospitals from Santa Rosa to Fresno, is the most popular vaccine-testing site in the nation . . . because of its military-like record keeping, and the fact that some 27,000 babies are born there very year," the *Mercury News* article continued. "Since 1990, the HMO has overseen 34 vaccine tests, for products developed by almost every major vaccine maker in the world."

"Hasidic Jews in New York" injected with the first hepatitis A vaccine, joined the short ethnically disparate list of test subjects that further included Navajo and White Mountain Apache Indians, and Alaskan Eskimos, besides Los Angeles's urban mix.

Internationally, the high-potency EZ measles experiment began at four major sites in the mid-1980s including Haiti, Senegal, Guinea Bissau and Mexico. Subsequent trials were conducted in Cameroon, Gambia, Bangladesh, Tono, Iran, New Guinea, Peru, Rwanda, Sudan, South Africa, Egypt, Philippines, Uzbekistan, Thailand, and Zaire. Primary funding came from USAID and the WHO. In Haiti, infants were given the experimental vaccine at 10 to 500 times the usual dose levels.

Kaiser attorney, Stan Watson, defended his organization's Institutional Review Board (IRB) saying that the committee worked hard to fulfill every federal requirement, but regarding the public's "recrimination" over how the Kaiser/CDC EZ measles vaccine experiments went, he argued, "People forget what disease was like. I saw polio. I saw people in iron lungs. The whole idea of what we do is a service to the community. We do it because it will benefit our patients and the world at large."[21]

As the next chapter reveals, Kaiser's direction in this community "service" field, and efforts to "benefit . . . the world at large," derives more from the Rockefeller–Royal Family-linked Committee of 300 and the Stanford Research Institute (SRI) than from the NIH, CDC, or WHO.[22] Moreover, their contributions to the field of public health derives less from a humanitarian spirit than from major investments in biospiritual (i.e., biological *and* electromagnetic) warfare for technotronic eugenics.

More Suppressed Facts and Therapeutic Alternatives

For the past half century, the Rockefeller–Farben directed Sloan and Kettering Foundations have not only led the cancer industry in the development and promotion of highly ineffective and risky chemotherapeutics, but they have, since the 1970s, consistently acted as a primary source of propaganda, in the truest sense of psychological warfare, insofar as covering the genocidal aspects of the cancer industry. The lead propagandist has been Laurance Rockefeller, not only the long term director and financial chief of the Sloan–Kettering Memorial Cancer Center, and the top contributor to the Sloan Foundation, but also the director of *Reader's Digest* "with 18 million circulation and *National Geographic* with 10 million circulation," according to author

Eustace Mullins. This meant that the Rockefeller Brothers Fund director personally influenced at least 28 million middle class American households per month. Further evidencing this fact, Mullins cited Dr. Ralph Moss, former public relations director of the Sloan–Kettering cancer center, as having acknowledged *Reader's Digest* as the reputable "barometer of orthodox thinking on the cancer problem."[23]

Similarly, the Sloan Foundation has heavily financed "public management" communications research, and supported pioneering developments in this field. The organization granted funds to famous propagandists including CIA-affiliated author Richard Preston (*The Hot Zone*) and *The Coming Plagues* writer Laurie Garrett to publish their deceptive efforts. Promoting such famous authors and best-selling publications, the cartel has thus managed to cloud the public's mind concerning the industrial and iatrogenic origins of most cancers, other immune system disorders, and a plethora of laboratory produced viruses now killing millions.[7] As detailed earlier, this propagandist function is a necessary central objective of non-lethal warfare.[24, 25]

Vital truths about many modern infectious diseases, including AIDS and Ebola, cancers, and most chronic illnesses, as well as low cost, no risk, highly effective treatment alternatives, have been effectively concealed by the global industrialists through their use of such propaganda.

Robert Guccione, the publisher of *Penthouse Magazine*, brought an excellent example of this offensive masquerade to light.[26] Motivated by the medical mismanagement of his wife, Kathy Keeton, for breast cancer, and her premature death from a "low risk" hospital procedure, Mr. Guccione initiated a class action lawsuit against the NCI that was announced in a feature story in his September 1997 issue. In "The $200 Billion Scam: Uncle Sam's Continuing Medical Genocide," author Jeff Kamen relayed the Guccione's story in which Kathy had been persuaded to forego promising alternative treatment with hydrazine sulfate for standard chemotherapy. The "inexpensive and effective cancer-fighting drug," hydrazine sulfate, proven life-saving in numerous studies in foreign countries, had been investigated and highly recommended by Joseph Gold, M.D., a former U.S. Air Force research physician, who later became Director of the Syracuse Cancer Research Institute in upstate New York.

The NCI-sponsored U.S. Government cover-up of hydrazine sulfate's utility began, according to congressional investigators, in 1976 when NCI officials wrote to Congressman James M. Hanley of New

York, "Hydrazine sulfate has been tested in the Soviet Union at the Petrov Institute. . . . No evidence of meaningful anti-cancer activity was reported." The following week, Congressman Hanley, who had launched the official inquiry, received the actual Petrov-study report that relayed just the opposite: "We observed a definite therapeutic effect of hydrazine sulfate in patients with Hodgkin's disease and malignant tumors of various localizations in far-advanced stages, when other measures of specific therapy have failed." Since then, Jeff Kamen reported, hydrazine sulfate became "an approved, first-line cancer drug in Russia, after 17 years of successful clinical testing there."[26]

Kamen reported that a large-scale clinical cancer trial of hydrazine sulfate was deliberately sabotaged by NCI investigators, who literally killed hundreds of women by neglecting to inform them about the known risks of combining the experimental drug with tranquilizers. Kamen wrote:

> In these [1989 and 1993] clinical trials the NCI failed to inform patients in its "informed-consent statements" that the combination of hydrazine sulfate with tranquilizers, barbiturates, and alcohol—in one of the NCI studies 94 percent of all patients were given tranquilizers alone—could not only deactivate the therapeutic action of the drug but could result in patient morbidity and mortality. The reason these severely ill cancer patients permitted the government to experiment on them with hydrazine sulfate was their hope that this drug might help them in the way it had helped the dozens of patients in smaller clinical trials conducted by Harbor–UCLA during ten years of testing.[26]

Later, in an effort to conceal the NCI's liability, a bogus United States General Accounting Office (GAO) investigation was published that stated the NCI's trials "were not flawed."

Undeterred by the obvious suppression of data and devious conclusion by the GAO, Mr. Guccione rallied his forces on Capitol Hill to further investigate the issue along with the GAO. On October 20, 1997, a Senate Subcommittee concluded that the NCI and the GAO had indeed erred. The Chief Minority Counsel who spoke for the hearings committee reported that the government agencies' conclusions about hydrazine sulfate were "plainly absurd" and "extremely misleading."[27]

Rockefeller Power Over the U.S. Government

By what mechanism(s) might Rockefeller family members have exerted such control over the U.S. Government and health science agencies? The answer is, through a hierarchy of privately financed and controlled entities described by Dr. John Coleman previously and diagramed in figures 15.2, 16.2 and 16.3.

For instance, following WWII, Nelson Rockefeller remained highly active in the politically powerful Council on Foreign Relations (CFR) directed by the Executive Arm of the Royal Institute for International Affairs under the Committee of 300. The CFR, an organization that many authors have effectively exposed,[7] deserves additional mention and updating here regarding their influence in setting international policy for administering non-lethal forms of population control.

According to the CFR's website,[28] at the time of this writing, the largely Rockefeller pioneered and American based organization promoted its global, allegedly "peacekeeping," services thusly:

Businessmen, bankers, and lawyers determined to keep the United States engaged in the world founded the Council on Foreign Relations in 1921. Today, the Council is composed of men and women from all walks of international life and from all parts of America, dedicated to the belief that the nation's peace and prosperity are firmly linked to that of the rest of the world. From this flows the Council's mission: to foster America's understanding of other nations—their peoples, cultures, histories, hopes, quarrels, and ambitions—and thus to serve our nation through study and debate, private and public.

The Council is a national membership organization and think tank with headquarters in New York, offices in Washington, D.C., and programs nationwide. Its widely respected and influential research staff—with backgrounds in government and scholarship in most international subjects—regularly meets with Council members and other leaders and thinkers. These exclusive sessions, known as study groups or roundtables, form the Council's intellectual core. The aim is to provide insights into international affairs and to develop new ideas for U.S. foreign policy, *particularly national security and foreign economic policy*. Council Fellows produce books, articles, and op-ed pieces and regularly contribute expert commentary on television and radio. [Emphasis added.]

The Council also publishes *Foreign Affairs*, the leading periodical in the field. This magazine has been host to the most important articles about world affairs in this century. [e.g., this was wherein Henry Kissinger published his nuclear weapon's thesis that ultimately directed the deployment of nuclear warheads throughout Europe largely on behalf of Nelson Rockefeller, who appointed Kissinger to lead the first CFR nuclear weapons study group in 1955.[29-31]]

The Council's 3,600 members are divided almost equally among New York, Washington, D.C., and the rest of the nation. They include nearly all current and former senior U.S. government officials who deal with international matters; renowned scholars; and leaders of business, media, human rights, humanitarian, and other nongovernmental groups. Council members choose new members, who aim to educate themselves and then others.[28]

In this way, the cult-like ideological consensus of CFR core members is evangelized throughout the growing organization to its affiliates. Their power ultimately moves media, politics, and policies, both foreign and domestic.

The next paragraphs provide a shallow disclaimer regarding the organization's stealth-like influence.

The Council is host to the widest possible range of views and advocate of none. It cultivates an atmosphere of nonpartisanship and nonideological engagement among members and staff. The views expressed in Council-sponsored independent task force reports, by members of study groups, or in articles in *Foreign Affairs* are solely the responsibility of the respective authors or groups.

This tradition of impartiality enables the Council to gather contending voices for serious and civil debate and discussion. That special convening power is unique in American society.[28]

"In keeping with its mission . . . and heritage," Council members consistently pursued three major goals, the website promoted. These included the provision of "new ideas for U.S. foreign policy," such as nuclear weapons deployment as directed by Rockefeller subordinate Dr. Henry Kissinger, and preparations for global bioterrorism, as directed by unrecognized white collar bioterrorist, Dr. Joshua Lederberg, representing Rockefeller University, and the American Type Culture Collection (ATCC).

Treasonous Foreign Policies

Dr. Lederberg was cited previously in Chapters 1 and 8, and in the media, for lying to Congressional investigators and the American people on behalf of the Pentagon regarding biological exposures of Gulf War troops. Sadam Hussein's preparedness to conduct biochemical warfare was largely due to the ATCC shipments of biological weapons cultures, including WNV, to Iraq prior to the Gulf War, and Dr. Lederberg knew it.

The NIH documents reprinted in figures 16.4 and 16.5 are even more stunning. The former contract shows that the ATCC committed acts that, at minimum, border on treason against the United States. These records show that *even leukemia-inducing and HIV-like retroviruses were shipped to Russian biological warfare labs during the Cold War*. The Senate Riegle Committee investigation of the ATCC failed to determine this fact. Thus, not only had Sadam Hussein received biological weapons shipments from the ATCC, including the West Nile virus, but also, so had the Russians!

Dr. Lederberg, it might be recalled from Chapter 8, had facilitated the biological weapons study group meeting at the CFR in 1997 with Richard K. Betts, Senior Fellow and Director of National Security Studies. Thus, the CFR, Betts, and other high level National Security officials are implicated by association, with Lederberg, to these reasonably treasonous acts against the United States, aside from the genocidal issues raised by these documents as discussed above.

In light of the USDHEW/NIH document reprinted in figure 16.5, citing the Russian recipients of America's most advanced viral cancer triggers, and other assorted biological weapons, the frequent allegation of American biowarfare "experts' that Russia led the biological weapons race might now be seen as grossly deceptive. According to the SVCP report of 1978, the Russians required and readily received, complete scientific assistance in developing their cancer virus and infectious disease laboratories and arsenals. Page two of the figure shows that in April, 1978, six years before Dr. Gallo was alleged to have discovered the AIDS virus, and just as the first GRID/AIDS cases were being diagnosed in New York, Dr. Gallo was delivering "large-scale production of human virus" methods and materials to the Russians at the Ivanovsky Institute in Moscow, the premier, previously Communist, biological weapons institute.[8]

The CFR's "Private" Policy Initiatives

Here's how the CFR articulated their first humanitarian goal. Emphasis has been added:

[To a]dd value by improving understanding of world affairs and by providing new ideas for U.S. foreign policy. The Council does this in many ways.

The Council will sponsor an independent task force when an issue arises of current and critical importance to U.S. foreign policy, and it seems that a group diverse in backgrounds and perspectives may nonetheless be able to reach a meaningful policy consensus through *private* and nonpartisan deliberations.

Council Policy Initiatives (CPIs) focus on current foreign policy issues of great importance where consensus seems unlikely. . . . [28]

It certainly would be next to impossible to develop a "consensus" regarding, for instance, the deployment of weapons of mass destruction. That is precisely why "nonpartisan deliberations" on such matters as nuclear and biological weapons are conducted in *"private."*

The CFR's second goal targeted organizational development. The membership was pledged to:

Transform the Council into a truly national organization to benefit from the expertise and experience of leaders nationwide. The Council aims to energize foreign policy discussions across the country. And as Council membership outside New York and Washington, D.C. continues to grow and diversify, the Council creates new ways to involve these members in intellectual dialogue. The four principal means of involvement are through a special members' area of the Council's website, at an annual National Conference, at dinner seminars based on Study Groups and independent task forces in key cities around the country, and through an interactive video-conferencing system.[28]

Finally, to assure its survival and future influence, the CFR pledged to:

Find and nurture the next generation of foreign policy leaders and thinkers. The Council does this primarily through a special term membership program for younger Americans and a "Next Generation Fellows" program that brings outstanding younger scholars onto the Council staff, as well as the International Affairs Fellowships and several other fellowship programs. These programs aim to spark interest and participation in world affairs and U.S. foreign policy.

In recent months, Council members have heard Madeleine K. Albright, Kofi Anan, James A. Baker III, Warren Christopher, Henry A. Kissinger, and George P. Shultz offer their views of challenges the United States will face in the next century; Charlene Barshefsky, Anatoly Chubais, Bill Clinton, Stanley Fischer, Paul Krugman, Lee Kuan Yew, George Soros, and James D. Wolfensohn discuss the global economy; William S. Cohen and the Joint Chiefs of Staff evaluate future defense policy . . .

Figure 16.4. American Type Culture Collection "Curatorial" Development & Distribution of Tumor Viruses Including "Leukemogenic" Retroviruses

CONTRACT REPORTS - OFFICE OF PROGRAM RESOURCES & LOGISTICS

Dr. Jack Gruber, Chief, OPR&L, VOP, DCCP
Dr. Garrett V. Keefer, Staff Scientist, OPR&L, VOP, DCCP
Dr. John S. Cole III, Staff Scientist, OPR&L, VOP, DCCP

AMERICAN TYPE CULTURE COLLECTION (NO1-CP-6-1047)

Title: Curatorial Preservation and Development of Reference-Grade Tumor Viruses

Contractor's Project Directors: Dr. Charles D. Aldrich

Project Officers (NCI): Dr. John S. Cole III
                        Dr. Garrett V. Keefer

Objectives: To biologically characterize and historically trace the origin of selected groups of tumor viruses, including avian, murine, feline, and primate, in order to develop and obtain reference-grade tumor virus materials. To serve as an archival repository for seed stocks of important virus materials from the Viral Oncology Program. To provide documented histories and characterizations of materials which have been provided in quantity to NCI collaborating investigators.

Major Findings: Receipt and characterization of oncogenic viruses from Program Resources and Logistics has continued. Data on RNA directed DNA polymerase of five murine and two primate viruses has been developed. Serological analysis of gs1 and gs3 antigen suggest a strong cross reactivity between squirrel monkey retrovirus and Mason-Pfizer Monkey Virus. The contractor reports a lack of correlation between in vitro assays of ecotropic viruses and leukemogenic activity in vivo, and an apparent transformation of euploid feline cells by Mouse Mammary Tumor Virus.

Significance to Biomedical Research and the Program of the Institute: Virus materials are supplied to investigators throughout the world by Program Resources and Logistics. It is important that highly characterized reference stocks of these viruses be available.

Proposed Course: This contract will continue for the duration of the approved project plan.

Date Contract Initiated: June 15, 1976

NIH document shows that the ATCC, linked to the Rockefeller-directed military industrial complex and cancer industry through Rockefeller University President, Dr. Joshua Lederberg, committed acts that might be considered treasonous by supplying biological weapons, including leukemia-inducing and AIDS-like retroviruses to potential enemies, including Russian labs, during the Cold War. Dr. Lederberg's organization, the Senate Riegle Report on the Gulf War syndrome stated, had shipped Sadam Hussein's biological weapons labs a broad array of viruses shortly before Iraq invaded Kuwait. Dr. Lederberg, a CFR study group director for "Non-lethal Warfare" and Biological Weapons planning, falsely denied, on behalf of the Pentagon, any biological weapons exposures to troops during the war. From: NCI Staff. *The [Special] Virus Cancer Program [SVCP].* U.S. Department of Health, Education and Welfare. Washington, D.C.: Public Health Service, National Institutes of Health, Division of Cancer Cause and Prevention, June 1978, p. 230. Library call number: E20.3152:V81/977 and 78-21195.

Figure 16.5. US–USSR Agreement Under Which Biological Weapons Including The Most Advanced Cancer Viruses Were Traded During the Cold War

US-USSR Agreement. A Memorandum of Understanding for cooperation in the study of the microbiology, immunology, and molecular biology of cancer viruses was first signed on November 18, 1972. The Memorandum established procedures for joint studies through the exchange of information, materials and scientists between the two countries.

Delegation Meetings: November, 1972   Moscow, USSR
November, 1973   Bethesda, USA (Subcommittee)
May, 1974   Moscow, USSR
May, 1975   Bethesda, USA
June, 1976   Sukhumi, USSR
October, 1977   Bethesda, USA
September, 1978   Riga, Latvian SSR

As agreed, the fifth meeting of the US-USSR Joint Working Group on Cancer Virology, Co-Chairmen Dr. J.B. Moloney and Professor V.M. Zhdanov, took place at the National Institutes of Health, Bethesda, Maryland, USA, on October 26-28, 1977. At a symposium held on October 27 and 28, members of both delegations and invited speakers presented recent studies in cancer virology. The main emphasis of this meeting was given to reviewing the progress of current cooperative efforts and assessing the problem of re-combinant DNA research. Dr. Michael Crawford (University of Kansas) presented preliminary results of a study to determine the role of genetic factors in an outbreak of leukemia in baboons. This work, conducted jointly by laboratories in the USA and in the USSR, is an excellent example of the cooperative research efforts sponsored under the US-USSR Agreement.

The Chairmen of both Sides reported on the recommendations made in the Memorandum of Understanding of the Joint Committee on Malignant Neoplasia held in Moscow, USSR, September, 1977. The recommendations included: (1) discussing, in depth, cooperative studies on recombinant DNA research, (2) increasing the program participation of other USSR institutions, in particular to include the Institute of Molecular Biology, Moscow, (3) conducting exchanges of scientists only under the auspices of the Cancer Virology Program under the topic of Malignant Neoplasia, USA-USSR Health Agreement, and (4) encouraging the use of small working group meetings on subjects of intense interest.

Delegates expressed interest in conducting collaborative studies in the following areas: (1) studies of viruses isolated from human tissues in cell culture or in animals and their possible role in the pathogenesis of human neoplasia; (2) continuation of studies on non-human primate viruses as they relate to human cancer; (3) studies on the role of viruses in the induction of human breast tumors, including continuation of studies on MPMV and related viruses; (4) studies on cocarcinogenesis--viral/viral, viral/chemical, and viral/hormonal; (5) characterization of nucleic acids and their role in the induction of animal and human cancers, particularly the detection of trans-forming sequences in cellular nucleic acids and molecular genetic studies with DNA from human tumor cells; (6) studies on viral proteins as probes for viral gene expression in animals and humans; and (7) studies on oncogenic viruses important to human ecology, e.g., those derived from bovine, avian,

Figure 16.5. US–USSR Agreement Continued

TO U.S. (continued)		INSTITUTIONS VISITED
Dr. I. Kryukova Gamaleya Inst., Moscow	February, 1976	M.D. Anderson Hosp. (Dr. Bowen); Michigan Cancer Fdn (Dr. Rich); NCI scientists; Rockefeller Inst. (Dr. Hanafusa)
Prof. S.M. Klimenko Ivanovsky Inst., Moscow	September, 1976	NCI scientists; Inst. Cancer Research (Dr. Blumberg)
Dr. E. Bagley Kiev Inst. Experimental and Clinical Oncology	March, 1977	NCI scientists; F. Hutchinson Cancer Ctr (Dr. Hakomori); Sloan-Kettering Institute (Dr. Sonnenberg)
Dr. Z. Butenko Kiev Inst. Experimental and Clinical Oncology	March, 1977	NCI scientists; laboratories of Drs. Spiegelman, Mayyasi, W. Moloney, E. Cronkite
Dr. S.A. Novakhatskiy Ivanovsky Inst., Moscow	May, 1977	NCI scientists; laboratory of Dr. R. Gallo, NCI; area laboratories involved in large-scale production of human virus
Dr. Felix Filatov Ivanovsky Inst., Moscow	September, 1977	University of Chicago (Dr. B. Roizman)
Dr. L.B. Stepanova Dr. O.B. Korchak Moscow Research Institute of Viral Preparations	November, 1977	NCI Laboratory of Viral Carcinogenesis, Viral Oncology Program
Prof. I.F. Seitz Petrov Institute of Oncology, Leningrad	April, 1978	NCI (Dr. Gallo); USC (Drs. McAllister and Vogt); UCLA (Baluda); Sloan- Kettering (Dr. Bendich)
Dr. Boris Lapin Director, Inst. for Experimental Pathology and Therapy, Sukhumi	September, 1978	NCI scientists; Sloan- Kettering Inst. (Dr. Moore- Jankowsky); Delta Regional Primate Ctr (Dr. Gerone)

Dr. Felix P. Filatov, Senior Scientific Researcher, Ivanovsky Institute of
Virology, Moscow, spent three-and-one-half months in the laboratory of
Dr. Bernard Roizman, University of Chicago. The purpose of his exchange
visit was to gain experience in (a) preparative purification of Herpes

The above agreement includes a partial list of researchers, including Dr. Robert Gallo of the NCI, who traded the most advanced methods and materials in the fields of molecular biology, bacteriology and virology during the Cold War. Included was the "large-scale production of human virus" transferred to the Soviets by Dr. Gallo. Might this have been the AIDS virus? Additionally, besides possible treason for trading biological weapons technical knowledge, and the weapons themselves, with the Russians, these documents clearly reflect the functioning of a global cryptocracy that superceded the geopolitical policies of the United States Government, and knowledge of the American people. From: NCI Staff. *Op. cit.,* 1978, pp. 36 and 39. Library call number: E20.3152:V81/977 and 78-21195.

As much as at any time during its nearly eight decades, the Council on Foreign Relations today serves its members and the nation with ideas for a better and safer world.[28]

Thus, council members may believe that we live in a "better and safer world" as a result of developing and deploying the biological, chemical, and nuclear weapons of mass destruction which the organization and its leading family has unofficially promulgated.

Indeed, most people cannot conceive of a conspiracy of such magnitude that might allow this virtually secret society, operating beneath a thin veil of public scrutiny, to dictate U.S. Government policies to the extent the CFR, and the Rockefeller family at its helm, does. Again, as Retired Pentagon Colonial Jack Kingston advised, the best covert operations occur in broad daylight, before everyone's eyes, without anyone seeing anything.

Rockefeller Befriends Kissinger

For the benefit of "devil's advocates," the following history documents the involvement of Dr. Henry Kissinger at the CFR on behalf of Nelson Rockefeller and their allies. The following facts might provide a suitable reality check, and explain why Dr. Kissinger, perhaps as much as anyone, deserves, as explained in the next chapter, the "mark of the beast"—666. The following should also be received as an adjunct to the article written by Christopher Hitchens in *Harper's*, March 2001, which explained why Rockefeller's protégé should be tried in an international court of law as a treasonous war criminal. (See figure 16.6)

In 1955, President Eisenhower's assistant for international affairs, Nelson Rockefeller, invited Dr. Kissinger to discuss national security issues at the Quantico (Virginia) Marine Base. Following their meeting, according to *Newsweek*'s Managing Editor, Walter Isaacson, Kissinger "the diplomat" became Rockefeller's "closest intellectual associate." Soon after, Kissinger authored several military proposals for Eisenhower to consider which, like his forthcoming nuclear weapons strategy, best served Rockefeller financial interests. Unimpressed, Eisenhower turned them down.[29,30]

As a result, Rockefeller sent Eisenhower his resignation and then launched a Special Studies Project that explored the "critical choices" America faced militarily in the coming years. Kissinger agreed to direct this new project along with a CFR study group, and as a result, published a 468-page book on his findings. The treatise proposed that tactical nuclear weapons be developed and "a bomb shelter [be built] in every house" in preparation for limited thermonuclear war. "The willingness to engage in nuclear war when necessary is part of the price of our freedom," Kissinger argued.[30]

Those old enough may recall the school "nuclear bomb drills," with fire alarms sounding as classes proceeded to the closest "fallout shelter"—typically the basement or beneath one's desk. The source of the intense anxiety felt by almost everyone might be best assigned to this Rockefeller/Kissinger CFR treatise. This was a practical expression of the dim view regarding prospects for world peace that Kissinger, on behalf of Rockefeller, articulated from at least the time he completed his Harvard doctoral thesis, *The Meaning of History*, according to Isaacson's biography.[30]

Eisenhower had warned America, without mentioning names, that the gravest threat to world security, democracy, and even spirituality, was the growing military–industrial complex directed by the Rockefeller family in partnership with IG Farben heirs. Kissinger became a leading proponent and propagandist for this unholy alliance and their globalistic intentions.

For more than ten years, Nelson Rockefeller's nuclear policy guru remained a well-paid Chase Bank consultant and Harvard faculty member. During that time, Kissinger continued writing numerous books and articles on subjects related to the practical application of his "realpolitik" in the nuclear and "Cold War" age. He also continued to provide favors and advice to White House dignitaries, and Rockefeller executives, until late 1968. After Nelson Rockefeller lost the Republican presidential nomination to Richard Nixon, Kissinger was appointed Nixon's chief of foreign policy and, as National Security Advisor, overseer of domestic and foreign intelligence by the FBI and CIA respectively.[29,30]

The National Security Council Job

During his 1968 Presidential campaign, Nixon became enamored with Kissinger's knowledge and loyalty. Kissinger had kept Nixon abreast of Vietnam War scuttlebutt within the Johnson camp for his campaign speeches and meetings with the press. In appreciation and respect for his powerful affiliations in the Rockefeller camp, Nixon rewarded him with the top position in national security.[30]

Fig. 16.6. *Harper's* Magazine Promotion, February 2001— "The Case Against Henry Kissinger: The Making of a War Criminal."

HARPER'S

MAGAZINE February 2001

ONLINE FEATURES
NEWSSTAND
READER SERVICES
ABOUT HARPER'S
CONTACT US
SUBSCRIBE

Photograph © Elliott Erwitt / Magnum Photos, Inc.

THIS MONTH IN HARPER'S MAGAZINE

THE CASE AGAINST HENRY KISSINGER
Part I: The making of a war criminal
by Christopher Hitchens

TABLE OF CONTENTS

WEEKLY REVIEW

January 30, 2001: Australian researchers, who were trying to use genetic engineering to sterilize mice, accidentally created a deadly, immune-system-destroying strain of the mousepox virus, a cousin of the human smallpox virus. Two biotechnology companies announced that they had sequenced the rice genome. Uganda's most recent outbreak of Ebola fever seemed to be over. Someone sent a letter filled with orange ...

The cover of *Harper's* magazine heralds the beginning of the end for the respected foreign policy diplomat Dr. Henry Kissinger. Curiously, and serendipitously, adjacent Kissinger's familiar forlorn face is a "weekly review" on the technology he politically and militarily helped to develop—the eugenic biological weapons race. The *Harper's* article covered Dr. Kissinger's Vietnam War and South American shenanigans, and said nothing about this even more heinous offense. In 1969, according to related Congressional testimonies by CIA directors Richard Helms and William Colby, Kissinger selected the military option to develop immune system ravaging "synthetic biological agents" like Ebola for germ warfare. He was also very interested in AIDS-like viruses for population control, particularly for Africa. Nixon's "War on Cancer" was largely inspired by Kissinger, on behalf of Rockefeller interests, and as a cover for the scientific race to develop more potent genocidal pathogens.

375

Nixon's aim in appointing Kissinger to be in charge of the National Security Council was to "run foreign policy from the White House."

As mentioned earlier, besides Kissinger, another candidate for the national security post, was Nixon intimate Roy Ash, the president of Litton Industries. Again, according to G. Edward Griffin, Rockefeller influence was heavily felt in directing Litton Industries.[9]

The realization that Roy Ash, Litton Industries, and Litton Bionetics, was part of a Rockefeller-led "good ole boy" network that included Henry Kissinger initially shocked me because of its implications concerning population control and the origin and initial transmission of HIV/AIDS.

According to testimonies by two previous CIA directors—Richard Helms and William Colby—it was Kissinger who must be credited for selecting the option to develop the exquisitely unique immune suppressive viruses that Litton Bionetics executives, including Robert Ting, John Landon, and NCI affiliate "Project Officer" Dr. Robert Gallo, had developed.[31] These viruses, Gallo later published, were closely related to HIV.

In other words, prior to 1978, with the first cases of AIDS appearing simultaneously and mysteriously in New York City and Central Africa, the unique leukemia–lymphoma–sarcoma cancer complex accompanied by opportunistic infections, was exclusively bioengineered only in cancer virus research labs. Chief among these were Litton's labs in Bethesda, Maryland and Northwest Uganda, associated with the Rockefeller-linked IARC. The NIH, another virtual Rockefeller proprietary, funded this "Special [i.e., Secret] Virus Cancer Program" beginning on February 12, 1962, after Merck Pharmaceutical Company vaccine officials realized they had just spread cancer viruses around the world in contaminated Salk and Sabin polio vaccines. Then in 1969, these types of viral agents were specifically requested by the military to serve as "synthetic biological agents" for germ warfare, and apparently population control, as docmented in figure 18.5.[32]

Ash had co-founded and directed the mega military weapons contractor from 1953 to 1972. In 1969, in lieu of having the National Security Council position go to Kissinger, Nixon appointed Ash to be Chairman of the President's Advisory Council on Executive Organizations, a post he held until 1971. Subsequently, Litton's principal was elevated to the rank of "Assistant to the President of the United States." He served the Nixon and Ford administrations in this capacity as well as directed the Office of Management and Budget for the White House until 1975.[33]

To the time of this writing, Ash's White House contemporary, Dr. Kissinger, has remained a leading advisor to Merck pharmaceutical company officials. Again, it was Merck's hepatitis B vaccine, partly prepared in Litton supplied contaminated chimpanzees, that is heavily implicated as the AIDS pandemic trigger.[7]

The CIA and Biochemical Warfare

As detailed in *Emerging Viruses: AIDS & Ebola—Nature, Accident or Intentional?*, from mid-1970 to mid-1973, the CIA operated without any interference from the Justice Department. Following the alleged assassination of FBI Director J. Edgar Hoover in 1972, the CIA grew in strength as the nucleus of foreign and domestic espionage operations. Despite the embarrassment of getting caught playing a central role in the infamous Watergate break-ins, the CIA, investigated by a Rockefeller chaired hearings committee, was hardly chastised by Congress.[34] Thereafter, it continued to expand agency operations at home and abroad under Kissinger by allegiance to Rockefeller.[35] These Nixon administration survivors, including Chief of Staff Alexander Haig, ran the CIA, State, and Defense departments. They reinstated COINTELPRO-like intelligence operations,[36] expanded CIA covert operations in Africa,[37] and increased biological as well as chemical weapons research, development, and testing.[38, 39]

In 1973, the CIA labored to maintain its positive public image. International condemnation over ongoing American biological warfare "experiments" was imminent. Anticipating this fallout, the Rockefeller Commission Investigation on CIA Wrongdoing began in the aftermath of Watergate. It was then that CIA director Richard Helms, succeeded shortly thereafter by William Colby, ordered Mr. Sidney Gottlieb, Chief of the CIA's Technical Services Division, and former head of its MKULTRA operation, to destroy all records pertaining to the "formulation, the development and the retention of" illegal biologicals that were used to wage wars and experiments on Third World populations. Helms's orders, he insinuated, came from his superior—Dr. Henry Kissinger.[40, 41]

By May 1973, in the wake of the Watergate scandal, as international attention focused on Nixon's fall from grace, a shadow government took control of America. The interim administration—which formed before President Ford was confirmed—was largely powered by Rockefeller, and commandeered by Kissinger and Alexander Haig.[41]

During the following presidential campaign, Zbigniew Brzezinski, Jimmy Carter's campaign manager and David Rockefeller's protégé, launched an embittered attack against the incumbent's foreign policy. Publishing in the CFR's *Foreign Affairs* he described Kissinger's tactics as:

> Covert, manipulative, and deceptive in style, it seemed committed to a largely static view of the world, based on a traditional balance of power, seeking accommodation among the major powers on the basis of spheres of influence.[42]

Cold and accurate as this criticism was, the irrefutable fact was that Kissinger, and by association, the Rockefellers' globalist cohorts at the CFR *including* Brzezinski, continued their genocidal activities.

While campaigning for the presidency, Jimmy Carter hailed Kissinger as the real "foreign policy . . . president of this country." "Under the Nixon–Ford administration," he said in a speech, "there has evolved a kind of secretive . . . closely guarded and amoral . . . , 'Lone Ranger' foreign policy, a one-man policy of international adventure." To these attacks, Carter added his standard refrain. "Our foreign policy should be as open and honest as the American people themselves."[42, 43]

One year later, under the more "open and honest" policies established by Carter, Brzezinski became National Security Advisor, and Joseph Califano became Secretary of the U.S. Department of Health, Education and Welfare (DHEW). Their more advanced genocidal policies are discussed in Chapter 18. Both men heavily supported Ray Ravenhott, the director of population control programs for USAID, who revealed his agency's intention to help sterilize one quarter of the world's women. He argued that this need stemmed from the administration's desire to protect U.S. corporate interests from the threat of Third World revolutions spawned by chronic unemployment.[38]

Today, thirty years later, with this sterilization goal having been achieved in the Third World, as well as in native Americans and urban dwelling Blacks, the political mischief, deceptions, and global genocide continues.

In this vein of U.S. Government sponsored genocide, in response to the same alleged "threat" of Third World revolutions and economic chaos, on April 30, 2000, the news media announced a National Security Agency (NSA) move to place AIDS science, and all public health agencies conducting it, under military intelligence command. The NSA and CIA were directed to oversee organizations such as the CDC, NCI, FDA, and National Institutes for Allergies and Infectious Diseases (NIAID). Curiously, this occurred directly following South African President's Thabo Mbeki's decision to include the testimonies of "dissident" scientists in a review of HIV/AIDS's origin, pathogenesis, and treatment. The National Intelligence Council (NIC) then advised President Clinton, to formally declare global AIDS a U.S. "national security threat."[44,45]

The CIA sponsored report warned, "The persistent infectious disease burden is likely to aggravate and, in some cases, may even provoke economic decay, social fragmentation, and political destabilization in the hardest hit countries. . . .

"The study defined 'instability,' as revolutionary wars, ethnic wars, genocides, and disruptive regime transitions. . . . Dramatic declines in life expectancy," the study said, is the strongest threat to national security simply because people revolt when they realize their lives are being genocidally threatened. Such "deterioration," intelligence analysts wrote, might be followed by only "limited improvement . . . owing to better prevention and control efforts, new drugs, and vaccines."[46]

The report posted many statistics reflective of this book's main hypothesis—that biochemical warfare is being conducted in the name of "public health" to covertly accomplish global genocide. For instance, the CIA summarized its intelligence on the "Number of 15-year-olds per 10,000 of that age group" who had "lost their mothers or both parents to AIDS." Uganda far surpassed other nations in this catastrophic parameter. Uganda, of course, was home to Litton Bionetics, the Rockefeller-linked IARC, the principle site of vaccine trials linked to the initial spread of HIV/AIDS, and at the time of this writing, more vaccine trials to allegedly combat the spread of HIV/AIDS. In essence, the CIA's AIDS report showed one victimized teenager out of every ten fell into this parentless group.[45]

According to U.S. Government watchdog groups and related policy analysts linked to JuriMed—a North American alternative medicine advocacy and legislative lobbying group—President Clinton's legislation empowered the CIA to act against scientific "dissidents" who raised concerns regarding the genocidal aspects of HIV/AIDS and related vaccination policies. As done in this book, such evidence might be considered a threat to U.S. National Security. The JuriMed communiqué heralded the likelihood of increased "mainstream [media] blackouts on AIDS dissident positions," and, as mentioned above, "global disease control" initiatives including "wide-ranging vaccination programs" becoming more coercive.[44] All business as usual for the Rockefeller directed military–medical–pharmaceutical cartel and propaganda mill.

References

1) Vergamo D. Who's teaching doctors? Drug firms sponsor required courses and see their sales rise. *USA Today*, Thursday, March 9, 2000, p. D1.

2) Starr P. *The Social Transformation of American Medicine: The rise of a sovereign profession and the making of a vast industry*. New York: Basic Books, Inc., 1982, pp. 338-341.

3) Simpson C. *The Science of Coercion*. London: Oxford University Press, 1996.

4) National Research Council. *Beyond Six Billion: Forecasting the World's Population*. Washington, D.C.: National Academy Press, 2000, p. iii.

5) Strickland S. *Politics, Science and Dread Disease: A Short History of United States Medical Research Policy*. Cambridge: Harvard University Press, 1958, pp. 1-14.

6) Lederman. R. Every child and senior to take West Nile vaccine. Published on the Internet at http://www.operair.org/alerts/artist/nyc.html. See also: http://baltech.org/lederman/spray.

7) Horowitz LG and Martin JW. *Emerging Viruses: AIDS & Ebola—Nature, Accident or Intentional?* Rockport, MA: Tetrahedron Press, 1998.

8) U.S. Department of Health, Education, and Welfare. Public Health Service, National Institutes of Health. The [Special] Virus Cancer Program. June, 1978. [Library call number: E20.3152:V81/977.] p. 118; For ATCC and Russian revelations see pp. 38-39 and 230.

9) Griffin E. *World Without Cancer*. Westlake Village, CA: American Media, 1997, pp. 235-236.

10) Mullins E. *Murder by Injection: The Story of the Medical Conspiracy Against America*. Staunton, VA: The National Council for Medical Research, 1995, pp. 73-101.

11) Starr, *Op. cit.* p. 340.

12) van Helsing J. *Secret Societies and Their Power in the 20th Century*, Gran Canaria, Spain: 1995, pp. 28-34; 39-40; for Bavarian Illuminati details see p.113; for Freemasonry in America see p. 120; for Clinton's life membership in the "Masonic Order of DeMolay" for boys see p.130; for Gary Allen's quote regarding Adam Weishaupt see p. 145; for Professor Quigley's quotes regarding Rhodes, The "Committee of 300," "The Round Table," and MI6 see pp. 145-147; for early "Brotherhood of the Snake" details see p. 374.

13) Loftus J and Aarons M. *The Secret War Against the Jews*. New York: St. Martin's Press, 1994, pp. 112-113, 142, 165; 168-169; for MI6 information see p. 182.

14) Quigley C. *Tragedy and Hope: A History of The World in Our Time*. New York: Macmillan Company, 1966, p. 952.

15) McLamb J. *Operation Vampire Killer 2000*. Phoenix, AZ: Police Against the New World Order, 1996, p. 16.

16) Goldwater B. *With No Apologies: The Personal and Political Memoirs of United States Senator Barry M. Goldwater*. New York: William Morrow and Company, Inc., 1979, pp. 278-279.

17) The Publishers. *What's Behind the New World Order?* Jemison, AL: Inspiration Books East, Inc., 1991. Backcover.

18) Brown RE. *Rockefeller Medicine Men: Capitalism and Medical Care in America*. Berkeley: University of California Press, 1979, pp. 3-4;119-30.

19) Borkin J. *The Crime and Punishment of I.G. Farben: The Unholy Alliance Between Hitler and the Great Chemical Combine*. New York: Barnes & Noble, 1997, pp. 131-133.

20) Kühl S. *The Nazi Connection: Eugenics, American Racism and German National Socialism*. New York: Oxford University Press, 1994, pp. 20-21; 165.

21) Eunjung Cha A. Minorities carry uneven burden in testing of vaccines: Tests in selected communities raise questions about ethics. *San Jose Mercury News*, Monday, December 20. 1999. p.1.

22) Coleman J. *Conspirator's Hierarchy: The Story of the Committee of 300*. Carson City, NV: American West Publishers, 1992, pp. 69-73.

23) Mullins E. *Op. cit.*, pp. 73-101.

24) Horowitz LG and Puleo J. *Healing Codes for the Biological Apocalypse*. Sandpoint, ID: Tetrahedron Publishing Group, 1999, pp. 125-180.

25) Keith J. *Mind Control World Control: The Encyclopedia of Mind Control*. Kempton, IL: Adventures Unlimited, 1997, pp. 264;267-269.

26) Kamen J. The $200 Billion Scam: Uncle Sam's Continuing Medical Genocide. *Penthouse Magazine*, September 1997, pp. 52-57.

27) Press release. Senate subcommittee counsel validates *Penthouse Magazine*'s accusation that a government agency deliberately sabotaged cancer drug tests. From the office of *Penthouse Magazine*'s Vice President, Al Freedman. Contact: 212-702-6000, ext. 1901.

28) The Council on Foreign Relations. Website description of organization. See: http://www.cfr.org/public/about.html

29) Kissinger H. Reflections on American diplomacy. *Foreign Affairs*, October, 1956.

30) Isaacson W. *Kissinger: A Biography*. New York: Simon & Schuster, 1992, pp. 90-93.

31) Horowitz and Martin, *Op. cit.*, pp. 299-301; 305-307; 358-362;

32) *Department of Defense Appropriations For 1970: Hearings Before A Sub-committee of the Committee on Appropriations House of Representatives, Ninety-first Congress, First Session, H.B. 15090, Part 5, Research, Development, Test and Evaluation, Dept. of the Army.* U.S. Government Printing Office, Washington, D.C., July 1, 1969, p. 129.

33) *Who's Who in America*, 49th Edition, Volume 1, A-K. New Providence, NJ., 1995, p. 123. Roy Ash's address for anyone wishing to write is: 1900 Avenue of the Stars, Suite 1600, Los Angeles, CA 90067-4407; Information on Alexander Meigs Haig, Jr. was found in the same publication on page, 1002.

34) Rockefeller NA, Connor JT, Dillon CD, Griswold EN, Reagan R, and Kirkland, *et al. CIA's Relation to Events Preceding the Watergate Break-in. Report to the President by the Commission on CIA Activities Within the United States.* New York: The Rockefeller Commission, 1975, pp. 193-197; 451.

35) Isaacson, *Op. cit.*, p. 491-495

36) Schaap B. Administration stonewalls while covert operations escalate. *Covert Action Information Bulletin* 1982;16:31

37) Agee P. The range of covert intervention. In: *Dirty Work-2: The CIA in Africa.* Secaucus, Ray E, Schaap W, Van Meter K and Wolf L eds. Secaucus, NJ: Lyle Stewart, Inc., 1979, pp. 47-49.

38) Lederer R. Precedents for AIDS? Chemical-biological warfare, medical experiments, and population control. *CovertAction Information Bulletin* 1987;28:33-42.

39) *Policy. Cong. Sess. 93-2, May 1-14, 1974*; *U.S. Senate Committee on Foreign Relations. Prohibition of Chemical and Biological Weapons: Hearing to Consider Definition and Ratification of Geneva Protocol. December 10, 1974*, Cong. Sess. 93-2. The hearings indicated that two years after Nixon allegedly forbade the development of chemical and biological weapons arsenals, additional ones were being produced and stockpiles had not been destroyed.

40) *U.S. Select Senate Committee to Study Governmental Operations with Respect to Intelligence Activities. Intelligence Activities. Senate Resolution 21. Vol. 1: Unauthorized Storage of Toxic Agents. September 16-18, 1975.* Cong. Sess. 94-1, pp 22-23.

41) Isaacson, *Op. cit.*, pp. 530-531; 491-495; 389.

42) *Ibid.* pp. 699-701.

43) Jimmy Carter speech, the Foreign Policy Association, Oct. 3, 1976.

44) Bolen T. AIDS dissidents now a threat to US National Security: An analysis of implications based on a CIA report circulated by the *Washington Post*. For

more information contact: http://www.aidsmyth.com/news/. To contact JuriMed e-mail:jurimed@yahoo.com.

45) Gellman B. AIDS is declared threat to security. *Washington Post* Online, Sunday, April 30, 2000; p. AO1. (See:

http://www.washingtonpost.com/wp-dyn/articles/A40503-2000Apr29.html)

46) National Intelligence Council staff. The Global Infectious Disease Threat and Its Implications for the United States. "[P]roduced under the auspicies of David F. Gordon, National Intelligence Officer for Economics and Global Is-sues," Lt. Col. (Dr.) Don Noah of the Armed Forces Medical Intelligence Center and George Fidas of the National Intelligence Council, chaired and submitted by John C. Gannon. NIE 99-17D, January 2000, pp. 4, 27, 29-30. (See: http://www.cia.gov/cia/publications/nie/report/nie99-17d.html) See also: Picard A. HIV deniers should be jailed: Head of AIDS body slams fringe movement. *Globe and Mail*, Monday, May 1, 2000.

Chapter 17.
Breaking Code 6
and the Heart of the Beast

"Power will gravitate into the hands of those who control information. . . . This will encourage tendencies
through the next several decades toward a technotronic
era, a dictatorship, leaving even less room for political
procedures as we know them. . . . Finally, looking ahead
to the end of the century, the possibility of biochemical
mind control, and genetic tinkering with man, including
beings which will function like men and reason like
them as well, could give rise to some difficult questions."

Zbigniew Brzezinski
National Security Advisor, Carter Administration,
from his book *The Technotronic Era*

According to biographers, Kaiser Wilhelm II of Germany was
widely known for his "saber rattling" and perceived war monger-
ing. He was crowned Emperor in 1888 and died in 1941. King
Frederick III of Prussia was his father, and Queen Victoria of Britain
was his grandmother. King Edward VII of England was his uncle, and
King George V, his cousin. He was born genetically handicapped with
a withered left arm, and quickly developed, "a military lifestyle. He
loved his numerous uniforms and surrounding himself with the elite of
German military society."[1] Thus, the German, Prussian, British, military, and even genetic roots of the Kaiser name foreshadowed what this
chapter reveals concerning the diversified Kaiser Industries.

In Dr. John Coleman's expertly documented, highly detailed, and
often cited book, *Conspirator's Hierarchy: The Story of the Committee
of 300*, Kaiser Industries was linked to the Stanford Research Institute
(SRI) which was founded by the Tavistock Institute for Human Relations immediately following WWII. SRI's initial purpose involved
public relations campaigning and administration on behalf of the Committee of 300 and Queen Elizabeth II's ARCO Oil Company which
desired to develop the Royal Family's Alaskan oil fields with the help

of Club of Rome member and international diplomat Robert O. Anderson who started the Aspen Institute think tank.[2] As documented previously, HAARP was constructed by ARCO and was linked to its European counterpart EISCAT, whose website text was copyrighted by Cold Spring Harbor (eugenics) Labs in New York, intricately tied to the Rockefeller Foundation, cancer industry, and "Human Genome Project."[3]

Dr. Coleman explained that by 1970, the Alaskan legislature had accepted SRI's plan to process and deliver Alaskan oil. The SRI grew from here to employ approximately 4,000 people with an operating budget of $160 million annually applied to social science research, primarily for public persuasion. Charles A. Anderson, the President of SRI, was linked through the scientific literature and the Tavistock Institute to Dr. Kurt Lewin—founder of the Harvard Psychological Clinic and the Institute for Social Research. According to Dr. Coleman, these three organizations have, more than any other, most profoundly affected the way in which Americans think, feel, and behave.[2]

"Although not on the Federal Contract Research Center lists, the SRI is today the largest military think tank, dwarfing Hudson and [the] Rand Corporation," Dr. Coleman wrote. Related to this book's main hypotheses, among "SRI's specialty departments are chemical and biological warfare centers" involved in human experimentation.

Dr. Coleman continued, "One of Stanford's more dangerous activities is counter-insurgency operations aimed at civilian populations—just the sort of '1984' things government is already using against its own people. The U.S. Government pays SRI millions of dollars each year for this kind of highly controversial 'research.' Following student protests against chemical warfare experiments conducted at Stanford, SRI 'sold' itself to a private group for just $25 million." Nothing really changed, Dr. Coleman submitted. The "SRI was still a Tavistock project and the Committee of 300 still owned it, but the gullible appeared to be satisfied by this meaningless cosmetic change."[2]

By the 1980s, Dr. Coleman recorded, Kaiser Industries was "among the TOP Committee of 300 companies" to partake in the RMA—Revolution in Military Affairs—discussed earlier. The SRI was at the forefront of engineering the RMA. "60% of SRI's contracts were devoted to 'futurism' with both military and civilian applications," Coleman wrote. "Its major clients were the U.S. Department of Defense–Directorate of Defense Research and Engineering [and its related Defense Advanced Research Products Agency (DARPA)], Office of Aerospace Research which dealt with 'Applications of the Behavioral Sciences to Research Management,' the Executive Office of the President, the Office of Science and Technology, the U.S. Department of Health. . . , the U.S. Department of Energy, the U.S. Department of Labor, the U.S. Department of Transportation, and the National Science Foundation (NSF)."

A significant document developed by the SRI for the NSF was discovered by Dr. Coleman, an intelligence agent with MI6. It was titled the "Assessment of Future and International Problems," and has direct relevance to the issues raised here.

SRI, with direction from the Tavistock Institute in London, assembled what Dr. Coleman called a "far reaching and chilling system"—the "Business Intelligence Program," in which Kaiser Industries was a "TOP" investor. From this program, Kaiser's companies, products, services, and affiliates gained the intelligence, motivation, and political support to develop the nefarious medical/biochemical/psychosocial operations befitting a conspiracy to commit global genocide. Included here is the use of advanced psychotronic methods and materials for optimal population control.[2]

Kaiser Industries and Psychotronic Eugenics

The "CHANGING IMAGES OF MAN" was "the most sinister of all SRI programs," according to Dr. Coleman, and his advisory appears to be accurate. A 1974 SRI "Contract Number URH (489)-2150 Policy Research Report Number 4/4/74," prepared by the Center for the Study of Social Policy, directed by Willis Harmon, "was one of the most far-reaching investigations into how man might be changed that has ever been conducted." Dr. Coleman credited this work for "doing tremendous damage in altering the direction" of American life and culture—"socially, morally, and religiously."

The report was instigated by Stanford's Charles F. Kettering Foundation—founded by Charles Kettering, the wealthy inventor of automobile essentials who joined Alfred P. Sloan, the president of the British royal family owned General Motors Corporation, and director of the Rothschild family controlled J.P. Morgan Bank, to form the Rockefeller controlled Sloan-Kettering Memorial Cancer Center. This circumstantially linked the Kaiser medical leadership to the Rockefeller directed cancer industry and the European oligarchy.

The Kettering Report was written by 14 "new-science scientists" supervised by Tavistock officials and 23 of the world's most esteemed social-psychologists and behavioral scientists that Dr. Coleman preferred to call "top controllers." The assemblage boasted Kurt K. Lewin, B.F. Skinner, Professor Hadley Cantril, Ervin Lazlo, Margaret Meade, Professor Derwin Cartwright, John Rawlings Reese, and Sir Geoffrey Vickers—a high-level British intelligence officer who, like Coleman, worked for MI6. "It will be recalled that his son-in-law, Sir Peter Vickers Hall, was a founding member of the so-called conservative 'Heritage Foundation,'" Dr. Coleman wrote. In 2000, The Heritage Foundation was commissioned by the Clinton Administration to develop the definitive report on the alleged necessity to "Revitalize space-based defense programs," that is, the Star-Wars program. This was featured on the Foundation's website.[4] "During the Second World War, there were over 100 researchers at work under the direction of Kurt Lewin, copying slavishly the methods adopted by Reinhard Heydrich of the SS that are linked to the modern Star-Wars program and to Kaiser Industries as you will soon read.

"The OSS," Coleman recalled, "was based on Heydrich's methodology and, as we know, the OSS was the forerunner of the Central Intelligence Agency." His point in detailing these relationships was to inform readers that by 1946, "the governments of Britain and the United States already had the machinery in place to bring us into line in a New World Order with only a slight modicum of resistance materializing." Each passing year, meanwhile, "has added new refinements."[2]

Following a lengthy review of this nation's psychosocial decline, Dr. Coleman concluded that this degradation was the apparent result of the massive social engineering efforts directed by these organizations against American citizens, primarily through the mass media. "America today can be compared with a soldier who falls asleep in the thick of battle," he argued. The general public's apathy regarding virtually anything substantive, an outcome of implementing Harmon's directives in "THE CHANGING IMAGES OF MANKIND," might be likened to sensory overload. What has occurred is a cultural and neurochemical shell-shocking into cognitive dissonance and chronic somatopsychosis. American behavior has been intentionally directed to, at best, approach political reality. Pain and pleasure motives have been effectively manipulated by these social engineers to direct the masses. All of this being done insideously as a designed outcome of the Committee of 300/SRI-directed cultural revolution.

The global elite's technical term for this, Dr. Coleman revealed, is "long range penetration strain." The art and science of directing large populations into ongoing "long range penetration strain," was pioneered by Dr. Lewin and perfected by the Tavistock Institute of Human Relations, the SRI, and the Rand Corporation whose scientists collaborated with "at least another 150 research institutions here in the U.S."[2]

Dr. Coleman summarized his view of the outcome of this cultural engineering and population management this way:

> This fiendish warfare has caused the average American . . . to fret over various conspiracy theories, leaving him/her with a feeling of uncertainty and insecurity, isolated and perhaps even afraid, as he searches, but fails to understand the decay and rot caused by "THE CHANGING IMAGES OF MANKIND," unable to identify or combat the social, moral, economic and political changes he/she deems undesirable and does not want, yet which increase in intensity on every hand.[2]

Returning to the Kettering and Kaiser connections to eugenically oriented psychotronic non-lethal warfare, Dr. Coleman revealed that in 1958, "a startling new development arose." DARPA requested the SRI direct a top secret program. In the words of Pentagon director John Foster, the SRI was to develop a proposal to insure America against "technological surprise." Foster requisitioned a weapon that used the environment for "technotronic warfare." The technology was planned, as discussed in Chapters 12 and 15, in Dr. Coleman's words, "to trigger volcanos and/or earthquakes." This was linked to "behavioral research on potential enemies and *minerals and metals* with potential for new weapons. The project was accepted by SRI and code-named 'SHAKY'." [Emphasis added due to the importance of certain minerals and metals discussed previously and below. See figure 17.4.]

SHAKY was to fulfill Committee of 300 member Zbigniew Brzezinski's vision described in *The Technotronic Era* in which he wrote about the materials and methods predicted to control the United States and its people. His book was commissioned by the Club of Rome. Moving into "an era unlike any of its predecessors," Brzezinski wrote, by the late 1970s, we were engaging "a technotronic era that could easily become a dictatorship." Besides heralding cloning and "robotoids," that is, people who acted like humans but were not, society was to become desensitized "in an information revolution based on amusement focus, spectator spectacles (saturation coverage by television of sporting events) which provide an opiate for an increasingly purposeless mass." A good example of this was the emergence of the heavily promoted XFL football league in 2001, with its focus on sexuality, crude language, and brutal contact. Another example is presented below—Ian Fleming's "James Bond" films.

Dr. Coleman reflected that Brzezinski's prose was not original, but merely recanted from "the Committee of 300's blueprint given to the Club of Rome for execution." In addition to the above, the execution order called for, in Coleman's words, the promotion of "unbridled sexual lusts, rock music, and a whole new generation of drug addicts . . . to distract people from what was happening all around them."[2]

Considering Brzezinski's prophetic vision, population management under "One World Government" was predicted to vastly increase "social and political control over the individual. . . . It will soon be possible to assert almost continuous control over every citizen," he wrote, "and to maintain up-to-date files, containing even the most personal details about health and personal behavior of every citizen in addition to the more customary data."[2]

> These files will be subject to instantaneous retrieval by the authorities. Power will gravitate into the hands of those who control information. Our existing institutions will be supplanted by pre-crisis management institutions, the task of which will be to identify in advance likely social crises and to develop programs to cope with them.[2]

Dr. Coleman added that this paragraph forecast the development and function of FEMA, as mentioned in Chapter 15. It also largely explains the function of the CDC, particularly concerning recurring threats of outbreaks and remedial measures such as the pesticide spraying programs conducted in the name of public health.

At the time Brzezinski wrote this, as well as the revealing quote that introduced this chapter, as President Carter's National Security Advisor, he was also penning National Security Memorandum–46 which secretly declared war on African and American Blacks. This document is considered in the next chapter insofar as population control issues are concerned.

Kaiser Aluminum, Maxxam Medical, and Psychotronics

Thus, these seemingly dissociated elements may be tied together, namely: Kaiser's diversified activities that fit perfectly with Brzezinski's "Technotronic Era" and psychotronic eugenics, and the SRI directives for the Committee of 300's "Business Intelligence Program."

The Kaiser Aluminum Corporation (KAC) of Houston, TX, and its wholly owned subsidiary, Kaiser Aluminum & Chemical Corporation (KACC) operated in "all principal aspects of the aluminum industry," according to their company profile, including the international supply of bauxite—earthy hydrous *aluminum oxides*.[5] This was most interesting for four reasons as detailed earlier: 1) William Thomas's discovery of the Hughes Aircraft patent promoting aluminum oxide usage for atmospheric spraying devices to help facilitate "weather modification" and likely Project HAARP as well; 2) William Winkler's report of extraordinarily high levels of seawater aluminum theoretically linked to numerous cases of neurotoxicity and even synthetic "jellyfish" with chemical absorbent properties; 3) the routine use of aluminum derivatives in vaccines which, like the mercury (thimerosal) compound (removed from the market in 2000), is a neurotoxin and immune suppressor; and 4) the company's location in, of all places, Houston, Texas, also home to TANOX Biomedical Systems with its links to the powerful Bush and Baker families, vaccine studies, and mycoplasma investigations preceding the emergence of Mycoplasma-linked Gulf War Syndrome and AIDS.

KAC and KACC, the Internet revealed, were reorganized in 1987, and then again in December of 2000 due to "bankruptcy" as "a subsidiary of MAXXAM, Inc." MAXXAM, Inc., Yahoo Finance Market Guide[6] reported, "is a company that conducts substantially all of its operations through its subsidiaries." In other words, it's a "front" company, such as those traditionally used by the Rockefeller–Farben petrochemical and pharmaceutical cartel to skirt antitrust and inside trading laws as explained by G. Edward Griffin.[7]

Besides maintaining MAXXAM Medical group businesses, the company operated in four principal RMA industries: 1) aluminum through majority owned KAC and KACC which controlled Kaiser Electro-optics, Inc., a Rockwell–Collins company largely dealing with microscopic and telescopic "applications in medicine, aerospace and defense,"[8] In this regard, a descriptive list of Kaiser subsidiaries and

Figure 17.1. Kaiser Aluminum and MAXXAM, Inc. Related Aerospace Companies and Technologies

Rockwell Collins   http://www.collins.rockwell.com
Kaiser Aerospace and Electronics http:/www.kaiseraerospace.com
Kaiser Electronics: Cockpit Display Systems, Head-up,
    Head-down, Helmet   http://www.kaiserelectronics.com
Kaiser Electro-Optics: Head-up, Helmet and
    Virtual Reality Displays   http://www.keo.com
Kaiser Electroprecision: Aircraft
    and Missile Products   http://www.kaiserep.com
Kaiser Fluid Technologies: Aircraft and Jet Engine Valves
    and Controls   http://www.kaiseraerospace.com
Polhemus: 3D Position Sensors
    and Trackers   http://www.polhemus.com
Vision Systems International: Military
    Helmet Mounted Displays   http://www.kaiseraerospace.com

List of Kaiser Aluminum, Electro-Optics, Inc., and Rockwell–Collins Company subsidiaries whose products largely fit the "technotronic era" of non-lethal population control. All the above are wholly owned by MAXXAM, Inc.—an apparent "front" for administering "Business Intelligence Program" operations advanced by the Stanford Research Institute think tank. From: http://www.kosi.com/main/coprofile/index.html

their websites is seen in figure 17.1. A definitive correlation was found between the Star Wars and psychotronic non-lethal weapons systems discussed earlier and Kaiser subsidiary developments including the surveillance and aerosol spraying technologies described in previous chapters. These were required for the RMA and electromagnetic projects to facilitate non-lethal warfare against both military and civilian populations and for population control; 2) Forestry products through MAXXAM Group Inc.'s wholly owned subsidiary, The Pacific Lumber Company and Britt Lumber Co., Inc., engaged in the controversial Headwaters Timberlands operation; 3) Real estate investments and developments, and 4) Horse racing operations, "including a Class 1 thoroughbred and quarter horse racing facility located in the greater Houston metropolitan area."[6]

James Bond, "A View to a Kill," and MAXXAM, Inc.

For those who might argue that these details approximate fictional cinema more than reality, the MAXXAM/Kaiser company description read so much like the James Bond Hollywood thriller, *A View to a Kill*, that I decided to screen the video again and take notes.

First, it should be recalled that James Bond's character was invented by Ian Fleming, born in 1908 into a wealthy Scottish *banking* family. Thus, according to biographer John Cork, "Ian Lancaster Fleming grew up the member of a rare class of Englishmen for whom all options are open. . . . Ian's father was a service-oriented land-owner in Oxfordshire and a member of Parliament." By 1939, following a brief career in journalism as a Reuters reporter, it appeared that "Fleming had become bored. . . . During his Reuters days, [he] had made friends in the Foreign Office, and maintained them even as a banker. In 1939, Fleming oddly took on an assignment for the *[London] Times* to return to the Soviet Union to report on a trade mission. It appears that Fleming, in fact, was all the time spying for the Foreign Office." By "May of 1939, Fleming started a more formal attachment to the intelligence service, working with Naval Intelligence." Soon, he became a full-time assistant to the director, . . . and later Commander. *Fleming became the right-hand man to one of Britain's top spymasters, Admiral John Godfrey.*"[9] [Emphasis added here and below.]

"The war was good to Fleming," continued Cork, "tapping his imagination, forcing him to work within discipline. Fleming schemed, plotted, and carried out dangerous missions. From the famous *Room*

39 in the Admiralty building in London's Whitehall, Fleming tossed out a myriad of off-beat ideas on how to confuse, survey, and enrage the Germans." Later his works would do the same globally.

Biographer Cork emphasized the "Fleming flair" that "proved to be his greatest strength in Naval Intelligence. . . . Yet, Fleming understood the business side of the war. . . . As assistant to Admiral Godfrey, Fleming wrote countless memos and reports. His style and elegant arguments, plus his seemingly limitless knowledge of his subjects made the usual dry missives a pleasure to read. Eventually, Fleming wrote memos to William "Wild Bill" Donovan on how to set up the OSS, apparently based on intelligence provided by Tavistock officials in *The Kettering Report.* For that bit of work, Fleming received a revolver engraved with the CIA director's thanks: "For Special Services."[9]

So Fleming was actually instrumental, along with Germany's Reinhard Heydrich, in helping to establish the OSS and CIA.

Thus, the truth about James Bond films is that they are indeed based on extensive accurate intelligence with names changed to protect "the business side of war." As entertaining propaganda, they provide a perfect venue for PSYOPs and population control C2W.

In the Hollywood movie "*A View to a Kill*" the film depicts virtually every major element discussed above. A eugenically engineered psychopathic humanoid named "MAX," the President of the "ZORIN Corporation," determined to establish a global cartel for the manufacture of *very special microchips.* Unlike normal silicone microchips that were susceptible to destruction by Star Wars weaponry, these innovations were electromagnetic radiation resistant. The KGB, MI6 and CIA wanted them. Together with his father, an ex-Nazi neuroendocrinologist, MAX dabbled in breeding "Class 1 thoroughbreds" from inferior stocks. Besides controlling government officials as desired, his ultimate plan included violating the environment as needed, including a nuclear strike on a fault line in Silicon Valley to accomplish his global Star Wars industry takeover.

Busting Code 6 and the Cryptocracy

Readers are advised to take note of the double "XX" at the center of MAXXAM, Inc.'s name as if to doubly reinforce that "'X' marks the spot." Likewise, the symbol for "adult entertainment"—"XXX"— and the sex and violence oriented XFL both contain three "Xs." With the XFL, two "Xs" were always seen in its logo, and a third "X" was always simultaneously seen in the station identification marker on the upper right corner of every television screen. The generally unrecognized code is commonly found highlighting the Rockefeller-directed EXXON company's logo as well.

As explained below, these symbols are numerologically encoded. A select few have been decoded here to reveal definitive, statistically significant, links between these companies and the sinister administration of modern forms of eugenics, population control, and technotronic warfare. Herein, the decoding methods advanced by Dr. Joseph Puleo in *Healing Codes for the Biological Apocalypse* were useful, but rather than the standard Pythagorean system as shown in figure 17.2, the multiples of 6, as shown in figure 17.3, appear to be most pertinent to exposing this global "beast."[3]

Quickly summarized, using Pythagorean mathematics, as the mystery schools have done for millennia, Dr. Puleo identified Bible codes used by Masonic globalists to obscure sacred knowledge, keeping it hidden from anyone not aware of the concealed codes. As discussed previously regarding Nikola Tesla's work in quantum physics and electromagnetism, the energy dynamics of the "3s, 6s, and 9s" were found to hold special energy and spiritual significance to the holders of this sacred arcana. Given this knowledge, by using the Pythagorean 1–9, 1–9, 1–8 numbering system and equivalents for the 26 letters of the English alphabet, as seen in figure 17.2, I was able to determine the origin, and largely the meaning, of the British Secret Service's alphanumeric code "MI6." It was apparent that England's "Military Intelligence" brand—MI6—derived from the Latin words's "MI-ra gestorum," meaning "MIracle" in English. Numerologically, mathematically and metaphysically, it derived from the third note of the ancient musical scale whose frequency was "528," and whose tone was MIddle "C." Stunningly, that precise frequency has been routinely used by leading military weapons contractors and world renowned genetic biochemists. Weapons engineers typically use that frequency and pitch to tune sophisticated military hardware. Geneticists use the same frequency to repair damaged DNA. These associations linking the military orientation of MI6 to its chief objective—to facilitate British colonialism and, when needed, eugenics—are definitive.[3]

The number "6" in MI6 was derived by determining the sum of the added numbers in "528," that is, 5+2+8=15, and again, 1+5=6, as was routinely done in the Pythagorean mystery schools. The number 6, central to the "3s, 6s, and 9s" power, has special significance in the fields of theology, metaphysics, alchemy, the occult, Islam, traditional Judeo-Christian religions, water science, organic chemistry, genetics, and medical science in general. It is no random "coincidence," for instance, that God took 6 days to create the universe, that organic molecules are all based on six-sided hexagonal carbon rings, and that the majority of clustered water rings forming the supportive electromagnetic frequency conducting matrix of DNA necessary for cellular "upregulation" of metabolic functions are 6 sided like the "Star-of-David" more accurately termed "Solomon's seal." This sacred geometric form, to this day, is renowned as an amulet associated with protective qualities that, according to *Webster's Dictionary*, are preventive against infectious diseases.[3,10]

Additional genetic research in this area of bioelectric science, as it relates to Atomic Energy Commission and population control objectives, is discussed in the final chapter of this book.

As shown in figures 17.3, and 17.4, the column of multiples of 6 provides the Pythagorean sequence of "6, 3, 9" and the base-ten 26 letter alphanumeric sequence shown (i.e., 6, 12, 18, 24, etc., etc.). These sequences include the codes most frequently used by the Illuminati or highest level secret society leaders. Using this knowledge for code-breaking, the word MAXXAM decodes for the number 15 or 1+5=6, as does the trade name EXXON. The alpha-numeric translation of EXXON using the Pythagorean single digit (1–9) sequence results in "5-6-6-6-5" wherein the "666" appears in the middle. The letter "X" in this Pythagorean skein also equals 6.

Relatedly, one of the chapters in Zbigniew Brzezinski's book, *The Technotronic Era*, described how new technologies were expected to strain social and nation-state accords. Further regarding "666," Dr. Coleman argued convincingly that "we are already under intense strains through surveillance" largely due to this designated name for a super computer housed in NATO headquarters in Brussels, Belgium. Here data storage and retrieval for earth's burgeoning population is 666's primary function. For instance, data retrieval "will be simple" in countries like America where social security numbers and/or drivers' license numbers are preassigned, Dr. Coleman predicted based on documents he examined while working for MI6. These files, he learned, "could simply be added" to the 666 computer "to provide the surveillance recording announced by Brzezinski and his Committee of 300 colleagues. The Committee already in 1981 warned governments, including the government of the USSR, that there 'will be chaos unless the Committee of 300 takes complete control of preparations for the New World Order. CONTROL WILL BE EXERCISED THROUGH

Fig. 17.2. Pythagorean Alpha-Numeric Code Chart

Letter & Number	Pythagorean Skein Equivalent	Sample Word Number Derivations
A 1	1⌐	E 5–5 + 0 = 5
B 2	2	X 24–2 + 4 = 6
C 3	3	X 24–2 + 4 = 6
D 4	4 ⌐1	O 15–1 + 5 = 6
E 5	5	N 14–1 + 4 = 5
F 6	6 9	82=1 82=1
G 7	7	
H 8	8	M 13–1 + 3 = 4 ⟍5
I 9	9⌐	A 1–1 + 0 = 1
J 10	1 + 0 = 1⌐	X 24–2 + 4 = 6
K 11	1 + 1 = 2	X 24–2 + 4 = 6
L 12	1 + 2 = 3	A 1–1 + 0 = 1 ⟍5
M 13	1 + 3 = 4 ⌐1	M 13–1 + 3 = 4
N 14	1 + 4 = 5	76=4 22=4
O 15	1 + 5 = 6 9	
P 16	1 + 6 = 7	X 24–2 + 4 = 6
Q 17	1 + 7 = 8	X 24–2 + 4 = 6
R 18	1 + 8 = 9⌐	X 24–2 + 4 = 6
S 19	1 + 9 = 10	72=9 18=9
T 20	2 + 0 = 2	
U 21	2 + 1 = 3 ⌐1	X 24–2 + 4 = 6
V 22	2 + 2 = 4	F 6–6 + 0 = 6
W 23	2 + 3 = 5 8	L 12–1 + 2 = 3
X 24	2 + 4 = 6	42=6 15=6
Y 25	2 + 5 = 7	The number 8
Z **26**	2 + 6 = **8**⌐	represents infinity.
		9 represents
		<u>completion</u>

The English alphabet and its equivalent numbers. Two or more digit numbers are reduced to single digit numbers to employ the Pythagorean skein. Thus, the numbers one through nine repeat. The number nine (9) represents completion. Using this system, "666" is found at the center of EXXON between 5s. Similarly, "66" lies at the heart of MAXXAM between 5s. Adapted from: Horowitz L and Puleo J. *Op. cit.*, 1999, p.28.

Fig. 17.3. Columns Showing Multiples of Three (3), Six (6), and Nine (9) Using the Pythagorean Skein

	Multiples of 3	Multiples of 6	Multiples of 9
A 1	1 X 3 = 3	1 X 6 = 6	1 X 9 = 9
B 2	2 X 3 = 6	2 X 6 = 12 – 3	2 X 9 = 18 – 9
C 3	3 X 3 = 9	3 X 6 = 18 – 9	3 X 9 = 27 – 9
D 4	4 X 3 = 12 – 3	4 X 6 = 24 – 6	4 X 9 = 36 – 9
E 5	5 X 3 = 15 – 6	5 X 6 = 30 – 3	5 X 9 = 45 – 9
F 6	6 X 3 = 18 – 9	6 X 6 = 36 – 9	6 X 9 = 54 – 9
G 7	7 X 3 = 21 – 3	7 X 6 = 42 – 6	7 X 9 = 63 – 9
H 8	8 X 3 = 24 – 6	8 X 6 = 48 – 3	8 X 9 = 72 – 9
I 9	9 X 3 = 27 – 9	9 X 6 = 54 – 9	9 X 9 = 81 – 9
J 1	10X3 = 30 – 3	10X6 = 60 – 6	10X9 = 90 – 9
K 2	11X3 = 33 – 6	11X6 = 66 – 3	11X9 = 99 – 9
L 3	12X3 = 36 – 9	12X6 = 72 – 9	12X9 = 108 – 9
M 4	13X3 = 39 – 3	13X6 = 78 – 6	13X9 = 117 – 9
N 5	14X3 = 42 – 6	14X6 = 84 – 3	14X9 = 126 – 9
O 6	15X3 = 45 – 9	15X6 = 90 – 9	15X9 = 135 – 9
P 7	16X3 = 48 – 3	16X6 = 96 – 6	16X9 = 144 – 9
Q 8	17X3 = 51 – 6	17X6 = 102 – 3	17X9 = 153 – 9
R 9	18X3 = 54 – 9	18X6 = 108 – 9	18X9 = 162 – 9
S 1	19X3 = 57 – 3	19X6 = 114 – 6	19X9 = 171 – 9
T 2	20X3 = 60 – 6	20X6 = 120 – 3	20X9 = 180 – 9
U 3	21X3 = 63 – 9	21X6 = 126 – 9	21X9 = 189 – 9
V 4	22X3 = 66 – 3	22X6 = 132 – 6	22X9 = 198 – 9
W 5	23X3 = 69 – 6	23X6 = 138 – 3	23X9 = 207 – 9
X 6	24X3 = 72 – 9	24X6 = 144 – 9	24X9 = 216 – 9
Y 7	25X3 = 75 – 3	25X6 = 150 – 6	25X9 = 225 – 9
Z 8	26X3 = 78 – 6	26X6 = 156 – 3	26X9 = 234 – 9
126 = 9	153 = 9	153 = 9	234 = 9

Columns show the numbers resulting from multiples of three, six and nine using the Pythagorean skein. Notice the resulting single digit numbers repeat forming patterns such as "6, 3, and 9" for the 6s column. Multiples of nine, the highest integer in the Pythagorean skein, consistently produces a "9"—completion. British intelligence, MI6, and globalists consistently use Pythagorean alphanumeric codes, particularly the multiples of 6. For instance, the RIAA (Royal Institute for International Affairs) code number is 6 (108+54+54+6=222=6) The code "666" or 6x6x6=18=9 or completion. From: Horowitz and Puleo, *Op. cit.*, 1999, p. 39.

Fig. 17.4. The Globalists' Alpha-Numeric Code

Multiples of 6	Sample Word Number Derivations		
A 1 X 6 = 6	E 30	K 66	
B 2 X 6 = 1 2	X 144	I 54	
C 3 X 6 = 1 8	X 144	S 114	
D 4 X 6 = 2 4	O 90	S 114	
E 5 X 6 = 3 0	N 84	I 54	
F 6 X 6 = 3 6	492=15=6	N 84	
G 7 X 6 = 4 2		G 42	
H 8 X 6 = 4 8		E 30	
I 9 X 6 = 5 4	M 78	R 108	
J 10X6=60	A 6	666=18=9	
K 11X6=66	X 144		
L 12X6=72	X 144	V 132	
M 13X6=78	A 6	A 6	
N 14X6=84	M 78	C 18	
O 15X6=90	456=15=6	C 18	
P 16X6=96		I 54	
Q 17X6=102		N 84	
R 18X6=108	S 114	A 6	
S 19X6=114	H 48	T 120	
T 20X6=120	A 6	I 54	
U 21X6=126	K 66	O 90	
V 22X6=132	Y 150	N 84	
W 23X6=138	384=15=6	666=18=9	
X 24X6=144		N 84	
Y 25X6=150		V 132	
Z 26X6=156		I 54	
		C 18	
		288=18=9	

Table shows the English alphabet and its equivalent numbers, and a related column listing the sums of the multiples of 6. The number 6 is central to Nikola Tesla's scientific discoveries and secret society coding methods. Some examples are provided above. These numbers and Tesla's technology, relate to creative spiritual forces explained by quantum physics. The above names are sociopolitically, mathematically, and statistically related. The number 666 in Bible prophecy relates to "mark of the beast," the name of a human global controller, and the "great tribulation" associated with massive deception, plagues, and death delivered largely by vaccination and its proponents. Adapted from: Horowitz and Puleo. *Op. cit.*, 1999.

OUR COMMITTEE AND THROUGH GLOBAL PLANNING AND CRISIS MANAGEMENT.'"[2] [Emphasis not added.]

In effect, the above details indicate that the British Secret Service's name obviously derived from forethought of this knowledge in mystery school metaphysics, electromagnetism, and genetics. More telling, it also substantiated MI6's mission centered on technotronics, psychotronics, and eugenics.

The Codes in Bible Prophecy

These codes also relate to scripture and Bible prophecy. The "XX" code in EXXON and MAXXAM, in fact, elucidates the final Bible prophecy regarding "666" and the number "144." In Revelation 13.18 and 14.1, these numbers are associated with spiritually resolving a Babylonian Old World of chaos to initiate a Divine New World Order. As seen in figure 17.4, X=144, where 1+4+4=9. Likewise, 2xX=288 where 2+8+8=18=1+8=9. Also, the number 666, where 3x6=18, similarly resolves to: 1+8=9. The number 9, as seen in figures 17.2 through 17.4, is reflective of completion, resolution, and/or finality.

Furthermore, the frequency "666" in Revelation (13:18) is "the mark of the beast," and the frequency "144" in Revelation's next verse (14:1) reflects the Famuli tuorum (i.e., the scholarly, spiritual, humble family of specially chosen attendants required to transact the business of humanity's salvation according to God's word and laws). The Bible refers to God as the creator of everything, including these numbers, and Satan only the great deceiver and destroyer. Thus, *these codes must also be utilized by powerful globalists to create, destroy, and fulfill their nefarious objectives.*

In fact, according to the Bible, the dawn of 1,000 years of world peace begins with the inspired "wisdom" in Revelation 13:18. This "understand[ing]" is recommended at the darkest time in earth's history during the "great tribulation" earmarked by unprecedented global plagues.

Reflecting on these Bible verses, the "wisdom" that is foremost advised includes an alphanumeric code that appears to be consistent with the one detailed in figure 17.4. The Bible prophesied that this wisdom would be required to "understand" and "count the number of the beast, for it is [also] the number of a person, and its number is "666." Who might be more deserving of this brand than Dr. Henry Kissinger?

In the context of this chapter's "revelations," these Bible verses are especially compelling. Quoting the verses from *The Complete Jewish Bible*'s direct Hebrew translation, Revelation 13:18 reads:

> This is where wisdom is needed [Other Bibles read: "Here is wisdom."]; those who understand should count the number of the beast, for it is the number of a person, and its number is 666.[11]

Obviously, to "count the number of the beast" or "the number of a person," an alphanumeric code is required. Figure 17.4 provides this unique code.

Daniel's related prophecy (8:23-25) reads:

> In the latter part of their reign, when the evildoers have become as evil as possible, there will arise an arrogant king skilled in intrigue. His power will be great, but not with the power the first king had. He will be amazingly destructive, he will succeed in whatever he does, and he will destroy the mighty and the holy ones. He will succeed through craftiness and deceit, become swelled with pride, and destroy many people just when they feel the most secure. He will even challenge the Prince of princes; but, without human intervention, he will be broken.[11]

Secondarily, this "wisdom" might be spiritually inspiring, if not lifesaving. "Knowledge is power." Here, awareness of the evildoers "craftiness," "deceit," "skilled intrigue," and "amazingly destructive power" may be liberating. This wisdom, coupled with Divine spiritual intervention was prophesied to halt the "End Times" genocide.

Resolving this "great tribulation," Revelation 14:1-4 reads:

> Then I looked, and there was the Lamb standing on Mount Tziyon; and with him were 144,000 who had his name and his Father's name written on their foreheads. I heard a sound from heaven like the sound of rushing waters and like the sound of pealing thunder; the sound I heard was also like that of harpists playing on their harps [HAARPS?]. They were singing a new song before the throne and before the four living beings and the elders, and no one could learn the song except the 144,000 who have been ransomed from the world.[11]

Figures 17.3 shows that 144=9 or completion. This, and figure 17.4, largely displays the "wisdom" needed to decipher both the number of the "beast," key agents within the beast, and a "person" who likewise carries the number 666. As shown in figure 17.4, the only suspected person bearing this number is Nelson Rockefeller's protégé, Merck pharmaceutical company's top advisor, and global depopulation's leading architect—Dr. Henry Kissinger. Kissinger's number, decoded using the multiples of 6 method preferred by the secret services, is 666. In keeping with this assessment, as shown in figure 17.4, the February 2001, issue of *Harper's*,[12] described Kissinger as a "treasonous" "war criminal" who should be brought to trial for his genocidal actions.

Such an allegation might be easily dismissed, if not broadly condemned, if not for fact that this code delivers a means to statistically test and establish conspiratorial associations. In other words, this code provides the "wisdom" to statistically prove a conspiracy. Now that this code is understood, by using the numbers and code names as correlational variables, it is now possible to statistically prove associations between implicated globalists and activities that reflect their genocidal and metaphysical orientations.

Clearly, the likelihood that these hypothetically correlated factors—mystery school code numbers and names linked by government documents to genocides, non-lethal technotronic warfare, and/or global depopulation—are significantly related beyond random chance is statistically astronomical!

In other words, using their alphanumeric code, numbers can now be assigned to their names to run statistical analyses testing the strength of these associations, and thus proving beyond a shadow of doubt that this is not simply a conspiracy theory, but a scientifically provable conspiracy. Simply, the likelihood that these associations have happened by chance is ridiculously remote.

To further reinforce this point, and disprove the null hypothesis—that is, the theory that all of these proposed associations are merely coincidental—figure 17.4 shows the word "VACCINATION" to be the alphanumeric equivalent of "the mark of the beast"—666—as well. Here, $3 \times 6 = 18$, which resolves to 9 or completion, as does vaccination's primary deceptive Astroturf organization, the NVIC, which likewise decodes to 18 or 9.

This may come as a shock to some, but it is reconcilable given the background provided, and secret society leaders' ritualistic compulsions reflecting sacred hidden wisdom. It stands to reason, then, as seen in figure 17.4, that VACCINATION might be cryptologically related to 666, the NVIC, Dr. Kissinger, and the world's leading vaccine maker—the Merck pharmaceutical company—all having socio-political ties to genocidal outcomes. Kissinger's consulting firm—Kissinger Associates—it may be recalled, directed Merck's Board of Advisors since the early 1970s, while their early hepatitis B and polio vaccines, implicated in initiating global AIDS, were being administered. In addition, numerous other programs like the EZ measles vaccination study conducted through Kaiser had genocidal outcomes. Likewise, the NVIC, which lobbied for the Vaccine Injury Act of 1986 which shielded pharmaceutical companies from liability, was largely funded and instigated by the vaccine industry, primarily directed by Merck. (Merck's name, meanwhile, using the same alphanumeric code, deciphers to "300," like the "Committee of 300.")

Thus, using this decoding method, we can begin to identify, and statistically prove, the beast's existence and conspiratorial associations.

Indeed, Revelation's references implicate the Rockefeller–Kissinger–Merck vaccination/biological weapons alliance. How? Through its "End Times" prophecy regarding Babylon's "Kings" who deceive the wealthiest men of all the nations. At this time, the Bible prophesied, everyone was to become deceived by the "sorcery" or "magic spells" practiced by the global dictators. The word "sorcery" derives from the Greek root word *pharmacopeia,* meaning "pharmacy." Thus, the sorcerers were pharmaceutical industrialists not only associated in the Bible with spilled and impure blood, but with the great plagues, and onslaught of deadly "beasts."

Strong's Concordance root word for "beasts" is the "Hebrew word #2416—chay—alive, raw flesh . . . appetite; in the Greek Lexicon, the Greek word #2342 for "beasts" is "therion"—"a little beast, little animal." Thus, the earth's greatest depopulation era is predicted to be associated with little beasts, impure blood, and great plagues. Could these "little beasts" be bacteria, viruses, or other pathogens—infectious microbes most insidiously spread throughout the world, precisely and extensively, in contaminated blood and vaccines? That is exactly what is occurring today.

Those who "fornicated" with the devil, and stole "the blood of prophets and of God's people," would surely be severely judged by God in the last days, Revelation 18:23-19:2 predicts. The Bible warns that around the time "Babylon the great" falls, its deadly wine, also symbolic of contaminated blood, will flow out full of impurities into the "rivers and streams" that the Bible says are earth's people. Might we be infected with agents—little "beasts"—associated with great plagues predicted, by scientists and religious scholars alike, to wipe out more than a third of the world's population.

A reasonable interpretation of these sections of Revelation include the suggestion that vaccine/pharmaceutical/blood industrialists, all largely directed by the Rockefeller family and their European cohorts, through Kissinger, have deceived international leaders, merchants, and the aristocracy.

Finally, in Revelation, God's judgement and great wrath comes upon those who have worshiped these Babylonian idols above the Lord. Revelation 18:4 urges people to turn away from such sorcery and deadly globalists saying, "Come out of her, my people, that ye be not partakers of her sins, and that ye receive not of her plagues."

"Curse or Cure: It's in the Numbers"

To additionally support the overwhelming probability that random chance *cannot* possibly explain these myriad associations, consider the findings of physicist and musicologist Joe DeBrouse. Published over the Internet, this developer of advanced music therapy equipment came to a similar conclusion of conspiracy to commit genocide. Mr. DeBrouse, immersed in the field of frequency science and technology for healing for two decades, likewise concluded that biological, chemical, and electromagnetic frequency weapons were being combined to conduct a new form of warfare against civilian populations. To relay his clinical concerns (which relate to several key biological and chemical warfare agents discussed previously) he wrote the following paragraphs reprinted with permission:

> There is an aggressive aerial spraying campaign that is being carried out worldwide without humanity's consent and for most, without their knowledge. The related chemicals and biological agents that have been verified through laboratory analysis have a sympathetic resonant signature and energy component with similarities that overshadow mere coincidence.
>
> Of the chemtrail/immune suppression-linked opportunistic pathogens, the Streptomyces fungus resonates at **333 Hz**. We find that the Mycoplasma median range of frequency is an octave higher ranging between **660 Hz** and **688 Hz** with a 4th harmonic at **2688 Hz**. The *Pseudomonas aeruginosa* bacteria have a complex of harmonics stemming from their fundamental frequencies of **660 Hz** to **663 Hz**. (3965 Hz and 5311 Hz yield the 6th and 8th harmonics respectively, with a decimal harmonic at 6646 Hz). As with *Brucella melitensis*, the bandwidth ranges from **643 Hz to 695 Hz**. Although this list is not all inclusive due to the pleomorphic aspect of each organism, *these findings illustrate a target zone of Sympathetic Resonant Frequencies, all of which can be activated and sustained through forced resonance by one Fundamental Frequency, 666 Hz*. An ominous number perhaps, yet **666 Hz** and

its harmonics are also relevant to several sarcomas and carcinomas (i.e., cancers [heavily investigated and widely induced by the biological weapons/NCI investigators discussed in previous chapters and below]). Anthrax, another significant pathogen, also resonates in the median range of **666 Hz**. The similarities linking these insidious constituents are apparent in their resonant frequency bandwidth and harmonics. [13]

The molecular weight (MW) of another component of proposed aerial attack, is the pesticide Malathion . . . [which] weighs in at 330.36.

One of the earliest chemtrail toxins revealed a bromide component of ethylene dibromide (EDB), a banned pesticide and fuel additive. Subsequently, barium was introduced into the mix. If barium and bromine are combined (barium bromide) the molecular weight (MW) is **333.17**.

Barium is also commonly used in conventional medicine for diagnostic purposes due to its extreme sensitivity to radiation and its radiopacity.

Barium is of significance when one considers its propensity to displace calcium and magnesium in human metabolism; all 3 elements share the similarity of their atomic valence energy level of 2. A myriad of physical and mental maladies are associated with the depletion of these vital nutrients. Muscular weakness, joint pain, and neurological dysfunction are just a few of the calcium deficient issues. The lack of magnesium will have a profound effect on the motility of the gastrointestinal tract causing cramps and bloating. Respiratory and cardiovascular complaints are also associated with the ingestion of barium along with the infectious organisms discovered in chemtrail laboratory analyses.

Regarding the metallic and reactive attributes of barium, also consider the similar enthalpy (i.e., measure of the energy content of a system per unit mass) of barium bromide (**333.17**) and Malathion (**330.36**). They have similar frequency signatures.

Malathion is genotoxic (damaging the genes of the DNA molecules), teratogenic (causing birth defects), and oncogenic (cancer causing).

Are we being chemically primed and inoculated with this highly reactive and conductive element to turn us into microwave and radio-wave receivers or worse?

Another question arises regarding the HAARP Project and the technology to reflect electromagnetic frequencies through our atmosphere potentially energizing these noxious elements and compounds, and once ingested by the unsuspecting populace, to induce DNA aberrations, physical sickness, and even mind control.

From a musician's perspective, both Malathion and barium bromide reside in the elemental octave range of A# (Malathion) and D natural (barium bromide), a complimentary major 3rd interval. Barium bromide's significant elemental harmonics include Strontium (38) and

405

Mercury (80), while Malathion is sympathetic to the halogen elements, fluorine (9), chlorine (17), bromine (35) and the radioactive element technetium (43), the first element to be created artificially.

Technetium is a by-product of the nuclear industry and is also a product of uranium decay. Technetium is used in many radioactive isotopes with the ability to chemically bind to many biologically active molecules.

Cause for concern? Perhaps, considering more recent reports regarding the irradiation of our food supplies. It is also interesting to note that some of the most poisonous elements and compounds that are prolific in consumer products, medicines, and our water supplies are harmonically related. Quite a composition for a HAARP, wouldn't you say?

Is there any hope for humanity having realized what now appears to be a totalitarian act of tyranny? With education, absolutely. However many refuse to recognize the criminals and their actions that are destroying our quality of life.

The bottom line is, 'Frequency vs. Frequency' as no entity can escape its own vibrational attributes; pathogens can be neutralized and destroyed by their own electronic signature. Electromagnetic technology is being utilized by alternative practitioners to treat acute symptoms and cure chronic end-stage diseases worldwide.

The greedy medical community refuses, however, to recognize electromedicine's efficacy and has ostracized its proponents for more than eighty years. They, with their decadent, costly, and outmoded procedures (most diagnostic and treatment modalities) must be held accountable for the iatrogenic diseases they have propagated and the countless lives they have destroyed.

While conventional medicine mostly fails to cure disease, there are several viable electromagnetic healing devices being distributed under innocuous names that have proven to be effective for myriad conditions. These relatively inexpensive machines have the capability to destroy the organisms associated with chemtrails when all antibiotic regimens have proven worthless. Also, the lives of terminally ill patients have been saved, at a fraction of the cost of conventional medicine, with non-invasive electromagnetic protocols. The empirical and scientific data supporting the effectiveness of electromagnetic therapy is irrefutable. There is also a synergistic aspect to this amazing technology that compliments and enhances the effectiveness of the protocols that devitalize parasites, bacteria, viruses, and fungi.

Immune function stimulation, improved circulation, hormonal balance, enhanced cognition, and emotional stability are the most immediate and pronounced beneficial side effects resulting from this safe cost-effective technology.

The advent of combining elemental harmonic frequencies is being researched regarding the potential to eliminate heavy metals and noxious compounds from intoxicated individuals.

As more people become enlightened, enabling them to make more educated choices, and take control of their health, positive changes can occur exponentially." Perhaps this is what the villains fear most.

Linking Hope's Suspected HAARP to Klaus Groenke

As discussed in Chapter 15, and as shown in figures 15.7 and 17.5, an aluminum wrapped building sits atop Lunch Peak near Hope, Idaho. It is believed by investigators to be an energy generator that may have sparked the lightning-triggered forest fires in the summer of 2000 in the Northwestern U.S. The site is marked on Forest Service maps as a "Permanent Lookout Station." It is surrounded by six "Horizontal Control Stations" mostly on the peaks of neighboring mountains. These were allegedly placed for standard geographic surveys. Almost directly west, approximately 18 miles, precisely situated on the North Parallel atop Baldy Mountain, sits one of three nearby "Electronic Sites." These are admittedly "microwave" installations such as those used during the Montauk Project that investigated earthquake production and population programming among sensitized individuals. (See figure 12.4.).

All of the sites described above overlook Lake Pend Oreille, the second largest lake west of the Mississippi. Broad rocky and denuded areas surround the building, protecting it from forest fires. Yet, NFS authorities cited a need to wrap the mostly concrete building with "aluminum" allegedly for protection against such fires.

A straight line connects this building with six more "Horizontal Control Stations" perpendicular to three triangulated Electronic Sites as shown in figure 17.6. The estate of international industrialist, Klaus Groenke, and the Navy's "Cutthroat" submarine base, also lie close to this axis.

If the "Horizontal Control Stations" were equipped to receive and transmit electromagnetic signals, then through such theoretic connections to the nearby "Electronic Sites," they would form the energy grid depicted in figure 17.7. Government officials have admitted ongoing U.S. Navy experiments in this area, but none pertaining to the use of microwave or grid pattern energy frequencies.

Lake Pend Oreille was reported in 2000 to be in use by the Navy for project "Cutthroat." On National Forest Service maps, the project boasts three more "Horizontal Control Stations" triangulated from the water and coastal edge to the Lunch Peak axis. The project was simply

Figures. 17.5. "Lunch Peak" Building, Hope, ID, Suspected Site of HAARP-like "Fire Starter"

Close range photograph of the mysterious building on "Lunch Peak" near Hope, Idaho reported associated with "lightning" strikes and suspected Phoenix II-type project theorized to have sparked forest fires during the summer of 2000 in areas geographically clustered around this region. Marked on forestry maps as a "Permanent Lookout Station," it is surrounded by six "Horizontal Control Stations" on the peaks of neighboring mountains and one restricted area named "Lightning Peak Administrative Boundary." West, approximately 18 miles, and precisely on the "North Parallel," sits one of three triangulated microwave "Electronic sites." A vector runs southwest from Lunch Peak through several Horizontal Control Stations ending at "Echo Bay" adjacent the Naval station as shown in figure 17.6.

All of these sites overlook Lake Pend Oreille—the second largest lake west of the Mississippi. The deep lake was reported in 2000 to be in use by the U.S. Navy for testing their 110 foot unmanned submarine named "Cutthroat." This project was described by authorities as using ultra-advanced electronics and satellite communications systems for twenty-first century military preparedness.

Centrally located within this energy grid is the home of a leading German real estate company executor, Mr. Klaus Groenke. Mr. Groenke, a diplomatic associate of Henry Kissinger, was a close friend and hearty benefactor to the deceased American–German artist Edward Kienholz, whose works speak volumes concerning the racist and genocidal exploits of leading global industrialists and militarists among which Mr. Groenke is privileged. Some of this "art" is incorporated in this book's gallery. Though it is not known what function, if any, Mr. Groenke's highly secure satellite-controlled home on Hope Point lends to either this suspected non-lethal warfare operation and/or the genocidal conspiracy documented in this book, he openly engages conspiracy theorists' imaginations by displaying three metal art lightning strikes on his property that code for the number "666," and form the double "X" symbol signifying "66," used by Exxon and Maxxam corporations whose operations under the Committee of 300 are central to ongoing eugenics and depopulation efforts. The Lunch Peak photos were obtained by *Idaho Observer* publisher Don Harkins from the National Forest Service.

Figures. 17.6. "Cutthroat" Naval Base and Surrounding "Horizontal Control Stations," and "Electronic Sites"

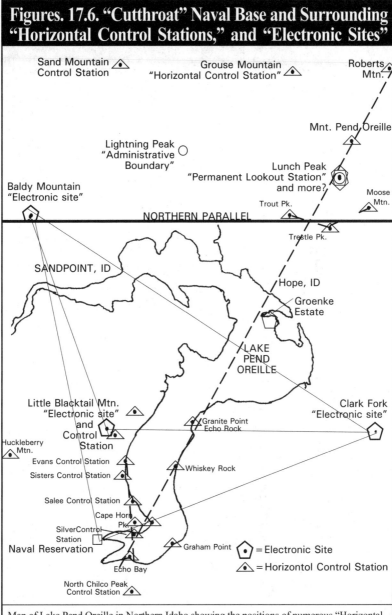

Map of Lake Pend Oreille in Northern Idaho showing the positions of numerous "Horizontal Control Stations" and "Electronic Sites" positioned in the vicinity of the U.S. Navy's "Cutthroat" project. The estate of global industrialist Klaus Groenke is stationed near the middle of the energy grid on the axis between Echo Bay and Roberts Mtn. The "Lunch Peak Lookout" on the same axis was reportedly associated with, and even possibly generating, the lightning strikes associated with "wildfires" clustered in the forests surrounding this area of Northern Idaho and Montana during the summer 2000.

Figures. 17.7. Theoretical Energy Grid From "Electronic Sites" and Stations Surrounding Lake Pend Oreille in Northern Idaho

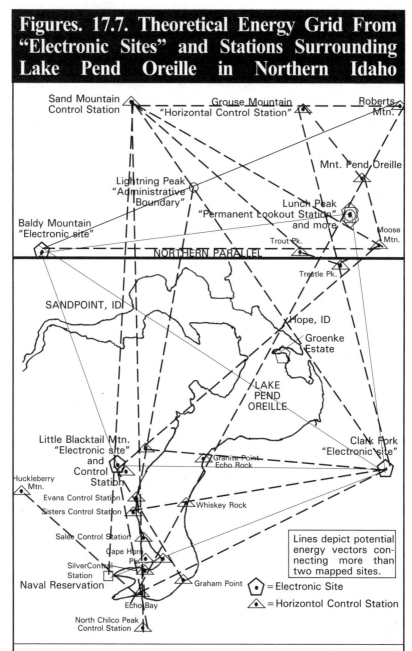

The same map as shown in figure 17.6 with the addition of lines connecting the area's "Electronic Sites" to "Lunch Peak" and the numerous "Horizontal Control Stations" in the vicinity of the U.S. Navy's "Cutthroat" project. The potential energy grid would make this area and Lake Pend Oreille resonate much like a large frequency transmitter.

described by authorities as using ultra-advanced electronics and satellite communications systems for twenty-first century military preparedness. The program highlights a 110 foot long unmanned deep water submarine that routinely cruises the lake. It is appropriately named "Cutthroat" to apparently reflect its military applications in a Technotronic Era of targeted depopulation.

The triangulation of the microwave "Electronic Sites" in particular suggests a Phoenix II (Montauk) type of project—those associated with geological, atmospheric, and/or electromagnetic non-lethal warfare applications. Such frequency triangulation, Montauk research established, creates a "Delta-T" rotational field and energy vortex that facilitates access to other dimensions of time and space. The limestone slabs brought to the Lunch Peak area, along with pure marble and chalk, are composed of triangular and hexagonal crystalline latices with primary angles of 51.51 degrees. The same is true for the great Pyramid of Giza. Using Pythagorean math, as the builders of the great pyramids had done, the 51.51 angle reflects sacred geometry wherein 5+1=6 twice or "66." The perfect triangle with three angles deciphers to "666."

During the mid-1990s, as the Navy's project was being established, a barge containing numerous large copper coils reportedly sank in Lake Pend Oreille. Montauk investigators have reported that such coils might be helpful in establishing the "X, Y, Z rotational vortex" required for some Phoenix II energy operations.

On March 8, 2001, the national cable television Discovery Channel aired a program entitled, "Would You Believe It." It broadcast the art and drawings of Adolf Hitler as displayed in the estate of deceased Lord Mountbatten, blood kin to the Royal Family of England. Hitler, an avid student of the occult, was shown to have drawn several sketches with two and three lightning bolts side by side. The two were symbolic of the his most feared Secret Service "SS." Using the Pythagorean math multiples of 6, and the British Secret Service's alphanumeric code, both MI6 and SS resolve into "66." (That is, M=78 and I=54 where 78+54=132, and 1+3+2=6; thus MI6=66. Similarly, the alphanumeric code for "S" using the column of 6s is 114 which yields 1+1+4=6, and 66 for SS.) Thus, the British Royal Family and English government's secret service used the same code as their greatest Nazi nemesis.

The Discovery Channel also broadcast, among Hitler's drawings, one sketch virtually identical to the triangulated energy grid with a perpendicular line running to it from Lunch Peak as shown in figure 17.6.

Figures. 17.8. American Academy in Berlin Governance including Henry Kissinger and Klaus Groenke

American Academy in Berlin Governance

Academy Officers at a "Berlin in New York" Conference (from left to right) Dr. Everette E. Dennis, president; Ambassador Richard C. Holbrooke, chairman; Gahl Hodges Burt, vice chairman; and Dr. Henry Kissinger, honorary chairman.

Honorary Chairmen
Henry A. Kissinger
Richard von Weizsäcker
Thomas L. Farmer

Chairman
Richard C. Holbrooke

Vice Chairman
Gahl Hodges Burt

President
Everette E. Dennis

Treasurer
Karl M. von der Heyden

Executive Director
Gary Smith

Trustees
Lloyd N. Cutler
Everette E. Dennis,
  ex-officio
Eberhard Diepgen,
  ex-officio
Richard B. Fisher
Jürgen Graf
Klaus Groenke
Thomas L. Hughes
Josef Joffe
Stephen M. Kellen
Horst Köhler
Otto Graf Lambsdorff
Baroness Nina von Maltzahn
Klaus Mangold
Erich Marx
Volker Schlöndorff
Jerry Speyer
Fritz Stern
Jon Vanden Heuvel

The association of Mr. Klaus Groenke, and the location of his home adjacent this axis is more intriguing. Mr. Groenke is the Managing Director and part owner of Trigon Holding GmbH, a Berlin based international real estate company. He is also reported to be a leading shareholder in the Coca Cola Company, and a Regional Board member of the Deutsche Bank Berlin/Brandenburg. Besides this, as shown in figure 17.8, he is officially linked to Honorary Chairman Henry Kiss-

Figures. 17.9. "Art" Sample From the Keinholz Collection Symbolizing the Themes in this Chapter

A detail from The Ozymandias Parade, 1985, by Klaus Groenke's beneficiary, Hope, Idaho neighbor, and long time friend, Edward Keinholz. The work depicts "war games," Star-Wars technology, and "porkbarrel spending." The black suitcase full of money symbolizes "black budget" financing and secret payoffs. This "art," and more in the gallery, was published with support from The Henry Luce Foundation, The Andrew W. Mellon Foundation, and others including Mr. Groenke.

inger as a fellow governor of the American Academy in Berlin, a diplomatic institute heavily funded by the Deutsche Bank, Coca Cola Foundation, Chase Manhattan and Citicorp banks, J.P. Morgan, David Rockefeller, and Kissinger himself. Mr. Groenke's estate lies near the center of the Lunch Peak–U.S. Navy submarine station axis, and not far from the easternmost "Electronic Site."[14]

Mr. Groenke displays a large slab of the Berlin Wall at the entrance of his Hope Peninsula complex. From the lake, passersby also view a series of three lightning strikes, similar to the three "S" elements in the U.S. Dept. of Energy (DoE) and ARCO affiliated INEEL logo shown in figures 15.9 and 17.11. The lightning strikes are identical to Hitler's art, like three Nazi "SS" symbols side-by-side coding for 666. As the winds change direction, the Ss pivot, and from various reference points these metal elements also overlap forming the double X symbol used by Exxon and Maxxam corporations whose operations under the global ruling elite are central to ongoing eugenics programs and applications of non-lethal warfare for planetary depopulation. As discussed above, the "XX," like SS and MI6, codes for "66" as in Phillips 66—an oil company merged with the Rockefeller family's Chevron Corporation in 2000 to form Chevron–Phillips. Only months earlier Phillips had purchased the Royal Family's Alaskan oil company ARCO, associated with Alaska's HAARP instillation and the DoE's project INEEL.[16]

Here again, primary indicators—documented evidence and associations—revolve around and consistently implicate the same two families that have economically led the world and global politics into genocidal operations for the past century—the Rockefellers and the Royal Family of England.

Visual confirmation of this most disturbing thesis is presented in the color gallery of this book. Here, the work of the deceased American–German artist Edward Kienholz is featured. Mr. Groenke was a close friend and principal benefactor to Mr. Kienholz. Much of Kienholz's work speaks volumes concerning the racist and genocidal exploits of leading global industrialists and militarists among whom Mr. Groenke is privileged. An example of his taste in "art" is displayed in figure 17.9. This is a detail from one large piece called "The Ozymandias Parade" that graphically depicts a Nazi-American warlord electronically controlling the wind (i.e., weather) over America, and, at the same time, Judeo-Christian genocide.

It is not known what function, if any, Mr. Groenke's highly secured home on Hope Peninsula lends to the suspected Montauk-like operation. His neighbors report that his estate is under heavy surveillance and is electronically controlled via *satellite* from Germany for Mr. Groenke's security and convenience. Likewise, it is not known what role, if any, Mr. Groenke plays in the genocidal conspiracy documented in this book. However, the fact that he is listed as a Trustee adjacent the Honorary Chairman Dr. Henry Kissinger of the American Academy in Berlin—a U.S. Diplomatic Corps affiliated institute, leaves less to the imagination and insinuates the worst. [14]

Historically, as documented in the 1905 edition of the *Northern Idaho News*,[17] mineral mining accounted for extensive tunneling in the area of the Groenke estate as detailed in figure 17.10. Electromagnetic

Figures. 17.10. Location of Mines, Pend Oreille Lake

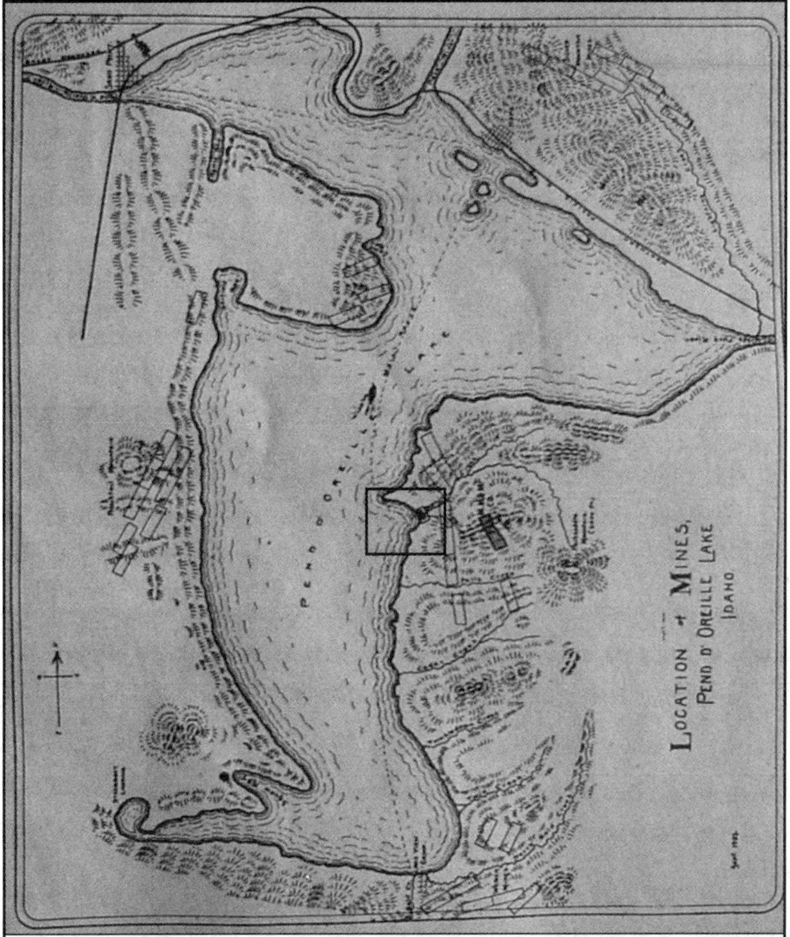

Map published in 1905 shows the mineral mining locations around Lake Pend Oreille, Idaho. Regarding the Groenke property located within the box, the *Northern Idaho News* quoted mining inspector Robert Bell who described the property thusly: "Among the best developed and most promising properties of this section are those situated near Granite creek on the east side of the lake." One of these mines, he stated, "is open on a well defined fissure vein in quartzite varying in thickness from one to eight feet in clean cut walls, carrying a free tale gorge, a condition that may be relied upon to carry its ores to great depth, and the vein is plainly traceable by surface workings through the property for nearly 2,000 feet.

"This property," he continued, "has several hundred feet of tunnels or drifts run on the vein, . . . The ore is a concentrating variety of lead-zinc sulphides, with some high grade gray copper, and makes a fine product that runs well in all the metals mentioned.'"
Source: Bonner County Historical Society. "The State of Idaho" in *Northern Idaho News: Industrial Souvenir Edition*. Sandpoint, Kootenai County, Idaho: July 1905, Vol VII, No. 37, p.7.

military consultant and HAARP expert Dr. Fred Bell reported in his book, *Rays of Truth–Crystals of Light,* that such tunneling, particularly in granite, quartz, and other conductive metals, predictably increases electromagnetic energy and/or signaling resonance for the creation of lightning storms and other technotronic control operations.[15]

A second extremely tall metal "art" structure dominates the Groenke estate shoreline as shown in figure 17.11. Might this be another "Electronic Site" and/or "Control Station?" It is unknown, though one thing is sure – these are perfect props and logistics for the villain in a James Bond film.

The Coca Cola company and Coca Cola Foundation is also linked to this conspiratorial consortium. The company was purchased in 1919 by Atlanta banker Ernest Woodruff for $25 million.[18] His son Robert W., took over the company in 1923. Since then, The Robert W. Woodruff Foundation has been a major contributor to Emory University and the Rockefeller-directed cancer industry. In 2000, for instance, The Woodruff Foundation contributed $82,676,563 to the Robert W. Woodruff Health Sciences Center Fund, Inc., of Atlanta, GA. in support of

Figures. 17.11. Metal "Art" Adjacent Idaho's Lake Pend Oreille on the Klaus Groenke Estate

Left photo shows three "Ss," similar to the DOE's INEEL project logo (inset), coding for "666." These lightning strikes, in a pivoting weathervane, also form the "XX" (i.e., "66") symbol as the elements move and overlap from various vantage points. Upper right structure appears to be a triangulated antennae. Lower right "art" depicts rams—alpha males (i.e., leaders) of the sheep species—walking the plank to their demise with additional sheep looking on.

Figures. 17.12. Yerkes Primate Center Irradiation Studies to Induce Sarcomas and Carcinomas

EMORY UNIVERSITY, YERKES PRIMATE CENTER (NO1-CP-3-3343)

Title: Maintenance of a Colony of Irradiated, Aging. Rhesus Monkeys

Contractor's Project Director: Dr. Harold McClure

Project Officers (NCI): Dr. Garrett V. Keefer
Dr. Lea I. Sekely

Objectives: To monitor the incidence of tumors in a unique group of irradiated, aging rhesus monkeys and to supply tissue from tumors to VOP collaborators for transplantation, tissue culture and virus isolation studies.

Major Findings: During this report period, a group of 56 aging and/or irradiated rhesus monkeys and progeny were monitored by daily observations and tri-annual physical and hematologic evaluation. These examinations specifically concentrated on the developing neoplasms. During the most recent survey, 17 animals were classified as slightly to moderately emaciated and skin and/or subcutaneous nodules or masses were present in 15 animals. One animal had a large mass in the thigh that has been characterized as a lipoma; two animals have basal cell carcinoma of the skin; two animals continue to have a very large mass in the lower abdomen in the region of the uterus; and one animal continues to have a palpable mass in the region of the liver.

Three of the four adult animals that died during the report period had tumors and one animal had two separate primary tumors. Neoplasms encountered included an intestinal adenocarcinoma, a transitional cell carcinoma of the kidney pelvis, a sarcoma of the hip region, and thyroid adenomas.

During this report period, 149 specimens were shipped to Viral Oncology Program investigators and collaborators. These specimens included 119 serum samples, six whole blood samples, and 24 tissue specimens (includes samples from one sarcoma). Preliminary data reported by these collaborators indicate that at least nine of these animals have demonstrable titers to Mason-Pfizer Monkey Virus.

Observations in this group of animals continue to confirm their value as a source of nonhuman primate tumor materials, as 17 of 36 animals (47.2%) that have died in this group have had neoplasms.

Significance to Biomedical Research and the Program of the Institute:
The VOP conducts collaborative projects for the study of relationships between the etiologies of tumors of various primates. This project provides tumor tissues and other important specimens from aging, irradiated subhuman primates for research within the VOP. Malignant changes in these irradiated primates may provide useful information which might be applied to humans, who are also subjected to similar physical stresses.

Proposed Course: The entire group of monkeys will continue to be monitored for neoplasia by physical and hematologic examinations. All tumors which develop will be evaluated by the contractor using light and electron-microscopy. Specimens of these tumors will be made available to VOP investigators. In addition, a program is underway to evaluate the incidence of leukemia or other tumors in infants with aging and irradiated parents.

Date Contract Initiated: May 1, 1971

417

the Winship Cancer Institute and other initiatives within the Woodruff Health Sciences Center. Mr. Woodruff and his beneficiaries at Emory University established the Yerkes Regional Primate Research Center tied to the Special Virus Cancer Program (SVCP), the cancer industry, the man-made origin of HIV/AIDS, as well as primate vaccines.[19,20]

Figure 17.12 reprints Emory University's Yerkes Primate Center SVCP contract to maintain a colony of irradiated aging Rhesus monkeys.[21] The study was ongoing between 1971 and 1978 in concert with allied cancer investigators, particularly those from the Atomic Energy Commission who were likewise involved in determining the effects of various radiations, including nonionizing frequencies, on the development of neoplasms and blood pathologies. Amazingly, carcinomas and sarcomas were the two types of cancer given most attention under this Yerkes contract. As Joseph DeBrouse relayed above, these two unique cancers were ominously associated with the "fundamental frequency" of 666 Hz.

Returning to Hope

All the birch trees surrounding Lunch Peak, and the majority of others throughout this region, had by 2000 suspiciously died. As already mentioned, citizens in this sparsely populated area reported, and documented, bizarre animal behavior and a strange absence of native birds, besides the unique "lightning" events in close proximity to this building. Security was reported as moderate surrounding this Forest Service acreage in 1999, but increased by early 2001 as reports such as this surfaced in alternative periodicals and on the Internet.

Authorities have claimed the Lunch Peak building stands abandoned, in disrepair, and in need of *aluminum* wrapping for fire protection which was accomplished in 2000. Might the aluminum be acting partly as a frequency conductor interacting with both toxic levels of aluminum sprayed into the atmosphere by the military in chemtrails and injected into humans through vaccines? Locals who inspected the building prior to the aluminum treatment stated the mostly cement building stood as strong as a fortress before officials wrapped it with the shiny metal.

Moreover, authorities have yet to explain the delivery of tons of energy conductive limestone slabs shipped from Portugal to the site as reported by area residents as documented earlier in figure 15.6. Geomagnetism experts have traditionally credited limestone, as well as granite naturally occurring under the Groenke estate, as among the most energetically conductive deposits.

References

1) Thumbnail bios at http://www.worldwarI.com/biokais.htm

2) Coleman J. *Conspirator's Hierarchy: The Story of the Committee of 300.* Carson City, NV: American West Publishers, 1992, pp. 69-73.

3) Horowitz LG and Puleo J. *Healing Codes for the Biological Apocalypse.* Sandpoint, ID: Tetrahedron Publishing Group, 1999.

4) The Heritage Foundation's website is http://www.heritage.org/issues/chap15.html

5) See Kaiser Aluminum company information at http://biz.yahoo.com/p/k/klu.html

6) See MAXXAM, Inc. information in the Yahoo Finance Market Guide at: http://biz.yahoo.com/p/m/mxm.html).

7) Griffin GE. World Without Cancer. Westlake Village, CA: American Media, 1997.

8) See information on Kaiser Electro-optics, Inc, a Rockwell Collins company at: http://www.keo.com/.

9) Cork J. The life of Ian Fleming (1908–1964). By the Editor of Goldeneye Magazine for the Ian Fleming Foundation. Available at: http://www.mcs.net/~klast/www/flem_bio.html.

10) Horowitz LG. *Healing Celebrations.* Sandpoint, ID: Tetrahedron Publishing Group, 2000.

11) *The Complete Jewish Bible.* Translated by David H. Stern. Clarksville, Maryland: Jewish New Testament Publications, Inc., 1998. Distributed by Tetrahedron Inc. 1-888-508-4787.

12) Hitchens C. The case against Henry Kissinger: Part I: The making of a war criminal *Harper's Magazine*, February 2001, p. 33.

13) Mr. DeBrouse's data concerning the specific resonant frequencies of certain microbes was gathered from standard Royal Raymond Rife manuals used by practitioners in this field. For more information in this regard, Mr. DeBrouse may be contacted by mail at: P. O. Box 878, Louisa, VA, 23093, or by e-mail at: vibes4you@hotmail.com.

14) Klaus Groenke's biographical data came by way of personal communications and documentation supplied by anonymous sources including his investments in the Coca Cola company. Mr. Groenke has been a partner in the Trigon international real estate company since 1978. In addition to his membership on the American Academy's Board of Trustees, he is a member of the Regional Board of the Deutsche Bank Berlin/Brandenburg. The Coca Cola Foundation is a heavy contributor to the American Academy in Berlin, as is the Deutsche Bank, Rockefeller's Chase Manhattan Bank, J.P. Morgan, Henry

Kissinger, who is "founding honorary co-chairman" of the organization, and David Rockefeller personally. Their website is linked to the U.S. Diplomatic Corps which also supports the academy which allegedly serves as "an institute for advanced independent study in the arts, culture, humanities, and public affairs." In other words, another think tank in the grand tradition of the Tavistock Institute, the SRI, and others that function to mold culture through strategic investments in the arts and media. See: http://www.chelsea.net/~cwhite/aaib/govern.html for documentation in this regard.

15) Bell F. *Rays of Truth–Crystals of Light: Information and Guidance for the Golden Age.* Laguna Beach, CA: Pyridine Press, 2000.

16) For Phillips 66 purchase of ARCO, and subsequent merger with the Rockefeller's Chevron Corporation see: http://www.phillips66.com/about/timeline.html. For additional details concerning the final selection, following the initial unspecified proposal to use "66" in the company's name, see: http://www.phillips66.com/about/why66.html.

17) Bonner County Historical Society. "The State of Idaho" in *Northern Idaho News: Industrial Souvenir Edition.* Sandpoint, Kootenai County, Idaho: July 1905, Vol VII, No. 37, p.7.

18) For early Coca-Cola Company history involving Ernest and Robert Woodruff, see: http://www.cocacola.be//about/index.cfm?fuseaction=about_main

19) For information about Robert Woodruff and the Robert Woodruff Foundation, see: http://www.woodruff.org/.

20) For information about the Yerkes Regional Primate Research Center's involvement in AIDS vaccine research, see Emery University's website at: http://www.emory.edu/WHSC/YERKES/NEWSROOM/robinson_990426.html.

21) NCI Staff. *The [Special] Virus Cancer Program [SVCP].* U.S. Department of Health, Education and Welfare. Washington, D.C.: Public Health Service, National Institutes of Health, Division of Cancer Cause and Prevention, June 1978, Library call number: E20.3152:V81/977 and 78-21195, pp. 236-37.

Chapter 18.
Public Health Politics, Eugenics and Population Control

> "Our position requires that we take immediate action at home and promote effective action worldwide. We must have population control at home, hopefully through a system of incentives and penalties, but by compulsion if voluntary methods fail. . . . We can no longer afford merely to treat the symptoms of the cancer of population growth; the cancer itself must be cut out."
>
> Professor Paul Ehrlich., 1968
> Author of *The Population Bomb*

On Friday, July 11, 1986, United Press International broke world news that the first human tests of an "anti-pregnancy vaccine," developed by doctors at Ohio State University in Columbus, was about to take place in Australia. The experimental vaccine, the article said, "would act as a contraceptive by immunizing women against a hormone necessary to maintain pregnancy."[1]

Dr. Vernon Stevens, Director of Reproductive Biology at Ohio State's Department of Obstetrics and Gynecology, credited with the vaccine's initial development, revealed that six years of pilot studies led to the 1980 development of the initial vaccine. He predicted that some form of the sterilizing preparation would reach the medical market by the mid-1990s.

The vaccine worked, the doctor explained, by attacking and neutering the female pregnancy hormone HCG—short for human chorionic gonadotrophin. The HCG, produced shortly after conception, facilitates placental development and the successful implantation of the fertilized egg into the uterine wall.

Vaccinating women with a foreign woman's HCG, researchers learned, prompted a powerful immune response against the natural pregnancy hormone. The end results included sterility, terminated pregnancies, and aborted fetuses.

Promoted for its benefits to "family planning," might this "breakthrough" in modern science be one of the more coercive methods heralded in the opening quote, and earlier by the CIA, for "wide-ranging vaccination programs" for "global population control?" Very likely, according to the Philippine Medical Association.

In the mid-1990s, hundreds of thousands of unsuspecting women began receiving "experimental" tetanus vaccines that contained this sterilizing hormone HCG.[2] Later reports confirmed that millions of women in other countries besides the Philippines, including South American nations, Mexico, and America, received the tainted vaccines as well. The Philippine Department of Health revealed that almost 20 percent of tetanus vaccines they sampled were positive for HCG.

"This study lends credence to what Human Life International (HLI) and some other groups have suspected all along," said Father Matthew Habiger, president of the international pro-life/family organization. "We first began to hear reports last year about tetanus vaccination campaigns in the developing world that targeted only women of childbearing or pre-child bearing years, and that they required multiple injections. The vaccination program is sponsored by the World Health Organization, an agency with a 20-year history of researching antifertility vaccines," Fr. Habiger said. "We brought our suspicions to the world's attention. This new study greatly heightens our concerns."

The WHO, and feminist organizations that claim to care about the health of women, publicly attacked HLI after it called for an investigation of the widespread allegations about the HCG contaminated vaccine.

"In light of the new Philippine study, it appears that these groups have squandered their credibility," Fr. Habiger said.

The Philippine Medical Association reported that nine of the 47 vaccine samples tested were found to contain HCG. They released a letter signed by the three Philippine physicians who actually tested the vaccines. The PMA president attested to the veracity of the letter and the testing process. All the vaccines sampled were taken from various health centers in Luzon and Mindanao. Almost all of them were labeled by one of two Canadian firms, Connaught (Aventis-Pasteur-

Hoechst) or Intervax. All the samples were tested with an immunoassay-based method developed by the FDA.

The tetanus vaccine tested in the Philippines was imported, allegedly, as part of a program against neonatal tetanus sponsored by the WHO. Similar vaccination protocols have also been observed in WHO programs administered in Mexico and Nicaragua, the Philippine Medical Association reported. Tests of the vaccine in Mexico yielded similar results, but none of those tests were performed as part of an actual investigation into the HCG contamination.

"We view the adulteration of tetanus vaccine with HCG to be a matter of grave concern," said Fr. Habiger. "It is absolutely essential that any country which has this program in place begin testing the vaccines for contamination."

Noting it is unlikely that contaminated vaccines would still be circulating after public concerns were raised, Fr. Habiger suggested that researchers acquire and test unused vaccines distributed prior to the public's outcry. He said it was even more important that women who previously received the vaccine be tested for the telltale presence of HCG antibodies in their bloodstream, and that the numbers of miscarriages experienced by vaccinated women be tabulated.

"We strongly suspect something is seriously amiss," Fr. Habiger complained. "And public confidence in these kinds of vaccination campaigns has been critically eroded in several developing nations. Only an objective, scientifically valid, study of this matter will lay public concerns to rest."[2]

A parallel story, written by Suzanne M. Rini, entitled "Open Season on Humanity: Abortion, Contraception, Sterilization, and the Coming Era of Coercion," appeared in the November, 1995 issue of *Celebrate Life*.[3] Like many pro-life articles, this too recalled the major affiliations and conflicts of interest between the Rockefeller family, the World Health Organization's depopulation and vaccination programs, the United Nations' "Fund for Population Activities," and their successful efforts at what appears to be global genocide.

An important "adjunct to the Rockefeller founded National Research Council," Ms. Rini wrote, was the Institute of Medicine (IoM). This most esteemed health science agency published a study entitled, "The Best Intentions: Unintended Pregnancy and the Well Being of Children & Families." The study was funded by several organizations with long term links to the eugenics movement. She included here: The with long term links to the eugenics movement. She included here: The Robert Wood Johnson Foundation, the Carnagie Corporation, the Annie E. Casey Foundation, and above all the U.S. Public Health Service. The IoM report was aimed at promoting policy change consistent with disseminating methods of long term contraception. Rini wrote that "antifertility vaccines," for example, "have long been linked to coercive reproductive social policy."

Looking back on the developmental history of this contemporary movement, in 1971, Edgar R. Chasteen—a national board member of Zero Population Growth, Inc., and also a member of the board of directors of Planned Parenthood of Greater Kansas City—predicted the development of a vaccine to prompt sterility. He wrote, "Assuming that we could soon have a vaccine to immunize against fertility, it would then be possible to inoculate all children. Permanent immunity to fertility could be established."[3]

Rini chronicled that during a 1978 meeting at Rockefeller University, vaccines were projected to deliver a "beyond the pill" strategy for depopulating the planet. This was said to be rationally consistent with earlier statements made by Dr. Allan C. Barne, head of the Rockefeller Foundation in 1973 when he stated, "Death control without birth control is pure folly."

"In the 1970s," Rini wrote, "a consortium was formed to develop the vaccines and other new long term contraceptives that would help cut the live birth rate in half, which is the stated goal of the global population group.

"The consortium consisted of: the WHO, the Population Council (supported by eugenics funding entities including the Andrew Mellon Foundation [that also helped fund the Whitney Museum of Art publication from which the stirring photos reprinted in this book's gallery were taken], the Dodge and Rockefeller Foundations, USAID, and the National Institutes of Health; The National Institute of Immunology in New Delhi, India, also funded in part by the Rockefeller Foundation; CONRAD—the Contraceptive Research and Development Program at Eastern Virginia Medical School at Norfolk; and the taxpayer funded National Institute of Child Health & Development, especially its Contraceptive Research and Development Branch in the Center for Population Research.

Another Birth Control Innovation

On September 29, 2000, the American news media heralded another birth control innovation—the FDA approved abortion pill, RU-486. The story, relayed in *USA Today* for instance, told that an organization called the "Population Council" had first applied for FDA approval on the drug in 1996. Following four years of negotiating a "U.S. regulatory maze," RU-486, also called mifepristone, was approved for the benefit of Danco Laboratories, "licensed by the non-profit Population Council, to distribute and market the drug under the name Mefeprex."[4]

The drug worked by blocking the vital hormone progesterone, a hormone required to maintain pregnancy. It was prescribed for use from "the time a woman knows she is pregnant until seven weeks after the start of her last menstrual period,"[4] the article said.

Mifepristone was credited for inducing about forty-percent of the abortions in France following its approval there in 1988. "It's impossible to predict" how many American women would opt for the pharmaceutical abortion over the surgical procedure, a Danco spokeswoman, Heather O'Neill, said.

About 120 of Planned Parenthood's 850 clinics planned to offer mifepristone as soon as it became available, added Gloria Feldt, President of the Planned Parenthood Federation of America. This was expected following initial shipments of the drug by the end of October, 2000.

Meanwhile, the National Abortion Federation (NAF) wasted no time in furthering the technology. The article mentioned the NAF had already trained "1,800 clinics or medical practices how to use Mifeprex," according to the organization's director, Vicki Saporta.

The limited side effects of the drug, according to the article, included "bleeding, cramping and nausea" that "almost all women experience."

A Feminist Majority Foundation (FMF) report transmitted over the Internet also promoted the drug not only as "safe and effective," but potentially therapeutic for a wide-array of female health concerns. "Mifepristone shows promise as a treatment for a wide range of serious diseases and conditions," the report stated. "Yet clinical trials on most of these uses in the U.S. have come to a standstill because of anti-abortion politics. In the absence of clinical trials, several dozen people with Cushing's Syndrome, meningioma, and breast cancer are currently being treated with mifepristone under compassionate use protocols."

The FMF article went on to report additional diseases and conditions that were likely to be improved or healed as a result of taking RU–486. These included: breast and ovarian cancers, meningiomas, endometriosis and fibroid tumors, Cushing's syndrome, AIDS-virus infections, depression, alcoholism, substance abuse, anorexia nervosa, ulcers, diabetes, Parkinson's, Multiple Sclerosis, and Alzheimer's.[5]

Neither of the "far left" or "far right" articles mentioned, however, the cornucopea of adverse reactions ascribed to RU-486 in the scientific literature. Nor were the medical questions yet to be answered concerning the drug's potential to cause harmful long-term side effects addressed.

A less biased report on "the side effects of a 'medical abortion'" came from the *Washington Post*. The article, by Caryle Murphy, stated, "On average, women experience varying degrees of bleeding for eight to nine days after a 'medical abortion,' compared with five days after a surgical abortion, according to information provided by the nonprofit Population Council, the drug's U.S. sponsor." The side effects "can include extensive bleeding, cramping, nausea and vomiting."[6]

Since, at the time of this writing, RU-486 had not been sufficiently tested to establish its full array of side effects, some articles noted most known adverse effects were caused by misopostol, which was sold under the brand name Cytotec and was additionally used to treat ulcers. The mifepristone caused the uterine wall to degenerate and as a consequence reject the developing fertilized egg or developing fetus. The misoprostol induced moderate to severe uterine muscle contraction, thus expelling, like an abortion, the rejected fetus. (Thus, the drug was appropriately named, "Are you for eighty-six?")

According to Ms. Murphy's article, "Clinicians must determine whether the woman has any medical condition that would preclude the use of mifepristone, such as high blood pressure or a history of heart disease. Also, a woman taking a nonsteroidal antiinflammatory drug (NSAID), such as Motrin, for arthritis or cramps, would have to stop that medication before a 'medical abortion,' because those drugs would inhibit the contraction-inducing effects of misoprostol."

Physicians were urged to counsel patients during the first visit about how the drug works, its possible side effects and the necessity for two more visits. "Patients who think they are not able to comply with returning for visits and taking the second medication on time are probably not good candidates," the article said.

Little Known Side Effects of RU–486

The above discussion concerning RU–486's publicized side effects and contraindications was provided to show the supreme suppression of facts with which we must contend in the "Technotronic Era" of global genocide.

The *Physician's Desk Reference* listed the generally undiscussed side effects and contraindications of misoprostol, though not mifepristone, since at the time of this writing they had not been fully determined. These included: "Gastrointestinal (GI) effects—risks of GI ulceration, bleeding and perforation. Serious GI toxicity, such as inflammation, ulceration, and perforation of the stomach, small intestine or large intestine, [that] can occur at any time, with or without warning symptoms, in patients treated with nonsteroidal antiinflammator drugs (NSAID). . . .

"Hepatic effects [included] . . . laboratory abnormalities . . . As with other NSAID products, if abnormal liver tests persist or worsen, if clinical signs and/or symptoms consistent with liver disease develop, or if systemic manifestations occur (eg., eosinphilia, rash, etc) . . . [the drug] should be discontinued immediately. . . . To minimize the possibility that hepatic injury will become severe . . . physicians should inform patients of the warning signs and symptoms of hepatotoxicity (e.g., nausea, fatigue, lethargy, pruritus, jaundice, right upper quadrant tenderness, and "flu-like" symptoms), and the appropriate action patients should take if these signs and symptoms appear. . . .

"Renal [i.e., kidney] effects . . . Caution should be used when initiating treatment in patients with considerable dehydration [which represents a majority of Americans drinking far less than their recommended daily allowance of pure water]. It is advisable to rehydrate patients first and then start therapy . . . Caution is also recommended in patients with preexisting kidney disease. As with other NSAIDs, long-term administration of diclofenac [added to misoprostol in the tablet formula] has resulted in renal papillary necrosis and other renal medullary changes. . . .

"Hematologic effects . . . [including] anemia is sometimes seen in patients receiving diclofenac or other NSAIDs. This may be due to fluid retention, GI blood loss, or an incompletely described effect upon erythropoiesis. . . . All drugs that inhibit the biosynthesis of prostaglandins may interfere to some extent with platelet function and vascular responses to bleeding. . . ."

Many other contraindications and side effects were listed in the *PDR* associated with the combination misopostol and diclofenac sodium in oral doses. Among these were cautions regarding rare cases of aseptic meningitis and fatigue, fever, infection, malaise, sepsis, arrhythmias—including atrial fibrillation, congestive heart failure, and hypertension; migraine, neuralgia, paresthesia, tremor, and vertigo, and musculoskeletal system disorders; respiratory problems including asthma, coughing, dyspnea, hyperventilation, pneumonia, and respiratory depression; skin ailments such as acne, eczema, bruising, and toxic epidermal necrolysis; urinary system problems including cystitis, dysuria, hematuria, proteinuria, papillary necrosis, urinary tract infections and renal failure; and vision troubles including blurred vision, conjunctivitis, diplopia, glaucoma, iritis, lacrimation abnormal, and night blindness.[7] In other words, virtually all the signs and symptoms of acute and chronic toxicity.

All in all, the "simple" birth control pill, RU–486, was not so simple, nor as "safe" as the mass media, or even pro-life and pro-choice groups, had people believing.

The mainstream media also neglected to mention that behind the allegedly "nonprofit" Population Council stood the Rockefeller Population Control empire, its ties to leading globalists, and its many historic investments in racial engineering (i.e., eugenics). Thus, the true nature of this non-governmental organization's "public interest" in RU–486 was insidious as well as deadly.

Early Roots of Contemporary Eugenics

The *British Medical Journal* reviewed the subject of "Eugenics and human rights" in its August 14, 1999, issue.[8] Author Daniel J. Kevles, a humanities professor at the California Institute of Technology in Pasadena, wrote that "modern eugenics was rooted in the social Darwinism of the late 19th century, with all its metaphors of fitness, competition, and rationalizations of inequality." It was pioneered by accomplished scientist Francis Galton, Charles Darwin's cousin, who coined the word eugenics. Galton advanced the idea of improving the human race by ridding the world of "undesirables" and multiplying the "desirables." In 1900, following the rediscovery of Mendel's theory that certain factors, later called genes, determined the biological development of organisms, eugenics began to flourish.

"Eugenic doctrines were articulated by physicians, mental health professionals, and scientists—notably biologists who were pursuing the new discipline of genetics—and were widely popularized in books, lectures, and articles for the educated public of the day," wrote Dr. Kevles. The movement was bolstered by reports pouring from institutes that studied "race biology," most notably the Rockefeller Institute. Here the race to unravel DNA, "the blueprint of life," was bolstered by the work of Dr. Phoebus Aaron Theodor Levene as early as 1909. (See figure 18.1.) Other race biology labs and eugenics institutes were established in several other countries including Denmark, Britain, Sweden, and Germany.[8]

"The experts raised the spectre of social degeneration, insisting that 'feebleminded' people (the term then commonly applied to people believed to be mentally retarded) were responsible for a wide range of social problems and were proliferating at a rate that threatened social resources and stability. Feebleminded women were held to be driven by a heedless sexuality, the product of biologically grounded flaws in their moral character that led them to prostitution and producing illegitimate children," Dr. Kevles noted. "Hereditarian" theory likewise attributed criminality and poverty to flawed genes rather than social development.[8]

In an effort to improve societies, eugenics swept through North America and western Europe during the early twentieth century. Many political reformers of that day felt that scientific eugenics might best serve their highest social aspirations. "Eugenics, of course, also drew appreciable support from social conservatives, concerned to prevent the proliferation of lower income groups and save on the cost of caring for them," Dr. Kevles recalled. "The progressives and the conservatives found common ground in attributing phenomena such as crime, slums, prostitution, and alcoholism primarily to biology and in believing that biology might be used to eliminate these discordances of modern, urban, industrial society."[8]

Race was most heavily weighed in the American and Canadian versions of the eugenics creed, more so than in Britain and Scandinavia. "North American eugenicists were particularly disturbed by the immigrants from eastern and southern Europe who had been flooding into their countries since the late 19th century. They considered these people not only racially different from, but inferior to, the Anglo-Saxon majority. Again, it was the WASPS that *American Journal of*

Public Health author Dr. Stephen Kunitz credited for the vast majority of twentieth century genocides discussed in Chapter 13 in relation to globalism. Eugenicists gained political advantage through fear appeals that criminals, slum dwellers, prostitutes, and the feebleminded were on the rise, and in many cities disproportionately high. "Eugenic reasoning in the United States had it that if deficiencies in immigrants were hereditary and eastern European immigrants out-reproduced natives of Anglo-Saxon stock, then inevitably the quality of the American population would decline," Dr. Kevles recalled.[8]

Positive and negative eugenics were promoted to increase the availability of "socially good" genes, and reduce the "bad genes." Positive eugenics implied bioengineering—breeding and/or human heredity experiments—to produce superior individuals. Alternatively, negative eugenics sought to eliminate or exclude biologically inferior people from society.

In the United States, during the 1920s, as shown in figure 18.2, "fitter family" competitions were held as a standard feature at many state fairs. In the "human stock" sections, winning families were awarded trophies in three categories—small, average, and large. "It is hard to know what made these families and individuals stand out as fit," pondered Dr. Kevles, "but the fact that all entrants had to take an IQ test and the Wasserman test for syphilis says something about the organizers' view of necessary qualities."[8]

Negative eugenics was more heavily promoted particularly with the passage of eugenic sterilization laws in two dozen American states by the late 1920s. "By 1933," Dr. Kevles wrote, "California had subjected more people to eugenic sterilization than had all other states of the union combined. Similar measures were passed in Canada, in the provinces of British Columbia and Alberta." These laws tended to discriminate against minority groups and poorer people. "In California, for example, the sterilization rates of blacks and foreign immigrants were twice as high as would be expected from their representation in the general population."[8] This is much the same today regarding disease rates more heavily affecting Black and Hispanic populations in the United States as is the case with AIDS. Moreover, the Kaiser–CDC "EZ measles vaccine" fiasco detailed earlier casts an ominous shadow on the fact that California has apparently remained at the forefront of eugenics efforts.

Much like the legal consensus concerning "mandatory vaccination" laws, the U.S. Supreme Court decided eight to one in 1927, in the

Fig. 18.1. Early Rockefeller Genetics Laboratory of Dr. Phoebus Aaron Theodor Levene, 1909

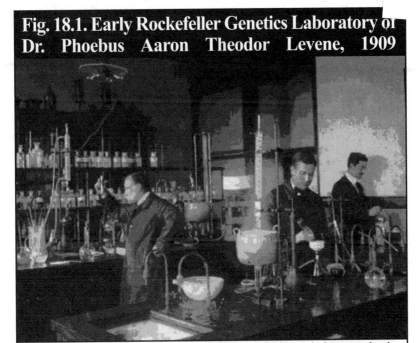

Pioneering the eugenics movement, this is one of several photographs detailing the earliest work in DNA/genetics conducted at the Rockefeller Institute beginning in 1909 by Dr. Levene and his students. Shown here are students (L-R) W. Jacobs, D. Slyke, G. Meyer. Courtesy of the Rockefeller Archive Center. From: http://vector.cshl.org/dnaftb/15/concept/

case of Buck versus Bell, to uphold eugenic sterilizations in Virginia. Justice Oliver Wendall Holmes summarized the majority's view that, "We have seen more than once that the public welfare may call upon the best citizens for their lives. It would be strange if it could not call upon those who already sap the strength of the State for these lesser sacrifices, often not felt to be such by those concerned, in order to prevent our being swamped with incompetence. It is better for all the world, if instead of waiting to execute degenerate offspring for crime, or to let them starve for their imbecility, society can prevent those who are manifestly unfit from continuing their kind. The principle that sustains compulsory vaccinations is broad enough to cover cutting the Fallopian tubes. . . . Three generations of imbeciles are enough."[8]

Likewise, Alberta's premier urged sterilization over segregation in advancing eugenics. He insisted that "the argument of freedom or right of the individual can no longer hold good where the welfare of the state and society is concerned."[8]

Regarding the political practicality of eugenic sterilizations from the depression era through the 1970s, Dr. Kevles wrote:

> Sterilization rates climbed with the onset of the worldwide economic depression in 1929. In parts of Canada, in the deep south of the United States, and throughout Scandinavia, sterilization acquired broad support. This was not primarily on eugenic grounds (though some hereditarian-minded mental health professionals continued to urge it for that purpose) but on economic ones. Sterilization raised the prospect of reducing the cost of institutional care and of poor relief. Even geneticists who disparaged sterilization as the remedy for degeneration held that sterilizing mentally disabled people would yield a social benefit because it would prevent children being born to parents who could not care for them.[8]

This argument, and related sociopolitical conditions supporting it, bears too close for comfort on contemporary geriatric and "baby boomer" populations straining social security and welfare economies. Reflecting on this history, the flu vaccine, particularly targeting the elderly, linked as it is to the Guillain Barré syndrome debacle of the mid-1970s and its ensuing claim of more than 10,000 mostly elderly lives, may be more utilitarian for population control, than sterilization was during the early eugenics period.

Dr. Kevles continued:

> In Scandinavia, sterilization was broadly endorsed by Social Democrats as part of the scientifically oriented planning of the new welfare state. Alva Myrdal spoke for her husband, Gunnar, and for numerous liberals like themselves when in 1941 she wrote, "In our day of highly accelerated social reforms the need for sterilization on social grounds gains new momentum. Generous social reforms may facilitate homemaking and childbearing more than before among the groups of less desirable as well as more desirable parents. [Such a trend] demands some corresponding corrective." On such foundations among others, sterilization programs continued in several American states, in Alberta, and in Scandinavia well into the 1970s.[8]

What Dr. Kevles failed to note was the heavy hand of Rockefeller influence behind both liberal and conservative eugenics promotions as chronicled in Chapter 16.

In conclusion, Dr. Kevles explained, that during the Nazi era, "eugenics prompted the sterilization of several hundred thousand people, then helped lead to anti-Semitic programs of euthanasia and ultimately,

Fig. 18.2. 1924 State Fair Eugenics Poster Attributing "Unfit Human Traits" to Breeding.

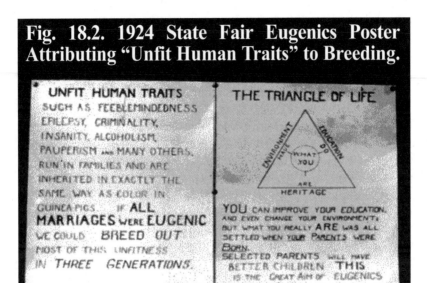

At state fairs across America during the 1920s, eugenics exhibits posting charts such as this were sponsored by organizations heralding the largely Rockefeller instigated eugenics movement. "Fitter family" competitions for "positive eugenics" were held during these events and winning families were awarded trophies in three categories—small, average, and large. The IQ test and the Wasserman test for syphilis was required for entry into the competition. At the same time, eugenic sterilization laws were enacted in two dozen American states. Source: Kevles DJ. Eugenics and human rights. *BMJ* 1999;319:435-438 (14 August).

of course, to the death camps." Eugenics was not, however, "unique to the Nazis. It could, and did, happen everywhere. . . . History at the least has taught us that concern for individual rights belongs at the heart of whatever stratagems we may devise for deploying our rapidly growing knowledge of human and medical genetics."[8]

"Competing interests: None declared," Dr. Kevles wrote tongue-in-cheek in his closing sentence. In other words, those who pioneered the eugenics movement, who are also the primary instigators of contemporary medical genetics, are not about to declare their opposition to individual rights over their current conducting of global genocide.[8]

Early Roots of Contemporary Population Control

As documented in *Emerging Viruses: AIDS & Ebola—Nature, Accident or Intentional?*, The Population Council of the City of New York, the chief instigator of Norplant and intrauterine device (IUD) contraception methods as well, was initially established by the Rockefeller family to aid and abet the modern eugenics movement for global depopulation.

In his detailed historic account of the United Nations, built and funded largely by the Rockefeller family fortune, author William F. Jasper, senior editor of *The New American* magazine, explained the current population control movement in terms of its chief architects. Highlighted was the "high oracle of the doctrine of overpopulation," Standford University biologist Paul Ehrlich and his landmark publication *The Population Bomb*. More than 20 million copies of this book have been sold since its debut in 1968, establishing the text as one of the top best sellers of all time. As Jasper pointed out, "it remains on high school and college required reading lists along with Professor Ehrlich's newest diatribe, *The Population Explosion*, a 1990 update of his famous doomsday message . . ."[8,10,11]

In *The Population Bomb*, Ehrlich advanced arguments consistent with those of early Rockefeller funded eugenicists. He wrote for instance the quote which began this chapter:

> Our position requires that we take immediate action at home and promote effective action worldwide. We must have population control at home, hopefully through a system of incentives and penalties, but by compulsion if voluntary methods fail. . . . We can no longer afford merely to treat the symptoms of the cancer of population growth; the cancer itself must be cut out.[10]

As Jasper revealed, despite Ehrlich's "radically pessimistic predictions of dying oceans and imminent global catastrophes" being refuted by many men of science, the biologist still became the leading spokesman for the population control/environmental movement. This was one more victory for politically correct "science."

In *The Population Bomb*, Ehrlich promoted abortion as "a highly effective weapon in the armory of population control," and advanced government mandated "compulsory birth regulation." Among his fascist suggestions in this regard was the addition of "temporary sterilants to water supplies or staple foods" that might be required by governments.[9,10]

Then, in the Winter 1968 issue of *Stanford Today*, closely followed by Texas Congressman George H.W. Bush's population control appeal in Washington, Ehrlich echoed these appeals and laid the foundation for contemporary birth control politics and policies. He said, "It must be made clear to our population that it is socially irresponsible to have large families." As a remedy, he called for "federal laws making instruction in birth-control methods mandatory in all public schools. . . . If these steps fail to reverse today's population growth, we shall then be faced with some form of compulsory birth regulation. We might institute a system whereby a temporary sterilant would be added to a staple food or to the water supply. An antidote would have to be taken to permit reproduction."[12]

Jasper discussed the global results of Ehrlich's political pronouncements. These were relevant to the subject of non-lethal military warfare wherein propaganda plays a vital role in perpetuating myths concerning the perceived *benefits* of exposing populations to toxic agents. Jasper wrote:

> Ehrlich's critical acclaim in the major media and his phenomenal book sales ushered in a doom boom that has fed, and in turn has been fed by, an ever-expanding proliferation of population control programs. They are funded by tax dollars funneled through national government agencies, the United Nations, and an international network of private anti-natalist organizations. Of the many ecological jeremiads following in the wake of *The Population Bomb*, two of the most influential were *The Limits to Growth* (1972), a report produced for the Club of Rome, and the *Global 2000 Report to the President of the United States* (1980), a federal government publication that gives legitimacy to the thoughts of a large assemblage of professional wailers from environmental/population control circles. . . .[13,14]

Jasper noted that these later publications were met with substantial scientific refutations. Concerning, for instance, in *The Limits to Growth* report for the Club of Rome—an organization controlled by the international banking community subservient to shadow governors in the Royal Institute for International Affairs, Committee of 300, and other groups such as the CFR wherein Rockefeller family members played guiding roles—the computer modeling was refuted. Massachusetts Institute of Technology (MIT) grantees, funded to deliver the same doomsday message, were likewise met with disdain by many scientists including Nobel Prize-winning economist Gunner Myrdal. Concerning the Club of Rome's haughty "science," Myrdal wrote:

> [T]he use of mathematical equations and a huge computer, which registers the alternatives of abstractly conceived policies by a "world simulation model," may impress the innocent general public but has little, if any, scientific validity. That this "sort of model is actually a

new tool for mankind," is unfortunately not true. It represents quasilearnedness of a type that we have, for a long time, had too much of. . . .[15]

There were many other scientists and academicians who took exception to population control proponents. Many professed that Ehrlich's conclusions better represented scientific fraud than sound research. In *The Resourceful Earth: A Response to Global 2000*, one group of academics and eminent scientists addressed the same premise and articulated a far more positive view of population densities and the resources available to sustain them. These experts optimistically concluded:

> Environmental, resource, and population stresses are diminishing, and with the passage of time will have less influence than now upon the quality of human life on our planet. These stresses have in the past always caused many people to suffer from lack of food, shelter, health and jobs, but the trend is toward less rather than more of such suffering. Especially important and noteworthy is the dramatic trend toward longer and healthier life throughout all the world. Because of increases in knowledge, the earth's "carrying capacity" has been increasing through the decades and centuries and millennia to such an extent that the term "carrying capacity" has by now no useful meaning.[15]

These authors explained that there was no rational basis for alarmist proclamations regarding overpopulation.

An additional review of the science of the matter by author Jacqueline Kasum, in *The War Against Population*, determined that the entire concept of overpopulation is a myth. Even considering China and India, countries most often cited as having severe population problems, in reality have similar population densities to Pennsylvania and the United Kingdom, respectively.[9,16]

As might be expected, such opposing scientific views and facts were highly suppressed, both academically and by the mainstream media.

Rockefeller Influence and Population Control PSYOPs

As previously introduced, Christopher Simpson documented the insidious manipulation of the social and physical sciences by the Rockefeller family in his book, *Science of Coercion: Communication Research and Psychological Warfare 1945-1960.*[16] Here, the control mechanisms behind American organizations, such as the United States

Public Health Service (USPHS), are elucidated. His evidence s
the powerful effects that "psychological warfare" has had on U.S. ᴜᴏᵥ
ernment politics and global policies. Simpson persuasively supported
his "heretical conclusion" that the "role of the United States in world
affairs during our lifetimes has often been rapacious, destructive, toler-
ant of genocide, and willing to sacrifice countless people in the pursuit
of a chimera of security that has grown ever more remote."[16]

Simpson astutely reasoned, "Rethinking psychological warfare's
role in communication studies, requires reconsideration of where contemporary Western ideology comes from, whose interests it serves, and
the role that social scientists play in its propagation. Such discussions
have always upset those who are content with the present order of
things. . . ."[17]

The origin of modern methods of applied coercion Simpson connected, once again, to the Rockefeller family. Aside from considering
the Rockefeller/IG Farben chemical/pharmaceutical cartel's support
for the pre-World War II, and later Nazi, psychiatrists upon which Josef
Goebbels, propaganda minister of the Third Reich, established his successful campaigns, Simpson documented the links between the Rockefeller family, the Rockefeller Foundation, and the CIA from its
inception.

Similar to Dr. John Coleman's findings, Simpson showed a
"wealth of evidence" indicating the first CIA-sponsored U.S. mass
communication manipulations derived from the work of Albert Hadley
Cantril, the renowned director of the Princeton Radio Project from
1937 to 1939, "a founder and longtime director of Princeton's Office
of Public Opinion Research, and a founder of the Princeton Listening
Center, which eventually evolved into the CIA-financed Foreign
Broadcast Information Service. . . . Cantril's career had been closely
bound up with U.S. intelligence and clandestine psychological operations since at least the late 1930s. . . . Cantril went on to serve as the
senior public opinion specialist of the Office of the Coordinator of Inter-American Affairs (an early U.S. intelligence agency led by Nelson
Rockefeller then focusing on Latin America) of the WWII Office of
War Information, and in a later period, as an adviser to President
Eisenhower on the psychological aspects of foreign policy. During the
Kennedy administration, Cantril helped reorganize the U.S. Information Agency."[18]

"According to the *New York Times*,"[19] Simpson recalled, "the CIA
provided Cantril and his colleague Lloyd Free with $1 million in 1956

to gather intelligence on popular attitudes in countries of interest to the agency. The Rockefeller Foundation appears to have laundered the money for Cantril, because Cantril repeatedly claimed in print that the monies had come from that source." The *Times*, however, along with Cantril's partner, Lloyd Free, confirmed that the CIA had been the source of the researcher's funding.[17-19]

Another example of the CIA's role in waging psychological warfare, cited by Simpson, "was the work of the Center for International Studies (CENIS)" at the Massachusetts Institute of Technology (MIT). "The CIA became the principal leader of this institution throughout the 1950s . . . [and] CENIS served as a conduit for CIA funds for researchers at other institutions, particularly the Center for Russian Research at Harvard."[17-19]

"CENIS," Simpson continued, "emerged as one of the most important centers of communication studies . . . According to CENIS's official account, the funds for its communications research was provided by a four-year, $850,000 grant from the Ford Foundation." Ford Foundation archives showed, however, that the foundation, with intimate links to the Rockefeller Foundation, had underwritten the costs of the CIA's principle propaganda project aimed at intellectuals—the Congress for Cultural Freedom. This grant cost $500,000 and was made at the CIA's request. The Ford Foundation's director, John McCloy, who is remembered for his World War II psychological warfare work, had "established a regular liaison with the CIA for the specific purpose of managing Ford Foundation cover for CIA projects," Simpson wrote. "Of the men on CENIS's communication studies planning committee, Edward Shils was simultaneously a leading spokesman for the CIA-backed Congress for Cultural Freedom project; [and] Hans Speier was the RAND Corporation's director of social science research . . . In short, CENIS communication studies were, from their inception, closely bound up with both overt and covert aspects of U.S. national security strategy . . ."[19]

The RAND Corporation, according to Simpson, also played a central role in administering psychological warfare projects for the CIA and the foundations which served as its cover. Today, the organization and its representatives remain at the forefront of U.S. counterintelligence and propaganda wars of various sorts.

Of particular relevance to this book, as will be addressed in the next section, the RAND Corporation, tied to the SRI and the Tavistock

Institute, has been instrumental in delivering propaganda concerning the nature and population risks of contemporary bioterrorism. By so doing, propagandists for RAND continue to shape public opinion on behalf of allied intelligence agencies and the globalists who control them and ongoing genocides.

Given this background on psychological warfare, even the notion that worsening environmental pollution is primarily linked to over-population, can be seen for what it is—a grave manipulation. Who, after all, besides the Rockefellers, have grossly monopolized the fossil fuel industries? Who more than the Rockefellers have made vast fortunes from wars conducted during the twentieth century to allegedly preserve cultural, religious and political freedoms, simultaneously safeguarding and expanding their precious oil reserves? Even OPEC nations' controls, like Saudi Arabian oil interests, have remained heavily influenced by the Rockefeller and royal families since their inceptions. Then, again, who has profited most by the burning of fossil fuels that, more than population desities per se, *actually cause* the environmental pollution, global warming, and ozone depletion. Thus, seen in this light, population control has became a convenient scapegoat for the fact that political, economic, and energy policy decisions have been orchestrated for decades by the Rockefeller/Farben cartel and the allied British oligarchs—those that became the derelict stewards of earth's power, energy, and natural resources.

Given the above history of the cryptocracy's interests and affiliates, it was not surprising that John Bongaarts of The Population Council of the City of New York directed the new millennium's consensus report from the Panel on Population Projections to conclude, like Dr. Ehrlich, that the world was severely over inhabited. Representatives on this panel included esteemed members of the National Academy of Sciences—National Research Council (NAS-NRC), the Institute of Medicine (IOM), the UN, World Bank, USAID, RAND, the Alfred P. Sloan Foundation, and more ideological clones representing academia. Dr. Bongaarts, vice president of the Population Council, together with experts from the Rockefeller directed Population Council and Rockefeller University, with funding primarily from (surprise, surprise) the Rockefeller Foundation and Andrew W. Mellon Foundation along with USAID, paid the National Academy of Sciences Press to produce *Beyond Six Billion: Forecasting the World's Population*—the most advanced scientific PSYOPs to command and control world

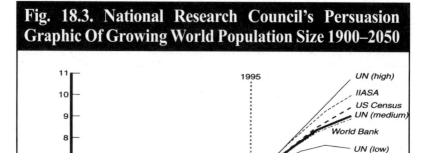

Fig. 18.3. National Research Council's Persuasion Graphic Of Growing World Population Size 1900–2050

Graph shows world population size estimates and projections by the United Nations (1999), World Bank (1999), U.S. Census Bureau (1999) and International Institute for Applied Systems Analysis—a think tank based in Austria (1996). From: National Research Council. *Beyond Six Billion: Forcasting the World's Population.* John Bongaarts and Rodolfo A. Bulatao, Eds. Washington, D.C.: National Academy Press, 2000, pp. 18.

opinion regarding the continued need to reduce world populations. Some of their "persuasion graphics" are reprinted in figures 18.3 and 18.4.[20]

The graphed projection in 18.3 of burgeoning populations through the year 2050 seriously conflicts with other reports cited earlier, and even the trend seen in 18.4 showing drastically reduced fertility rates in industrialized and developing nations.

An additional spin was added by World Population Projections (WPP)—a UN agency that published its propaganda in Henry Luce's *Time* magazine on June 29, 1998. Here the depopulationists wrote:

7.7 billion: The peak that world population will reach in 2040, according to latest estimates. The total is projected to fall to 3.6 billion by 2150, less than two-thirds of today's population.[21]

The NAS–NRC experts and *Time* failed to explain why populations were expected to fall so precipitously. Obviously, they held intelligence they were not sharing such as the NAS—NRC's knowledge of

Fig. 18.4. National Research Council's/United Nations Data on Projected Fertility in Low-Fertility Countries

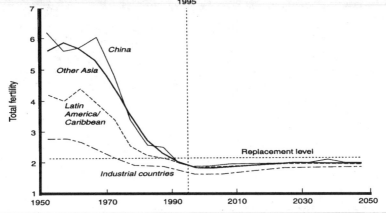

Graph shows below "replacement level" growth, that is, depopulation occurring in "Low-fertility" nations according to the U.N. and National Academy of Sciences—National Research Council. This same Rockefeller-controlled scientific think tank advised the U.S. Department of Defense in 1969 that "synthetic biological agents," descriptively identical to HIV/AIDS could be developed by 1974 for $10 million. (See figure 18.5.) From: National Research Council. *Op. cit.*, p. 86.

"synthetic biological agents" for germ warfare the organization helped to develop. These, in fact, were predicted to reduce targeted populations dramatically. Figure 18.5 shows the NAS—NRC was precisely the organization that advised U.S. Defense Department officials that they could develop an AIDS-like virus for merely $10 million spent between 1970 and 1975.[22]

RAND's Analysis of Domestic Bioterrorism

Besides educators like James P. Smith of RAND in Santa Monica, California espousing world depopulation requirements, others from RAND have been traveling throughout North America promoting biological terrorism preparedness.

"'Astute observation' begs the question: 'Who are the real bioterrorists?'" asked Don Harkins, Editor of the *Idaho Observer*, in his September 2000 issue.[23]

Mr. Harkins, along with emergency management directors from northern Idaho, attended an official government workshop conducted by the RAND corporation's Washington, D.C. Office Director, Dr.

Fig. 18.5. NAS–NRC Advises U.S. Military on the Development of HIV-like Biological Weapons in 1969

SYNTHETIC BIOLOGICAL AGENTS

There are two things about the biological agent field I would like to mention. One is the possibility of technological surprise. Molecular biology is a field that is advancing very rapidly and eminent biologists believe that within a period of 5 to 10 years it would be possible to produce a synthetic biological agent, an agent that does not naturally exist and for which no natural immunity could have been acquired.

Mr. SIKES. Are we doing any work in that field?

Dr. MACARTHUR. We are not.

Mr. SIKES. Why not? Lack of money or lack of interest?

Dr. MACARTHUR. Certainly not lack of interest.

Mr. SIKES. Would you provide for our records information on what would be required, what the advantages of such a program would be, the time and the cost involved?

Dr. MACARTHUR. We will be very happy to.

(The information follows:)

The dramatic progress being made in the field of molecular biology led us to investigate the relevance of this field of science to biological warfare. A small group of experts considered this matter and provided the following observations:

1. All biological agents up to the present time are representatives of naturally occurring disease, and are thus known by scientists throughout the world. They are easily available to qualified scientists for research, either for offensive or defensive purposes.

2. Within the next 5 to 10 years, it would probably be possible to make a new infective microorganism which could differ in certain important aspects from any known disease-causing organisms. Most important of these is that it might be refractory to the immunological and therapeutic processes upon which we depend to maintain our relative freedom from infectious disease.

3. A research program to explore the feasibility of this could be completed in approximately 5 years at a total cost of $10 million.

4. It would be very difficult to establish such a program. Molecular biology is a relatively new science. There are not many highly competent scientists in the field, almost all are in university laboratories, and they are generally adequately supported from sources other than DOD. However, it was considered possible to initiate an adequate program through the National Academy of Sciences-National Research Council (NAS-NRC).

The matter was discussed with the NAS-NRC, and tentative plans were made to initiate the program. However, decreasing funds in CB, growing criticism of the CB program, and our reluctance to involve the NAS NRC in such a controversial endeavor have led us to postpone it for the past 2 years.

It is a highly controversial issue and there are many who believe such research should not be undertaken lest it lead to yet another method of massive killing of large populations. On the other hand, without the sure scientific knowledge that such a weapon is possible, and an understanding of the ways it could be done, there is little that can be done to devise defensive measures. Should an enemy develop it there is little doubt that this is an important area of potential military technological inferiority in which there is no adequate research program.

The above document proves the interest of the U.S. military/CIA and Rockefeller directed National Academy of Sciences–National Research Council (NAS-NRC) in developing "synthetic biological agents" that were descriptively and functionally identical to HIV/AIDS in 1969. This hearing evolved from directives issued by National Security Advisor, and Rockefeller protégé, Dr. Henry Kissinger, according to testimony provided Congress by previous CIA directors Richard Helms and William Colby. According to *Newsweek*'s Managing Editor, Walter Isaacson, Kissinger was seeking alternatives to nuclear weapons in 1969 just prior to articulating his most extensive depopulation policy report—National Security Memorandum 200. Nixon's "War on Cancer" began the following year, largely as a cover for this new biological weapons race for "yet another way of massive killing of large populations." Source: Classified portion of Department of Defense Appropriations for 1970, Hearings Before a Subcommittee of the Committee on Appropriations House of Representatives, Ninety-First Congress, Tuesday, July 1, 1969, p. 129. Washington, DC: U.S Government Printing Office, 1969.

Bruce Hoffman, on August 24, 2000. RAND's terrorism researcher David Brannon, and international security specialist, Peter Chalk, spoke at the one-day program entitled, "Understanding What Terrorism Means to Rural Idaho." The seminar was hosted by the State of Idaho Military Division Bureau of Disaster Services (BDS). According to BDS official, Fred Heywood, who welcomed the 50 city and county employees and law enforcement officers from all parts of north Idaho, the seminar was held to "put into proper perspective" the threats posed by various types of domestic terrorism.

Harkins reported that almost immediately after being introduced, Dr. Hoffman stated that, though he, Chalk, and Brannon work for RAND, all three of them were allegedly speaking for themselves and were *not* representing RAND. This afforded their organization the ability to claim "plausible denial" should their agents err or be exposed.

Dr. Hoffman opened the seminar by giving an overview of what he referred to as, "the changing face of terrorism," and attempted to explain the meaning of terrorism through distinctions rather than definitions. As part of an on-going slide presentation he provided the audience an orientation to terrorism. The FBI definition of terrorism was presented as, "the unlawful use of force or violence against persons or property to intimidate or coerce a government, the civilian population, or any segment thereof, in furtherance of political or social objectives."

The Department of Defense's definition of terrorism, as presented by Dr. Hoffman, was "the calculated use of violence or the threat of violence to inculcate fear; intended to coerce or try to intimidate governments or societies in the pursuit of goals that are generally political, religious, or ideological."

"All acts of terrorism are politically motivated," Dr. Hoffman stated.

Though terrorists have always been "politically radical," they are "operationally conservative," explained Dr. Hoffman. Since most terrorists have limited resources they must carefully plan and carry out acts of terrorism with maximum impact at minimal expense.

Terrorists have traditionally used acts of terrorism to gain attention and sympathy for their causes. Dr. Hoffman stated that only 12 terrorist incidents in the last 9,000 have killed more than 100 people.

Traditionally, terrorists have announced their intentions in advance of an attack or have publicly claimed responsibility for an attack after it has occurred because their main objective is publicity, that is, public opinion. Most of the 12 incidents mentioned were recent and no one had stepped forward to claim responsibility for them.

Dr. Hoffman referenced the Oklahoma City bombing and Timothy McVeigh several times as exemplary of modern terrorism. He also used the 1995 nerve gas attack in a Tokyo subway and the bombing of Pan Am 103 over Lockerbie, Scotland, to illustrate the "changing face of terrorism."

Dr. Hoffman admitted that "conspiracy theories" abound in the absence of credible claims of responsibility for terrorist attacks.

He also said that he and his colleagues at RAND anticipated incorrectly that an era of copycat bombings would follow in the wake of the 1995 bombing of the Murrah Federal Building in Oklahoma City which killed 168 people.

According to Dr. Hoffman, the new face of terrorism was more murderous and "calls into question the most basic assumptions" regarding terrorists. That is, they may not be "fundamentally rational" and solely interested in publicity.

Defense Secretary Cohen's Unprecedented Hype

Defense Secretary William Cohen had proposed earlier in 2000 on national television a chemical and/or biological attack scenario that virtually sparked a new antiterrorism industry.

The threat of chemical or biological attacks by domestic terrorists was not as great as the American public had been lead to believe, Dr. Hoffman stated. Conditions must be perfect for biological weapons of mass destruction (WMD) to be effective. The sheer volume of chemical agents that would be needed to effect a massive terrorist attack diminishes the likelihood that chemicals will be weapons of choice among modern terrorists. Dr. Hoffman stated that chemical and biological attack scenarios proposed by Defense Secretary William Cohen, and political intrigue author Tom Clancy, were not reality based.

Since Defense Secretary Cohen held up a five-pound bag of sugar in 1997 and said that a similar amount of anthrax released in the air above the nation's capitol would kill approximately 300,000 people, antiterrorism has become one of the nation's fastest growing industries.

To support this claim, Mr. Harkins reported the following:

• The number of FBI agents assigned to counter terrorism has grown from 550 in 1993 to nearly 1,500 in 2000.

• According to Chalk, a native of Australia, the U.S. devoted $89 million to WMD preparedness in 1998.

• The Clinton administration had requested that $566 million be budgeted for WMD preparedness for 2001.

• In November 1999, President Clinton proposed a $10 billion antiterrorism package, which is up from the antiterrorism budget of $6.5 billion in 1998.

• Since Cohen instilled the fear of chemical and/or biological attack into the collective mind of the American public in 1997, WMD preparedness spending alone increased by 536 percent since 1998.[23]

"Why would Cohen, who had access to all chemical/biological weapons intelligence data, including that disseminated by RAND, want to frighten the public with the imminence of a chemical/biological threat? Was he not mirroring the intent of 'terrorists' to leave a specific impression on a gullible public," asked Mr. Harkins for a response destined to be published in the *Idaho Observer*.

Chalk gave a thoughtful and lengthy answer to Harkins's question. Chalk explained that Cohen's public announcement was undoubtedly prompted by lobbyists who used the Clinton cabinet member as political leverage to fund their antiterrorism programs and research.

"Earlier today Dr. Hoffman stated that 'all terrorist acts are politically motivated.' What you just described to me was that Cohen's threat of imminent chemical or biological attack was politically motivated. How, then, is Defense Secretary Cohen's behavior different from what you have described as that of a domestic terrorist?" Harkins asked.

With a wry smile that seemed to say, "touchet," Chalk said, "Your observation is very astute."[23]

Another Ehrlich For Population Control

As detailed in *Emerging Viruses*, the Paul Ehrlich Institute in Frankfort/Main, Germany, was among the first vaccine research and development facilities to receive a shipment of contaminated monkeys associated with the first outbreak of the Marburg virus—the mother of Ebola—in 1967. The institute was named for a pioneer in immunology and pharmaceutical therapy, Dr. Paul Ehrlich.

In 1899, Paul Ehrlich moved to Frankfurt to work at the Institute of Experimental Therapy. He was later appointed the director there, and much later the institute took his name. He worked initially on cancer, but eventually began a successful career in identifying synthetic chemical substances that would be toxic to disease causing microorganisms, and likely humans as well. His pioneering work in this field heavily influenced the pharmaceutical industry. He, in fact, paved the way for the discovery of the sulfonamides and non-synthetic antibiotics. After the course and means of transmission of syphilis was recognized, a specific chemical agent against this disease became Ehrlich's main ambition. He was awarded the Nobel Prize for Medicine in 1908. In 1909, Ehrlich and Hata discovered the antibiotic salvarsan. The following year, his experiments on the synthetic drug arsphenamine for spirochaetal infections including syphilis and yaws was reported at the "Internisten-Kongreß" in Wiesbaden.

Was it serendipitous that two Dr. Paul Ehrlichs made it to the forefront of their interrelated fields—depopulation and vaccination? Yet, there was a third Dr. Paul Ehrlich with whom we must contend. *Emerging Viruses: AIDS & Ebola—Nature, Accident or Intentional?* documents showed this Dr. Paul Ehrlich to be a central figure in covert U.S military biological weapons testing, cancer virus research, and human experimental vaccine developments, particularly in Third World countries.[24]

Dr. S. Paul Ehrlich, Jr., rose to power in the United States Department of Health Education and Welfare (DHEW), to finally become the acting Surgeon General of the United States under Joseph Califano, Secretary of the DHEW with intimate links to population control, the CIA, and Zbigniew Brzezinski's documented war on African Americans and Blacks abroad.[24]

In 1976, this Dr. Ehrlich was Surgeon General of the United States when the U.S. Congress investigated Department of Defense (DoD) open air biological weapons experiments conducted on unsuspecting human subjects in San Francisco, New York, Pennsylvania, and elsewhere. These tests were later determined to be lethal for many elderly people and children with suppressed immune systems. Ehrlich's department then defended the Army by issuing a false statement that read: "We do not know of any evidence that would indicate an association between the deaths reported in the press . . . and the organisms reported to have been used in the atmospheric tests."[24]

Vaccine Production, Ebola, AIDS and Other Outbreaks

As detailed in *Emerging Viruses*, the Paul Ehrlich Institute vaccine production facility was struck by the Ebola virus *bioweapon* initially tested on monkeys in Litton Bionetics labs in 1965. It might be recalled that Litton Bionetics was the Army's sixth top biological weapons contractor during the late 1960s and early 1970s, and was linked through high level parent company officials to the Rockefeller-directed cancer and depopulation industries. I say *bioweapon* because Ebola is recognized as among the most ideal biological warfare agents as discussed by David Baltimore in *Biological and Toxin Weapons Today* (Oxford University Press, 1986).[25]

Dr. Baltimore became President of the California Institute of Technology as a leading expert in the field of molecular biology, recombinant virology, and biological warfare. Evidence linking him to the 1969 military requisition for AIDS and Ebola-like viruses is shown in figures 18.5 and 18.6, and discussed below.

Figure 18.6 proves Dr. Baltimore directed MIT studies beginning in 1971 that sought to "define the role of these [HIV/AIDS-like viruses] in malignant cell transformation." The manmade HIV/AIDS origin link was further reinforced, if not proven, by his 1978 statement of his project's "Proposed Course: [In the] Analysis of genetic control of viral replication . . . Mechanism of DNA proviral synthesis by reverse transcriptase and the function of RNAase H will be explored. . . . In vitro translation will be used to determine precursor [gene] sequences and cleavage sites." For AIDS scientists, this technical language is familiar. It simply proves that Baltimore, an esteemed member of the NAS-NRC at that time, was reporting on the primary mechanism of HIV/AIDS *before* anyone knew it existed. Plus, his lab was actually doing sophisticated genetic viral engineering studies *long before* even scientists believed this was possible.

According to two experts discussing the mysterious Marburg virus outbreak, Dr. Rudolph Siegert of the Hygiene Institute of the Philipps University in Marburg, and Dr. Seymour Kalter—the National Cancer Institute's leading diagnostician of viruses that were believed to be "emerging" from labs—the Marburg virus was "manmade." Siegert reported in 1972 that the Marburg virus shared the closest similarity to a family of viruses known as *Rhabdovirus simian*. These included the culprits responsible for rabies initially found in rodents, and then transferred to monkeys before "jumping species" to humans at the Paul Ehrlich Institute for vaccine production.

Fig. 18.6. David Baltimore HIV/AIDS-like Virus Study at MIT During the SVCP, 1971-1978

MASSACHUSETTS INSTITUTE OF TECHNOLOGY (N01-CP5-3562)

Title: Studies on the Leukemia Virus DNA Polymerase and Terminal Deoxynucleotidyl Transferase

Contractor's Project Director: Dr. David Baltimore

Project Officer (NCI): Dr. Edward Scolnick

Objectives: (1) Carry out a detailed analysis of DNA polymerases from RNA tumor virus particles and from normal and neoplastic cells. (2) Study the mechanism of double-stranded DNA synthesis by the avian myeloblastosis virus DNA polymerase and the functions of the subunits of the enzyme in infected cells and variation in DNA polymerases in various stages of cell growth.

Major Findings: Studies of reverse transcription in virions of MuLV showed that under defined conditions, very long molecules of complementary DNA could be made. These DNA molecules were infective in NIH/3T3 cells but actinomycin D blocked synthesis of infective molecules. The longest DNA made in the presence of actinomycin D lacked sequences from the .5'-end of the viral RNA as shown by heteroduplex analysis with 21S RNA that was presumably the mRNA for the glycoprotein of the virion. This RNA was shown to be a composite of 5'- and 3'-proximal sequences.

In other studies, it was shown that reverse transcriptase was made as a 180,000 molecular weight precursor that was cleaved in virions to the 85,000 molecular weight reverse transcriptase. The 180,000 protein had antigenicity of both gag and pol proteins and was made by a by-pass of UAG codon at the end of the gag gene. This codon could be suppressed in vitro with yeast amber suppressor tRNA but the in vivo mechanism remained unknown.

Studies of terminal deoxynucleotidyl transferase (TdT) continued to define it as a marker of maturing lymphoid cells probably of both the T and B lymphocyte series. In patients with blastic chronic myelogenous leukemia, occurrence of TdT was a very good indicator that remission induction with vincristine and prednisone would be successful.

Significance to Biomedical Research and the Program of the Institute: Fundamental studies on oncogenic virus replication are necessary to define the role of these viruses in malignant cell transformation. In vitro synthesis of infectious nucleic acid and in vitro translation of proteins allows first level mechanistic studies which can logically be expected to provide means for controlling the infections and/or transforming processes.

Proposed Course: Analysis of genetic control of viral replication will be analyzed. Mechanism of DNA proviral synthesis by reverse transcriptase and the function of RNase H will be explored. In vitro translation will be used to determine precursor sequences and cleavage sites.

Date Contract Initiated: May 1, 1971

David Baltimore, NAS–NRC member and the nation's leading expert in biological warfare using immune suppressive viruses such as HIV and Ebola, is believed to have advised DoD officials in 1969 regarding the development of HIV-like "synthetic biological agents" for "massive killing of large populations." In 1998, Dr. Baltimore became President of California Institute of Technology, heavily invested in genetic biotechnology. Source: NCI Staff. *The [Special] Virus Cancer Program [SVCP]. Op cit.,* 1978, p. 204.

Their documents showed that Litton Bionetics's director, John Landon, beginning July 1965—preceding the first Marburg virus outbreak by two years—began experimenting with *Rhabdovirus simian.* He reported to the NCI in 1971, that nine of the original eighteen monkeys he had injected had either "died," or were "transferred." Monkeys that had survived the biological injections/infections had developed immunity and antibodies required for vaccine production. Thus, they were routinely "transferred" to Europe's premier Paul Ehrlich vaccine production lab wherein the Marburg outbreak initially occurred in 1967.

On March 19, 1975, during a cancer virus research and safety symposium, Dr. Kalter, director at the Southwest Foundation's primate labs, obviously frustrated by the scientific impropriety of avoiding the truth about the mother of Ebola, testified: "I believe simian-hemorrhagic fever is *important.* It appears to be a *manmade* disease."[26]

Hellman at the Helm of Airborne Studies

Directing the meeting was Dr. Alfred Hellman, a previously introduced U.S. Navy Biological Research Laboratories (NBRL) official, and the chairman of the NCI's section on Biohazards Control and Containment. Following Dr. Kalter's stunning but accurate diagnosis of the "manmade" origin of Marburg/Ebola, Hellman, at the helm of the conference, felt compelled to redirect discussion to less troubled waters.

Dr. Hellman, Special Virus Cancer Program reports revealed, was one of the world's leading experts in airborne viruses. Contrary to mainstream media reports, the Ebola virus may spread through aerosols. With his links to the Atomic Energy Commission (AEC), discussed in greater detail below, as well as his work at the U.S. Navy that included airborne biological warfare research and developments, his intimate links to the CIA and their top secret bioweapons program called Project: MKNAOMI can be surmised.

As discussed and documented in *Emerging Viruses: AIDS & Ebola,* Hellman served as the executive project officer for the NCI in their effort to test the "Aerosol Properties of Potentially Oncogenic Viruses" with the Navy. Hellman, oversaw the NBRL studies in which viruses were spread through the air in an effort to study "virus-host interaction considering both the hazard to humans and animals and the potential for cross contamination."[27] These studies, similar to what had been conducted on the USS Coral Sea and the USS F. D. Bailey in

1950, were apparently a follow-up to the studies conducted by the Special Operations Division of the Army in cooperation with the Navy and the CIA.[28] This time, in 1971, instead of exposing unwitting servicemen to aerosols containing relatively mild, *Serratia marcescens* and *Bacillus globigii* bacteria, humans and animals were exposed to carcinogenic viruses. In these reports, Hellman and his colleagues wisely chose to keep the identity of their human and animal test subjects classified.[27]

Figure 18.7 reprints the contract that Dr. Hellman administered from 1976–1978 for the NCI and U.S. Navy through a privately owned entity—Enviro Control, Inc.—in Rockville, Maryland. It was benignly titled, "Monitoring of Biohazard Containment Facilities." Yet, its primary function was to oversee "virus production facilities which provide resources to NCI . . . [to promote] the integrity of experimental systems by protecting them from contamination; . . .[and provide] support to the NIH Recombinant DNA Research Program." As stated earlier in this 1978 SVCP report, Dr. Hellman's studies, similar to Dr. Baltimore's, "stress[ed] endogenous type C virus [HIV/AIDS-like RNA retrovirus] interaction[s] with immunological defense mechanisms, reproductive process and chemical [co-]carcinogens. . . . To achieve these goals . . . humans and baboons are being examined for immunological evidence of endogenous [genetic] or exogenous [environmental] infection with baboon virus M7 or cross reacting viruses. . . . The most significant advance during this year has been the isolation and purification of a type C viral associated protein, which modifies the *in vitro* [cell culture] and *in vivo* [live primate, including human] cellular immune mechanism."

As documented in *Emerging Viruses: AIDS & Ebola—Nature, Accident or Intentional?*, Dow Chemical Company had administered a parallel contract beginning in 1965.

All of these studies, biological developments, and testing programs, conducted under the guise of "cancer research," "disease prevention," "vaccine development" and/or military "defense" were, as discussed in the U.S. *Congressional Record*, parts of the CIA's Project: MKULTRA for population control including depopulation. This insidious outcome was the ultimate goal of this vast covert biomedical effort. Aspects of this that have impacted the public's health through

Fig. 18.7. Dr. Alfred Hellman's Viral Hazard and Containment Contract During the SVCP, 1976-1978

ENVIRO CONTROL, INC. (NO1-CP-6-1021)

Title: Monitoring of Biohazard Containment Facilities

Contractor's Project Director: Dr. Robert W. McKinney

Project Officer (NCI): Dr. Alfred Hellman

Objective: In collaboration with the Viral Oncology Office of Biohazard Safety (OBS), NCI, the contractor: performs safety inspections of virus production facilities which provide resources to NCI to determine compliance with relevant safety standards; performs biological safety and environmental control surveys to contract research facilities for the purpose of providing guidance in biohazard control technology with aim of reducing accident potential and promoting the integrity of experimental systems by protecting them from contamination; evaluates the effectiveness and accomplishments of previous OBS safety program and recommends means to improve the OBS control program; provides safety, environmental microbiology, and engineering consultation to NCI laboratories and to other parties seeking assistance from OBS; and procures and installs essential safety equipment needed by Program scientists involved in cancer research. Through requests from the Office of Research Safety, OD, NCI, the contractor also assists other parties by providing technical safety information and guidance.

Major Findings: During the period covered by this report, 20 site visits were were conducted, which involved 26 separate contracts. Five of the contracts were resources efforts and 19 were research. In addition, visits were made to provide consultation regarding renovations to a facility as well as a consultation to a Food and Drug Administration laboratory.

Support was provided to the Office of Research Safety, NCI and the Research Facilities Branch, NCI in the review of plans and specifications for ten proposed or active laboratory construction projects. In addition, two courtesy consultations were provided. These reviews and consultations were conducted for the purpose of evaluating the adequacy of design and specifications in relation to biohazard containment and environmental control.

Work was continued on the development of modifications for two items of safety equipment. These were: (1) a primate containment system; and, (2) a small animal necropsy cabinet. The preparation of review documents was continued and during this report, reviews were initiated in the subject areas of: (1) Face Velocity Criteria for Chemical Type Fume Hoods; (2) Constant Air Volume Control Systems; (3) Incineration; and, (4) Storage of Chemicals.

Support to the NIH Recombinant DNA Research Program was continued. This has been expanded to include the development of Class III cabinet systems utilizing surplus units from the Ft. Detrick laboratories. These cabinet systems will be installed in laboratories of the NCI.

Significance to Biomedical Research and the Program of the Institute: This contract contributes biological safety and environmental control expertise to the VOP and to the general scientific community. This expertise is used to improve the quality and safety of the cancer research laboratory environment. The contractor functions as an important support to the NCI Office of Biohazard Safety.

Proposed Course: The contractor will continue to provide technical assistance to the VOP contractors on problems of environmental control, personnel safety, and product protection. All recommendations will be based on compliance with accepted engineering design, biological safety and environmental control practices.

Date Contract Initiated: September 29, 1976

Dr. Hellman, chief of airborne biological weapons research and containment for the U.S. Navy is shown here overseeing special HIV/AIDS-like virus production facilities from 1976 to 1978 *before* HIV/AIDS was known to exist. Source: NCI Staff. *Op cit.,* 1978, p. 238.

The Hellman *et al.* activities described above and others documented below, along with the U.S. Navy and AEC's links to the military–medical–pharmaceutical globalists that hype the dangers of
burgeoning populations and administer the depopulation programs described in this chapter, lend credence to the thesis developed in this
book. That is, that growing modern epidemics are the result of well
studied, intentionally administered, biological and chemical exposures,
that produce a non-lethal "Russian Biological Cocktail" method of reducing undesired populations while raising minimal suspicions and
maximizing pharmaceutical and "defense" industry profits.

Figure 18.8 provides additional evidence in this regard. It docu-
ments the U.S. Department of Energy and AEC (previously linked to
Rockefeller influentials and in figure 15.9 to British royalty-directed
ARCO) conducted just such early research into the development and
testing of HIV-like retroviruses and related illnesses, along with other
cancers that tend to target minorities, especially Jewish populations.
This list of Energy Department investigators and study titles include:
"HOST CELL CONTROL OF RETROVIRUS EXPRESSION" by Dr.
R.W. Tennant et al., with the RNA Tumor Virus Section; "IN VITRO
INTERACTION OF CHEMICAL CARCINOGENS WITH PRI-
MATE CELLS," directed by Dr. George Lavelle et al. of the "Co-carcinogenesis Section of the SVCP; "IN VIVO RADIATION-
ACTIVATION OF ENDOGENOUS SARCOMA VIRUS GENOME."
Earlier, sarcomas were determined to strike predominantly immune
suppressed elderly Jewish males of European descent before the cancer suddenly began to affect young gay males in New York City during
the 1970s. It should be noted that virus activation by "radiation" in
these studies likely included low-level nonionizing electromagnetic
frequency radiation such as that emitted by HAARP generators besides
the better known ionizing radiation associated with X-ray equipment
and nuclear weapons. Additional studies in this domain included, "HU-
MAN MAMMARY TUMOR VIROLOGY" by Dr. A.J. Hackett et. al.,
which likewise concerned Jewish woman more than other minorities.

Relatedly, Oak Ridge Nuclear Laboratory (ORNL) Senior Staff
official, Dr. J.E. Phelps, has linked environmental pollution with fluoride, beryllium, and other toxic metal oxides (including aluminum oxide
discussed in Chapter 10 related to chemtrails), to human immunodeficiency and autoimmunity in numerous contemporary illnesses wherein
chronic fatigue is a prominent symptom. According to Dr. Phelps, "this
key effect has not been reported by the ORNL and suppressed [by the
E] since 1986 due to . . . liabilities from toxic emissions."[24] The 1978
CP DoE contracts for the ORNL are listed in figure 18.8.

Fig. 18.8. Viral, Chemical, and Radiological Co-Carcino-genesis Studies By U.S. Department of Energy With Special Emphasis on AIDS-like and Minority Diseases

```
INSTITUTION  :   ENERGY, DEPARTMENT OF                                    (CP 6-0500)
ADDRESS      :   BIOLOGY DIVISION
                 OAK RIDGE NATIONAL LABORATORY
                 P.O. BOX Y
                 OAK RIDGE, TN, 37830
TITLE        :   NCI-ERDA VIRAL CARCINOGENESIS PROGRAM:
                 HOST CELL CONTROL OF RETROVIRUS EXPRESSION
PRINC INVEST :   DR. R.W. TENNANT
                 DR. WEN YANG
PHONE        :   615-483-8611
PROJ OFFICER :   DR. CHARLES J. SHERR, BLDG. 37, RM. 1B22, 496-6135
CONTRACT SPEC:   MR. THOMAS LEWIN, LANDOW BLDG., RM. 4C09, 496-1781
SECTION      :   RNA VIRUS STUDIES


INSTITUTION  :   ENERGY, DEPARTMENT OF                                    (CP 7-0503)
ADDRESS      :   DIV. OF BIOMEDICAL & ENVIRONMENTAL RES.
                 OAK RIDGE NATIONAL LABORATORY
                 P.O. BOX Y
                 OAK RIDGE, TN, 37830
TITLE        :   IN VITRO INTERACTION OF CHEMICAL CARCINOGENS WITH PRIMATE CELLS
PRINC INVEST :   DR. GEORGE C. LAVELLE
PHONE        :   615-483-8611
PROJ OFFICER :   DR. STEVEN R. TRONICK, BLDG. 37, RM. 2C07, 496-6462
CONTRACT SPEC:   MR. JACQUE LABOVITZ, LANDOW BLDG., RM. 4C09, 496-1781
SECTION      :   COCARCINOGENESIS STUDIES


INSTITUTION  :   ENERGY, DEPARTMENT OF                                    (CP 7-0504)
ADDRESS      :   DIV. OF BIOLOGICAL & MEDICAL RES.
                 ARGONNE NATIONAL LABORATORY
                 9700 SOUTH CASS AVENUE
                 ARGONNE, IL, 60489
TITLE        :   IN VIVO RADIATION-ACTIVATION OF ENDOGENOUS SARCOMA
                 VIRUS GENOME
PRINC INVEST :   DR. EMERSON W. CHAN
                 DR. CHRISTOPHER A. REILLY
PHONE        :   312-739-7711
PROJ OFFICER :   DR. JOHN DAHLBERG, BLDG. 37, RM. 1C21, 496-1478
CONTRACT SPEC:   MR. JACQUE LABOVITZ, LANDOW BLDG., RM. 4C09, 496-1781
SECTION      :   COCARCINOGENESIS STUDIES


INSTITUTION  :   ENERGY, DEPARTMENT OF                                    (CP 7-0510)
ADDRESS      :   PERALTA CANCER RESEARCH INSTITUTE
                 3023 SUMMIT STREET
                 OAKLAND, CA, 94609
TITLE        :   HUMAN MAMMARY TUMOR VIROLOGY
PRINC INVEST :   DR. ADELINE J. HACKETT
PHONE        :   415-451-4900
PROJ OFFICER :   DR. JOHN DAHLBERG, BLDG. 37, RM. 1C21, 496-1478
CONTRACT SPEC:   MR. JACQUE LABOVITZ, LANDOW BLDG., RM. 4C09, 496-1781
SECTION      :   BREAST CANCER VIRUS STUDIES


INSTITUTION  :   ENVIRO CONTROL, INC                                      (CP 6-1021)
ADDRESS      :   11300 ROCKVILLE PIKE
                 ROCKVILLE, MD, 20852
TITLE        :   MONITORING OF BIOHAZARD CONTAINMENT FACILITIES
PRINC INVEST :   DR. ROBERT W. MCKINNEY
PHONE        :   301-468-2500
PROJ OFFICER :   DR. ALFRED HELLMAN, BLDG. 41, RM. A108, 496-6758
CONTRACT SPEC:   MR. JAMES DOYLE, LANDOW BLDG., RM. 4C09, 496-1781
SECTION      :   PROGRAM RESOURCES & LOGISTICS
```

Energy Department cofactor studies suspiciously consistant with the "Revolution in Military Affairs," showing a suspicious focus on viral diseases and cancers that have placed minority populations, particularly Jewish people, at higher than normal risk. Source: NCI Staff. *Op cit.,* 1978, p. B-8.

Also contained herein is Dr. Hellman's "viral hazard control" contract in which project officers submitted some of the most chilling government documents in the history of planet earth. In one report it was clearly admitted that experimental vaccines had delivered laboratory cancer virus hybrids "with known oncogenic properties" to "more than one million people." On the audiocassette program, "Horowitz 'On Vaccines,'" I reported that far more people, mostly Russians, likewise received the monkey cancer virus SV40 through contaminated polio vaccines.[24] The NCI authors' precise words regarding this horrifying revelation were:

> A further complication was introduced when it was discovered that the oncogenic [African green monkey] papovavirus SV40 acquired from the simian cells used for propagation of the [rodent/human] adenoviruses, was present as a major contaminant in these vaccine preparations. Since hybrid viruses with a spectrum of biological functions have been isolated from mixed adenovirus-SV40 populations, these adenovirus vaccines undoubtedly contained such recombinant viruses. Thus, *more than one million people were inoculated with representative members of two groups of DNA viruses with known oncogenic properties.*[27] [Emphasis added.]

An equally horrifying revelation concerning adenovirus vaccine trials was contained in these investigators' following statement:

> The role of DNA viruses as etiologic agents of proliferative cellular diseases in several animal species is now well accepted. Early reports describing the capacity of certain murine [rodent] and simian [monkey] papovaviruses to induce malignant tumors in animals and transform cells in tissue culture provided the impetus for examining the relationship between various human DNA viruses and cancer in man.
>
> The first class of viruses considered in this context were human adenoviruses which have been shown to act as biological carcinogens in selected rodent systems. Prior to this demonstration, various live, attenuated adenovirus vaccines were administered to selected human populations as a control measure for debilitating respiratory tract infections.[27]

In other words, some unfortunate, possibly Russian or African, population with chronic respiratory disease was provided euthanasia by American cancer researchers in an apparent effort to keep the victims' respiratory illness from spreading.

Given the close ties between the viral investigators involved in these studies and NBRL airborne biological weapons investigators Dr. Hellman was overseeing, it is not unreasonable to suspect the "selected human populations" reported above with "debilitating respiratory tract infections" obtained their chronic infectious lung disease in the same manner in which they received free euthanasia, courtesy of the global eugenicists and population controllers at the highest levels of the U.S. "cancer research" establishment.

In the 1978 SVCP report, there were unfortunately additional admissions of contaminations, and human error bordering on sloppy deadly science. Dr. W. Peterson's contract summary report from the Child Research Center of Michigan stated that 17.6% of the 23 different species of cell cultures he tested "were found to be contaminated by cells of different species or different donor origin."

The University of Michigan and the Michigan Department of Public Health, it may be recalled, managed the Michigan Biologic Products Institute (MBPI)—the only licensed U.S. manufacturer of anthrax vaccine. Sloppy record keeping and potential vaccine contaminations caused the FDA to threaten revoking their license. Miraculously, a few months later, the company was bought at the brink of bankruptcy by Bioport Corporation of Lansing, Michigan, directed by the former chairman of the Joint Chiefs of Staff, Adm. William J. Crowe. ABC news reported that Adm. Crowe took control of the troubled company with financial assistance from the Pentagon and German investors, and soon received approximately $50 million in military orders. The huge vaccine contract was a direct result of the Admiral's closed door meeting with President Clinton. Due to the heroic efforts of antivaccination forces that rallied nationwide to alert military personnel concerning the scam, the U.S. Congress demanded the Pentagon cease and desist administering the grossly unproven, questionably effective, and clearly risky anthrax vaccine.[28]

A similar report concerning laboratory contamination was submitted by Dr. Walter Nelson-Rees *et al.*, from the Department of the Navy. He documented a 15% cell culture contamination or mislabeling rate.[27]

The above data certainly supports the "accidental theory of AIDS and other disease transmissions." Such knowledge, that high rates of contamination were linked to human error, might always be used in defense against claims that deadly outbreaks and epidemics have been perpetrated for population control. These data, again, establish "plausible denialability" to safeguard those primarily responsible for these risky programs as a cover for global depopulation efforts.

Pfizer's Role in Viral Reproduction

It may be recalled from the *Congressional Record* (See figure 1.2.) that Pfizer drug company was among the leading biological weapons contractors. Given the records of the SVCP, including the Pfizer "new special virus" supply contract shown in figure 18.9, along with the company's connection to the Rockefeller–I.G. Farben petro-chemical cartel detailed below, the outbreak of HIV/AIDS was not likely an accident.

Other important 1978 reports raising the spectre of genocide included the Litton Bionetics/Robert Gallo contract seen in figure 18.10. All of this new knowledge raises the possibility of provable liability, if not genocidal criminality, in seeking justice for such crimes against humanity.

Such is the argument of Attorney Boyd Ed Graves. He explained to justices, U.S. Senators, and the press beginning in 1998 why it is appropriate to take such a case to court. Figure 18.11 shows his complaint against Defense Secretary William S. Cohen, *et al.*

Under Pfizer's 1977 contract seen in figure 18.9, officiated by chief NCI cancer virologist Jack Gruber, NCI/pharmaceutical company investigators developed "large volumes of selected" cancer-causing viruses, and others suspected of triggering cancer, along with their associated vaccines. Dr. Sami Mayyasi, at Pfizer, reported the year's production of "over 28,000 liters of virus harvest fluids." These infected fluids were "distributed in over 400 shipments to approximately 140 laboratories throughout the world." The major viruses included several monkey virus strains, feline leukemia virus (believed by some investigators to be linked to HIV/AIDS), the RD-114 cat/human hybrid virus, the Epstein-Barr virus known to be a cofactor in accelerating HIV/AIDS pathogenicity, and others.

"More than 50% [of these viruses] were grown on human cells" to get them to readily jump species and be infectious for humans. Much contamination with foreign viruses was reported in this study as well.[27]

The Rockefeller-linked International Agency for Research in Cancer (IARC) based in Lyon, France, with labs experimenting on Black Africans in the West Nile region of Northwest Uganda, collaborated with Pfizer under this contract.

Possibly related to the 1978 initial simultaneous emergence of HIV/AIDS cases in New York and this region of Central Africa, these experimental cancer virus and vaccine production officials described "a major new effort" to produce and supply three new "animal retroviruses with *special* characteristics. Production concerned preparation of high molecular weight RNA-containing BeV [baboon endogenous virus], SSV-1 [simian sarcoma virus], and FeLV [feline leukemia virus]

Fig. 18.9. Pfizer Contract for "Large-Scale . . . Virus Production for Cancer Research"

PFIZER, INC. (NO1-CP-3-3234)

Title: Large-Scale Tissue Culture Virus Production for Cancer Research

Contractor's Project Director: Dr. Sami Mayyasi

Project Officer (NCI): Dr. Jack Gruber

Objectives: To provide a service facility for the production of large volumes of selected oncogenic and suspected oncogenic viruses, cellular antigens, tissue culture cell lines, and specific antisera to various oncogenic viruses. Production of these materials is supported by appropriate laboratory groups whose activities include process improvement, product standardization, quality control testing, and applied developmental research.

Major Findings: The current annual rate of large-scale tissue culture production results in over 28,000 liters of virus harvest fluids and over 1,200 grams of cells being processed to fulfill the needs of VOP collaborating investigators. During the past 12 months these materials were distributed in over 400 shipments to approximately 140 laboratories throughout the world. The major viral products generated included: Mason-Pfizer monkey virus (MPMV), which accounted for approximately 20% of the contractor's output; baboon endogenous virus (BeV), 26%; woolly monkey sarcoma virus (SSV-1), 18%; feline leukemia virus (FeLV), 17%; RD-114 virus, 13%; and Epstein-Barr virus. Of all viruses produced, more than 50% were grown on human cells (i.e. NC-37 lymphoblastoid line, A204 rhabdomyosarcoma line). The production of EBV in the P3HR-1 and B95-8 cell lines account for only approximately 1% of the total volume production effort, but the manipulation and concentration of these agents requires a disproportionate amount of time and effort as compared to the RNA type C virus production, and EBV preparation is a significant activity. Additionally, in support of collaborative studies being conducted at the IARC, Lyon, France, slides of concentrated P3HR-1 cells and RAJI cells are being produced and supplied to IARC for EBV epidemiologic titrations.

During this report period a major new effort was included in the workscope. This involved the production and supply to Program of three animal retroviruses with special characteristics. Production concerned preparation of high molecular weight RNA-containing BeV, SSV-1, and FeLV for a specially coordinated molecular epidemiology study. This laboratory helped coordinate the overall virus production effort and the distribution to the collaborating research laboratories.

A major effort was also initiated during this year to modernize the production methodology and improve the quality of product. Roller bottle tissue culture systems were introduced for growth of several of the primate retroviruses, growth of cells on microcarriers is now being studied, and new equipment was purchased to monitor the separation of viruses and viral components in gradients to enhance the purification and concentration procedures. The former tedious procedure for preparing concentrates of infectious EBV will be replaced by simpler procedures as a result of developmental studies on methods to process large volumes of this virus. New facilities to house the DNA

457

Fig. 18.9. Pfizer Virus Production Contract Continued

A number of valuable cell lines of tumor origin have been received from other laboratories and processed at CCL for distribution; among these were four of human origin. Approximately 20 laboratories have submitted 101 individual cell cultures for analysis of species and cell line purity. Of these 96 could be studies. Of these 15% were as purported, three cases were HeLa contaminants. others involved intra- and inter-species contamination. Activities of this nature are projected to continue at the same level for the remainder of the contract year.

Morphologically abnormal cell lines are being compared to morphologically normal cells in terms of growth pattern, cell· doubling time, saturation density, clonal growth on various substrates, karyology, and tumorgenicity in nude mice. Clonal growth studies are in progress on a variety of low passage, nonHeLa, human cancer cell lines in an effort to define the optimum nutrition and environmental conditions for culture of such cells.

Techniques for isoenzyme analysis by acrylamide gel electrophoresis have been improved and used to assay for glucose 6-phosphate dehydrogenase (G6PD), 6-phosphogluconic dehydrogenase (6PGD), and alkaline phosphatase isoenzymes in a variety of cell structures. A commercial preparative-scale electro-phoresis apparatus is being investigated with a view to possible performance improvement and its subsequent utilization in the examination of growth factors associated with various tissue culture media components.

Karyologic characterization of all cells maintained in the repository continues and specific collaborative programs requiring the use of karyologic data are in progress.

Significance to Biomedical Research and the Program of the Institute:
The contractor has an excellent tissue culture facility and is supplying cell cultures for cancer research studies to NCI investigators, to VOP contract laboratories, and the general scientific community. The contract continues to develop techniques for the identification and study of tumor cells oriented toward a study of the fundamental biology of tumor cells and the interaction between tumor cells and viruses of oncogenic importance.

Proposed Course: Continue to develop cell reagents as substrates for human carcinogenesis; continue a reference laboratory for karyology of cells in culture; continue repository and distribution functions.

Date Contract Initiated: October 1, 1977

This 1977 contract shows that Pfizer, Inc., officiated by chief NCI cancer virologist Jack Gruber, developed "large volumes of selected" cancer-causing viruses, and others suspected of triggering cancer, along with specific vaccines. That year, Pfizer produced "over 28,000 liters of virus harvest fluids." These infected fluids were "distributed in over 400 shipments to approximately 140 laboratories throughout the world." The major viruses included several monkey virus strains, feline leukemia virus (believed to be linked to HIV/AIDS), the RD-114 cat/human hybrid virus, the Epstein-Barr virus known to be a cofactor in enhancing HIV/AIDS pathogenicity, and others. The Rockefeller-linked International Agency for Research in Cancer (IARC) with labs in the West Nile region of northwest Uganda collaborated with Pfizer under this contract.

for a *specia*lly coordinated molecular epidemiology study." Emphasis on the word special, used twice in this sentence, was added. The word is generally understood in military circles such as this as meaning "secret."

A "specially coordinated molecular epidemiology study," implies that human populations and human blood was to be studied for the presence of these "special" manmade recombinant viruses or hybrid viral gene sequences. For this to occur, humans would *first* have to be inoculated, or exposed in some other way, to these special viruses. The location of Pfizer, Inc. in Maywood, New Jersey—close to New York City, and the IARC in the African AIDS belt, presents the grave likelihood that this "specially coordinated" study may have triggered, or helped to trigger, the international AIDS pandemic.[27]

This document is a "smoking gun" insofar as the iatrogenic theory of HIV/AIDS.

As of 1992, Pfizer was the sixth leading drug company in the world. It did more than $4 billion in sales annually according to Standard and Poor. The company banked with the Rockefeller's Chase Manhattan Bank while its chairman, Edmund T. Pratt, Jr., graduated from Pfizer to become the bank's director during the mid-1990s. Other contemporary Pfizer directors linked to the Rockefeller controlled cancer industry included Paul A. Marks, the chief officer of the Sloan–Kettering Memorial Cancer Center from 1980 to the mid-1990s, director of treatment regimens at the National Cancer Institute, and director of the American Association for Cancer Research.

Robert Gallo's "Effective Control Measures"

In 1996, the Gallo–Litton connection to AIDS-like virus development was first made in *Emerging Viruses: AIDS & Ebola—Nature, Accident or Intentional?* Figure 18.10 presents stunning new documentation. Here, Gallo—the alleged 1984 HIV "discoverer"—and Bionetics's Project Director, Dr. Marvin Reitz, conducted studies in which "fresh human" blood producing cells were "successfully" infected with various combinations of simian sarcoma virus, ape leukemia virus, baboon endogenous virus, cat leukemia virus and Epstein–Barr virus to produce coinfected dysfunctional human cells. It may be recalled that Epstein–Barr virus coinfections prompt accelerated immune suppression and more rapid disease onset than cancer virus infections alone. Thus, Epstein–Barr has been implicated as a

Fig. 18.10. Stunning 1977 Documentation Linking Robert Gallo and Litton Bionetics to Human Immune Virus (HIV-like) Cellular Disease Inductions Through Recombinant Infections with Cat Leukemia, Monkey Sarcoma and Epstein-Barr Viruses

LITTON BIONETICS, INC. (NO1-CP6-1029; successor to NO1-CP3-3211)

Title: Studies on Molecular Events Leading to Transformation by RNA Oncogenic Viruses

Contractor's Project Director: Dr. Marvin Reitz

Project Officer (NCI): Dr. Robert Gallo

Objectives: To characterize virus-like particles in human leukemic cells with respect to DNA polymerase and nucleic acids and characterize and purify viral reverse transcriptases from mammalian viruses, especially primate type C RNA tumor viruses.

Major Findings: It was found that some human DNA samples were capable of forming nuclease-resistant complexes with single-stranded nucleic acid probes from simian sarcoma virus (SiSV) and murine leukemia virus (MuLV). These complexes had a thermal stability and kinetics of formation consistent with the presence within the DNA samples of a set of DNA sequences related to but not identical with a portion of the viral genome. These sequences were found more frequently in leukemic than nonleukemic DNA samples, particularly with chronic myelogenous leukemia (CML). This type of distribution of sequences was not found with labeled probes from feline leukemia virus (FeLV), endogenous rat virus (V-NRK) and the Hall's Island strain of gibbon ape leukemia virus (GaLV-H). Some DNA samples, including a normal placental DNA and a CML cell line (K562), had a high level of these sequences, and were characterized in greater detail for specificty of these sequences.

A nonleukemic gibbon ape which had been exposed to a viremic animal and was persistently positive for GaLV antibody, but from whom no virus could be recovered, was examined for GaLV-related DNA sequences. The spleen, kidney and liver, but not the marrow or other tested tissues, appeared to contain an incomplete set of proviral sequences.

Fresh human hematopoietic cells were infected successfully with SiSV, GaLV, baboon endogenous virus (BaEV) and FeLV. In the case of the first two viruses, the cells were induced to grow independent of added growth factor, became tumorigenic in nude mice and were able to form colonies in semisolid media. All these induced cells were EBNA-positive, suggesting that Epstein-Barr virus (EBV) and SiSV-GaLV were acting synergistically.

Significance to Biomedical Research and the Program of the Institute: The knowledge acquired is applied to the determination of the etiological relationship of viruses to leukemia in humans, to the development of diagnostic and prognostic modalities for human cancer, and ultimately, to the development of more effective control measures.

Proposed Course: This contract terminates June 30, 1978.

Date Contract Initiated: September 1, 1972

Document proves the development of mutant viruses functionally identical to HIV were developed, tested and then mass produced under the direction of NCI project officer Robert Gallo and Litton Bionetics personnel years before he allegedly "discovered" the rapidly mutating HIV-1. Source: NCI Staff. *Op cit.,*1978, p. 202.

primary cofactor in several forms of cancer including the leukemia/ sarcoma/lymphoma AIDS cancer complex. Thus, the date in which this work was done is most incriminating. Between 1972 and 1977—that is, long before Dr. Gallo had alleged the HIV/AIDS virus "discovery"—he had worked to engineer these highly unique types of viruses and complex illnesses that were never before seen on planet earth in any species.

According to this document, this work was done to determine "the etiological relationship of viruses to leukemia in humans," to develop "diagnostic and prognostic modalities for human cancer, and ultimately, to" develop "more effective control measures." Given the Rockefeller links to Litton Industries, population control programs, and NIH/NCI industry overseers, the unspecified "effective control measures" Gallo *et. al.*, advanced here might best explain the "effective *[population]* control measures" effected by these viruses and related diseases including HIV/AIDS.[27]

The above information adds to the documentation advanced in *Emerging Viruses: AIDS & Ebola—Nature, Accident or Intentional?* linking the early hepatitis B virus (HBV) and vaccine experiments to HIV/AIDS. In brief, the U.S. Army contractor Dr. Saul Krugman, while working for another confirmed biological weapons contractor— the New York University Medical Center—during the 1960s, bioengineered strains of HBV from the original "Australian Antigen" to make his pilot vaccines. In keeping with earlier eugenicists, Dr. Krugman subsequently injected these new strains of HBV and pilot vaccines into mentally retarded children. Later recipients included gay men in New York, and Blacks in central Africa during the 1974–5 Merck HBV vaccine pilot studies linked to AIDS's origin.

Integrating this old and new knowledge, it is most reasonable to contend that HIV-1 may be linked to the simian sarcoma virus/baboon endogenous virus/feline leukemia viruses initially produced and tested in the Gallo–Bionetics affiliated labs, likely retested at Ft. Detrick or elsewhere, and then mass produced at Pfizer under the contract reproduced in figure 18.9. From here, HIV-1 or its progenitors apparently entered the Merck vaccines given to dozens of gay men in NYC and Central African Blacks involved in the early HBV pilot studies that may be what Gallo *et al.* referred to in the Pfizer contract as their "specially coordinated molecular epidemiology study" during the SVCP.

Fig. 18.11. U.S. Court of Appeals AIDS Case of Boyd E. Graves, et al. v. DoD Secretary William Cohen , et al.

IN THE UNITED STATES COURT OF APPEAL
FOR THE SIXTH COURT

BOYD E. GRAVES, et. al.,
    Lead plaintiff-appellants,

v.

Appeal No.: 99-4476
(Dist.Ct. #:98CV2209)

WILLIAM S. COHEN, et. al.,
    Defendants-appellees.

APPEAL FROM THE FINAL ORDER ENTERED ON 10/27/99

(MAJOR) QUESTION ON APPEAL:

Did the district court abuse its discretion and commit other reversible errors when it "set aside" Graves' evidence in support of his allegations of AIDS bioengineering, in which to reach a finding of "frivolity" under 28 USC 1915(e)?

SUMMARY OF THE APPEAL:

Between 1995 until the present, plaintiff-appellant, Boyd E. Graves ("GRAVES") faces federal employment discrimination relative primarily to his disability (HIV/AIDS). During the course of his research into HIV/AIDS, Graves discovered a 1971 flowchart, part of an ultra-secret federal program entitled, "Special Virus." The "special virus" began officially in 1962 and produced 15 yearly progress reports. The archives of the National Cancer Institute houses some of the reports. The 'research logic' reveals the program was seeking to isolate, stabilize, develop and proliferate a synthetic biological agent (a "human" retrovirus). SEE Graves v. Cohne, Exhibit One, filed September 28, 1998. On September 28, 1998, Graves brought suit against the named (and yet named) federal defendants pursuant to final proceedings before the EEOC, Department of Justice and the little known, Office of Special Counsel. On October 28, 1998, the district court dismissed Graves' allegations of AIDS bioengineering as frivolous. Graves believes the district court can not "set aside" direct evidence in which to reach a finding of frivolity under 28 USC 1915(e). The district court's final Order represents an abuse of discretion for a number of reversible reasons: 1) There is an identifiable class, 2) Graves has met the standard for appointment of counsel, 3) Graves' activities call for no curtailment or injunctive restrictions, 4) His complaint and exhibits, filed on September 28, 1998 meet and exceed the federal rules, 5) The district court erred in not allowing service of process. As a direct result of the court's action, Graves' constitutional rights and health continue to suffer, because of the excessive delay created by the district court's errant judicial activism. Graves believes this matter should be immediately returned to a neutral district court for service of process and appointment of counsel.

NATURE OF THE CASE

On October 28, 1998, the district court dismissed as frivolous Graves' claims of AIDS bioengineering against defendant-appellee, U.S. Pentagon, et. al. In order to do so, the district court convenienty "set aside" Graves' Exhibits. Exhibit One is page 129 of U.S. House Resolution 15090, Part VI, of the Ninety-First U.S.Congress. Exhibit One is sworn Congressional testimony by the U.S. Pentagon given on June 9, 1969. The heading listed in the Congressional Record is "SYNTHETIC BIOLOGICAL AGENT." On June 9, 1969, the U.S. Pentagon informed the U.S. Congress of it's involvement in the development of

Fig. 18.11. Boyd E. Graves Complaint Continued

a "Special Virus." In consideration of the credible history of the "special virus" program, it is reasonable to believe the program was well underway prior to 1969. This fact is thoroughly supported by the record of the program. SEE: Progress Report #8 at 2 (1971). Under the leadership of (yet named) defendant, Robert C. Gallo, a project officer for the program, the "special virus" isolated a "human" retrovirus and co-mingled it with animal viruses.[1] Graves believes the district court is not free to set aside his evidence of AIDS bioengineering, nor enjoin him from further filings. Graves has sufficiently demonstrated that his claims of AIDS bioengineering are not frivolous and are worthy of an ANSWER from the United States. With regard to Graves' motion for certification of the class, in his capacity as lead plaintiff, he sincerely believes there exists a live controversy worthy of further adjudication.

THE COMPLAINT FILED ON SEPTEMBER 28, 1998
IS SUFFICIENT FOR SERVICE OF PROCESS

Graves' complaint meets and exceeds the federal requirements for sufficiency under Fed. R. Civ. P. 3(a). Additionally, Graves' motion for reconsideration (amended complaint) filed on November 2, 1998, clearly cures every (if any) defect identified by the district court on October 28, 1998. The sworn Congressional record, the flowchart and progress report of the ultra secret program, and the substantial, credible scientific evidence require an ANSWER, consistent with every other legitimate demand of the U.S. Constitution. Equally, the October 13, 1999 press release of Dr. Len Horowitz (Appeal Exhibit "A," herein) identifies the Chairman of the National Security Advisory Board ([Ret.]Colonel Jack Kingston as a significant professional objection to the district court's determination.[2] Graves believes his timely filed motion for reconsideration on 9/27/99, best exemplifies the totality of the substantial evidence against the United States.

CONCLUSION

The district court has abused its inherent powers and has 'actively' sought to thwart or preclude this appellant from well established Constitutional rights of due process and equal access, inter alia. The appellant and the class are both entitled to service of process and an ANSWER. Graves believes the United States should be compelled to ANSWER the credible claims of AIDS bioengineering. The judicial activism exhibited by the district court is akin to the current "wall of silence" permeating the medical and scientific communities. The 1971 flowchart of this grotesque federal program is the indisputable "missing link" in the etiology of AIDS. The people can now 'easily' duplicate the program's experiments. The people can now prove conclusively the AIDS virus is a chimera. As the attached letter from Senators DeWine and Voinovich indicates (Appeal Exhibit "B," herein, the legislative branch of our government is indeed spineless with regard to any investigation of the "Special Virus." Perhaps it is because NONE of them have AIDS. Please return this matter immediately to a "fair-minded" district court. The people have a Constitutional right to accountability for the appalling state conduct of Dr. Gallo, Dr. Carlton Gajdusek, Dr. Robert Manaker, Dr. Paul Kotin, et al.,

Respectfully submitted,

Boyd E. Graves, pro se

Accumulating Incriminating Evidence

However circumstantial the evidence may seem, the fact that the key players described above, and in the preceding chapters, were all administratively and/or financially linked to CIA sponsored population management activities, and by association, to Rockefeller population controllers, deserves serious investigation and reconciliation. In summary, David Baltimore played a leading role in the Rockefeller-linked National Academy of Sciences–National Research Council in 1969 when his unique expertise was apparently called upon to advise DoD officials and the Congressional appropriations committee, of the feasibility of developing viruses that were descriptively and functionally identical to HIV. Figure 18.12, also reprinted from the NCI's Special Virus Cancer Program report, showed studies prior to 1971 involving mutant biological agents including the "mad cow" disease prion agent initially called "kuru," and recombinant influenza (flu) and leukemia viruses. Other than population control, much like that being accomplished by HIV/AIDS, there is no more conceivable use for these hybrids. Indeed, the cruelest examples of this use of early biotechnology, currently sickening humanity, is seen on this summary list of lethal biologicals. Under investigation at that time was the airborne recombinants of "acute lymphocytic leukemia" and "influenza" and "parainfluenza" viruses.[24, 27]

In other words, spreading leukemia like a common flu would better suit a depopulation objective than it would either cancer research or biological warfare objectives. After all, leukemia kills too slowly for use in traditional biological warfare applications. Not so, however, for "non-lethal" applications for gross population reduction. Additionally incriminating is the fact that these appropriations hearings and investigative efforts occurred immediately following Henry Kissinger's request for clarification by the Secretary of Defense, Melvin Laird, concerning America's biological weapons capabilities. Kissinger was formulating depopulation policies particularly targeting Third World nations as U.S. National Security Advisor at that time.

Kissinger's foreign policy objectives for central Africa then included massive depopulation.[24] His ordering of the CIA to release deadly biologicals in this area is not unrealistic. Nelson Rockefeller's protégé had, after all: 1) instigated the Zaire/Angola war by initially dispatching CIA agent-provocateurs into the area to foment unrest; 2) arranged for payments and "soft loans" to President Mobutu of Zaire who, for an additional $250 million, leased approximately 30,000 square miles of Eastern Zaire (home to approximately 760,000 African villagers) to Atomic Energy Commission-linked scientists. These men included Third Reich V2 missile project aces including: Dr. Kurt H. Debus, who subsequently became director of the Cape Canaveral space program until 1975, Richard Gompertz—a specialist on V2 engines who later directed NASA's Chrysler space division, and Lutz Thilo Kayser—also known as "Dadieu's young man," in reference to Armin Dadieu, his mentor and prominent SS officer who reported to the infamous Nazi commander and art thief, Hermann Goering, on a special program for storing uranium; 3) directed the exfiltration of Nazi scientists, like those mentioned above, from Germany to the United States. These Project Paperclip inductees included Erich Traub—Hilter's top biological weapons developer; 4) formulated and prompted the deployment of nuclear weapons around the world to serve Rockefeller's "national security" interests. In this regard, the association of U.S. Navy/ NIH official Alfred Hellman to the secret testing of immune suppressive airborne biologicals, Kissinger's alternative to costly nuclear weapons, is additionally disturbing, if not incriminating; and 5) served as a leading consultant on the Board of Advisors of the Merck Pharmaceutical Company, the firm that developed the 1974-75 hepatitis B vaccine given to gay men in New York City and Blacks in Central Africa that much evidence indicates triggered the international AIDS pandemic.[24]

Considering the substantial wealth of the Merck family, and its obvious role in the centuries-long development of the international chemical–pharmaceutical cartel, it is astonishing that so little is written or discussed about them. Since its establishment more than 300 years ago in Darmstadt, Germany, when the Merck family purchased their first apothecary, their history, along with George W. Merck's biography as U.S. biological weapons industry director, has been shrouded in secrecy.

"Au Ag" and the Precious Results of the Hepatitis B Vaccine

Given the above suggested links between the hepatitis B vaccine, AIDS, and the individuals and organizations profiting through global genocide, particularly the World Bank leadership, it may not be a random coincidence that the initial name given the hepatitis B virus, as shown in figure 18.12, was "Au Ag," short for "Australian Antigen." It

Fig. 18.12. Litton Bionetics List of Infectious Agents and Mutant Viral Recombinants Being Used in 1971 Primate Inoculation and Disease Induction Studies

transferred are real numbers. The dates present in the tabulations refer to the time the animals were placed on study.

1. Material inoculated

    a. Origin

        A   avian
        B   bovine
        C   chemical
        E   equine
        F   feline
        G   guinea pig
        H   human
        M   murine
        O   ovine
        R   rabbit
        S   simian

    b. Diagnosis

        A12S40   Adenovirus 12 + SV-40
        A2S40   Adenovirus 2 + SV-40
        Ad2P   Adenovirus 2 + parainfluenza
        Ad 7   Adenovirus 7
        AL   Acute leukemia
        ALL   Acute lymphocytic leukemia
      ● ALL I   Acute lymphocytic leukemia + influenza
      ● ALL PI   Acute lymphocytic leukemia + parainfluenza
        AM BL   American Burkitt's lymphoma
        AML   Acute myelogenous leukemia
        AM MOL   Acute myelogenous leukemia + monocytic leukemia
        AMOL   Acute monocytic leukemia
        Arbo   Arthropod-borne virus
        AT MON   Atypical monocytosis
      ● Au Ag   Australia antigen
        Bac Agt   Bacterial agent
        BL   Burkitt's lymphoma
        BOL   Bovine leukemia
        CA   Condyloma acuminatum
        CCHy   Congenital cerebral hyperplasia
        CF   Control familial
        C-H   Chediak-Higashi
        Chondr   Chondrosarcoma
        CLL   Chronic lymphocytic leukemia
        CML   Chronic myelogenous leukemia
        CMV   Cytomegalovirus
        CSCL   Congenital stem cell leukemia
        DC   Disease control
        D Enc   Dawson's encephalitis
        Echo 9   Echovirus 9
        EL   Erythroid leukemia

279

466

Eosinp	Eosinophilia
Fibro	Fibrosarcoma
GB	Glioblastoma
H-1	H-1 virus
Herp/G	H. genitalis
Herp/S	H. simplex
HD	Hodgkin's disease
HV	Herpesvirus
I	Influenza
IM	Infectious mononucleosis
* Kuru	Kuru
L	Leukemia
Liposar	Liposarcoma
L lymph	Lymphocytic leukemia
LRL	Leukemoid reaction of the liver
LS	Lymphosarcoma
Lymph	Lymphoma
Mamm T	Mammary tumor
Mening	Meningitis
MH	Malignant histiocytosis
Misc L	Miscellaneous leukemia
Misc V	Miscellaneous virus
ML	Malignant lymphoma
MM	Multiple myeloma
MSV	Moloney sarcoma virus
MSV AV	Moloney sarcoma virus + arbovirus
MSV L	Moloney sarcoma virus + leukemia
MSV MT	Moloney sarcoma virus + monkey tumor
Osteo S	Osteosarcoma
P	Papilloma
PI	Parainfluenza
PIA C	Pia mater control cell culture
Plyctm	Polycythemia
∧ PPLO	Mycoplasma
R	Rubella
Rau Vi	Rauscher virus
RCS	Reticulum cell sarcoma
Reo 1	Reovirus 1
Reo 3	Reovirus 3
■ Rhabd L	Rhabdomyosarcoma + leukemia
Rhabdo	Rhabdomyosarcoma
RTC	Rous transformed cells
S	Sarcoma
S20S40	SV-20 + SV-40
SA 7	Simian agent 7
SCL	Stem cell leukemia
Sq S	Squamous cell sarcoma
SV-5	Simian virus 5
SV-20	Simian virus 20
SV-40	Simian virus 40
T	Thrombocytopenia

● = Airborne flu/leukemia viral recombinant for no more reasonable explanation/use than depopulation

✱ = "Mad cow disease"/Creutzfeldt–Jakob disease agent

∧ = AIDS, Gulf War syndrome, and upper respiratory agent

■ = Marburg and Ebola virus progenitor

♠ = Hepatitis B vaccine—most likely trigger for HIV/AIDS

From: NCI Staff, *Op. cit.*, 1971 pp. 279-280.

is common scientific and metaphysical knowledge these symbols also represent the precious metals—"Au" for gold, and "Ag" for silver. The documents compiled in *Emerging Viruses: AIDS & Ebola—Nature, Accident or Intentional?* proved the Australian Antigen was crudely bioengineered with modifications to form various strains of the virus to faciliate "cancer research" and "vaccine development." The evidence compiled here suggests that "Au Ag," along with its related HBV vaccines, may have been initially developed to serve as genocidal weapons.

Symbolically, the AuAg vaccine delivered the most precious payload for global depopulation and eugenic managment.

This might be considered an outlandish series of speculations, suggestive of paranoia, were it not for the obvious display of these symbols of wealth and power precisely between Denver Airport's murals of a Nazi–gas-masked–alien committing global genocide and the Masonic tribute to the extinct species including Blacks, Indians, Hispanics, Jews and Christians. The gold (or bronze) inlay of the mining cart containing "Au Ag," pictured in figure 18.13, is centrally located between these most shocking images and other paintings depicting the resolution and celebration in a New World Order. These murals, shown in the gallery section of this book, were commissioned by the "New World Airport Commission" and dedicated by Colorado's leading racially segregated secret Masonic societies.

One might ask, "Why on earth would they have exposed themselves in this manner?"

There are two possible explanations: The first is best explained by researcher David Icke who has carefully examined the compulsive, cult-like, ritualistic attention to symbolic details and publicly displayed symbols that reflect the history and influence of Freemasonry. The fact that their lodges are part of a network of secret societies, Icke and others explained, means their symbols are only understood by people privy to their secrets. Others would simply bypass this "art" unassuming.

The second reason has to do, presumably, with the "craft" of Freemasonry, and a law in the Luciferous occult, to herald devilish undertakings and demonic deeds. It has been proposed that this exhibitionism reflects, in a sense, the perverted pleasure in conducting Satanic rituals and assignments, breaking social norms, yet remaining immune to societal justice. In effect, while violating the Ten Commandments, devildoers take pleasure in taunting their prey.

Fig. 18.13. Abbreviations for Gold and Silver and the "Australian Antigen" in Denver's "New World Airport"

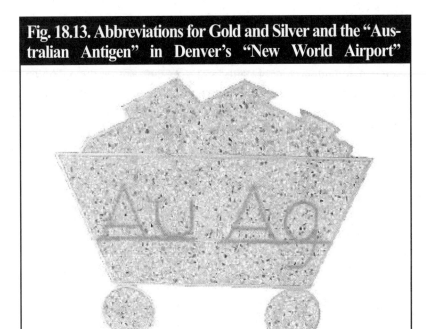

This floor inlay in Denver's "New World Airport" displays the symbols for precious metals gold (Au) and silver (Ag). "Au Ag" also represents wealth, power, and the hepatitis B virus linked through contaminated vaccines to the AIDS pandemic. It is located between murals of a Nazi–gas-masked–alien committing global genocide and the Masonic tribute to eugenics and the extinct species. The airport was dedicated by Colorado's racially segregated secret Freemasonry societies.

Genocidal Testing of Racial Theory

Relevant to the discussion of genocidal vaccine experiments linking contemporary eugenicists to U.S. Navy biological weapons experts and Atomic Energy Commission (AEC) officials, was an article by investigative journalist Paul Brown, circulated among Gulf War veterans. The text reviewed the research of Cornell University Professor Terry Turner who learned that "thousands of South American Indians were infected with measles," killing hundreds, so American scientists could "study the effects on primitive societies of natural selection.[29, 30]

"In its scale, ramifications, and sheer criminality and corruption," Professor Turner wrote, "this study is unparalleled in the history of anthropology." His letter, submitted to Louise Lamphere, the president of the American Anthropology Association (AAA), accused James Neel—the geneticist who directed the 10-year investigation of the Yanomami people of Venezuela—of using a deadly measles vaccine to trigger an epidemic that killed possibly thousands.

Once the epidemic began, according to Turner's text, Neel's research team "refused to provide any medical assistance to the sick and dying Yanomami, on explicit orders from Neel. He insisted to his colleagues that they were only there to observe and record the epidemic, and that they must stick strictly to their roles as scientists, not provide medical help."

Turner's words, put to print by journalist Patrick Tierney in *Darkness in El Dorado* were cosigned by Leslie Sponsel, another anthropologist working at the University of Hawaii.

"One of the most controversial aspects of the research which allegedly culminated in the epidemic," Brown wrote, "is that it was funded by the AEC, which was anxious to discover what might happen to communities when large numbers were wiped out . . . ." Professor Turner believed the only rational explanation for the experiment is that Neel was attempting to test "controversial eugenic theories like the Nazi scientist Josef Mengele. . . .

"Mr. Tierney's analysis is a case study of the dangers in science of the uncontrolled ego, of lack of respect for life, and of greed and self-indulgence," continued Brown. "It is a further extraordinary revelation of malicious and perverted work conducted under the aegis of the AEC."

Professor Turner revealed that Neel had used a virulent vaccine called "Edmonson B" on the Yanomami, which was known to produce symptoms virtually indistinguishable from cases of measles.

Tierney explained that "medical experts, when informed that Neel and his group used the vaccine in question on the Yanomami, typically refuse to believe it at first, then say that it is incredible that they could have done it, and are at a loss to explain why they would have chosen such an inappropriate and dangerous vaccine.

"There is no record that Neel sought any medical advice before applying the vaccine. He never informed the appropriate organs of the Venezuelan government that his group was planning to carry out a vaccination campaign, as he was legally required to do."

Professor Turner explained that Neel's view of "natural" human society consisted of small, genetically isolated groups in which dominant genes predicted "leadership" or "innate ability," thus providing a selective advantage.

"In such an environment," Brown summarized, "male carriers of this gene would gain access to a disproportionate number of females, reproducing their genes more frequently than less 'innately able' males. The result would supposedly be a continual upgrading of the human genetic stock."

Neel, according to the deceased professor Turner, believed that in modern societies "superior leadership genes would be swamped by mass genetic mediocrity . . . The political implication of this fascistic eugenics is clearly that society should be reorganised into small breeding isolates in which genetically superior males could emerge into dominance, eliminating or subordinating the male losers in the competition for leadership and women, and amassing harems of brood females."

In Turner's memo to AAA president Lamphere, he wrote of the "startling" revelation "that the whole Yanomami project was an outgrowth and continuation of the AEC's secret programme of experiments on human subjects.

Adding to the bulk of evidence linking early Rockefeller-directed genetics and eugenics experiments to more recent DoE and AEC investigations into biological, chemical, and radiological methods of reducing undesired populations, Turner wrote, "Neel, the originator of the project, was part of the *medical and genetic research team attached to the AEC since the days of the Manhattan Project.*" He was widely known for his investigation into the effects of radiation exposures on Hiroshima and Nagasaki bomb survivors. [Emphasis added.]

According to Professor Turner, Neel's group also secretly conducted experiments on American citizens. These included radioactive plutonium injections into people without informed consent.[30]

Califano on World Health and Population Control

Shortly before the AIDS epidemic began, in May 1978, Joseph A. Califano, Jr., Secretary of the DHEW, headed a U.S. delegation to the 31st assembly of the WHO in Geneva.

Califano's role as government lawyer and "public health policy educator" began shortly following his receipt of a law degree from Harvard in 1955—the same year Dr. Kissinger defended his Harvard thesis entitled *The Meaning of History*. Kissinger was then appointed by Nelson Rockefeller to direct the CFR's nuclear weapons study group. Over the next decade, Califano served as special assistant to the general counsel of the DoD, special assistant to the secretary of the Army, general counsel for the Army, and then between 1964 and 1965, Califano became special assistant to the secretary, and ultimately, deputy secretary of the Defense Department.[31]

"It is my honor to speak today," the chief public health official said, "as the first Cabinet officer ever to head the U.S. delegation to the World Health Assembly. I come as President Carter's personal emissary to underscore the commitment of the government and people of the United States to the World Health Organization (WHO)."[32]

The expert in public health and military justice then reviewed the WHO's achievements and challenges. The achievements, he said, "striking as they are, are dwarfed by the unmet challenges that confront us."

Chief among these unmet challenges, besides food and water shortages and infectious diseases, was rapid population growth, which Califano said, "retards social and economic progress in many nations and burdens many families and communities."[32]

To help resolve these woes, he pledged activities that "will be conducted in close cooperation with international agencies, and in partnership with other nations." The emphasis, he said, "will be on prevention of ill health, including malnutrition and infectious diseases. Our own national resources will be more fully mobilized—our universities, industries, and private organizations—and we will coordinate more closely the various international health activities within our government."[32]

Regarding America's role in international health, "President Carter announced publicly his intention to strengthen the role of the United States in international health," Califano said. "We want to commit new resources to the battle against infectious diseases. . . . To this end, we are conducting significant work to develop a malaria vaccine . . ."

Califano continued his address explaining it was his intention to improve research in countries where tropical diseases were a problem. The NIH and the WHO, he said, would collaborate in developing a "global epidemic surveillance service," and that this was "indispensable" for public health.

The plan was initially advanced by Rockefeller University officials according to Sloan Foundation grant recipient Laurie Garrett. The author of *The Coming Plague*—another best-seller that conveniently fit the bioterror genre of books funded by the Rockefeller/Sloan cancer consortium—conveniently omitted the Special Virus Cancer Program from discussion. Naturally applauding her benefactors with subtle propagandist finesse, Garrett detailed their concept of developing "fifteen surveillance clinics" on the fringes of tropical rain forests as a defense against the "coming plague." Dr. Stephen Morse at Rockefeller University had pioneered the notion. More incriminating, Morse had discussed the matter with Rockefeller University President and CFR bioweapons study group leader, Joshua Lederberg. This occurred "in 1988 while planning the historic 1989 'Emerging Viruses' conference." The Program for Monitoring Emerging Diseases (ProMED), in essence, resurrected Morse's proposed "network of tropical laboratories," that had been previously administered by the CDC and the Rockefeller Foundation.[24]

Califano assured that America stood ready to "help the World Health Organization develop a program for training physicians and field officers from developing countries." Then he mentioned that "Tropical Disease Research Centers" would be established in two countries in particular—Ndola, Zambia and Kuala Lumpur, Malaysia.[32]

Zambia lies between the Congro (previously Zaire) and Angola, just below the militarily active Shaba region. This is essentially the heart of the "African AIDS belt."

Yaws, a spirochetal disease amenable to Dr. Ehrlich's arsphenamine treatments, Califano said, had resurged in several African and Asian countries. In one African country, reported cases had risen "from less than 3,000 in 1969 to more than 70,000 in 1976." It appeared to be increasing in 12 other African nations.[32] This admission contrasted with expected results from increased USAID and WHO public health research, education, and vaccination programs conducted here during this period. One might have expected less of this most treatable disease, especially with such a sharp focus on African health at that time. The huge increase in morbidity and mortality reflected medical sociologist Stephen Kunitz's obervation that Third World genocides commonly followed USAID, U.S. Geological Survey, and World Bank "aid" to "underdeveloped nations."[33]

Then Califano said:

> The expanded program on immunization is an endeavor we believe highly important. . . .

> In the developing world, despite the fact that effective vaccines exist, less than 10% of the children receive immunizations against preventable diseases. . . . Our concern for these preventable diseases abroad has led us to develop bilateral immunization programs in cooperation with the World Health Organization—programs designed to help countries strengthen their own preventive health capacities.

We stand ready to go beyond our present participation in WHO's immunization program by increasing the numbers of our epidemiologists and other international health workers available to join in the efforts of developing nations. Moreover, I can announce that, in addition to the services we are already providing, we will make available a further $200,000 in direct support to the WHO expanded program on immunization through a contribution to the Voluntary Fund for Health Promotion [VFHP]. Our Agency for International AID [USAID], in cooperation with my own Department, is exploring with WHO the possibility of undertaking a multiyear immunization program for the African region.[32]

Califano then called for joint efforts to achieve one overriding objective—"to immunize the children of the world by 1990." There could be no greater gift to the next generation," he cheered, than to celebrate this event as it came to pass.[32]

The public celebration Califano anticipated, however, never occurred, but there were those in 1990 who found cause to celebrate. AIDS, believed by a growing concensus of scientists to have been spread by WHO vaccines, had devastated many of the most populated areas of central Africa.[33]

At the time of this writing, very few people could recall that Joseph Califano, prior to becoming Secretary of the DHEW in the 1970s had served as Alexander Haig's superior at the Pentagon. During the Nixon administration, it was Califano who recommended Haig to serve on Henry Kissinger's National Security Council. Then in 1977, as the large scale Merck hepatitis B (HB) vaccine trials began in gay Americans and Black Africans, Califano took over as Secretary of the DHEW overseeing Dr. S. Paul Ehrlich, Surgeon General, and the entire public health communty. Evidence referenced in *Emerging Viruses: AIDS & Ebola—Nature, Accident or Intentional?* indicated that Califano then authorized USAID money in support of this HB vaccine program in Africa, while his other employer, Columbia University's School of Public Health, was collaborating through their Division of Epidemiology with the Rockefellers' New York City Bood Council and their Blood Bank concerning these HB vaccine trials.

Given this background on Califano as it relates to the "gift" of vaccinations, military affairs, U.S. National Security, and population control, the following sections are disturbingly relevant.

National Security Memorandum–46:
Motivation for African–American Genocide

National Security Memorandum–46[34] is one of the most disturbing documents you will ever read. Never officially declassified, Zbigniew Brzezinski's report virtually declared covert war against the Black people of Africa *and* America. In fact, this is the grossest certification of U.S. Government hypocrisy, propaganda, and state-sponsored genocide the world has ever seen. The top secret report, publicly shown for the first time in figure 18.14, was sent to all top Carter administration cabinet members *less than two months before* Joseph Califano, as "President Carter's personal emissary," with top intelligence briefing, pledged the "American People's" commitment to help the people of the Third World. (Africans especially were to receive the special "gift" of "immunization.") Held in the context of what follows, NSM–46, Califano's words issued a virtual death sentence.

Brzezinski, discussed previously as the author of *The Technotronic Era,* described various measures to produce total psychosocial submission through non-lethal forms of optimal political and population control. He wrote that the President had directed the National Security Council (NSC) to conduct a "comprehensive review . . . of current developments in Black Africa from the point of view of their possible impacts on the black movement in the United States." The report was to have been "forwarded to the NSC Political Analysis Committee by April 20th [1978]." Primary concerns focused on the "danger of being deprived of access to the enormous raw material resources of southern Africa which" were said to be "vital for our defense needs." Additionally, it was allegedly feared that losing tactical advantage over "the Cape sea routes" would impact the supply of *oil.* Finally, NSM–46 alleged that unless measures were taken to undermine, if not assassinate, Black leaders and suppress Black political movements, the African continent might fall under Russian communist control. Ironically, these directives were issued at the precise time that America's most advanced biological weapons—immune system destroying viruses— were flowing from the NCI labs to bioweapons centers globally, particularly into the Soviet Union (as documented in figure 16.5). Thus, expressed concern over the "Communist military menace" in NSM– 46, and elsewhere, is somewhat specious, if not overtly deceptive.

"Moreover," the report said, Communism's expansion in Africa "may bring about internal political difficulties by intensifying the activity of the black movement in the United States itself."

The report cited political, economic, and public health instabilities of African nations, and reasoned that $4 billion in investments and exports might be lost by American corporations in the absence of covert actions.

"Apart from the above-mentioned factors adverse to U.S. strategic interests," the NSM–46 added, "the nationalist liberation movement in black Africa can act as a catalyst with far-reaching effects on the American black community by stimulating its organizational consolidation and by inducing radical actions. Such a result would be likely if Zaire [the Congo] went the way of Angola and Mozambique.

"A recurrence of the events of 1967–68 would do grievous harm to U.S. prestige, especially in view of the concern of the present [Carter] Administration with human rights issues. Moreover, the Administration would have to take specific steps to stabilize the situation. Such steps might be misunderstood both inside and outside the United States."

Concerning domestic risks from Black nationalism, Brzezinski's report continued:

"In elaborating U.S. policy toward black Africa, direct weight must be given to the fact that there are 25 million American blacks whose roots are African and who consciously or subconsciously sympathize with African nationalism.

"The living conditions of the black population should also be taken into account . . . , [including] a long-lasting high rate of unemployment, especially among the youth, and by the poverty, and traditional dissatisfaction with government social welfare standards.

"These factors taken together may provide a basis for joint actions of a concrete nature by the African national movement and the U.S. black community. Basically, such actions would take the form of demonstrations and [political] protests. But the likelihood of violence cannot be [ruled out.] There would also be attempts to coordinate their political activity both locally and in international organizations. . . .

"Internationally, damage could be done to the United States by coordinated activity of African states designed to condemn U.S. policy toward South Africa and to initiate discussion on the U.S. racial issue at the United Nations where the African representation constitutes a powerful bloc with about one third of all the votes.

Fig. 18.14. National Security Council Memorandum–46
Brzezinski's Plan for African–American Genocide

NATIONAL SECURITY COUNCIL
MEMORANDUM–46

(SECRET) March 17, 1978
Presidential Review Memorandum/NSC-46
TO: The Secretary of State
The Secretary of Defense
The Director of Central Intelligence
SUBJECT: Black Africa and the U.S. Black Movement

The President has directed that a comprehensive review be made of current developments in Black Africa from the point of view of their possible impacts on the black movement in the United States.
The review should consider:
1. Long-term tendencies of social and political development, and the degree to which they are consistent with or contradict the U.S. interests.
2. Proposals for durable contacts between radical African leaders and leftist leaders of the U.S. black community.
3. Appropriate steps to be taken inside and outside the country in order to inhibit any pressure by radical African leaders and organizations on the U.S. black community for the latter to exert influence on the policy of the Administration toward Africa.
The President has directed that the NSC Interdepartmental Group for Africa perform this review.
The review should be forwarded to the NSC Political Analysis Committee by April 20th.

Zbigniew Brzezinski

cc: The Secretary of the Treasury.
The Secretary of Commerce
The Attorney General
The Chairman, Joint Chiefs of Staff

See 'FBI Division 5', For Cong-mssge Gentls:
March 4, 1978 on David Garrow,
The FBI & Martin Luther King Jr: P. 187

SECRET
NATIONAL SECURITY COUNCIL
INTERDEPARTMENTAL GROUP
FOR AFRICA
STUDY IN RESPONSE TO PRESIDENTIAL SECURITY
REVIEW MEMORANDUM / NSC-46
BLACK AFRICA AND THE

This "(SECRET) March 17, 1978" document was never declassified. It articulated a U.S. National Security apparatus coordinated effort to commit genocide against Black people in Africa and America. It is part of the documentation advanced by Black attorney Boyd Ed Graves in pursuing a class action lawsuit against the U.S. Government on behalf of those with HIV/AIDS.

Fig. 18.15. National Security Council Memorandum–46 "Recommendations" for African–American Genocide

RECOMMENDATIONS

In weighing the range of U.S. interests in black Africa, basic recommendations, arranged without intent to imply priority, are:

1. Specific steps should be taken with the help of appropriate government agencies to inhibit coordinated activity of the black movement in the United States.

2. Special clandestine operations should be launched by the CIA to generate mistrust and hostility in American and world opinion against joint activity of the two forces, and to cause division among black African radical national groups and their leaders.

3. U.S. embassies to black African countries specially interested in southern Africa must be highly circumspect in view of the activity of certain political circles and influential individuals opposing the objectives and methods of U.S. policy toward South Africa. It must be kept in mind that the failure of U.S. strategy in South Africa would adversely affect American standing throughout the world. In addition, this would mean a significant diminution of U.S. influence in Africa and the emergence of new difficulties in our internal situation due to worsening economic prospects.

4. The FBI should mount surveillance operations against black African representatives and collect sensitive information on those, especially at the UN, who oppose U.S. policy toward South Africa. The information should include facts on their links with the leaders of the black movement in the United States, thus making possible at least partial neutralization of the adverse effects of their activity.

The above national security policy was advanced by President Jimmy Carter's NSC Advisor Zbigniew Brzezinski in 1978, at least four years after HIV-like viruses had been prepared for population control under the leadership of Brzezinski's predecessor Henry Kissinger. This evidences a coordinated Black genocidal effort during the Nixon and Carter administrations.

"A menace to U.S. economic interests, though not a . . . critical one, could be posed by a boycott by black African states against American companies which maintain contracts with South Africa and Rhodesia. If the idea of economic assistance to black Americans shared by some African regimes could be realized by their placing orders in the United States mainly with companies owned by black [as the Japanese had successfully done to their economic advantage,] they could gain a limited influence on the U.S. black community.

"In the above context, we must envisage the possibility, however remote, that black Americans interested in African affairs may refocus their attention on the Arab–Israeli conflict. Taking into account the African descent of American blacks, it is reasonable to anticipate that their sympathies would lie with the Arabs who are closer to them in spirit and, in some cases, related to them by blood. Black involvement in lobbying to support the Arabs may lead to serious dissension between American blacks and Jews. The likelihood of extremist actions by either side is [serious.]"[34]

"Recommedations" for Covert Actions Against Blacks

As shown in figure 18.15, the recommendations Brzezinski advanced to deal with the above concerns—a "black solution"—included:

1) "Specific steps . . . to inhibit coordinated activity of the black movement in the United States."

2) "Special clandestine operations . . . by the CIA to generate mistrust and hostility in American and world opinion against joint activity of the two forces, and cause division among black African radical national groups and their leaders."

3) Placing U.S. embassies on alert.

4) FBI mounted "surveillance operations against black African representatives" to "collect sensitive information on those, especially at the U.N., who oppose U.S. policy toward South Africa." Such intelligence might be used to blackmail certain leaders as well as make available "at least partial neutralization of the adverse effects of their activity."

NSM–46 stated under "Trends in the American Black Movement" that "considerable changes" in the Black movement had occurred for the benefit of U.S. national security. These included the "fragmentation and a lack of organizational unity" among African Americans, a "decrease of influence in the movement's extremist groups," "social stratification of the black population, lack of policy options which could reunite them," and the lack of "a national leader of standing comparable to that of Martin Luther King."[34]

"The Range of Policy Options" the NSC advanced included: a) social and economic welfare programs designed to reduce the aforementioned risks; b) "to elaborate and bring into a special program designed to perpetuate division in the black movement to neutralize the most active groups of leftist radical organizations representing different social strata of the black community; to encourage divisions . . . ;" c) "to preserve the present climate which inhibits the emergence from within the black leadership of a person capable of exerting nationwide appeal," (e.g., the promotion of the completely ineffective if not completely corrupt Black "leader" Jesse Jackson); d) to exercise "preventive operations in order to impede durable ties between U.S. black organizations and radical groups in African states;" e) "to support actions designed to sharpen social stratification in the black community, which would increase the widening and perpetuation of the gap between successful educated blacks and the poor, giving rise to growing antagonism between different black groups, weakening . . . the movement as a whole;" f) "to facilitate the greatest possible expansion of black business by granting government contracts and loans with favorable terms to black businessmen [to assure the previous option];" g) to "counteract the increasing influence of black labor organizations . . . ;" h) "to support the nomination at federal and local levels of loyal black public figures to elective offices, to government agencies and the court . . ." to give the appearance of black leadership and enhance the stratification of social classes among American blacks. (This best explains the appointment of a Black Surgeon General of the U.S., David Satcher, who has shunned the evidence I personally presented to him documenting worldwide Black genocide.)[34]

Reflecting on the socioeconomic and political transitions within Black America since the issuance of NSM–46 to the time of this writing, all of Zbigniew Brzezinski's "options" have obviously been exercised. Relevant signs of this ongoing attack on Black America is the demonizing and disappearance of inspirational civil rights leaders like Martin Luther King. This is coupled with the rise of contemptuous characters like Jesse Jackson to speak for America's Blacks, the election of political impotents like Black National Caucus leader Maxine Waters, and San Francisco's Mayor Willie Brown, both of whom have skirted the AIDS issues I personally relayed to them. In addition, the appointment of Black figureheads including Secretary of State Colin Powell and Chief Justice Clarence Thomas precisely fit Brzezinski's written objectives. All of these are pathognomonic of African–American genocide, making these, and other high profile Black "leaders," virtual puppets for PSYOPs and C2W waged against their own people.

Repackaging Population Control

During the Fall of 1994, in a newsstand adjacent Fisherman's Market in San Francisco, I came across an issue of *Covert Action Information Bulletin* that contained a fascinating article by British journalist Helen Simons entitled "Repackaging Population Control." The article, explained that despite official claims to the contrary, African overpopulation was not a prime motivation behind family planning and maternal and child health programs.[33-36] Nor was population control even a desire among African women.

As Nicholas Eberstadt, foreign policy analyst for the American Enterprise Institute for Public Policy Research noted, "in most of sub-Saharan Africa it is infertility—not unwanted pregnancies—that women rank as their top priority." The fate of barren women throughout the region, he continued, "is a pitiable one. . . . While fertility enhancement in the industrialized north is a multi-billion dollar industry, little attention is accorded to the population problems that most concern Africans themselves."[36]

For almost four decades, Third World countries had held American population control policies accountable for diverting attention from the central problem—too much poverty, not over-population.[37] Many leaders charged that such policies were "nothing short of blackmail and coercion directed against the people of the Third World."[33]

This was likewise argued by Linda Gordon, author of *Woman's Body, Woman's Rights: A Social History of Birth Control in America.* She wrote, "Coercive population control is stimulated and then made acceptable by racism. . . . Nonsensical ideas about the cheapness of life among Asians [and Africans] and highly documented analyses of the different structure of the black family such as matriarchal theory have served to justify coercion to reduce non-white birth rates."[38]

This view predominated during the first United Nations conference on population control held in Bucharest in 1974. The meeting ended in shambles after delegates from Africa, Latin America, and

Russia denounced the entire concept of Third World population control as imperialistic and racist.[38]

To further her point, Simons quoted Pentagon consultant, and National Defense University Associate Dean, Gregory D. Foster, who wrote:

> [P]olicy makers and strategic planners in this country, have little choice in the coming decades but to pay serious attention to population trends, their causes and effects. Already the United States has embarked on an era of constrained resources. It thus becomes more important than ever to do those things that will provide more bang for every buck spent on national security. . . . [Policy makers] must employ all the instruments of statecraft at their disposal (development assistance and population planning every bit as much as new weapons systems).[39]

Thus, the horrific notion of conducting non-lethal warfare through various forms of "public health assistance," particularly vaccination campaigns, for "national security" in providing "more bang for the buck" is reconciled, and more completely substantiated, in this context.

Alternative Views of Population Policy

The State Department hailed the 1974 Bucharest population conference as consensus building, but in reality it was an "embarrassing failure." In its wake, U.S. policymakers scrambled to reformulate population control strategies as discussed in another secret National Security Council report published four months later.[35, 40]

The document suggested new language be used. It warned against actions that gave the appearance that "the policy was directed against the Less Developed Countries." Instead, it recommended the use of leverage through more neutral organizations like the U.N. and NGOs to assist developing countries "in integrating population factors in national plans, particularly as they relate to health services [e.g., vaccination], nutrition [e.g., infant formula], agriculture [e.g., to undermine family farming], education [e.g., "sex education" and contraception], social services [e.g., family planning], organized labor, women's activities [e.g., Norplant contraception and "maternal and child health"] and community development [e.g., racial and ethnic class stratification]." In essence, population control was repackaged to overcome the opposition.[35, 40, 41]

The report revealed the true motives underlying the representational changes in U.S. foreign population control policy. "The U.S. can help minimize charges of an imperialist motivation behind its support of population activities by repeatedly asserting that such support derives from a concern for: a) the right of the individual to determine freely and responsibly their number and spacing of children. . . . and b) the fundamental and economic development of poor countries," the report stated.[41]

Thus, the tarnished image of U.S. population control policies in the Third World was polished and repackaged. The perception that America sought only to promote basic rights for women was promoted. In doing so, it became possible to present population control as a legitimate concern for developing countries. International feminist groups, NGOs, and foreign leaders all endorsed the principals and practices of "family planning."[35]

Over the next two decades, U.S. population policymakers repeatedly refined their messages so that all of these activities were more broadly accepted. A USAID commissioners' report urged that population activities "should be integrated with maternal and health care delivery." The move was motivated by concerns that USAID programs "only increase suspicion in the host country" if they were too narrowly focused on family planning.[34,41,42]

"Since the mid-1970s," Simons wrote, "much of the aid from Western governments, the World Bank, and the European Union has been channelled through" NGOs that "are prepared to toe the line on population control."[33] Thus, American-backed donor agencies, including USAID and the World Bank, have used their economic power to influence NGO policy.[44,45]

The World Bank was represented in full force at the September 1994, Cairo, Egypt "International Conference on Population and Development" meeting. It "emerged as a major funder of population control. During 1969-70, it only spent $27 million on population programs. In 1987, the then president promised to increase the amount to $500 million by 1990. In 1993, it had already shot up to $1.3 billion."[35] Additional funds were then promised to the tune of $2.5 billion by 1995 for depopulation.

A position paper transmitted over the Internet entitled, "Was Cairo a step forward for Third World women?" by Drs. Vandana and Mira-Hiva, warned that the World Bank had "cleverly redefined the 'population and development' sector as 'population and women,' thus making invisible the destructive impact of its policies on the lives of Third World women and ironically appearing as a champion of women's rights."[35]

Simons also noted, when appeals for stricter "maternal and child health policy" failed, environmental concerns were then successfully used to "dress up old racist rantings."[35] Their argument was eloquently expressed in an article in *Atlantic Monthly* by author, Robert Kaplan:

> Mention "the environment" or "diminishing natural resources" in foreign-policy circles and you meet a brick wall of skepticism or boredom. To conservatives especially the very term seems flaky . . . [but] it is time to understand "the environment" for what it is: the national security issue of the early twenty-first century. The political and strategic impact of surging populations spreading disease, deforestation and soil erosion, water depletion and possibly rising sea levels in critical overcrowded regions like the Nile Delta and Bangladesh—developments that will prompt mass migration and in turn incite group conflicts—will be the core foreign policy challenge from which most others will ultimately emanate.[46]

Thoreau's warning that, "Nothing is so much to be feared as fear," has relevance here.[47]

"Wrapped up in the language of women's empowerment and environmental" fears, Simons concluded, "the establishment's old arguments about there being too many non-white babies in the world have finally won the day."[35]

Regarding the effects of such political applications in America, a review of the "medical history of African Americans and the problems of race" was published in 2000 by Harvard's Black professors W. Michael Byrd and Linda A. Clayton.[48] These authors more diplomatically concluded that "a roller-coaster ride to nowhere" might best describe the genocidal treatment of Blacks by the American medical and public health communities.

RAPID Disinformation and Deterioration

Betsy Hartmann, Director of the Population and Development Program at Hampshire College and author of *Reproductive Rights and Wrongs: The Global Politics of Population Control and Contraceptive Choice* (New York: Harper and Row, 1987), noted the World Bank's key device for administering population policy was "leverage over other forms of development finance." She noted that governments often burdened by massive foreign debt are persuaded to "devalue their currency, privatize their industries, open their doors to foreign investment, freeze wages, raise food prices, slash social services *and* implement Bank-sanctioned population programs."[33,36,49]

Consistent with the vital need to conduct PSYOPs and C2W in support of non-lethal military efforts, Hartmann reported that the Futures Group, a Washington, D.C.-based consulting firm was funded by USAID to develop RAPID (Resources for the Awareness of Population Impacts on Development).[33] RAPID analyses urged Third World economies to follow a Western-style development model and thus become dependent on external markets and Western technology. For example, in Zaire's eastern neighbor, Tanzania, a RAPID study concluded the country must abandon traditional labor-intensive farming for more "scientific and commercial agriculture." The report warned that the ensuing population growth and "entry of large numbers of new workers into the agricultural sector" hinder the country's development since "traditional patterns of small holder production with land-intensive and resource-intensive cultivation" are probably not "the most feasible means of employing so many additional people."[50]

Unfortunately, RAPID consultants intentionally overlooked this policy's most tragic outcome in their own backyard—the heartland of America. American family farmers were once bonded by their labor and service to society. Generally speaking, family farmers maintained a great sense of purpose. Their social, religious, and economic environments supported farming and their family values. Families depended on one another to survive. When automated farming methods forced many small farm owners to sell their land, the vast majority of family owned farms were lost. Children left home to seek employment elsewhere. This added to the country's political turmoil.[51] Dr. Lambo, Africa's most outspoken critic of public health colonialism, correctly predicted this outcome before the WHO in 1970 when he prophesied global capitalism would bring mass disillusionment accompanied by the destruction of traditional cultures, a preoccupation with money, and a weakened dependence on "family, clan, shrine, and community."[52]

For this exact reason—the socially engineered loss of traditional family values—the Rockefellers determined to have the "National Security State" promote the new "National Purpose" for all Americans linking "guns, butter, and the new technology of . . . weapons production to the cause of Freedom and the Free World."[53,54]

Human Rights, Malthusian Eco-Fascism, and Population Control

Before concluding, Hartmann provided an example of USAID's "cavalier" approach to population control in disregard of health and safety.[33] As this chapter began, I noted the association between the Rockefeller/ IG Farben linked Population Council and the ongoing pharmaceutical induced genocide. In this regard, Hartmann also disparaged the use of Norplant:

> Developed by the *Population Council in New York*, Norplant is a progestin implant system inserted under the skin of a woman's arm, which prevents pregnancy for at least five years. Common side effects of Norplant include menstrual irregularity, headaches, nervousness, nausea, acne and weight gain. Both insertion and removal require local anesthesia and medical skill. Ethical use of the drug depends on adequate medical screening and follow-up, and most importantly on access to removal on demand.

> An internal Population Control report provides chilling evidence of how Norplant has been misused in the Indonesian population program. Nearly a half million women have had Norplant inserted, often without counseling on side effects, alternative contraceptive options, pregnancy screening, or proper sterilization of equipment. Many have not even been told that the implant must be removed after five years to avoid increased risk of life-threatening ectopic pregnancy.

> Moreover, removal on demand is not guaranteed, not only because of lack of trained personnel, but more importantly to serve the . . . government's demographic objectives. According to the Population Council report, "Recent government policy encourages use of Norplant for the duration of the full five years of effectiveness, which is communicated to the client as a form of commitment. . . ." Or as one Indonesian population official put it, "People are told it has to last five years, they give their word . . . and rural people don't go back on their word. If they request removal, they are reminded that they gave their word."[43,55] [Emphasis added]

Hartmann then noted, "coercive use of Norplant is not restricted to the Third World." Similar programs in California, Kansas and Texas have been proposed or sanctioned for use in special populations.[43,56]

Finally, she addressed what she termed "Malthusian Eco-Fascism." Hartmann considered the moral decay of population strategists, among whom Dr. Maurice King established prominence in Britain. King, in *The Lancet*, endorsed what Hartmann adversely labeled "a 1990s variant of triage: try family planning, but if it doesn't work, let the poor die because they are an ecological menace."[33]

According to King, in countries where there is unsustainable pressure on the environment from overpopulation, "such desustaining measures as oral rehydration [a simple lifesaving method of treating diarrheal disease] should not be introduced on a public health scale," he concluded, "since they increase the man-years of human misery, ultimately from starvation. . . . Such a strategy needs a name," he wrote. "Why not call it HSE 2100—health in a sustainable ecosystem for the year 2100?"[33, 43]

Why not call it "MEF—Malthusian Eco-Fascism," Hartmann rebutted after contacting Dr. King in Leeds to confirm that his statements in *Lancet*—believed by some to have been a parody—were "dead serious."[43]

Hartmann concluded, "In much of Africa where AIDS threatens tragic human and demographic consequences, the present emphasis on population control and de-funding of health systems amount to indirect triage—no less morally repugnant than Dr. King's twisted vision."[33]

Some extremist U.S. ecologists go so far as to see AIDS as a blessing. According to a letter from "Miss Ann Thropy" printed under an open-letter policy in *Earth First!* journal, "If radical environmentalists were to invent a disease to bring human population back to ecological sanity, it would probably be something like AIDS." In this context, "We can see AIDS not as a problem, but a necessary solution. . . ." brought to fruition by world banking strategists, corporate philanthropists, NGOs, and misguided medical specialists, all for the benefit of a few global elitists.

This conclusion was also intimated by the consensus panel from the National Academy of Sciences–National Research Council who wrote about high fertility rates among poor Sub-Saharan Africans and "ultraorthodox Jews in Israel." These people simply fornicated and conceived too much as a cultural liability professed the esteemed council members. Though AIDS had interrupted "mortality transitions" in some developing countries, "[n]evertheless, population size has not declined in these countries and is not projected to do so."

In classic rhetorical fashion designed to leave even the scientifically astute trapped in the Hegelian dialectic, Bongaarts et al., admitted their own population projection weaknesses. They wrote:

> The traditional scenario method for calculating and communicating uncertainty, which is still common practice for official national and some international projections," they concluded "has many serious problems. No probability is attached to high-low intervals. In fact, probabilities would be difficult to assign because they would vary for different projected variables, such as population size and the old age dependency ratio. As indicators of uncertainty, high-low scenarios are internally inconsistent. Furthermore, the bundling of assumptions about population growth components (high fertility with low mortality, for instance) is arbitrary and affects the uncertainty attached to outcomes, which are therefore also arbitrary. Finally, scenarios for regions and for the world do not take account of the correlations among the forecast errors for national populations, which determine whether country errors cancel or reinforce each other when countries are combined into an aggregate.[20]

If you finished the above paragraph with a higher level of confusion or frustration, that was by design—the global elite's and mine. The result of a cleverly guided PSYOP, *Beyond Six Billion*, like the untold volumes of other works designed to distract and confuse, is what distinguishes *Death in the Air: Globalism, Terrorism and Toxic Warfare* from the counterintelligence efforts to which you have likely grown accustomed. This book relays the truth, reprinted in black and white, versus the Hollywood fiction that plays on your fears and imagination in living color. Their methods are a lot sexier than mine. They have a lot more money to spend to facilitate their agenda—non-lethal warfare for effective global governance. My agenda is simply to open your eyes, ease the confusion, and save more than a small remnant of civilization.

The Human Eugenics Program:
Future Prospects for Population Control

One might ask, "What are the prospects for human health given all of the above?"

Earlier, the AEC was shown to play a dual role in investigating radiological as well as biological threats and weapons of mass destruction. Their research contracts covered "co-carcinogenesis" studies linking viral research and genetic engineering to nuclear radiation studies and risks from the full spectrum of electromagnetic radiations including non-ionizing frequencies that fall within the transmission capability of the CIA's Phoenix II and Montauk projects. HAARP, likewise, was more directly linked to the Rockefeller/Royal Family-directed Human Genome Project through Cold Spring Harbor (Eugenics) Laboratory's copyrighted material published in *Healing Codes for the Biological Apocalypse.*[57] Thus, there seems to be a suspicious, if not highly disconcerting, connection between the most advanced genetic and radiological (including frequency) research—including "death ray" technologies, and several agents and agencies historically linked to Malthusian eco-fascism. What are the implications of this multidisciplinary subject, including its ramifications to the RMA, non-lethal warfare capabilities, and population control in general?

In *Healing Codes for the Biological Apocalypse*, and in greater detail in *Healing Celebrations*, I reviewed the impressive research provided by a number of authorities in these fields including Nikola Tesla, Royal Raymond Rife, Russian investigators A.G. Gurvich and V.F. Kaznachayev, and genetic hydration experts including University of California at Berkeley, Chemistry Department Chairman, Ron Saykally *et al.* As seen in figure 18.16 Saykally *et al.*, largely proved that DNA electromagnetic status, and subsequent intracellular upregulation of structural integrity and metabolic functions is critically dependent on clustered water hydration at the molecular level.[58] Simply put, three of five Nobel Prize winners in medicine during the 1990s won their awards based on the discovery that DNA's primary function, is not as a template for RNA and protein synthesis, but as an electromagnetic receiver and transmitter of "biospiritual" energy. In fact, authorities determined that *only 0.1-2 percent of DNA functions as genetic material. The vast majority of the helical strand not involved in coding for protein synthesis is believed to function electromagnetically.*

489

Approximately ninety-three (93) percent of the function of DNA is "photon/phonon emissions for intra- and intercellular communications." Photon is light and phonon is sound. Both are part of the electromagnetic spectrum of energy resonating with, or potentially damaging, the bioelectric and bioacoustic properties and functions of cells.

Based on the evidence presented in this book, it can be safely assumed that AEC investigators, project HAARP scientists, and Human Genome Project principals, all coordinated at the highest levels of the cryptocracy invested in eugenic advances for optimal population control, are well aware of the primary function of DNA, and its potential use and abuse during military and medical manipulations. This bioenergetic domain represents the cutting edge of science. For those in the national security field, who leave no stone unturned in efforts to develop advanced "defense" systems and weapons that deliver "more bang for the buck," this area is critical.

In 1923, for instance, Russian anatomy professor, Dr. A. G. Gurvich, advanced a theory that ultraviolet light was essential to one of life's greatest mysteries—cell division. He had pointed the root tip of a growing onion toward the side of a second proliferating onion root. He noticed that the cells of the latter, in the area of the root tip, divided much faster. He theorized that ultraviolet light, or some other electromagnetic "mitogenetic radiation," was likely responsible for the biological change later called the "Gurvich Effect."[59]

During the following decade teams of mostly German and Russian scientists attempted to confirm the "Gurvich Effect" without success. After more than 500 research papers were published in this field of study, the subject was dropped. Then it was resurrected in the 1950s with the development of the photon-counter photomultiplier. This technology, aided by cryogenic techniques, enabled photodetectors to be cooled to very low temperatures, and allowed researchers to confirm the "Gurvich Effect"—the effect of mitogenetic radiation on cells.

Central to "biospiritual warfare," by 1974, Dr. V.F. Kaznachayev and his associates showed that *ultraviolet light frequencies could transmit viral induced infections between cell cultures*. These researchers arranged "pairs of sealed glass tubes containing healthy cell cultures end to end separated only by a sheet of quartz." After inoculating one culture with a deadly virus, the investigators were surprised to learn the adjacent sterile culture had also become infected.[59]

Fig. 18.16. Electromagnetic Functions DNA and Clustered Water On Cellular Metabolic and Structural Upregulation

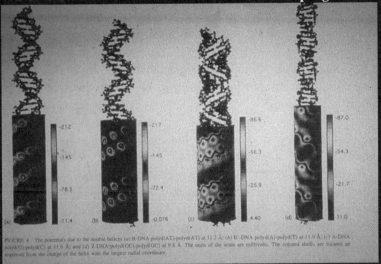

FIGURE 4   The potentials due to the double helices (a) B-DNA polyd(AT)-polyd(AT) at 11.2 Å; (b) B'-DNA polyd(A)-polyd(T) at 11.9 Å; (c) A-DNA polyd(G)-polyd(C) at 11.6 Å; and (d) Z-DNA-polyd(GC)-polyd(GC) at 9.8 Å. The units of the scale are millivolts. The colored shells are located as negatives from the charge of the helix with the largest radial coordinate.

Electrical potentials in millivolts of adequately hydrated DNA are shown in the figures above. Saykally et. al, showed small clustered water rings, mostly six-sided, facilitate electromagnetic transmissions to and from the double helix.

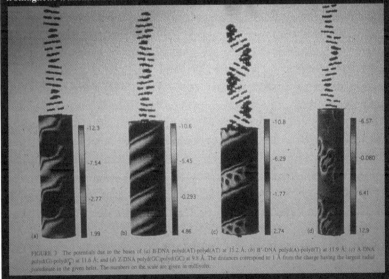

FIGURE 3   The potentials due to the bases of (a) B-DNA polyd(AT)-polyd(AT) at 11.2 Å; (b) B'-DNA polyd(A)-polyd(T) at 11.9 Å; (c) A-DNA polyd(G)-polyd(C) at 11.6 Å; and (d) Z-DNA polyd(GC)polyd(GC) at 9.8 Å. The distances correspond to 1 Å from the charge having the largest radial coordinate in the given helix. The numbers on the scale are given in millivolts.

The figures above show the results of cellular dehydration on DNA, and resulting drops in millivolt charges for electromagnetic cell signaling (i.e., frequency upregulation for structural integrity and metabolic functioning). The upper figure clearly shows more pronounced frequency transmissions reflected in the well formed patterns in the associated radial photographs. Source: K Liu, JD Cruzan and RJ Saykally. Water Clusters. *Science* (16 Feb) 1996;271:929-931.

When they duplicated the experiment with the quartz sheet removed, the sterile culture adjacent to the infected one remained unaffected. The glass tubes alone could not transmit the electromagnetic frequencies required to communicate the disease. In other words, special disease frequencies were *transmitted by the quartz crystal* and these alone were sufficient to infect the sterile cell cultures.

After repeatedly reproducing these results, the Russian team surmised that when the infected cells in culture died, they emitted UV light which was transmitted through the quartz to the adjacent cell cultures. These electromagnetic frequency transmissions then induced, like progressive crystal growth in prion diseases, progressive cell death in the initially healthy cultures.[57, 59]

Kaznachayev's team also showed that with the introduction of a virus into cell cultures, a change in the photon emissions of the cells was seen even before cell degeneration and death occurred.

Then, as the cell cultures died, they were observed to change their UV frequency radiations again. This suggested to Dr. Kaznachayev and his colleagues, that disease processes could possibly be altered by determining the dying cell frequency emissions and intercepting or neutralizing them before they had a chance to kill adjacent cells or tissues within their energy field. Additional support for this theory came from the observation that yeast cell reproduction (wherein prion transmissions and/or shape transformations have been observed,[57]) could be slowed using specific UV light frequencies. Alternatively, these findings suggested military applications beyond most people's worse nightmares.

Dr. Schjelderup, a Norwegian doctor suggested that viruses might emit lethal electromagnetic (EM) radiations, and thus kill cells in culture. He added that viral infections might thereby transmit disease by specific frequency emissions besides physical or genetic contact.

This explains the great interest shown by the AEC since at least the 1970s in this interdisciplinary field merging cancer and disease virology with radiological analyses. Based on these discussions, it is most reasonable to conclude much of the motivation behind the Human Genome Project is not for prevention, as alleged through the identification of genes that specifically predispose mostly minority persons to certain diseases, but rather for eugenics through advances in bioelectric, more aptly called "biospiritual," warfare.

Summary and Conclusion

In this book I have explained the abuse of science, medicine, and the public's trust to further political and population control agendas. Several non-lethal methods of conducting depopulation as a substitute for traditional warfare to sustain military-based economies were also documented.

The earliest chapters provided unbiased expert testimonies that the spraying of toxic pesticides to control vector insects, such as mosquitoes in New York for the West Nile virus, better serves to control human "pests." The middle chapters gave cold hard examples of genocide carried out in the name of public health primarily involving biological and chemical weapons largely developed and tested during World War II. More revealing was the almost twenty-year-long "Special Virus Cancer Program," beginning in the early 1960s, that paved the way for contemporary cancer research, genetic biotechnology, and modern eugenics. Major racial hygienists were exposed most vividly in the final chapters of this book along with their methods, materials, and administrative mechanisms for successfully waging psychotronic war and Malthusian eco-genocide in the "Technotronic Age."

Distinguished chemtrail commentator Diane Harvey summed up this book's thesis and purpose better than I might when she wrote: "It is beginning to look as if the actual purpose of all that we have been investigating is nothing less than the actual physical transformation of the earth's atmosphere in order to provide a platform for the latest chemical/electromagnetic technologies of warfare, communication, weather control, and control of populations through non-lethal chemical electromagnetic means. And what this portends for the future in terms of any meaningful retention of human freedom, and even the very life of the planet itself, is entirely unknown. Therefore it is not beyond reason to suggest that, unless this project is forced into the light of public scrutiny by means of a relatively few dedicated citizens, human freedom itself and perhaps even all life on this planet may be at risk."[60]

Consequently, I hope this book will serve as a wake up call, particularly for health professionals, public health servants, and policy makers who believe they are applying sound scientific principles in their practices. As strong opinion leaders, I thought it best to attempt awakening this segment of society first. My message here is not unlike James Bryant Conant's contention in *Science and Common Sense* when he explained, "The stumbling way in which even the ablest of the scientists in every generation have had to fight through thickets of erroneous observations, misleading generalizations, inadequate formulations, and unconscious prejudice is rarely appreciated by those who obtain their scientific knowledge from textbooks."

Given the full accounting in this book, we have all been similarly victimized, continue to be, and therefore need to respond as a community of concerned citizens to this alarm.

First, while considering your personal options, be advised that, "You're either part of the solution or part of the problem" as William Winkler insisted in Chapter 9. His actions might best serve as a model for the public at large. Despite his ailments, his family and business responsibilities, his ongoing scientific and political investigations, and battles with state and federal authorities, he managed to get an important piece of this information to the public. By getting truth out every way possible, he wrote, more people "are likelier to join in the effort to right serious wrongs" and save additional lives. He urged, "The power of pens remains mightier than swords. Write your truths for public consumption. Call radio talk shows to defend 'justice for all.' Consistently pressure your legislators to make needed changes, and demand honest and complete answers to pressing questions. Ask *hard* questions like 'Who did the testing [and are they biased, in any way, by conflicts of interest]?' Ask for copies of test results. Keep the pressure up until you achieve your goals. If a significant minority of people did this, we might all live a lot healthier and be better off."

I also recall the quote by Massachusetts evangelist Reinhold Niebuhr, "God, give us grace to accept with serenity the things that cannot be changed, courage to change the things which should be changed, and the wisdom to distinguish the one from the other." I believe I speak from the *Wisdom of Solomon* by refusing to accept global genocide masquerading as public health for my family and this world's future. This can, must, and will be changed, mostly by Divine intervention as I concluded in *Healing Codes for the Biological Apocalypse*, but in the meantime, you too can save some lives by spreading these shocking truths. Consistent with Niebuhr's counsel, I have expressed here a certain amount of courage that I hope will inspire a mustard seed of faith and trust in you too. May this book inspire the courageous to help right some wrongs, and save, if we can, one life at a time.

"In Germany they came first for the Communists. Then they came for the Jews, and I didn't speak up because I wasn't a Jew," confessed Martin Neimoeller. Today they are coming for Jews and Christians, Blacks and gays, Hispanics and Muslims, the aristocracy, the middle class, and poor whites as well. They are virtually coming for all of us in the age of non-lethal warfare, and because of the nature of this beast, and of psychotronic warfare, very few people remain awake enough to protest. That makes your individual efforts even more meaningful.

I have seen the difference my protests have made in people's lives around the world. A simple sharing about vaccine risks today can save an infant, a child, or a parent's life tomorrow.

For the most part, we are not *required* to blindly follow medical advice, consume toxic chemically treated foods and drinks, or even breathe polluted air. My family, for instance, has chosen to rely on alternative health professionals and self-care practices. We do not pay for costly health insurance, but invest our savings in healthy lifesyles. We have learned to treat ourselves with periodic fasting, detoxification, deacidification, immune boosting, oxygenation, and bioelectric and bioacoustic therapies. These strategies are published in *Healing Celebrations,* and summarized on tape in "Horowitz 'On Healing.'"[61]

The fact that we are locally challenged by high powered energy transmitters wielding waves of technotronic warfare caused us to investigate, and purchase, reasonably priced preventive technologies. How have we made them more affordable? We live comfortably, but we don't spend a lot of money on liquor, fashions, extravagancies, brand new cars, and we don't smoke. Still, life is far from boring. It's amazing how much money people spend on consumables, such as microwave ovens and color TVs, which experts warn are detrimental to physical and mental health, but refuse to invest in personal products and services for prevention and health maintenance. Who needs health, happiness, or enhanced well-being when you can vicariously live imagined lives on television, the silver screens, and on the Internet?

Our family of five watches less than an hour of television per day compared to the national average of six hours per person. We substitute art, music, singing, games, crafts, socializing, outdoor sports and reading. We routinely exercise. Beyond this we have been blessed with enough land to grow a significant part of our food. For this we labor in the garden with love. We live where well water is still fresh and clean, not chlorinated or fluoridated, but if we didn't, we'd use the best filtration systems available.

Most of these lifestyle choices can be made by the majority of people. It simply requires personal will to find better ways.

Last, but certainly not least, the best advice for people and population controllers alike, in this age of non-lethal technotronic war, was given by General Omar Bradley during his Armistice Day address in 1948. "The world has achieved brilliance without conscience. Ours is a world of nuclear giants and ethical infants. . . . We have grasped the mystery of the atom and rejected the Sermon on the Mount."

Ultimately, the choice to assimilate this knowledge and intelligence, is both practical and spiritually uplifting. Arguably, in this age of "biospiritual warfare," it is not against flesh and blood with whom we do battle. Faith and trust in a better future includes the knowledge that "it's always darkest before the dawn." The subtitle of this book—"globalism, terrorism, and toxic warfare"—relays the methods used by humanity's greatest adversaries to control or destroy what they apparently do not love. They coerce and enslave people through the insidious use of fear-based propaganda, and intoxicate large populations that lack "eyes to see and ears to hear" these truths. By applying this knowledge and responding to these warnings we will, in fact, facilitate the Darwinian notion of evolution of the species and survival of the fittest. Surely, those most knowledgeable will be most capable of responding and surviving.

The best news is that this war between good and evil is restrained by the same forces that balance nature. Although this factual account may seem overwhelmingly bad, if not horrifying, these revelations have come in cadence with the greatest spiritual renaissance in history. The spirit of humanity, as mediated through everyone's DNA, is responding to the greatest challenge in history. For God clearly wants a New World Order too. How long it will be controlled by corporate fascists remains to be seen.

References

1) UPI staff. Vaccine against pregnancy now being tested on humans. *St. Louis Globe-Democrat*, Friday, July 11, 1986, p. 32.

2) HLI staff. Philippine Medical Association study indicates that women were injected with contaminated tetanus vaccine. Human Life International website posting. E-mail distributed by: media@hli.org.

3) Christine M. Anti-Immunities in Vaccines. *News & Views*, April 1997;14;3:1-2. For reprints contact: Betty Tannenbaum, Editor, 8520 Bryan Avenue, Richmond Heights, MO 63117; 314-721-7818.

4) Rubin R. RU-486 met with praise and condemnation. USA Today, Friday-Sunday, Sept. 29-Oct. 1, 2000, p. 1.

5) Anonymous author. Feminist Majority Foundation Reports on Mifepristone: A Chronology in brief. From: http://www.feminist.org/gateway/ru486one.html

6) Murphy C. RU 486: Abortion by pill is not as simple as it seems. The Washington Post, Tuesday, February 4, 1997 P. Z10. Available from: http://www.w-cpc.org/news/post2-97.html

7) *Physicians' Desk Reference*. Arthrotec (diclofenac sodium and misoprostol [Cytotec]). Montvale, NJ: Medical Economics Company, Inc., 2000, pp. 2888-2891.

8) Keveles DJ. Eugenics and human rights. *British Medical Journal* 1999 (August 14);319:435-438.

9) Jasper WF. *Global Tyranny: Step by Step*. Appleton, Wisconsin: Western Islands Press, 1992, pp. 158-170.

10) Ehrlich PR. *The Population Bomb*, 1st ed. New York: Ballantine Books, 1968.

11) Ehrlich PR and Ehrlich AH. *The Population Explosion*. New York: Simon & Schuster, 1990.

12) Ehrlich PR. World population : Is the battle lost? *Stanford Today*, Winter 1968, p. 9.

13) Donnela H and Meadows DL, et al. *The Limits to Growth, a report for the Club of Rome's Project on the Predicament of Mankind*. New York: Universe Books, 1972.

14) Barney GO. *Global 2000: Report to the President of the United States: Entering the Twenty-First Century*. New York: Penguin Books, 1982.

15) Simon JL and Kahn H. *The Resourceful Earth: A Response to Global 2000*. New York: Basil Blackwell, Inc., 1984, pp. 34-35;45.

16) Kasum J. *The War Against Population.* San Francisco: Ignatius Press, 1988, p. 50.

17) Simpson C. *Science of Coercion: Communication Research & Psychological Warfare 1945-1960.* Oxford: Oxford University Press, 1994, pp. 116-117; 60-61.

18) Simpson references works by Cantril, Albert Hadley. "See also collection of Psychological Strategy Board correspondence with Cantril, including Cantril's oblique reference to what appears to be clandestine CIA sponsorhip and editing of his pamphlet 'The Goals of the Individual and the Hopes of Humanity' (1951; published by Institute for Associated Research, Hanover, NH) in Cantril note of October 22, 1951; in Hadley Cantril correspondence, Psychological Strategy Board, Truman Library, Independence, MO."

19) Crewdson JM and Treaster J. Worldwide propaganda network built by the CIA. *New York Times*, December 26, 1977.

20) National Research Council. *Beyond Six Billion: Forecasting the World's Population.* John Bongaarts and Rodolfo A. Bulatao, Eds. Washington, D.C.: National Academy Press, 2000, pp. ix, 8, 18, 86-87, 214.

21) Staff writer. Numbers. *Time*, June 29, 1998 p. 16.

22) Department of Defense Appropriations for 1970, Hearings Before a Subcommittee of the Committee on Appropriations House of Representatives, Ninety-First Congress, Tuesday, July 1, 1969, p. 129. Washington, DC: U.S Government Printing Office, 1969.

23) Harkins D. RAND analyst admits Defense Secretary fits profile of domestic terrorist? The Idaho Observer, September, 2000. For copies write to: P.O. Box 457, Spirit Lake, Idaho 83869; Phone: 208-255-2307; Email: observer@dmi.net; Web: http://proliberty.com/observer/

24) Phelps JE. Final diagnosis: Evironmental toxic pathway analysis and immune system cytokine modality provide key insight into chronic fatigue syndrome mechanism and etiology of varied pathogen driven illnesses. Published on the Internet at: http://members.aol.com/magnu96196/cfs.html; For SVCP references and notes see: Horowitz LG and Martin JW. *Emerging Viruses: AIDS & Ebola—Nature, Accident or Intentional?* Rockport, MA: Tetrahedron Press, 1998.

25) Geissler E. (with contributions by D. Baltimore). Biological and Toxin Weapons Today. Stockholm and London: Stockholm International Peace Research Institute; Oxford University Press, 1986, p. 31.

26) Simmons ML. *Biohazards and Zoonotic Problems of Primate Procurement, Quarantine and Research: Proceedings of a Cancer Research Safety Symposium.* March 19, 1975, Conducted at the Frederick Cancer Research Center, Frederick, Maryland. DHEW Publication No. (NIH) 76-890, pp. 27; 50-52.

27) NCI staff. *The Special Virus Cancer Program: Progress Report #8.* Office of the Associate Scientific Director for Viral Oncology (OASDVO). J. B. Moloney, Ed., Washington, D. C.: U. S. Government Printing Office, 1971. pp. 224-225;376. See also: NCI Staff. *The [Special] Virus Cancer Program*

[SVCP]. U.S. Department of Health, Education and Welfare. Washington, D.C.: Public Health Service, National Institutes of Health, Division of Cancer Cause and Prevention, June 1978, Library call number: E20.3152:V81/977 and 78-21195; See p. 19 for contaminated vaccine admissions, pp. 231, 254 and 255 for contaminated cell culture reports, pp. 257-258.

28) Rosenberg HL. Anthrax cloud's silver lining: Bioport Copr. lands exclusive license to produce vaccine. ABCNEWS.com. March 12, 1999. Article is available from: http://www.tetrahedron.org/articles/anthrax/Anthrax_Vaccine_Crowe_Bristish.html.

29) *Hearings before the Subcommittee on Health and Scientific Research of the Committee on Human Resources, United States Senate, Ninety-fifth Congress, First Session, on Examination of Serious Deficiencies in the Defense Department's Efforts to Protect the Human Subjects of Drug Research, Biological Testing Involving Human Subjects by the Department of Defense.* Washington, D.C.: U.S. Government Printing Office, March 8 and May 23, 1977, pp. 125-127.

30) Brown P. Geneticist accused of letting thousands die in rainforest: Scientist "killed Amazon indians to test race theory." Gulf-Chat, Saturday, September 23, 2000, Internet article distributed by gulf-chat@structured.net. Originally posted at http://www.guardianunlimited.co.uk/international/story/0,3604,372067,00.html

31) 17. *Who's Who in America*, 49th Edition, Volume 1 A-K. New Providence, NJ: Marquis Who's Who, 1995, p. 552.

32) Califano, Jr. JA. Health: U. S. Initiatives in International Health. *Department of State Bulletin.* September, 1978, pp. 35-38.

33) Hartmann B. Population control as foreign policy. *Covert Action Information Bulletin.* Winter 1991-92;39:26-30.

34) Brzezinski Z. National Security Council Memorandum–46: National Security Council Interdepartmental Group For Africa. Study in Response to Presidential Security Review Memorandum 1 NSC–46: Black Africa and the U.S. Black Movement, (SECRET) March 17, 1978.

35was). Simons H. Repackaging population control. *Covert Action Quarterly* 1994;51:33-44.

36) Eberstadt N. *Foreign Aid and American Purpose.* Washington D.C.: American Enterprise Institute for Public Policy Research, 1988, p. 104.

37) Porrit J. Birth of the Brave New World Order. *Guardian Weekly* (London), September 11, 1994.

38) Gordon L. *Woman's Body, Woman's Rights: A Social History of Birth Control in America.* New York: Grossman, 1976. pp. 400-401.

39) Foster G. quoted in "Global Demographic Trends to the Year 2010: Implications for U.S. Security," Washington Quarterly, Spring 1989, and *Information Project for Africa, Population Control and National Security.* Washington, D.C.: U. S. Government Printing Office, 1989, p. 54.)

40) *National Security Study Memorandum 200 (NSSM 200). "Implications of Worldwide Population Growth for US Security and Overseas Interests."* U.S National Security Council Report, December 10, 1974.

41) *Ibid.*, pp. 21-22;115.

42) Robinson, Jr LH. *Report to Africa Bureau, Office of Regional Affairs, Agency for International Development.* Battelle Human Affairs Research Centers, November 6, 1981, pp. 15-16; Also see *Ambassadors of Colonialism: the International Development Trap. An essay on the Benevolent Superpower, Sustainable Development, and Other Contemporary Myths*, (Washington, D.C., Information Project for Africa, Inc.) 1993.

43) Knowles JC. *"Tools for Population Policy Development OPTIONS for Population Policy Project"* (AID-funded project), 1988, p. 23.

44) In 1982 a U.S. General Accounting Office report cautioned that many NGOs in the U.S. were becoming overly dependent on USAID for financing their projects. See, "Voluntary Aid for Development: the Role of NGOs," OECD (Paris: OECD, 1988), p. 113.

45). NGO Review 1993. *The well-spent pound: an assessment of aid agencies's priorities for population activities.* London: House of Commons, March, 1994, p. 48. Author Helen Simmons reviewed this work and footnoted, "While UNICEF was set up by the U.N. and so is not strictly an NGO, it increasingly operates in and is treated as one in the development circles. Even relatively modest NGOs still have fantastic incomes in African terms. The Save the Children Fund's (SCF) income of over $149 million in 1991-92 outstrips that of the Eritrean government five times over."

46) Kaplan R. The coming anarchy. *Atlantic Monthly* February, 1994, p. 58.

47) Thoreau HD.*Journal [1906].* September 7, 1851

48) Byrd WM and Clayton LA. *An American Health Dilemma: A Medical History of African Americans and the Problem of Race.* New York: Routledge Press, 2000.

49) Sai FT and Chester LA. The role of the world bank in shaping Third World population policy. In: *Population Policy: Contemporary Issues*, G. Roberts, Ed., New York: Praeger, 1990, p. 183.

50) The Futures Group. The United Republic of Tanzania: Population and Development. Washington, D.C., 1980, p. 45. For more information on the use of RAPID presentations, see Sai and Chester, *op. cit.*

51) Associated Press. HRS can't do everything for everybody, task group's chief says. *The Orlando Sentinel*, Tuesday, January 8, 1991. The position articulated here by Janet Reno, prior to becoming attorney general in the Clinton administration, was that social reforms were needed to respond to "the failed family institution." The breakdown of the family, she said was the chief cause of crime and drug use in the United States.

52) Lambo TA. The African mind in contemporary conflict: The Jacques Parisot Foundation Lecture, 1971. *World Health Organization Chronicle* 1971;25;8:343-353.

53) Rockefeller Brothers Fund, *Prospect for America: The Rockefeller Panel Reports*. Garden City, New York: Doubleday & Company, 1961.

54) Raskin M. *Keinholtz: A Retrospective*. New York: Whitney Museum of American Art, 1997, p. 38.

55) Ward SJ, Poernomo I, Sidi S, Simmons R and Simmons G. *Service Delivery Systems and Quality of Care in the Implementation of Norplant in Indonesia*. New York: Population Control Council, February, 1990, pp. 45, 50-51.

56) Allen C. Norplant—Birth control or coercion? *Wall Street Journal*, September 13, 1991, p. 10.

57) Horowitz LG and Puleo J. *Healing Codes for the Biological Apocalypse*. Sandpoint, Idaho: Tetrahedron Publishing Group, 1999, p. 398.

58) Lui K, Cruzan JD and Saykally RJ. Water clusters. *Science* (16 Feb) 1996;271:929-931.

58) Horowitz LG. *Healing Celebrations*. Sandpoint, Idaho: Tetrahedron Publishing Group, 2000, pp. 135-137.

60) Harvey D. quoted in *The Idaho Observer*, September, 2000. PO Box 457, Spirit Lake, Idaho 83869, (208) 255-2307; observer@dmi.net; www.proliberty.com/observer.

61) Horowitz LG. Horowitz "On Healing." Sandpoint, ID: Tetrahedron Publishing Group, 2000. For a free catalog of all of Dr. Horowitz's books and tapes, please call 1-888-508-4787 or link to: http://www.tetrahedron.org

Epilogue

"Attorneys commissioned by the Centers for Disease Control and Prevention (CDC) in Atlanta have advanced health policy legislation that dramatically suspends civil rights in case of a declared biological emergency. The "Model State Emergency Health Powers Act," according to the *Boston Globe*, would give public health officials and states governors the power to arrest, transport, quarantine, drug, and vaccinate anyone suspected of carrying a potentially infectious disease."

Press Release, Tetrahedron Publishing Group,
Based on the official document available at:
www.publichealthlaw.net/MSEHPA/MSEHPA.dpdf.
November, 2001

This book was published months before the September 11, 2001 "terrorist" attacks on America's financial and military icons—the World Trade Center and the Pentagon. Since then, people worldwide have been heralding this book as shockingly prophetic. The horrifying social, economic, and political realities that have unfolded in the wake of these events have left people dazed and the world forever changed.

I hate to say, "I told you so," but the preceding pages prove it.

Herein lies the intelligence to accurately interpret everything that has transpired since that fateful day. From the heightened threats of biological and chemical attacks relayed through the mail and media, to the companies profiting from, if not instigating, these assaults. This book precisely forecasts and explains these tragedies, and more to come, in the sociopolitical and economic context in which they have arisen.

Most readers of this book will concur, these tragic events, demonstrating the Machiavellian theory in military–medical practice, are best explained using the information relayed in earlier chapters concerning the CIA, the "Revolution in Military Affairs," "non-lethal warfare," and the widespread psychological operations (PSYOPs) required to effect mass mediated mind control and population management.

Thus, this work sounds an alarm that will ring eternal in readers' ears—that while most of the world slept, the "beast," particularly well defined in Chapters 17 and 18, struck Metropolis U.S.A. and forever changed the world stage. As a result, global attention was effectively focused on CIA-funded, trained, and apparently orchestrated "religious fanatics" called "terrorists," and "America's New War" in Afghanistan set the stage for World War III. Meanwhile, the distracted masses never saw the ongoing genocide effected by myriad other methods. These, include vaccinations, blood transfusions, petrochemical sprayings, and oral (food and water) intoxications, and genetic manipulations, agendas all accelerated by fabricated policy rationales for "national security" and "public health."

Military Intelligence Viewpoint

It may be recalled that "the best covert operation is one that takes place in broad daylight, in front of everyone's eyes, yet no one sees it." These words by Joint Chiefs of Staff, Special Operations specialist, Retired Col. Jack A. Kingston, best describe the alleged "terrorist" attacks on America. To reinforce his point, Col. Kingston, in 1997 as Chairman of the National Security Advisory Board in Washington, provided a "critical analysis" on my previous book, *Emerging Viruses: AIDS & Ebola—Nature, Accident or Intentional?*[1] His words foreshadowed, and further clarified, the fateful 9-11. Much like the ghastly attack on Pearl Harbor that historians claim triggered World War II, the "terrorist" attacks on New York and Washington expressed a covert operation intended to promote a new world war mentality, global economy, and social controls consistent with the long developing globalistic agenda described earlier. Col. Kingston wrote that "the reality of U.S. covert operations," like the use of "biological warfare during the American Revolutionary War, would stretch the credulity of the average person.

"In John Toland's comprehensive historical nonfiction work, *Infamy*, and an earlier 1954 book exposing the *Final Secret of Pearl Harbor* by Rear Admiral Robert Theobald (USN-Ret'd), [the authors] actually concluded that FDR painstakingly engineered the Japanese attack on December 7, 1941. Taken together with more recently available and substantive works on the ULTRA, ENIGMA and MANHATTAN projects, it is plausible to develop a comprehensive declassified picture of America's most secret, and most devastating, strategic covert operations. . . .

"It is also obvious," Col. Kingston continued, "that unrelenting wars, and the rapidly changing military technology of the twentieth century, have steadily increased the demand for strategic operations that 'do not reveal the hand of the U.S. government,' as well as, vastly increased the scope and lethality of the secret bureaucracy. Just as evident is the actuality that the vast American intelligence community must then employ several hundreds of thousands of secret 'agents for things' and daily conducts inter-service operations, utilizing inter-agency task forces worldwide. . . .

"Additionally, although the final approval authority for U.S. covert operations now rests solely with the President, with oversight by Select Committees of Congress, these safeguards may be illusory. That is because small covert activities, in support of major operations already approved by the Chief Executive, may be approved at lower levels within the CIA, and these 'supporting activities' constitute the majority of all CIA covert operations. Furthermore, low-risk parent projects may evolve into high-risk supporting functions. . . .

"In closing, it is exceptionally noteworthy that Len Horowitz doesn't force his readers to accept or conclude what the overwhelming evidence he has amassed clearly indicates. He wisely knows what he can prove, what he can disprove, and what he should leave to the reader's wisdom. In my estimation he has unearthed a covert operation run amok that is bigger than any secret operation in U.S. history, and more momentous in it's implications to humanity than the atomic weapons 'Manhattan Project' of World War II."[1]

Col. Kingston's report raises a spectre consistent with the evidence relayed herein. That criminal cells operate within our own intelligence hierarchy, as was apparently the case with the Kennedy assassination, and 9-11. In observance of Machiavellian mentality, these CIA "supporting activities" have consistently produced ends that justify their deadly means. Serious investigators are thus compelled to critically analyze the social, economic, and political outcomes of 9-11 in relation to the agents and agencies who benefit most by this, apparently managed, chaos. Indeed, if Ret. Col. Kingston's sources are correct, then we might expect to find ample evidence of foreknowledge and even complicity by our president and cryptocracy regarding 9-11, which we do.

On September 13, 2001, following an editorial I circulated over the Internet that the 9-11 attacks were obviously planned,[2,3] I received an e-mail from Dr. Garth Nicolson, Director of the Institute of Molecular Medicine, whose internationally esteemed scientific reports in the field of Gulf War syndrome, as reviewed earlier in this book, are greatly respected. In response to my communicated foreknowledge of the attacks, Dr. Nicolson wrote:

> Dear Len, we actually gave the Pentagon the correct date of Sept. 11 for an attack on the Pentagon, but they disregarded our messages. We did not know the method or that other attacks would precede the Pentagon attack. But the NSC was warned.

I then requested that Dr. Nicolson supply his source(s) of this intelligence. Based on reports from family members involved with organized crime, he replied:

> We received the information from multiple sources, but it was confirmed in a conversation with the head of state of a North African country when we were visiting midyear after speaking at the 13th International Conference on Integrative Medicine in Malta. The information was passed on to the Director of Policy of the Department of Defense, the Inspector General of the US Army Medical Corps and the National Security Council. Unfortunately, it was ignored.

> I believe that you are correct that many people may have known about this, and we find it interesting that of four targets, two were secretly owned by 'Fat Tony' Salerno. Now we hear that the largest towers in the world will replace the WTC towers. What a way to get insurance to put up new buildings![2]

Indeed, growing evidence suggests that, much like FDR's complicity in the attack on Pearl Harbor, President George W. Bush and several administration officials, including members of the CIA, were privy to foreknowledge of, if not party to, the 9-11 attacks. Much of this intelligence has been posted by multiple reputable sources on the Internet.[3] This is much like Klaus Groenke's "Big Double Cross" when considered in light of the blame shifted from the CIA and military–industrialists to the "Muslim people" in general for what the oligarchy obviously instigated. (See Figures E-1 and E-2.)

For those still inclined to believe in the lone villain excuse for every major unnatural catastrophe in the last century, if not beyond, I posted twenty-six (26) reasons why Osama bin Laden was not as heavily implicated in the attacks as our shadow governors and spy networks wish us to believe.[3] Figures E-1 and E-2 graphically depict these more than coincidental sickening elements of this "Big Double Cross."

The anthrax mailings mystery that occurred in the weeks following 9-11 provides an excellent example of the manner in which these

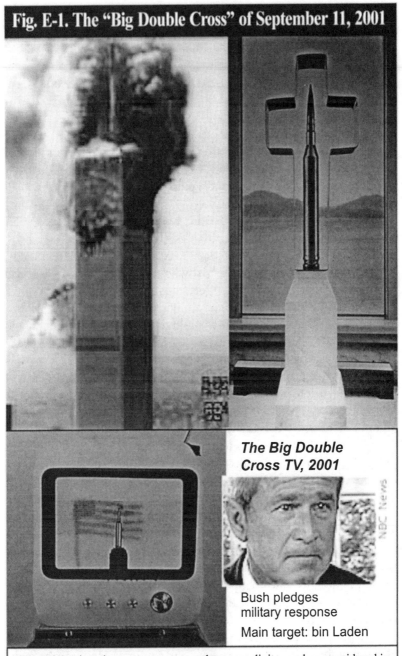

Fig. E-1. The "Big Double Cross" of September 11, 2001

The Big Double Cross TV, 2001

Bush pledges
military response
Main target: bin Laden

These sickening elements seem more than serendipitous when considered in light of the religious angles, and reported Bush administration officials' fore-knowledge of 9-11. (See color gallery and Chapters 17 and 18 for details.)

"terrorist" events and outcomes reflect the Machiavellian practices of the global elite, and the economics of population control.

In an effort to help solve the anthrax mystery I advanced a viable, yet unspeakable, "industrial espionage" theory, and forwarded the evidence to more than 1,500 F.B.I. personnel and every member of Congress beginning on Oct. 1, 2001. The resulting avoidance of my controversial theory angered political observers, grassroots activists, and news investigators alike as it became increasingly clear that F.B.I. officials were politically incapable of solving the case. I later learned that bureau directors were given "back off" orders from the Bush administration in keeping with their culpability and the theories I advanced in this book.

In the past I had used the F.B.I.'s own methods and materials for investigating serial killers beginning with the federal government cover-up of the facts concerning the 1990 Florida dental AIDS tragedy. This famous case involved a dentist who transmitted his disease to at least six patients. I published three scientific articles in this regard, exposing Dr. David Acer and other similarly deranged individuals who spread HIV—the AIDS virus—as biological weapons to frighten and kill victims. To date, despite my efforts in broadly disseminating the concealed evidence in this matter, like the anthrax mailing case, important truths have been suppressed and the issue remains a "mystery."[4, 5]

A serial killer's motivation, I learned, is always paramount in every search and profiling of suspects. Yet, with the widely publicized anthrax mailings, F.B.I. officials suddenly seem disinterested in this criminology edict. Even on television, homicide investigators begin by asking who profits most by murder. Closest kin and wealth recipients are typically scrutinized. So why hadn't official investigators, or the mainstream media, held anthrax and related smallpox profiteers up to this customary scrutiny? Some of the chief suspects were even operating near Trenton, NJ where the anthrax letters originated.

I asked why, with more than two dozen biologicals to choose from in state-run weapons laboratories, had America's incessant focus been limited to anthrax and smallpox threats? Could the drug-makers who produced the only state-sanctioned remedies for these agents be economically and politically related to policy-makers?

I explained that standard F.B.I. serial killer investigations, like that of "Unibomber" Ted Kaczynski, who sent explosives through the mail, were supported by analyzing the "developmental histories" of suspects. Might the histories of implicated drug companies, including those that demanded court warrants for F.B.I. access to their labs, reflect those historically linked to murder, or even mass genocide?

Developmental History of the Fourth Reich

In fact, the only FDA endorsed anthrax antibiotic, Cipro, and the government purchased smallpox vaccine, was produced by companies that evolved directly from Germany's infamous WWII military–industrial cartel—I.G. Farben. Cipro was produced by Bayer AG, discussed in Chapter 1, while the smallpox vaccine's newly formed producers were announced as Acambis (previously OraVax), partnered with Baxter and Aventis—created in 1999 by parent companies Hoechst and Rhone-Poulenc. All have severely jaded histories.

Bayer and Hoechst were two of "The Big Three" companies formed following the "decartelization" of I.G. Farben. The CIA immediately took over their corporate headquarters in Frankfurt, which had curiously escaped allied bombings. Historians explain that the Farben complex had been protected by military officials obligated to John D. Rockefeller's Standard Oil Company—half owner of the Farben cartel.[5]

Soon after the CIA began operations in the Farben building, Bayer and Hoechst were reorganized in 1951 under the direction of the Allied High Commission, largely influenced by U.S. High Commissioner John J. McCloy—a lawyer and banker from Philadelphia, with intimate ties to Rockefeller banking and oil interests. After "decartelization," the I.G. Farben labor camps were consolidated into "The Big Three" holding companies—Bayer, Hoechst, and BASF—for the benefit of the stockholders.

Hermann Schmitz, president of Bayer A.G and I.G. Farben during WWII, who also largely directed the Deutsche Bank, "held as much stock in Standard Oil of New Jersey as did the Rockefellers," according to former CBS News war correspondent Paul Manning who thanked CIA director Allen Dulles for his historic accounts. On August 10, 1944, the Rockefeller-Farben partners moved their "flight capital" through affiliated German/French, American, British and Swiss banks "for the new Germany," according to Manning. This secured "the sophisticated distribution of national and corporate assets to safe havens" throughout the world, and assured the continuation and further development of the "Neuordnung" (new [world] order) for both global petrochemical–pharmaceutical and banking cartels.[5]

Historic records showed in the legal battle of Standard Oil (NJ) et. al., v. Clark, in 1947, that U.S. Circuit Court Judge Charles Clark found this "unholy alliance" between America's wealthiest company and the Farben cartel was nothing short of "an enemy national." The judge wrote that the Rockefeller plaintiffs "became enemy nationals [i.e., traitors] after the outbreak of the war, since their concealment of I.G. assets continued thereafter." Such underhanded manipulations for war profits prompted President Dwight D. Eisenhower, in his Farewell Address to the Nation in 1961, to urge diligence regarding the "military–industrial complex" and "the potential for the disastrous rise of misplaced power."[6]

More Modern Machinations

As discussed in Chapter 18, in 1998, a lucrative defense department contract was granted to a new company, Bioport Corporation, for the production of a largely untested anthrax vaccine. The firm was formed principally by Saudi financier Fuad El-Hibri, reportedly connected to Bin Laden family businesses and investments. Bioport's predecessor, the failing Michigan Biologic Products Institute (affiliated with Michigan State University) failed to secure FDA approval on their anthrax vaccine for several reasons, including excessive contaminations and poor record keeping. Others joining El-Hibri on the Board of Directors of Bioport included Reagan staffer and Clinton advisor Admiral William J. Crowe, Jr., former Chairman of the Joint Chiefs of Staff, and Senior Advisor for Global Options—an industrial think tank whose members included former Director of Central Intelligence, R. James Woolsy. In recent years Mr. Woolsy has been a leading financial consultant who lectures extensively on "industrial espionage."[7]

Howard L. Rosenberg of ABC NEWS reported in March, 1999, that Bioport's exclusive $29 million contract with the U.S. Department of Defense to manufacture, test, bottle and store the anthrax vaccine was overtly specious. "According to former Central Intelligence Agency military analyst Patrick Eddington, the estimated $60 million worth of anthrax vaccine Bioport is expected to produce for the Defense Department over the next five years could just be the beginning. The Pentagon has a $322 million, 10-year program to develop at least three, and perhaps as many as a dozen additional biological warfare vaccines [smallpox, no doubt, included]. . . . These have never really been tested, and most importantly, no one has provided data to validate the threat."[8]

Another major stockholder of Bioport, Corp., according to Chicago judicial system investigator Sherman Skolnick and others,[9,10] is The Carlyle Group—a $12 billion private investment firm and the 11th leading defense contractor. This group's Chief Executive Officer, Frank C. Carlucci, III, was a key CIA operations director implicated in the initial Sub-Saharan Africa AIDS outbreak,[10] and was National Security Advisor during the Iran-contra scandal. Other Carlyle Group officials include former cabinet members of the George H.W. Bush administration such as Secretary of State James A. Baker, III, and members of the Bin Laden family.[9,10]

Mr. Baker and the senior Bush are likewise linked to another experimental vaccine producer—Tanox Biomedical Systems of Houston, Texas. As briefly detailed in Chapter 1, and more extensively elsewhere,[11] this Baylor College of Medicine affiliated lab is currently a defendant in a class action lawsuit filed on behalf of Huntsville, TX prisoners and civilians who received Mycoplasma contaminated vaccines and/or resulting infections. Their diseases are astonishingly similar to those seen in the Gulf War Syndrome, even though these vaccine experiments began years before Operation Desert Storm.[11]

Updating the international intrigue visiting these military vaccine producers, according to the *Wall Street Journal*, (Sept. 28, 2001), "The father of President Bush, works for the Bin Laden family business in Saudi Arabia through the Carlyle Group . . ."[10]

Exposing the Powerful Bioterror Cartel and F.B.I. Impotence

The likelihood that today's widely heralded biological threats such as smallpox, though potentially real, are orchestrated by multinational corporations. This best reflects "industrial espionage" activities. The media targeted anthrax mailings that effectively "wagged the dog" for drug-makers' profits is a classic example of this new form of bioterrorism and military-medical profiteering.

Retired L.A. Police Department investigator-turned-journalist Michael Ruppert agrees. He has published numerous articles exposing or implicating Bush administration and CIA officials in profit-making from various forms of terrorism following September 11. Reinforcing the Carlyle Group connection, Mr. Ruppert wrote that "The senior Bush had met with the Bin Laden family at least twice in the last three years—1998 and 2000—as a representative of Carlyle, seeking to expand business dealings with one of the wealthiest Saudi families, which some experts argue, has never fully severed its ties with black sheep Osama."[10]

The political strength and identity of these unsavory parties connected to Bush, the Bin Ladens, Bioport, and possibly other recently formed vaccine and drug companies conveniently positioned and illegally contracted to take advantage of anthrax and smallpox "bioterrorism," bodes badly for the F.B.I. The bureau's apparent unwillingness to follow my anthrax mailing leads is best reconciled by the following facts:

Fig. E-2. The "Changing Images of Man" and "Long Range Penetration Strain"

AMERICA'S DAY OF TERROR

The global elite determined to produce, according to British Secret Service agent, Dr. Coleman, "long range penetration strain" for America's psychosocial decline. Global colonialists directed the arts and sciences to control large populations by way of ongoing sensory overload. This effort was pioneered by Willis Harmon and perfected by the Tavistock Institute of Human Relations, the Stanford Research Institute, and the Rand Corporation whose scientists collaborated with "at least another 150 research institutions here in the U.S." The Rand Corporation has been the principle contractor for "terrorism education" serving U.S. Government agencies and emergency preparedness personnel in the fifty states.

According to a recent BBC report instigated by investigative reporter Greg Palast for Britain's premier Sunday Newspaper, *The Observer*, "F.B.I. and [U.S.] military intelligence officials in Washington say they were prevented for political reasons from carrying out full investigations into members of the Bin Laden family in the US before the terrorist attacks of September 11. . . . [T]he F.B.I. files were closed in 1996 apparently before any conclusions could be reached on either of the Bin Laden brothers . . . They said the restrictions became worse after the Bush administration took over this year. The intelligence agencies had been told to 'back off' from investigations involving other members of the Bin Laden family, the Saudi royals, and possible Saudi links to the acquisition of nuclear weapons by Pakistan. 'There were particular investigations that were effectively killed,'" F.B.I. and intelligence officers in Washington told Palast and the BBC.[12]

Conflicts of Interest, Illegalities, and Lies

According to Dr. Sidney M. Wolfe, health director at Ralph Nader's Public Citizen Health Research Group, illegal meetings were routinely conducted between Bush administration officials, including Secretary of the Department of Health and Human Services (HHS), Tommy Thompson, and principals of the Pharmaceutical Research and Manufacturers of America (PhRMA). Their covertly managed Emergency Preparedness Task Force, in violation of federal transparency laws for such decision-making bodies, touted in November, 2001 its orders for enough drugs and vaccines to protect every American against the threats of anthrax and smallpox. The PhRMA task force was directed by Aventis executive and anthrax mailing conspiracy suspect Richard Markham at that time.[13]

Apparent illegalities did not deter Secretary Thompson from ordering more than $100 million worth of Bayer's Cipro, at the "bargain price" of $.90 per tablet when other companies offered equally effective and lower risk substitutes for a few pennies each, and later for free.

Predictably, given the preceding background, on October 25, 2001, Mr. Thompson asked Congress for another $500 million to produce enough of the Acambis/Aventis smallpox vaccine "so every American will be assured there is a dose with his or her name on it if it is needed." This, despite CDC official admissions that people already vaccinated probably shouldn't take it, and that the new smallpox vaccine will require extensive testing.[14,15]

Meanwhile, much like Bioport, Acambis's rapid and suspicious evolution from the failing OraVax corporation described in "West Nile Virus in New York City"—Chapter 8—leaves many observers wondering.[16] You might recall that OraVax had been likewise linked to shady back-room dealings with Clinton administration officials in 1998 regarding government orders for the (yet to be tested) West Nile Virus vaccine. These earlier writings recorded a stealth meeting between Dr. Thomas Monath, the Vice President of OraVax (now Acambis), President Clinton, Janet Reno, CIA Director John Deutsch, and American Type Culture Collection (ATCC) curator Dr. Joshua Lederberg—the same former Rockefeller University President and Council on Foreign Relations bioterrorism study group leader discussed in Chapters 8 and 16. [17]

What concerns me is not that a business deal was struck, albeit illegally, but that Dr. Lederberg had falsely assured the American military and public that no biological weapons were used during the Gulf War despite his knowledge that the ATCC, under his watch, sent nineteen shipments of various strains of anthrax suitable for weapons production to Sadam Hussein in the years leading up to Desert Storm, and that tens of thousands of vets may have suffered and died from Gulf War syndrome as a result. Consequently, these people who are largely directing the public health response to bioterrorism today, are downright liars and traitors.

These allegations are solidly documented in the U.S. *Congressional Record* from Don Reigle's committee hearings concerning Gulf War syndrome. The Reigle report exposed ATCC as the chief supplier of biological weapons strains to virtually anyone with a lab, including pharmaceutical companies.[18] Returning to the mystery of the mailed anthrax, since the mailed anthrax strain was certified American, it likely originated from ATCC.

The *New York Times* (November 9, 2001) reported ATCC vice president Nancy Wysocki saying, "We have a very close working relationship with many of the federal agencies, including the F.B.I." Then, the "conspiracy of silence" I experienced at the F.B.I., since my October 1st efforts to rally the bureau, made even more sense.[19]

Given this history, it is not particularly reassuring that the nation's chief law enforcement agency and the ATCC have a "close working relationship."

Nor was I pleased to learn that the new unlawful and untrustworthy biotech firms were financed by Bush and Bin Laden family members and associates. This does explain, however, why even after hand delivering urgent requests for F.B.I. officials to investigate these white-collar criminals for possible industrial espionage in the anthrax mailings, they never had the courtesy to respond.

"Federal Bungling Incompetents" or Pawns for Global Genocide

In fact, I hand-delivered my report, and this book, to my regional F.B.I. office, as mentioned, on October 1, 2001, almost two weeks before the first anthrax letter was sent from Trenton, New Jersey to the American Media building in Boca Raton, Florida. My action was prompted by reading the Oklahoma City bombing grand jury investigation, *The Final Report*, commissioned by then State Representative Charles Key. It stated that German-based neo-Nazis were known to have "masterminded" both airline hijackings and U.S. military installation bombings by the PLO. This matched what the F.B.I. had reported, and reinforced the German connection to what was obviously a Cipro and smallpox vaccine sales "scam." The Cipro scam reported by Kelly O'Meara on November 5, in the *Washington Times*, was based on my leads—the information I shared with the F.B.I.[7]

The F.B.I. reported that the silica-mixed anthrax powder required expensive equipment, as well as a bioweapons savvy microbiologist, to produce. By early November, they had ruled out Islamic terrorist groups, but not "state-sponsored" criminals. This likewise suggested a "white collar" gang operating within our own cryptocracy.[19]

The *New York Times* (November 11, 2001) also reported that F.B.I. agents were denied access to "some pharmaceutical companies in New Jersey." These companies demanded agents "present a subpoena before they would grant access to their files."[19] I found this additionally suspicious, if not seriously incriminating, especially since Aventis, one of my primary suspects, had two plants within forty-five minutes drive of Trenton.

"I should think that any company with nothing to hide would welcome the bureau's inquiry," I thought, "especially at this time of national emergency." To me, the drug firms' response seemed like Gestapo tactics rather than amiable support.

In summary, I asked the F.B.I. to thoroughly investigate the possibility of industrial espionage being perpetrated by Bayer corporate officials as well as possibly Dr. Thomas Monath, the Vice President of OraVax/Acambis, and affiliated officials at Aventis. I also urged an inquiry into ATCC curator Dr. Joshua Lederberg, and the financial interests he represents, including Rockefeller pharmaceutical and banking interests.

The trouble is, in the real world of power politics, economic espionage, and bioterrorism, this level of investigation and mainstream exposure is admittedly impossible. I concluded that in this New World Order, our great American law enforcement agency, under restraints posed by British loyalists and banking globalists in the Bush administration and the CIA, has been reduced to a group of Federal Bungling Incompetents.

What Can You Do?

I urge you, the readers of this book, to not to get caught up in the media hype and political spins aimed at generating religious and interracial hate and warrior mentalities. Instead, pray for preventive knowledge, guiding wisdom, and above all, world peace.

Given that it is always darkest before the dawn, and these times appear to be disastrously dismal for most Americans and people worldwide, we can rest assured we're on the verge of something special. After all, even if you don't believe in God, anyone with moderate intelligence recognizes there is balance in nature.

In my humble opinion, the devil-doers discussed and exposed in this book are on their last legs. This planet is destined for a spiritual renaissance which the ruling elite are unable to extinguish, despite their best efforts.

The end result is much like the illuminating power of walking into the darkest room with a lit candle or match. The light—the truth—instantly dispels the darkness and sends evil to a place where no man dwells.

Much like this metaphor, I have experienced my own work changing the course of history, the anthrax mailing mystery detailed above is one example. Within days of my e-mailing my report to 1,500 F.B.I. agents, more than 7,500 members of the national press, and close to 135,000 Americans, the "anthrax-in-the-mail" story suddenly disappeared from the news.

Imagine what would happen to the villains, and their ability to operate covertly if just 2,000 people did the same to help save America—relaying this message of truth to 144,000. The entire nation's population of more than 250 million would be affected. Then their light would illuminate the darkness, making such devil-doing extremely difficult, if not impossible.

Clearly, the light of truth and love can not be extinguished no matter how much hate, fear, or man-made threats tyrants generate. The global elite are simply no match for the Power of Peace and Divine Will. The Sacred Harmony and Holy Vibration that is building in people's hearts worldwide will not be deterred. Nor will a peaceful resolution to our generalized madness be postponed beyond its time.

In this spiritual context, especially considering there are at least six spiritual dimensions beyond our physical three—that's two-to-one proof that our battles and destinies are more spiritual than physical— the blessings and curses of humanity include the correlates and antecedents to healthy human development and Divine transcendence. These are principally pain, loss, and threatened survival. So given you are more spirit than body, you have nothing to worry about!

"No pain, no gain," the saying goes. This is especially clear when considering personal and spiritual development. The greater the pain one is willing (or required) to embrace or suffer before being moved to repentance or positive change, the greater the opportunity for significant lasting gain.

Consider the example, the pain and lasting gain of Christ, or even Mahatma Gandhi. They took on this same challenge.

These labors reflect a Divine Will operating in the world. As previously mentioned, God too intends a New World Order, though not likely run by petrochemical fascists. Given the already high and rapidly increasing intensity of biospiritual warfare pervading this planet and targeting humanity, this exciting, albeit challenging, time foreshadows a spiritual renaissance unprecedented in the annals of philosophy and religion.

As you can gather from my writings, I respect knowledge as power, and consider ignorance deadly. Thus, in this rapidly changing and dangerous world, I have worked to relay warnings for the wise in efforts to save lives and souls. I recommend you do the same—jump in, the water is *fine*.

In fact, wholehearted engagement in political outreach is what I perceive is tied to enlightenment. Political activism and enlightenment are certainly linked by their common utility. Political activism helps secure physical protections while enlightenment offers spiritual ones. Both enable and empower human service—the thread with which our social fabrics are knit.

Now it appears urgent and critical to be aware of, and share, this book's alerts. Then use this knowledge and my earlier recommendations[20] to protect yourself, your family, and community against new biological and chemical threats, to strengthen immunity through healthier habits, and to pray for a peaceful planet and leaders with loving hearts. This wisdom and activity is obviously needed to direct a righteous lasting victory.

Begin by making the changes and choices in your own life that your children may thankfully inherit. Whether you like it or not, you are currently making the choice to be herded, like masses of ignorant "sheeple" to slaughter, or alternatively, to march freely to a different melody of spirituality that relays protection and peace. Your future, and that of our entire civilization, rests now in your hands as an empowered kindred spirit.

References

1) Kingston J. A critical analysis of *Emerging Viruses: AIDS & Ebola—Nature, Accident or Intentional?* Unpublished report. December 13, 1996.

2) Nicolson G. Personal communication. September 13, 2001.

3) Horowitz LG. "26 reasons why "white collar terrorists" are to blame for "America's New War" and the impending World War III." Article available on the Internet at: http://www.tetrahedron.org/articles/apocalypse/ 26_reasons.html. For more details, see: http://www.tetrahedron.org/articles/ apocalypse/. For instance, the Federal Emergency Management Agency (FEMA) had been dispatched enmasse to New York City to direct the September 11, 2001 emergency response *on September 10th!*

4) Horowitz LG. *Deadly Innocence: The Kimberly Bergalis Case—Solving the Greatest Murder Mystery in the Annals of American Medicine.* Tetrahedron Press, 1993. This book was based on the following scientific reports: Horowitz LG. Murder and cover-up could explain the Florida dental AIDS mystery. *British Dental Journal* 1994;1;24:423-427; See also: Horowitz LG. Sexual homicide with HIV in a Florida dental practice? *Journal of Clinical Pediatric Dentistry* 1994;19;1:61-64; See also: Horowitz LG. Correlates and predictors of sexual homicide with HIV in the Florida Dental AIDS tragedy. *AIDS Patient Care*, 1994;8;4:220-229.

5) Letters to F.B.I. officials and members of Congress are available at http:// www.tetrahedron.org/articles/apocalypse/FBI_Anthrax_mailings.html and http://www.tetrahedron.org/articles/anthrax/letter_to_fbi.html

6) Borkin J. *The Crime and Punishment of I.G. Farben: The Unholy Alliance Between Hitler and the Great Chemical Combine.* New York: Barnes and Noble, 1997.

7) Woosey J. Former CIA Director Woolsey delivers remarks at foreign press center. March 7, 2000. Available at http://cryptome.org/echelon-cia.htm

8) Mr. Rosenberg's ABC News article is available at: http:// www.tetrahedron.org/articles/anthrax/Anthrax_Vaccine_Crowe_British.html

9) Skolnick SH. Overthrow of the American Republic: Bioport and The Anthrax Commissars. Available from: Citizen's Committee to Clean Up the Courts, 9800 South Oglesby Ave., Chicago, IL 60617-4870.

10) Ruppert M. The best enemies money can buy. Available at: http:// www.tetrahedron.org/articles/terrorism/economics_behind.html; for background on Frank C. Carlucci, III in relation to HIV/AIDS see: Horowitz LG and Martin WJ. *Emerging Viruses: AIDS & Ebola—Nature, Accident or Intentional?* Rockport, MA: Tetrahedron Press, 1998.

11) Horowitz LG and Puleo JS. *Healing Codes for the Biological Apocalypse.* Tetrahedron Publishing Group, 1999, pp. 270-281.

12) Palast G and Pallister D. FBI and US spy agents say Bush spiked Bin Laden probes before 11 September. *The Guardian* (London), Wednesday, Nov. 7, 2001. Available at: http://www.gregpalast.com/ detail.cfm?artid=103&row=0.

13) Wolfe SM. Letter to HHS Secretary on Pharmaceutical Research & Manu- facturers of America Emergency Preparedness Task Force (HRG Publication #1600). *Public Citizen.* Available at http://www.citizen.org/publications/ release.cfm?ID=7101.

14) O'Meara KP. Investigative Report: Government rip-off on the Cipro deal. *Washington Times*, Insight Magazine, Nov. 26, 2001. Available at http://insightmag.com/main.cfm?include=detail&storyid=138294.

15) Charlotte D. Rules relaxed in rush for a new smallpox vaccine. *The Guardian*, Thursday, Oct. 25, 2001.

16) See: http://www.oravax.com/

17) Horowitz LG. Death *in the Air: Globalism, Terrorism and Toxic War- fare.* Tetrahedron Publishing Group, 2001, pp. 105-109.

18) U.S. Senate, 103rd Congress, 2d Session. *U.S. Chemical and Biological Warfare-related Dual Use Exports to Iraq and Their Possible Impact on the Health Consequences of the Persian Gulf War: A Report of Chairman Donald W. Riegle, Jr., et. al.* May 25, 1994, pp. 39-47.

19) Broad WJ, Johnston D, Miller J and Zielbauer P. Experts see F.B.I. Missteps Hampering Anthrax Inquiry. *New York Times*, No- vember 9, 2001. Available at http://www.nytimes.com/2001/11/09/ national/09INQU.html?todaysheadlines.

20) Horowitz LG. *Healing Celebrations: Miraculous Recoveries Through Ancient Scripture, Natural Medicine and Modern Science.* Sandpoint, ID: Tetrahedron Publishing Group, 2000. Go to: http:// www.healingcelebrations.com

Acknowledgments

I am extremely grateful to the following people who have given me tremendous support over the past few years.

First and foremost, I would like to publicly acknowledge my wife of sixteen years, Jackie, who besides being a superior companion, has labored continuously behind the scenes to help me organize my research, administer my schedule, manage Tetrahedron Publishing Group, oversee our great staff, edit my books and articles, challenge my errors, and still find the time and energy to be a fantastic mother, and chauffeur, to our three blessed children. Without her special contributions, this work and my other earlier books and tapes would not exist.

The staff at Tetrahedron, Inc.—a nonprofit educational corporation—deserve special mention for their long and hard labors. I have often demanded more from Elaine Zacky and Sue Shafer than perhaps I should, but they have consistently risen to the occasions. Without their dedication and dependability, this work would not exist.

In a world where too few share the politically damning perspectives provided in this book, Don and Ingri Harkins, publishers of *The Idaho Observer*, receive my heart-felt appreciation for their close friendship, consistent support, commitment to improving public health, raising vaccine risk awareness, and ongoing efforts to battle against violations of human rights that most people seem content to let fall to the machinations of "public health," "law enforcement," and "national security."

Moreover, on a planet thoroughly steeped in deceptions, it is gratifying to know and acknowledge my friend, colleague, and gifted physician, Dr. Joseph Puleo, who has an uncanny knack for research, perceiving the largest truths, and healing his mostly destitute patients. The loving example and enthusiasm that he displays daily in his healing ministry and clinical practice is awe inspiring. Besides this, the manner in which I was able to decipher the oligarchy's "Special Service" codes herein—perhaps this book's greatest contribution—would not have come to pass without Dr. Puleo's earlier contributions in *Healing Codes for the Biological Apocalypse*.

To those who have made other great contributions to this book: Betsy Russell–Manning (mentioned in the Preface) for her kindness, direction, and concern for public health and safety; Robert Lederman for his heroism in heralding the truth about the West Nile virus in New York; William Thomas for his tenacity in investigating and articulating the chemtrail issue across North America; William Winker for an equal amount of hutzpah in taking a Delaware demon by the horns and not letting it wrestle loose; and Dr. Nick Begich for his alerts regarding the misuse of power by the cryptocracy. To all of the above, I praise you.

Last, but not least, I wish to thank the hundreds of people who have been my eyes, ears, and clipping servers over the past five years sending a steady stream of intelligence from which my books and tapes largely derive. Their prayers and efforts uplift me in the knowledge that many average people can, and do, make a *big* difference.

Index

Index

107, 113, 121, 137, 154, 179-182, 195, 198, 200, 207, 209, 210, 213-218, 222, 223, 226-229, 289, 310-321, 341, 342, 350-353, 354, 464, 490, 492; and chemical warfare, 185; See also: *biological weapons, biowarfare, bioweapons,* and *bioweapons centers.*

biological weapons, 2, 3, 7, 9, 11, 12, 15, 16, 47, 83, 104, 107, 111, 210, 213, 216, 368, 404, 465; airborne, 465; and immune system, 475; testing, 182, 185, 214; Title 1520 of the United States Code Annotated T, 214; See also: *biological warfare, biological weapons tests,* and *biowarfare.*

Bionetics, 2, 4, 5, 6, 12, 16, 47, 48, 49, 157, 171, 195, 210, 250, 256, 262, 264, 266, 270, 357, 376, 379, 447, 449, 456, 460, 461, 466

Bioport Corporation, 455, 510, 511, 513

biospiritual warfare, 489, 492, 495

bioterrorism, 1, 13-15, 17, 199, 367, 438, 511, 515

biowarfare, 107, 153, 154, 159

bioweapons, 104

bioweapons centers, 475

birth defects, 58

Bjerklie, David, 244

Black people, 118, 119, 468; covert actions against, 479; and Hispanic, 118, 119; in central Africa, 461, 465; and Jewish women investigated for cervical cancer, 195; *genocide* against 475, 480; movement, 479; organizations, 240; population, 476; covert war against the Black people of Africa and America, 475; See also *genocide.*

black helicopters, 79

"black mold" Nigrospora, 155

Blair, James, 85

blowback, 77

BLUEBIRD, 217

Bluhm, Agnes, 357

Bobst, Elmer, 5, 8

Boeringer, Richard, 66

Bolling, General Alexander, 7

Bond, James, 393

Bongaarts, John, 439

Borkin, Joseph, 356

Bormann, Carolyn, 104

Bowart, Walter, 218

Bradley, Omar, 495

Bradshaw, Thornton , 317

Brain Research Institute, 222

Brannon, David, 441

breakdown products, 57

breast cancer, 425

Brenner, 26

Brenner, Loretta, 24

breve, Gymnodinium, 124

brevetoxin, 132

brevetoxins, 131, 133; See also *red tide(s).*

Brian Edward Mountain, 317

British Broadcasting Company (BBC), 511

British Royal Family, 11, 136, 298, 316, 317, 387

British Secret Service (MI6), 317, 350, 395; See also *MI6.*

Britt Lumber Co., Inc., 393

Brown, Candace, 152

Brown, Paul, 469

Brown, Willie, 480

Brucella melitensis, 404

Brzezinski, Zbigniew, 9, 158, 240, 354, 378, 385, 389, 390, 396, 446, 475, 478-480; prophetic vision, population management, 390

Burkitt's lymphoma, 195

Burns, Glen, 149

Burton, Dan, 16

Bush, George H. W., 8, 9, 10, 11, 13, 14, 20, 21, 80, 108, 294, 354, 391, 434, 510

Bush, George W., 294, 506, 507, 511

Bush, Prescott, 11, 346

Byrd, W. Michael, 484

C

C-130 scandal, 156

C2W (Command and Control Warfare), 394, 481, 485

CACTUS (Citizens Against Chemtrails U.S.), 170

Cadesporium, 169

Calabrese, Kevin, 116

Caldeira, 163

Caldeira, Ken, 163

Califano, Joseph, 378, 446, 471, 472, 473, 474, 475, 499

California Academy of Sciences, 88

California Department of Food and Agriculture (CDFA), 60, 73, 86, 87, 88

California Department of Health Services (DHS), 26, 60, 66, 73

California Department of Pesticide Regulation, 24

California Health Evaluation Systems and Information Service (HESIS), 66, 68, 74

California Institute of Technology, 428, 447

California State University, 85

Caltex, 100

cancer, 152, 347-349, 356, 363-365, 368, 370, 376, 382, 386, 387, 405, 417, 421, 425, 434, 445, 446-472, 492, 493; carcinomas, 404; industry, 5, 356; See

Index

Index

Index

immune system, 38, 43, 71, 72, 74, 103;
   dysfunction, 246; suppression 2, 43,
   toxicology, 72
immunization, 473; program, 473, 474
immunological functions, 180
Indians, 468; See also *genocide*.
industrial espionage, 85, 506-515; See also
   Central Intelligence Agency (CIA).
"inert" ingredients, 56; See also *Malathion*
   and *pesticides*.
Infectious crystalline agent, 213
Infectious Diseases Society of America, 291
influenza, 171; and leukemia viruses, 464;
   influenza-like illness, 147; See also:
   flu-like illness and *chemtrails*.
inoculation of diseases, 201, 255
Institute for Associated Research, 498
Institute for Molecular Medicine, 152
Institute of Medicine (IoM), 287, 288, 290,
   293, 423. 439
Institute of Psychiatry in Munich, 357
Inter-American Development Bank, 235, 236
Intermountain Aviation, 79, , 80, 81, 110; See
   Evergreen Helicopters and *CIA*.
International Agency for Research on Cancer
   (IARC), 2, 12, 195, 376, 379, 456, 458,
   459
International Conference on Population and
   Develop, 483
International Labor Organization, 236
International Monetary Fund, 158
International Panel on Climate Change
   (IPCC), 163, 164, 167, 177
Intervax Corporation, 423
IR radiation, 164; See also *electromagnetic*.
Iraq's "Yellow Rain", 113; See also *chemical
   warfare*.
iron oxide, 161
Isaacson, Walter, 7, 373
Islam, 395
isomalathion, 69: See also *Malathion*.
Ivanovsky Institute, 368

J

J&J–Merck Consumer, 136
J. P. Morgan, 349, 353, 387, 412, 419
J. P. Morgan & Co., 352
Jackson, Jesse, 480
James Bond, 390, 417; truth about James
   Bond films, 394
Japanese encephalitis (JE), 104, 106, 185.
Japanese subway system biological attack,
   117
Jasper, William F., 434
Jefferson, Thomas, 352
jellyfish, 131, 132, 134, 136, 138, 391; "type-

I" and "type-II" jellyfish, 136
jet fuels, 102; See also *Chevron*.
Jewish, 195, 347, 359, 452, 468; and
   Christians, 468; military intelligence,
   359; males of European descent, 452;
   scientists, 347; women were investi-
   gated for cervical cancer, 195
John Foster and Allen Dulles, 5
John Glenn, 216
JP-8 jet fuel, 98, 157
Judeo-Christian, 414, 395; genocide, 414;
   religions, 395 See also *Jewish*.
JuriMed, 380

K

Kaczynski, Ted ("Unibomber"), 508
Kahn, Ephraim, 67-69, 74, 261
Kaiser Aluminum Corporation (KAC), 391,
   392, 419; & Chemical Corporation
   391;
Kaiser Electro-optics, Inc., 391
Kaiser Industries, 385-388; subsidiary
   developments, 393; See also *Kaiser
   Aluminum Corporation (KAC)*.
Kaiser medical leadership, 387; Kaiser
   connection, 389
Kaiser Permanente, 360, 362
Kaiser Wilhelm Institute for Anthropology,
   Eugenic, 357, 358; Kaiser connection,
   389
Kaiser Wilhelm Institute for Psychiatry, 357
Kaiser Wilhelm Society, 357
Kalman, Sumner M., 30, 32
Kalter, Seymour, 447
Kamen, Jeff, 364, 365, 382
Kaplan, Robert, 484
Kasum, Jacqueline, 436
Kayser, Lutz Thilo, 465
Keeton, Kathy, 364
Keith, Jim, 180
Keith, Kenneth , 317
Kettering, Charles, 387; Kaiser connection,
   389; Foundation, 363; See also *Sloan-
   Kettering Memorial Cancer Center*.
Kevles, Daniel J, 428; 428-433
Key, Representative Charles, 514; Oklahoma
   City bombing report, 514-515
Khamisiyah, 107, 197; See also *Gulf War*.
Kienholz, Edward, 325, 331, 332, 414
King Edward VII of England, 385
King George V, 385
King, Martin Luther, 480
King, Maurice, 487
Kingston, Jack, 31, 373, 504, 505
Kissinger, Henry A., 4, 7-9, 19, 20, 171, 209,
   240, 241, 252, 325, 331, 332, 351, 354,

National Academy of Sciences–National
Research Coucil (NAS–NRC), 439,
464, 487
National Aeronautics and Space Administration (NASA), 144, 161, 173, 246, 247,
250; Chrysler space division, 465
National Broadcasting Company (NBC), 317
National Cancer Control Society, 27
National Cancer Institute (NCI), 2, 6, 12, 30,
38, 39, 45, 47-49, 84, 196, 250, 256,
264 , 347, 348, 364, 365, 370, 372,
376, 379, 404, 420, 447-467, 475, 498;
Biohazards Control and Containment
section, 449
National Childhood Vaccine Injury Act of
1986, 290, 292, 293
National Defense University, 482
National Forest Service (NFS), 325, 326,
329, 332, 333, 407
National Foundation for the Chemically
Sensitive, 29
National Immunization Program (NIP), 285
National Institute for Allergy and Infectious
Diseses (NIAID), 288, 379
National Institute for Occupational Safety
and Health (NIOSH), 25
National Institute of Child Health &
Development, 424
National Institute of Health (NIH), 47, 49, 95,
106, 264, 287, 288, 347, 360, 362, 363,
368, 370, 376
National Oceanographic and Atmospheric
(NOAA), 124
National Pollutant Discharge Elimination
System, 94
National Press Club, 202
"National Purpose" for America, 204, 205
National Research Council (NRC), 289, 345,
346, 423, 439, 440, 442, 448; See also
National Academy of Sciences.
National Science Foundation (NSF), 387
National Security Agency (NSA), 8, 9, 379
National Security Council, 376, 480, 482,
506
National Security Memorandum–46, 9, 307,
390, 475, 476, 479, 480
National Security Special Memorandum–200,
national security state, 204, 205, 504
National Socialists, 358
National Vaccine Advisory Committee, 284,
286
National Vaccine Information Center (NVIC),
290, 291, 292
Native Americans, 81; Navajo, 363; See also
Indians.
Naval Biomedical Research Laboratories
(NBRL), 449, 454; See also *U.S. Navy.*
Nazi(s), 7, 9, 11, 19, 20, 176, 237, 252, 261,

289, 347, 357, 359, 360, 382, 394, 411,
413, 414, 432, 437, 465, 468, 469, 470
Neel, James, 469
Negative Population Control, Inc., 90; See
also *Population Council.*
Neimoeller, Martin, 494
Nelson, Fred, 29
Nelson-Rees, Walter, 455
neo-Nazis, 514
nerve agents, 194; pretreatment drugs, 194
neuroendocrine, 103, 180
Neurolinguistic Programming (NLP), 76
neurological dysfunction, 29
neurotoxicity, 29, 114, 122-133, 356, 391;
pesticide poisoning, 44, 133; pollution,
131; and Infectivity of Aluminum, 167;
See also *neurological dysfunction.*
New World Airport Commission, 468; See
also *Denver Airport.*
New World Order, 14, 89, 100, 198, 200,
231, 232, 317, 319, 341, 354, 382, 388,
396, 400, 496
New York City Blood Council, 474
New York City Department of Health
(NYCDoH), 91, 92, 95 101
New York City Department of Emergency
Management, 105, 106
New York University Medical Center, 461
Niblack, Twila, 27
nickel, 70; See also *heavy metals.*
Nicolson, Garth, 152, 505
Niebuhr, Reinhold, 494
Nixon, Richard, 4, 5, 9, 76, 77, 209, 214, 238,
240, 354, 374, 376, 377, 378, 383, 474,
478
NOAA, 124, 137
NOEL (No Observable Effect Level), 57
Non-governmental organizations (NGOs),
236, 237, 238, 314, 482, 483, 487, 500;
involved in genocide, 238
non-lethal activities, 17, 43, 48, 85, 89, 95,
100, 103, 111, 159, 179, 180, 181, 182,
185, 189, 194, 195, 198, 199, 203, 209,
213, 217, 244, 251, 283, 299, 300, 301,
302, 304, 305, 306, 309, 319, 321, 323,
325, 331, 338, 339, 341, 450, 493;
devices, 182; for law enforcement, 180;
military warfare, 121, 217; technological slavery, 319; to genetically control
humanity, 358; warfare for population
control, 114, 159, 179, 180, 182, 185,
189, 195, 198, 199, 203, 209, 213, 217,
389
non-lethality doctrine, 179, 194, 198
nonsteroidal antiinflammatory drug
(NSAIDs), 426, 427
Norplant, 433, 482, 486, 501
North Atlantic Treaty Organization (NATO),
250, 314, 317, 396

Index

Index

Index

Weber, Kim, 170
Weidner Environmental and Natural
    Resources Law Clinic, 133
Weishaupt, Adam, 352
Wellington House "social conditioning", 350;
    See also the *Royal Institute for
    International Affairs, Committee of
    300, propaganda, social sciences,* and
    Stanford Research Institute.
Welsbach materials, 164; oxides of metals,
    164
West Nile encephalitis, 15, 110
West Nile region of Northwest Uganda, 2,
    456
West Nile virus (WNV), 1-4, 10-12, 14, 15,
    17, 23, 25, 38, 52, 55, 82, 91, 100, 101-
    120, 131, 185, 189, 192, 195, 244-246,
    250, 288, 333, 368, 513; vaccine, 107,
    513
western medical modes, 234
Westinghouse, 317
Whitney Museum of Art, 203, 424
Wilhelm II of Germany, Kaiser, 11, 360, 385
Williams, Frank, 114
Williams, Kathy, 290
Winker, William J., 95, 122, 123, 125, 127,
    132, 134, 140, 167, 391, 493
Winship Cancer Institute, 417
Wiseman, William, 317
Wisdom of Solomon, 494
Wolfe, Sidney M., 192, 513
Woodruff, Ernest, 417
Woodruff Health Sciences Center, 417
Woodruff, Robert W., 417
Woodward, Bob, 77
Woolsy, James, 10, 82, 83, 510
World Bank, 158, 235, 236, 238, 240, 243,
    439, 440, 465, 473, 483, 484
World Health Organization (WHO), 58, 150,
    171, 202, 233, 234, 363, 422, 423, 424,
    471, 472, 473, 474, 485; immunization
    program, 474; World Health Assembly,
    472; World Population Projections
    (WPP), 440
World Research Foundation, 34
World Trade Center, 503, 506, 507,512
World War II, 7, 11, 35, 43, 100, 232, 237,
    242, 289, 345, 350, 357, 366, 385, 437,
    438, 493
World War III, 504
World Wildlife Fund, 99, 317

X

XFL, 394
XX, 394
XXX, 394

Y

Yacca, Joe, 115
Yale University, 107
Yanomani society, 236, 469
yeast, 229, 492
yellow rain (component called DAS), 113
Yerkes Primate Center, 417

Z

Zaire, 485
Zanus Corporation, 92
Zero Population Growth, Inc., 424
ZORIN Corporation, 394
Zyclone B, 261

Death in the Air

About the Author

Leonard G. Horowitz, D.M.D., M.A., M.P.H., is a Harvard graduate, independent investigator, and an internationally known authority in behavioral science and public health education. He earned his doctorate in medical dentistry from Tufts University, a master of arts degree in health education from Beacon College, and a master of public health degree in behavioral science from Harvard University.

One of healthcare's most captivating motivational speakers, Dr. Horowitz has served on the faculties of Tufts University, Harvard University, and Leslie College's Institute for the Arts and Human Development. He has served as a consultant to several leading healthcare corporations and national associations. His works have prompted interviews on every major television and radio network throughout North America and England.

Dr. Horowitz, recipient of the 1999 "Author of the Year Award," by the World Natural Health Organization, has published more than 125 articles in scientific and lay periodicals, two dozen audio and videotape programs, and thirteen books including the American bestseller, *Emerging Viruses: AIDS & Ebola—Nature, Accident or Intentional?* In 1999, he coauthored *Healing Codes for the Biological Apocalypse*, a landmark publication revealing sacred Bible codes intimately involved with creation, destruction, and miracles, including miraculous healings. In 2000, based largely on these revelations, he authored *Healing Celebrations* which demystifies the steps required to produce miraculous healings.

Dr. Horowitz lives in northern Idaho with his wife and three children. He is a fitness buff who spends his free time skiing, hiking, swimming, sailing, snorkeling, singing, and playing guitar.

Death in the Air

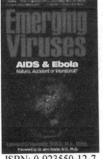

ISBN: 0-923550-39-9

An urgent and inspired work for global salvation!

One half of the world's current population has been targeted for death by the global elitists. Dr. Len Horowitz and Dr. Joseph Puleo reveal 2000 years of religious and political persecution and disclose the latest technologies being used to enslave, coerce and kill, billions of unsuspecting people. This work, precisely timed for the spiritual and natural healing renaissance, returns the most precious spiritual knowledge, power, and Bible "healing codes" to humanity. A must read for every serious devotee of ultimate truth and holistic healing.

517 Page Hardcover Book $26.45
4 Hour Video $39.50
4 Hour Audio $24.65

Divine Harmony CD - by Al Harris

Music that can empower, uplift and celebrate our loving human relationships and connection to God. It can increase Divine anointing through which pure love and healing powers flow.

Six inspirational compositions $19.25

The Lost Chord - by Jonathan Goldman

Entering the next stage of sonic exploration, Jonathan Goldman introduces the world to The Lost Chord that includes exact tones, revealed in *Healing Codes for the Biological Apocalypse*, chanted by monks accompanied by musicians. Among the most scientifically and spiritually uplifting records ever released. For inspiration and transformation. The Lost Chord will enhance any healing work being done. Great background music for congregational meetings, clinics or therapy sessions.

75 Minute CD $16.55

Solfeggio Healing Tones - by Dan Kunkel

Precise sound frequencies designed to nourish and uplift spirits to their source. These sounds, based on the Bible codes uncovered in *Healing Codes for the Biological Apocalypse* may create harmony and balance and may even effect miraculous healings.

Healing Tones CD $15.65
Audio $12.50

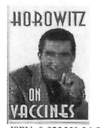

ISBN: 0-923550-26-7

Horowitz 'On Vaccines' - This best seller is our favorite!

If you have questions about the safety and efficacy of vaccines, then this tape is for you. Are vaccines truly "mandated by law" or can you and your children be exempt from vaccine programs if so desired? How effective are vaccines? What risks do they pose? Why have so many vaccines suddenly become required? Join Dr. Horowitz as he answers these questions and more. Dr. Horowitz tells the whole story regarding vaccine side effects. He explains how vaccines are delivering a host of autoimmune diseases including AIDS, chronic fatigue, many types of cancer, Gulf War Syndrome, fibromyalgia, MS, lupus, Guillain Barre, asthma, allergies, and even hyperactivity and attention deficit disorders and autism. Every family with young or coming children need to hear this tape.

90 Minute Audio $14.75

ISBN: 0-923550-19-4

Taking Care of Yourself - Gain powerful immunity! - A Priceless Guide to the Best Investment you'll ever make - YOU!

Optimal health, happiness, and success are yours to enjoy by following the breakthrough steps detailed here by public health education authority, Dr. Len Horowitz. This interactive package provides easy to follow instructions to succeed in your quest for powerful immunity against common illnesses and the coming plagues. By making Dr. Horowitz's common sense recommendations part of your daily routine, you will dramatically improve your quality of life. Let the miracles begin! This package includes: *Nutritional Supplements for Immunity, Energy and Acuity, Horowitz 'on Healing'* and *Survival Water: pH and Oxygen.* **A terrific value!**

9 Hour Audio Program with Workbook $69.65

ISBN: 0-923550-03-8

Horowitz 'on Healing'- Outlines 5 critical steps for building immunity now!

Reviews the critical five steps required to defend against the current and coming plagues. This audiotape explains how to: detoxify your body through colon cleansing, fasting, diet, and exercise; deacidify your body terrain and shift your blood chemistry to prevent and reduce bacterial, viral, and fungal growth; boost your immune system every way possible - physically, mentally, emotionally, socially, environmentally, and above all spiritually; oxygenate your body and blood to kill off invading germs and empower your cells to heal; and bioelectrically treat infectious diseases and chronic illnesses. These disciplines for optimal health are simple yet profound in their effect. Use it - these keys to health - or lose it.

90 Minute Audio $14.75

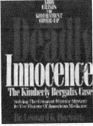

ISBN: 0-923550-13-5

Deadly Innocence - The Kimberly Bergalis Case

Dr. Horowitz reads his critically acclaimed book that exposes the government investigators for covering up virtually all of the incriminating evidence against the Florida dentist responsible for infecting Kimberly Bergalis and at least five other patients with the AIDS virus. Learn what Dr. Acer was really like, how his personality profile matched those of thirty-six serial killers studied by the FBI, why he likely committed serial homicide, and why the government investigators covered up the evidence to leave the case an "unsolvable mystery". Here is the unbelievable truth about the case which rocked the American health care system, and panicked patients and healthcare professionals around the world. There's great drama in this true story of unthinkable politics and economics that took precedence over the public health and safety of Americans.

3 Hour Audio $19.25   2 Hour Video $19.25

ISBN: 0-923550-23-2

Gulf War Syndrome: The Spreading Epidemic Cover-up

Gulf War Syndrome affects more than 200,000 veterans now. It is an infectious disease related to biological warfare, contaminated vaccines, and chronic fatigue. And it's spreading to civilian populations! As the CIA and Pentagon spread disinformation and doubt, children, health professionals, and even pets are becoming infected, ill, and are dying. This video presents the unnerving truth and documented facts, about this spreading plague. Four internationally known experts - Dr. Len Horowitz, Dr. Garth Nicholson , Captain Joyce Riley, and Lieutenant Louise Richard share the stage and their knowledge about the politics and propaganda surrounding the issue. See for yourself the real story on one of the greatest military-medical cover-ups in history.

3 1/2 Hour Video $24.65

The Nazi–American Biomedical/Biowarfare Connection

If you think the Nazi agenda for world control, disposing of undesirable populations, and experiments to genetically develop a master race ended with World War II, you are in for a shocker! Learn about the links between Hitler's top medical and biowarfare researchers and U.S. and British intelligence, allied pharmaceutical and population control interests, the Rockefellers, the Bushes, and the British Royal Family! Dr. Horowitz and Dave Emory, nationally syndicated talk show host, reveal how Merck, Sharp and Dohme - the world's largest vaccine producer - was a principle recipient of the Nazi war chest, as part of a scheme to create a monopoly over the world's chemical and pharmaceutical industries, for the expressed purpose of creating a "New World Order" and giving rise to "The Fourth Reich." If you really want to know the "straight skinny on the deep doo doo", this is required listening.

ISBN: 0-923550-22-4

3 Hour Audio $19.25

Virus Makers of the CIA - Absolutely Riveting!

Nationally syndicated talk show host, Dave Emory interviews four heroic authors on the most controversial and horrifying facts about why we now have epidemics of cancer, AIDS, chronic fatigue, Gulf War Syndrome, and more. Dr. Alan Cantwell recounts the hepatitis B vaccine experiments that most likely brought AIDS to the world. Dr. Horowitz implicates the Defense Department's top biological weapons contractors, the National Cancer Institute, and the world's leading pharmaceutical companies in the development and transmission of AIDS and Ebola. Ed Haslam reveals the documented connection between the CIA, the secret monkey virus mutation lab in New Orleans, and those implicated in the assassination of John F. Kennedy. Dr. Garth Nicholson describes the horrors of Gulf War syndrome and its origin from U.S. produced biological weapons and contaminated vaccine experiments. Forget conspiracy "theories"; here's the cause and core.

ISBN: 0-923550-29-1

3 Hour Audio $19.25

End Times: Preparedness, Prophecy & Propaganda

Dr. Len Horowitz interviews Pastor Norm Franz—a leading expert on Bible prophecy. They discuss how to: prepare mentally, physically and spritually for the great tribulation and the Messianic Age; understand "alien" phenomena; and see through the "New World Order" and its spiritual implications. Pastor Franz challenges you to be "doers of the word" and not just believers at a time when unprecedented levels of propaganda may deceive you and cause you to become complacent. This is a powerful inspirational message. There is a Higher Power. "Own it" for peace of mind.

ISBN: 0-923550-28-3

90 Minute Audio $14.75

Survival Water: pH and Oxygen

Your body is more than 70% water. Drinking the wrong kind of water may cause problems. Not only is water contamination a common problem, but the pH and oxygenation levels of the water is foundational to your health or disease status.
This is a very important master key to your optimal health. Discover this missing link from Jim Karnstedt, as he is
interviewed by Dr. Len Horowitz.

ISBN: 0-923550-02-X

90 Minute Audio$ 14.75

ISBN: 0-9609386-4-8

Freedom From Headaches & TMJ

This package provides a complete selfcare program to help analize, mitigate and prevent headaches. This audiocassette helps you to creatively eliminate your aches and pains from migraines, tension headaches & TMJ.

90 Minute Audio & 72 Page Book $14.75

ISBN: 0-923550-27-5

Why It's Time Jews and Christians Unite

Dr. Weinstein, author of *The Christ Killers: The Story of How Jews Were Blamed For The Crucifixion*, interviewed by Dr. Horowitz, presents convincing evidence to urge reconciliation between Jews and Christians. Pastor Norm Franz, one of the nation's leading experts on Bible prochecy, gives his interpretations on tape three. Powerful insight for overcoming the divide-to-conquer agenda challenging the unity-in-diversity of our Judeo-Christian heritage.

4 1/2 Hour Audio $24.65

ISBN: 0-9609386-8-0

Freedom From Teeth Clenching

This program, recommended by dentists and psychologists, will help you to stop grinding your teeth. The tape, ideally suited for bedtime listening, will put you to sleep fast and help you achieve positive results. The booklet gives nutritional, exercise, and self massage instructions for powerful relief.

60 Minute Audio & 32 Page Book $14.75

ISBN: 0-9609386-7-2

Freedom From Desk Job Stress

This program provides relaxation and stress management exercises, a mini-course in communication, physical exercises, nutritional programs, self-massage and acupressure instructions, and a guide to improve office ergonomics and occupational hazards. Great for computer users.

60 Minute Audio & 70 Page Book $14.75